Jewish Culture and Society in North Africa

T0369806

INDIANA SERIES IN SEPHARDI AND MIZRAHI STUDIES
Harvey E. Goldberg and Matthias Lehmann, *editors*

Jewish Culture and Society in North Africa

Edited by
Emily Benichou Gottreich
and Daniel J. Schroeter

INDIANA UNIVERSITY PRESS
BLOOMINGTON AND INDIANAPOLIS

This book is a publication of

Indiana University Press
601 North Morton Street
Bloomington, Indiana 47404-3797 USA

www.iupress.indiana.edu

Telephone orders   800-842-6796
Fax orders   812-855-7931
Orders by e-mail   iuporder@indiana.edu

Library of Congress Cataloging-in-Publication Data

Jewish culture and society in North Africa / edited by Emily Benichou Gottreich and
Daniel J. Schroeter.
p. cm. — (Indiana series in Sephardi and Mizrahi studies)
Includes index.
ISBN 978-0-253-35509-6 (hardcopy : alk. paper)
ISBN 978-0-253-22225-1 (pbk. : alk. paper)
1. Jews—Africa, North. 2. Judaism—Relations—Islam. 3. Islam—Relations—Judaism. I.
Gottreich, Emily, 1966- II. Schroeter, Daniel J. III. Series: Indiana series in Sephardi and
Mizrahi studies.
DS135.A25J49   2011
305.892'4061—dc22   011008989

Contents

14

Sol Hachuel, "Heroine of the Nineteenth Century": Gender, the
Jewish Question, and Colonial Discourse
Sharon Vance 201

15

Searching for Suleika: A Writer's Journey
Ruth Knafo Setton 226

Part V. Gender, Colonialism, and the Alliance Israélite Universelle

16

Corresponding Women: Female Educators of the Alliance
Israélite Universelle in Tunisia, 1882–1914
Joy A. Land 239

17

Education for Jewish Girls in Late Nineteenth- and Early Twentieth-
Century Tunis and the Spread of French in Tunisia
Keith Walters 257

18

"Les Temps Héroïques": The Alliance Israélite Universelle in
Marrakesh on the Eve of the French Protectorate
Jonathan G. Katz 282

**Part VI. North African Jews and Political Change in
the Late Colonial and Post-Colonial Periods**

19

Jewish-Muslim Relations in Tunisia during World War II:
Propaganda, Stereotypes, and Attitudes, 1939–1943
Fayçal Cherif 305

20

The Emigration of Moroccan Jews, 1948–1956
Jamaâ Baïda 321

Acknowledgments

A s is the case with all books, but especially edited volumes that grow out of conferences, this publication is the result of the tremendous assistance and goodwill of many. The editors wish to take this opportunity to thank the following individuals and institutions in particular.

First and foremost, the American Institute for Maghrib Studies (AIMS), which sponsored the conference; the Tangier American Legation Institute for Moroccan Studies (TALIM); and Thor Kuniholm, then director of the museum, which hosted it at its splendid building in the Tangier madina. AIMS officers Keith Walters, Jim Miller, Donna Lee Bowen, and Mark Tessler were especially helpful, as was the staff at TALIM (especially Assistant Director Yhtimad Bouziane) and CEMAT (Centre des Études Maghrébines à Tunis) (especially Assistant Director Riadh Saadaoui).

The conference "Rethinking Jewish Culture and Society in North Africa" would not have happened, let alone been successful, had it not been for the active participation of our overseas colleagues. We are especially grateful to André Azoulay, Counselor to His Majesty Mohammed VI, who opened the conference with characteristic insight and charm. Khalid Ben Srhir and Jamaâ Baïda helped organize the Moroccan delegation, as did Farid Benramdane in Algeria and Jim Miller and Riadh Saadaoui in Tunisia. Simon Lévy, director of the Musée du Judaïsme Marocain in Casablanca, and the late Edmond Amran El Maleh contributed greatly to the conference proceedings in ways uniquely their own.

Additional support for the conference came from the Center for Middle Eastern Studies (CMES) at the University of California, Berkeley, the home institution of Emily Benichou Gottreich, and Research and Graduate Studies of University of California, Irvine, the former home institution of Daniel Schroeter. Grants for the preparation of the book were generously offered by the International Center for Writing and Translation and the Humanities Center of UC Irvine. The comments of the anonymous reviewer were extremely useful. We are likewise thankful to Priscilla Minaise at UC Berkeley's CMES for help assembling the manuscript, and to Allan MacVicar for translations. Whatever faults and inconsistencies remain are ours alone.

JEWISH CULTURE AND SOCIETY IN NORTH AFRICA

PART I

Introduction

1

Rethinking Jewish Culture and Society in North Africa

EMILY BENICHOU GOTTREICH AND DANIEL J. SCHROETER

THE CHAPTERS IN this volume grow out of the proceedings of the 2004 annual conference of the American Institute for Maghrib Studies (AIMS), held at the Tangier American Legation Museum in Morocco. It was co-directed by the editors of this book and included thirty-four participants from Morocco, Algeria, Tunisia, Israel, and the United States. Its goal, seemingly simple enough at the time, was to rethink the older work of the first generation of scholars on the Jews of the Maghrib and in the process try to shed light on questions not previously considered. The chapters in this volume do this and much more; if nothing else, they clearly demonstrate that Jewish culture and society in North Africa continue to be a major focus of scholarly and popular interest, not only in France and Israel, where, not coincidentally, the vast majority of Maghribi Jews settled, but also, and increasingly, in North Africa and the United States, where a new generation of scholars from a variety of backgrounds has begun to grapple with the complexities of the Judeo-Islamic experience. Not only do these authors raise new questions, but in many instances they do so by challenging the very categories out of which traditional and even many contemporary scholarly inquiries about North African Jews emerged, causing us to reconsider conceptualizations of identity ("Berbers Jews," "Arab Jews," "Sephardim"), historical junctures (pre-Islamic versus Islamic, colonial versus postcolonial), and religious experience (popular versus orthodox) that have all but defined the field to now.

The conference in Tangier was an encounter that in itself merits some comment. Obviously this was not the first formal academic conference on the Jews of the Maghrib or on Jews of a specific country in the Maghrib to result in the publication of valuable research. The first such meeting, which took place in Jerusalem in 1977 and was organized by Hebrew University professor Michel Abitbol, included scholarly contributions in French, English, and Hebrew by (for the most part) Israeli scholars.[1] Subsequent conferences devoted to the same or similar themes followed over the next several decades, and their proceedings were also frequently published.[2] The great majority of the participants in these conferences were Jews from the Maghrib who had emigrated to Israel or Europe. One of the first major meetings to gather both Muslims and Jews (including scholars and public figures) from Morocco, Israel, and Europe took place in Paris in 1978 and focused on Moroccan Jewry.[3] It was organized by Identité et Dialogue, an association of Moroccan Jewish intellectuals, most of whom lived in France, that sought to recover and maintain a Moroccan Jewish identity as an integral part of the Moroccan patrimony and to advance the cause of Jewish-Muslim dialogue and peace. The co-founder and leader of the Identité et Dialogue movement was André Azoulay, who subsequently served as advisor in the Moroccan royal cabinet, beginning in 1991 under King Hassan II, and currently serves in the same capacity under Mohammed VI. As the most prominent Jew living in the Arab world today, André Azoulay spoke eloquently about his identity as an Arab Jew in Morocco in the opening session of the AIMS conference in Tangier.

Because most of the meetings focusing on the Jews of the Maghrib, academic or otherwise, have been held outside the place of origin, often in Israel and France,[4] it was particularly meaningful and symbolically important that the 2004 conference was held in Morocco. Though again this was not the first time that an international academic conference on the Jews of the Maghrib was held in a North African country—significantly, one was held in Tunis in 1998[5]—the meeting in Tangier was nonetheless unique in a number of ways. Scholars of the Maghrib from North America, where there has been a small but growing interest in North African Jews in recent years from a variety of interdisciplinary perspectives, had been largely absent from previous meetings. Of particular interest in Tangier were the exchanges between scholars from Tunisia, Algeria, Morocco, and Israel. This was noteworthy not only for the open and lively discussions that were had on a subject of great sensitivity that all too often becomes entangled in differences over Israeli-Palestinian conflict but also because intra-Maghrib exchanges are surprisingly rare in North Africa, stymied by a history of sensitive borders and political conflict between countries, most pointedly between Algeria and Morocco.

No less problematic are the obstacles that stand in the way of exchanges between the United States and the Arab and Muslim world, which have only become more daunting in the post-9/11 era, particularly in light of the ongoing conflict in the Middle East. Looming even more closely in the background of the conference were the synchronized bombings in Casablanca the previous spring that had targeted Jewish and foreign institutions. And just a few months before our meeting the Madrid bombings occurred, some of the perpetrators of which were traced back to Tangier, which was being widely reported in the American press as a hotbed of fiery preaching imams and a breeding ground for extremists who used the city as a transit point between the Islamic world and Europe.[6] In the wake of these incidents and increasingly dangerous developments in Afghanistan and Iraq, the meeting proceeded with some trepidation and concern; a conference on the theme of Jewish culture and society in the Maghrib, symbolically held under the auspices of an American institution, seemed to some to constitute a potential target for the frustrations and discontent brewing in the region and in Tangier specifically.

And yet Tangier proved a particularly appropriate setting for such a meeting. Throughout its history, the city has served as a crossroads of cultures, civilizations, and religions. Its Jewish community reflects the realities of Jewish communities elsewhere in the Maghrib: cosmopolitan and local, ambulatory but also rooted in the environment, polyglot yet maintaining the particular linguistic characteristics of the region. Although the Jewish community has always been identified as a distinct religious group from the dominant Muslim majority, this mutually recognized separation, often more symbolic than practical, is what has enabled coexistence in daily life, allowing the culture of the Jews to reflect the larger Maghribi culture, even in its specificities. Tangier, historically and in the contemporary period, exemplifies both the ambivalence and openness, the interconfessional tensions and the cultural hybridity that anchored the themes and debates raised during the meeting. Given the potentially contentious nature of the subject, what was striking was the total absence of rancor, apologetics, or propaganda on a subject that had clearly come of age as an academic field. With the near-total disappearance of Jews from the Maghrib and their rapid fading even from memory, participants, with some objective distance from the subjects, felt no need to rationalize or defend the study of Jews and recognized the intrinsic importance of understanding the history of the Jewish presence in the Maghrib. Perhaps it is precisely their absence that makes the Jews' once-integral role in society and culture an important countervailing symbol for conceptualizing a more pluralistic and progressive North Africa, which is currently threatened by forces that reject cross-cultural and interconfessional exchange.

Historiographical Considerations

The chapters in this volume present new research on topics whose chronology stretches from late antiquity to the twenty-first century and that examine the role of memory throughout the long Jewish presence in North Africa. Taken as a corpus, they suggest fruitful new directions for research in the history, anthropology, language, and literature of the Jews of the Maghrib. It is particularly noteworthy that Maghribi scholars include senior scholars trying out Jewish topics for first time and younger scholars for whom the study of Jews is their primary focus. This group of scholars has introduced new texts and sources, deploying language skills not only in European languages and Arabic but in some cases in Berber (Tamazight)[7] and Hebrew. These chapters suggest a careful rethinking and revising of the existing scholarship on North African Jewish themes. A brief review of that literature is perhaps warranted.

The earliest attempt to write a comprehensive history of the Jews of the Maghrib dates to colonial Algeria in the nineteenth century. Based on an investigation of primary sources, Abraham Cahen, the chief rabbi of the province of Constantine, surveyed the history of North African Jews, beginning in antiquity and concluding prior to the colonial period.[8] In 1888, a scholarly survey on the history of the Jews of Tunisia was published by David Cazès,[9] a Moroccan-born teacher of the Alliance Israélite Universelle (AIU) in Tunis. It goes without saying that both works must be understood within their colonial context; they support the colonial project while advancing an agenda of modernization and emancipation for the Jews of the Maghrib.[10]

The most systematic research on the Jews of the Maghrib, however, dates from the first decade of the twentieth century. The work of Nahum Slouschz, the Russian-born, French-educated Orientalist, combines a wide variety of sources—texts, epigraphy, oral narratives, and so forth—and includes ethnographic observations based on his extensive travels throughout North Africa, from Libya to the Atlas Mountains in Morocco.[11] His observations and many monographs are invaluable repositories of information, though they are to be used with great caution since they were compiled with little critical analysis of the texts and are replete with anachronisms, including the use of personal observation of contemporary subjects as a basis for dubious historical reconstructions. Slouschz was a complicated individual who played multiple roles in the drama of colonial North Africa. He got his start as a researcher for the Mission Scientifique in Morocco and subsequently worked for French resident general Hubert Lyautey, who employed Slouschz for a period of time to devise a plan for the reform of the Moroccan Jewish community but abruptly let him go when his services were no longer desired.[12] Slouschz's body of scholarship reflects his identity as an individual who was both a part of and marginal to colonial rule; it is also deeply informed by his support for Zionism and the personal and professional ambitions he pursued in North Africa, the United States, and eventually Palestine, where he settled. Despite these caveats, it remains an important work. A third systematic effort to research the history of the Jews in the Maghrib in the colonial period is worth mentioning: *Les Juifs de l'Afrique du Nord; démographie & onomastique*, written by Maurice Eisenbeth, who served as chief rabbi in Algeria in the 1930s.

This culmination of his earlier work on the Jews of Constantine was published in 1936.

The pioneering and often erudite works on North African Jewish history produced in the colonial era, despite their methodological and sometimes ideological shortcomings, remain useful, as evidenced by the fact that they are cited repeatedly in contributions to this volume. Critical scholarship on the topic, however, began to appear in the postcolonial period only after the mass emigration of the Jews was well under way.

In the 1960s, Haim Zeev Hirshberg, an Israeli Orientalist, wrote the most comprehensive history of the Jews of North Africa to date. Like Slouschz, Hirshberg traveled widely in North Africa, albeit at a very different time and with a very different purpose. Hirschberg's observations during a semi-official mission to North Africa for several months in 1956, just prior to Moroccan and Tunisian independence, are particularly valuable since he was able to visit numerous smaller communities on the eve of their disappearance; his is the last glimpse on these Jews in situ.[13] In the 1960s, he published a two-volume history of the Jews of North Africa.[14] Unlike Slouschz, Hirschberg drew few historical conclusions from his encounters with the Jewish communities of the Maghrib; instead, he stuck to published sources and manuscripts in multiple languages, which he quoted liberally. While Hirschberg challenges some of the older hypotheses, most notably the theory of the Berber origins of Jews developed by Slouschz, the book as a whole is nonetheless undertheorized and is in many ways is a compilation of texts—some of doubtful historical value—rather than a rigorous historical analysis. This is particularly the case with the second volume, which treats each country of the Maghrib separately, tracing the political and diplomatic history of the Maghrib as it pertains to the region's Jews from the sixteenth century onward. Hirschberg's first volume is more directly concerned with the cultural, religious, and intellectual life of the Jewish communities, but he has little to say on these subjects after the Middle Ages, following common practice among most scholars of the Islamic world at the time, who typically understood cultural and intellectual life after the "classical" period as being in decline.

The analysis that Hirschberg's work lacks is precisely the focus of Haïm Zafrani's oeuvre. A Moroccan-born and -educated scholar and a leading educator for the Alliance Israélite Universelle in its transitional period following Moroccan independence, Zafrani pursued an academic career in France, though he always remained influential in Morocco, where his contributions were celebrated by a generation of scholars. Zafrani's work focused on post-Andalusian/post-expulsion Judaism and Jewish culture of the Maghrib, especially in Morocco in the period prior to colonial rule. Zafrani's first series of studies, which he pub-

lished in 1972 at a time when Morocco's Jewish community was steadily diminishing, was an effort to record the intellectual, cultural, and religious life of what
could be called the Moroccan Jewish patrimony as it was constituted in the years
following the expulsion of the Jews from Spain.

Though Zafrani's work was most influential in France and Morocco, it also
provided inspiration for the research on North African Jewry that was eventually undertaken in Israel. Of greatest interest to Israeli scholars were the Jewish communities that had emigrated to Israel from the more remote regions of
the Maghrib, particularly the rural Jews who lived among Berbers in the Atlas
Mountains in Morocco and the cave dwellers of the Gharian mountainous region
of Libya. Moshe Shokeid, Shlomo Deshen, Alex Weingrod, and Harvey Goldberg
were some of the more prominent scholars working in this area.[15] While their initial studies were informed by their own observations of the challenges of settlement and absorption in a new society, increasingly these scholars turned from
the ethnography of immigrants to historical ethnography, reconstructing Jewish
cultures and societies in the Maghrib, not only through the recollections of their
informants but also through the close and critical reading of texts: Harvey Goldberg's detailed account of Tripolitanian Jewry, which was based on the text of
Mordecai Cohen, who had once served as Nahum Slouschz's guide,[16] and Shlomo
Deshen's reconstruction of precolonial "mellah society," which was based on the
juridical writings of Morocco's well-known rabbis.[17]

Both Goldberg and Deshen were influenced by the work done by anthropologists, mainly Americans, working in Morocco and elsewhere in North Africa in the 1960s and 1970s. Although Jews were generally not the primary focus
of such research,[18] Muslim-Jewish relations was nonetheless an important component of these investigations, leading to interesting observations about still-
existent (though diminished) Jewish communities. Especially important was the
work of Clifford Geertz, who wrote about the complex interactions and inter-
dependencies between Jews and Muslims in Sefrou,[19] Lawrence Rosen, who stressed
the network of "dyadic" ties (over ethnic categories) in which personal connections between individuals facilitated cordial relations,[20] and Kenneth Brown,
who analyzed networks of social relations in the urban setting of Salé.[21]

The introduction of an anthropological perspective on Muslim-Jewish relations in Morocco generated a constructive debate with historians, including
most notably Norman Stillman, who takes anthropologists to task for ignoring
historical change and elaborates on the deep-rooted beliefs that shaped Muslim
attitudes toward Jews (as reflected in texts, popular culture, language, etc.)[22] or,
as anthropologist Henry Munson puts it, their inattention to "the distinction between belief and behavior."[23] Historical context as well as the great differences in
regions and within regions and between rural areas and major cities also proved

problematic in the attempt to construct a general model for Muslim-Jewish relations in Morocco or elsewhere in the Maghrib, for that matter. And yet Geertz was able to make a significant observation that Jews were simultaneously embedded in Jewish and Moroccan cultures.[24] Lucette Valensi and Avraham Udovitch make a similar observation in their historical and ethnographic study of the two Jewish communities on the island of Jerba, whose nuanced communal identities remained largely intact even after the departure of most Jews from Tunisia.[25]

In the 1970s and 1980s, linguistic and literary studies of the Jews in the Maghrib flourished, pioneered by a handful of North African–born Israeli scholars, many of whom had moved from other topics to the study of the Maghrib, thus introducing areas of inquiry that until then had been all but absent from the Eurocentric Israeli educational system at all levels. Their efforts reflected the changing cultural and political landscape in Israel itself, in which Jews of "Oriental" or "Mizrahi" (as Jews from the Middle East and North Africa are called, not unproblematically, in Israel)[26] background, who had long remained outside the mainstream of the dominant political culture in Israel, finally surpassed Ashkenazi Jews demographically; among the so-called Mizrahim, the Jews of the Maghrib formed the largest single segment. From the margins of Israeli society, Maghribi Jews, whose culture had been assigned little value beyond the exotic by the dominant Ashkenazi ethos, now began to explore their own rejected heritage, and they were soon joined by other groups from Asia and Africa. The hallmark of this new field was the founding of the journal *Pe'amim*, whose first issue was published in 1979.[27]

While in the past—and especially in the nineteenth century—the culture and society of the medieval Islamic world, especially Islamic Spain, occupied an important place in the development of modern Jewish studies as a whole, a connection between the present moment and the people who inhabited the Middle East and North Africa in the last several centuries was rarely made. As this new generation of scholars began to explore the more recent centuries of Jewish life in the Middle East and North Africa, they connected their individual backgrounds to a new collective understanding of the past. Illustrating this shift in emphasis is the work of Michel Abitbol, who authored and/or edited several works on the Jews of the precolonial and colonial Maghrib.[28] Taking a somewhat longer view, both Richard Ayoun and Paul Sebag, working on Algeria and Tunisia respectively,[29] began their inquiries in antiquity but focused on the modern period, especially on the transformations of colonial rule and the resulting political changes of the twentieth century. The history of the Jews of the Maghrib thus slowly began to be integrated into the history of Jews as whole: these studies explored how North African Jews were affected by the major forces that shaped the history of the Jews more generally in the modern world by examining the impacts of westernization,

modernity, Zionism, and even the Holocaust on the local level. While much progress was made during this period toward integrating non-Ashkenazi narratives
into broader history of the Jews, the task of completing the picture by connecting their stories to the larger history of the Maghrib still remained.

The Alliance Israélite Universelle was arguably the most influential agent
of change within the Jewish communities of the Maghrib in the nineteenth and
twentieth centuries. With a network of schools and educators that spanned the
Mediterranean basin, the AIU was able to inculcate most (though far from all)
members of the local Jewish communities with its radical plans for transform-
ing Jewish life in the various countries where it pursued its mission. Equally significant, at least for scholars, the AIU's headquarters in Paris maintains the most
important archive on the Jewish communities of the Mediterranean, which has
been much utilized by historians for decades. Michael Laskier wrote the first important work on Moroccan Jews that was based on the AIU archives.[30] More than
simply a study of the organization, Laskier wrote a history of the Moroccan Jewish communities in the modern period and their transformation as a result of
the AIU's intervention. Laskier later extended his research to North Africa as a
whole (including Egypt), examining the range of forces affecting Jewish communities and inexorably leading, in his view, to their mass departure in the twentieth century: westernization, pan-Arab nationalism, decolonization, Zionism and
the creation of the State of Israel.[31]

While the challenges of modernity and the changing political landscape were
certainly determinant factors in the history of the Jews in the Maghrib in the
nineteenth and twentieth centuries, researchers in the 1980s and 1990s began to
probe beyond the AIU's view of agency and regeneration, as reflected in their archives, as well as beyond the teleological narrative implicit in "the end of the tradition," as Bernard Lewis titles the last chapter of his book, *The Jews of Islam*.[32]
In his various studies of Maghribi Jewry from the eighteenth through the twentieth centuries, Yaron Tsur offers a more nuanced view of social transformation
of North African Jewish society during this period. Through an analysis of Jewish leadership in Tunisia, he has demonstrated that the transition from the precolonial to the colonial period was not a linear process but rather one that was
marked by continuities and ambivalences.[33] Other scholars, often of North African origin and equipped with the necessary linguistic skills and training in religious traditions to analyze pious and popular literature in Hebrew and Judeo-
Arabic—notably, Joseph Chetrit[34] and Moshe Bar Asher[35] in the area of language
and culture and Yossef Charvit[36] in the area of rabbinic discourse—began to explore the continuities, as opposed to the ruptures, of Maghribi Jewish culture in
the modern period, focusing on the ways that modernity interacted, coexisted,
and was assimilated into the quotidian culture of North African Jews rather than

simply replacing it, thus moving discussion on this theme beyond binary views of tradition and modernity.

Beginning in the 1970s, researchers in North Africa's national archives (in Morocco and Tunisia in particular) finally began to integrate the history of the Jews, especially the role they played in the economy, into regional narratives. While not typically the central focus of such studies, Jews nonetheless began to appear in works of North African historians as an important component of society in both rural and urban environments.[37] As Mohammed Kenbib mentions in his chapter in this volume, in the Muslim world, Moroccan scholars have led the way in studying the role Jews played in their country's history (which partly explains why this volume is bracketed by introductory and concluding chapters that focus on Morocco). This is not altogether surprising, given the fact that Morocco historically had the largest Jewish population in North Africa, in both absolute and proportional terms.[38] As elsewhere in the Islamic world, Moroccan Jews often played important intermediary roles in diplomacy, foreign commerce, and government finances in the precolonial period. Hence they appear frequently in records of the affairs of state. Previously such activities had been examined exclusively from foreign sources, but research in the state archives in Morocco has led Moroccan scholars to new interpretations of the roles Jews played in the history of their country.[39]

The distancing of Maghribi Jews from indigenous cultures, their identification—though always ambivalent and multivalent—with the colonial power, and their ultimate departure from the Maghrib has led some North African scholars to look deeper into the causes of this uprooting, particularly the impact of foreign penetration and the larger colonial project on Muslim-Jewish relations, revisiting some of the earlier questions from a nationalist perspective.[40] Yet research focusing specifically on the Jews remained, until very recently, the preserve of only a few North African scholars,[41] foremost among them Mohammed Kenbib. In several works,[42] Kenbib has problematized the rising tensions between Muslims and Jews in the modern era as an asymmetrical process that was instigated by colonization and catalyzed by the widening gap between the Western-looking *"alliancists"* and the mass of their "indigenous" co-religionists. Seen from the perspective of the Maghrib, the assumptions are reversed; the Jews did not necessarily "choose" to identify with Europe. Rather, Europe, in effect, chose them: the imposition of colonialism and modernity on the Maghrib directly led to the ultimate detachment and uprooting of Jews from these societies.

As Kenbib acknowledges in chapter 2 of this volume, major obstacles remain for Moroccans studying the Jewish history of their country—difficulties with sources, languages, methodology, and interpretation. There is also a pressing need to rethink the colonial historiography, which is still prominently featured in research on Moroccan Jews, and develop a more deeply contextualized understanding of Moroccan history in order to better understand its Jewish dimensions while at the same time avoiding falling prey to timeworn generalizations that often ignore difference and diversity within the Jewish communities.

In some sense the chapters in this volume confront the challenges that Kenbib has outlined for Morocco, extended to the region as a whole. They are written by a new generation of scholars that is studying communities that have all but disappeared from the Maghrib yet have hardly been forgotten. This was amply demonstrated by the passionate dialogue at the conference in Tangier, particularly the interventions by André Azoulay and the writer Edmond Amran El Maleh (in whose honor a Moroccan national foundation was created). Both men are important national figures in Morocco who have sought in their own unique ways to preserve a place in the national consciousness for this surviving Jewish community in the Maghrib. It is a community that is at once insulated yet dependent on Muslims, that is politically weak but able to maneuver in such a way as to cultivate a sense of superiority, and that has complicated relationships to France and Israel yet is unwavering in its Moroccanness.[43] Although the fact is shocking to any Moroccan over the age of 50, there are practically no Muslims living in the Maghrib today who interact with Jews. In fact, whole generations of North Africans have never even met a Jew; for these generations, the very notion of Jews as indigenous is an alien concept. Jews have become almost invisible in the Maghrib, yet for a new generation of researchers, they are everywhere part of the landscape: the objects of memory, nostalgia, and research.

It is striking how little we know about the origins and the early history of the Jewish presence in the Maghrib. Yet many of the chapters in this volume by North African historians reflect a deep engagement with the land, suggesting a more immediate connection to the spaces and places where Jews once lived and where their memory is still inscribed for those who care to look for it. As Farid Benramdane reveals, the traces of biblical names throughout the Algerian landscape suggest just how much the expansion of Islam was facilitated by the presence and influence of Jewish and Christian traditions. Sources on the ancient and medieval history of Jews in North Africa are likewise very sparse, and much of what has been written on these earlier periods is highly speculative, failing to disentangle myths of origin, legends, and anachronisms from the context in which they were produced. And yet Mabrouk Mansouri's illuminating study on Ibadi-Jewish relations in the early centuries of Islam in North Africa resourcefully examines new sources (or old sources in a new light), revealing the extent to which cultural and religious lines between Islam and non-Muslims were not initially as clearly drawn as they later became. Mansouri examines the conversion of indigenous Berbers to the Ibadiyya, a branch of the sectarian Kharajite movement in Islam, and their maintenance of a particular local cultural identity and, as a result, their complicated relationship with "orthodox" Arab Muslims. Within this context, his analysis of images of Jews in Ibadi texts unsettles conventional understandings of the transition to a "normative" Islam by highlighting Jewish cross-pollination and grounding it in North Africa's long and definitive experience of Kharijism.

As Islam spread throughout the Maghrib it encountered Jewish communities in every corner, often with origins dating from antiquity. Some had come from Palestine and points further east. Others, particularly in the far west, al-Maghrib al-Aqsa, had long thrived alongside Berber sectarian movements, as in Sijilmassa in southeastern Morocco. As the Maghrib and the Iberian Peninsula became more closely linked under Islamic rule, Jews emerged as an important component of the urban milieu, particularly in the dynastic centers where the usefulness of their transregional ties to their coreligionists in Europe was recognized and rewarded by Muslim authorities. We are generally better informed about the Jews in the earlier centuries of Islamic rule in the Maghrib, especially the tenth through the twelfth centuries, than in the centuries immediately following, thanks in large part to the Cairo Geniza. The extant documentation found there contains extensive correspondence from Qayrawan, Sijilmassa, and elsewhere in the Maghrib during this period. The Maghrib is of course an important setting in S. D. Goitein's *Mediterranean Society,* a work that inspired a generation of his own students as well as other scholars who have undertaken research on the medieval Maghrib based on the Geniza, including Norman Stillman,[44] Menahem Ben Sasson,[45] and Hmida Toukabri.[46]

Yet there are whole centuries during which we know very little about the actual lives and activities of the Jews. In the twelfth century, the rise and expansion of the Almohad dynasty, infamous for enforcing an intolerant Islam that prohibited Jews and Christians from practicing their religion in violation of the pact of protection (*dhimma*) accorded to the People of the Book, is a period about which little is known and few sources about Jews exist. While the Almohads are often held responsible for the extinction of indigenous Christians from the Maghrib and the forced conversion of the Jews (many of whom still practiced secretly), neither the duration of the persecution nor its geographical reach can be confirmed.[47] It is plausible that some Jews took refuge in the rural hinterlands of the western Maghrib, as is suggested by the existence of numerous communities throughout southern Morocco a few centuries later. But any attempt to trace the history of the many rural Jewish communities ends in a vacuum; we know little of their origins and history, the continuities of specific communities, migration patterns, and so forth. The many legends and myths of origin tell us more about the identity of Jews, Muslims, and others at the time the stories were produced than the actual experience or social conditions of these communities in earlier times.

Yet the histories of these rural communities and their complex relations with Muslims (at least during the last 200 years) are slowly becoming better known. Abdellah Larhmaid's study of the question of Jewish land ownership—or lack thereof—in the Sous region in southwest Morocco reveals how Jews rooted themselves to the local environment through their efforts to acquire land and resources or their associations with local religious figures. Yet the Muslim population perceived them as foreign migrants, as evidenced by the authorities' attempts to divest Jews of their property. But in just what sense were they foreigners? Larhmaid also shows how the authorities often buttressed their own Muslim identity through their control of Jewish property (or, in the case of the sultan, through the institutional control of the *jizya*) as guarantors of the pact of protection (*dhimma*). Through a close reading of new sources, Larhmaid is able to make fine distinctions between landownership in the residential quarters of towns (where Jews sometimes owned property) and landownership in agricultural areas, where Jewish property ownership was much more rare and precarious. In the nineteenth century, the growing influence of European commercial houses on Morocco's coasts and the efforts of the sultans to control the Sous and its trade facilitated an enhanced role for Jewish intermediaries, who were able to use their new influence to obtain land, a development that challenged the authority of both tribal and municipal leaders.

These changes were taking place in the Moroccan rural south just as Jews were being "discovered" by European travelers, such as John Davidson,[48] René Caillié,[49] and, most famously, Charles de Foucauld,[50] who left the most detailed account of the southern communities to date. The nature of these European sources was, of course, quite different from the local accounts, since these travelers' underlying purpose was reconnoitering as a prelude to conquest and as such they were linked to colonialist strategies. As Aomar Boum notes, nationalist historians have often dismissed the utility of these accounts because of their obvious biases and agendas. And yet if we ignore these sources and rely exclusively on nationalist histories of the southern regions, especially those of the prolific Mukhtar al-Susi, who published many volumes on the history and leading personalities of the Sous in the period after Moroccan independence, we are left with only silence about the Jews. In grappling with these gaps, Aomar Boum reflects on his own journey to southern Morocco—and to Akka in particular— where he discovers three distinctive yet interlocking voices seeking to represent Jews in southern Morocco: the colonial, the postcolonial nationalist, and the local tradition. These are not necessarily separate things: as Boum describes, local accounts reflect a clear recollection and understanding of the colonial production of knowledge.

From the countryside we move to the cities, the premier sites of cultural exchange and transition. These chapters build on an existing body of scholarship on Jewish-Muslim relations in the urban sphere, including work on Essaouira[51] and Marrakesh[52] by the present editors as well as notable studies on Sétif[53] and Batna,[54] among others already mentioned. While these studies are all historical or anthropological, the city is also considered from a literary perspective in this volume. In Philippe Barbé's study of Tunisian Jewish writer Albert Memmi, public spaces are revealed as a stage where all the ambivalences of Jewish-Muslim coexistence could be played out. A sense of confinement and isolation pervades Memmi's autobiographical novel *The Pillar of Salt,* which delves into the great difficulties of coexistence in the context of colonialism and anti-Semitism in the interwar years and during the German occupation of Tunis. And yet elsewhere Memmi admits to a kind of cultural syncretism, which is apparent in the very structure of his writing. As Barbé explains, it is often from fragmented identities that a truer image of coexistence can emerge.

Nowhere is this idea more clearly manifest than in Tangier, a cosmopolitan city with a long tradition of religious intermingling. As Susan Gilson Miller's study shows, the tremendous entrepreneurial growth that Tangier witnessed in the late nineteenth and early twentieth centuries drew heavily from an entrenched experience of intercommunal living. Moving to Fez, Stacey E. Holden's study hones in on a specific segment of urban economic life, namely the meat markets, and demonstrates that even in the realm of religious practice—the ritual slaughter of meat was performed by both Jews and Muslims—a space for interfaith coexistence and interdependency emerged. Finally, Saddek Benkada's study of the tumultuous history of Jewish life in Oran presents North African cities as both crossroads and frontiers. Oran was an integral part of the early modern Sephardi network. It harbored Sephardi refugees from 1492, including those fleeing the persecutions of Mawlay al-Yazid in North Morocco as well as those fleeing from Gibraltar. Whatever persecutions Jews suffered were always mitigated by their vital services to the economy, whether for the Spanish Crown or the western beylik of the Regency of Algiers. Hence, as Benkada shows, Jews were a crucial element in the Muhammad al-Kabir's policy of resettling Oran after the city was reconquered from the Spanish in 1792.

As Yaron Tsur's chapter shows, it was in this period of revival, the thriving decades after the reconquest of Oran and before the French colonial conquest, that the Western Sephardi diaspora of the Maghrib reached its peak, especially in Algeria. His argument persuasively overturns the often-cited hypothesis that the southern Mediterranean branch of this diaspora declined; the continued relevance of this group is often overshadowed by the global scope of the Europe-centered Western Sephardi network. Yet it was precisely during the period when the Hispanic Atlantic world was being eclipsed that this Western diaspora, located along the southern shores of the Mediterranean in the precolonial period, thrived most.

The social repercussions of Jews' prominence in large-scale trade registered particularly strongly in cities as centers of culture and places of contact with the larger Maghribi population. In Hadj Miliani's study of the careers of celebrated Jewish musicians in Algeria in the twentieth century, the cultural crossings are striking. Jewish musicians and their Muslim counterparts in Algeria (and the same could be said for Morocco and Tunisia) were bearers of a common heritage of Arabo-Andalusian music at the same time that they were mediators of culture in the traumatic encounter with colonialism. Even after Algerian Jews were naturalized by the Crémieux Decree of 1870 and many of them embraced Western habits as a means of distinguishing themselves from the Muslim masses, they remained integral to local Maghribi culture, especially in the world of music. Close cultural affinities and convivial personal relations existed between Muslims and Jews simultaneously with the recognition of religious limits and even alongside the collective disdain for the other, a mutual ambivalence that remained a constant theme throughout the history of the Maghrib and that cannot be whitewashed or willed away. Yet the contributions of Jews to the Maghribi musical tradition have endured, both in the Maghrib and in the diaspora communities where North African Jews continue to produce music in the Maghribi style. The incontestable Jewish element in this profoundly North African musical tradition stakes perhaps the strongest claim in Muslims' collective memory of Jews.

The simultaneity of inclusion and exclusion is dramatically borne out by the story of Sol, a.k.a. Suleika Hachuel, the martyr of Tangier, who continues to exert influence over imaginations both scholarly and literary. As Yaëlle Azagury shows in her analysis, a symbolic separation often existed between Jews and Muslims—a kind of imaginary mellah even in the absence of a physical boundary. The tragic story of Sol warns of the dangers of crossing these boundaries and serves as a cautionary tale. But at the same time, the story only makes sense and is only truly poignant if one recognizes how closely Jews and Muslims actually lived together, particularly in Tangier. Sharon Vance's chapter views the story of Suleika through a broader prism constructed not only of Jewish hagiographies but also of Spanish and French literature in which Sol's story was a lightning rod for contemporary debates about gender, anti-Semitism, and the so-called Jewish question while at the same time reflecting prevailing European attitudes toward Muslims and colonial expansion. While Suleika may no longer be remembered in the non-Jewish Mediterranean world, she remains firmly implanted in Moroccan Jewish consciousness (and perhaps in a more limited way among Moroccan Muslims as well). Even in the diaspora she continues to inspire, as writer Ruth Knafo Setton's insightful search for Suleika shows: the author's own border crossings and the challenge of reconstituting her identity from within the fragmented world of exile clearly resonate with Sol's experience.

The onslaught of colonialism and the imposition of Western-style modernity, which the AIU schools wrought with particular efficacy in Morocco and Tunisia and the secular French educational system wrought in Algeria, transformed all aspects of the Jewish communities of North Africa: religious expression, vocational patterns, culture, language, gender conventions, and relations with Muslims. The AIU has received considerable attention, yet the three studies in this volume reveal that there is still much to say. The significance of gender and the AIU, first introduced in an earlier article by Susan Gilson Miller,[55] is here drawn out in detail in the respective contributions by Joy A. Land and Keith Walters. Land underscores the radical change brought by the women of the AIU in Tunisia, who constituted the community's first cadre of modern female Jewish professionals and withstood the ramifications, some surprising, of that status. Walters, meanwhile, focuses on gender roles as reified through language. Drawing from Bourdieu's notion of symbolic capital, he investigates the value of French, the language of the colonizer, to Jews as they positioned themselves in relationship to the Muslim population.[56] In the process he shows how Jewish women served as a conduit for the spread of French among Muslim women. Jonathan G. Katz, finally, takes an in-depth look at one particular AIU school in Marrakesh, painstakingly tracing points of resistance to the Alliance, showing that the path of the AIU's penetration of Morocco was more bumpy than many have assumed and that its links to the colonial enterprise were likewise far from uncomplicated.

Jews' longstanding habit of maneuvering between local authorities and foreign powers persevered in the colonial period but in the context of new conjunctures and ruptures with the past. World War II was a particularly crucial turning point, as we see in Fayçal Cherif's study. Tensions between the Muslim and Jewish communities in Tunisia, already simmering over French colonial policy and the Tunisian nationalists' position on the Palestine question, were greatly exacerbated by the war. Whereas Jews had everything to lose by the arrival of Nazism, some Muslims saw the potential for a new order that might liberate them from the grip of colonization. The events of the war can be seen as a turning point in Muslim-Jewish relations elsewhere in the Maghrib as well. Against the backdrop of the struggle for Palestine and the emergence of the State of Israel in 1948 and national liberation struggles and decolonization processes closer to home, many Jews were forced to make the difficult choice between emigration and an uncertain future in the nascent independent states. As Jamaâ Baïda's chapter asks with respect to Morocco, do not the Jews, in their presence as well as their absence, test the limits and legitimacy of national identity in the postcolonial context, not just for minorities but for all citizens?

Nowhere in the Maghrib does the uprooting of Jews appear to be so complete as in Algeria, where for all intents and purposes the entire Jewish community was "repatriated" to France in the wake of Algerian independence in 1962. Yet the political turmoil at the end of the twentieth century awakened a sense that Algeria was in fact a much more pluralistic country than the postindependence rhetoric of the Algerian state would lead one to believe. Belcacem Mebarki shows, quite amazingly, that Jews remained in Algeria after independence to a much greater extent than is conventionally believed. Mebarki offers a touching and humorous portrait of Zouzef Tatayou (Joseph the Taylor), the last Jew in the small city of Nedroma in western Algeria, who quite simply refused to leave.

In passing, Mebarki notes that the Jews' "excessive" veneration of saints was well known in Nedroma, and as Benramdane shows, many of these figures were of biblical origin. As Oren Kosansky shows in the Moroccan context, the rhetorical way this particular aspect of Judeo-Islamic hybridity is represented deserves further scrutiny; indeed, he finds that it has been an important element in imagining and constituting the Moroccan nation under French rule and as an independent liberal nation-state in the postcolonial era. In the colonial context, the more pagan aspect of the religious syncretism of saint veneration became a symbol of Moroccanness in line with the French project of privileging the Berbers as the "original" Moroccans and displacing Arab-Islamic identity. In independent Morocco, the idea of joint Jewish and Muslim pilgrimage became emblematic of a liberal and religiously tolerant nation, one that emphasizes Jewish-Arab coexistence (while simultaneously supplanting the Berber element). New pilgrimages developed into a symbol of Moroccan authenticity. Mebarki and Benramdane also seem to imply that Judeo-Muslim syncretism is a means through which contemporary Algerians can imagine a more pluralistic country. Kosansky's chapter constitutes a significant exception to one of the more dramatic trends in the direction of scholarship about North African Jews: interest in ritual and the sacral life, once a central concern of scholars, has clearly waned, even as the North African Jewish diaspora itself exhibits ever-increasing levels of religiosity and adopts new forms of practice (particularly the embrace of Hasidism). In the capable hands of Kosansky, however, what was once treated as the topic of salvage anthropology or included in ethnographic lists of "exotic" Jewish practice becomes a powerful argument that transnational Moroccan Judaism continues to be relevant.

* * *

This volume is intended to contribute equally to the fields of Jewish studies and Maghribi studies, which, not coincidentally, constitute our own areas of specialization. But that is not to say it is intended as a bridge between two separate disciplines or fields, for that initial goal has, for the most part, already been met. Whereas only a generation ago scholars interested in such topics had to choose whether to pursue careers in Jewish *or* Middle Eastern Studies, the intrinsic link between the two is finally receiving institutional recognition in the United States and elsewhere. Although still in its infancy, the study of Judeo-Islamic societies and cultures is growing, along with new faculty and students who no longer need to suppress one part of their academic profiles in favor of another. Historically on the margins of both Middle Eastern Studies and Jewish Studies, scholars of the Maghrib have been perhaps less constrained by the boundaries that still often obscure the obvious connection between the two fields. The contributions in this volume begin from the premise that the most fruitful inquiry is one that integrates the study of Muslim and Jewish culture in a shared historical space.

That said, this volume might usefully address important research agendas specific to each field. In terms of Jewish history, an obvious goal is to continue to integrate more of the non-European narrative into what is still a decidedly Ashkenazi-centric field, particularly in relation to the modern period. Along these lines, this volume pays considerable attention to the encounter between European and North African Jews in the colonial era. Understanding just what bound and what separated Jews as they moved into uncertain futures provides us with a fuller view of the multiple trajectories of Jewish history. The same holds true in North African studies: recognizing that Jews were an influential minority population on both sides of the imperial equation unsettles common assumptions about how colonial hegemony actually became established and functioned in the region. In Morocco particularly, as postcolonial scholarship begins to give way to postnationalist sensibilities, a transition evident in the chapters by Kenbib and Boum, the concerns have become even more immediate: What does memory of the Jews consist of in a land now bereft of them, and what about the minorities who remain, such as the Berbers, who once coexisted with Jews but now help signify their present absence?

Far too many books, articles, and movies begin with a gerund these days, but in this case we are consciously hopeful for the continuity the title of our introduction suggests. We are gratified by the contributions here yet remain convinced that there is still much left to think, and rethink, about Jewish culture and society in North Africa.

NOTES

1. Some of the papers presented at this conference were published in Michel Abitbol, ed., *Judaïsme d'Afrique du Nord aux xixe–xxe siècles* (Jerusalem: Institut Ben-Zvi, 1980) (in French and Hebrew).

2. Michel Abitbol, ed., *Communautés juives de marges sahariennes du Maghreb* (Jerusalem: Institut Ben-Zvi, (1982) (in French and Hebrew); Michel Abitbol, ed., *Relations judéo-musulmanes au Maroc: perceptions et réalités* (Paris: Stavit, 1997).

3. *Juifs du Maroc: identité et dialogue: actes du colloque international sur la communauté juive marocaine: vie culturelle, histoire sociale et évolution, Paris, 18–21 décembre 1978* (Grenoble: La Penseé sauvage, 1980).

4. Since the meeting of the American Institute for Maghrib Studies in Tangier, another major meeting on the Jews of the Maghrib took place in Paris in November 2008, organized by La Société d'Histoire des Juifs de Tunisie, on the theme "Les Juifs du Maghreb de l'époque coloniale à nos jours: Histoire, mémoire et écritures du passé."

5. *Histoire communautaire, histoire plurielle: la communauté juive de Tunisie. Actes du colloque de Tunis organisé les 25–26–27 février 1998 à la faculté de la Manouba* (Tunis: Centre de Publication Universitaire, 1999).

6. See, e.g., Craig S. Smith, "A Long Fuse Links Tangier to Bombings in Madrid," *New York Times*, 28 March 2004.

7. The term Tamazight also refers specifically to the Berber dialect spoken in the Middle Atlas and parts of the High Atlas Mountains, but increasingly it is being used more generically for Berber. It is derived from the term Amazigh (pl. Imazighen), the indigenous term used to refer to Berbers. Both terms are used throughout the following chapters.

8. Abraham Cahen, *Les Juifs dans l'Afrique septentrionale* (Constantine, 1867).

9. David Cazès, *Essai sur l'histoire des Israélites de Tunisie* (Paris: Librairie Armand Durlacher, 1888).

10. Colette Zytnicki, "David Cazès (1850–1913), historien des Juifs de Tunisie: un 'métis culturel'?" *Outre-Mers* 94, nos. 352–353 (2006): 97–106; Colette Zytnicki, "Entrer dans l'histoire: les premiers historiens des Juifs d'Afrique du Nord (milieu XIXe siècle–début XXe siècle)," in *Enjeux d'histoire, jeux de mémoire: les usages du passé juif*, ed. Jean-Marc Chouraqui, Gilles Dorival, and Colette Zytnicki (Paris: Maisonneuve & Larose, 2006), 301–314.

11. Of Nahum Slouschz's many publications, see especially *Un voyage d'études juives en Afrique* (Paris: Imprimarie Nationale, 1999); and "Hébræo-Phéniciens et Judéo-Berbères," *Archives Marocaines* 14 (1908).

12. Daniel J. Schroeter and Joseph Chetrit, "Emancipation and Its Discontents: Jews at the Formative Period of Colonial Rule in Morocco," *Jewish Social Studies* 13, no. 1 (2006): 181–187. On Slouschz's various activities, see Harvey Goldberg, "The Oriental and the Orientalist: The Meeting of Mordecai Ha-Cohen and Nahum Slouschz," *Jewish Culture and History* 7 (2004): 1–30.

13. H. Z. Hirschberg, *Me-erets mevo ha-shemesh; ʿim yehude Afrikah ha-tsefonit be-artsotehem* (Jerusalem: Ha-Maklakah le-ʿInyene ha-Noʿar veha-Haluts shel ha-Histadrut ha-Tsiyonit, 1957).

14. Haim Zeev Hirshberg, *Toldot ha-Yehudim be-Afrikah ha-Tsefonit*, 2 vols. (Jerusalem: Mosad Bialik, 1965); translated as *A History of the Jews in North Africa*, vol. 1, *From Antiquity to the Sixteenth Century* (Leiden: Brill 1974) and *A History of the Jews in North Africa*, vol. 2, *From the Ottoman Conquests to the Present Time* (Leiden: Brill, 1981).

15. Alex Weingrod, *Reluctant Pioneers: Village Development in Israel* (Ithaca, N.Y.: Cornell University Press, 1966); Shlomo A. Deshen and Moshe Shokeid, *The Predicament of Homecoming: Cultural and Social Life of North African Immigrants in Israel* (Ithaca, N.Y.: Cornell University Press, 1974); Moshe Shokeid, *The Dual Heritage: Immigrants from the Atlas Mountains in an Israeli Village* (Manchester: Manchester University Press, 1971); Harvey E. Goldberg, *Cave Dwellers and*

Citrus Growers: A Jewish Community in Libya and Israel (Cambridge: Cambridge University Press, 1972).

16. Mordekhai Ha-Cohen, *The Book of Mordechai: A Study of the Jews of Libya.* = *Selections from the Highid Mordekhai of Mordechai Hakohen: Based on the Complete Hebrew Text as Published by the Ben-Zvi Institute Jerusalem*, ed. and trans. with intro. and commentaries by Harvey E. Goldberg (Philadelphia, Pa.: Institute for the Study of Human Issues, 1980).

17. Shlomo Deshen, *The Mellah Society: Jewish Community Life in Sherifian Morocco* (Chicago: University of Chicago Press, 1989).

18. A noted exception is the study of the Ghardaia Jewish community of the Mzab region by Lloyd Cabot Briggs and Norina Lami Guáede: *No More Forever: A Saharan Jewish Town*, Papers of the Peabody Museum of Archaeology and Ethnology, Harvard University 55, no. 1 (Cambridge: Peabody Museum of Archaeology and Ethnology, 1964). The study was conducted shortly before the community's disappearance, and this exercise in "salvage ethnography" tends to treat the community as "exotic" and lacks a broader or comparative perspective. For a critical discussion of this work, see Harvey E. Goldberg, "Tripolitanian Jewish Communities: Cultural Boundaries and Hypothesis Testing," *American Ethnologist* 1, no. 4 (1974): 619–621.

19. Clifford Geertz, "Suq: The Bazaar Economy in Sefrou," in *Meaning and Order in Moroccan Society: Three Essays in Cultural Analysis*, ed. Hildred Geertz, Clifford Geertz, and Lawrence Rosen (Cambridge: Cambridge University Press, 1979), 164–172.

20. Lawrence Rosen, *Bargaining for Reality: The Construction of Social Relations in a Muslim Community* (Chicago: University of Chicago Press, 1984), 148–163.

21. Kenneth L. Brown, "Mellah and Madina: A Moroccan City and Its Jewish Quarter (Salé ca. 1880–1930)," in *Studies in Judaism and Islam*, ed. Shelomo Morag (Jerusalem, 1981), 253–281.

22. Norman A. Stillman, "The Moroccan Jewish Experience; A Revisionist View," *Jerusalem Quarterly* 9 (Fall 1978): 111–123.

23. Henry Munson, "Muslim and Jew in Morocco: Reflections on the Distinction between Belief and Behavior," *Poznan Studies in the Philosophy of the Sciences and the Humanities* 48 (1996): 357–379.

24. Geertz, "Suq," 164–165.

25. Abraham L. Udovitch and Lucette Valensi, *The Last Arab Jews: The Communities of Jerba Tunisia* (Chur: Harwood, 1984).

26. Ella Shohat, "The Narrative of the Nation and the Discourse of Modernization: The Case of the Mizrahim," *Critique* 10 (Spring 1997): 3–18; H. Hever, Y. Shenhav, and P. Motzafi-Haller, eds., *Mizrahim in Israel: A Critical Observation into Israel's Ethnicity* (Tel Aviv: Van Leer Jerusalem Institute and HaKibbutz HaMeuchad Publishing House, 2002).

27. On these historiographical questions in Israel, see Yaʿakov Barnai, "Yehude artsot ha-Islam be-'et ha-hadasha ve-ha-'eskolah ha-Yerushalmit'," *Peʿamim* 92 (2002): 98–99; Yaron Tsur, "ha-Historiografyah ha-Yisraelit ve-ha-baʿayah ha-ʿedatit," *Peʿamim* 94–95 (2003): 26–33; Norman Stillman, "Me-Heker ha-Mizrah u-mehokhmat Yisrael le-rav-tahumiyut: hitpathut mehkar Yehadut Sefarad ve-ha-Mizrah," *Peʿamim* 94–95 (2003): 66–71.

28. See note 1 above; and Michel Abitbol, *The Jews of North Africa during the Second World War* (Detroit, Mich.: Wayne State University Press, 1989); Michel Abitbol, *Tug'ar al-sultan: ʿilit kalkalit Yehudit be-Maroko* (Jerusalem: Institut Ben-Zvi, 1994); Michel Abitbol, *Le passé d'une discorde: Juifs et Arabes depuis le VIIe siècle* (Paris: Perrin, 1999).

29. Richard Ayoun and Bernard Cohen, *Les Juifs d'Algérie: deux mille ans d'histoire* (Paris: Jean-Claude Lattès, 1982); Paul Sebag, *Histoire des Juifs de Tunisie: des origines à nos jours* (Paris: L'Harmattan, 1991).

30. Michael M. Laskier, *The Alliance Israélite Universelle and the Jewish Communities of Morocco, 1862–1962* (Albany: State University of New York Press, 1983). Aron Rodrigue also included material on Morocco in his study of the correspondence of AIU teachers: *Jews and Muslims: Images of Sephardi and Eastern Jewries in Modern Times* (Seattle: University of Washington Press, 2003).

31. Michael Laskier, *North African Jewry in the Twentieth Century: The Jews of Morocco, Tunisia, and Algeria* (New York: New York University Press, 1994).

32. Bernard Lewis, *The Jews of Islam* (Princeton, N.J.: Princeton University Press, 1984).

33. See, e.g., Yaron Tsur, "L'époque coloniale et les rapports 'ethniques' au sein de la communauté juive en Tunisie," in *Mémoires juives d'Espagne et du Portugal*, ed. Esther Benbassa (Paris: Publisud, 1996); Yaron Tsur, "Haskala in a Sectional Colonial Society: Mahdia (Tunisia) 1884," in *Sephardi and Middle Eastern Jewries: History and Culture in the Modern Era*, ed. Harvey E. Goldberg (Bloomington: Indiana University Press, 1996), 146–167; Yaron Tsur, "Jewish 'Sectional Societies' in France and Algeria on the Eve of the Colonial Encounter," *Journal of Mediterranean Studies* 4 (1994): 263–277; and Yaron Tsur, "Yehadut Tunisya be-shilhe ha-tekufah ha-teromkolonialit," *Miqqedem Umiyyam* 3 (1990): 77–113.

34. Joseph Chetrit has published numerous articles on the Jews of the Maghrib, including in a journal he founded and edited, *Miqqedem Umiyyam* [*mi-Kedem u-Miyam*]. Volume 8 is a monograph devoted to Jewish marriage in Morocco: Joseph Chetrit et al., *Ha-Khatunah ha-yehudit ha-mesortit be-Maroko: perake 'iyun ve-te'ud* (Haifa: Universitat Hayfa, ha-Fakultah le-Mad'e ha-Ru'ah ve-ha-Merkaz le-Heker ha-Tarbut ha-Yehudit be-sefarad u-be-Artsot ha-Islam, 2003). Other studies by Chetrit on North African Jewish culture and its transformation include "Moderniyut le'umit ʿivrit mul moderniyut tsarfatit: ha-haskalah ha-ʿivrit be-Tsefon Afrika be-sof ha-me'ah ha-19," *Miqqedem Umiyyam* 3 (1990): 11–76; Joseph Chetrit, *Piyut ve-shirah be-yahadut Maroko: asupat mehkarim ʿal shirim ve-ʿal meshorerim* (Jerusalem: Mosad Bialik; Ashkelon: ha-Mikhlalah ha-Ezorit, 1999); Joseph Chetrit, "Discours et modernité dans les communautés juives d'Afrique du Nord à la fin du XIXᵉ siècle," in *Transmission et passages en monde juif*, ed. Esther Benbassa (Paris: Publisud, 1997), 378–400; and Joseph Chetrit, "ha-Teʾatron ha-yehudi, perek be-naftule ha-modernizatsiyah shel Yehadut Maroko," in *Maroko*, ed. Haim Sadoun (Jerusalem: Makhon Ben-Tsevi le-Heker Kehilot Yisra'el be-Mizrah, 2003), 213–226.

35. Moshe Bar-Asher, *La composante hébraïque du judéo-arabe algérien: communautés de Tlemcen et Aïn-Témouchent* (Jerusalem: The Hebrew University Magnes Press, 1992); Moshe Bar-Asher, *Masorot u-leshonot shel Yehude Tsefon-Afrikah* (Jerusalem: Mosad Bialik; Ashkelon: Ha-mikhlalah Ha-ezorit, 1999). Bar-Asher's studies also appear in the journal *Massorot*, which he edited.

36. Yossef Charvit, *La France, l'élite rabbinique d'Algérie et la Terre Sainte au XIXe siècle: tradition et modernité* (Paris: Champion, 2005); Yossef Charvit, *Elite rabbinique d'Algérie et modernisation, 1750–1914* (Jerusalem: Editions Gaï Yinassé, 1995).

37. For Morocco, see Ahmad Tawfiq, *al-Mujtamaʿ al-Maghribi fi al-qarn al-tasiʿ ʿashar: (Inulatan, 1850–1912)*, 2nd ed. (Rabat: Kulliyat al-Adab wa-al-ʿUlum al-Insaniya, 1983); ʿUmar Afa, *Mas'alat al-nuqud fi tarikh al-Maghrib fi al-qarn al-tasiʿ ʿashar: Sus, 1822–1906* (Agadir: Jamiʿat al-Qadi 'Iyad Kulliyat al-Adab wa-al-'Ulum al-Insaniya, 1988); ʿUmar Afa, *Tarikh al-Maghrib al-muʿasir: dirasat fi al-masadir wa-l-mujtamaʿ wa-l-iqtisad* (Rabat: Manshurat Kulliyat al-Adab wa-al-ʿUlum al-Insaniya, 2001); and ʿUmar Afa, *al-Tijara al-Maghribiya fi al-qarn al-tasiʿ ʿashar: al-binyat wa-l-tahawwulat, 1830–1912* (Rabat: Dar al-Aman, 2006). For Tunisia, see, e.g., Abdelhamid Larguèche, *Les ombres de Tunis: pauvres, marginaux et minorités aux XVIIIe et XIXe siècles* (Paris: Arcantères; Tunis: Centre de Publication Universitaire, 2000).

38. In the twentieth century, Morocco had a Jewish population of 250,000–280,000, more than any other Arab state and more than the rest of the Maghrib combined.

39. For example, in studying British-Moroccan relations. See Khalid Ben Srhir, *Britain and Morocco during the Embassy of John Drummond Hay, 1845–1886* (London: RoutledgeCurzon, 2005) (translated from Arabic).

40. The most trenchant critique of the colonial historiography from a nationalist perspective is by Abdallah Laroui, *Les origines sociales et culturelles du nationalisme marocain (1830–1912)* (Paris: Maspero, 1977).

41. It is also worth noting that several films have recently been made in North Africa that deal with the topic of indigenous Jews and intercommunal relations. These include *Goodbye,*

Mothers, directed by Mohamed Ismail, and *Where Are You Going, Moshe?* written, directed, and produced by Hassan Benjelloun.

42. Mohammed Kenbib, *Juifs et Musulmans au Maroc, 1859–1948* (Rabat: Université Mohammed V, Publications de la Faculté des Lettres et des Sciences Humaines, 1994); Mohammed Kenbib, "Les relations judéo-musulmanes au Maroc, 1860–1945: essai bibliographique," *Hespéris-Tamuda* 23 (1985): 83–104; Mohammed Kenbib, "Recherches sur les Juifs du Maroc. Esquisse de bilan," in *Les sciences humaines et sociales au Maroc. Etudes et arguments* (Rabat: Institut Universitaire de la Recherche Scientifique, 1998).

43. André Levy, "Notes on Jewish-Muslim Relationships: Revisiting the Vanishing Moroccan Jewish Community," *Cultural Anthropology* 18, no. 3 (2003): 365–397.

44. Norman A. Stillman, "East-West Relations in the Islamic Mediterranean in the Early Eleventh Century: A Study of the Geniza Correspondence of the House of Ibn 'Awkal" (Ph.D. diss., University of Pennsylvania, 1970).

45. Menahem Ben-Sasson, *Tsemihat ha-kehilah ha-yehudit be-artsot ha-Islam: Kairawan, 800–1057* (Jerusalem: Magnes, 1996).

46. Hmida Toukabri, *Les Juifs dans la Tunisie médiévale, 909–1057: d'après les documents de la Geniza du Caire* (Paris: Romillat, 2002).

47. See Menahem Ben Sasson, "On the Jewish Identity of Forced Converts: A Study of Forced Conversion in the Almohad Period," *Pe'amim* 42 (1990): 16–37 (in Hebrew). The presumed disappearance of indigenous Christians during the Almohad period is not well substantiated by sources either. For an argument against the notion that persecutions were of long duration, see David Corcos, "Le-Ofi yahasm shel shalite ha-Almohadun le-Yehudim," *Tsion* 32 (1967): 137–160, republished in David Corcos, *Studies in the History of the Jews of Morocco* (Jerusalem: Rubin Mass, 1976), 319–342.

48. John Davidson, *Notes Taken during Travels in Africa* (London: J. L. Cox and Sons, 1839).

49. René Caillié, *Travels through Central Africa to Timbuctoo; and across the Great Desert, to Morocco, Performed in the Years 1824–1828* (London: H. Colburn and R. Bentley, 1830).

50. Charles de Foucauld, *Reconnaissance au Maroc, 1883–1884* (Paris: Challamel, 1888).

51. Daniel J. Schroeter, *Merchants of Essaouira: Urban Society and Imperialism in Southwestern Morocco, 1844–1886* (Cambridge: Cambridge University Press, 1988); Daniel J. Schroeter, *The Sultan's Jew: Morocco and the Sephardi World* (Stanford, Calif.: Stanford University Press, 2002).

52. Emily Gottreich, *The Mellah of Marrakesh: Jewish and Muslim Space in Morocco's Red City* (Bloomington: Indiana University Press, 2007).

53. Joëlle Bahloul, *The Architecture of Memory: A Jewish-Muslim Household in Colonial Algeria, 1937–1962* (Cambridge: Cambridge University Press, 1996).

54. Elizabeth Friedman, *Colonialism and After: An Algerian Jewish Community* (South Hadley, Mass.: Bergin and Garvey, 1988).

55. Susan Gilson Miller, "Gender and the Poetics of Emancipation: The *Alliance Israélite Universelle* in Northern Morocco, 1890–1912," in *Franco-Arab Encounters,* ed. L. Carl Brown and Mathew Gordon (Beirut: AUB Press, 1996), 229–258.

56. Joëlle Bahloul makes similar observations about language as a mechanism for cultural distancing among Jews in Algeria in *The Architecture of Memory,* 85–89.

2

Muslim-Jewish Relations in Contemporary Morocco

Mohammed Kenbib

A few preliminary remarks should be made about contemporary Moroccan history and the prevailing disequilibrium between the considerable number of doctoral dissertations dealing with precolonial times and the low levels of interest in the protectorate era among Moroccan scholars.[1] First, it is obvious that not much can be said about the Jewish dimensions of Moroccan history and culture during the nineteenth and twentieth centuries if no attention is paid to the general historical context. The second remark concerns researchers' interest in the positions held and roles played by the Jewish communities of Morocco throughout the centuries. Most researchers in the field of Moroccan history have encountered this topic in one way or another, whatever the period they are dealing with. They inevitably "come across" Jews when dealing with subjects such as tribes, urban history, makhzan (Moroccan government) institutions, trade, drought and epidemics, foreign relations, reforms, printing, presses, modernization, colonial penetration, shifts in natives' perceptions of "Christians," and so on.

Nevertheless, one can wonder whether enough attention has been paid to actual events concerning the Jews in particular and their relationship to the Muslim environment in general. In other words, have the social functions and roles of Jews as part of Moroccan society been sufficiently and objectively examined and assessed? Even though it seems difficult to answer such a question, a quick evaluation of the dissertations available at the Faculté des Lettres in Rabat and elsewhere in Morocco shows that these aspects of Moroccan history have not been completely neglected.[2] Yet they have been approached with a great deal of caution.

The scholarly encounter with Jews and acknowledgment of their contribution to Morocco's history are important achievements. Since the end of the 1960s and early 1970s, Moroccan scholars have played a pioneering role in these areas.

They have paved the way for historians and other scholars in the rest of the Arab and Muslim world. Tunisian scholars, for example, are following in their path and have started to explore the intercommunal past of their country.³ Nevertheless, studies dealing with the Jewish dimensions of Moroccan history and culture will have to overcome methodological, conceptual, and technical obstacles.

First of all, researchers must solve the problem of locating the sources they need and accessing archives. Most of the relevant sources are inaccessible to Moroccan scholars beginning their research. Dispersion is, indeed, one of the striking features of sources about Moroccan Jews. While bibliographies do exist, no precise or exhaustive inventory enumerating bibliographical and other data required for such studies is available.⁴ Linguistic obstacles are also a challenge for researchers. Sources exist in numerous languages, another hallmark of Moroccan Jewish studies. Texts in Moroccan Judeo-Arabic written in the Hebrew alphabet and Hebrew-language works require considerable technical linguistic knowledge, which a diminishing number of people possess. Although a small but gradually growing number of Moroccan scholars have competence in Hebrew, many important sources that could help better integrate the study of Jews in Moroccan history remain untranslated and inaccessible to most.⁵

Even for scholars familiar with Hebrew, obstacles remain for exploiting highly specialized texts, such as responsa literature. According to Shlomo Deshen, author of an important book on the Jews of precolonial Morocco,⁶ "the usage of rabbinical responsa material is fraught with problems of interpretation. . . . Since it is written in the language and terminology of Talmudic scholasticism, interpreting the responsa requires specific literary skills. One common pitfall of rabbinical responsa research is the failure to recognize the appearance of stylized expressions. . . . The responsa are replete with stock phrases, which superficially seem to express particular circumstances of time and space, and apparently constitute grist for the social historian's mill."⁷

Parallels can be drawn between responsa literature and the way Muslim clerics and their like—ʿulama (clerics or scholars), fuqaha (jurists), and other talaba (scholars or students)—used to think and write about the Jews. Their fatwas (formal legal opinions), nawazil (compilations of legal rulings), letters, and books present a second, related group of difficulties contemporary Moroccan researchers encounter. Issues concerning the dhimmis are examined in the writings of the religious elite from a perspective (and using a terminology) in which religious discourse is prominent. In pre-protectorate Morocco, the emphasis on the legal condition of the Jews in works by the ʿulama, the qadis (judges), the muhtasibs (market superintendents), and scholars with a traditional background may be confusing. The fatwas and other texts referring to intangible stipulations and rigid exegesis written in specific contexts can often be misleading. They remain ahistorical and obscure the gap that has existed throughout history between Islamic scriptural provisions and the real conditions of daily life. Close scrutiny of the different eras of Moroccan history shows that the interpretations and implementation of the original text known as the "Pact of ʿUmar" (the model for the theoretical legal status of non-Muslim "people of the book") was constantly fluctuating and that little uniformity existed in the views and behavior of the rulers and the ʿulama. Changing political, economic, social, and environmental conditions (e.g., drought, epidemics, and other calamities) shaped the foundations and features of Muslim-Jewish relations. Even in holy cities such as Fez and in *zawiyas* (or pilgrimage centers) such as Ouezzane, Boujad, and Iligh, the conditions that shaped the relationship between the interpretation of the legal status of Jews and the realities of daily life varied depending on local circumstances and exigencies.[8]

Taking such texts at face value may lead to ahistorical understandings. It would certainly be wrong to conclude on the basis of some quotations and the sophisticated arguments they refer to that Jews in Morocco were simply a "tolerated" minority living at the margins of the community of "true believers" and therefore had no impact or influence on politics, society, and culture.[9]

Misinterpretations of this kind are common in Europeans' historical writing in the precolonial and colonial periods and in writings dealing with Moroccan Jews. Charles de Foucauld, for instance, and some other ethnographers presented Jewish realities in Morocco through clichés and caricatured profiles, the product of their own latent of explicit anti-Semitism combined with a static understanding of Moroccan Jewish history.[10] However, such "distortions" do not mean that their descriptions and comments were systematically incorrect or inappropriate.

For these fundamental reasons, rethinking Jewish culture and society in Morocco means necessarily revisiting the well-known and often-cited texts of the precolonial period that often became an integral part of colonial historiography. This is a sine qua non if one is to avoid the stereotypes and biases found in the scholarly and popular writings about Moroccan Jews dating from the precolonial and colonial period. Otherwise, parts or fragments of anachronistic and irrelevant perceptions and ideas will continue to be conveyed, nolens volens, in our writings.

It should be added that such a rethinking implies as a preliminary step not only an accurate assessment of the importance of the Jewish dimension of Moroccan history and culture throughout the ages but also greater insight into the general historical context in order to shed light on Jewish communities. That is, an internal, or domestic, investigation of Moroccan history is necessary in order to understand and hopefully explain the Jews' preoccupations and perspectives from within—how the so-called mellah (the name for the Jewish quarter and by extension the Jewry of a given community) societies functioned. However, if we consider the institutional and other constraints hampering historical research in Moroccan universities, we realize that the ability to achieve this kind of comprehensive insight is limited. How can we hope to deepen our understanding of the place of Jews within their native society in the absence of an internally focused approach?

The fact that Jews did not constitute a homogeneous or even monolithic ethnic and religious bloc is one of the difficulties that makes such a task even more complicated. Unlike the conventional understandings of national histories that tend to blur internal differences, socioeconomic and even ethnic and linguistic diversity is perhaps the most striking feature of the Jewish communities. Quick or partial descriptions of the mellahs usually do not mention that for centuries a feeling of difference existed between the *toshavim* (indigenous Jews) and the *megorashim* (lit. those expelled), namely Jews who fled from Spain after the fall of Granada in 1492. In the sixteenth and seventeenth centuries and even later, the mutual prejudice between these two groups was so intense that in some places they refused to pray in the same synagogues.[11] Later, even when the cultural gap between "natives" and descendants of the Sephardi exiles had diminished, other forms of social differentiation remained. During the eighteenth and nineteenth centuries, for instance, a clear distinction existed between the merchant elite and the popular masses. Matrimonial alliances and common business interests helped lend cohesion to the upper classes, whose members felt that they were forming a sort of oligarchy through such acts.[12]

The intervention or interference of European and American Jewish associations was part of the process of change that Moroccan Jewish communities underwent from the nineteenth century onward. Of crucial importance in this regard was the philanthropic assistance these associations provided to the impoverished populations of overcrowded mellahs.[13] Perhaps even more influential was the establishment of a network of schools throughout most of the country by the Paris-based Alliance Israélite Universelle (AIU, founded in 1860). The first school was established in Tetuan in 1862, immediately after the Spanish occupation of the city (1860–1862).[14]

It is undoubtedly thanks to the modern education introduced in the AIU schools that Jewish traditional culture began to change. Such changes affected not only the minds and mentality of the people and generations who learned the French language, French history, and "Enlightenment thought" but also social relations in the mellahs and long-established and previously unchallenged hierarchies. The *evolués,* as modern Jews educated in the AIU schools were called, started to develop feelings of superiority and to contest the traditional social order within their own *kehillot* (communities) and with regard to their relations with Muslims. Unlike their parents, they refused to obey blindly the "natural" leaders of their communities. They rejected, on similar grounds, their legal condition as *dhimmis*. To enjoy a status similar to that of their co-religionists in Algeria, who in 1870 benefited from the promulgation of the Crémieux Decree, which granted Algerian Jews French citizenship en masse, became their dream.[15]

The hope of gaining French nationality (or Spanish nationality in the northern part of the country) and the claims made toward that end were part of the political ideology that almost all the *evolués* followed vis-à-vis the French and Spanish authorities after the establishment of the protectorate regime (1912). Only a tiny minority of modern educated Jews were suspicious about the colonial authorities' intentions. Based on a sense of premonition and close scrutiny of the true nature of colonialism, these Jews had no positive expectations and feared the socioeconomic consequences of foreign domination. "The new era which begins nowadays for Morocco," wrote Haim Toledano, chair of the AIU Alumni Association, in 1913, "is pregnant with a new life. . . . Except for those who managed to build (strong) positions . . . , the native Jewish masses will soon feel the economic pressure of the new regime. . . . I refrain from mentioning) social issues, or rather and more precisely I should say, racial issues closely linked to economic facts."[16]

Toledano's warning had no impact. Most of the *evolués* continued to call for the extension of French nationality to Moroccan Jews. They stigmatized Zionist activists and depicted their movement and program as "utopian." They paid almost no attention to the Muslim nationalists who were asking them to join in a common struggle aimed at improving the social condition of Moroccans regardless of their faith. French nationality and assimilation remained their credo until World War II. Even if the Vichy laws had not been implemented in Morocco, they would have destroyed Jews' confidence in France—a country they had considered the *patrie adoptée* (adopted motherland). After the war, Zionism emerged as an alternative for an increasing number of disappointed *evolués* and their like.[17]

The dramatic shift that took place during World War II and after the creation of the state of Israel was an important and complex turning point. It still requires further investigation.[18] Understanding the process and its causes may help explain why the Jewish modern elites joined the masses who prepared to flee for spiritual as well as for economic reasons and saw no future in independent Morocco.

The massive emigration of Moroccan Jews in 1948, 1956, and 1967 was an unprecedented and irreversible process in Morocco's history. Under the cumulative impact of the Israeli-Arab wars in the Middle East, the multidimensional change that had undermined the traditional foundations of Muslim-Jewish relations since the mid-nineteenth century and the transformations generated by the protectorate regime, deeply rooted Jewish communities began to vanish from different parts of the country, a process that took less than twenty years. Their exodus was a fatal blow to the Jewish presence in the country and to its historic ethnoreligious and cultural diversity.

Rethinking the social life and culture of Jewish communities requires an exhaustive investigation into the ways their members interacted with their immediate environments. We need well-planned and carefully conceived programs of research that assess studies already undertaken, especially the complicated legacy of historical writings during the colonial period, and a methodical evaluation of topics that have yet to be thoroughly studied. It is obvious that when necessary even subjects that have already been dealt with need to be revisited with an eye to new perspectives and research. While in recent years the Jews of the post–World War II era have received some attention by historians, this period in Moroccan history as a whole remains largely unexplored.[19] New perspectives on the history of the Jewish communities can rely not only on official archives (whenever accessible) but also on oral sources and other materials still not commonly used by historians. A global approach that is open to comparisons with the other Muslim countries, starting with Algeria, Tunisia, and Libya, would certainly help open new horizons.

NOTES

1. *Dalil al-utruhat wa-l-rasa'il al-jami'a: al-musajjalah bi-kulliyat al-adab bi-l-Maghrib*, ed. 'Umar Afa (Rabat: Jami'at Muhammad al-Khamis, Kulliyat al-Adab wa-al-'Ulum al-Insaniya, 1996–); Mohammed Kenbib, "Ecriture et réécriture de l'histoire contemporaine du Maroc. Acquis, interrogations et perspectives," in *Du protectorat à l'indépendance. Problématique du temps present*, ed. Mohammed Kenbib (Rabat: Publications de la Faculté des Lettres et des Sciences Humaines, 2006), 19–46.

2. See Mohammed Kenbib, "Recherches sur les Juifs du Maroc. Esquisse de bilan," in *Les sciences humaines et sociales au Maroc. Etudes et arguments* (Rabat: Institut Universitaire de la Recherche Scientifique, Rabat, 1998), 169–183; Mohammed Kenbib, "Les relations judéo-musulmanes au Maroc, 1860–1945. Essai bibliographique," *Hespéris-Tamuda* 23 (1985): 83–104.

3. Al-Hadi Timumi, *al-Nashat al-sahyuni bayna 1897 wa-1948* (Tunis, 1982); Abdelkrim Allagui, "La minorité juive de Tunisie face à la décolonisation au cours des années cinquante," in *Processus et enjeux de la décolonisation en Tunisie (1952–1964)*, ed. Habib Belaid (Tunis: Université de Manouba, Publications de l'Institut Supérieur d'Histoire du Mouvement National, 1999), 305–320; Abdelkarim Allagui, "Les Juifs du Maghreb dans les années vingt," in *Les années vingt au Maghreb*, ed. Hédi Jallab (Tunis: Université de Manouba, Publications de l'Institut Supérieur d'Histoire du Mouvement National, 2001), 151–164; Amira Aleya Sghaier, *La droite française en Tunisie entre 1934 et 1946* (Tunis: Université de Manouba, Publications de l'Institut Supérieur d'Histoire du Mouvement National, 2004), 113–120 and 193–224.

4. Two detailed bibliographies on Moroccan Jews have been published: Robert Attal, *Les Juifs d'Afrique du Nord: Bibliographie* (Jerusalem: Ben-Zvi Institute and the Hebrew University of Jerusalem, 1993) (in French and Hebrew); and Arrik Delouya, *Les Juifs du Maroc: bibliographie generale* (Paris: Librairie Orientaliste Paul Geuthner, ca. 2001). Delouya's bibliography provides short summaries of books he considers essential; however, he makes no clear distinction between academic and non-academic works. Attal's bibliography, which contains extensive references to academic and non-academic works, is not annotated at all.

5. Georges Vajda's *Recueil de textes historiques judéo-marocains* (Paris: Larose, 1951), also published in *Hespéris* 35 (1948): 311–358 and *Hespéris* 36 (1949): 139–188, remains a classic achievement. See also R. Abner Sarfaty, "Yahas Fas (Chronique de Fès)," published by Y. D. Semach in *Hespéris* 19 (1934): 79–94. Another significant contribution is that of Haïm Zafrani, especially *Études et recherches sur la vie intellectuelle juive au Maroc de la fin du 15e au début du 20e siècle*, Part 1, *Pensée juridique et environnement social économique et religieux* (Paris: Geuthner, 1972). On Zafrani's studies, see Nicole S. Serfaty and Joseph Tedghi, eds., *Présence juive au Maghreb. Hommage à Haïm Zafrani* (Paris: Bouchène, 2004).

6. Shlomo Deshen, *The Mellah Society: Jewish Community Life in Sherifian Morocco* (Chicago: University of Chicago Press, 1989).

7. Ibid., 11.

8. Roger Le Tourneau, *Fès avant le protectorat* (Casablanca: Société Marocaine de Librairie et d'édition, 1949); Lhachemi Berradi, "Les chorfas d'Ouezzane, le Makhzen et la France, 1850–1912" (Ph.D. Thesis, Université d'Aix-en-Provence, 1971); Dale F. Eickelman, *Moroccan Islam: Tradition and Society in a Pilgrimage Center* (Austin: University of Texas Press, 1976).

9. Examples of this type of clerical discourse can be found in ʿAbd al-Rahman Ibn Zaydan, *Ithafaʿlam al-nas bi-jamal akhbar hadirat Miknas*, 5 vols. (Rabat: al-Matbaʿat al-Wataniya, 1929–1933), 2:235, where the author quotes the fatwa issued by the ʿulama after the sultan asked them to consider a case that arose after the "Jews of Fez set up a triumvirate to settle their disputes" with no regard to the makhzan's authority. See also Ahmad b. Khalid al-Nasiri, *Kitab al-istiqsa li-akhbar duwal al-Maghrib al-Aqsa*, 2nd ed., 9 vols. (Casablanca: Dar-al-Kitab, 1954–1956), 9:112–115, where the author comments on the "Jews' violations of the limits they should not trespass in the immediate aftermath of Moses Montefiore's visit to Marrakesh and the edict issued to him by the sultan" (Muhammad b. ʿAbd al-Rahman, 1859–1873). Other texts treating such violations are found in Paul Paquignon, "Documents sur les Juifs du Maroc," *Revue du Monde Musulman* 9 (1909): 112–124. See also Daniel J. Schroeter, *The Sultan's Jew: Morocco and the Sephardi World* (Stanford, Calif.: Stanford University Press, 2002); Nicole S. Serfaty, *Les courtisans juifs des sultans marocains, XII–XVIII siècles. Hommes politiques et hauts dignitaries* (Paris: Bouchène, 1999); Michel Abitbol, *Témoins et acteurs. Les Corcos et l'histoire du Maroc contemporain* (Jerusalem: Institut Ben-Zvi, 1977); and Samuel Romanelli, *Travail in an Arab Land,* trans. Yedida K. Stillman and Norman A. Stillman (Tuscaloosa: University of Alabama Press, 1989).

10. See for instance the impressions and remarks of Joseph Dalton Hooker and John Bell in *Journal of a Tour in Morocco and the Great Atlas* (London: Macmillan, 1878). See also Charles de Foucauld, *Reconnaissance au Maroc, 1883–1884* (Paris: Challamel, 1888); Robert Cunninghame Graham, *Moghreb El-Aksa: A Journey in Morocco* (London: W. Heinemann, 1898); and Edmond Doutté, *Missions au Maroc: En tribu* (Paris: P. Geuthner, 1914). See also chapter 6 in this volume, by Aomar Boum.

11. On the differences between the Spanish exiles and their descendants and the native Jews, see Deshen, *The Mellah Society*, 8, 99; Zafrani, *Études et recherches*, 103, 126; Vajda, *Recueil de texts*; and Lucette Valensi, "La Tour de Babel: groupes et relations ethniques au Moyen-Orient et en Afrique du Nord," *Annales ESC* 4 (1986): 817–838.

12. Jean-Louis Miège, *Le Maroc et l'Europe, 1830–1894,* 4 vols. (Paris: Presses universitaires de France, 1961–1963). On the merchant elite in Essaouira, see Daniel J. Schroeter, *Merchants of Essaouira: Urban Society and Imperialism in Southwestern Morocco, 1844–1886* (Cambridge: Cambridge University Press, 1988), 21ff.; Daniel J. Schroeter, *The Sultan's Jew: Morocco and the Sephardi*

World (Stanford, Calif.: Stanford University Press, 2002), 17–20; and Michel Abitbol, *Les commerçants du roi, tujjār al-sultān: une elite économique judéo-marocaine au xixe siècle* (Paris: Maisonneuve & Larose, 1998).

13. Mohammed Kenbib, *Juifs et Musulmans au Maroc: 1859–1948* (Rabat: Université Mohammed V, Publications de la Faculté des Lettres et des Science Humaines, 1994).

14. Michael M. Laskier, *The Alliance Israélite Universelle and the Jewish Communities of Morocco: 1862–1962* (Albany: State University of New York Press, 1983).

15. On these changes, see Kenbib, *Juifs et Musulmans au Maroc,* 309–320, 405–426.

16. Haïm Toledano, *Le Maroc nouveau et les Israélites* (Tangier: Imp. Marocain, 1913), 6–9.

17. Kenbib, *Juifs et Musulmans au Maroc,* 508–601; Michel Abitbol, *Les Juifs d'Afrique du Nord sous Vichy* (Paris: Maisonneuve & Larose, 1983), 59–111.

18. A new generation of Moroccan scholars has conducted research on these questions. See Abdellah Larhmaid, "Jamaʿat yahud Sus, al-majal wa-l-tamathulat al-ijtimaʿiya wa-siyasiya, 1860–1960" (Doctoral diss., Faculty of Letters and Human Sciences, Université Mohammed V-Agdal, Rabat, 2002); Mohamed Bouras, "al-Ahzab al-wataniya wa-l-yahud al-maghariba bayna khususiyat al-wadʿ al-mahalli wa-muʿaththirat al-qadiya al-filastiniya, 1934–1967" (Doctoral diss., Faculty of Letters and Human Sciences, Université Mohammed V-Agdal, Rabat, 2004); and Muhammad Hatimi, "al-Jamaʿat al-yahudiya al-maghribiya wa-l-khiyar al-saʿb bayna nida al-sahyuniya wa-rihad al-maghrib al-mustaqil, 1947–1961" (Doctoral diss. [*utruh al-dawla*], Faculty of Letters, Université Mohammed V-Agdal, Sais-Fès, 2007). On this period in general, see Daniel Rivet, *Le Maghreb à l'épreuve de la colonization* (Paris: Hachette Littératures, 2002), 352–374. *Editors' note:* For Israeli scholarship on these questions, see Yaron Tsur, *Kehila keruʿa: Yehude Maroko veha-le'umiyut, 1943–1954* [A Torn Community: The Jews of Morocco and Nationalism, 1943–1954] (Tel Aviv: Universitat Tel Aviv, ha-ʿAmuta le-heker maʿrkhot ha-haʿpalah ʿa. sh. Sha'ul Avigor, ʿAm ʿOved, 2001); and Michael M. Laskier, *North African Jewry in the Twentieth Century: The Jews of Morocco, Tunisia, and Algeria* (New York: New York University Press, 1994).

19. See especially Hatimi, "al-Jamaʿat al-yahudiya al-Maghribiya," and Tsur, *Kehila keruʿa.* On postcolonial Morocco more generally, see Pierre Vermeren, *Histoire du Maroc depuis l'indépendance* (Paris: La Découverte, 2002); and Mohammed Kenbib, "Le Maroc indépendant 1955–2005: Essai de synthèse," in Royaume du Maroc, *Commission du Cinquantenaire, Rapports transversaux,* available at www.rdh50.ma/fr/transversaux.asp.

PART II

Origins, Diasporas, and Identities

3

Place Names in Western Algeria

Biblical Sources and Dominant Semantic Domains

Farid Benramdane

Translated by Allan MacVicar

This chapter focuses on the linguistic customs and semantic traditions of monotheistic religions and mystical place naming in a region where different cultures, religions, and languages were in constant contact. Rather than attributing exegetical values and meanings to secular customs, I will instead try to answer the following questions: within a traditionally oral society, how do place names bear evidence of a naming tradition with biblical origins? What are the number and proportion of names with religious and mystical connotations in the general nomenclature of toponyms in western Algeria? Which biblical names recur most in the Algerian toponymy? What pragmatic dimensions might be attributed to a place bearing a name of biblical origin?

The corpus of place names used here was formed by a systematic notation of toponyms in western Algeria comprising 20,060 terms collected orally and/or from written documents. They have been classified according to morphological and semantic criteria.

In onomastic studies, causal relationships are not necessarily evident on a purely semantic level. Historical developments do not necessarily determine the discursive and linguistic aspects of proper names. In Algeria, for example, French proper names did not fall into disuse after the end of French colonization, even those whose linguistic formations were very unusual and foreign to the local environment. Likewise, place names of biblical origin remain embedded in the landscape of Western Algeria.

Naming and Cultural Contact

In his study of languages in contact, Albert Dauzat has emphasized that "place names rarely penetrate the new language as is. If their meaning is or seems to be clear, they are generally translated. One could say that there is a substitution of forms, but in reality, it is a question of semantic assimilation."¹ Along these lines, one might identify different forms of expression, articulation, and production of meaning in an interconnected space such as North Africa, where numerous civilizational, symbolic, religious, and cultural currents intersect and where the naming of places, persons, human groups and establishments, and cultural and linguistic entities remains an ongoing process. Such naming processes reveal how identities and symbolic repositionings are constructed and reconstructed. Names are thus a powerful means of identification and social recognition in North Africa, as elsewhere.²

My approach here is guided by the desire to understand, in both linguistic and anthropological terms, how meaning is produced through the attribution of proper names, the reinforcement of such names through oral expressions of memory, and the synchronic and diachronic dimensions of the discursive manifestations of these names. The linearity of the classic linguistic approach, according to which linguistic and cultural data are perceived only fragmentally, is ineffective when dealing with contact and variation, factors in all inter- and translinguistic processes. These dynamics exist in all established cultural spheres, whether past and present, multiple or complex, initiatory or ritualized.

In many human societies, the purpose of a name is "to win the favor of a divinity, to put the child to whom the name is attributed under divine protection. This idea has guided Egyptian, Assyrian, Jewish, Christian, and Muslim populations as well as the religious peoples of the Far East."³ According to anthropologist Charles Bromberger, "In many societies, proper names echo the foundational myth. Such is the case with theophoric names, as demonstrated in the ancient Semitic world by 'Yohannan,' or 'John,' meaning, 'God has manifested his grace,' or still today in the Muslim world by "Abdallah,' meaning, 'the servant of God.'"⁴ Proper names present new materials for considering culture and language precisely because they exceed the scope of a single geographical area, religion, or language or family of languages. The intensive relations between North Africa and the Eastern and Western worlds have helped weave together, from a diachronic perspective, a single onomastic custom. This idea is underpinned not by linguistic conflict but by the fact that both Eastern and Western peoples lay claim to a single mental representation,⁵ like the two poles of a single truth, in spite of the fact that historical events have created distance between these cultures, obscuring the significant cultural and linguistic mixing that one finds when examining the proper names. As Bromberger notes, "As such, the proper name can have a double status, that of classificatory reference point which then assigns the named individual to one or more positions within the social structure, or that of a symbol participating in a vision of the world, an organized system of representations and beliefs."⁶

Naming, Foreign Contributions, and Semantic Assimilation

Arthur Pellegrin discovered in the course of his macro-toponymic study of Algeria and Tunisia that in the Maghribi context there are a significant number of place names of Arabic origin that "seemed to have hidden, in some cases, the successive linguistic contributions that preceded the Arabic conquest. It may be that some toponyms are simply a translation from a primitive Berber."[7] After the Muslim conquest of North Africa in the seventh century, a profound transformation of onomastic customs occurred. More specifically, two toponymic systems, Berber and Arabic, converged, instituting a complex process of substitution and hybridization for naming places. Thus it is possible to determine whether or not established onomastic practices represent a rupture or merely gradual change over time and whether the transformations are morphological or semantic.

Elsewhere, I have shown that the most effective substitution occurs when the names of locally venerated saints are used to replace original appellations, whereby terms of Berber extraction refer to pagan, Jewish, and Christian worship in the new nomenclature.[8] By far the most frequent process of hybridization is that of composition. For example, a determinant with a macro-toponymic value is attached to all names of a religious and mystical nature: "Sidi" is a form derived from the classical Arabic *"sayyid,"* meaning "sire, your lordship, mister," and refers particularly to a moral value, to respect for one's ancestors, the *murabits*, and the *tulaba'*. "Si," a more rarely used toponymic form, is a truncated form of "Sidi" and has approximately the same meaning.

Religious Names and Spatial-Temporal Continuity

Hagionomy (from *hagios*, the Greek word for sacred) has faithfully preserved this rich deposit of religious accumulation by bringing together the disparate religious practices and mystical beliefs of the region. As Tadeusz Lewicki has noted, Arab authors of the Middle Ages (including Ibn Khaldun, al-Bakri, al-Yaqubi, al-Idrissi, al-Muqaddasi, and others) discussed the religious practices of the Berbers of the Muslim era until the fourteenth century in terms of "the worship of rocks, stones, and water, the faith in tutelary genies and in other mythic, demonic beings, the worship of footprints and bloodstains, and finally the magical prohibitions and recommendations."[9]

Other place names related to religion make up an important part of the microtoponymy. They are rarely found in isolation; rather, they usually exist in compound appellative formations: as determinants, determinatives, or in a medial position. Examples include: *sidi jahil* ("His lordship the polytheist"), *jabal b. shirk* ("mountain of the heathens"), and so forth.

I now examine a series of toponyms with religious and mystical connotations, including the names of persons, institutions, and places of worship. Of the 20,060 western Algerian place names studied, approximately one-fifth refer to religious and mystical semantic fields, either directly, such as the place names formed with hagionyms (Sidi, Lalla, Maqam, Rajm), or indirectly, when one of the components in a medial or final position makes a general Jewish or biblical reference, as is shown in table 3.1.

This table shows that seven names predominate: Musa, Yahiya, Ibrahim, Sulayman, Yusuf, ʿIssa, and Yaʿqub. Together they constitute 82 percent of the local nomenclature. Musa and Yahya together constitute 31 percent. Three hundred and six of the terms in this group are composed with "Sidi."[10] The remainder feature different ethnonymic formations, for example using "Awlad" and "Bani," Awlad Bu Daud, Sidi ʿAli Ben Yahya, Kudiat Si ʿIssa, Sidi Yaʿqub Musa, Sidi Musa al-Mazuzi, Wad Sidi Musa, and so forth. The most representative toponymic base hagionomy is "Sidi": 2,797 terms begin with Sidi and then have proper names of biblical origin as their second or third component.

The toponyms in Table 3.1 and Figure 3.1 and all the other toponymic categories of a religious and mystical nature, such as Lalla, Maqam, Rajm, Kuba, are dispersed more or less equally across the different regions of western Algeria.

The Relationship between Hagionymy, Anthroponymy, and Toponymy

Honorific designations are ethnographic evidence of veneration of the dead, as François Decret and Mhamed Fantar note: "Berbers did not fail to revere persons who were particularly gifted in power or the Divine. Maraboutism and its broad dissemination in the countries of the Maghrib could be understood as the vestiges of Lybic anthropolatry."[11] With its combination of earlier practices and assimilated foreign contributions, notably Muslim and Arabic, the onomastic system and its categories (ethnomyny, anthroponymy, hagionymy, toponymy) are intimately related to the social system in North Africa. As Pierre Bourdieu notes, the social system "is conceived of according to a genealogical model, which, at least ideally, allows ramified and dispersed groups to find common ancestors."[12] Thus, in terms of the hybridization of linguistic and cultural forms, it is worth mentioning again that terms with the base "Sidi" or "Lalla" are derived from ancient Berber or Arabic eponyms. For example, Sidi Muhammad Gazul, Sidi Mrhila, Sidi ʿAbd al-Qadir Madrissa, Lalla Akarma, Gezuld, Mrhila (Mghila), and Lalla have Berber roots that are known to have existed before the arrival of Islam in the Maghrib.

The terms al-Yahudi or Yahudi, the Arabic equivalent of "Jew," appear in a very small number of toponyms: Makabarat al-Yahudi, Shabit al-Yahudi, Jabal al-Yahudi, Hammar al-Yahudi, Khanag al-Yahudi, Kharbat al-Yahudi. They desig-

Table 3.1. Biblical Names in Algerian Toponyms

Name	Number of Place Names	%
Musa (Moses)	84	16.00
Yahya (John)	83	14.61
Ibrahim (Abraham)	75	13.20
Sulayman (Solomon)	61	10.74
Yusuf (Joseph)	61	10.74
ʿIssa (Jesus)	48	8.45
Yaʿqub (Jacob)	48	8.45
Daud (David)	28	4.93
Shuʿayb(Jethro)	14	2.46
Idris (Enoch)	14	2.46
Ismaʿil (Ishmael)	11	1.94
Ayyub (Job)	10	1.76
Naʿim (Naʿim)	9	1.58
Sadiq (Zadok)	7	1.23
Maryam (Miriam)	5	0.88
Yunis (Jonas)	5	0.88
Ishuʿa (Joshua)	5	0.88
Total	568	100

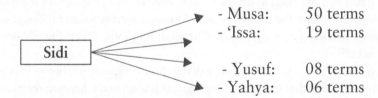

Figure 3.1. Occurrences of the Hagionymic Base "Sidi."

nate topographical entities, not religious or symbolic ones (except perhaps Makabarat, meaning "cemetery"), as is also the case with Musa, ʿIssa, and Yusuf.

Islam, Judaism, and Christianity and Their Mental Onomastic Representations

The triumph of Islam set in motion extensive toponymic creativity with regard to names of biblical origin. Earlier prophets, such as Ayyub (Job), ʿIssa (Jesus), Shuʿayb (Jethro), Musa (Moses), and so forth are recognized by Muslims, which explains their inclusion in the local onomastic field. Most of the traces of earlier

religions in the micro-toponymy predate the arrival of Islam. The adoption of
the new religion effectively integrated the contributions made by the religious
practices that preceded it, either by making a straightforward translation of place
names or by introducing a system of hybrid composition.

While the medieval period was witness to the development of the final Libyco-
Berber formations, it also saw the birth of the first Muslim toponyms. This process took place within the context of the development of a Maghribi Islam with
strong mystical tendencies. According to Charles-André Julien, "The Sufism that
spread in the Maghrib beginning in the eighth century increased in scale in the
fifteenth century. . . . At the leaders' urging, the [Sufi] orders of Qadiriyya, Shad-
haliyya, Jazuliyya, Rahmaniyya, Darqawa, and Sanusiyya were formed and continued to develop until the nineteenth century."[13]

Although it is true that beginning with the founding of the Rustumid state
at Tahart in 761, Islamization and Arabization spread more rapidly across the Saharan plains and high plains than elsewhere,[14] it is nonetheless important to note
that the hagiographic practices surrounding this process have not received the
recognition they deserve.

The fact that a very high percentage of the terms were of a religious nature,
noted in part of the corpus (Figure 3.1), and the fact that they were most densely
used in the territories of Berber tribes such as the Maknassa, Luwata, Maghila in
the eighth century suggest that Islamization and Arabization also spread quickly
in regions where Jewish and Christian monotheistic religious traditions were
found. Latin authors attest to this fact. Thus, even areas in medieval Tahart or ancient Tingartia where the Islamized and Arabized territories and tribes were located were bordered by a significant Christian religious center: the bishopric of
Columnata.[15]

Considering the common heritage of the three religions, it is not an exaggeration to hypothesize that territories located near Jewish and Christian religious institutions favored conversion to Islam and subsequent Arabization.

Biblical Anthroponymy and Place Names

Muslim personal names began to spread in the wake of the arrival of Islam
in North Africa. The Libyco-Berber substrate is the least visible language group
in North Africa, and as a result, Arabization was successful in this region. It
is worth noting that at this time toponymic configurations had also begun to
change. Land and other property were given the names of their owners. The process of Arabization was accelerated by the fact that the regions in question were
located on fertile soil at the axes of much tribal movement (Sersou, Nador, Chel-
lala, Aflou, Ouargla, etc.).

Onomastic assimilation is also linked to the development of typically Maghribi Muslim practices, such as the rise of the religious brotherhoods in the fifteenth century. The Arabization process, meanwhile, shows the direct link between toponymy and anthroponymy through the exchange of forms between the two. Conversion to Islam thus involved changing one's name to a name from the Arabic language, a well-known requirement for new Muslims.[16]

In 1882, French colonial administrators noted "a certain similarity in pronunciation with regard to European names: *Cayla–Hirsh –Hamel –Maury –Sassi –Farre –Noir –Ruis*."[17] Knowledge of the origins of so-called Arabic and French names could have resolved many misunderstandings when French colonial administrators gave civil status to the Muslims of Algeria and attempted to Gallicize apparently Algerian names by changing Naʿima to Noémie, Farid to Alfred, Qasi to Kassis, and so forth.[18] Many of the principal biblical names were used by at least two if not three of the major religious groups in Algeria (Christians, Muslims, and Jews): examples include Adam/Adam, John/Yahya, Abel/Habil, Moses/Musa, Anne/Hanna, Zadoq/Sadiq, Elijah/Elyas, Zachariah/Zakariya, Esau-Joshua-Jesus/ ʿIssa, Naomi-Noayma/Naʿima, Isaac/Ishaq, and Ishmael/Ismaʿil. In monotheistic religions, the concept of the name and its contribution to the person who bears the name is the same. In the biblical tradition, "the name that a person bears is not an arbitrary designation. The name expresses something of the person; . . . The name of God is equivalent to the divine person. The sanctification of the name reaches the person."[19]

For Pierre Rossi, there is no doubt as to the Eastern origin of Judeo-Christian and Muslim names. He writes, "The east and the west are in no way antinomic, but are in fact the opposite ends of a single truth, a single culture, and a single history. The Greeks were eastern. The Romans claimed to originate from Aeneas."[20]

Let us also consider the biblical origin of names of persons, "the term *biblical* having a much greater affinity with the term *rab* (Aramaic, which amounts to the same thing). By replacing Noah with its Arabic name, Nuh, Job with Ayyub, Jonah with Yunus ben Matta, Shem with Sam bin Nuh, Abraham with Ibrahim, David with Daud, Aaron with Harun, Solomon with Sulayman, Goliath with Jallud, Jesus with ʿIssa, and bringing it to full circle, the Christian name Mary, derived from Miriam, becoming Maryam, we can rediscover the primitive freshness of the Bible and its real presence."[21]

Naming, the Power of Speech, and the Written Tradition

It is clear that the conceptual tools and the methodological approaches used to analyze linguistic phenomena are regulated by historical and symbolic factors susceptible to interpretation within a descriptive, synchronic, multilingual, and

dynamic model. The conditions of production of such onomastic linguistic practices and their modes of reception as well as linguistic, social, and symbolic interactions open up new theoretical and methodological perspectives. Orality is an
equally important intrinsic, discursive, and organic component.

Inevitably, the problem of naming, aptly emphasized by Koskas and Kremin,
can be structured along three lines: "First, the line of the naming subject; second,
the line of linguistic actualization as such and of the social interaction that this
implies; and third, the line of linguistic status in relation to the extra-linguistic,
empirical data."[22] Oral practice creates its own space of historical, social, and
symbolic legitimation, especially of lexical creativity. This affects all onomastic
aspects of religion: Daud, Bu Daud, Ibn Daud, Daudi, Daudiya, ʿAbd al-Qadir,
ʿAbdaqa, Daqa, Qad, Qaddur, Qadiriya, and so forth. However, onomastics is, to
put it mildly, characterized by significant linguistic stability. Orality produces
linguistic flexibility, even in the sacred realm of religious and mystical proper
names. For Cheriguen, it is a matter of a simplification process that follows the
law of linguistic economy: "It is produced by the difference between a sacred
classical Arabic of North Africa and a more secular, popular, Algerian Arabic....
There may also be other reasons behind this secularization of the name, such
as prolonged contact between Arabic and Berber. With regard to the question
of belief, Berber is less rigid since it is polytheistic."[23] The pragmatic dimension
of these Maghribi onomastic practices is also interesting, insofar as the users
themselves were mostly unaware of the meaning of the names they bore or gave
their children. By examining these contexts of enunciation it is possible to distinguish the projective character of orality in naming. In addition, lexical creativity,
or more precisely neology (from ʿAbd al-Qadir to Biqa, from ʿIssa to ʿAyssawa),
makes it possible to see how oral tradition can remove the original meaning and
replace it with a new meaning in order to reach the most basic level of nomination, the identification of a person in a group. For Calvet, "the *power of speech* is
prevalent in oral societies while societies with a written tradition are more ac-
quainted with the *power of the text*. In the latter case, people are governed by laws,
decrees, and treaties, while in the former, they are governed by an ancestral tradition that is not inscribed in books but in the social memory."[24]

Conclusion

From the perspective of pragmatic linguistics, any discussion of multilingualism in onomastics is problematic when one tries to analyze how such a diverse patrimony was received. Underpinning this kind of examination is a uni-
versalist and humanist symbolism: Jewish names, Greek names, and others have
become universal. The meaning of the Hebrew roots is ignored. No one knows

what John-Yahya, Yusuf-Joseph, Zakariya, Jallud, Nawil, Ishuʿa, Samuel, Rabiʿa, Naomi, Hanna, or Sadik mean, but they remain popular nonetheless. For some, all that remains is a name's musicality, as is the case with the dramatic recent return of given names like Sarah and Yos in Algeria, "words which please or displease." For others, mythical references to a prophetic space-time common to the three religions linger.[25]

NOTES

1. Albert Dauzat, *Les noms de lieux: origines et évolution et la toponymie française* (Paris: Delagrave, 1972), 72.

2. Paul Siblot, "Appeler les choses par leur nom. Problématique du nom, de la nomination et des renominations," in *Noms et re-noms: la dénomination des personnes, des populations, des langues et des territoires,* ed. Salih Akin (Rouen: Publications de l'Université de Rouen-CNRS, 1999), 12.

3. Eugène Vroonen, *Le noms de personnes dans le monde. Anthroponymie universelle comparée* (Bruxelles: Éditions de la librairie encyclopédique, 1967), 231.

4. Charles Bromberger, "Pour une analyse anthropologique des noms de personnes," *Langages* 66 (1980): 120.

5. Pierre Rossi, *La cite d'Issis: l'histoire vraie des Arabes* (Algiers: ENAG, 1980).

6. Bromberger, "Pour une analyse anthropologique des noms de personnes," 122.

7. Arthur Pellegrin, *Les noms d'Algérie et de Tunisie. Etymologie et interpretation* (Tunis: SAPI, 1949), 146.

8. Farid Benramdane, "Espace, langue et identité au Maghreb. Du nom au symbole," *Insaniyat* 9 (1999): 5–18.

9. Tadeusz Lewicki, "Le monde berbère vu par les écrivains arabes du Moyen Age," in *Congrès d'études des cultures méditerranéennes d'influence arabo-berbère, Actes du 1er Congrès d'Etudes des cultures méditerranéennes d'influence arabo-berbère* (Algiers: SNED, 1973), 39.

10. The toponymic base "Sidi" occurred 2,796 times.

11. François Decret and Mhamed Fantar, *L'Afrique du nord dans l'antiquité. Des origins au V siècle* (Paris: Payot, 1981), 257.

12. Pierre Bourdieu, *Sociologie de l'Algérie* (1956; Paris: Presses universitaires de France, 1974), 87.

13. Charles-André Julien, *L'Afrique du Nord en marche,* 3rd ed. (Paris: René Julliard, 1972), 18.

14. Salem Chaker, *Imazighen Ass-à: Berbères dans le Maghreb contemporain* (Algiers: Bouchène, 1990), 11.

15. "They [the Sanhaja or Zanata Berbers] were certainly prepared for the absolute monotheism of Islam by the recent development of Christianity"; Gabriel Camps, *Les Berbères. Mémoire et identité* (Paris: Errance, 1987), 136.

16. Daniel Gimaret, *Les noms divins en Islam. Exégèse lexicologique et théologique* (Paris: Éditions du Cerf, 1988), 88.

17. Elie Tabet, *Notes sur l'organisation des tribus et étymologie des noms propres* (Oran: Heintz, Chazeau et Cie, 1882), 25.

18. See Farid Benramdane, "Violence et état civil. De la destruction de la filiation ou elements pour un onmacide sémantique," *Insaniyat* 10 (2000): 79–87.

19. Louis Monloubou and François Michel du Buit, *Dictionnaire biblique universel* (Paris: Desclée, 1984), 509–510.

20. "Thus, it would make sense that not only Judaism, Christianity, and Islam, but also that Zoroastrians, Solar and Orphic religions, religions of mystery and salvation, and Greek and Roman religions all derive, like brothers and sisters, from the eastern cosmos as it reign over the region between the Nile and the Indus, made possible by a common language, Aramaic living on in present-day Arabic." Rossi, *La cite d'Issis*, 10.

21. Ibid., 16.

22. Eliane Koskas and Helgard Kremin, *La Dénomination* (Paris: Larousse, 1984), 1.

23. Foudil Cheriguen, *Toponymie algérienne des lieux habités. Les noms composés* (Algiers: Dar El Ijtihad, 1993), 65.

24. Louis-Jean Calvet, *La tradition orale*, 2nd ed. (Paris: Presses universitaires de France, 1997), 114.

25. Abdelghani Belhamdi and Jean-Jacques Salvetat, *Les plus beaux prénoms du Maghreb. Avec l'étymologie des prénoms français correspondants* (Paris: Éditions du Dauphin, 2000), 7.

4

The Image of the Jews among Ibadi Imazighen in North Africa before the Tenth Century

Mabrouk Mansouri

The history of the Jews in North Africa has captured the attention of many scholars.[1] But many gaps remain in our knowledge, especially in the still-unexplored period of the early centuries after the Arab conquest in North Africa. We take for granted that the formation of a religious experience is determined both by the context where it appears and the setting(s) in which it gains ground, an idea equally applicable to Islam and Judaism. Yet neither Islam nor Judaism can be said to be the "original" religion of North Africa. The North African religious experience is multifaceted and may be approached in many ways, including through the complicated relationship between the three monotheistic faiths: Judaism, Christianity, and Islam. Yet rethinking North African Jewry as a component of the North African monotheistic landscape also requires considerable knowledge of Amazigh culture and society before and after the spread of Islam in North Africa.[2] The diversity of North African ethnicity and religious sects in particular should be taken into account and be grounded in a particular social and cultural context in any attempt to reinterpret the North African religious landscape.

With this in mind, I will analyze the Muslim-Jewish relationship in a specific North African community in the Middle Ages: the Imazighen (Berbers; sing. Amazigh), the indigenous North African people who converted to the Ibadi Islamic sect.[3] In the following discussion I survey some images of the Jews in Ibadi texts, particularly those that illustrate a fundamental trust between the two communities. The corpus examined is the Ibadi biographies of religious leaders (siyar). The central text is that of Abu Zakariya (471/1078), *Kitab siyar al-a'imma wa-akhbarihim* (The Biographies of the Ibadi Imams). Sources that date from the tenth century in-

45

clude two well-known unpublished tenth-century collections, *Diwan al-masha'ikh* and *Diwan al-ashyakh,* found in private libraries of Ibadi shaykhs. These two collections are rarely used for reasons other than religious purposes. Later Ibadi writers depended heavily on these early materials as representations of what they believed to be the characteristics of the formative period of North African Ibadism. However, from a different analytical perspective, the anecdotes found in these texts can be understood as authentic representations of the collective imaginary before they were written down for the first time by Abu Zakirya less than a century after the events to which they referred had taken place. The anecdotes recorded by the Ibadi writers described institutions and practices during the formative period of Islam in North Africa until the tenth century, expressing a social reality of a long and peaceful coexistence between the two communities before and after the arrival of Islam in the Maghrib.

The Arabs came to North Africa initially as invaders but quickly transformed themselves into pastoralists who spread the Arabic language and the call to Islam. Many indigenous North Africans converted to Islam and adopted its new traditions and customs. Nevertheless, most of the North African societies preserved their own cultural identity in various ways.[4] This was first expressed by the revolutions during the seventh and eighth centuries, then by the adoption of the two Kharijite sects, Ibadism and Sufrism.[5] These two sects produced a local "Amazigh Islam" that preserved their local culture and identity but were considered heretical by orthodox Muslims.

Two major questions arise from this historical conceptualization: First, can we apply the Imazighen experience to Jews? Did Jews follow the same cultural processes? Did they succeed in preserving their Jewish identity? Second, how did the Imazighen who converted to the Ibadi Islamic sect during the formative period of Islamic religious experience in North Africa portray their Jewish neighbors?[6]

The Imazighen-Jewish relationship in North Africa during the first four centuries of Islamic rule can be explained in the context of the historical and religious structures of the larger Jewish experience under Islamic domination. To that end, I will propose a model of ethnicity/religiosity and of minority/majority relations.

A first case to consider is that of Dihya "al Kahina,"[7] the legendary Amazigh queen of Jirawa, who successfully fought the Arabs and resisted their conquest and who some scholars have portrayed as a Jewish leader.[8] Assigning a Jewish origin to Dihya is controversial, and contemporary historians have not reached agreement on this subject. Some consider it a later fiction but without providing a satisfactory alternative explanation. Whatever the historicity of the story, it does not deny the very important influence of Jews among the Imazighen and reflects the specificity of Islam in North Africa. Even if the story of "al-Kahina" is a later fiction,[9] the tradition itself reveals the Judaization of Imazighen tribes before Islam.[10]

Second, in (122/740), the leader of the Barghawata religious movement and state, Tarif ibn Sham'un ibn Ishaq (whom some Arab historians claim was Jewish),[11] participated with his son Salih in the Amazigh Sufrite revolt of the Matghara tribe under the leadership of Maysara al-Matghari in 739–740 against the Arab authorities. Both subtribes belonged to Masmuda, the strongest tribe of the Atlas region. Their attempt to hold the Sunni orthodox capital of Qayrawan was a failure. Two years later, Salih presented himself as a prophet teaching a mixture of Islamic, Judaic, and astrological beliefs. He preached that Muhammad was a true prophet but was only for the Arabs. Salih came to be regarded as the Imazighen prophet, sent for all humankind. His name, it was believed, was declared in the Quran in Sura 66:4.[12] He gave himself Arabic, Tamazight, and Hebrew names; his Arabic name was Salih, his Hebrew name was Yariba, and his Tamazight name was Wiryawri, the meaning of which was that no prophet should come after him. His religion survived more than five centuries, based on his innovation of an Amazigh Quran, local religious practices, and veneration of the local god "Yaqush."[13]

If we accept the claim of some Arab historians that the Jirawa, Madiyuna,[14] and Barghawata were Jewish tribes, we can infer that Jews were present everywhere from the Nefusa to the Atlas Mountains. Given their powerful position in society, they did not act like a typical minority group; indeed some of the strongest tribes of North Africa were Jewish. Hence the model of minority-majority for understanding the relationship between Jews and non-Jews is meaningless. As Clifford Geertz has argued, "A majority-minority kind of model for the relationship is wrong; . . . the whole ethnic group notion . . . does not fit the Moroccan [and the entire North African] situation. . . . I think it is rather too easy to arrange symbolic materials in such a way as to present a model of a dominant oppressive majority, and a subdominant, oppressed minority. This does not fit the situation, which is not to say that there is not oppression but that is not the form it takes and that is not a proper model to understand what is going on."[15] The situation of Jews should be compared to other ethnic groups in North Africa. Not only were the populations of Nefusa, Jerba, and Wargla diverse, but those of Ghadames Matmata, Gabes, Hama, Tozeur, and Gafsa were diverse as well.[16] Among the Imazighen we find Arabs (Hijazi, Yemeni, Shami, Omani, Iraqi), Persians, Sudanese, Jews,[17] and the Imazighen. While the Persians and the Arabs shared political roles, the Jews played especially important economic roles.[18] The Iraqis (mainly from Basra) monopolized the religious and intellectual domains. Indeed, foreigners founded all the Muslim dynasties that arose in North Africa in the eighth through the tenth centuries. However, the Imazighen did not consider these foreigners to be ethnic minorities. This is also true for their attitude toward the Jews.

The Imazighen Ibadis viewed the Jews as a religious rather than an ethnic group. However, this cannot be well understood without first asking how perceptions of the Jews of North Africa in the pre-Islamic period changed over time. Was there a total or partial transformation of the Jews' image in North Africa after the arrival of Islam? Did the Islamization of the Imazighen and their conversion to Ibadism affect their view of the Jews? Did the coming of Arabs profoundly change the status of the Jews under the Imazighen local tribes prior to the tenth century?

The model for Jewish-Muslim relations in the Arab world prior to the tenth century should also be taken into account. In Arabic literature Jews are often portrayed as untrustworthy individuals who had evil intentions toward Islam and Muslims. This image is portrayed in some Quranic passages and in the biography of the Prophet. But how reflective of Muslim attitudes toward Jews are such images in the context of North Africa?

It would be difficult to establish that concepts that were developed in the Quran and Sunna really affected the Imazighen vision of the Jews. We know that the Quranic image has to be understood in the context of its Hijazi background,[19] which is very different from the North African situation. North African Ibadi sources reveal that the concepts and attitudes of the Ibadi Imazighen were far more complex than has previously been assumed. The process of Arabization and Islamization were only partial in North Africa. Furthermore, Arabic culture and Islamic learning spread through translators. It is worth noting that the most important component of Islam—prayer—was not practiced in many Imazighen areas until the tenth century and even later. In his fourteenth-century travel notes, al-Tijani stated that none of the inhabitants of Ghumrassen (in southern Tunisia) knew the terms for prayer (*salat*) or how to practice it. He stated that during his stay among them he had not heard any call for prayer (*adhan*).[20]

In addition, even if the Quran clearly states that non-Muslims should be humbled (Sura 9:29),[21] the situation in North Africa was quite unique until the end of the eighth century. In the imperial cities and orthodox religious centers of North Africa, such injunctions were understood in the most literal sense, but they applied to Ibadis, Sufrites, and Mu'tazilites, not just Jews and Christians. Indeed, even though members of these groups were Muslims, the Maliki judge Suhnun Ibn Sa'id (240/854) expelled them from the mosque of Qayrawan, punished them, and made them homeless. To justify his deeds, he claimed that their presence was an unquestionable danger to public life.[22] The Ibadis were an outcast community, and they formed a very separate world of their own in the south.

The Arabs saw all North Africans, including the indigenous Imazighen and the Jews, as inferior. Thus the Imazighen and the Jews found themselves in the same situation, albeit for different reasons. Adherents of the Maliki school of jurisprudence considered themselves to be the real representatives of "true" Islam, that of Muhammad and the *rashidun* ("rightly-guided" caliphs who ruled directly after Muhammad). Arabic literature, meanwhile, portrayed the Amazigh as *kafir* (infidels), *mushrik* (polytheists), *shaytan* (devils), and *haqir* (contemptible).[23] The Arabs denied the Imazighen most rights and worked to isolate them socially, politically, and economically. They refused to pray with them in daily and *janaza* (funeral) prayers. In fact, Ibadi communities from Nefusa to Wargla were denied the right to be part of the so-called *dar al-Islam*. These attitudes contrasted with those of the Ibadis, who were more tolerant than orthodox Muslims.[24]

Application of the term *dhimmi* is complicated in the early centuries of Islam, for it was used not only to designate Jews and Christians but also Amazigh Muslims: Arabs considered the Imazighen to be *dhimmis* until the late ninth century. Though the Imazighen had converted to Islam, they were obliged to pay the *jizya* (obligatory per capita tax for non-Muslims). Two examples illustrate this. First, ᶜAmr ibn al-ᶜAs (the Muslim conqueror of North Africa) ordered the Imazighen of Lawata in Barka to pay the *jizya* even though they had converted to Islam.[25] Second, before his rebellion against Arab rule, Maysara, an Amazigh Sufrite leader, visited Damascus and told the *wazir* (minister) of Hisham ibn 'Abd al-Malik that the Umayyad governors of North Africa obliged them to give their daughters as a *jizya* tax even though they were Muslims.[26] Clearly, the Ibadi-Jewish relationship must be approached in light of the specific circumstances in North Africa and the Maliki-Ibadi relationship in particular. Continuing along these lines, is it possible to say whether the Imazighen Muslims' relationships with the Arabs affected their attitudes toward the Jews?

The first use of the term *dhimmi* in Ibadi texts appears as a synonym for the word Yahudi (Jew) and dates from eighth-century Tahart: "We rejoice at the sun when it shines, as the *Dhimmi* rejoices on the Sabbath."[27] In Ibadi legal theory of the eleventh century, as reflected specifically in the legal works *Diwan al-masha'ikh* and *Diwan al-ashyakh*, we consistently find *"ahl al-kitab"* (people of the book) or *"ahl al-tawhid"* (monotheists). The term ᶜabd (slave; pl. ᶜabid) is used for blacks from the "Sudan" (sub-Saharan Africa); for the Jews, the term Yahudi typically appears not with the connotation of 'abd or of *dhimmi* but rather as "servant." Thus we find it even in a verbal form: "he had Jews serving (lit. "Jewing") him" (*wakana ᶜindahu yahudiyyun yakhdimuhu wa-yaqdi hawa'jahu*).[28] *"Ahkam al-dhimma,"* referring to rules regarding *dhimmis* as such, are not a big part of these two *diwans*. Ibadi Siyar writers almost always used the word Yahudi (pl. Yahud) and its different connotations instead.[29]

The status of *dhimma* in Ibadi thought is made clear in the short passages that we find in the two *diwans*. A Muslim (male) could shake hands with any *dhimmi*: male and female, free and slave, young and old. He could embrace them and they could eat side by side. He could enter a *dhimmi*'s house with the owner's permission. On social occasions, they could exchange gifts and visit each other. Ibadi legal theory reflects the sense of friendship and regular contact between the Imazighen and the Jews as two peoples belonging to a single community. It is based on Qur'anic teaching but also reflects social ties based on a long coexistence that had existed for centuries before the arrival of Islam. In the early Ibadi texts, the Ibadi-Jewish relationship can be analyzed according to three patterns or models: (1) the model of friendship and neighborliness; (2) the model of the clever helper; and (3) the model of the opponent.

The Model of Friendship and Neighborliness

This model is the first and hence the oldest model to appear in the Ibadi texts. It indicates the existence of a harmonious relationship between a Jew and an Ibadi shaykh, a relationship governed by good manners, coexistence, respect, and mutual help. The Ibadi writers focused on the tiny details that best described their religious leaders, including their relationships with the Jews and Christians. In fact, portraits of Jews in Ibadi texts were qualitatively more detailed and quantitatively much more numerous than portraits of Christians.

Several anecdotes found in early Ibadi texts portray the relationship between Ibadis and Jews. One anecdote that supposedly took place in the middle of the ninth century suggests a pleasant and perfect relationship. Two Ibadi shaykhs from Nefusa, Abu al-Muhasir al-Ifatmani and ʿUmrus ibn al-Fath, went to the forest. Abu al-Muhasir picked some fruit to bring back home, which he shared with his relatives and neighbors. He also gave some to a Jew (who may have been a neighbor or friend). That affectionate act had a strong influence on the Jew, who called for God's mercy based on the kindness he had received: "O my God be merciful to him as he was to me," said the Jew. Abu-l-Muhasir replied, "That is, indeed, what I wanted you to do," and he thanked him.[30] This anecdote reinforces the understanding among both groups that God is unique, refuting claims of fundamental religious difference between Jews and Muslims; they call on the same God for forgiveness for them both.

A second anecdote is also revealing. When the Ibadi *qadi* (judge) of Nefusa, Abu Yahya al-Arjani, had a new son, the Nefusi Jews collected forty dinars and offered it to him as a present. The *qadi* refused the offer because it was not *jizya* and in return offered them grapes and thanked them. The Jews thereby understood that Nefusa was a safe place with a fair and just ruler who refused to take their money. Thereafter the Jews bought farms and settled down in Nefusa.[31] This event reveals that economic rather than religious issues were at stake. Religious freedom was already guaranteed; thus, the situation of the Jews in Nefusa was implicitly open to comparison with the situation of Jews in other North African cities, prompting Ibadi historians to portray Nefusa as a land of peace where different religions could coexist.

Another anecdote reveals that Imazighen-Jewish friendship had few limits and that neither religious nor economic factors hampered its survival. A rich Jew in Nefusa visited his Ibadi friend, a poor man who shared his meager food with him. For the Jew, the historians tell us, it was a very delicious meal, the likes of which he had never tasted before.[32] This story reveals the depth of friendship, harmony, and mutual help that prevailed between both groups in what was regarded as a single community. These and other stories indicate that Ibadis and Jews were on good terms: they visited one another; they offered each other help on important occasions such as births, marriages, and deaths; and they shared food and housing. They were friends, neighbors, and partners in business and commerce.

The Model of the Clever Helper

One model for this relationship is rooted in universal ethics, which present a social reality based on tolerance, love, and peace without racial discrimination or religious persecution. All people are presented as equal, and differences in ethnicity or religion are not seen as a determinant factor in defining social interaction between Ibadis and Jews in North African society. The conversion of the Imazighen to Ibadism affirmed these humanistic traits and principles of tolerance.[33]

However, a second model may be less utopian and hence more fitting, one in which the Jew is seen as an essential element in the Ibadi community who uses his wit and cleverness for the benefit of the entire community. Consider the following examples:

1) After the founding of the Fatimid dynasty in North Africa, ʿUbayd Allah decided to kill the Wargla inhabitants and destroy their city. Yet, with a clever idea, a Jew succeeded in avoiding the catastrophe and saved the people and the city from total destruction. Abu Zakariya al-Wargilani wrote:

> ʿUbayd Allah sent a big army to destroy Wargla. When the Wargilani heard about the conquest they left the oasis and ascended a huge unreachable mount called Karima. Among them were a large number of Jews. The Shiʿi militants could not reach them. Therefore, they blockaded them with seven circles of troops so they would die from lack

of water. Some days later, the Ibadi were suffering from a shortage of water and food. A Jew had a good idea to protect the life of his Ibadi friends. He put olive oil in many big vessels. When the camels saw the oil they thought that it was water, so they began to sip it. When the militants saw them from the bottom of the mount, they thought that they were really drinking water. They said: "We are blockading them to be killed out of thirst and they had enough water to give to their camels." Therefore, they left them.[34]

This story was very appealing to the Ibadi writers, who were proud of the stratagem that saved Wargla and protected its people. The Jew is portrayed as a protector, a savior of a whole community. The Jew was seen as a significant member of a united society free from ethnic or religious discrimination.[35]

In addition to being a savior of a whole Ibadi community, the Jew is also seen as a protector of individuals. The following story conveys how the Jews contributed to protecting the Ibadi shaykhs.

When al-Mu'izz al-Din Allah decided to leave North Africa to settle in Egypt, he ordered the Ibadi shaykh of Jerba, Ibn Zinghil, to accompany him. Ibn Zinghil was upset because he did not want to leave his native land and his Ibadi community, but he could not refuse the invitation or he would be killed. A Jewish servant-friend advised him to drink barley bran water and wash his face with it, so that everyone who saw him would think that he was ill and could not travel. When al-Mu'izz was told that Ibn Zinghil was ill, he did not believe it, so he asked to see him. When he saw his yellow face, he trusted him and allowed him to stay in bed.[36] In this story, the Jew was willing to help the Ibadi keep their leader, Ibn Zinghil, who was the most important Ibadi theologian of the tenth century. A similar story, in which the Ibadi scholar Yaghla ibn Ziltaf was obliged to go with the Fatimids to Egypt, serves to underline how important the Jew's role was in Ibn Zinghil's case. Ibn Ziltaf was the writer of the first North African Ibadi theological treatise, *al-Rad 'ala jami'i al-mukhalifin*.[37] The story reveals that with no Jewish intercessor to foil the plan to force his departure, he would have been lost to the Ibadis of North Africa.

The Model of the Opponent and the Ibadi's Reaction

This third model contradicts the former models. Jews lived under the Fatimid dynasty in Mahdiyya and Qayrawan and sided with the Fatimids against the Ibadi shaykhs. So what was the Ibadi shaykhs' reaction to the Jews who lived among them?

One story tells us that Ibn Zinghil had participated in the revolt against the Fatimids along with Ibn Ziltaf and Ibn Mukhallad after the failure of the revolt by Abu Yazid ibn Qaydad. He wrote a letter of support offering to form a confederation with the Umayyad caliphate in al-Andalus.[38] The Fatimids discovered this letter, and someone told al-Muʿizz that it had been written by Ibn Zinghil. Ibn Zinghil was arrested without being told why. A Jew then told al-Muʿizz that he could help him find out if the letter had been written by Ibn Zinghil or not. He visited Ibn Zinghil in jail and requested that he write a letter asking al-Muʿizz why he had been imprisoned and demanding his freedom. He did, but he altered his handwriting, remembering the letter that he had sent to the Umayyads. When the calligraphers compared the two letters, they told al-Muʿizz that it was not written by the same person. The Jew's intercession had no effect, and Ibn Zinghil was let out of prison.[39]

A second story deals with a Jew who informed al-Muʿizz about the other leader of the revolt, Ibn Mukhallad. No sooner did al-Muʿizz hear about the shaykh then he ordered the Shiʿi governor of al-Hamma to kill him.[40]

Despite the underlying message of these two stories, the Ibadi writers refrained from mentioning any repercussions for the Jews in their societies, and there was no hint in any *fatwa* of the period that communication with Jews might have been prohibited. In fact, what the Ibadi writers consistently record is that the Jews lived in peace; they experienced neither marginalization nor exclusion. If the religious authorities had issued a *fatwa* against them, the Ibadi writers would have certainly mentioned it.

The latter two stories tell us that the Jews had a role in the Shiʿi Fatimid dynasty similar to their role in Ibadi society, namely, working for the benefit of the community in which they were living. In Ibadi localities, we have discovered two models: a model of friendship and a model of protector of the community or individuals. In non-Ibadi localities, the Jew is an opponent: Ibn Zinghil was condemned to death and Ibn Mukhallad was killed. The two models are completely different. The image of the Jew as a figure of opposition is in no way similar to that of the helper. The reaction of Ibadis is also different: in their localities, a Jew is respected and treated as a friend or neighbor, as seen above; in other localities, he is untrustworthy. However, the image of the "other side's" Jew as trickster did not damage the image of local Jews as friends or neighbors. Rather, these Jews were perceived as belonging to two different moral categories: their ethnic and religious identity did not lead the Ibadis to adopt a single stereotypical image.

To conclude, in Ibadi societies until the tenth century, Jews were seen neither as outcasts nor as ethnically, religiously or economically humbled. Rather, Jews were "the motor of Ibadi communities," as the Ibadi shaykh of Tunisia, Professor Farhat al-Jabʿiri, has proposed.[41] It is probably appropriate in my final analysis to note that these three models are based on the only images of Jews to be found in the Ibadi *Siyar*. As discussed, most were positive. Moral values determined the type of the relationship that existed between all members of the community: religious tolerance, protection, respect, peace, and mutual help prevailed in Imazighen-Ibadi societies.

Ibadi writers never hesitated to document and describe how Jews behaved as true friends and helpers toward individuals or toward the whole Ibadi community. They also described how Jews might also hamper good relations. However, even when Ibadi writers wrote of incidents when Jews worked against Ibadi goals, the stories they told made it clear that no punitive or discriminatory measures were taken against the Jews. The purpose of these texts was to reflect the situation through the writers' perceptions of social reality. Avraham Udovitch claimed that the Ibadis of Ghardaïa allowed the Jews to say the *shahada,* to say *"La 'ilaha 'illa Allah, Muhammadun Rasulu Allah"* and to add "but not for us" (Muhammad is the apostle of God, but not for us). The Ibadis accepted this formulation.[42] This *shahada* is similar to the one attributed to Salih ibn Tarif, the prophet of Barghwata in the eighth century, whom some writers believed was Jewish. This North African *shahada* is adopted by the ʿUmayriyya, a Nefusi Ibadi sect. Its leader, ʿIsa ibn ʿUmayr, stipulated that only knowledge of God is required for a Muslim to be a true believer, thus denying the necessity to acknowledge the Prophet Muhammad as Imam. In his view, only knowledge of the one God was essential for the *shahada.*[43]

Can the Ibadi formulation of the *shahada* be a result of Jewish influence in North Africa? Only by consulting the Jewish sources, if they exist, could we find an adequate answer to this problematic issue.

Moreover, the Amazigh name for God, *"yaqush,"* which for both the allegedly Jewish tribe of Barghawata and the Ibadi was a synonym of the Arabic name "Allah," was the subject of long theological debates among the Ibadi shaykhs until the eleventh century. The majority proclaimed that *yaqush* is Allah and Allah is *yaqush.* If a Muslim says *"yaqush* is not God he is an infidel (*kafir*)." If he utters the expression *"yaqush* is the turtle," then "he is a polytheist (*Mushrik*)."[44]

Whether the term *"yaqush"* is found in North African Jewish sources requires further research. But it is certain that the Imazighen-Jewish relationship cannot be fully grasped without reference to the image of the Imazighen in Hebrew, Judeo-Berber,[45] and Judeo-Arabic sources. Was the tradition of tolerance reciprocal? Was the image of the Imazighen in Jewish sources positive or negative? Finally, the larger question of the influence of Jews and the Hebrew language on North African Muslim culture and society awaits further investigation.

In conclusion, the scholarly analysis of the Muslim-Jewish interaction in the early centuries of Islam can shed light on many problematic issues related to the characteristics of North African Jewry as foundational to North African monotheism.

NOTES

I would like to thank the Ibadi shaykh of Tunisia, Professor Farhat al-Ja'biri, and Professors Galit Hasan Rokem and Daniel Boyarin for their fruitful help.

1. See, e.g., André Chouraqui, *Histoire des Juifs en Afrique du Nord* (Paris: Rocher, 1998); Paul Sebag, *Histoire des Juifs de Tunisie; Des origines à nos jours* (Paris: L'Harmattan, 1991); Michel Abitbol, ed., *Communautés juives des marges sahariennes du Maghreb* (Jerusalem: Institut Ben-Zvi, 1982); and Jacob Oliel, *Les Juifs au Sahara: Le Touat au Moyen Age* (Paris: CNRS, 1994).

2. F. Valderrama Martínez, "El Islam en el Mundo Beréber," *Boletín de la Asociación Española de Orientalistas* 5 (1991): 5–24; and F. Valderrama Martínez, "Mitos y leyendas en el mundo Beréber," *Boletín de la Asociación Española de Orientalistas* 30 (1994): 11–20.

3. Al-Ibadiya (Ibadis) is one of the earliest Islamic sects. It was founded in the first half of the seventh century and is considered to be a moderate branch of the Kharijite movement. Adherents of this school have formed a number of communities that hold fast to its teachings in Oman and Muscat in Southeast Arabia, Zanzibar on the East Coast of Africa, Jabal Nafusa and Zuwara in Libya, the island of Jerba in Tunisia, and in the Mzab in Algeria. Non-Ibadi Muslim scholars regarded Ibadis as extreme Kharijites and heretics and consequently did not pay serious attention to their doctrine. Only recently have the Ibadiya been included among the other Islamic schools represented in encyclopedias of Islamic law published in Egypt and Kuwait. See Amr Khalifah Ennami, "Studies in Ibadism (al-Ibadiyah): Accompanied by a Critical Edition of: 1. Section II, part 1 of K. Qawa'id al-Islam of Isma'il b. Musa al-Jitali; 2. K. Usul al-Din of Tabghurin b. Dawud b. 'Isa al-Malshuti; 3. Ajwibat Ibn Khalfun by Abu Ya'qub Yusuf b. Khalfun" (Ph.D. thesis, University of Cambridge, 1971); M. H. Custers, *Ibadi Publishing Activities in the East and in the West, c. 1880s–1960s* (Maastricht: M. H. Custers, 2006).

4. Mabrouk Mansouri, "Jamaliyat al-jasad wa-tuqusuhu al-ihtifaliyatu fi al-a'yad fi shamal Ifriqiya," *Majallat dirasat Andalusiya* 24 (July 2000): 73–93; Tadeusz Lewicki, "Survivances chez les berbères médiévaux de cultes anciens et de croyances païennes," *Folia Orientalia* 8 (1967): 5–37; Tadeusz Lewicki, "Culte du bélier dans la Tunisie Musulmane," *Revue des Études Islamiques* 9 (1935): 195–199; E. Laoust, "Noms et cérémonies des feux de joie chez les berbères de haut et de l'anti-Atlas," *Hesperis* 1 (1921): 53–65; D. Jacques-Meunié, "Sur le culte de saintes et les fêtes rituelles dans le moyen Dar'a et la région de Tzarine," *Hespéris* 38 (1951): 365–380.

5. Mohamed Talbi, "La conversion des Berbères au Harigisme Ibadito-sufrite et la nouvelle carte politique du Maghreb au II et IIIème siècle," *Etudes d'histoire Ifriqiyenne et de civilisation musulmane médiévale* (Tunis: Publications de l'Université de Tunis, 1982), 13–80; Ulrich Rebstock, *Die Ibaditen im Magrib, Die Geschichte einer Berberbewegung im gewand des Islam* (Berlin: Klaus Schwarz Verlag, Berlin, 1983); Werner Schwartz, *Die Anfänge der Ibaditen in Nordafrika; Der Beitrag einer islamischen Minderheit zur Ausbreitung des Islams* (Wiesbaden: Otto Harrassowitz, 1983).

6. M. I. Fierro, "El derecho maliki en Al-Andalus; siglos II–V/VIII–XI," *Al-Qantara* 12 (1991): 121.

7. T. Fahd, *La divination arabe, études religieuses sociologiques et folkloriques sur le milieu natif de l'Islam* (Paris: Sindbad, 1987); H. Z. Hirschberg, *A History of the Jews in North Africa*, vol. 1, *From Antiquity to the Sixteenth Century* (Leiden: Brill, 1974), 88, 95.

8. Chouraqui, *Histoire des Juifs en Afrique du Nord*, 84–86.

9. S. D. Goitein, "The Origin and Historical Significance of North African Jewry," in *Proceedings of the Seminar on Muslim-Jewish Relations in North Africa* (New York: World Jewish Congress, 1975), 8.

10. M. Simon, "Le Judaïsme berbère dans l'Afrique ancienne," *Revue d'Histoire et de Philosophie religieuse* 26 (1946): 1–31, 105–145.

11. Whether or not Salih ibn Tarif was a Jew is a controversial subject. His sacred genealogy as Salih son of Tarif son of Simeon son of Jacob son of Isaac and genealogies of subsequent

Barghwata leaders after his death, such as Yunus (Jonah) and al-Yasa' (Elisha), appeared for the first time in al-Bakri (d. 1094), and most Maghribi historians after him claimed this Jewish genealogy. Modern historians are divided on this subject. See J. Iskander, "Devout Heretics: The Barghawata in Maghiribi Historiography," *The Journal of North African Studies* 12, no. 1 (2007): 37–53. Those who reject the Jewishness argument claim that this genealogy was a way to give legitimacy to the Barghwata line. Ibn Khaldun, who claims that Salih was an Amazigh of the Masmuda tribe, applies his theory of group feeling (*ʿasabiya*) to argue that common descent is necessary for one to be accepted as a leader. By this logic, Salih could not have been an outsider and stranger but must have been a member of the Barghwata. Ibn Khaldun's theory has been accepted uncritically by many modern historians. However it can also be argued that this genealogy is more than a tool to claim legitimacy and that it is not plausible that a North African Muslim in the tenth century would have known the Hebrew Bible well enough to construct this genealogy. This chapter adopts the position, in reference to Ibadi writings of the tenth century, that a Jew can assume a leadership position.

12. Quran, Surat al-Tahrim, 66:4: "And the righteous one among those who believe and furthermore, the angels will back (him up) (*wa-Salihu al-muʾminin wa-l-malikahu baʿda dhalika zahir*). Literally, with reference to what Salih understood from this Quranic verse, it could be translated "and the Salih (good man) among the angels and the believers will appear."

13. Mabrouk Mansuri, "Zahiratu al-tanabbuʾ fi biladi al-Maghrib ila nihayat al-qarn al-sadis al-hijri," *Mawarid: Revue de la Faculté des lettres et des Sciences Humaines de Sousse* 5 (2000): 67–115; Mohammed Talbi, "Hérésie acculturation et nationalisme des berbères Bargwata," in *Actes du premier congrès d'études des cultures méditerranéennes d'influence arabo-berbère* (Algiers: Société Nationale d'Édition et de Diffusion, 1973), 217–233; Tadeusz Lewicki, "Prophètes divins et magiciens chez les berbères médiévaux," *Folia Orientalia* 7 (1965): 3–27; G. Marcy, "Le Dieu des Ibadites et de Bargwata," *Hespéris* 21, Fasc. 1 (1936): 33–56.

14. Gabriel Camps, "Réflexions sur l'origine des Juifs des régions Nord Sahariennes," in *Communautés juives des marge sahariennes du Maghreb,* ed. Michel Abitbol (Jerusalem: Institut Ben-Zvi, 1982), 64.

15. "Discussion," in *Proceedings of the Seminar on Muslim-Jewish Relations in North Africa* (New York: World Jewish Congress, 1975), 52.

16. Jean Despois, *Le Djebel Nefousa* (Paris: Larose, 1935); Abraham L. Udovitch and Lucette Valensi, "Etre Juif a Djerba," in *Communautés juives des marge sahariennes du Maghreb,,* ed. Michel Abitbol (Jerusalem: Institut Ben-Zvi, 1982), 199–225; Abraham L. Udovitch and Lucette Valensi, *Juifs en terre d'Islam: les communautés de Djerba* (Montreaux: Éditions des Archives Contemporaines, 1984), 8–14; bibliographical notes in Pessah Shinar, "Réflexions sur la symbiose judeo-ibadite en Afrique du Nord," in *Communautés juives des marge sahariennes du Maghreb,* 81–84; Michel Abitbol, "Juifs maghrébins et commerce transsaharien au Moyen-Age," in *Communautés juives des marge sahariennes du Maghreb,* 234, citing S. Assaf, *Sources et Etudes d'Histoires d'Israël* (Jerusalem, 1946), 141 (translated from Hebrew).

17. Nehemia Levtzion, "The Jews of Sijilmasa and the Saharan Trade," in *Communautés juives des marge sahariennes du Maghreb,* ed. Michel Abitbol (Jerusalem: Institut Ben-Zvi, 1982), 259.

18. Abitbol, "Juifs maghrébins et commerce transsaharien," 229–251; Tadeusz Lewicki, "Pages d'histoire du commerce trans-Saharien: les commerçants et les missionnaires Ibadites au Soudan central et occidental aux 8ᵉ–12ᵉ siècles," *Przegląd Orientalistyczny* 3 (1961): 3–18; Tadeusz Lewicki, "L'état nord-africain de Tahert et ses relations avec le Soudan Occidental à la fin du 8ᵉ et au 9ᵉsiècle," *Cahiers d'Études Africaines* 2 (1962): 513–535.

19. Fazlur Rahman, "Islam's Attitude toward Judaism," *The Muslim World* 72, no. 1 (1982): 1.

20. Muhammad Ibn Ahmad al-Tijani, *Rihlat al-Tijani,* ed. Hasan Husni ʿAbd al-Wahhab (Tunis: Kitabat al-Dawla lil-Maʿarif, 1958), 187.

21. "Fight those who believe not in Allah nor the last day, nor hold that forbidden which hath been forbidden by Allah and his Messenger, nor acknowledge the religion of truth, from

among the people of the Book until they pay the jizya with willing submission and feel themselves subdued." Qur'an, Surat al-Tawba, 9:29.

22. ʿIyad ibn Musa, *Tartib al-Madarik,* ed. 'Ahmad Bakir Mahmud (Beirut: Dar al-Hayat, 1968), 2:600.

23. A Maliki legend tells us that the Maliki jurist al-Buhlul ibn Rashid invited his Maliki friends to dinner only after he asked about their origin and was told that they were not Imazighi.

24. See, e.g., *Diwan al-ashyakh,* 10, 26, 27, 35, 49, 119, ms., Library of Sh. Farhat al-Ja'biri, Tunis.

25. In practice, this usually meant sending Amazigh sons and daughters to the East as servants in place of actual monetary payment. Al-Baladhuri, *Futuh al-buldan,* ed. ʿAbdallah and ʿUmar at-Tabba' (Beirut: *Dar al-Nashr li-al-Jamiʿiyyin,* 1957), 315–316.

26. Ibn al-Athir, *Al-Kamil fi al-Tarikh* (Beirut: Dar Sadir & Dar Beirut, 1979), 5, 192–193.

27. Hirschberg, *A History of Jews in North Africa,* 1:97; Al-Barradi, *Al-Jawahir al-muntaqat,* ed. Ibrahim Talay (Ksantina: Imp. Al Baʿath, n.d.), 173.

28. Al-Barradi, *Al-Jawahir al-muntaqat,* 138; Abu Zakariya, *Kitab siyar al-a'imma wa-akhbarihim,* ed. Ismaʿil al-ʿArabi (Beirut: Dar al-Gharb al-Islami, 1982), 229.

29. Abu Zakariya, *Kitab siyar al-a'imma* (Algiers: Diwan al-Matbu'at al-Jami'iyah, 1984), 248.

30. Ahmad ibn Saʿid al-Shammakhi, *Kitab al-siyar,* ed. Muhammad Hasan (Tunis: Kulliyat al-ʿUlum al-Insaniya wa-l-Ijtimaʿiya, 1995), 114.

31. Ibid., 171.

32. Ibid., 172.

33. *"Sans nul doute, l'égalitarisme des tenants des Kharijiyya et tout spécialement, leur esprit de tolérance à l'égard des Gens du livre encouragèrent de nombreux Juifs à venir s'installer dans ces nouveaux carrefours qui, bien souvent d'ailleurs avaient été habités par des Juifs depuis les temps les plus reculés"* (Without a doubt, the egalitarianism of the Kharijites and especially their spirit of toleration with regard to the People of the Book, encouraged many Jews to come settle in these new crossroads which, very often, had since long ago been inhabited by Jews); Abitbol, "Juifs Maghrébins et commerce transsaharien au Moyen-Age," 231. To make a similar point, Nehemia Levtzion cites two tenth-century witnesses, one Orthodox Sunni, the other an agent of the Fatimids (hence considered to be unbiased). Ibn al-Saghir, who resided at Tahart, described it thus ca. 902–903: "No foreigner stayed among them but made his permanent home among them and built among them because of the opulence he saw in the town, the laudable conduct of its Imam and his justice towards his subjects and the security of their person and property. . . . The roads to the land of the Sudan and all the countries of east and west were brought into use for trade and all kinds of goods" (quoted in Levtzion, "The Jews of Sijilmasa and the Saharan Trade," 257–258). Ibn Hawkal, who visited Sijilmasa in 951–952, was likewise impressed: "There is at Sijilmasa an uninterrupted trade with the land of the Sudan and other countries, abundant profits, and the constant coming and going of caravans. The inhabitants, too, are well bred in their actions and perfect in their morals and deeds. In their manners, they do not share the pettiness of the other people of the Maghrib in their dealings and customs, but act with great frankness. They are known for their ready charity and show manly concern for one another. . . . I saw there more than anywhere else in the Maghrib, shaykhs of blameless conduct and devotion to scholars and scholarship combined with lofty broad-mindedness and elevated and pure ambition" (quoted in Levtzion, "The Jews of Sijilmasa and the Saharan Trade," 258).

34. Abu Zakariya, *Kitab siyar al-a'imma,* 172.

35. We may take into consideration that the Fatimid conquest of Sijilmasa in 909 took place before the conquest of Wargla and ended a period of about 150 years of tolerance and peaceful coexistence. This conquest began with the persecution of Jews. It was a Jew who had pointed out the fugitive *mahdi,* 'Ubayd Allah, to the ruling Midrar prince, al-Yasa'. So when 'Ubayd Allah recounted to his compatriot, the Ismʿaili missionary (*daʿi*) Abu ʿAbdallah, what had happened to him, Abu ʿAbdallah rescued him and killed all the rich people among the Jews, first

torturing them and seizing their wealth. Saʿd Zaghlul ʿAbd al-Hamid, ed., *Kitab al-Istibsari fi ʿajaʾib al-amsar* (Alexandria: Matbaʿat Jamiʿat al-Iskandariya, 1958), 202. See also Levtzion, "The Jews of Sijilmasa and the Saharan Trade," 261.

36. Zakariya, *Kitab siyar al-aʾimma*, 229; Al-Barradi, *Al-Jawahir al-muntaqat*, 138.

37. Yaghla Ibn Ziltaf, *al-Rad ʿala jamiʿi al-mukhalifina*, ms., Library of Sh. Farhat al-Jaʿbiri, Tunis.

38. E. Lévi Provençal, "La política africana de ʿAbd al-Rahman: El conflicto entre las influencias Omeya y Fatimi en el Magrib," *Al Andalus* 11 (1946): 351–378.

39. Abu Zakariya, *Kitab siyar al-aʾimma*, 221; Al-Shammakhi, *Kitab al-siyar*, 317.

40. Abu Zakariya, *Kitab siyar al-aʾimma*, 210–213; Al-Shammakhi, *Kitab al-siyar*, 313–314.

41. Farhat al-Jabʾiri, communication with the author, 2004.

42. "Discussion," 35.

43. Abu ʿAmmar al-Wargilani, *Sharh al-jahalat li-tibghurin*, ed. Wanis b. al-Tahir Ibn ʿAmir (Tunis: Kulliyat al-Zituna, 1985), 163, 255.

44. Abu Zakariya, *Kitab siyar al-aʾimma*, 124; Al-Wargilani, *Sharh al-jahalat li-tibghurin*, 15–16; al-Wasiyani, *Kitab al-siyar*, ms., Library of Sh. Farhat al-Jaʿbiri, Tunis, 447–448.

45. Camps, "Réflexions sur l'origine des Juifs des régions Nord Sahariennes," 66; P. Galand-Pernet and Haïm Zafrani, *Une version berbère de la Haggadah de Pesah, texte de Tinrhir du Todrha (Maroc)* (Paris: Librairie orientaliste P. Geuthner, 1970).

5

Jewish Identity and Landownership in the Sous Region of Morocco

Abdellah Larhmaid

MUSLIM JURISTS ONCE conceptualized and developed the rights of Jews to control property in Morocco's southwestern region of the Sous according to whether the land in question was part of a residential quarter or an agricultural plot. In most Moroccan cities, Jews lived in a mellah, an urban quarter surrounded by a wall and endowed with a gate.[1] In most villages of the Sous, some Jews managed to control property, transmitting it from one generation to the next. At the turn of the twentieth century, however, 90 percent of this region's approximately 6,300 Jews lived in rural villages.[2] In these villages, Jews gathered in small hamlets, which, though physically separate from Muslim neighbors, did not have walls. The exploitation of property in these small hamlets differed from the system established in urban centers. In rural hamlets, Muslim chiefs transmitted the land on which Jews built their houses and (if they were farmers) earned their keep. To understand the experiences of Moroccan Jews over the past three centuries, it is important to study the differences in Muslim-Jewish interaction not only in urban centers and rural areas, a fairly standard division, but also with respect to residential quarters and agricultural lands.

The issue of property rights in residential quarters and agricultural lands has obvious implications for the study of the regional economy, but it also provides a way to show how relations with the land affected the cultural sphere of collective memory. When it came to owning land, Jews in the Sous were subject to the rulings of Muslim jurists as implemented by Muslim political leaders. Muslims in the Sous conceptualized Jews as foreign migrants who therefore had fewer rights to land than the religious majority, who they idealized as indigenous peoples. If Jews in Moroccan villages of the Sous did not have the right to control land, then how did they express the idea of belonging to a place? Juridical texts and royal correspondence as well as interviews with residents of the Sous provide a way to analyze the political and economic stakes of landownership in a way that defines the social identity of Jews in relation to their Muslim neighbors. Muslim authorities in the Sous tried to divest Jews of the property that might have ensured that they had a sense of regional belonging. However, Jews asserted their right to land.

Between Juridical Rhetoric and Political Practice

Jurisprudence focusing on the construction of non-Muslim sites of worship in territories controlled by Muslims makes it clear that Islamic scholars have never agreed on whether or not *dhimmis,* a term that signifies Jews or Christians (and in the Maghrib, Jews specifically), can control land. Scholars in the Sous who penned *nawazil* (juridical consultations based on interpretations of Islamic law) advance arguments by evoking *hadith* and the *sunna* as well as the texts of their predecessors, especially Ibn Sahl of Andalusia and al-Wansharisi.[3] Most arguments regarding the construction of non-Muslim sites of worship in an Islamic land center on the question of whether or not the *dhimmis*—in the case of Morocco, the Jews—had already constructed a synagogue before they became tributaries of a Muslim ruler. Most Islamic scholars authorized the continued maintenance of a synagogue that had been constructed before the Muslim conquest provided that a contract of *jizya* was signed, whereby the *dhimmis,* who continued to practice their religion, agreed to pay a ruler in exchange for their protection. In the case of non-Muslim sites of worship that postdate conquest, however, there is no consensus. Some Islamic scholars believe that Muslim rulers could authorize the construction of a new synagogue, while others believe that they had to prevent the spread of sites of worship that serviced a non-Muslim religious minority.[4]

The actions of ʿAli Bu Damiʿa of Iligh in the Sous region suggest that the political and economic concerns of Muslim rulers superseded the theoretical considerations of the Islamic scholars who addressed the right of a Jewish community to control land. ʿAli Bu Damiʿa was a descendant of the Sidi Ahmad U-Musa, the most important *murabit* worshipped in the region of Tazarwalt, located sixty kilometers from the city of Tiznit. Bu Damiʿa established local power just when the ʿAlawi dynasty was emerging in Tafilalt, located southeast of Sous. By leaning on the symbolic power of his holiness, he came to control a vast swath of the Sous during the period 1612–1670. During the first ten years of his rule, he set up a new Jewish colony in Iligh, which Bu Damiʿa himself founded approximately five kilometers from the sanctuary of Sidi Ahmad U-Musa as a new settlement.[5] The merchants in this Jewish colony, who came from Ifrane (or Oufrane), fifty kilometers to the south, were charged with expanding the trans-Saharan trade on which Bu Damiʿa based his power.

After Bu Damiʿa set up the new colony of Jews in Iligh, he decided to consult the Islamic scholar ʿAysa al-Suktani, then *qadi* of Marrakesh, about whether or not he could allow a new synagogue to be constructed and a Jewish cemetery to be created in a Muslim land under his jurisdiction.[6] If Bu Damiʿa hoped to ensure the religious legitimization of his commercial venture, he must have been sadly disappointed. Basing his arguments on those of his legal predecessors, al-Suktani ruled that Maliki law prohibited the establishment of new sites of non-Muslim worship that Morocco's *dhimmis* occupied only after the arrival of Islam.[7]

Ultimately, Bu Damiʿa disregarded al-Suktani's unfavorable ruling. Although the Jews in Iligh had already constructed a synagogue when al-Suktani wrote his response to Bu Damiʿa, Bu Damiʿa did not order that the synagogue be destroyed. Furthermore, he granted the Jews the land they needed for their cemetery.[8] In superseding al-Suktani's ruling, it seems that Bu Damiʿa favored his own political and economic interests, not the religious convictions of Islamic scholars; it is clear that political practice sometimes trumped juridical rhetoric. Bu Damiʿa's actions provide evidence that some Muslim rulers buttressed their temporal authority by overruling the legal interpretations of established scholars, instead transferring some property rights to Jews.

This event demonstrates the economic and political stakes of Jewish communities in the struggle for power. Under ʿAlawi rule, the authorities often supported their political legitimacy by reinforcing their Muslim identity. Since the Muslim identity of sultans was best expressed through the fact that they had Jewish subjects (indeed, having Jewish subjects accentuated Muslim identity and gave it value), the *jizya* played a critical role in the Moroccan political system. The sultans as guarantors of protection gained both monetary support and the support of their loyal subjects. On a symbolic level, however, the guarantor of the *jizya* gained religious legitimacy for his political power because he assumed a responsibility that reflected the role of the imam, a reflection of the role of the Prophet Muhammad as described in the canonical texts of Islam. By reinforcing the Muslim identity of their guarantors, the *jizya* put sultans in a better position in the context of the larger struggles for power in Morocco. The sultan, as imam, was theoretically the sole authority who could sign the pact of *dhimma*.[9] As far as I know, it was not typical for contracts of *jizya* to be signed between Jews and local authorities in the Sous; the only one I know of was signed on 1 October 1864 between the Bayruk brothers and the Jewish residents of Goulimime, a village in the southwestern region of the Sous.[10]

However, according to local customs, the leaders of tribes protected some Jews through other means. The act of *dhabiha* (ritual slaughter of a sheep) is one of the most common traditions of sacrifice used as a symbol of spiritual relationship; as part of the ritual, Jews had to present material gifts in order to guarantee their security.[11] This kind of act was practiced not only by Jews but also by Muslims, who used it to gain the political protection of patrons of other tribes.[12]

Beginning in the seventeenth century, Muslim authorities in the Sous acted as guarantors of Jewish property rights in residential quarters. In 1774, for example, the Jews of Tamanart, located in an oasis seventy-five kilometers east of Akka, signed a contract with local chieftains whereby they agreed to provide dung from their livestock.[13] The Jews there were not farmers, so they did not need the dung to fertilize their own fields. In exchange for this dung, Muslim authorities permitted them to establish residential quarters in their village. This contract is important because it shows that Jews in Tamanart had no inherent right to control residential properties; instead they rented that right from indigenous Muslim inhabitants.

The designation of Jews as "outsiders" continued into the modern era, indeed, as witnessed in the village of Tintazart, up until the present day.[14] Tintazart is located ten kilometers south of Tata. In 1883, French explorer Charles de Foucauld visited Tintazart with his Jewish guide, Mardochée Aby Serour, who told de Foucauld that the Jews who lived there had migrated from Akka, Aby Serour's own birthplace.[15] Mohamed Lamine, who was born in Tintazart approximately forty years after de Foucauld's visit, is now this village's *muqaddam,* or administrative representative. In discussing Jewish property rights in Tintazart, Lamine makes it clear that this region's political leaders still conceptualize Jews as protégés installed on Muslim lands, in this case those of his forebears. Lamine highlights the fact that Muslim inhabitation of this area predates Jewish settlements. He says that Jews originally constructed homes with planks taken from the roofs of the homes of Muslim residents. Lamine says that his family bequeathed the lands on which the Jewish quarter was built. His ancestors "donated" this land to the Jewish community in exchange for the dung of their livestock, which the chieftains used as fertilizer in his family's fields.[16] Lamine's explanation of the relations between Muslims and Jews in his village demonstrates that providing Jews with land constituted, and continues to constitute, a symbol of a Muslim ruler's temporal authority.

The Transfer of Property in Residential Quarters

The documented action of Bu Damiʿa and the oral tradition of Lamine show how early settlement in an area strengthened Jews' claims to property rights.[17] Jews of the Sous, however, unlike their counterparts in the region of the Draa valley, could rarely claim to be original settlers. In the Draa, oral tradition maintains that Jews settled in Zagora in the sixth century BCE.[18] Further, this tradition maintains that rabbis from Ktawa, a district near Zagora, founded Tidri, Morocco's first city.[19] Legends claim that Jews even established their own kingdom after a great struggle with the Kushites, black Berbers who were Christians.[20] The Jews of Ifrane, a town on the border between the Sous and the Draa, claim that their ancestors came from Palestine in the sixth century BCE, thereafter founding their own kingdom.[21] Except for the settlement in Ifrane, however, most Jews in the Sous migrated to this region from the Draa. Although their ancestors in the Draa had legitimate claims to settlements that predated Islamic conquest, the rights associated with such claims did not translate to the movement of Jewish migrants into the Sous.

Despite fragile claims to property rights, Jews in the Sous maintain oral traditions that reveal a cultural struggle regarding claims that they belonged to this region. Both Jews and Muslims tried to prove their role as early settlers, often through tales of mythical religious figures. The amnesia that characterizes the collective memory of Jews in the Sous and their Muslim neighbors is demonstrated by a lack of precision in dating the first settlements of this land. The stories, however, provide a window for viewing the life that the Jewish minority experienced in relation to the Muslim majority.

A system did evolve that gave some Jews the right to control property. Some Jews in residential quarters, especially in the urban mellahs, transferred land from generation to generation. In the residential quarters, rabbis usually oversaw the transfer of land between Jews, acting on behalf of a Muslim authority. This management led to the development of a customary right called *hazaqa*[22] by which a Jew who purchased the lease of a property from religious endowments or royal domains could transfer the right to exploit that property from one generation to the next.[23] The *hazaqa* gave the right to bequeath control of leased land without outright ownership, thus sharing some elements associated with private property.

In some instances, Jews actually owned land in residential quarters, for some contracts registered the outright sale of properties that named a Jewish buyer or seller. For example, in the fifteenth century, members of the Katiriyya family became Muslim chieftains in the village of Tamanart. At an unspecified date, a member of this family was in dire economic straits, so he sold some land to Jews.[24] Also in Tamanart, Jews sold land to Muslims. In 1720, for example, one Muslim resident, Shaykh Ibrahim, son of the *qa'id* Muhammad b. ʿAbdallah b. Mansur al-Tamanarti, purchased a garden from Rabbi Shlomo Ben Bihi and another Jew named Haga Ben Yaʿish.[25] This evidence shows that some Jews experienced economic autonomy from the dominant local Muslim authority. Outright ownership of land, however, was at best a precarious right. According to the historian Jacques-Meunié, the Sultan Mawlay Ismaʿil (r. 1672–1727) prohibited the right to own land, probably noting control of land by Jews such as Ben Bihi and Ben Yaᶜish.[26]

Regional land ownership patterns reflect cultural and social identity patterns, not just economic organization. The founding of some villages in the Sous was linked to the emergence of an Islamic saint who played a political and cultural role in regional settlements.[27] In and around Akka during the reign of the Saᶜdi dynasty (1511–1659), one Muslim family, the Mubaraks, played a primordial role in settling the residential quarters in this area and in the subsequent political development of those areas. Akka was founded at the start of the twelfth century and was enlarged three centuries later, after the destruction of the nearby town of Tamdult. The expansion of this city led to the ascendance of the Mubarak family.[28]

In Akka's hinterland, members of the Mubarak family were not only political leaders but were also popularly recognized as saints, thereby reinforcing the family's political power.[29] Before his death in 1518, for example, Muhammad b. Mubarak Aqqawi founded the village of Fum Akka, where he constructed his eponymous *zawiya*.[30] After his death, his four sons shared regional power. One son succeeded his father as head of the *zawiya* and another son was a religious figure, though in this instance a hermit in the Bani Mountain, where he founded the village of Agadir U-Zeru.[31] Leo Africanus, known in Arabic as al-Hasan b. Muhammad al-Wazzan (ca. 1494–ca. 1552), referred to the political activities of this family's saints when he visited the region at the beginning of the sixteenth century. He recorded that the region's inhabitants had fought among themselves until a saint established a truce.[32] The Mubarak family made their hometown of Akka the focal point of the region, and it became a key commercial outpost on the trans-Saharan trade route.[33] The establishment of new villages helped the family translate local power into national influence. For example, before his death in 1607, Shaykh ᶜAbdallah b. Mubarak was a regular presence at the court of Sultan Mawlay al-Mansur (r. 1578–1603).[34]

Jews in this region reinforced their sense that they belonged to the land through religious figures with mythical powers, although they never made them the focal points of new settlements. Rabbi Yissakhar Baᶜal Ha-Maᶜayan, for example, claimed ancestral origin in the Draa, although he had been born in the Sous. The rabbi led a group of Jews on a mythical journey out of Tagdirt n U-Shaᶜib, a village that had been founded in 1731, when Muslim inhabitants of nearby Irhalen had decided to establish a new settlement.[35] The name Tagdirt n U-Shaᶜib reflects the relative newness of the village, for it is a Berber word that means "nomads."

In their memories of Rabbi Yissakhar Baᶜal Ha-Maᶜayan, Jews focus on the journey from Tagdirt n U-Shaᶜib to Akka. In 1945, a French officer recorded the following story:

Two or three centuries ago, the Rabbi Chaffar Bal, who came from the South, headed toward Akka during a day of extraordinary heat. Still some hours from Akka, the people escorting him began to complain of thirst, and they refused to go any further. The rabbi gathered them and told them that he would allow them to drink on one condition, which was that they would not carry water with them as they continued along the route. Having all promised to respect this condition, Rabbi Chaffaar Bal struck the ground with his foot and made gush forth a spring that exists in the place called Talgha'cht, between Akka and Ait Oubelli. After all the men and the animals drank their fill, the caravan once again began to advance. At this moment, however, the rabbi saw that one black conductor of the convoy had, despite giving his word, carried a vessel (*guerba*) filled with water before leaving Talgha'cht. Rabbi Chaffar announced that this lack of confidence would cause his ruin, and so he died several hours later.[36]

Setting aside, for the purpose of this chapter, the implications of the wrongdoer's race, the story of this rabbi has both a cultural and an economic component. It is the tale of Jewish migration seemingly ordained by God, thereby offering a cultural argument that favors the notion that Jews belong to the land. Further, the rabbi controlled the key natural resource of water, a precious commodity in these semi-arid lands.[37]

As distinct from the activities of Muslim saints, however, the rabbi's holy action and subsequent death never led to the establishment of a new village. By transferring this oral tradition from generation to generation, Jews in this part of the Sous point to the sanctity of the idea that they belong to the region while also highlighting their economic claims to control of the land's resources. The rabbi's tomb is a site of pilgrimage for many Jews in and around Akka even though it never became the focal point for a village. Located near Talgha'isht, only nine kilometers from Tagadirt n U-Sha'ib, the tomb is in a Jewish cemetery that is rather far from any residences. The rabbi's story continues to be told until this day and, as revealed even by one present-day Muslim resident of Akka, he is widely known throughout the region.[38] Jews and Muslims in this region differed in how they constructed sociocultural identity. Muslim saints often founded new villages, while Jewish saints never fostered permanent settlement, even though their actions indicated an attachment to the land.

Since many Jews in the Sous were merchants, the nineteenth-century rise of trade networks with Europe increased their economic influence. The regional economy extended into Europe during the reign of Sidi Muhammad b. ʿAbdallah (r. 1757–1790), who ordered the construction of the port of Essaouira, where many Jewish and a few European merchants established commercial firms for trade with Europe. After this sultan's death, a struggle for power took place among

ʿAlawi contenders for royal succession. It took Mawlay Sulayman (r. 1796–1822) six years to secure power, but, once he became sultan, he clearly wanted to establish royal control of the Sous and maintain stability there. In 1807, he led an army into the Sous to ensure that fractious tribes there respected his authority.[39] Mawlay Sulayman engaged in a policy of indirect negotiations with the merchants who had flocked to Essaouira, a policy that allowed this Jewish community to thrive.[40] In fact, his successor, Mawlay ʿAbd al-Rahman (r. 1822–1859) relied on Jews as "merchants of the Sultan." These commercial agents, who worked in Essaouira[41] and other southern ports, did business with foreigners on behalf of the royal Muslim leaders of the region.[42]

Because Jews played such an important economic role, it is no surprise that Muslim rulers, perhaps fearful that Jews would develop too much independence, reaffirmed their role as guarantor of the religious minority's property rights. ʿAlawi sultans who perceived themselves as ultimate guarantors of Jewish rights did not intend to harm the interests of Jewish merchants, merely to ensure that merchants did not exceed the traditional limits placed on them by Muslim authority. Mawlay Sulayman's military intervention, after all, led to new prosperity for the Jews of Tarudant, and Sulayman consequently enlarged the mellah.[43] When Sulayman sent ʿAbd al-Malik b. Bihi b. Mulud al-Hahi to Tarudant as head of his army,[44] the latter ordered his representative Muhammad b. Yahya Aghnaj to conquer Hashim b. ʿAli Bu Damiʿa's fortress in Iligh, which he did in 1811.[45] He also moved the Jews of Iligh to Tarudant, although some of them chose to leave for Essaouira and Ifrane.[46] They returned to the Iligh mellah when Hashim regained his position just after Aghnaj left the government in 1816.[47] Meanwhile, in 1824, Tarudant's Jews had bought the right to exploit properties bequeathed as charitable endowments (*hubus*) in order to further expand their mellah.[48] In this way, the combination of regional unrest and expansion of trade increased the rights of Jews to express the notion that they belonged to the region through their control of urban properties.

Jews and Agricultural Lands

The newfound economic power of some urban Jews in the early decades of the nineteenth century led them to make claims to control agricultural properties, thereby touching directly on the issue of representation of Muslim power. In the Sous, cultivated lands held both a symbolic and material value that provided a means of distinguishing social categories. The Arabic term *asl*, or "origin," designated any lands inherited from one's forebears. In the Sous, local customs allowed Jews to obtain only the *manfaʿa*, the extended use of agricultural properties for a period of no more than thirty years. In the nineteenth century, for example, each family in the mellah of Tahala, located in the Anti-Atlas territory of Shtuka, paid one *riyal hasani* (a silver coin) for the right to use an agricultural plot.[49] In the minds of the religious majority, Muslims were indigenous inhabitants and Jews were outsiders, and the new claims of Jews that they owned agricultural land as private property—that is, as *asl* rather than *manfa'a*—provoked the ire of some Moroccans.

According to local custom, Jews, even those who purchased the extended use of a property, never touched the land, instead hiring Muslims to do agricultural work for them. They entrusted the work to tenant farmers, in this instance the *haratin* (dark-skinned agriculturalists).[50] They cultivated narrow plots of land between the palm trees of oases, where they grew cereals (barley, wheat, and maize) or fruits (figs, grapes, and pomegranates). The limited amount of water in these oases was shared among the owners of the parcels of land, and a *muqaddam* oversaw the system of irrigation. He decided how many hours water would flow to a certain property.[51]

As in Tarudant, however, new trade networks with Europe led to the commercialization of agriculture, which, in turn, led some Jews to seek a more direct means of control over farming land. With Essaouira nearby, Jewish merchants in Tarudant began to set up a trade in olives. During the reign of Mawlay Sulayman, they requested agricultural land outside the city's wall, just downstream from the Tamalalt canal. The contract they eventually signed provides insight into the relative value of local and foreign commerce; Jews in this city clearly favored the latter. Jewish merchants exchanged the right to use seven shops that were controlled as a religious endowment for the right to possess agricultural land that would produce foodstuffs sought in Europe.[52]

Jews in the Sous, however, were not content to possess the right to use properties, for they could actually own such properties through the practice of *rahn* (which means pledge or security), whereby wealthy Jewish and Muslim merchants accepted the deed to the land of a struggling property owner for a determined period of time in exchange for what was, in effect, a loan. If the borrower did not pay his debt, the lender had no need to take him to court since he already possessed the deed to the property.[53] This practice was widespread in the Sous, though many Islamic scholars questioned its legal validity.[54] By 1890, one royal official, Tarudant's governor, was complaining that several Moroccan Jews in Essaouira had become owners of an enormous expanse of property through their partnerships with Muslims living in that city.[55] Two years later, Sultan Mawlay al-Hasan (r. 1873–1894), clearly concerned about the shifting forces of economic influence, ordered his officials in Tarudant to prohibit *rahn* transactions.[56] The response of these officials to this royal order, however, proves that Moroccan sultans were sometimes subject to the "will of the people." The *qa'id* Sa'id Ja'idi al-Yahyawi informed Mawlay al-Hasan that the practice was far too ingrained to ban.[57]

Muslim rulers at the turn of the twentieth century expressed their increasing frustration over the fact that a number of Jews had come to own land through the mechanism of *rahn,* thus gaining economic independence. In 1901, the *qadi* of Tarudant expressed frustration about Jewish merchants in a letter to Sultan Mawlay ʿAbd al-ʿAziz (r. 1894–1908):

> In this form, their transactions have spread. They put their hand on prop-
> erties which would be difficult, if not impossible, to recuperate. This situa-
> tion is due to the indulgence of the official previously occupied with lands
> of this region. He did not send Muslim notaries (ʿudul) to ensure that what-
> ever might provoke this situation would be avoided. He did not assign no-
> taries to conclude transactions between the aforementioned people of the
> *dhimma* and their associates. He did not prevent the signing of any contract
> except to make sure that it was drawn up according to existing rights.[58]

In this letter, this royal official perceived the new economic power of Jews in the Sous as a threat to the Muslim sultan's political authority, which had pre-viously been based, at least in part, on his role as guarantor of Jewish property rights.

The environmental crises Moroccans experienced during the twentieth cen-tury only seemed to increase Jews' access to property ownership, which, in turn, increased their claims that they belonged in the Sous. When drought and sub-sequent famine struck southern Morocco in 1945, some Muslims in and around Akka who were struggling to survive sold agricultural land to Jews. In one in-stance, the courts recorded the sale of a parcel of agricultural land in Tagadirt U-Shaʿib to a Jew who thereafter assumed full possession of the land. This parcel of land was located just next to the mellah. The history of this property reflects the complexity of Jewish relations to land in the Sous. According to the contract that transferred ownership, the Muslim owner had himself purchased the prop-erty from a Jewish woman.[59] In this way, circumstances allowed Jews in the mel-lah to recuperate property that had once been owned by Jews.

Conclusion

Prior to concluding, it is perhaps necessary to acknowledge that the fore-going socioeconomic study of Jewish property rights requires broader historical contextualization to address several questions. Which rulers, whether they were sultans or local chieftains, enlarged Jewish property rights and which did not? When did Jews gain more social leverage through increased property rights? At what period did Muslim authorities make an effort to rescind these rights? Was it during times of economic prosperity, as when trade with Europe increased during the nineteenth century? Or was it during times of economic hardship, such as the crisis brought on by drought in the twentieth century? And how did colonial rule change or regulate land tenure and Jews' access to land? In defining patterns of Jewish property rights over an extended period of time, we can understand not only the internal dynamics of Muslim-Jewish relations but also their broader agency.

And yet in this short essay, I have shown how Muslims of the Sous perceived Jews as outsiders without inherent rights to land ownership, thereby defining them as a distinct social group. Despite this Muslim conceptualization, Jews struggled to assert the notion that they had belonged to the lands of the Sous over the course of the previous 400 years. Oral tradition offers one means of providing a counternarrative to the dominant discourse of the Muslim majority, and Jews recount stories that suggest that they were the first occupants of the territory, well before Islam arrived in North Africa, or that their mythical religious figures exercised divine control over the natural resources supplied by the very land they could not legally own. The establishment of new legal traditions that reflected their economic influence also provided a means for Jews to claim a literal belonging to the land. Whether through the right of *hazaqa*, whereby some Jews transferred to their children the right to urban properties, or later, by developing contracts with European merchants that permitted them direct control over agricultural properties, Jews made an effort to sidestep Muslim control over all of the lands of the Sous.

NOTES

1. On the topic of creation of mellahs, see Haïm Zafrani, "Mallāḥ," *Encyclopedia of Islam*, 2nd ed. (Leiden: Brill, 1991); Emily Gottreich, "Mallāḥ," in *Encyclopedia of the Jews in the Islamic World*, ed. Norman A. Stillman (Leiden: Brill, 2010); Kenneth L. Brown, "Mellah and Madina: A Moroccan City and Its Jewish Quarter (Salé ca. 1880–1930)," in *Studies in Judaism and Islam*, ed. Shlomo Morag, Issachar Ben-Ami, and Norman A. Stillman (Jerusalem: Magnes Press, 1981), 253–281; Emily Gottreich, "On the Origins of the Mellah of Marrakesh," *International Journal of Middle Eastern Studies* 35 (2003): 287–305; David Corcos, *Studies in the History of the Jews of Morocco* (Jerusalem: Rubin Mass, 1976), 64; ʿAbd al-ʿAziz al-Khamlishi, "Hawla masʾala binaʾ al-millahat bi-al-mudun al-maghribiyya," *Dar al-Niyaba* 4 (Spring 1987): 21–28; and Susan Gilson Miller, Attilio Petruccioli, and Mauro Bertagnin, "Inscribing Minority Space in the Islamic City: The Jewish Quarter of Fez (1438–1912)," *Journal of the Society of Architectural Historians* 60, no. 3 (2001): 310–327.

2. De la Porte des Vaux, "Notes sur le peuplement juif dans le Souss," *Bulletin Economique et Social du Maroc* 15, no. 55 (1952): 448–459.

3. A. Abel, "La Djizya: tribut ou rançon?" *Studia Islamica* 32 (1970): 5–19.

4. Antoine Fattal, *Le statut légal des non-Musulmans en pays d'Islam* (Beirut: Imprimerie Catholique, 1958), 266.

5. Paul Pascon and Daniel Schroeter, "Le cimitière juif d'Iligh, 1751–1955: Étude des épitaphes comme documents d'histoire démographique," in Paul Pascon et al., *La maison d'Iligh et l'histoire sociale de Tazerwalt* (Rabat: Société Marocaine des Editeurs Réunis, 1984), 121.

6. Bibliothèque Nationale (al-Khizanat al-Wataniya), Rabat (henceforth BN), *dal* 2814, *Nawazil al-Suktani*, 414.

7. For the argument of the Andalusian *qadi*s, see Bibliothèque Nationale et Archives (henceforth BGA), Rabat, *dal* 464. See also Thami Elazemmour, "Les nouazil d'Ibn Sahl," *Hespéris-Tamuda* 14 (1973): 40–41; E. Amar, "La pierre de touche des Fétwas d'Ahmed al-Wanscharisi: Choix de consultations juridiques des synagogues juives de Touat," *Archives Marocaines* 12, no. 1 (1908): 231–268; Ahmad b. ʿAbd al-Munʿim Damanhuri, *Iqamat al-hujja al-bahira ʿala hadm kanaʾis Misr wa-al Qahira,* manuscript no. 1930, BGA.

8. Pascon and Schroeter, "Le cimitière juif d'Iligh," 113–140.

9. Susan Gilson Miller, "*Dhimma* Reconsidered: Jews, Taxes, and Royal Authority in Nineteenth-Century Tangier," in *The Shadow of the Sultan: Culture, Power, and Politics in Morocco,* ed. Rahma Bourqia and Susan Gilson Miller (Cambridge, Mass.: Harvard University Press, 1999), 103–126.

10. Abdellah Larhmaid, "Collecting Jizya: Commerce, Power and Religious Identity in Goulmime, 1859–1893," paper presented at the conference Islam in Africa, Binghamton University, Binghamton, New York, 19–22 April 2001.

11. Daniel Schroeter, *Merchants of Essaouira: Urban Society and Imperialism in Southwestern Morocco, 1844–1886* (Cambridge: Cambridge University Press, 1988), 91.

12. A. Sebti, "Insécurité et figures de la protection au XIXe siècle: La 'ztata' et son vocabulaire," in *La societe civile au Maroc* (Rabat: Signes du Present, 1992), 47–69.

13. Lease contract, Ramadan 1188 (November 1774), family archives in possession of Karim al-Bashir, a descendant of the Katiriyya family of Tamanart.

14. The concept of "outsiders" is used here not in a way that means exclusion but to describe how some groups identify themselves as long established in contrast to others. See Norbert Elias, "Introduction," in Norbert Elias and John L. Scotson, *The Established and the Outsiders: A Sociological Enquiry into Community Problems* (London: Sage, 1994).

15. Charles de Foucauld, *Reconnaissance au Maroc* (Paris: Challamel, 1888), 145.

16. Mohamed Lamine, interview with author, 16 August 1996.

17. The Jewish tradition maintains an attachment to Ifrane (or Oufrane) as an ancient Jewish settlement dating from before the Islamic period. In contrast, other Jewish communities, even if they were indigenous to the region, had to move to new neighborhoods following the establishment of new Muslim communities. See Vincent Monteil, "Les Juifs d'Ifran," *Hespéris* 35 (1948): 151–161.

18. J. Gattefossé, "Juifs et Chrétiens du Draa avant l'Islam," *Bulletin de la Société de Préhistoire du Maroc* 3–4 (1935): 39–66.

19. Dominique Jacques-Meunié, *Le Maroc saharien, dès origines au XVIe siècle* (Paris: Librairie Klincksieck, 1982), 1:180–185.

20. Ibid.

21. Ibid.

22. In biblical and Talmudic texts, the Hebrew term "*hazaqa*" refers to the right of a previous owner of land/property/real estate to intervene in decisions about transmitting ownership of the property. *Hazaqa* was applied in Morocco in a number of different ways. For example, if land was sold by one Jew to another, the previous owner still had the authority to object to its transfer to a foreign person. His possession of the right of the *hazaqa* would allow him to object, using what is called in Jewish law *modaʾa,* caveat emptor. This law was used to protect the community and assure that it would be protected from interested neighbors. See Haïm Zafa-

rani, *Études et recherches sur la vie intellectuelle juive au Maroc,* Part 1, *Pensée juridique et environ-nement, social éconnomique et religieux* (Paris: Geuthner, 1972), 188–195.

23. Paul Decroux, *Droit foncier marocain* (1937; reprint, Rabat: Edition La Porte, n.d.), 454.

24. Family archives in possession of Karim al-Bashir.

25. Bill of purchase, 1 Rajab 1132 (9 May 1720), family archives in possession of Karim al-Bashir.

26. Jacques-Meunié, *Le Maroc saharien,* 1:188.

27. Villages also developed when religious lodges expanded in the sixteenth century in the Draa Valley. See Remco Ensel, *Saints and Servants in Southern Morocco* (Köln: Brill, 1999), 48–52.

28. Anonymous, *Tarikh al-dawla al-Saʿdiya al-Tagmadartiya,* ed. ʿAbd al-Rahim b. Hadah (Casablanca: ʿUyun al-Maqallat, 1994), 56.

29. Muhammad Habib Nuhi, "Aqqa," in *Muʿallamat al-Maghrib,* vol. 2, ed. Muhammad Hiji (Salé: Matabiʿ Sala, 1989–2000), 578–579.

30. Jacques-Meunié, *Le Maroc saharien,* 1:430.

31. Ibid., 428.

32. Leon l'Africain, *Description de l'Afrique,* trans. A. Epaulard, vol. 2 (Paris: Maisonneuve, 1956), 422.

33. Nuhi, "'Aqqa," 578–579.

34. Ibid.

35. Ibid.

36. "Texte recueilli par le Capitaine Jouin, chef de l'annexe d'Akka," 1945, 3H 2126, Ar-chives du Ministère de la Guerre, Vincennes, Paris.

37. The saint was known in Jewish tradition as Rabbi Yissakhar Baʿal Ha-Maʿayan (Rabbi Yissakhar, Master or Owner of the Spring). The title "Chaffar" referred to by the French officer is probably a corruption of *shafaʿ,* which means to flow (abundantly). *Shafaʿ ha-maʿayan* has the sense of a spring gushing forth. The symbolic significance is the idea that the saint is like Moses, who drew water from a rock. I am grateful to Daniel Schroeter for this interpretation.

38. Ibrahim Nuhi, interview with author, 20 August 1996.

39. *Hawalat ahbas Tarudant,* no. 145, 11, BN.

40. Mohamed El Mansour, *Morocco in the Reign of Mawlay Sulayman* (Wisbech, Cambridge-shire: MENAS Press, 1990), 57–60.

41. Schroeter, *Merchants of Essaouira,* 24–26.

42. On the role of *tujjar al-Sultan* in Morocco in the late eighteenth and early nineteenth centuries, see the example of Meir Macnin, analyzed by Daniel Schroeter in *The Sultan's Jew, Morocco and the Sephardi World* (Stanford, Calif.: Stanford University Press, 2002).

43. Jacques Caillé, *La mission du capitaine Burel au Maroc en 1808* (Paris: Arts et Métiers Graphiques, 1953), 106–107.

44. Muhammad al-Duʿayyif, *Tarikh al-Duʿayyif, tarikh al-dawla al-Saʿida,* ed. Ahmad Al-ʿAmari (Rabat: Dar Al-Maʾthurat, 1986), 151–161.

45. Muhammad al-Mukhtar al-Susi, *Illigh qadiman wa-hadithan* (Rabat: al-Matbaʿat al-Wata-niya, 1966), 242–243.

46. Ibid.

47. Ibid.

48. BN, *Hawalat al-ahbas Tarudant,* no. 145, 11.

49. Pierre Flamand, *Diaspora en terre d'Islam: les communautés israélites du Sud marocain* (Casablanca: Presses des Imprimeries Réunies, n.d. [1959]).

50. Chafik Arrefag, "Al-Mujtamʿa al-Tamanarti: Mulahazat awaliya hawla al-bina al-ijti-maʿiya," in Wahat Bani: *Al-ʿUmq al-tarikhi wa-muʿahhilat al-tanmiyah: aʿmal nadwat Tata, 15–17 March 1995* (Agadir: Jamiʿat Ibn Zuhr, Kulliyat al-Adab wa-al-ʿUlum al-Insaniya, 1998), 70. As most of *haratin* in the southern Morocco were landless, they were nicknamed *khamasa,* or share-

croppers, the term used in the whole of Morocco to designate men who work in service of the owner in exchange for one-fifth of the harvest. See Hasin Ilahiane, *Ethnicities, Community Making, and Agrarian Change: The Political Ecology of a Moroccan Oasis* (Lanham, Md.: University Press of America, 2004), 60; and Remco Ensel, *Saints and Servants in Southern Morocco* (Leiden: Brill, 1999), 83–124.

51. Nuhi, "Aqqa," 578–579.

52. *Hawalat ahbas Tarudant,* no. 145, 11, BN.

53. Decroux, *Droit foncier marocain,* 46.

54. Muhammad al-Mukhtar al-Susi, *al-Maʿsul,* vol. 7 (Casablanca: Matbaʿat al-Najah, 1963), 51.

55. Bibliothèque Royale (al-Khizanat al-Hasaniya), Rabat, Registre 166, governor of Tarudant to Mawlay al-Hasan, 6 Shawwal 1307 (26 May 1890).

56. Direction des Archives Royales (Mudiriya al-Wathaʾiq al-Malakiya), Rabat, Mawlay al-Hasan to Qaʾid Muhammad b. ʿAli al-Shibani, 19 Hijja 1309 (15 June 1892).

57. Direction des Archives Royales, Qaʾid Saʿid Jaʿidi al-Yahyawi to Mawlay al-Hasan, 21 Hijja 1309 (17 June 1892).

58. Direction des Archives Royales, Muhammad b. ʿAbd al-Rahman, Qaʾid of Tarudant, to Mawlay ʿAbd al-ʿAziz, 26 Shawal 1318 (16 February 1901).

59. Archives du Tribunal de Premiere Instance, d'Akka Sale Contract, 1945.

6

Southern Moroccan Jewry between the Colonial Manufacture of Knowledge and the Postcolonial Historiographical Silence

Aomar Boum

In the absence of an abundance of archival documents on the Jews of southern Moroccan rural communities, the European travel narrative[1] became one of the key sources in the production of Jewish history in this part of the Islamic world.[2] European travelers reported a large body of information about southern Moroccan Jewry during the nineteenth and twentieth centuries,[3] writing from a imperial perspective on both Moroccan Jewry and Moroccan society. These perspectives make European travel narratives interesting historical sources of colonial and postcolonial writings about the Jews of southern Morocco.

Since many European travelers were associated with European geographical societies, which were themselves linked to the military,[4] postindependence historiography questioned the credibility of the travel narrative as an "authentic" source. European travelers were thought to have negative motives in writing about Morocco since they "all shared sentiments of hatred and racial discrimination" in their writings about Morocco.[5] Therefore, a group of Moroccan historians called for a reevaluation of colonial sources and a reappraisal of colonial Moroccan historiography.[6] Some historians went as far as advocating the total rejection of non-Western sources and their basic historiographical premises.[7] For instance, according to El Mansour, Germain Ayache advocated that European sources be rejected, claiming that the usefulness of European archives was "dubious since their authors merely reflected European interests and preoccupations."[8]

By rejecting the use of European sources, including travel narratives, these historians called into question the premises of what has been called the French colonial vulgate, which was primarily developed in Algeria before it was used in Morocco.[9] The colonial vulgate rests on a racial paradigm that "provided an ideological basis for absorbing the Kabyles into French colonial society to the detriment of the Arabs."[10] Lorcin argues that French colonial authorities did not have a preexisting policy that would create this divide on religious or sociological grounds and that it was "formed due to the circumstances of conquest and occupation coupled with the intellectual, social and political background of the Frenchmen (and in a very few cases, women) who observed, analyzed and recorded data on the peoples residing in Algeria during their colonization."[11]

Although this racialized paradigm was never codified into law in Algeria, it largely influenced the intellectual environment of North African colonial historiography. In Morocco, French colonial authorities drew from the Algerian vulgate to establish an ideological divide between Arabs and Berbers. Accordingly, they managed to "convince themselves that Morocco was in a state of semi-permanent rebellion."[12] In time, they elaborated a theory of a country divided into two political areas, *bilad al-makhzan*, the Arabic-speaking plains and cities whose denizens obeyed the sultan, and the *bilad al-siba*, the mountains and deserts inhabited by Berber-speaking people who did not.[13]

This chapter raises issues related to the use of travel narratives as colonial sources in the production of Moroccan Jewish history. I argue that historians of rural Moroccan Jewry must seek common ground about how to use Arab sources and European archives. Certain nationalist historians have called for the rejection of European sources in their entirety because they feel that European authors are unable to comprehend Moroccan society or the country's customs.[14] If we assume the validity of such a blanket claim and dismiss colonial historical works outright for their particularly biased sources and representation of Moroccan social groups, we are largely left with a vacuum of silence about southern Jewry, a group that receives scant attention in nationalist accounts but is more widely discussed in colonial documents.

This historical silence contradicts the very basis of postindependence nationalist ideology, which argues for the inclusion of all social groups, including minorities. While historians such as Germain Ayache and Muhammad al-Mukhtar al-Susi[15] critiqued colonial historiography for its biased sources, they themselves ignored the very Jewish subtext that colonial historians tried to highlight in the historiographical map of Morocco. Although some modern Moroccan historians have broken this silence in the past decade, the historical scholarship about rural Jewry remains very limited.[16]

A Personal Ethnographic Note

In January 2004, after spending three years in the United States, I enthusiastically returned to southwestern Morocco, my native region, to carry out dissertation fieldwork on the memories of Muslims about their erstwhile Jewish neighbors. For almost a year, I followed the historical traces of Jewish peddlers, visiting many villages located at the foot of the southern Anti-Atlas region. The ways lo-

cal informants constructed the social and economic historical relationships between Jews and Muslims in the region captured my attention. In particular, I was
interested in the intersections between the local memories of Jews and the recorded local, national, and colonial histories about Jews.

In the absence of a long recorded historical tradition about Jews in southwestern Morocco, historians have relied on local legend and myth.[17] Oral tradition became the key source in historical writing on southern Moroccan Jewry.
For instance, in his study of Kahina, the Jewish North African queen, Abdelmajid
Hannoum argues that "when historiography borrows a theme from oral tradition, the theme is no longer likely to be forgotten, but is henceforth part of the
memory of history."[18] If that is the case, are the accounts provided by European
travelers and colonial ethnographers and local Muslim historians similar in nature?

The local tradition is replete with stories about colonial divide-and-conquer
policies. During my ethnographic encounter with the local population of southwestern Morocco, I understood the history of southern Jewry as a web of discourse emanating from three distinctive voices: that of the French colonial vulgate, an edited postindependence national historical narrative, and local oral
traditions and memories.

For example, during my sojourn in the oasis of Tissint, some local elders in-
sisted on showing me—for a small fee—the houses where the French traveler
Charles de Foucauld (1858–1916) had stayed in 1883–1884. More than a century
ago, de Foucauld came to Akka with Rabbi Mardochée Aby Serour, a learned
Moroccan trader who was born in southern Morocco in 1826 and served as de
Foucauld's guide.[19] De Foucauld provided a relatively detailed description of the
area, including its tribes, villages, and Jewish population. Despite the fact that de
Foucauld's *Reconnaissance au Maroc* includes historical information, many villag-
ers remarked that Muhammad al-Mukhtar al-Susi had provided a social history
of southwestern Morocco and that I should be content with his version of the region's historiography.[20] The locals rejected the European (especially French) narrative of Moroccan history and its Jewish subtext. During my fieldwork, I had
many conversations with local people about local histories and historians. Although locals generally recognize the importance of the colonial historical writing in the form of travel narratives and historical monographs and military reports, they generally tended to challenge these histories of southern Morocco as
politically motivated and therefore lacking historical legitimacy and "authenticity." Idir, one of my informants from the region of Akka, remarked:

> French historians and travelers have *invented* texts with the intention of in-
> stigating social chaos and turning communities against each other: I mean
> Berbers against Arabs, powerful lords against one another, and Arabs against
> Jews. Unfortunately we believed their stories and *marginalized* our Islamic
> historiographical writing about the region and its Jewish communities. I

am not claiming that Muslim historians have highlighted the Jewish history of Morocco[,] but at least they did not *invent* it. Their only mistake is that they *ignored* it. [My italics.]

This vignette gives a summary of the main issues in this chapter, which center on the concept of the truth or fiction of the historical narratives and the silences within the historical text about Jews in southern Morocco because of how power operates in the construction and recording of history. In the absence of any recorded history, how can we produce a history of the Jews of rural southern Moroccon? I do not claim that this chapter demonstrates an adequate theory of how histories of rural Moroccan Jews should be produced. Instead, my main objective is to raise some of the questions inherent in the production of histories of Jews of rural communities in Morocco in general given the relative absence of relevant historical texts.

Idir's statement is reminiscent of Trouillot's discussion of the idea of history as one "among many types of narratives with no particular distinction except for its pretence of truth."[21] My informant argues that the history of southwestern Morocco as we know it today is the result of a premeditated colonial policy built upon a preexisting French strategy in Algeria. This strategy, which revolves around what Lorcin calls the "mechanics of marginalization and the formation of social hierarchies," is the basis of the French colonial vulgate in Algeria and later in Morocco. The French introduced the colonial vulgate in Morocco by using "sociological differences and religious disparities between the two groups to create an image of the Kabyle [and Jew] which was good and one of the Arab [Muslim] which was bad and, from this, to extrapolate that the former was more suited to assimilate than the latter."[22] On another level, Idir's statement highlights the silences about Jewish history in texts written by Muslims; he points out the absences of narratives about Jews in Muhammad al-Mukhtar al-Susi's local history.

Jews of Saharan Oases: Akka as a Case Study

Akka is one of the major Jewish settlements in the Anti-Atlas. The word Akka refers to the valley of palm groves, which opens at the mouth of Oued (*wadi*) Akka, one of the tributaries of the Draa River. Akka is an aggregate of villages that include a variety of ethnicities. Traditionally, it was under the control of the Ait Mrabat, the largest tribe in the oasis. Today, it is one of the main communes of the province of Tata and has a population of around 20,000 people. It borders the communes of Issafan (to the north), Foum Lahsen (to the west), Tata (to the east), and the Draa River (to the south). It is unclear when Moroccan

Jews first arrived in Akka. Jewish narratives describe Jewish settlements from the sixth century BCE in the city of Vaqqa near the Draa,[23] but no evidence of such an ancient city exists. Some historians maintain that the oasis was populated in the twelfth century CE and that it became important after the breakup of the Idrisid city of Tamdult in the fourteenth century.[24]

Akka is the home of one of the oldest religious brotherhoods in the Anti-Atlas, which was founded by Muhammad b. Mubarak al-ʿAqqawi (d. 1518/924), a disciple of al-Jazuli. His son ʿAbdallah b. Mubarak al-ʿAqqawi (d. 1563/971) retreated to the foot of the mountain, and his home became the village of Agadir Azru.[25] Many travelers, both Moroccan and Western, were interested in Akka. They left valuable descriptions and data about its social, political, and economic life. Al-Hasan al Wazzani and Muhammad al-Mukhtar al-Susi described the villages there and the feuds between their populations from the sixteenth century until descendants of Muhammad b. Mubarak al-ʿAqqawi, one of the main supporters of the Saʿdi dynasty, restored peace between the factions. The rise of the Saʿdis to power was greatly facilitated by an alliance with the *zawiya* of Akka against the Portuguese, the Spanish, and the Wattassids (1399–1554). Until the nineteenth century, Akka was one of the main caravan ports that linked sub-Saharan Africa and northern Morocco. After the collapse of the Saʿdi dynasty, Akka came under the control of Hassun al-Samlali, who controlled Tafilalt until he was defeated by al-Rashid b. al-Sharif al-ʿAlawi after the latter assumed power in 1664.[26]

Although their history is less well documented than that of Jews in other parts of Morocco, the Jews of the Moroccan Anti-Atlas were involved directly in trade and indirectly in agriculture. Legends and oral stories recount a long historical coexistence of Berbers and Jews characterized by complexities and paradoxes. The Anti-Atlas was historically home to a large Jewish population, whose members traveled from one weekly market to another to conduct trade. Jewish and Muslim merchants of Akka also navigated extensive commercial networks between Iligh, Ifrane, and Essaouira and other rural and urban centers. In the nineteenth and twentieth centuries, the Jews of Akka and other parts of southwestern Morocco were key actors in trade between the cities of Iligh, Marrakesh, Essaouira, Goulmime, and Tindouf and interior and sub-Saharan African communities.[27] The French were not able to control the region until 1934, at which time they established the current commune. Akka is still one of the most important and largest settlements of the Anti-Atlas, but the Jewish community of Akka ceased to exist after the second half of the twentieth century. Some Jews migrated to other urban Moroccan centers, while others left for Israel, Canada, and France. The descendants of the Jews of Akka are currently living elsewhere in Morocco, in France, and in Israel.

Figure 6.1. Shrine of Sidi Shanawil, Tamdult. Aomar Boum, 2004.

Figure 6.2. A view of the largest
mellah of Akka, Tagadirt.
Aomar Boum, 2004.

Figure 6.3. A view of the mellah of Taourirt, Akka. Aomar Boum, 2004.

The Limitation and Strength of the Travel Narrative as a Historical Source

In the process of their historical encounter with North Africa, European colonial powers subordinated, domesticated, and constructed colonized subjects through various forms of agency, including the production and dissemination of travel narratives. This dominant European representation of the colonized lingered in postcolonial texts. After independence formerly colonized subjects began to challenge the colonial narrative. Mary Louise Pratt uses the term "auto-ethnography" to refer to "instances in which colonized subjects undertake to represent themselves in ways that *engage with* the colonizer's own terms. If ethnographic texts are a means by which Europeans represent to themselves their (usually subjugated) others, autoethnographic texts are those the others construct in response to or in dialogue with those metropolitan representations."[28]

Using European travel narratives as a source for the rewriting of nineteenth- and twentieth-century Moroccan history remains a difficult enterprise; the native interpretation of history is not as independent as it claims to be from the colonial texts. Indigenous historians unconsciously appropriate idioms of the colonial texts, and indigenous modes of representation have unconsciously appropriated elements of colonial knowledge. Pratt suggests that colonial narratives should no longer be seen as one-dimensional sources in which "imperial eyes passively look out and possess." Instead, she invites us to see this encounter through the framework of the concept of the "contact zone." The "contact" perspective, Pratt argues, "emphasizes how subjects are constituted in and by their relations to each other. It treats the relations among colonizers and colonized, or travelers and 'travelees,' not in terms of separateness or apartheid, but in terms of copresence, interaction, interlocking understandings and practices, often within radically asymmetrical relations of power."[29]

Some travelers were aware of their fellow Europeans' misrepresentations and listed a series of rules for "objective" representations of the land of Barbary. James Grey Jackson, who spent around seventeen years in the region at the turn of the nineteenth century, wrote:

> It must be obvious to every one, that a considerable portion of time and study is requisite to obtain a thorough acquaintance with the moral and political character of any nation, but particularly with one which differs in every respect from our own, as does that of Marocco; *he therefore, who would be thoroughly acquainted with that country, must reside in it for a length of time; he must possess opportunities of penetrating into the councils of the State, as well as of studying the genius of the people; he must view them in war and in peace; in public and in domestic life; note their military skill, and their commercial system; and finally, and above all, he must have an accurate and practical knowledge of their language, in order to cut off one otherwise universal source of error, misconception, and misrepresentation.* [Italics in original.][30]

The European travelers who pioneered in breaking the ethnographic silence about slaves and the conditions of Jews were ideologically motivated,[31] and travelers' descriptions were not detailed enough to provide a clear idea about the realities of Jewish-Muslim relations in the pre-Saharan oases. James Grey Jackson acknowledges this:

> The greater part of the compositions respecting North Africa, are narratives of Journeys of Ambassadors, . . . generally for the purpose of redeeming captives, compiled by some person attached to the embassy, who, however faithfully he may relate what passes under his eye, is, nevertheless from his situation, and usual short stay, unable to collect any satisfactory information respecting the country in general, and what he does collect, is too often from some illiterate interpreter, ever jealous of affording information to Europeans even on the most trifling subjects.[32]

A similar passage in Graf Sternberg's *The Barbarians of Morocco* reads:

> I accompanied Count Sternberg on this little journey to Fez, not for the pur-
> pose of wringing concessions from the Sultan, but to learn something of
> the people and the country. . . . To speak with authority and true under-
> standing of Morocco and its people requires sympathy and a life long resi-
> dence amongst them. . . . Although we cannot claim to have lived amongst
> the Moors for more than a few months, we started our journey in a sympa-
> thetic mood, and returned with still more sympathy for these misunder-
> stood people. To say that we thoroughly understand the Moorish character
> would be to adopt a presumptuous attitude. . . . Tourists flock to Tangier,
> and, after a conversation with a low-caste guide and a donkey-ride on the
> sands, take [a] boat to England or America, and speak with the authority of
> ignorance on Morocco and its mysteries.[33]

Many historians caution us against blindly assuming the "academic merit
and truthfulness" of these narratives and descriptions.[34] They argue that the
travel narrative should be contextualized and analyzed within the ideology of the
French colonial occupation of Morocco. Mohammed Kenbib argues that many of
these French explorations coincided with social crises, revolts, social insecurities,
famine, and droughts. Accordingly,

> Multiple distortions were the result. Among them, a good number already
> have been the object of various re-readings. . . . These stereotypes have been
> revived since the 1950s. They have in particular served to paint a "profile
> of the oppressed in North Africa," creating a kind of "black legend of the
> Jew" in the land of Islam. And in this proclaimed revisionist perspective,
> which almost exclusively centers on the canonical obligations of the Jews
> of Morocco, practically no attention is paid to the diverse foundations and
> manifestations of cohabitation between different religious communities in
> this country.[35]

Within this context, it is logical to take the descriptions of de Foucauld and
other European travelers such as Lenz, Rohlfs, and Harris with a grain of salt.
Joffe sees Walter Harris's writings on the Rif as

> charming literary sketches of Morocco, valuable for their insights but of-
> fering little by way of real analysis of the political complexities through
> which the author lived. As literature, they are works of the imagination in
> which the author is the hero. As literary texts, they reveal the dominance
> of the author's European and imperial assumptions over the reality of the
> pre-colonial Morocco and the anticipated triumph of modernism over in-
> digenous values.[36]

Although I agree with critiques that point to the limited analysis of the travelers, I disagree with the recommendations that such descriptions be discarded

as viable sources of historical representation. The travel narrative as a literary work can be pregnant with historical significance. Historians can use it as a reference as they rewrite their historical subjects with the condition that the colonial ideologies behind it are acknowledged and dealt with. European travel narratives should be used cautiously as one component of what might have taken place in the historical writing about the less-documented and marginalized Jews of southern Morocco.

Michel-Rolph Trouillot provides a critical theoretical model for analyzing historical narratives. Trouillot confesses that human agency interferes with the narrative's plot. Narratives "necessarily distort life whether or not the evidence upon which they are based could be proved correct. With that viewpoint, history becomes one among many types of narratives with no particular distinction except for its pretence of truth."[37] By implementing a constructivist perspective with regard to travel narratives, the historian can expose the "tropes of power" within the process of producing the text. That is to say, the historian has the ability to recognize and sort out the potentially fictional aspect of the historical narrative from its "facts."

However, the issue here is not limited to whether the narrative represents truth or fiction. Instead, it is about rethinking a historiographical paradigm that acknowledges that the historical narrative's claims to "truthfulness" are linked to the position of the narrator as a winner or loser. Therefore the new model of historical writing of southern Moroccan Jewry should not profess a dogmatic relativist approach that claims that "nothing can serve as evidence about past events because they are unobservable."[38] Many historians are divided between realist empiricism and instrumentalism in the way they write history. Realist empiricism "sees the historian as first collecting his evidence and then building his account of the past on the basis of this sound foundation. [Instrumentalism] takes objects in the present and constructs an account of the past in order to explain the presence of these objects."[39] Both theories face the problem of the actual nature of the evidence. Jack W. Meilland has described historical writing as a "fable." For Meilland, historical accounts are a creation and a construction of the writer, not "objective" reports. Some Moroccan nationalist views, perhaps unconsciously, followed this view with regard to colonial writing, and a new nationalist and revisionist history, part of an effort to decolonize the past, emerged as an alternative to the old French historical paradigm. However, as Abdallah Laroui and others have pointed out, the revisionists' contributions were very limited and usually degenerated into abstract refutations.[40] Besides, the majority of these historians, who lacked solid training in historiography, were not interested in initiating a new model of history. They contented themselves with challenging the ideological basis of colonial discourse. Post-independence Moroccan historical writing tended to focus on the moral and ideological basis of ethnographic and historical literature on Morocco. In Smail's words, they were more concerned with the "moral view" of colonial discourse than with the "perspective" of this history.[41]

Following A. C. Danto's concept of historical instrumentalism,[42] I believe that in a socio-religious context, where relations between two social groups— Muslims and Jews—are strained, it is hard to provide reliable evidence regarding the nature and workings of group interactions. The social animosities, manifest or hidden, affect group perceptions and create long-lasting biases. Thus, neither the European traveler nor today's historians/anthropologists can provide all-encompassing statements about possible Jewish-Muslim realities. However, unlike Danto, I consider that *all* sources written on Jewish-Muslim relations in rural and urban Morocco can provide an explanatory piece of the puzzle, no matter how biased the writer is.

In my argument against an instrumentalist theory of Jewish-Muslim relations, I assume that historical descriptions of these relations can emanate from limited views, constructions of the writer's imagination, and/or hypotheses that may be culturally influenced. At the same time, histories are rarely the sole inventions, constructions, and creations of the historian. My approach is double-pronged: I propose to the post-independence historian of Moroccan Jewry a model in which the travel narrative can be used as a point of departure that reports and documents the situation of southern Moroccan Jews from an eyewitness perspective. At the same time, I ask that historians arm themselves with a concept that Arjun Appadurai calls the "debatability of the past."[43] Historians should question the veracity of the categories travelers constructed about Jews in southern Morocco because the travelers were part of a French colonial vulgate that was already established in Algeria.

European Travelers and the Construction of a Colonial Knowledge about Jews

Until the first quarter of the twentieth century, travel writings remained what they had always been: eyewitness reports from European travelers who imperfectly struggled to recount their meetings with Middle Eastern societies for their governments.[44] Despite their shortcomings, the reports European travelers produced played a major role in the colonial enterprise from the early period of the nineteenth century. From early 1800, many European travelers had tried to reach sub-Saharan Africa through the southern Moroccan desert. It was no surprise that the local population of Morocco saw Christian travelers as spies whose intention was to prepare the ground for France's ultimate invasion of Morocco after it had gained complete control of neighboring Algeria. Many travelers were aware of this risk and traveled in Muslim territories in disguise as a Jew or a Muslim. Charles de Foucauld described the dangers of the enterprise in the preface of his travel narrative:

> Five-sixths of Morocco . . . is entirely closed to Christians; they can only enter there by subterfuge and by risking their lives. This extreme intolerance is not caused by religious fanaticism, rather, it stems from a common sentiment of all the indigenous people. For them, a European traveling in their country can only be an emissary sent to reconnoiter: he comes to study the land with the intention of invading. He is a *spy*, and is killed as such, and not as an infidel. [My italics.][45]

This interest in exploration was largely linked and supported by European geographical associations, such as those of Paris, London, and Berlin. These institutions became instrumental in colonial expansion. In France, the Société de Géographie de Paris was founded in 1821, drawing "its initial membership mainly from the military and the aristocracy. Its stated aim was to achieve a greater knowledge of the globe and its inhabitants and to establish communication among scholarly societies, travelers and geographers."[46]

At the height of European explorations during the nineteenth century, Morocco was still inaccessible. Algeria, Senegal, and Tunisia were already under French control, and European powers had their eyes set on the southern Moroccan territories. Europeans, driven by the spirit of colonial exploration, managed to explore parts of southern Morocco and reach as far as Timbuktu, although some met their death at the hands of tribal lords. Réné Caillié (1799–1838) was one of the few French travelers who explored some of the areas de Foucauld later visited. Caillié described the Jewish communities he encountered during his 1828 journey through the Anti-Atlas and Tafilalt, giving a general picture of the Jews of southern Morocco:

> Throughout the districts of el-Drah and Tafilet are found Jews, who inhabit the same villages with the Musulmans; they are in a pitiable condition, wandering about almost naked, and continuously insulted by the Moors; these fanatics even beat them shamefully, and throw stones at them as at dogs: the smallest children may abuse them with impunity, since they dare not revenge themselves, and cannot expect protection from authority. . . . The Jews of Tafilet are excessively dirty, and always go barefoot, perhaps to avoid the inconvenience of frequently taking off their sandals, which they are compelled to do in passing before a mosque or the door of a sheriff. . . . Some are pedlars, others artisans; they manufacture shoes and mats from palm-leaves; some of them also are blacksmiths. They lend their money upon usury to the merchants trading in the Soudan, whither they never

go themselves. Their only visible fortune consists of their houses, but they often take lands as a guarantee for the money which they lend. Money is always plentiful with the Jews: yet they affect the utmost] poverty; because the Moors, who ascribe to them greater riches than they really possess, often persecute them for the purpose of extorting their gold: besides which, they not only pay tribute to the emperor and his agents, but are moreover harassed by the Berbers.[47]

Caillié's report on the state of southern Morocco and its Jews is relatively accurate because of his approach to the exploration of the region. He spent many years learning Arabic, familiarizing himself with local customs, and studying the Islamic religion before his travel. Caillié's adoption of Muslim disguise began a tradition for Europeans that was later followed by Oskar Lenz and other travelers. (Alexander Gordon Laing, who did not take sufficient precautions, was killed.) Caillié outlined a set of steps that future explorers of Morocco and the Saharan desert should take:

> To ensure success, the traveler should, I think, make no sort of display; he should externally adopt the worship of Mahomet, and pass himself off for an Arab. A pretended convert would not enjoy so much liberty, and would be an object of suspicion to such distrustful people. Besides, I am of opinion that a converted Christian would not be tolerated among the negro tribes. The best plan would be, I think[,] to cross the great desert of Sahara in the character of an Arab, provided with adequate but concealed resources. After remaining for some time in the Musulman town selected by the traveler as his starting point, where he might give himself out as a merchant, to avoid suspicion, he might purchase some merchandise in that town, under the pretence of going to trade further on, carefully abstaining from all mention of the city of Timbuctoo. Let us suppose Tangiers or Arbate [Rabat] to be the place chosen as the point of departure; mercantile business at Fez might be alleged as an excuse for setting off. Still adopting the same pretence, the traveller might proceed from Fez to Tafilet and, thence to Timbuctoo. At Tafilet there would be no danger of speaking of Timbuctoo, for there a journey to the Soudan is an affair of frequent occurrence and it excites no attention.[48]

Another European traveler who contributed information about the Jews of southern Morocco is John Davidson, a British doctor who was killed in a region of southern Morocco not far from Akka. Davidson claimed that the Jews of southern Morocco were different from those who lived in the plains among the Arabs. He argued:

> The Jews of the Atlas are far superior, both physically and morally, to their brethren residing among the Moors. Their families are numerous, and each

of these under the immediate protection of a Berber . . . patron, or master. They have, however, their own sheik, a Jew, to whose jurisdiction all matters are referred. Differing from the Jews residing amongst the Moors, who are punished by the Mussulman laws, they are not in the same state of debasement or servitude; their case is one of patron and client, and all enjoy equal privileges, and the Berber is bound to take up the cause of the Jew upon all emergencies. They all carry arms, and serve by turns with their patrons.[49]

The third major European traveler who gave an account of the state of Jews in southern Morocco is Charles de Foucauld. Although de Foucauld had familiarized himself with previous explorations while in Algeria preparing for his southern Moroccan exploration, his knowledge of Morocco and local customs was very meager and his understanding of Islam was almost nonexistent. MacCarthy, the curator of the national library in Algiers, advised de Foucauld against wearing an Arab disguise and counseled him instead to pass himself off as a Jew. According to Preminger, MacCarthy saw Jews as "rootless people who came from many lands and spoke many languages, all with a foreign accent. . . . Furthermore, the Jews were a small minority in Morocco; with centuries of abuse and persecution behind them, they would instinctively protect Foucauld from Moslems, even though they saw through his masquerade."[50] Through MacCarthy, Charles de Foucauld was introduced to Mardochée Aby Serour.

De Foucauld's ability to survive his dangerous exploration has provided colonial and postcolonial historians with one of the most detailed accounts about the Jews of the rural communities of southern Morocco. He wrote:

> The Jews of Bilad al-Siba are no less despicable [than those of Bilad al-Makhzan] but they are miserable: attached to their plot of land, each having their Muslim Lord to whom they are considered property, immeasurably oppressed, seeing all that they toil for taken away from them every day, without security for their persons or property, they are the most unfortunate of men. Lazy, avaricious, greedy, drunkards, liars, thieves, especially heinous, and without faith or goodness, they have all the vices of the Jews of Bilad al-Makhzan, minus their cowardice. I write about the Jews of Morocco with less rancor than I actually feel.[51]

With these different accounts in mind, modern Moroccan historians who share the perspective of Ayache are left with the following question: did these German, British, and French travelers accurately describe the situation of the Jews of southern Morocco? Certain features of their historical accounts are repeated today by Muslim and Jewish observers, which testify to their persistence in the popular imagination. Yet the limited access the travelers had to Jewish,

Berber, and Arab families suggests that European representations of the latter are inadequate and biased. While doing fieldwork among the Berber and Arab populations of Akka I was able to hear testimonies—supported by family records—that the relationship between local Jewish and Muslim families was intricate and complex, an idea that reverberates in the folktales and myths reported by Muslims and Jews whom I myself interviewed. Hence, given the limited nature of the reports of de Foucauld and other travelers, we need to draw upon a variety of sources if we are to understand the history of intercommunal relations in this region.

Interrogating the Postcolonial Historiography

Abdallah Laroui provides a critical analysis of historical writing on the Arab Maghrib, arguing that the region's past has been imprisoned within a colonial model of history. Laroui points out that: "All [colonial] historians refer the reader back to each other and invoke each other's authority. The consequence is a conspiracy which puts the most adventurous hypotheses into circulation and ultimately imposes them as established truths."[52]

These colonial historical "established truths" were ideologically constructed by colonial administrative officers, missionaries, and travelers and found their way into colonial writing to justify France's *mission civilisatrice* in the Maghrib.[53] The engulfing power of these ideological constructions can be seen in postcolonial historical literature, which finds itself repeating the same colonial jargon. Colonial knowledge thus became an unchallenged, quasi-sacred reference that escaped analytical scrutiny. The absence of historical documents in certain regions left the historian with no alternative but to use these ideologically biased sources.

In post-independence historiography, skepticism surfaced about colonial sources of information regarding Moroccan Jews. Few historians stopped to consider the viability of the travel narrative as a legitimate paradigm and model of historical writing on southern Moroccan Jews. While a number of Moroccan historians, including Mohammed Kenbib, Aomar Afa, Khalid Ben Srhir, and Jamaâ Baïda have joined American and European scholars to study the Jewish communities of Morocco, very few histories of the rural Jewries of the south have been produced to date.

The rejection of colonial historiography did not automatically lead to the production of successful regional histories. Muhammad al-Mukhtar al-Susi, for example, is considered by many Moroccan historians to be one of the pioneers of the revisionist history of southern Morocco.[54] He called for the production of a "regional social history" of the Sous.[55] Yet he ignored the Jewish communities of Sous and their relations with powerful Muslim Berber and Arab families. Despite his treatment of the economic relationships between Jews and Muslims in Sous, al-Susi did not actually document this part of the local history of southern Morocco. Muhammad Da'ud, on the other hand, the historian of Tetuan, included copies of the documents he collected about the Jews of Tetuan.[56]

Da'ud and al-Susi were among the earliest nationalist figures to recognize the importance of challenging colonial narratives of Moroccan history. They believed in writing local history as the first stage before producing national histories. However, while Da'ud's multivolume book on the history of Tetuan included many narratives about the Jews of that city, al-Susi ignored them even though historical documents about the Jews of the Anti-Atlas were available.[57]

In his review of Trouillot's *Silencing the Past: Power and the Production of History*, William Roseberry notes that "[many] different kinds of silence enter into the production of history at each moment in its production: certain knowledge and experiences are never written down or are written in ephemeral forms and never become potential sources of 'historical' knowledge; certain sources are defined as less significant and thus never collected in archives; certain collections never gain status as archives; certain events, persons, and connections drop out of historical narratives, grand and small."[58] In the historiography of southern Morocco, many silences are at play not only in terms of the history of the regions but also in the historical themes covered. The most pertinent can also be explained by the general orientation of North African social history by which Jews and other marginal groups were not considered worthwhile historical topics.

Conclusion

In the postcolonial era in Morocco, local narratives about the French protectorate are still ingrained in the southwestern Moroccan imagination. The elders of the farthest Saharan oases remember French agents and their role in maintaining colonial control in the region. Colonial memories are not outside their daily frame of reference. My ethnographic encounter with the local population triggered some of those dormant views of the colonial officers, missionaries, and travelers who once visited the area disguised as local Jews or Muslims. In the post-9/11 era, my study of the Jewish communities of Morocco has brought back those memories of spies and the lack of trust and questions surrounding the production of knowledge. For some locals, I am part of the Western tradition of knowledge. By comparing my work with de Foucauld's narrative, I am already part of a continuing colonial legacy of knowledge. By studying the Jews of Morocco, I am in the process of writing another reconnaissance of Moroccan Jewry.

But what kind of reconnaissance do historians of Moroccan Jews need to produce? Should it be based on a colonial genealogy of knowledge or on other sources of knowledge? Should I reject the claims of colonial narratives in their entirety, as Germain Ayache suggested? De Foucauld's study of Moroccan society in the nineteenth century has as many strengths as it has flaws. My own ethnographic encounter corroborated information de Foucauld reported more than a century ago. And there are other sources that could complement de Foucauld's study: legal manuscripts, personal Muslim narratives, and local myths. In any postcolonial revision of Moroccan national historiography, we have to accept the fact that colonial knowledge is an interpretation of local reality. This interpretation, like any other, is open to deconstruction. It should be analyzed, critiqued, and appreciated as a phase of our national history and not rejected in its entirety because of its link with a colonial power. Following the same line of thought, de Foucauld's narrative should be used despite its apparent biases about Jews and Muslims because each narrative is told from the perspective of the moral and intellectual climate of its century. While absolute truth may not be available to humankind, knowledge and deliberate ignorance are incompatible.

NOTES

1. Hundreds of travel narratives were written about North Africa before and during the early stages of the French conquest. Some examples are James Grey Jackson, *An Account of the Empire of Morocco and the Districts of Sus and Tafilelt*, 3rd ed. (London: Printed by William Bulmer and Co., 1814), James Grey Jackson, *An Account of Timbuctoo and Housa* (London: Longman, Hurst, Rees, Orme and Brown, 1820); J. B. Ginsburg, *Account of the Persecution of the Protestant Mission among the Jews at Mogador, Morocco* (London: E. G. Allen, 1880); George Beauclerk, *Journey to Morocco* (London: Printed for Poole and Edwards, 1828), Stephen Bonsal, *Morocco as It Is* (New York: Harper and Brothers, 1893); John Buffa, *Travels through the Empire of Morocco* (London: J. J. Stockdale, 1810); Arthur Leared, *Morocco and the Moors* (London: S. Low, Marston, Searle, & Rivington, Ltd., 1891); Donald Mackenzie, *The Khalifate of the West: Being a General Description of Morocco* (London: Darf, 1987); Frances Macnab, *A Ride in Morocco among Believers and Traders* (London: E. Arnold, 1902); Arthur De Capell Brooke, *Sketches in Spain and Morocco* (London: Henry Colburn and Richard Bentley, 1831); and Charles de Foucauld, *Reconnaissance au Maroc* (Paris: Challamel, 1888).

2. On the uses of travel narratives for the writing of Moroccan Jewish history, see Mohammed Kenbib, *Juifs et Musulmans au Maroc 1859–1948: Contribution à l'histoire des relations intercommunautaires en terre d'Islam* (Rabat: Faculté des Lettres et des Sciences Humaines, 1994); ʿAbd al-Nabi Dakir, *Al-Waqiʿi wa-l-mutakhayyil fi al-rihla al-urubiya ila al-Maghrib* (Casablanca: Matbaʿat Manshurat Kawtar, 1997); El Houcine Bouchama, "Les sources étrangères et l'histoire du Maroc," in *Dirasat tarikhiya muhdat li-l-faqid Jarman Ayyash*, ed. Afa ʿUmar (Rabat: Kulliyat al-Adab wa-al-ʿUlum al-Insaniya, 1994); *Mémorial Germain Ayache* (Rabat: Faculté des Lettres et des Sciences Humaines, 1994); Khalid Lazaare, "Le Maroc dans les récits de voyages allemands du

xixe siècle, in *Al-Rihla bayna al-sharq wa-l-gharb,* ed. Muhammad Hammam (Rabat: Kulliyat al-Adab wa-l-ʿUlum al-Insaniya, 2003), 113–131; Selwa Idrissi Mounjib, "Les Voyageurs allemands/germanophones au Maroc de 1830 à 1930 entre aventure, impérialisme et exotisme," in Hammam, *Al-Rihla bayna al-sharq wa-l-gharb,* 133–147; Rabia Hatim, "Voyage au Rif: à la recherche de la vérité," in ibid., 149–158.

3. For a discussion of the representation of Moroccan Jews in travel narratives, see Bat Yeʾor, *The Dhimmi: Jews and Christians under Islam* (Rutherford, N.J.: Fairleigh Dickinson University Press, 1985), and Dakir, *Al-Waqiʿi wa-l-mutakhayyil fi al-rihla al-urubiya ila al-Maghrib.*

4. Patricia Lorcin, *Imperial Identities: Stereotyping, Prejudice and Race in Colonial Algeria* (London: I. B. Tauris Publishers, 1995).

5. Hayat Diyen, "Jewish Migrants in Morocco in the 18th Century," in Hammam, *Al-Rihla bayna al-sharq wa-l-gharb,* 103.

6. C. R. Pennell, *Morocco since 1830: A History* (New York: New York University Press, 2000), xv–xxvii; Mohamed El Mansour, "Moroccan Historiography since Independence," in *The Maghrib in Question: Essays in History and Historiography,* ed. Michel Le Gall and Kenneth Perkins (Austin: University of Texas Press, 1997), 109–120.

7. Germain Ayache, *Etudes d'histoire marocain* (Rabat: Société Marocaine des Éditeurs Réunis, 1979), 22–23.

8. El Mansour, "Moroccan Historiography since Independence," 115.

9. Edmund Burke, III, "The Image of the Moroccan State in French Ethnological Literature: A New Look at the Origins of Lyautey's Berber Policy," in *Arabs and Berbers: From Tribe to Nation in North Africa,* ed. Ernest Gellner and Charles Micaud (London: Duckworth, 1972).

10. Lorcin, *Imperial Identities,* 2–3.

11. Ibid., 3.

12. Pennell, *Morocco since 1830,* 28.

13. Ibid. Also see Burke, "The Image of the Moroccan State in French Ethnological Literature."

14. El Mansour, "Moroccan Historiography since Independence."

15. Al-Mukhtar al-Susi, *Khilal Jazula,* 4 vols. (Tetuan: Al-Matbaʿa al-Mahdiyya, n.d.), 3:25; 4:59–60.

16. Modern studies of the Jews of southern rural Morocco have been limited to a few native historians. See ʿUmar Afa, *Tarikh al-Maghrib al-muʿasir: dirasat fi al-masadir wa-l-mujtamaʿ wa-l-iqtisad* (Rabat: Manshurat Kulliyyat al-Adab wa-l-ʿUlum al-Insaniya, 2002). Two dissertations on rural Jewish communities have recently been completed: Aomar Boum, "Muslims Remember Jews in Southern Morocco: Social Memories, Dialogic Narratives and the Collective Imagination of Jewishness" (Ph.D. diss., University of Arizona, Tucson, 2006); and Abdellah Larhmaid, "Jamaʿat yahud Sus: al-majal wa al-tamatulat al-ijtimaʿiya wa-l-siyasiya 1860–1960" (Doctoral diss., University of Mohammed V, Rabat, 2002).

17. The most extensive research was carried out by Pierre Flamand; see *Diaspora en terre d'Islam: les communautés Israélites du sud marocain* (Casablanca: Presses de Imprimeries Réunies, n. d. [1959]).

18. Abdelmajid Hannoum, *Colonial Histories, Post-Colonial Memories: The Legend of the Kahina, a North African Heroine* (Portsmouth, N.H.: Heinemann, 2001), 22.

19. On Aby Serour and his relationship to De Foucauld, see Jacob Oliel, *De Jérusalem à Tombouctou: L'odyssée saharienne du rabbin Mardochée 1826–1886* (Paris: Editions Olbia, 1998); and Jacob Oliel, *Les Juifs au Sahara: Le Touat au Moyen Âge* (Paris: CNRS, 1994).

20. Al-Susi has a vision of Moroccan history that starts with the writing of the regional history of Sous and then the production of a national history. His main works include *Al-Maʿsul,* 20 vols. (Casablanca: Matbaʿat al-Najah, 1973); *Khilal Jazula,* 4 vols. (Tetuan: n.d.); *Sus al-ʿalima* (Mohammedia: Matabaʿat Fadala, 1960); and *Iligh qadiman wa hadithan* (Rabat: Al-Matbaʿat al-Malakiya, 1966). Al-Susi's regional histories focus on historical specificities and rely on mul-

tiple historical sources. His historical methodology places local historical events within the national context.

21. Michel-Rolph Trouillot, *Silencing the Past: Power and the Production of History* (Boston, Mass.: Beacon Press, 1995), 6.

22. Lorcin, *Imperial Identities*, 2.

23. Thomas Park and Aomar Boum, *Historical Dictionary of Morocco* (Lanham, Md.: Scarecrow Press, 2006), 39. See also Vincent Monteil, "Choses et gens de Bani," *Hespéris* 33 (1946): 385–405.

24. Al-Yaᶜqubi, *Les pays,* trans. G. Wiet (Paris, 1937), 225. See also Abu Oubeid al-Bakri, *Description de l'Afrique sepentrionale,* trans. MacGuckin de Slane (Paris: Maisonneuve, 1965); Al-Susi, *Khilal Jazula,* 3:86–88; Bernard Rosenberger, "Tāmdult: Cité minière et caravanière pre-saharienne IXᵉ–XIVᵉ siècles," *Hespéris-Tamuda* XI (1970): 103–141; Patrice Cressier, "Du sud au nord du Sahara: la question de Tamdult (Maroc)," in *Du nord au sud du Sahara: Cinquante ans d'archéologie française: bilan et perspectives,* ed. Andres Bazzana and Hamady Bocoum (Paris: Editions Sépia, 2004); and Jean-Michel Lessard, "Sijilmassa la ville et ses relations commerciales au XI siècle d'après El Bekri," *Hespéris-Tamuda* 10 (1969): 5–36.

25. Al-Susi, *Khilal Jazula,* 3:75. Also see D. Jacques-Meunié, *Le Maroc saharien des origines à 1670,* vol. 1 (Paris: Librairie Klincksieck, 1962), 70–72.

26. Park and Boum, *Historical Dictionary of Morocco,* 39.

27. Daniel J. Schroeter, *Merchants of Essaouira: Urban Society and Imperialism in Southwestern Morocco, 1844–1886* (Cambridge: Cambridge University Press, 1988), 90ff.

28. Mary Louise Pratt, *Imperial Eyes: Travel Writing and Transculturation* (London: Routledge, 1992), 7.

29. Ibid.

30. Jackson, *An Account of the Empire of Morocco and the Districts of Sus and Tafilelt,* vii–viii.

31. Muhammad al-Dahan, "Al-rihla al-itnugrafiya al-istiᶜmariya bi-l-Maghrib, namudaj ᶜasfar bi-al-Maghrib li-al-mu'alif de Segonzac," in Hammam, *Al-Rihla bayna al-sharq wa-l-gharb,* 303–317.

32. Jackson, *An Account of the Empire of Morocco and the Districts of Sus and Tafilelt,* vi.

33. Graf Sternberg, *The Barbarians of Morocco* (New York: Duffield, 1909), v.

34. See, e.g., Kenbib, *Juifs et Musulmans,* 2.

35. Ibid., 2.

36. E. G. H. Joffe, "Walter Harris and the Imperial Vision of Morocco," *Journal of North African Studies* 3 (1996): 263.

37. Trouillot, *Silencing the Past,* 6.

38. B. C. Hurst, "The Myth of Historical Evidence," *History and Theory* 20 (1981): 278.

39. Ibid.

40. Abdallah Laroui, *The History of the Maghrib: An Interpretive Essay* (Princeton, N.J.: Princeton University Press, 1977), 3–4.

41. John R. Smail, "On the Possibility of an Autonomous History of Modern Southeast Asian History," *Journal of Southeast Asian History* 2 (1961): 75–82.

42. A. C. Danto, *Analytical Philosophy of History* (Cambridge: Cambridge University Press, 1965), 80.

43. Arjun Appadurai," The Past as a Scarce Resource," *Man* 16 (1981): 218.

44. Dakir, *Al-Waqiᶜi wa-l-mutakhayyil fi al-rihla al-urubiya ila al-Maghrib,* 351.

45. De Foucauld, *Reconnaissance au Maroc,* xv–xvi.

46. Lorcin, *Imperial Identities,* 147.

47. Réné Caillié, *Travels through Central Africa to Timbuctoo and across the Great Desert to Morocco Performed in the Years 1824–1828,* 2 vols. (1830; London: Frank Cass, 1968), 2:84–85.

48. Ibid., 84.

49. John Davidson, *Notes Taken during Travels in Africa* (London: J. L. Cox and Sons, 1839), 188.

50. Marion Mill Preminger, *The Sands of Tamanrasset: The Story of Charles de Foucauld* (New York: Hawthorn, 1961), 61.

51. De Foucauld, *Reconnaissance au Maroc,* 395.

52. Laroui, *History of the Maghrib,* 3.

53. Bouchama, "Les sources étrangères et l'histoire du Maroc," 81.

54. See Al-Susi, *Al-Ma^csul,* 20:272–278; and Al-Susi, *Kitab min afwah al-rijal* (Tetuan: al-Matba^ca al-Mahdiya, n.d.), 4. See also Ali Oumlil, "Al-Sulta al-^cilmiyya wa al-sulta al-siyasiya," in *Al-Mukhtar al-Susi: al-dhakira al-musta^cada* (Casablanca: Matba^cat al-Najah al-Jadida, 1986); and Muhammad al-Hatimi, "Al-Bu^cd al-watani fi rihlat 'Khila Khilal Jazula' li-Muhammad al-Mukhtar al-Susi," in Mustafa Jawhari, *al-Rahalat al-maghribiya al-dakhiliya 1912–1956* (Salé: Matba^cat Bani Yaznasan, 2005).

55. Al-Susi, *Khilal Jazula,* 2:1; 3:1.

56. Muhammad Da'ud, *Tarikh Titwan* (Tetuan: Krimadis, 1957).

57. Al-Susi's silence about southern Moroccan Jewish communities cannot be ascribed solely to his Salafiyist and pro-nationalist position and training. He was a *salafi,* a sufi, and a historian. He was the son of the founder of the Zaouia Darqawiya in Sous and was trained from an early age under his father and his disciples. As a *salafi,* he called for a social, economic, and political reform movement that would restore the traditional beliefs and practices of the former companions of the Prophet. However, his mystical training differentiates his religious thinking from the "pure" *salafi* thought of other nationalist reformers, especially Allal al-Fassi. As a local historian, al-Susi focused on writing the local history of his region. See Al-Susi, *Al-Ma^csul,* 1:31–33.

58. William Roseberry, "Review Essay: On Historical Consciousness," *Current Anthropology* 38, no. 5 (1997): 927.

7

Dating the Demise of the Western Sephardi Jewish Diaspora in the Mediterranean

Yaron Tsur

Discussing Jewish communities in the Maghrib as a whole has certain advantages when the region is viewed as having historical connections that distinguish it from other parts of the Mediterranean and beyond. However, as with elsewhere in the Jewish world, the specificity of a given region can be better understood by examining the extensive supracommunity networks in which it was located. This chapter will discuss in brief the history of such networks in the Muslim Mediterranean on the brink of modern times. My interest focuses on a network whose boundaries reached far beyond the region of Islam and had important centers in Western Europe and on the American continent—the so-called Western Sephardi diaspora. But I will refer also to a second network whose boundaries were confined to the Ottoman Empire, North Africa, and the Middle East. The comparison between these two networks constitutes the chief contribution of the chapter.

Jonathan Israel, one of the more important historians of Europe in the early modern era, devoted much of his research to the Western Sephardi diaspora. Several years ago, he published *Diasporas within a Diaspora*, a collection of his essays on the topic.[1] One of his conclusions is that the diaspora weakened and disintegrated around the middle of the eighteenth century.[2] I would like to examine his conclusion and dating with respect to the Mediterranean arena. However, before turning to the end of the diaspora, it is worth examining its beginnings and development.

The Western Sephardi diaspora originated with both the Jews who were expelled from Spain and part of the families of converts, or "New Christians," who remained in the Iberian Peninsula and lived after 1492 in Spain and Portugal or in their colonies in the New World of America. Family and social connections across the religious divide derived from special circumstances: in Portugal, Jewish refugees were forced to convert to Christianity in 1497, but some of the New Christians continued to practice Judaism covertly as crypto-Jews, and in some cases their descendants fled the Inquisition and returned to normative Judaism in Jewish communities abroad. The 1492 expellees founded some communities in North Africa but they mainly went to communities in the Ottoman Empire, the Balkans, and the Levant, from where they later sent out an offshoot to Italy. In Italy the "Levantines" (Sephardim who came from the East) met up with the "Ponentines," Sephardim and former Portuguese crypto-Jews who had immigrated directly from the West to cities such as Venice and Livorno. Other branches developed from the communities of "New Christians" in Portugal, including those of Antwerp and the Spanish and Portuguese colonies in the New World.

In the sixteenth century, the main lines of the Western Sephardi network ran between Salonika in the Balkans and Venice in Italy, between Lisbon in the Iberian Peninsula and Antwerp in the Lowlands, and between Antwerp and Venice. The network also spread out from Lisbon and Antwerp across the Atlantic to Brazil and Peru in South America. These centers sufficed to connect the two continents of Europe and America. But Jonathan Israel's primary argument is that the Western Sephardi diaspora was unique in connecting *all* the continents by both primary channels and secondary lines from the Ottoman Empire in Anatolia and the Fertile Crescent to North Africa, the Sahara, India, and even Indonesia and China, linking Asia and Africa as well as Europe and America. He contends that though other non-Jewish commercial diasporas existed in this period (Armenian, Greek, Huguenots), those diasporas merely spanned *parts* of the worldwide wings—*part* of the cultures and *part* of the religions. Only the long-term Sephardi network joined up all the continents across both religious and cultural divides.[3]

The title of Israel's book, *Diasporas within a Diaspora,* may seem misleading at first glance if "diaspora" is taken to mean all Jewish communities as a whole. Actually, Israel means only the Spanish-Portuguese diaspora centered in the West, and the term "diasporas" relates to its secondary branches. The assumption behind the designation is that the Western Sephardi network consisted of secondary networks that were integrally related to it socially, culturally, and commercially, in contrast to other Jewish networks of the time. Israel thus differentiates between the overall religious diaspora and the commercial networks made up of Jewish co-religionists that were delineated by clear boundaries of cultural and economic origin. In the early development of the Western Sephardi network in the sixteenth century, Ottoman Sephardi communities constituted an important part of the commercial diaspora, displaying its characteristic feature of long-distance sea trade within the Empire, for example, between Safed and Peloponnesus. By the last quarter of the century, however, its economic status had sharply deteriorated, accompanied by chiefly local centralizations of labor and commercial resources.[4] From this point on, Israel does not discuss the broad Sephardi, or Judeo-Spanish-speaking, public in the Ottoman Empire, implying that it was distinct from the commercial diaspora that interests him. He does not explain what the new status of Ottoman Sephardim was, though clearly they no longer relied on long-distance commercial routes and increasingly resembled other Jewish communities of the world. Such communities may be defined as "static" in order to differentiate them from communities in which most of the members maintained social and economic ties with supraregional networks.

The study of commercial diasporas has made significant strides in recent decades, though it has had little influence on the historiography of modern Jewish history.[5] The topic undeniably deserves study, as a glance at the Mediterranean arena confirms: it was a distinct meeting point between the Western Sephardi commercial diaspora and "static" Jewish communities and, apparently, between other Jewish transregional networks as well. Israel attributes a central role to the Salonika-Venice axis in the Western Sephardi diaspora, but only until the end of the sixteenth century. The network's other offshoots in the lands of Islam never achieved the status of key channels in *any period*. Livorno replaced Venice as the network's chief Italian city sometime in the seventeenth century.[6] Tunis, for example, where Jewish Livornese immigrants and their descendants prospered and were major players in foreign trade, does not appear in the index of Israel's book.[7] This omission may be pardonable, considering that his point of departure is Western Europe and the trans-Atlantic commercial diaspora. To him, the only unique feature of the Western Sephardi diaspora network was that it connected the continents of America, Europe, Asia, and Africa. It was Amsterdam and the communities of crypto-Jews in the Iberian Peninsula and its empires that assured the bonds between the Western Sephardi network and the Atlantic routes in the seventeenth century. Without these links, as Israel sees it, the Livornese of the Mediterranean would have been of little importance. In his model, the decline of Holland's commercial empire and the disappearance of "New Christians" from the leading stratum of the Iberian economy resulted in the withering of the entire Western Sephardi diaspora. Since these processes matured toward the mid-eighteenth century, this was when the network ended.[8]

An examination of the history of the Western Sephardi branches on the northern shores of Africa reveals that though the Egyptian branch fits in nicely with Israel's chronology, the North African westward extensions do not.[9] In fact, the Jewish commercial diaspora continued to thrive, reaching its peak of power around 1800 in the autonomous province of Ottoman Algeria and maintaining its importance in the ʿAlawi sultanate of Morocco. Jews attained unprecedented positions of economic and political strength in the Maghrib, networking in what may be termed the vestiges of the Western Sephardi diaspora in Europe. A recent book by Daniel Schroeter, *The Sultan's Jew*, revolves around just such a Jewish figure, Meir Macnin. Virtually unknown to scholars, Macnin was charged by the sultan with overseeing most of Morocco's foreign trade and diplomatic contacts in the 1820s. He spent years in London and other European commercial centers.[10] Similar figures can be found in the joint commercial association of the Bujnah and Cohen Bacri families in Algeria, which has long been known to researchers due to the deep involvement of the two families in the conflict that led to that country's conquest by the French in 1830. Family members did not just move along the channels of the Western Sephardi diaspora; a number of them set down roots in Livorno and Marseille.[11] Their counterparts in Tunisia, members of the Grana elite, as the Livornese community was called locally, apparently lost much of their power around 1800 but later regained it and remained fairly strong until the 1880s. Jean-Pierre Filippini wrote three volumes on the history of Livorno in the eighteenth century, of which a large part is devoted to the city's Jews.[12] He is quite explicit about their role in trade with North Africa in the second half of the eighteenth century: the channels between Livorno and Tunis, Algiers, Tetuan, Tangier, and Essaouira (Mogador) buzzed with activity in which the Jewish network played a major role.[13]

Care must be taken not to turn the secondary channels in the Western Sephardi diaspora—its Maghribi extensions into newly flourishing foci of the entire network. Israel rightly says that the special force of that Jewish diaspora lay in its global dimension. In the early centuries after the discovery of the Americas as well as in accelerated contacts with the Far East, only the Spanish-Portuguese Jewish network spanned the four continents and the religious and cultural centers throughout the world. In the eighteenth century, the Western Sephardi diaspora lost this uniqueness and power. The Grana (Livornese Jews) in Tunis, Cohen Bacri and Bujnah in Algiers, and Macnin in Morocco were not engaged in trade with India and America. Their business axis lay between North Africa and Europe and, in some cases, between North Africa and the Levant. They bridged two and sometimes three continents and two religious and cultural regions, Islam and Christianity. The late blooming of the North African channels of the Western Sephardi diaspora seems to confirm the network's decline as a whole, its truncated arena of action, its retreat inward. The partial Jewish network was now reminiscent of its sixteenth- and seventeenth-century competitors, the non-Jewish commercial diasporas.

Nevertheless, the blooming of the non-European North African channels cannot be ignored, even though they happened late in the diaspora process. Nor can developments in the Middle East. One such example that relates directly to the Western Sephardi diaspora is the case of Aleppo in Syria. Here, the local extension of the commercial diaspora did not weaken. Aleppo's Livornese were known in the Levant as Francos. One Franco family, the Picciotos, showed similarities with the powerful Western Sephardi families of North Africa, and its members were integrated into the diplomatic network of the Habsburg Empire. They, too, at this stage enjoyed greater power than before.[14] In the 1780s there were negotiations about granting an official diplomatic role to a member of another Western Sephardi family with roots in Istanbul: the renowned Camondo family. The talks led nowhere and some of the members ended up fleeing the Ottoman capital to Trieste. But anyone familiar with the history of the Camondos and their position in nineteenth-century Istanbul cannot fail to discern here the seeds of their approach to the European powers, which was the key to their ascendancy in that century.[15]

These were isolated cases, however, for the overall economic activity of the Western Sephardi diaspora in the Middle East was clearly in decline. This picture emerges more lucidly from Filippini's analysis of commercial movement in Livorno. While the North African branches thrived, those drawn to Ottoman business centers—Egypt, the Balkans, Anatolia, and Syria—weakened considerably.[16] In other words, their situation corroborates Jonathan Israel's general diagnosis and chronology. However, the *overall* picture of the Jewish elite's economic and political power in the Middle East rules out any interpretation of "decline." If, as said above, its prosperity deserves attention, then the reference should not be primarily to the Picciotos in Aleppo but to the Farhis in Damascus.[17] They apparently belong not to the Western Sephardi network but to another Jewish commercial and political network that had developed in the Middle East and may be termed "Eastern Sephardi." It, too, appears to have originated with the Spanish expellees who migrated to the Ottoman Empire. Their mercantile families were involved in setting up a connection between Venice and Salonika, the first channel of the Western Sephardi diaspora. This axis ensured contact between Western Europe and the East in the sixteenth century.[18] The Levantines, as the members of this network in Venice were called, played a key role in the first century of the Western Sephardi diaspora, but their importance waned. They yielded their place as a vibrant hub between European and Ottoman commercial centers to the Francos or the Livornese.

In other words, in terms of influence, the merchants of the first wave of expulsion in 1492 and other Iberian-Jewish settlers in the Ottoman Empire were replaced by Western Sephardim who had been based in Christian Europe. What happened to the Ottoman Sephardi elite? Some of them integrated into the Ottoman merchant class, sometimes serving in key administrative economic positions that were allowed to non-Muslims and thereby founding a kind of new Jewish milieu: an economic-political network with links to almost every important

Ottoman center—Istanbul, Salonika, Izmir, Baghdad, Basra, Aleppo, Damascus, Tyre, Acre, Jerusalem, and Cairo, among others. The main languages of communication used in this Eastern Sephardi network were Judezmo (Judeo-Spanish) and Hebrew and probably also Judeo-Arabic in the Ottoman centers located in the Arabic-speaking regions.[19] Members of this elite group would have had to converse in Ottoman Turkish as well, because unlike most sectors of the Jewish public, they were in regular contact with the imperial Muslim elite. If the source of economic strength of the Western Sephardi diaspora was its integration into the trans-Atlantic trade of the new maritime powers, then the Eastern Sephardi network relied on integration into the Ottoman economic system and regime.[20]

Obviously, the two Jewish networks were mutually supportive; a large part of the success of each derived from internal cooperation and religious and legal contacts as well as issues of identity that could well have spilled over into additional social spheres. At the same time, a look at specific encounters between the two networks raises questions about competition, boundaries of identity, institutions, and other matters. The issue of identity boundaries becomes more pertinent in the context of increasing deviation from traditional patterns of Jewish/non-Jewish relations in Western Europe, which was the pivot of the Livornese branches. In any case, the Western Sephardi and Eastern Sephardi networks had different geopolitical, cultural, and economic foci and there is no reason to suppose that their history or their fates were similar. Indeed, to the extent that one can judge, the waning of the Livornese branches in the Ottoman Empire was not accompanied by a comparable decline of the Eastern Sephardi network. On the contrary, there, too, as in North Africa, one detects signs of prosperity at the turn of the nineteenth century in Syria, Istanbul, Tyre, Basra, and Baghdad. In fact, Ottoman Empire prosperity deserves attention not so much in regard to the Picciotos in Aleppo but primarily to the Farhis in Damascus.[21]

Even more interesting than the boundaries that separated the Jewish supra-regional networks in the Mediterranean basin at the start of the modern period are the gray areas between them and the transitions from one network to another. In the New World's Jewish communities and on Europe's Atlantic coast, Spanish and Portuguese Jews enjoyed ethnic dominance until the eighteenth century. Their numbers were few; demographically, the Western Sephardi diaspora peaked at about 15,000 people.[22] Nonetheless, most of the Jews in these communities in the West were Western Sephardim. Hamburg was an exception, and in Amsterdam the minority Ashkenazi community gradually became the majority, but only in the eighteenth century.

In contrast, wherever Livornese or Francos arrived in the lands of Islam, they were a minority and usually a tiny one at that, while the bulk of the Jewish population was Judeo-Arabic or Ottoman-Sephardi. In Istanbul, the largest Jewish community in the Mediterranean basin in the eighteenth century, there were 30,000–40,000 Jews, more than twice the number of the entire Western Sephardi diaspora worldwide.[23] Most of the local Jews constituted a "static" community. Apart from them, however, there was an Eastern Sephardi transregional network whose members spoke the languages of the Jewish public alongside Ottoman Turkish. In order to function in the local political and economic arena, Livornese and Francos also had to adapt culturally to the local languages, and they learned to speak Judeo-Spanish, Turkish, or Arabic while retaining Italian and holding on to other elements of their European heritage. Like Janus, they faced two directions, looking to both their original Western European and Ibero-Latin environments and to their new Muslim and Balkan surroundings. They can perhaps be seen as the new Levantines of the Western Sephardi diaspora. The old Levantines, originally the expellees who had settled in the Ottoman Empire and migrated to Italian cities, developed a complex cultural identity on Christian European soil over time but ultimately they merged with their new surroundings. In contrast, though the new Levantines (the immigrants from Italy to Muslim cities on Middle Eastern and North African soil) also developed a complex cultural identity, they retained their dual cultural identities.[24]

Moreover, the new Jewish Levantines constituted a rather open sector of Jewish society. Members of Eastern networks, whether Sephardi-Ottoman or local Judeo-Arab (as in Morocco), were attracted to and were able to integrate into the Western Sephardi network. This sort of mobility does not seem to have developed in the lands of Islam; it only happened in centers of the Western commercial diaspora in Europe, especially Livorno. In the seventeenth and eighteenth centuries, this Tuscany port became a Western Sephardi "melting pot," so to speak. Judeo-Arabs and Eastern Sephardim moved to Livorno for shorter or longer periods and attempted to integrate socially.[25] The immigrants from the lands of Islam were not interested merely (or even chiefly) in cultural assimilation or business connections. They coveted the legal status of Western Sephardim under the patronage of a European power. At first, it was France that lent its patronage to the Livornese subjects of the Duke of Tuscany, then Austria and other powers. After acquiring foreign patronage in Livorno, these new Levantines returned to their original communities with an entirely different cultural, economic, and political status from their fellow local Jews.

The dual cultural character of the new Jewish Levantines may help explain why Jewish elites in the lands of Islam were thriving during the period that the Western Sephardi diaspora declined overall. The decline of the Jewish commercial centers that had the advantage over Christian (Armenian and Greek) competitors in Islamic regions at the start of modern times was due to, among other things, the change in status of the supranetworks of the European powers. Although many, following Immanuel Wallerstein, would date the incorporation of much of the globe into a capitalist world system dominated by Europe from the sixteenth century onward, recent research on Asian and Middle Eastern regions challenges the idea of the hegemonic and linear European capitalism from this earlier period and suggests the end of the eighteenth century as the real turning point in Western penetration.[26] In the latter half of the eighteenth century, the European powers entered a new stage in the expansion of a world market, each concerned with strengthening its own political and commercial networks and with stretching its influence as far as possible. The lands of Islam as a geopolitical region went on the defensive against this new Western momentum. But the Christian diasporas—Armenian, Greek, and Catholic Syrian—reaped the benefits of the Western momentum and gained the advantage over Jews in the new international balance of powers.[27] As a result, the Livornese branches in the Middle East grew weaker at this stage in history, evincing similar general symptoms to those found in the network's foci on the Atlantic shore.

But other parts of the Jewish Mediterranean elite did not necessarily share the fate of the Livornese Jews. At this time, before Europe gained much greater control of the Muslim world, local rulers were able to maneuver and gain power through familiar strategies and resources. Some governmental bodies in the Ottoman capital or provinces chose to include Jews in these measures. Consequently, during this period, some magnates of the Eastern Sephardi network were able to grow stronger.[28] Members of the local Livornese branches were keen to take advantage of these efforts, adapting themselves to autochthonous cultural practices. However, it was clear to many that in the balance of world or even of just Mediterranean forces, the scales were noticeably tipping toward Europe. This tendency would have encouraged the fostering of Western identities and cultural accoutrements and, indeed, found prominent expression in North Africa. In this region, Jews were the only non-Muslim dispersed minority. This was the heyday of the Livornese in Algeria and Tunisia, who had meanwhile become bicultural, and it enabled Sephardi families in Morocco to develop their multicultural potential. Witness, for instance, Meir Macnin, the hero of Schroeter's book,[29] and the magnate Eliahu Halevy of Meknes, the villain of Romanelli's wonderful travelogue *Massa be–ʿArav* [Travail in an Arab Land].[30] Halevy in the second half of the eighteenth century and Macnin in the 1820s roughly mark the period's chronological boundaries in Morocco. Their stories demonstrate that for half a century and more, Moroccan sultans strove to cope with diverse international conditions by promoting local Jewish families in order to augment revenues of the makhzan. The Jews, for their part, were ready to hitch the services of the declining Western Sephardi diaspora to the sultan's wagon.[31]

On the whole, the picture Israel described is insightful. But it misses one of the fascinating chapters in the history of the Jewish (religious) diaspora, particularly of the Western Sephardi diaspora: the flowering of a secondary, complex, and hybrid branch of that commercial diaspora at the precise juncture when the central stalk withered. The parting of the ways between the center of the Western Sephardi diaspora and its southern Mediterranean periphery was the fruit of a new phase of globalization. The Portuguese-Sephardi pioneering network had thrived in the early modern period, but as new political and national networks emerged and Iberian predominance in the Atlantic waned, the Western Sephardi diaspora was eclipsed. In the lands of Islam, new strategies and tactics enabled the network's secondary wing to continue functioning, albeit not for long. The day of the Francos in the Ottoman regions of the Middle East passed close to the time when the Sephardi Jewish community in Amsterdam and the New Christians in Lisbon waned. As for North Africa, the decade marked by the colonial invasion and conquest of Algiers (the 1830s) began with what might have seemed like the necessary conditions for the continued functioning of the diaspora's local offshoot. Later, however, the French presence in Algeria destroyed this group along with the rest of the local elites. In Tunisia, the Livornese were able to persist and even flourish until the last quarter of the century. There too, the French conquest in 1881 spelled the end of the central role this group played in finance and international trade. In Morocco the prominent role of the Jews in international trade was evident through the first half of the nineteenth century. Later, Western companies took over the country's foreign trade, long before the colonial conquest of 1912.[32]

The West's accelerated takeover of regions outside Europe set in motion processes and created basic conditions that contributed to the withering of the Atlantic centers of the Western Sephardi diaspora in the mid-eighteenth century. The southern Mediterranean branch, however, lasted until the third quarter of the nineteenth century, about a hundred years after the demise of its center.

NOTES

This research was supported by the Israel Science Foundation (Grant no. 814/02).

1. Jonathan I. Israel, *Diasporas within a Diaspora: Jews, Crypto-Jews, and the World Maritime Empires, 1540–1740* (Leiden: Brill, 2002).
    2. Ibid., 38–39.
    3. Ibid., 2–3.
    4. Ibid., 12–13.

5. Abner Cohen, "Cultural Strategies in the Organization of Trading Diasporas," in *The Development of Indigenous Trade and Markets in West Africa*, ed. C. Meillassoux (Oxford: Oxford University Press, 1971), 266–281; Philip D. Curtin, *Cross-Cultural Trade in World History* (Cambridge: Cambridge University Press, 1984); Francesca Trivellato, "Juifs de Livourne, Italiens de Lisbonne, hindus de Goa: Réseaux marchands et échanges interculturels à l'époque moderne," *Annales HSS* 58, no. 3 (2003): 581–603. Trivellato's article includes references to recent research on commercial diasporas.

6. For Israel's overall analysis of Livorno, see *Diasporas within a Diaspora*, 16, 34, 36–39; see also Jonathan I. Israel, *European Jewry in the Age of Mercantilism, 1550–1750*, 2nd ed. (Oxford: Clarendon Press; New York: Oxford University Press, 1989), 49, 58, 60–61, 113, 156–158, 161–162, 175, and 206. On the Jewish community of Leghorn, see Renzo Toaff, *La Nazione Ebrea a Livorno e a Pisa 1591–1700* (Florence: L. S. Olschki, 1990). For studies on the Livornese migrations to the Levant and North Africa, see H. Z. Hirschberg, *A History of the Jews in North Africa*, vol. 2 (Leiden: Brill, 1981), 14–32, 82–104; Jean-Pierre Filippini, "Livourne et l'Afrique du Nord au 18ᵉ siècle," *Revue d'Histoire Maghrébine*, no. 7–8 (January 1977): 146–147; Simon Schwarzfuchs, "La 'Nazione ebrea' Livornaise au Levant," *La Rassegna Mensile di Israel* 50 (1984): 707–724; Richard Ayoun, "Les Juifs livournais en Afrique du Nord," *La Rassegna Mensile di Israel* 50 (1984): 650–706; Minna Rozen, "Tsarfat veYehudei Mitsrayim: anatomia shel yehasim (1683–1801) [France and the Jews of Egypt: An Anatomy of Relations, 1683–1801], in *Ha-Yehudim be-Mitsrayim ha-Otomanit (1517–1914)* [The Jews in Ottoman Egypt (1517–1914)], ed. Jacob M. Landau (Jerusalem: Misgav Yerushalayim, 1988), 421–470 (in Hebrew); Yaron Tsur, *Yehudim bein Muslemim: ʿal saf ha-ʿIdan ha-moderni 1750–1830* [The Jews in the Land of Islam at the Dawn of the Modern Age 1750–1830] (Tel Aviv: Open University, forthcoming) (in Hebrew).

7. On the Livornese in Tunis, see Hirschberg, *A History of the Jews in North Africa*, 2:82–104; Yitshak Avrahami, "Yehudei Livorno ve-kishrehem ʿim Tunis ba-meot ha-17–18" [The Jews of Leghorn and Their Relations with Tunis in the XVII–XVIII centuries] (M.A. thesis, Bar-Ilan University,1979); Yitshak Avrahami, *Pinkas ha-kehilah ha-yehudit ha-portugezit be-Tunis 1710–1944* [The Register of the Jewish Portuguese Community in Tunis 1710–1944] (Lod: Orot Yahadut ha-Magreb, 1997); Minna Rozen, "Les Marchands juifs livournais à Tunis et le commerce avec Marseille à la fin du XVIIe siècle," *Michael* 9 (1985): 87–129; Lionel Lévy, *La nation juive portugaise, Livourne, Amsterdam, Tunis (1591–1951)* (Paris: L'Harmattan, 1999); and Rhida Ben Rejeb, "Al-Nukhub al-yahudiya fi Tunis wa-mawqifuha min al-iqtisad wa-l-sulta 1685–1857" [The Jewish Elites in Tunis and Their Attitude toward the Economy and the Government 1685–1857] (Doctoral diss., University of Tunis, 2003).

8. Israel, *Diasporas within a Diaspora*, 38–39.

9. In Egypt, the local Jewish economic elite, which enjoyed Venetian protection, was destroyed in the years 1768–1770 and its place was taken by Syrian Catholics. See John W. Livingstone, "Ali Bey al-Kabir and the Jews," *Middle Eastern Studies* 7 (1971): 221–228; and Thomas Philipp, *The Syrians in Egypt, 1725–1975* (Stuttgart: Steiner, 1985), 25–34.

10. Daniel J. Schroeter, *The Sultan's Jew: Morocco and the Sephardi World* (Stanford, Calif.: Stanford University Press, 2002).

11. Françoise Hildesheimer, "Grandeur et décadence de la Maison Bacri de Marseille," *Revue des Etudes Juives* 136 (1977): 389–413; Jean-Pierre Filippini, "Una famiglia ebrea de Livorno tra le ambizioni mercantili e le vicissitudini del mondo mediterraneo: i Coen Bacri," *Richerche storiche* 2 (1982): 287–333.

12. Jean-Pierre Filippini, *Il porto di Livorno e la Toscana (1676–1814)*, 3 vols. (Napoli: Edizioni Scientifiche Italiane, 1998).

13. Filippini's chapters on this subject were formerly published as follows: Jean-Pierre Filippini, "Livorno e gli Ebrei dell'Africa del nord nel settecento," in *Gli Ebrei in Toscana dal Medioevo al Risorgimento, Fatti et momenti*, ed. Bruno Di Porto (Florence: Olschki, 1980), 21–32; Jean-Pierre Filippini, "Le rôle des négociants et des banquiers juifs de Livourne dans le grand commerce international en Méditerranée au XVIIIe siècle," in *The Mediterranean and the Jews; Banking, Fi-*

nance and International Trade, XVI–XVIII Centuries, ed. Ariel Toaff and Simon Schwarzfuchs (Ramat Gan: Bar Ilan University Press, 1989), 123–149; Jean-Pierre Filippini, "Il posto dei negozianti ebrei nel commercio di Livorno nel Settecento," *La Rassegna Mensile di Israel* 50 (1984): 634–649; Filippini, "Livourne et l'Afrique du Nord."

14. B. Le Calloc'h, "La Dynastie Consulaire des Picciotto (1784–1894)," *Revue d'Histoire Diplomatique* nos. 1–2 (1991): 135–175; Yaron Harel, "Maʿamadam ve-tadmitam shel benei Pigoto be-ʿenei ha-moshava ha-tsarfatit be-Haleb, 1784–1850" [The Status and Image of the Piccoto Family in the Eyes of the French Colony in Aleppo], *Michael* 14 (1997): 171–186.

15. Correspondence of September 1785 from the Austrian State Archives (Nota der Vereinigten Hofkanzlei d. 16 Septembris 1785, Nobilitisirungsgesuch des Camondo in Triest, Haus-Hof- und Staatsarchiv) was supplied by Dr. Michael Silver. On the Camondo family, see Aron Rodrigue, "Abraham de Camondo of Istanbul: The Transformation of Jewish Philanthropy," in *From East and West: Jews in Changing Europe, 1750–1870,* ed. Frances Malino and David Sorkin (Oxford: Basil Blackwell, 1991), 46–56; Nora Şeni and Sophie le Tarnec, *Les Camondo, ou l'éclipse d'une fortune* (Arles: Actes Sud, 1997).

16. Filippini, "Il posto dei negozianti ebrei," 647.

17. On the Farhis, see especially Thomas Philipp, "The Farhi Family and the Changing Position of the Jews in Syria, 1750–1860," *Middle Eastern Studies* 20 (1984): 37–52; Thomas Philipp, *Acre: The Rise and Fall of a Palestinian City, 1730–1831* (New York: Columbia University Press, 2002); Julie D. Bouchain, *Juden in Syrien; Aufstieg und Niedergang der Familie Farhi von 1740 bis 1995* (Hamburg: Lit, 1996).

18. For further information about the Levantines, see Israel, *European Jewry in the Age of Mercantilism,* 37; Benjamin Arbell, *Trading Nations: Jews and Venetians in the Early Modern Mediterranean* (Brill: Leiden, 1995); B. D. Cooperman, "Venetian Policy towards Levantine Jews and Its Broader Italian Context," in *Gli ebrei e Venezia,* ed. Gaetano Cozzi (Milan: Edizioni Comunità, 1987), 65–84; and Israel, *Diasporas within a Diaspora,* 61–62, 69–70, 73–74, 76–77. This channel had offshoots in other commercial centers as well, for example in the Balkans and in Italy's commercial cities, but its most stable center was between the Ottoman Empire and Venice, Italy's main port in this period.

19. Careful scrutiny may unearth channels from Istanbul to Tunis and Algiers as well.

20. For an extensive discussion of this Ottoman Jewish diaspora, see Tsur, *Yehudim bein Muslemim,* part A.

21. Ibid. See also Yaron Tsur, *'Al hashivutam shel ha-mosadot ha-semuyim min haʿayin: gvirei Kushta ve-ha-intisab* [On the Importance of Unseen Institutions: The Jewish Notables of Istanbul and the Intisab], in *Turkiya: he-ʿAvar ha-Otomani ve-ha-hove ha-Republikani. kovets Maamarim likhvod Professor Mordekhai Shmuelevitz* [Turkey: The Ottoman Past and the Republican Present; Collection of Articles in Honor of Prof. Mordekhai Shmuelevitz], ed. Michael Winter and Miri Shefer (Tel Aviv: Tel Aviv University, 2007), 121–138.

22. Compare the demographic data supplied by Jonathan Israel for main communities of the Western-Sephardi diaspora in *Diasporas within a Diaspora,* 18, 28, 34. Yosef Kaplan suggested this general figure in an oral communication.

23. Halil Inalcik, "Istanbul," in *Encyclopedia of Islam,* 2nd ed. (Leiden: Brill, 1978), 4:242–243.

24. Tsur, *Yehudim bein Muslemim,* part A, especially the chapters on Aleppo and Tunis. See also Matthias B. Lehmann, "A Livornese 'Port Jew' and the Sephardim of the Ottoman Empire," *Jewish Social Studies* 11, no. 2 (Winter 2005): 51–76.

25. Much information on this immigration is found in Toaff, *La Nazione Ebrea;* and Filippini, *Il porto di Livorno.*

26. Immanuel Wallerstein, *The Modern World System; Capitalist Agriculture and the Origins of the European World-Economy in the Sixteenth Century* (New York: Academic Press, 1974). See also the short but illuminating discussion of research trends in Abdullah Thabit, *Merchants, Mamluks, and Murder: The Political Economy of Trade in Eighteenth-Century Basra* (Albany: State University of New York Press, 2001), 4–8.

27. On the Jews and other diasporic minorities in the Ottoman Empire, see Benjamin Braude and Bernard Lewis, eds., *Christians and Jews in the Ottoman Empire: The Functioning of Plural Society,* 2 vols. (New York: Holmes & Meier, 1982); Avigdor Levy, ed., *The Jews of the Ottoman Empire* (Princeton, N.J.: Darwin Press, 1994); and Bruce Masters, *Christians and Jews in the Ottoman Arab World: The Roots of Sectarianism* (New York: Cambridge University Press, 2001). For the respective roles of Jews and Christians in Aleppo, see Bruce Masters, *The Origins of Western Economic Dominance in the Middle East: Mercantilism and the Islamic Economy in Aleppo, 1600–1750* (New York and London, 1988); and A. Marcus, *The Middle East on the Eve of Modernity: Aleppo in the Eighteenth Century* (New York: New York University Press, 1988). For Egypt, the most spectacular example of the deterioration of the Jewish "Italian" elite, see Livingstone, "Ali Bey al-Kabir and the Jews"; and Philipp, *The Syrians in Egypt,* 25–34.

28. Tsur, *Yehudim bein Muslemim,* part A.

29. Schroeter, *The Sultan's Jew.*

30. Samuel Romanelli, *Travail in an Arab Land,* trans. Yedida K. Stillman and Norman A. Stillman (Tuscaloosa: University of Alabama Press, 1989).

31. As evidenced in Schroeter, *Sultan's Jew;* and Schroeter, *Merchants of Essaouira: Urban Society and Imperialism in Southwestern Morocco, 1844–1886* (Cambridge: Cambridge University Press, 1988).

32. Though this perspective on the Western Sephardi networks and elites is absent in the historiography of the nineteenth-century Maghrib, their respective evolutions have been described in several studies. For Algeria, see Claude Martin, *Les Israélites algériens de 1830–1902* (Paris: Éditions Herakles, 1936), 40–74; and Charles André Julien, *Histoire de l'Algérie contemporaine,* vol. 1, *La conquête et les débuts de la colonisation (1827–1871)* (Paris: Presses universitaires de France, 1964). For Tunisia, see Paul Sebag, *Histoire des Juifs de Tunisie des origines à nos jours* (Paris: L'Harmattan, 1991), 109–134; Jean Ganiage, "La crise des finances tunisiennes et l'ascension des Juifs de Tunis (1860–1880)," *Revue Africaine* 99 (1955): 153–173; Abdelhamid Larguèche, *Les ombres de la ville: pauvres, marginaux et minoritaires à Tunis, XVIIIème et XIXème siècles* (Manouba [Tunis]: Centre de Publication Universitaire, Faculté des Lettres de Manouba, 1999), 370–382; and Ben Rejeb, "Al-Nukhub al-yahudiya fi Tunis wa-mawqifuha min al-iqtisad wa-l-sulta 1685–1857." For Morocco, see Schroeter, *The Sultan's Jew;* Schroeter, *Merchants of Essaouira;* and Mohammed Kenbib, *Juifs et Musulmans au Maroc, 1859–1948* (Rabat: Publications de la Faculté des Lettres et des Sciences Humaines, Université Mohammed V, 1994).

PART III

Communities, Cultural Exchange, and Transformations

8

Jewish-Muslim Syncretism and Intercommunity Cohabitation in the Writings of Albert Memmi

The Partage* *of Tunis*

Philippe Barbé

Translated by Allan MacVicar

Although Judaism's "golden age" in Andalusia reached its apogee during the period of intense Islamization of the Mediterranean basin, Jewish-Muslim *"convivencia"* was also marked by harassment and (less often) massacres. In spite of such incidents, and at a time when Jews in Europe were undergoing the worst of persecutions, North African Jews lived in a state of relative (but not permanent) peace.[1] With the notable exception of the ruthless Almohad dynasty that came to power in the twelfth century in Morocco, Muslim authorities in the Maghrib only rarely forced Jews living under their protection to convert to Islam and never engaged in a policy of systematic expulsion or extermination. As Bernard Lewis admits, "There is nothing like Auschwitz in Islamic history."[2] The religious history of the Mediterranean shows instead that the "Abode of Islam" (Dar al-Islam) was the only real asylum open to the Jews who had been persecuted and exiled by the Catholic kings of France, Spain, and Portugal. During the period before French colonization, the daily lives of Jewish communities in the Maghrib were officially governed by the laws of the *dhimma,* that is, the "protection treaty" Muslim authorities accorded only to "People of the Book," principally Christians and Jews. The exceptional legal status of *dhimmis* was based on a central ambivalence between a willingness to protect non-Muslims and a desire to make them feel inferior. That is, while it was socially discriminatory, *dhimmi* status nonetheless al-

---

*The word *partage* denotes both division and sharing in French.

lowed Jewish communities to thrive and to leave an enduring mark on the plural identity of the Maghrib.

As the work of Tunisian writer and essayist Albert Memmi shows, the profoundly ambivalent nature of the *dhimma*—between protection and humiliation—continued to shape the Jewish and Muslim imaginary centuries after its first appearance. The aim of this chapter is to show that the past life of the Jewish community in North Africa, particularly in the multiethnic city of Tunis, can be fully reevaluated only by a prudent examination of both the positive and negative aspects of a fragile Jewish-Muslim cohabitation. In so doing, I hope to avoid reducing the analysis of cultural proximity and religious difference to the logic of either a golden age or martyrdom. Instead, I want to show that it is possible to imagine an admittedly ambivalent form of coexistence between two communities and two religions that today find themselves deeply divided in spite of their common cultural heritage.

Representation of the Jewish Quarter in *The Pillar of Salt:* Between Protection ("Hara-Refuge") and Discrimination ("Hara-Darkness")

Even though the Jewish minority only made up approximately 3 percent of the total population of the Maghrib in the middle of the nineteenth century, its presence was much greater in the capitals, urban centers, and large port cities along the southern and eastern coasts of the Mediterranean. The concentration of Jews in urban areas was particularly obvious in Tunis, where more than half of the Jewish community lived mainly in and around the Jewish quarter, known as the *hara*. In the mid-twentieth century, Jews represented close to 20 percent of the total population of 100,000 of the city.[3] As Abdelhamid Larguèche reminds us, it is impossible to write the thousand-year history of Tunis without according a dominant role to the Jewish community, whose presence was "as old as the city itself."[4] Albert Memmi's first autobiographical novel, *The Pillar of Salt,* published in 1953, is a valuable document for its portrayal of the role Tunis played in the complex history of Muslim-Jewish relations in the Islamic world. As Albert Camus notes in his short preface, *The Pillar of Salt* describes the difficulty, or rather "the impossibility for a Jewish Tunisian of French culture to be anything precise."[5] Twice removed from the Arab-Muslim culture because he was a Jew of French nationality, Albert Memmi endeavors in his first novel to describe the untenable position of his native community, rooted as it is in diverse heritages and split between several allegiances. During an interview with Victor Malka in 1976, Memmi explained that he had chosen to write novels to recount his life and essays to try to understand it.[6] This necessary passage through an autobiographical account was a source of authenticity for both his literary and critical work and represented, in his eyes, the "only guarantee, a safeguard against madness and abstraction."[7] Like the majority of colonized writers of the Maghrib, Albert Memmi thus began his novel-writing with the publication of a "ledger" that allowed him "to evaluate the active and the passive, the negative and the positive" of his existence.[8] This willingness to root his fiction in his own experience led Memmi to make a more subtle distinction between the "truth of facts" and the "symbolic truth."[9] Well before it was formalized in *Le Scorpion ou la confession imaginaire*, this tension between factual and literary truth determined the narrative structure of *The Pillar of Salt*.[10] This dialectic tension is particularly embodied in the complementary figures of the two main characters in the novel: Alexandre Mordekhai Benillouche, the autobiographical double of the author, and his companion, Bissor, a fictional character Memmi created. Through Bissor and through the process of "condensation" and "dramatization," Memmi reaches a higher level of "symbolic truth," which, for all of its apparent falseness, in the end becomes more universal than the "true truth."[11]

Born in the heart of the ghetto, Bissor stands apart from Alexandre and the other Jewish kids by his corpulence and stoutness; he was built "like a plough-horse."[12] As a symbol of the inability of Jews and Muslims to live together peacefully, Bissor will eventually be "killed" by Memmi in an elliptical "pogrom" scene.[13] As numerous critics have noted, the pogrom Memmi mentioned (but did not describe) took place not in Tunis but in Constantine, Algeria, in 1934.[14] Forty years after the publication of his first novel, Memmi himself admitted that there were never any pogroms in Tunis, only "attacks and panics."[15] *The Pillar of Salt*, however, should not be rejected because of its numerous approximations, spatio-temporal distortions, and other novelistic licenses. Such manipulations (or adjustments) of historical truth allowed Memmi to evoke with greater intensity the feeling of alienation and claustrophobia that affected his childhood in Tunis. Harassment, insults, and other forms of humiliation continued to dominate the daily lives of Tunisian Jews well after the official abolition of *dhimmi* status in the middle of the nineteenth century.[16] This deep-seated feeling of communal confinement and alienation is not limited to Memmi's writings. It constitutes a recurring trope in Jewish North African literature produced in Tunisia throughout the first half of the twentieth century. As Guy Degas notes, Jewish North African writers have traditionally represented the Tunisian Jew in such works as J. Véhel's *La Hara contée* (1929), Ryvel's *Les Lumières de la Hara* (1935), or Nine Moati's *Les Belles de Tunis* (1983) as a humiliated or marginal figure dominated by a Muslim majority:

> While specialists tell us that the North-African hara or mellah displayed
> none of the confinement and segregation that characterized the European

ghetto, one has to admit that this is what certain North African Jewish writers, like those of the Tunis school, experienced. Theirs was a crowded, miserable world cut off from a frightening exterior (the image of heavy doors
closed each night recurs in a considerable number of stories) in a universe
apart, on the one hand rich and reassuring, based on an illusion of protection in its isolation, and on the other, deeply shameful, since it expressed
the misery of its inhabitants.[17]

As the literary double of the author, the character of Alexandre corresponds
more explicitly to "the truth of facts" Memmi sought. The events that mark his
journey in *The Pillar of Salt* seem to have been primarily inspired by events that
greatly affected the author through childhood and adolescence. For example,
the Tronja alleyway where the young Memmi grew up on the edge of the Jewish ghetto of Tunis reappears as the Tarfoun impasse. Alexandre, just like Albert
Memmi, is able to go to a French high school because of a scholarship financed
by a rich Jewish pharmacist. The young Alexandre's stay at a summer camp, his
leaving the alleyway, his relocation outside the Jewish quarter, and his traumatic
participation in an exorcism performed on his mother are all events based on the
author's own childhood. In the first chapter of the second part of *The Pillar of Salt*,
Memmi presents to his readers the most explicitly negative and segregated description of the *hara*, the name given to Jewish quarters in Tunisia. In this chapter, entitled "The City," Alexandre describes his lost relationship with the city of
his birth. Alexandre, who lives in proximity to the enclosed space of the *hara*, describes his childhood as being cut off from both the French and the Muslim communities. His strongest reproach for Tunis generally and the *hara* specifically
is that it reflected his own image. Isolated at the very center of this degenerate,
"stinking city," full of "filth" and "untidiness," the Jewish quarter in Tunis was
nothing more than a closed, unhealthy, and overpopulated space—a world paralyzed by its phobias and withdrawn into its ancestral fears:[18]

> My native city is after my own image. . . . I discovered I was doomed for-
> ever to be an outsider in my own native city. And one's home town can no
> more be replaced than one's mother. . . . I am my city's illegitimate son, the
> child of a whore of a city whose heart has been divided among all those to
> whom she has been a slave. . . . Slowly, painfully, I understood that I had
> made a mess of my own birth by choosing the wrong city.[19]

The portions of the book that best exemplify the insurmountable isolation
of the Jewish community are almost always connected to Bissor, while the rare
attempts at reconciliation between Jews and Muslims are usually initiated by
the literary double of Albert Memmi. An episode at the cinema demonstrates
what Memmi later described in his memoirs as "Hara-anxiety, Hara-darkness,

Hara-obscurantism."[20] Each Saturday afternoon, Bissor and Alexandre would religiously go to the Kursaal cinema, which showed Westerns and other adventure films. It was during these rare excursions that the two young boys would have the barest sense that fraternization with the other communities in Tunis might be possible. Once plunged into the darkness of what Marguerite Duras described, in the context of colonial Indochina, as "the great democratic night,"[21] the movie theater would be transformed into a magical place where the different communities found themselves in a common and festive space: "For a few minutes, we all forgot our individual fears and hatreds and became a single unit in the noisy expression of our emotions."[22] For the duration of the film, they all inhabited the same room; Sicilian laborers at the top of the social scale along with "the ragged bootblacks" and "the Maltese cabbies."[23] This unity was, however, very fragile. After a fight with a Sicilian spectator who had dropped a lit cigarette into Bissor's hair, the two young boys were violently kicked out of the theater even before the film began. As they headed to the docks, Bissor explained to Alexandre that this incident only confirmed their own marginality and the Jew's inability to live in peace with the other inhabitants of Tunis:

> "You see how they hate us?" said Bissor, hopelessly convinced. They: the young Sicilians, the Arab policeman, the French newspaper owner, our classmates at the lycée, the whole city in fact. And it was true that our native city was as hostile to us as an unnatural mother. We had been disappointed at one blow; it was final and couldn't be healed.[24]

On 24 November 1973, twenty years later, and less than a month after the Yom Kippur war, Albert Memmi reiterated the impossibility of being Jewish among Arabs at a Paris conference.[25] Closely following the arguments Bissor made, Memmi used the following terms to describe the dual hostility that Tunisian Jews faced from Europeans and Arabs: "In my novel, *The Pillar of Salt*, I have told how the French authorities coldly abandoned us to the Germans. But I must add that we also lived amidst a hostile Arab population."[26] From this, Memmi concluded that the inability to be an "Arab Jew" lies (exclusively) in the fact that Muslim Arabs have made such an alliance impossible: "*Jewish Arabs*—that's what we would have liked to be, and if we have given up the idea, it is because for centuries the Moslem Arabs have scornfully, cruelly, and systematically prevented us from carrying it out. And now it is far too late to become Jewish Arabs again."[27]

Unlike the episode at the cinema, which allowed Memmi to underscore the absence of a Jewish-Muslim dialogue and especially of a peaceful intercommunal cohabitation, the scene of a journey Alexandre took on a streetcar presents a more positive and nuanced description of the "*hara*-refuge."[28] Unused to walking about in the European and Muslim quarters, Alexandre is particularly sensitized to his travels by streetcar, during which bodies come into contact with one another and voices become intertwined in a polyphonic and harmonized space. Following a trajectory that cuts across the geographical boundaries that separate the primary ethnicities of the city, Alexandre sees the streetcar as one of the rare places where the different communities of Tunis are forced to interact and meet each other. He describes in minute detail the new arrivals that surge onto the streetcar at every stop. The first impression the young man notes is that of a collective well-being, a human warmth that stands in stark contrast to the cold rain falling on the city of Tunis:

> Each new passenger who boarded the car arrived among us wet and covered with mud, hurriedly slamming the sliding door behind him. The car itself, all warm from its human load and saturated with the steam of our breath, was acquiring an odd kind of intimacy as the passengers felt drawn together by a common feeling of well-being that contrasted with the storm beating against the windows. A mysterious sense of communion was thus born among us.[29]

This "mysterious sense of communion" should not, however, lead one to infer that this produced a new community, a community like the generous but problematic "Mediterranean race" Audisio dreamed of in his idealized description of the physical union of the different Mediterranean peoples.[30] As opposed to this intensely intimate model of a *patrie Méditerranée*, Memmi, through Alexandre, presents the image of a mosaic of peoples living next to one another without, however, managing to come together:

> All the races of our city were represented there. Sicilian workers in patched blue overalls, with their tools at their feet, were arguing noisily; a French housewife, conscious of her own dignity, was on her way to the market; in front of me a [Muslim] sat with his son, a tiny little boy wearing a miniature fez and with his hands all stained with henna; to my left, a Djerban grocer from the south, off to restock his store, with his basket between his legs and a pencil over his ear.[31]

Alexandre's eyes then fall on a Bedouin with "the stink of a stable and of stale cooking fats"[32] who faces the wrath of the other passengers when he forgets to close the door of the compartment behind him. Stung by the icy wind that filled the car, the Sicilian bricklayers yell at the Bedouin, telling him to close the door. Unlike the scene at the cinema, Alexandre notes that this time the altercation does not degrade into a real fight. He fails to detect the slightest trace of spitefulness or "clannish animosity" and is relieved to discover that this incident that might have led to another intercommunal confrontation diffuses itself in a familial and Mediterranean atmosphere:

"Close the door!" the Sicilian masons shouted, though apparently without any hostility or clannish animosity. The Muslims in the car all pricked their ears up. For a while, the little game stopped. But the Sicilians had really intended no harm and we were quite clearly, one and all, a big family of Mediterraneans. One of the Muslims, to show that he appreciated it, even decided to join in the fun: "Close that door! Don't they have doors, back home on your mountainside?" The Bedouin smiled foolishly and, without giving an answer, finally closed the door.[33]

In order to better understand the importance of this anecdote, one needs to remember the historical and sociocultural uniqueness of Tunis. Situated at the juncture between East and West, this coastal city was known to be a geographical node where different religions and Mediterranean peoples came together but also spread out. From the first Arabized Berbers to the Maltese Christians as well as the Andalusians, the Turks, the Portuguese, and even the Jews of Livorno, the diversity of Tunis grew through a slow process of sedimentation at various social, ethnic, racial, and religious levels. Unlike the "melting pot" model of integration, the social structure of Tunis corresponded to a "mosaic" in which the mechanisms of juxtaposition and cohabitation did not necessarily imply a mixing of communities. As Roberto Berardi notes in his topo-sociological reading of the map of old Tunis, the historic urban center was made up of a complex system of "interwoven enclosures" that were segregated but nonetheless allowed a significant degree of cultural solidarity and socio-professional complementarity to be maintained.[34] While in some rare passages of *The Pillar of Salt* Memmi recognizes that a Mediterranean fraternity may be possible, he is very careful not to represent the cohabitation of the different ethnicities, nationalities, and religions as a perfect fusion. Such a fusion would synthesize, on the smaller scale of Tunis, all of these idiosyncrasies into a new Mediterranean identity. Alexandre brings up this interethnic cohabitation several times when he describes the segregated urban topology of Tunis. He notes that one would only have to "walk five hundred steps" to literally "change civilizations."[35] Beginning from the Arab town, with "its houses like expressionless faces, its long, silent, shadowed passages leading suddenly to packed crowds," Alexandre continues his exploration of Tunis by pushing into "the busy Jewish alleyways, so sordid and familiar, lined with deep stalls, shops and eating houses, all shapeless houses piled as best they can fit together."[36] On the edge of the Arab town and the *hara*, Alexandre travels up and down other ethnic enclaves: the poverty-stricken "Little Sicily"; the *funduqs* of the Maltese, "those strange Europeans with an Arab tongue and a British nationality"; and the European quarter filled with "the little homes of retired French *rentiers*."[37] Through the veil of human diversity, it was possible to see how each community had withdrawn into itself and was deeply segregated. However, any latent hostility toward the other communities was expressed through avoidance, indifference, or spite rather than with direct confrontation.

Hara-Madina: The Division of the City in the Jewish-Muslim Imaginary

Unlike the main European ghettos, the *hara* in Tunis, the first archaeological traces of which date back to the thirteenth century, was never a clearly defined zone. Some historians thus question the designation of this area as a ghetto, since it was probably never delimited by walls or doors.[38] It may be difficult to clearly discern the boundary of the *hara* partly because of the diverse origins of its inhabitants. The inhabitants of the Jewish quarter of Tunis were by no means homogeneous because the area developed slowly, following several large waves of migration: the Jews of Qayrawan escaping from the destruction of that city in the eleventh century, the Jews fleeing the Almohad dynasty in the thirteenth century, the Jews driven out of the Iberian peninsula at the end of the fourteenth and fifteenth centuries, and even the exodus of European Jews from Livorno in the sixteenth and seventeenth centuries. The arrival of each new set of immigrants caused the quarter to become overpopulated and extend beyond its historical borders. As the richer inhabitants (primarily Jews from Livorno) began to leave during decolonization, the Jewish quarter opened up to the poorest segment of the Muslim population.

In the modern period, the borders of the *hara* fragmented and Jews and Muslims began to intermingle. In his 1950s study of urban ethnology in the *hara*, Sebag noted that socioeconomic imperatives increasingly undermined sectarian segregation: "But in neighboring stalls, Jews and Muslims work the same jobs; on the patios, their wives help one another in different ways; on the esplanade, their children play together, without there being the slightest incident."[39] A detailed reading of the statistical charts, graphs, and tables Sebag reproduced in the appendix of his book confirms the socioreligious complexity of the human mosaic in the *hara*. The streets of the Jewish and Muslims quarters belonged to a wider network of alleyways, main roads, and arteries that were in turn connected to other lanes or cul-de-sacs. It was, therefore, almost impossible to distinguish physical borders that would clearly separate the Jewish from the Muslim quarter. In this way, certain impasses or sections of the streets Muslims or Europeans inhabited became a part of the streets that were inhabited almost exclusively by Jews.[40] This difficulty in physically delimiting the Jewish and Muslim sectors was further reinforced architecturally; Jewish and Muslim houses were built based on the same model of a courtyard home.[41] The *hara*'s topological complexity is central to Memmi's writings and thought, from his earliest novel to his latest autobiographical account.[42] Several times in *The Pillar of Salt*, Alexandre remembers that unlike Bissor, his family did not live at the center of the *hara:* "I was not born in the ghetto. Our alleyway was at the frontier of the Jewish quarter of Tunis, but this was enough to satisfy my father's pride."[43]

The testimonies of numerous Western travelers throughout the nineteenth century emphasized the great poverty of the Jews of Tunis, who were crammed into unhealthy slums. A more refined sociohistorical study shows, however, that far from being socially homogeneous, the Jewish community was not entirely segregated in a clearly delineated Jewish quarter. This social heterogeneity becomes clear when we retrace the topological boundaries that divided the communal space of the *hara*. First, it should be noted that the center of the Jewish quarter was mainly inhabited by the poor as well as by workers, employees, and beggars. This pauperized social space was bordered by a middle class composed of shopkeepers and craftsmen who worked as silversmiths, weavers, garment makers, carpenters, and leatherworkers. Finally, in neighborhoods farther out lived a small, Europeanized, bourgeois elite made up of merchants, financiers, doctors, and lawyers. Memmi's family chose to live in the intermediate space at the junction of Jewish and Muslim worlds because of the father's occupation as a saddler. The main clients of the family shop were the Babesian carters who lived and worked primarily in the Muslim quarter. Because of the location of the Tronja alleyway (the real name of the Tarfoune alleyway) on the edge of the quarter, Memmi played with local Muslim youths from a very young age and thus came into direct and apparently fraternal contact with them: "Because of this topographical location, I played as much with the Arab Muslim children as I did with Jewish children. This had an additional consequence: I am now very familiar with the accent of the Muslim community."[44] In *Le Nomade immobile,* Memmi explains again that his father, who worked mainly for an Arab clientele, had voluntarily chosen to "live in this no man's land, *between* the Arab quarter and the Jewish quarter."[45] Rather than being a negative space, for Memmi this "no man's land" represented a chance to belong to several spaces and border cultures: "The advantage of the no man's land is that one is simultaneously an inhabitant of the border and a neighbor, regardless of the problems or tragedies of cohabitation."[46] This frontier zone is both a place of discord and separation and a space of mediation and meeting, an inclusive frontier, a bridge, a place of passage.

The question of topological mediation between the Jewish and Muslim communities is also the focus of the correspondence between Abdelkebir Khatibi (a Moroccan Muslim sociologist and novelist) and Jacques Hassoun (an Egyptian Jewish psychoanalyst and novelist).[47] After having read a richly illustrated work by J. Toledano on the Jewish quarters of Morocco (the mellah), Khatibi expresses his difficulty with the word "labyrinth" to Jacques Hassoun.[48] The Moroccan writer considers it an error to think of the Muslim *madina* and the Jewish mellah as labyrinthine spaces where the other, the outsider, is condemned to become lost.[49] In Khatibi's estimation, these two spaces do not oppose one another but rather converge in a "logical spatial order."[50] In problematizing the notion of labyrinth, he would prefer to speak of a "reading path" ("*un chemin de lecture*") with rules, codes, landmarks, referents, passages, and doors as well as centers. The mellah and the *madina* are thus described as spaces where the observer, Jewish or Muslim, can find "a psychology and a strategy of walking, meeting, avoidance, combat, escape, and of all the movements of the body when it is caught in this kind of social network."[51] To learn how to move about in these rhizomic spaces, the observer has to adapt to the topographical fluidity and allow him or herself to be carried along by the unsettling "flexible movement of the mind."[52] Khatibi then notes that these microspaces, in spite of the religious differences of their inhabitants, participate in the same labyrinthine logic of wandering that disrupts the colonial rationalizing and domesticating urban space. The *hara-madina* labyrinths, understood simultaneously as mazes, impasses, and crossroads, thus came together as counterspaces on the fringes of colonial neighborhoods. This proximity between the urban spaces Jewish and Muslim communities inhabited is even more clearly seen after reading Orientalist accounts written throughout the nineteenth century by European travelers passing through Tunis. Travelers such as N. Davis (1840), L. Frank (1850), and V. Guérin (1860), cast an ambivalent eye on the Tunisian capital.[53] While they recognized the splendor of this great, thousand-year-old city of the Mediterranean, these authors do not hide their discomfort with and inability to understand a city whose apparent urban anarchy contrasts so sharply with their perception of the rationality and geometric perfections of the Western metropolises. For example, V. Guérin notes that "the interior of Tunis is a confused and irregular network of streets and alleys that are poorly laid out, poorly built, and even more poorly maintained. There seems to have been no planning in the construction of this city, where there are nonetheless three main arteries that traverse it . . . which become reference points for the foreigner who ventures into this almost inextricable maze without a guide."[54] He adds, "This inability to find rationality—a logic regulating the urban topology of Tunis—troubles the Western gaze when confronted by a city that it can only be perceived as a negative, incoherent, and dangerously chaotic space."[55] French colonization further obscured indigenous urban patterns. As Frantz Fanon emphasized in *The Wretched of the Earth,* the commonality of Jewish and Muslim quarters was reinforced by their shared isolation and opposition to the urban worlds of the colonizers. While the frontiers that separate the urban spaces occupied by the colonized populations (Jewish and Muslim) remain extremely permeable, the frontier between the indigenous quarters and the colonial world is an insurmountable barrier, a pure line of separation rendering any overlap or encounter impossible: "The 'native' sector is not complementary to the European sector. The two confront each other, but not in the service of a higher unity. Governed by a purely Aristotelian logic, they follow the dictates of mutual exclusion: there is no conciliation possible, one of them is superfluous."[56] The topography of the labyrinth thus reveals the "reflection of a common history" that unifies Arab-Muslim and Arab-Jewish space in their resistance to the colonial enterprise and its rigid compartmentalization of urban space.[57] Faced with French colonization, Jews and Muslims thus rediscovered within urban space a "micro-structure" of resistance based on a "counter-apprenticeship" and a "strategy of contours."[58] It is through this "psychology of the detour" that Jews and Muslims continued to share a common North African imaginary, in what admittedly remains the "same topological fiction."[59]

A Torn Identity: From the Hyphen (Arab-Jew) to the Comma (Arab, Jew)

As a "torn writer," (*écrivain de la déchirure*), Memmi dedicated the bulk of his writing to the exploration of the different facets of his North African, colonized-decolonized, Jewish identity.[60] Because of the richness and analytical depth of Albert Memmi's imagination, his work remains an essential testimony to the difficulty of living in a Mediterranean world ravaged by colonialism and anti-Semitism. The acceptance of such a difference can only arouse suffering and a wounded identity. Instead of glorifying the thousand-year-old coexistence of the three monotheistic religions, Memmi's writing allows us to rethink the tensions as well as the dialogues undertaken in the Mediterranean and around the Arab-Jew hyphen across the centuries. From his first autobiographical novel in 1953 until the publication of his *Portrait du décolonisé* in 2004, the author of *The Pillar of Salt* has constantly oscillated between two contradictory positions: the temptation of discord and the promise of reconciliation.[61] The wildest dreams of reconciliation or fusion as well as the greatest disappointments came about because of a desire to establish this hyphen. Memmi responded to the question "What is an Arab-Jew?" in 1974 by saying that such an identity had been rendered irreparably impossible because of the unilateral rejection of the Jews by the Arabs: "The Jews lived very badly in the Arab-dominated countries. . . . The Arabs never did more than tolerate the existence of the Jewish minorities. . . . The Arabs want Israel destroyed."[62] As Jacques Derrida showed in the analysis of his own French–North African identity (and of his Jewish–French–North African wound), the hyphen betrays "a disorder of identity" rather than "a surfeit of richness of identities, attributes, or names."[63] In the postcolonial context of the Mediterranean, Arab-Jewish memory, like French–North African memory, is still too affected by disunions, desertions, and betrayals for a simple hyphen to suffice for reconciliation:

"The silence of that hyphen does not pacify or appease anything, not a single tor-
ment, not a single torture. . . . A hyphen is never enough to conceal protests, cries
of anger or suffering, the noise of weapons, airplanes, and bombs."[64] Memmi's inability to define the "Arab-Jew" does not, however, result in an insurmountable
and permanent discord. Memmi refused to believe that the Jew and the Arab are
condemned to deny or destroy each other and tried to rethink the splitting of his
identity based on what Deleuze and Guattari defined in another context as the
"logic of the AND."[65] As Memmi tells us in his autobiographical essay entitled
Ce que je crois, as soon as he arrived in France he tried to reconstruct his identity
according to the notion of the supplement: being Jewish *and* Arab, French *and*
North African, Eastern *and* Western. In a key passage in this book, Memmi recalls the response he tried to give to a naïve question Edmond Fleg posed concerning the former's Jewish-Tunisian origins. After listening to Memmi, Fleg replied, "In summary, you are Jewish, Tunisian, and French, and you hold to all
three. . . . Well then, be Jewish, Tunisian, and French."[66] While appreciating the
comforting kindness of this declaration, Memmi had the painful impression that
by wanting to be Jewish, Tunisian, and French, he would unfortunately end up
being "neither one nor the other. . . . It was difficult wisdom, but I was unable to
think any other way; it remains the same today."[67]

Faced with this acknowledgment of disunity, Memmi did manage, however,
to look upon his childhood as a Mediterranean Jew living on Muslim soil with
greater ambivalence in other texts. In fact, in his two latest autobiographical accounts, published in 1995 (*Le Juif et l'autre*) and 2000 (*Le Nomade immobile*), Memmi
most explicitly recognized the possibility of a mediation between the three monotheistic religions of the Mediterranean. While Memmi continues to describe Judeo-
Muslim relations in terms of opposition and noncommunication, he does recognize, and with less hesitation than in his early books, that the Jews and Muslims
of Tunisia have effectively lived through "suspicious but inescapable kinships,
daily sliding one against the other like oiled ball bearings."[68] North African and
Tunisian identities were effectively built over a long period through a process of
cultural contamination, infiltration, sedimentation, and transvaluation. In spite
of the fact that these different populations never really intermingled, Memmi
nostalgically remembers that his childhood in Tunis was truly marked by an
Arab-Jewish symbiosis:

> For us, the Arabs were both brothers and enemies, hostile cousins: there
> were, of course, common customs. Like them, we ate couscous, we liked
> fish, we went to the beach . . . but to each their own; there were no mixed
> marriages, or very few. These occurred later, but at the beginning, there
> were absolutely none. Things were rigorously kept apart. We had, however,
> the same sensibilities, the same songs, the same singers.[69]

Memmi found that Mediterranean culture did not fit well with the more or-thodox aspects of religion, and this led him to rediscover the power of religious and cultural syncretism that would allow for more fruitful exchanges between Islam, Judaism, and Christianity. Memmi's recognition of this syncretism reveals that his work is centered on what might be described as a logic of suspension and of the comma. By not seeking to reduce or erase fractures, the comma allows a more modest recognition of the wounded identity shared by the colonized-decolonized. In the tracing of this comma, the "Jew, Arab" then preserves an in-terior alterity, which, as long as it is identified and accepted as such, would as-sure within a subtle distance in proximity the respect for the Other and thereby protect it from the devouring and often destructive passion of the One.[70]

Toward a Recognition of Arab-Jewish Syncretism in Tunisia

Whether it be in the area of magical and religious beliefs and practices, the Judeo-Arabic dialect, culinary traditions, or the type of clothing worn, the daily life of the Jewish and Muslim communities in Tunis have borrowed a great deal from the culture of the Other. As Abdelhamid Larguèche writes, it was probably in Tunis, more than any other city in the Maghrib, that these symbioses made the creation of a common heritage between Jews and Muslims possible:

> Besides the attitudes towards rejection or cohabitation, it would also be in-teresting to look into the mutual influences and conjunctions. Even if the Jewish community lived autonomously and to a certain degree focused only on its values and the enclosed space of the [*hara*], it was still affected by the surrounding area. Even though the two communities were separated by the insurmountable barrier of religion, the strong worship of saints and certain beliefs and customs that affected the popular Jewish mindset in Tunis were not foreign to the prevailing culture of the city. The worship of saints and maraboutism were the most widespread expressions of popular religiosity in Tunisia and all the Maghrib.[71]

The Jewish customs practiced in the *hara* of Tunis seemingly resembled the ones found in all other Jewish communities around the world. In matters of cir-cumcision, joining the religious majority (the Bar Mitzvah), or wedding ceremo-nies, the Jews of Tunis practiced the main rites of Judaism very diligently. The significant Jewish holy days such as Sukkot, Shavuot, Yom Kippur, Hanukkah, Rosh Hashanah, Passover, and Purim all structured life in the *hara*. Besides these official celebrations, the Jews of Tunis remained deeply attached to more spe-cifically Tunisian holidays as well as to other superstitious beliefs that the rab-binical tradition formally condemned. Never confronted in Tunisia by the "west-ern Hassidim with their black robes, their untrimmed beards, their curls, and their large black hats or furs," Memmi remembers that the Judaism of his youth was a "friendly religion" and was quite close to Catholicism as it was practiced by his Sicilian friends:

> The Italians, I knew them well, I had many little Italian friends, in class, on the street, in the sports clubs. And we were influenced by the Italians, no doubt, almost as much as by the French. When the Italians were happy, they thanked the Madonna for what she had done for them; but if they were angry and she had not done what they had asked, they would insult her. It was 'Putana la Madone,' 'Goddamn Madonna[,]' . . . a very popular expression. . . . The Sicilians had something similar. It was not a gloomy religion, but one that took account of the light, of the sun, a "good-natured" religion.[72]

It was, however, on the margins of monotheism, in "a vast zone of cultural syncretism," that the Jewish and Muslim communities were able to share, mostly unconsciously, an archaic heritage of common superstitions.[73] The belief in evil spirits (*jnun*) as well as the protective hand of the "evil eye" (*'ayn hara*) could be found among both Jewish and Muslim Tunisians. When this protection against the evil eye and the evil spirits was not effective, Tunisians turned to healers. The common struggle against the evil spirits reinforced a Judeo-Islamic syncretism. As Sebag has noted, the Jews and the Muslims almost always consulted with a female Muslim soothsayer (*deggaza*) when they needed to find out where an evil had originated, and then they went to a Jewish healer for it to be exorcised.[74] The exorcism session almost always began with a handful of salt methodically encircling the sick body. Once the evil spirit was captured, the salt was violently thrown into the fire. This gesture was accompanied by a series of offerings (mainly of nuts, almonds, and raisins) strategically placed near doors and in the corners of windows. These offerings were to appease the evil spirits and encourage them to release their prey. Finally, the ceremony ended with a magical dance to the sound of an Arab-Andalusian orchestra or, if the family had the financial means, of a "black orchestra."[75] To the ancestral rhythms and sounds of bagpipes, tom-toms, and other tambourines, the hypnotized participants would abandon themselves to the mystical trance of an invocatory dance.

This ritual constitutes a central passage in *The Pillar of Salt.* As an involuntary witness to the exorcism of his Aunt Maïssa, Alexandre describes and condemns with disgust "this collective seizure of epilepsy."[76] He appears particularly troubled by the presence of "savage" and "terrifying Negro musicians" coming from "some tribes of the deep South, a strange offshoot of Negro Africa sent out toward the luminous Mediterranean shore."[77] Their "dreadful music," described as a "weird mixture of hysterical flutes, wild cymbals, tom-tom drums, and *dar-*

bouka bagpipes," seems to cast a spell on the women attending the exorcism.[78] At the center of the ceremony, Alexandre eventually notices that "a woman, dressed in gaudy veils, was dancing wildly, throwing out her arms, jerking her head back and forth with so violent a motion that it hurt my neck to watch her."[79] It was only after having recognized "the orange-colored *djebbah* gown strewn with red and green sequins, the gaudy artificial silk *fouta* veil, brilliantly colored and gaudy, orange, yellow, green, and red, and the green and yellow scarf decorated with Fatima's hand and a fish" that the young Alexandre identifies behind "this primitive mask, glazed with sweat, with its disheveled hair, eyes tightly closed, [and] lips all bloodless" the transfigured face of his own mother.[80] After the traumatizing scene of the maternal trance, he then seeks to distance himself from the ancestral traditions of his mother's tribe throughout the rest of *The Pillar of Salt*. Memmi's ambivalence with regard to the question of Judeo-Islamic syncretism crystallizes around the figure of the mother. With a certain detachment tinged with incomprehension and (perhaps) contempt, Memmi describes his mother as an illiterate and superstitious "Bedouin," an "oriental" woman whose "fine Berber face" betrayed a worrisome primitive splendor.[81]

Fifty years after having described this scene for the first time, he returns, in *Le Nomade immobile*, to the importance of this traumatic incident in the construction of his personality and imagination. In those areas where his mother was effusive and superstitious, Memmi would be reserved and reasonable. Without explicitly denying that he does so, he presents a particularly Orientalist image of his own mother. He even goes so far as to say that he wrote more essays than novels for fear of being overwhelmed by a nostalgia for a childhood dominated by Eastern tradition and old-fashioned folklore: "Spurred on by History, no doubt I gave too great a place to essays. I was probably also afraid of being overwhelmed; I didn't want to imitate the magical dances of my mother and of the women of my youth, which always ended in trances—they would fall on the ground, overcome by veritable hysterical fits, successfully swayed by the music that led them in and then out. I compelled myself to follow a rigid style, and to it being transparent."[82] Memmi's ambivalence about his mother summarizes the rending of an identity irreducibly split between an Eastern heritage and Western aspirations. As a negative horizon to his desire for the West, the Eastern figure of the mother continues to haunt Memmi's life, work, and imagination: "A simple, illiterate, almost primitive woman, my mother was central to the constitution of my person."[83]

An Imaginary of Judeo-Islamic-Christian Mediation

In less than fifty years after the creation of the State of Israel in 1948, the national independence movements in the 1950s and 1960s, the policy of Arabization, the thorny Palestinian question, and numerous Arab-Israeli wars, the Jewish presence in North Africa that had endured for over 2,000 years came to an end. While the Jews have virtually disappeared from Algeria and Egypt, today an aging community of approximately 5,000 Jews remains in Morocco and a little more than 2,000 in Tunisia (mainly in Tunis and Jerba). It is now too late to dream of a return of North African Jews to the land where their ancestors lived and died. Like almost all the areas populated by a Muslim majority, the southern coast of the Mediterranean has probably lost its Jewish population forever. In the particular case of Tunis, the disappearance of the Jewish presence has become even more definite because at the end of the 1950s, the *hara* was declared unfit for habitation and underwent a long process of rehabilitation, demolition, and reconstruction, which reshaped beyond recognition the topography of the traditional Jewish quarter.[84] As Memmi states, "Geographically, nothing remains of the [*hara*]."[85] While recognizing that "the ghetto has been demolished" and that "the people have all left," Memmi acknowledges that it is hard for him to turn the page and to erase this "essential soil" from the memory around which he has (re) built his Judeo-North African imaginary:

> The [*hara*] is my inner land. . . . I became a kind of chronicler of the [*hara*], the depository of the collective memory of the [*hara*], that is being yielded back to me a hundredfold. . . . Because of my subsequent history, I became a nomad, I have no ties, but at the same time, I'm firmly anchored. In a certain way for the rest of my life—as a writer at least—I continue to live in the [*hara*], an imaginary [*hara*]. . . . The [*hara*] is my radium, my uranium 236, my inner, portable, and unquenchable sun. . . . I am sure that it will continue to shine in me until my death.[86]

The slow but irreversible disappearance of the Jewish presence from North African soil does not mean that the memory of this community will be completely erased. On the contrary, North African Jews are exhibiting a renewed interest in rediscovering their roots. From Fez to Tetuan to Tangier and Tunis, many synagogues are being restored and visited by a growing number of tourists and pilgrims in search of their origins. Since the beginning of the 1990s, organizations like the Foundation of Judeo-Moroccan Cultural Heritage (FPCJM) and the association of Arts and Popular Traditions of the Jews of Tunisia (ATPJT) have increased their activity with the goal of keeping the Judeo-North African memory alive.[87] As Patrick Simon and Claude Tapia have shown, memory still structures the relationship between Jews and Muslims of Tunisian origin transplanted in Paris. The *quartier tune* (Tunisian quarter, in French slang) of Belleville is one of the principal sites of memory of Tunisian identity in France, and it is here that the imaginary of an Arab-Jewish syncretism as it existed in the *hara* in Tunis can be found. It is important to note that this attachment for Belleville came about not simply because a few exiles were nostalgic for a lost world. In fact, a "second generation of Jews of Tunisian origin born in France find Belleville to be an idealized, certainly, but also material representation of the environment in which their grandparents lived."[88] At a time of increasing tensions between Israel and the Arab world, this return to an idealized past where both communities cohabited harmoniously offers an optimistic model of Jewish-Muslim relations based on the recognition of and respect for the Other.

NOTES

1. The massacres and forced conversions of Andalusian Jews in Spain began to increase in 1391, putting an end to what today is often considered the "Golden Age" of Judaism. A century later, during the Reconquista of the summer of 1492, more than 200,000 Jews were brutally expelled from Christian Spain. Four years later, the Jewish community fled from Portugal.

2. Bernard Lewis tempers his statement about the tolerance of Islam, however, by recalling that while there was no real Muslim Hitler, "it would not be difficult to name Muslim rulers or leaders worthy to rank with Cotton Mather or Torquemada." *The Jews of Islam* (Princeton, N.J.: Princeton University Press, 1984), 7.

3. For a more detailed statistical presentation of the Jewish presence in the Maghrib, in Tunisia, and in Tunis, see Lucette Valensi, "Multicultural Visions: The Cultural Tapestry of the Jews of North Africa," in *Cultures of the Jews: A New History*, ed. David Biale (New York: Schocken Books, 2002), 890–891.

4. Abdelhamid Larguèche, *Les Ombres de Tunis: pauvres, marginaux et minoritiés aux XVIIIe et XIXe siècles* (Paris: Arcantères Éditions, 2000), 13.

5. Albert Camus, "Preface" in Albert Memmi, *La Statue de sel* (Paris: Éditions Gallimard, 1966), 9.

6. Published in Albert Memmi, *La Terre intérieure* (Paris: Éditions Gallimard, 1976), 140.

7. Ibid., 217.

8. Memmi, *La Terre intérieure*, 108. Much francophone literature by authors from North Africa or of North African origin displays the tendency to begin a literary lifework by an autobiographically inspired account in which the author returns in a more or less hidden way to key events of his or her childhood. Examples include Mouloud Feraoun, *Le Fils du Pauvre* (Paris: Éditions du Seuil, 1954); Mouloud Mammeri, *La Colline oubliée* (Paris: Plon, 1952); Abdelkebir Khatibi, *La Mémoire tatouée* (Paris: Éditions Denoël, 1971); and even Kateb Yacine, *Nedjma* (Paris: Éditions du Seuil, 1956).

9. Memmi, *La Terre Intérieure*, 163.

10. Albert Memmi, *Le Scorpion ou la confession imaginaire* (Paris, Éditions Gallimard, 1969).

11. Memmi, *La Terre intérieure*, 9.

12. Memmi, *The Pillar of Salt*, trans. Edouard Roditi (Boston: Beacon Press, 1955), 98.

13. Ibid., 98, 254, 256. It is important to note that the notions of "ghetto" and "pogrom" that Memmi uses are in fact expressions that originated in Europe and not in the Maghrib. This choice of terminology remains highly problematic when one recognizes that anti-Semitic violence was historically much greater in Europe.

14. In spite of its violence, the pogrom in Constantine did not irreparably divide the Jewish and Muslim communities in this city, which its Jewish inhabitants proudly described as the "Je-

rusalem of the Maghrib." As Benjamin Stora notes in his autobiographical essay, "Une enfance à Constantine," the real frontier was situated (in spite of the 1934 pogrom) between the Jewish/ Muslim and European communities: "Two cities were effectively juxtaposed: the Jewish-Arab old city, where an extremely high number of people lived right on top of one another, and were completely mixed together, and the European Saint-Jean, on the other side of the city" (236). It was only after the beginning of the Algerian war that this "communal and urban complicity" between Jews and Muslims living in the working-class neighborhoods of Constantine was permanently broken. Benjamin Stora, "Une Enfance à Constantine," in *La Méditerranée des Juifs: exils et enracinements*, ed. Paul Balta, Catherine Dana, and Régine Dhoquois-Cohen (Paris, Éditions L'Harmattan, 2003), 236–242.

15. Memmi, *Le Juif et l'Autre*, 76. While the death toll from the Constantine pogrom on 3–5 August 1934 is known (twenty-three Jews and three Muslims killed), the cause has proven much more difficult to ascertain. Memmi seems to accept a little too quickly that this pogrom was the result of profoundly anti-Semitic feelings on the part of the Muslim community. However, as Michael Laskier reminds us, the exact causes of the Constantine pogrom are still unknown, though it does seem that the anti-Semitic campaign orchestrated by Algerians of European (and not Muslim) origin played a central role. Michael Laskier, *North African Jewry in the Twentieth Century: The Jews of Morocco, Tunisia, and Algeria* (New York: New York University Press, 1994), 56–57.

16. North African Jews' sense of alienation and inferiority was expressed in day-to-day life rather than on a strictly politico-legal level. As A. Larguèche notes, the status of the *dhimma*, in spite of its importance, "was historically only a theoretical framework or a referential model. In practical terms, the respect of its statutes depended largely on the circumstances, events, states, and social and cultural relations, as well as on the mood of the princes." Larguèche, *Les Ombres de Tunis*, 351.

17. Guy Degas, "Ni paradis perdu, ni terre promise: le juif dans le regard du musulman, le musulman dans le regard du juif à travers leurs littératures de langue française," in *Juifs et Musulmans en Tunisie: fraternité et déchirements*, ed. Sonia Fellous (Paris: Somogy éditions d'art, 2003), 280. See also Guy Degas, *La Littérature judéo-maghrébine d'expression française* (Paris: Editions l'Harmattan, 1990).

18. Memmi, *The Pillar of Salt*, 97.

19. Ibid., 96, 98.

20. Memmi, *La Terre intérieure*, 17.

21. Marguerite Duras, *Un Barrage contre le Pacifique* (Paris: Éditions Gallimard, 1950), 188. For a more detailed study of the liberating dimension of cinema in the colonial context, see Philippe Barbé, "Hétérotopies et cartographie existentielle: des lieux de Marguerite Duras," in *Origins and Identities in French Literature*, ed. Buford Norman (Amsterdam: Rodopi, 1999), 183–196.

22. Memmi, *The Pillar of Salt*, 100

23. Ibid., 99–100.

24. Ibid., 102–103.

25. Memmi, "What Is an Arab Jew?" in Albert Memmi, *Jews and Arabs*, trans. Eleanor Levieux (Chicago: J. Philip O'Hara, Inc., 1975), 19–29.

26. Ibid., 23.

27. Ibid., 20.

28. Memmi, *La Terre intérieure*, 27.

29. Memmi, *The Pillar of Salt*, 166.

30. "We are all brothers, from Algeciras to Marseille to Messina. This is what is called a race"; Gabriel Audisio, *Jeunesse de la Méditerranée* (Paris: Éditions Gallimard, 1935), 10.

31. Memmi, *The Pillar of Salt*, 166–167.

32. Ibid., 168.

33. Ibid. (my translation).

34. Roberto Berardi, "Signification du plan ancient de la ville arabe: la Médina de Tunis," in *La Ville arabe dans l'Islam: histoire et mutations: Actes du 2ème colloque de l'A.T.P. "Espaces socio-culturels et croissance urbaine dans le monde arabe," Carthage-Amilcar, 12–18 mars 1979,* ed. Abdel-wahab Bouhdiba et Dominique Chevallier (Tunis: Université de Tunis, Centre d'études et de recherches économiques et sociales; Paris: Centre national de la recherche scientifique, 1982), 165–190.

35. Memmi, *The Pillar of Salt,* 97.

36. Ibid.

37. Ibid.

38. Regarding this topic, Paul Sebag found strikingly contradictory evidence, preventing a definitive answer to this question. During a trip to Tunis in 1865, A. de Flaux noted that the Jewish quarter in Tunis strangely was not bordered by doors or walls; *La Régence de Tunis au XIXème siècle,* cited in Sebag, *La Hara de Tunis: l'évolution d'un ghetto nord-africain* (Paris: Presses universitaires de France, 1959), 17. However, Sebag discovered that in an 1888 letter, written by a certain Chalom Flah and published in Hebrew in Warsaw in the periodical *Haasif,* there is a description of the *hara* that speaks of "a kind of enclosure with four doors" (Flah cited in Sebag, *La Hara de Tunis,* 17).

39. Ibid., 88.

40. For example, the impasse des Bracelets was inhabited by twenty-eight people, of whom twenty-four were Muslim (86 percent), three were Jewish (11 percent), and 1 was Catholic (3 percent). Fifty-seven people lived in the Sidi Mardoum alleyway, forty-eight of whom were Muslim (84 percent) and nine of whom were Jewish (16 percent). These small cul-de-sacs with Muslim majorities, however, opened on to streets inhabited almost exclusively by Jewish families: the impasse des Bracelets opens onto rue du Palmier, which, out of a total population of 148 inhabitants, included 118 Jews (79.7 percent), eight Catholics (5.4 percent), and twenty-two Muslims (14.8 percent). The Sidi Mardoum impasse opened onto rue Sidi Mardoum, which, out of total population of 159 people, included 132 Jews (83 percent), eighteen Catholics (11.3 percent), and only nine Muslims (5.6 percent). These percentages were calculated based on the 1956 census of the city of Tunis as well as from the detailed chart of the *hara* reproduced in Sebag, *La Hara de Tunis,* Appendix 1.

41. Jallel Abdelkafi notes regarding this that "the first concrete trait in the planning of the *madina* in Tunis is that all levels of society use the same basic architectural unit, the courtyard house." Jallal Abdelkafi, *La Médina de Tunis, espace historique* (Tunis: Alif, 1989), 43.

42. Albert Memmi, *Le Nomade immobile* (Paris: Editions Arléa, 2000).

43. Note that in this frontier location it is difficult to know whether the father's pride expresses the satisfaction of living near the Jewish ghetto or outside it. Memmi, *The Pillar of Salt,* 20.

44. Memmi, *Le Juif et l'Autre,* 13. This description contrasts sharply with some statements made by Alexandre in *The Pillar of Salt,* including this one: "Sometimes I crossed a Moslem quarter as if I were fording a river" (96).

45. Memmi, *Le Nomade immobile,* 13.

46. Ibid., 16.

47. Abdelkebir Khatibi and Jacques Hassoun, *Le Même livre* (Paris: Editions de l'éclat, 1985).

48. Ibid., 130. See also Joseph Toledano, *Le temps du Mellah: une histoire des juifs au Maroc racontée à travers les annales de la communauté de Meknès* (Jerusalem: Editions Ramtol, 1982).

49. Sebag also noted such a topographical link between the Jewish and Muslims quarters in Tunis: "The street of the *hara* can hardly be distinguished from that of the *madina.* Each is characterized by an extremely irregular route. It bends, straightens out, and then makes a sudden right angle turn. The outsider finds it difficult to not confuse the road he is trying to follow with the numerous impasses that open on to it. The width of the roads, which is never wider than four meters, even on the largest arteries, is as capricious as their course. The tight streets may widen but also narrow"; Sebag, *La Hara de Tunis,* 23.

50. Khatibi and Hassoun, *Le Même livre,* 130.

51. Ibid.

52. Ibid., 132.

53. N. Davis, *A Voice from North Africa; or, A Narrative Illustrative of the Religious Ceremonies, Customs, and Manners of the Inhabitants of That Part of the World* (Edinburgh: Paton and Ritchie, 1844); L. Frank, *Tunis, description de cette regence,* in *l'Univers: histoire et description de tous les peoples: Algérie, Etats Tripolitains Tunis,* ed. J. J. Marcel (Paris: 1850).

54. Victor Guérin, *Voyage archéologique dans la Régence de Tunis,* vol. 1 (Paris: H. Plon 1862), 15, cited in Larguèche, *Les Ombres de Tunis,* 27. It would be interesting to compare the unsettling similarities between this colonialist and Orientalist description of Tunis and the postmodern and neo-Orientalist description of the *madina* in Tangier by William S. Burroughs in *Interzone* (New York: Penguin Books, 1989). Exiled in Tangiers at the end of the 1950s, Burroughs described the city of Tangier as a place without place, a disconnected space in which any ontological stabilization is impossible for anyone who becomes lost in its labyrinth: "The Native Quarter of Tangier is all you expect it to be: a maze of narrow, sunless streets, twisting and meandering like footpaths, many of them blind alleys. After four months, I still find my way in the Medina by a system of moving from one landmark to another" (56). "Tangier extends in several dimensions. You keep finding places you never saw before. There is no line between 'real world' and 'world of myth and symbol.' Objects, sensations, hit with the impact of hallucination" (58).

55. Guérin, *Voyage archéologique dans la Régence de Tunis,* 1:15.

56. Franz Fanon, *The Wretched of the Earth* (New York: Grove Press, 2004), 4. Like Fanon, Khatibi contrasts the fussy geometry of the colonial quarters with the heterotopic opening of the indigenous quarters: "'One has to create rational gardens, geometric cities, a soaring economy, one must create Heaven on earth,' 'God is dead, long live the colonist.' These are the words of the colonist drawing up the city like a military map. . . . We know the colonial imagination: juxtapose, compartmentalize, militarize, cut the city into ethnic zones, silt up the dominated people's culture. When this people discovers that it is disoriented, it will haggardly wander into the broken space of its history. And there is nothing more dreadful than the rending of memory. But this rending is common to colonized and colonial, since the medina resisted by its maze"; Abdelkebir Khatibi, *La Mémoire tatouée* (Paris: Éditions Denoël, 1971), 53–54.

57. Khatibi and Hassoun, *Le Même livre,* 130.

58. Ibid., 131–132.

59. Ibid., 131.

60. Guy Degas, *Albert Memmi: Écrivain de la déchirure* (Sherbrooke, Quebec: Éditions Naaman, 1984).

61. Albert Memmi, *Portrait du décolonisé arabo-musulman et de quelques autres* (Paris: Éditions Gallimard, 2004).

62. Memmi, *Jews and Arabs,* 28.

63. Jacques Derrida, *Monolingualism of the Other; or, the Prosthesis of Origin* (Stanford, Calif.: Stanford University Press, 1998), 14.

64. Ibid., 11.

65. Paraphrasing the authors of *A Thousand Plateaus,* we could say that the quest for identity Memmi undertook at the beginning of the 1950s expressed the same willingness to "move between things, establish a logic of the AND, overthrow ontology, do away with foundations, nullify endings and beginnings." Gilles Deleuze and Félix Guattari, *A Thousand Plateaus: Capitalism and Schizophrenia,* trans. Brian Massumi (Minneapolis: University of Minnesota Press, 1987), 25.

66. Albert Memmi, *Ce que je crois* (Paris: Éditions Graset et Fasquelle, 1985), 47.

67. Ibid.

68. Memmi, *Le Nomade immobile,* 104.

69. Albert Memmi, *Le Juif et l'autre* (Paris: Editions Christian de Bartillat, 1995), 61.

70. In 1986, during a talk at the Hebrew University of Jerusalem on "negative theology," Jacques Derrida discreetly confessed that his most autobiographical discourse comes from rec-

ognizing his divided identity of *Jew comma Arab*: "From lack of ability, competence, or self-authorization, I am still unable to speak of the most intimate thing my birth should have given me: the Jew, the Arab" [*Je n'ai encore jamais pu, faute de capacité, de compétence ou d'auto-autorisation, parler de ce que ma naissance, comme on dit, aurait dû me donner de plus proche: le Juif, l'Arabe*]. Jacques Derrida, "Comment ne pas parler," in *Psyché: Inventions de l'autre* (Paris: Éditions Galilée, 1987), 362.

71. Larguèche, *Les Ombres de Tunis*, 348.

72. Memmi, *Le Juif et l'autre*, 17.

73. Jacques Taïeb, *Être Juif au Maghreb à la veille de la colonization* (Paris: Éditions Albin Michel, 1994), 75.

74. Sebag, *La Hara de Tunis*, 84.

75. Ibid., 82. While traditional music remains one of the most obvious contributions by Jews to North African culture, Jewish communities that originated in North Africa continue to maintain a strong cultural identity within Israel that is based on their Arab-Andalusian heritage. The singer Shlomo Bar (originally from Morocco) and his group Habréra ha-tivʿit were largely responsible for introducing and popularizing Mediterranean and North African music among Israeli youth. Shlomo Elbaz, "Les Marocains en Israël: une aventure équivoque," in *La Méditerranée des Juifs: Exodes et Enracinements*, ed. Paul Balta et al. (Paris: l'Harmattan, 2003), 221–233.

76. Memmi, *The Pillar of Salt*, 162.

77. Ibid., 161, 159–160.

78. Ibid., 158.

79. Ibid., 159.

80. Ibid., 161.

81. Ibid., 44, 27.

82. Memmi, *Le Nomade immobile*, 99.

83. Memmi. *Le Juif et l'autre*, 29. In *Le Nomade immobile*, Memmi wonders if his decision to marry a European woman was not a reaction to his mother's identity as an Arab Jew: "But was not my choosing a wife done equally against her? My wife has blue eyes because my mother's were black; she is blond because my mother was a brunette; not very talkative, restrained in her movements because my mother was crazy" (61).

84. On the transformation of the *madina* of Tunis and especially the *hara*, see François Vigier, *Housing in Tunis* (Cambridge, Mass.: Harvard University Graduate School of Design), 1987.

85. Memmi, *La Terre intérieure*, 46.

86. Ibid., 70–71.

87. Regarding this topic, see Simon Lévy's essay, "Il y a encore des Juifs au Maroc," in Balta, Dana, and Dhoquois-Cohen, *La Méditerranée des Juifs: exils et enracinements*, 210–211; and the richly illustrated book by Jean-Pierre Allali, *Juifs de Tunisie* (Paris: Editions Soline), 2003.

88. Patrick Simon and Claude Tapia, *Le Belleville des Juifs tunisiens* (Paris: Éditions Autrement, 1998), 177.

9

Making Tangier Modern: Ethnicity and Urban Development, 1880–1930

Susan Gilson Miller

Tangier is unusual in every sense, but especially in the way the city grew in the late nineteenth century. A walk around the old *madina* offers proof enough of that. The jostling of a Baroque-style bank against an Art Nouveau entryway, the proximity of an Italianate palazzo to a Spanish-tiled post office, a gargoyle peering out of a rainspout tell us that the old city is a palette of the builder's imagination, a sketchpad for whatever stylistic fantasy Europe was offering at the time. Unlike other traditional Moroccan *madinas*, where the urban fabric maintains a certain uniformity, Tangier's is discontinuous. Modernization began at an early date, and extensive transformations were already taking place in the mid-nineteenth century, long before the rest of Morocco's *madinas*. The effects of this growth process are evident in the eclecticism and variety of building types found within its concentrated space. The physical diversity of the Tangier *madina* has become emblematic of the city itself; a babble of architectural voices that somehow creates a music of its own.

The streets also proclaim a confessional variety that now belongs to a distant past. On the Siyaghin, the main thoroughfare of the old *madina*, the Cathedral of the Immaculate Conception is only a few steps away from the Great Mosque, and just around the corner is the Street of the Synagogues. However, in one respect, this diversity speaks with a single voice, enunciating the vision of the builders that made them. This is a story about some of the people who took part in making modern Tangier and of the monuments they created that are witnesses to another time, when the city lived according rhythms of an "international" age marked by a cultural multiplicity that is no longer in the air.

This chapter in Moroccan history, like so many others, has been occulted by the ideological mindset of another era. Mainly, it has been buried in the discourse of imperialism, according to which the historically determined process of "European penetration" created an economic and social "crisis" in Morocco at the end of the nineteenth century that undermined its equilibrium. Casting the story of the country's modernization within a colonialist framework, historians have viewed Europe's economic influence as all powerful, ignoring the extent to which other forces were also at work, operating according to processes that were purely local in nature. Furthermore, they often invoke the phrases "Jewish urban capital" and "the Jewish oligarchy" in tones of rebuke and portray "Jews" as an undifferentiated category acting as the willing tools of a gluttonous Europe.[1]

One cannot deny the reality that in Tangier a group of influential men, Jews among them, enthusiastically joined the new capital-based economy, acting aggressively (and sometimes selfishly) to further their own interests. Just as other Mediterranean port cities such as Salonika and Alexandria were undergoing a major transition, Tangier too was in the throes of a rapid remaking along European lines, resulting in the reconfiguration of space, society, and economic life.[2] Within this framework, the notion of an essentialized "Jewish capitalism" that came into being as a result of contact with the West in which "the Jews" as a group were uniquely engaged does not fit with the historical reality. A more balanced picture sees in Tangier a high degree of cooperation across communal lines among moneyed interests, both Jewish and non-Jewish, for the purpose of profit and status, as the sources will indicate. How this new capitalism was mobilized and deployed to make the city modern is the subject of this inquiry.

The chosen site for examining these ideas is the sphere of architecture and urban planning. In the late nineteenth century, ideas about modernizing the built environment infiltrated Tangier at many levels from the grandiose building schemes of world-famous architects such as the Catalan Antonio Gaudí[3] and the Scottish master builder R. Rowand Anderson,[4] both of whom brought their exuberant talents to Tangier. Buildings are expressions of the imagination, and in the construction projects achieved at the turn of the last century, we read the aspirations of individuals who saw themselves at the center of an expanding universe of influence and personal power. The focus of this discussion is the connections between entrepreneurship, architecture, and urban change, with special attention to the role that individual Jewish and non-Jewish investors played in the larger story.

A City in Flux

Tangier was a city of immigrants, of people who came from elsewhere. During the 200 years of foreign occupation the city endured from the late fifteenth until the end of the seventeenth centuries, native Muslims and Jews fled the town. After the city was retaken by Moroccan arms in 1682, Moroccan Muslims—mainly rustic Rifian warriors and their chieftains—drifted back, closely followed by a handful of Moroccan Jews. The two groups quickly established a détente: the Rifian militia provided government and civic order, while the Jews filled the essential functions of traders, skilled artisans, and moneychangers who oiled the wheels of commerce. Migrating mainly from nearby Tetuan and Meknes, Tangier's Jews spoke a particular dialect of Judeo-Spanish called *Haketia,* enjoyed their own distinctive cuisine, and adhered to their own special melodies in the synagogue. In sum, they felt and acted quite differently not only from Moroccan Muslims but also from other Moroccan Jews, especially those of "the interior," whom they disdainfully dismissed as *foresteros,* or strangers.

Another peculiar feature of Tangier was the mixing together of its population. In most Moroccan towns, Jews were coerced to live in a separate quarter, called the mellah, but in Tangier, Muslims, Jews, and Christians lived together in an unregulated coexistence. Since the late eighteenth century, and perhaps even earlier, Jewish life had been centered in the Beni Ider quarter, evidenced by the high concentration of synagogues there.[5] But the Beni Ider was not strictly a Jewish quarter; rather, it was a mixed neighborhood where Jews, Christians, and Muslims lived side by side, close to the main commercial street. As one observer noted in 1909, "In Tangier, the word *'mellah'* is practically unknown."[6]

This mixing intensified in the nineteenth century with the arrival of Europeans, led by representatives of the foreign powers eager to open Morocco for business. At the end of the eighteenth century, by order of the sultan, they were obliged to live in Tangier so as to minimize the threat of moral contagion they posed to Morocco's heartland.[7] Not an unpleasant banishment, for Tangier was blessed with pure air, panoramic views of the strait, and a temperate climate conducive to gardening, horsemanship, and other outdoor sports, all favorite diplomatic pastimes. When not in their country estates, the consuls, many of whom were displaced aristocrats fleeing Europe's crumbling caste system, lived in town and rubbed elbows with the rest of the population, creating new paradigms of social hierarchy in this provincial center that had previously known little class differentiation, and certainly none on the European scale.

In Tangier, a long tradition of intermingling in the tight confines of the *madina* had made the art of living together a requirement of daily life. At certain times of the day, the call of the muezzin, the sound of church bells, and the melodies of the *ma'ariv,* the Hebrew evening prayer, blended in an impromptu chorale that filled the nearby streets. In the recollection of former inhabitants, life in the *madina* was characterized by intercommunal tranquility. Isaac Assayag, who grew up in the Beni Ider quarter in the 1930s, wrote about the lack of social distance, saying that "all the inhabitants, Christians, Muslims and Jews, lived in close harmony" (*tous les habitants, chrétiens, musulmans et juifs vivaient en étroite amitié*).[8] The *madina* was a place where ethnicities, religions, and social classes mingled; where the lessons of living in a pluralistic society were learned; where a sociability born of proximity was carried forward when residents eventually migrated to other parts of town.

When Europeans arrived in force after 1850, Tangier society evolved rapidly. Native Jews made themselves indispensable to Europeans baffled by Arabic and the arcane court protocol. The *dragoman*, or interpreter, occupied a vital position in every consular establishment, acting as translator, procurer, and conduit to the surrounding society and power structure. A handful of Jews moved in a rapid trajectory from translator to moneychanger and trader to international banker and businessman in a transformation in the space of one generation that was nothing short of remarkable. Jews as a group constituted more than a fourth of the entire population before 1912.[9] Like their Muslim neighbors, most of them were occupied with the daily struggle for existence. However, a small coterie of outstanding Jewish personalities rose above the rest and took their place alongside leading Muslim and European men of affairs in shaping Tangier's growth, wielding ideas, capital, organization, and sheer bravura to remake the face of the city.

The vicissitudes of famine, plague, and war kept Tangier's population stable for centuries, but by the late 1800s, after nearly a century of rapid growth, Tangier had achieved the status of Morocco's leading port, surpassing Essaouira while not yet challenged by Casablanca. As its commercial role grew, Tangier's relations with the makhzan attenuated. Weakened by internecine conflicts and growing dependency on Europe, the sultanate was preoccupied with its own internal crisis. In the period just before the French and Spanish occupations of 1912, the absence of official oversight gave Tangier's business class an unusual degree of autonomy. As the influence of the state diminished, two groups took charge at the local level and provided the momentum for urban expansion: the foreign representatives on the one hand and the small but rising native bourgeoisie on the other. Three periods in Tangier's growth are important for our story: 1880 to 1906 (from the Madrid Convention to the Treaty of Algeciras), when the first *extra-muros* housing was built; 1906 to World War I, when largely local capital engaged in frenzied development; and 1914 to 1930, when investments in urban planning laid the groundwork for the growth burst of the forties and fifties.

The Making of the Garden City

The process of growth in Tangier is the classic one of expansion beyond the old urban core into periurban areas. Land beyond the walls was absorbed into the city through extensions in the street pattern, the opening and dismantling of gates, and the creation of new *extra-muros* housing on terrain that had for-

merly been agricultural. At the same time, the fabric within the city walls became denser by the additions of second and even third stories to *madina* houses.
New European-style apartment houses were built along principal thoroughfares,
and land once considered unsuitable for building was filled in. In 1890, a tourist
guidebook noted that "there are few good houses in Tangier, the generality being small, and of one story only. . . . A few larger houses have been built of late
years, and the number doubtless will increase as Tangier becomes more popular
as a winter station."[10]

The increase in population spurred by a steady influx of Europeans and
rural migrants produced a doubling of Tangier's population in the period 1860–
1888 and a second doubling by 1904. The *madina* became overcrowded and the
value of land increased many times. Scarcity of building plots was compounded
by the fact that the *hubus* (waqf, or Islamic pious foundation) controlled a large
percentage of the *intra-muros* property, making it off limits to foreigners, at least
in theory. Almost the entire main street of Tangier belonged to the *hubus* of the
Great Mosque (*al-jamiᶜ al-kabir*).[11]

Despite these constraints, it became increasingly difficult for Moroccan authorities to prevent foreigners from buying land. Foreign investment in Tangier
real estate was not new; in fact, non-Muslims had been acquiring land and property in and around the town since the early nineteenth century. At first, foreigners were required to buy land with a Muslim partner who provided the legal "cover" for these transactions, but after the Madrid Conference of 1880 this
kind of subterfuge was no longer necessary. The ensuing growth spurt saw the
transfer of considerable property from old Muslim landowning families to Europeans, and this new situation in which Europeans were increasingly in control
raised expectations about a more disciplined use of public space.[12]

Taking the lead in organizing public space was the Hygiene Commission,
whose forbear was the Conseil sanitaire, or Sanitary Commission, formed early
in the nineteenth century by the foreign consuls as an oversight body to prevent the spread of disease from ships arriving in the port. The Hygiene Commission was interested in all aspects of urban affairs, and by 1890, its base of support extended widely into the community, operating as a vocal citizens' interest
group and raising funds through public subscription to improve urban infrastructure. By 1910 more than 900 residents of Tangier, including Jews, Muslims,
and Christians—the rising tide of a new middle class—had become subscrib-
ers. Its membership was multinational and multiethnic, crossing family, class,
and religious lines. The commission was active in paving roads, digging drains,
and installing street lighting. Its meetings and circulars stirred up interest about
the management of municipal services and created an open forum for discus-

sion about the development of urban space. Announcements in the local press in English, French, and Spanish made people aware of its activities and nourished a new cult of civic awareness. In fact, the commission was a harbinger of the changing power structure in a community that increasingly saw itself as separate and distinct from the rest of Morocco. The terms "international" and "cosmopolitan" began to appear with increasing frequency in the local press, acknowledging this sense of Tangier's difference.

As the population grew, the territory outside the walls gradually became integrated into the city plan. By 1906 security had improved to the point where fear of brigands such as the notorious Ahmad al-Raysuni, who snatched well-heeled foreigners from their country villas and demanded huge ransoms in return for their freedom, was a memory.[13] Other evidence of rampant growth was the shack colonies that began to appear on the beach, perhaps the first *bidonvilles* in Morocco. They were inhabited by Spanish workers, fugitives from the anarchist uprisings in Andalusia in the 1870s. The Spaniards brought with them a taste for radical politics, red wine, and *jambon*.[14] To the disgust of their Jewish and Muslim neighbors, they raised pigs that roamed the nearby streets, offending native sensibilities and causing periodic uproars in the press.[15]

Tourism flourished, drawing escapees from northern Europe's sooty winters, and new hotels appeared in the Outer Market and along the seafront with names like Villa de France, Hotel Cecil, Hotel Cavilla, and Hotel Valentina. Some had enclosed gardens designed to appeal to vacationers seeking reminders of home. Foreign legations gradually abandoned their properties in the crowded *madina* and reestablished themselves in park-like settings outside the walls. The royal regent Ba Ahmad, acting as agent for Sultan ʿAbd al-ʿAziz (reigned 1895–1907) bought a huge tract of land on the Marshan, the spacious plateau to the west of the town, and launched its development by building a series of sixteen modern villas.

Even more distant from the town, the mountain (*al-jabal*) became the *quartier résidentiel deluxe*. Villa Idonia, the baronial estate of Greek-American tycoon Ion Perdicaris, set deep in an oak forest overlooking the sea, marked the outermost limits of "civilized" Tangier. With its half-timbered façade and turreted entryway, it implied a nobility that was appreciated in snobbish Tangier. A new pattern of growth emerged: an inner core centered on the old *madina* that was predominantly Muslim, Jewish, and Spanish working class; an intermediate *extramuros* belt along the old walls of newly built villas and hotels; and an outer circle of open country, rapidly becoming suburban, that was still owned by wealthy old Muslim families but was gradually moving into Christian hands. The new urban extensions resembled a "garden city" in the English sense, with winding,

tree-lined streets and luxurious villas in park-like settings that formed an emer-
ald ring around the traditional *madina* core.[16]

Who were the agents of this unprecedented wave of development? In the absence of state intervention, overseas banks, and organized international capital,
local investors had to rely on themselves. Tangier's modernization, unlike that of
some other Mediterranean towns, was based not on industry but on wealth generated from its port and the trading and distributive opportunities that nodal
point afforded. Some local investment went into goods and services, to be sure,
but the most attractive target of investment was land and real estate. Even those
with a little bit of money invested in property, making it the main status symbol
and measure of success. In the 1950s, Claude Verdugo captured this sentiment
when he wrote: "In the heart of every citizen is a landlord in the making" [*Il y a
dans le coeur de chaque habitant un propriètaire foncier qui sommeille*].[17] Seeing the opportunities for making money in construction, especially in housing, Tangier's
new mercantile elite coalesced into private consortia of investors that cut across
religious, ethnic, and national lines.

The history of the real estate holding company Rentistica offers a rare insight
into the secretive world of Tangier private capital. Founded by Yorkshireman
Ernest Waller in 1894, it was the biggest landholding company in Tangier in the
early twentieth century. Waller was a trained horticulturalist who had come to
Tangier in the employ of Sir R. Rowand Anderson, Scotland's preeminent architect, who was fond of wintering there in the 1880s along with other titled friends.
Anderson set Waller up in the nursery business and sericulture, but Waller soon
realized there was more money to be made in buying and selling land than in
raising silkworms. Around 1909, in association with Jewish bankers Isaac Abensur and Salvador Hassan, British journalist Walter Harris, and a German banker
named Haessner, Waller launched his own real estate company with the purchase of a large property in the Emsallah, the old prayer ground (*musalla*) outside
the city walls.[18]

This consortium became a model for future real estate ventures in Tangier.
Each partner brought different assets: Abensur, the leading Jew of the town, was
well connected to the local Muslim administration, respected by the *qadi*, *ʿudul*
(notaries), and other officials whose assent was critical to completing legal property transfers; Hassan, the banker, was vice-consul for Spain and Italy and had
ties to influential Spanish sources; and Harris, the literary gadfly, had access to
the Moroccan court through his friendship with Kaid Maclean, a British officer in
the sultan's army.[19] This consortium of access, money, and talent (and others like
it) financed the most notable buildings of Tangier erected before World War I, including the new British consulate, the Café Central, the Bristol Hotel in the Outer
Market, and the Eastern Telegraph office.

Building beyond the Walls

But the main investment opportunity was in housing outside the city walls. Overcrowding provided the push to leave the *madina,* while the desire to express a newfound social and economic power offered the pull. For the newly affluent, the lure of a more modern domestic style that emulated European standards of comfort was irresistible, and when given the choice, wealthy Moroccans of every background opted for private residences that were distant from the old *madina* core. They built luxurious private villas in outlying places, replicating the *madina's* pattern of coexistence on a grand scale. This migration was not only a step up in material terms; it also confirmed new social hierarchies introduced by an expanding capitalism. Those who could afford it moved to the Marshan, where you had only to look at your neighbors—Moroccan royalty, Jewish bankers, the sharif of Wazzan, British lords and ladies—to know that you had finally "arrived."

The elite reinforced these horizontal ties by supporting activities and joining clubs that also defined class membership. Cricket matches, horse races, boar and fox hunts, *soirées musicales, tombolas,* carnivals, balls, consular dinners, and visits from royalty filled the social calendar and were amply reported in the local press. For the men, there were the Chamber of Commerce and the Freemasons, and for the ladies, societies of *bienfaisance.* Sports, charity, music, and games of chance provided the framework for new forms of social expression. Associational life entered the public sphere and provided a framework for displaying class solidarities that cut across ethnic lines.

Meanwhile, as the Marshan was being transformed into the *quartier de luxe,* other spaces become the building sites of more modest proportions. The rue de Tetuan is an example of housing built for members of the new middle class. It was Morocco's first "planned" community, built in 1905 over a garden, or *huerta,* owned by a local Spaniard. It took the form of a single gated street ending in a cul-de-sac, lined on both sides by identical row houses. The financiers of the project were David Benelbas and the brothers José and Mimoun Bendahan, originally from Tetuan, who had amassed considerable capital in Latin America. Like other Jewish émigrés, they returned home with full pockets, eager to invest, but soon recognized that the possibilities for gain in bustling Tangier were far greater than in their birthplace. After purchasing the land for the enormous sum of 150,000 *hassani* duros from the landowning Muslim al-Ghassal family, they decided to name the project after their hometown.[20]

The construction of rue de Tetuan was assigned to contractor Antonio Cano and the foreman was Antonio Ramírez, both members of the Spanish community that monopolized the building trades. The project, which was completed in stages, included sixty apartments and fourteen shops. Although each house was

Figure 9.1. The rue de Tetuan was the first planned housing *extra-muros* in Tangier. Photograph from the early twentieth century. Collection of the author.

separate from the other on the inside, the uniformity of the façade, with its long, continuous lines and shared cornices, created the impression of one extended mansion. Modern amenities were much in evidence: water was furnished by means of a pump that served the entire street and night lighting was provided by acetylene lamps, lit by the Jewish concièrge of the complex, Leon Elbaz. Various commercial establishments filled the shops at the street level, such as a branch of the Banque d'Etat, a gym, and the local offices of the Parisian newspaper *Le Temps*. At the end of the street a *café maure* opened its doors.[21]

The rue de Tetuan provided a logical transition from life in the *madina* to a more modern residential style. The feeling of the street was that of "one big family," a self-contained social unit where residents engaged in constant visiting, celebrations, and meetings in stairways and on the street, creating a closeness usually associated with *madina* space. Even marriages were contracted among the residents. While the intimacy of the old neighborhoods was preserved, more modern practices were evident everywhere: in the design and furnishing of the houses, in the behavior and dress of the residents, and in the way the residents spent their leisure time. Every afternoon, Mlle. Conchita Vera, a Spanish piano teacher, arrived to give lessons to the young ladies of the neighborhood. At night, the gates were locked, reinforcing a sense of separation from the rest of the city.[22]

Another, even more European-like form of modern housing was introduced in the extended apartment block on the nearby rue d'Italie, which was built around the same time as the rue de Tetuan. Flanking the outer wall of the old town, this complex was a complete departure from the rest of the urban fabric. Built in the first decade of the twentieth century by Salomon Buzaglo, the site was reclaimed by clearing away shacks that had been illegally constructed against the city wall. Buzaglo himself was the product of a rapidly westernizing Jewish Tangier. Son of a modest rabbinical family, Buzaglo was educated at the Tangier branch of the Alliance Israélite Universelle School in modern languages and accounting and then worked his way up the social and economic ladder by apprenticing himself to Benjamin Braunschvig, an Alsatian Jewish trader who made a fortune by supplying the Moroccan court with luxury goods.[23] Buzaglo's success led him to the bold decision to invest in a completely new housing form.[24]

Economic and social factors made apartment living attractive to the new bourgeoisie of Tangier, especially to its Jewish population. It was cheaper than living in a private villa, since less maintenance and fewer servants were required, yet it offered many of the same amenities as the private house: light and air through open windows, improved plumbing, and a secure domesticity without having to endure the isolation of country living. Apartments presented a comfortable transition out of the *madina,* since they were close to the old neighborhood with its shops, services, and schools, while they eliminated the crowding and poor sanitation that the *madina* house imposed. Apartment dwelling also posed certain challenges, because it called for a rethinking of the boundaries between public and private. The apartment dweller had to concede to others space that he had formerly considered his own, such as entranceways, hallways, and rooftops. But the costs of cohabitation were more than compensated for by the benefits the apartment building provided. The interior plan was roomy, with a long narrow interior corridor leading from the vestibule to the parlor, the dining room, bedrooms, and finally, at the rear, the kitchen and maid's quarters. Unlike the gated rue de Tetuan, these buildings opened directly onto the street. The contemplation of the street from above was one of the benefits of apartment living; to see without being seen, to observe life below—especially for women—without being observed in return. The ground floor was planned as commercial space. Not only did rents from the shops make the buildings economically viable, but the shops themselves contributed to a feeling of animation around the building.

The mix of commercial and residential space, the innovative design, and the suggestion of both economy and luxury made the apartment buildings along the rue d'Italie a huge success, inserting into the urban fabric a type associated in

Figure 9.2. The elegant façade of the rue d'Italie apartment building, still in use. Susan Gilson Miller, 2006.

the popular mind with housing in the capitals of Europe. The facade articulated a firm attachment to a European sense of design. The long front with its rhythmic balconies and delicate ironwork, the placement of the windows, and the hierarchy of decorative elements announced that the building was the product of a modern architectural sensibility, as opposed to the typical *madina* house, which was built by traditional craftsmen without a plan. While the name of the architect of this complex is now forgotten, his personality is marked on its surface. A feeling of grandeur distinguishes it even today: its scale in comparison with that of the rest of the *madina* and its elaborate surface decoration arrest our attention. In the 1920s, this style of building was replicated along the main avenue, the Boulevard Pasteur, and became the dominant housing type in the *ville nouvelle*.[25]

Transformations in housing types were accompanied by new uses of public space. As the home increasingly became the refuge of the family, shut off from outside view, public space grew in importance as a site of sociability. Efforts by the Hygiene Commission to clean up beaches, parks, and thoroughfares indicate a heightened sense of awareness of their value to the town. The newspapers chastised the public about offensive behaviors, smells, and noises, circumscribing and drawing attention to the existence of a commons, a new concept in Tangier. At the same time, popular attitudes about the use of open space underwent a change. Walks in the countryside, which had once been frowned upon as dangerous and morally dubious, became popular. Some of the bolder Jewish women even took up bathing. The pleasures of the beach were a thrilling novelty: "The beach has become the favorite promenade of Tangerinos, the meeting place of the European and native high life, especially on a Sunday afternoon. . . . Near the bathing cabins, two grand open-air cafés offer the chance to rest and take some refreshment. . . . A little further on, a merry-go-round, something we saw for the first time in Tangier just a few months ago," a Jewish teacher wrote in 1889.[26]

Cafés in the European style became a feature of everyday life, frequented by all groups and social classes. Located mostly in the Inner Market, or Socco Chico, cafés were quickly woven into the urban fabric, becoming places where news was made and transmitted. Located near the various *bureaux de poste* and the newspaper offices, they were an additional link in Tangier's growing network of communications, along with the telephone, the telegraph, and improved mail service. Innovations in the use of public space underscored the fact that mixing and heterogeneity among religions and classes were becoming a leitmotiv of urban life.

1906–1914: A Period of Frenzied Growth

The Treaty of Algeciras (1906) removed all remaining restrictions on foreign purchase of property and created new institutions, such as the Banque d'Etat and the Dette Marocaine, or Dar al-Salaf, aimed at controlling Moroccan finances and repaying the makhzan's swollen foreign debt. This office administered the customs house at the port, *hubus* properties, and urban "gate" taxes. It was housed in a modern building built to the southeast of the town along a sandy track renamed Boulevard de la Dette, later to become Boulevard Pasteur, the principal thoroughfare of today's Tangier. Recognizing its development potential, the Jewish Toledano brothers, Tangier-born importers of tea, bought up much of the land along both sides of the new artery. Paying the small sum of two francs a square meter, the Toledanos saw its value increase many times over the course of the next few decades.[27]

This period also saw the creation of several large international *syndicats de initiative*, groups of foreign venture capitalists on the lookout for large public works contracts. Backed by impressive resources, they were soon competing with local entrepreneurs for the choicest and most profitable projects. The Society for Public Works for Morocco, established in Paris on 15 February 1910, was capitalized at 2 million francs, with France holding 50 percent, Germany 30 percent, and all other countries 20 percent.[28] But these foreign groups were not as successful in their bid to make inroads into the local real estate market as local investors were. They lacked the know-how that was essential to getting things through the administration and its thicket of overlapping laws of ownership, the still-important role of the Muslim courts in matters of property, and the ingrained suspicion of Moroccan officials toward foreigners. Local societies, such as the International Syndicate for the Development of Tangier, led by longtime Spanish resident Ricardo Ruiz, Jewish banker Isaac Abensur, and an enterprising French lawyer, Daniel Saurin, fared much better. They promoted ideas such as beautification, the development of an urban plan, and the preservation of historical sites in order to attract business and capital investment while maintaining ties to traditional Muslim functionaries who still had control over property transfers.

The coming of the protectorate in 1912 gave the homegrown entrepreneurs a new sense of purpose. Now removed from the rest of Morocco, Tangier openly redefined itself as an "international city," a "paradise" for investment with its modernizing infrastructure, an enlightened population, and a well-developed public sphere that was used to governing itself. A sense of unbridled optimism permeated the air. The local English-language newspaper trumpeted that unlike cities in the French zone that required a "rigid discipline . . . backed by . . . pains and penalties" in order to achieve urban growth, Tangier was now a place where "progress and reform are not likely to proceed much faster than the sense of the public desires."[29] But the coming of the World War I left many of these plans stillborn as Tangier waited out the war years. The privations in supply and disruption in communications with Europe turned the local economy inward, while the chaos on the international level left the city in suspense for almost a decade.

The War Years and After

During the war, tourism and trade dried up and food stocks fell so low that the town had to be provisioned by sea. The old consular regime sprang to life once again, filling the vacuum in the absence of a governing body, and the foreign representatives enjoyed a momentary reemergence on center stage. After the war, recovery was slow. While the French and Spanish zones were being reorganized by draconian colonial rule, Tangier was left in limbo awaiting an "international" solution to its political status. Meanwhile, the loss of maritime trade to Casablanca had heavy repercussions for Tangier's role as a center of international commerce.

The most important development in this period was the continued expansion of the town to the southeast. Urbanist Henri Prost, who planned most of the new towns of French Morocco, drew the master plan for Tangier "while in an airplane," according to Ernest Waller, who added that "nine times out of ten," new building projects followed the outlines of Prost's plan.[30] His scheme had the support of property owners as well as the administration. His plan for Tangier was strikingly like the one he had created for Casablanca, which featured a strong central commercial axis, a luxurious residential quarter to the west, and the old *madina* at its core. He envisioned an enlarged port of over 100 hectares and a beach area reserved for hotels. Tangier's destiny, according to Prost, was to be a *"station climatique,"* a resort town with a port large enough to accommodate tourists but not so large as to compete with Casablanca.

In the immediate postwar years, private capital continued to dominate the real estate market but few Muslims took part, reluctantly ceding their place to European and Moroccan Jewish investors. French sociologist Edouard Michaux-Bellaire wrote in 1921 that "there is no longer a native economy to speak of. In reality, all business is in the hands of Europeans and Jews, with local Muslims playing only a subordinate role [*un rôle subalterne*]."[31] The gradual movement of choice property into Jewish and Christian hands caused great resentment in the Muslim community. Muhammad Skirij, the historian of Tangier, singled out Tangier's Jews for vehement criticism, finding them directly responsible for the decline in Muslim fortunes:

> The commerce of the *madina* is entirely in the hands of the Jews who have ingratiated themselves with the foreigners and thrown themselves into the role of go-between because of their familiarity with other lands. They think this is their right because they insinuated themselves from the beginning with the foreigners when they began interfering in the affairs of the country; also because of their natural disposition to be subservient to whomever they deem worthy. They gravitate to them as one and take sides with the foreigners in their rivalries. They are in the forefront of learning

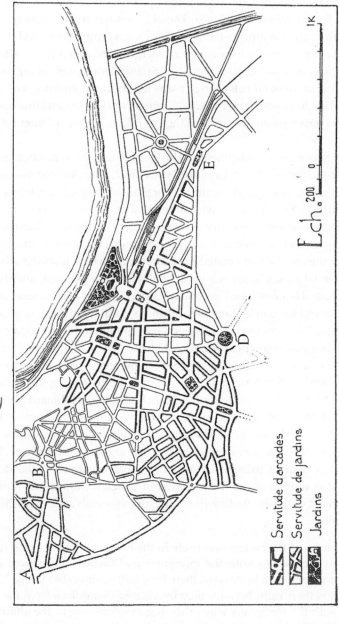

Figure 9.3. Prost's plan for the new town of Tangier, drawn during the 1920s, the basis of the urban form today. Present locations include: A) Sahat al-Kuwayt, B) Sahat Faransa, C) Shariʿa Pasteur, D) Sahat al-Jamiʿa al-ʿArabiya, and E) Sahat Suède. Sources: Prost's map: Jean Royer, *L'urbanisme aux colonies et dans les pays tropicaux*, 2 vols. (Nevers: Fortin, 1932) 1, 107; locations are taken from the map Tanger: Plan urbain (Rabat: Ministère de l'Agriculture et la Réforme Agraire, Direction de la Conservation Foncière et des Travaux Topographiques, 1986).

their languages and in reading the latest information while taking advantage of the ignorance of the people of the country who played into their hands. They are in need of the judgment of Allah upon their deeds. There are those who say that the Jews are the most fitting mediators between outsiders and the people of this land in matters of politics, but they are mistaken and speak without thinking, for the Jew is only interested in his own profit, and in lighting the spark of alienation between groups in order to extend his own advantage and to preserve his proximity to those in charge. For in truth, access by itself is power . . . and the first to report the news is always one of them.[32]

The seeds of intercommunal conflict, ever-present in a multiethnic society, remained dormant throughout the boom years that seemed to benefit all. But tensions reemerged after the war, fed by jealousy and harsh competition in the economic sphere, where Muslims were clearly the losers. These tensions came into full view in the decades that followed, as Moroccan society polarized into competing groups and ethnicities, encouraged by nationalist sentiments that superseded the cosmopolitan consciousness that so typified Tangier.

Meanwhile, habits and practices continued to favor the ascendancy of Tangier's business elite, who were accustomed to untrammeled self-rule. This group, which was still constructed on the basis of personal and familial ties, had profited from a weak governing authority, the absence of foreign competition as a result of the war, and the political stalemate following the war that lasted until agreement was finally reached in 1925 on an international statute that allowed for a multinational administration independent of the neighboring French and Spanish protectorates. Business practices in Tangier in the interwar years prospered under the rubric of a long-awaited "internationalization," a reference not only to the source of Tangier's particular sovereignty but also to the belief in the dominance of unrestricted free enterprise over regulatory principles.[33] The contrast between the tightly controlled state-sponsored capitalism of the French zone and the economic free-for-all of Tangier could not have been greater.

Understanding the Role of Private Capital

Building arts is a complex social and economic phenomenon that cuts across many fields. Taste and aesthetics are one component, but also important are topography, land use, availability of water and building materials, zoning laws and municipal regulations, and social and political knowledge. No single set of factors brings about change in the built environment. The complexity that produces a particular cityscape is daunting. Elements that influenced decisions about how Tangier developed and the role that entrepreneurial individuals played in accelerating the processes that have been identified here.

The picture that emerges is that of an ambitious local elite that was adaptable to new ideas and (for the most part) attentive to matters of taste. The formation of this elite was part of a worldwide emergence of new urban moneyed classes in the late nineteenth century whose members shared common interests and ways of living. Cities everywhere, in Europe and in the non-European world, became the "great stages" on which a rising entrepreneurial class enacted practices and discourses related to their own gathering sense of what constituted "the modern."[34] In Tangier, the freewheeling local economy and the absence of state controls helped the local elite in this endeavor. Yet these factors would not have been sufficient had it not been for the willingness of these elites to mobilize, innovate, cooperate, and make use of capital in all its forms.

While capital in premodern times was the "sum of tangible wealth," in the modern age it took on more abstract forms that included a variety of assets in addition to goods and money. Capital became, in the words of Robert Heilbroner, "an abstract sum of infinitely flexible use whose value was its capacity to earn interest or profits."[35] The accumulation of capital among Tangier's mercantile elite came from different sources, roughly but not strictly applied: land ownership for the Muslims, banking and money changing for the Jews, the new industrial economy for the Europeans. The genius of Tangier's entrepreneurial class was its ability to leverage these various forms of capital in crosscutting associations whose sole purpose was the pursuit of profit.

A series of economic innovations helped the real estate boom. Individuals who wished to buy or build could usually find the money to do so through an informal lending process. Banks were operating in Tangier from the 1860s onward, but they were not the sole source of credit or even a reliable one. Funds could be acquired more easily by borrowing from a friend or business associate at a lower rate than that offered by banks if one could put up sufficient collateral in the form of cash or other property. Usually investors sought a mix of bank and private funds. If they failed to meet the bank payments, the associate, already in effect a part owner, would purchase the property at a favorable rate and pay off the bank loan. This method of acquiring property was the principal means Waller used to build his company's fortunes, according to his own account.[36]

Another innovation was the rationalization and routinization of building through the introduction of architects, plans, construction experts, and organized work crews. The old method of calling in a native builder (*mu'allim*) who made the plan using his eye and his hands was no longer possible on large building sites, where costs were estimated at the outset and architects were responsible for the outcome. The creation of a real estate company such as Waller's Rentistica with its multinational group of investors was key to this operation. It brought together architects, builders, speculators, and buyers, giving the construction business a degree of rationality and stability it had previously lacked. The management of large construction jobs by "experts" helped minimize risk and assured that the results would be marketable and of high quality.

Other mechanisms that might have spurred urban growth were less well developed, such as the long-term lease that was so instrumental in developing parts of London in the nineteenth century. Waller believed it would be "good business" to rent out land on long-term lease because the capital needed to develop big sites was very large. But his company did not engage in this business. His comment was: "Tangier is probably not ripe for this yet," but in fact it was Waller and his associates who shunned uncertain deals.[37] He bought, sold, and improved land but rarely invested in a project that did not promise a quick return. The main business of Waller and his business partners was collecting rents on properties they owned, both land and buildings; foreclosing on mortgages; and recycling properties back into the system after taking their share of the profit. He summed up his success succinctly when he said, "Fortune favored me . . . and many properties passed through my hand, some properties two or three times."[38]

Other entrepreneurs managed to find the capital to both buy and develop land without resorting to long-term leases. The Toledano brothers are an example of this variety of more adventuresome entrepreneurship. Their speculative investment in the wasteland known as the Boulevard de la Dette proved to be a wise one.[39] In the 1920s, they hired the Spanish architect Don Diego Gimenez to design and build many of the elegant apartment buildings that still line the main street.[40] At first these buildings remained empty because the gap between supply and demand was so huge. But the Toledanos held on, hoping that the modern apartments and commercial space constructed along the length of the boulevard would eventually become profitable, which indeed proved to be the case. By 1930, much of the space was filled, and the boulevard was well on its way to becoming "*un lieu privilégé*," the domain of the newly rich of all ethnicities.[41] Built with an eye to the future, the Toledano's investment in the Boulevard Pasteur eventually paid off. An unusual willingness to assume longer-term risk was a primary factor that held their effort together. It allowed a tightly knit Jewish family of investors like the Toledanos to borrow and build in advance of the market, to weather the cycles of boom and bust that inevitably interrupted it, and to sustain a forward if uneven pace of development.[42]

Freedom from state control, a weak public sector, and habits of cooperation within a mixed business community help explain the phenomenal growth of Tangier in the early decades of the twentieth century. But economic factors alone do not explain the dynamism of Tangier's development in this period. Other, less tangible ingredients helped to shape Tangier's upwardly mobile bourgeoisie: a yearning for European standards and lifestyles, a perfect understanding of

the rules of the game, and a sophistication based on generations of intercommunal living in the confines of the *madina*. A cultural apparatus honed over decades
of mixing created a local type, the *tanjawi*, whose ethnic and religious proclivi-
ties were deeply and privately felt but whose public persona was avidly inte-
grative.[43]

For the Jews of Tangier in particular, jealously guarded boundaries of private life inscribed privileged spheres where "others" did not enter, such as home,
family, marriage, and birthright. Business, on the other hand, belonged to a world
where intermingling, give and take, negotiation, and compromise were admired
and promoted. This facility of living among several different worlds at once often
baffled outsiders. How, in this corner of Africa, did Jews manage to preserve their
communal integrity while engaging fully in the social and economic life of the
town? It was a source of wonderment, especially to those more familiar with the
stark alternatives presented to Jews in the European context: the stifling confinement of the ghetto, on the one hand, and the perilous path to assimilation, on the
other. The genius of Tangier's Jews, and of Moroccan and Maghribi Jews in general as they entered the modern period, was their consummate ability to pass
from an inner world to an outer one and back again while maintaining a whole-
ness of outlook.

This navigation of borders was especially pronounced in the economic sphere,
where a native capitalism was born that brought Jews into lucrative partnerships
with Muslims and Europeans. The resulting concentration of wealth energized a
wave of growth that made Tangier a jewel of Morocco's northern coast in the first
half of the twentieth century. Regardless of ethnic origin, the person of Tangier
knew his or her exact location in the larger frame of the city. This acute sense of
place and the balancing of individual and communal interests were the foundations of Tangier's flourishing associational life and the source of its dynamism.

NOTES

My thanks to Lucette Marques-Toledano, a great lady of Tangier, for her insights and recollections that helped me develop this topic. Also I am grateful to M. Bouzid, who gave me a
photocopy of "A History of CIA Rentistica S. A. by Ernest Waller" and to Tangier friends Rachel
Muyal and Sonia Azagury, who offered me a personal vision of their city. This research was
conducted with the support of the Graham Foundation for Advanced Studies in the Fine Arts
and the Moroccan Studies Program at the Center for Middle Eastern Studies, Harvard University.

1. For examples of this mindset, see Jean-Louis Miège, *Le Maroc et L'Europe (1830–1894)*, 4
vols. (Rabat: Editions La Porte, 1989), 3:29; and Abdallah Laroui, *Les origines sociales et culturelles du nationalisme marocain (1830–1912)* (Paris: François Maspero, 1977), 310–314.

2. A Mediterranean example that places the Tangier case in comparative perspective is Mark Mazower, *Salonica: City of Ghosts, Christians, Muslims, Jews, 1430–1950* (New York: Knopf, 2005).

3. Gaudí was commissioned to build a Franciscan mission in Tangier in 1892–1893, but the project was never realized. The plan for a chapel with many towers seems to have been the inspiration for the famous Barcelona church of the Sagrada Familia. George R. Collins, *Antonio Gaudí* (New York; G. Braziller, 1960), 12–13 and Plate 44.

4. Sir Robert Rowand Anderson (1834–921) was Scotland's leading architect at the end of the nineteenth century. Anderson's public buildings included the Scottish National Portrait Gallery and the Medical School for the University of Edinburgh. He also designed the Eastern Telegraph Office in Tangier. Sam McKinstry, *Rowand Anderson: The Premier Architect of Scotland* (Edinburgh: Edinburgh University Press, 1991), 144–146.

5. Susan Gilson Miller, "Apportioning Sacred Space in a Moroccan City: The Case of Tangier, 1860–1912," *City & Society* 13 (2001): 69–72.

6. Moïse Nahon, "Les Israélites du Maroc," *Revue des études ethnographiques et sociologiques* 2 (1909): 262.

7. On Tangier's place as Morocco's "diplomatic capital," see Ramón Lourido Díaz, "Le Sultan Sidi Muhammad b. ʿAbd Allah et l'institution de la représentation consulaire à Tanger," in *Tanger, 1800–1956: Contribution à l'histoire récente du Maroc* (Rabat: Université Mohammed V, Faculté et des Sciences humaines, 1991), 9–28.

8. Isaac Assayag, *Tanger . . . Regards sur le passé. Ce qu'il fut* (Casablanca: Imp. Najah El Jadida, 2001), 129.

9. Population statistics varied in the absence of an "official" census. One source estimates that in 1905, of a total population of 44,115, there were 24,000 Muslims, 9,115 Europeans, and 10,000 Jews (clearly an approximate number). Albert Cousin and Daniel Saurin, *Annuaire du Maroc* (Paris: Comité du Maroc, 1905), 408.

10. *Murray's Handbook for Travellers: Part 1. Mediterranean*, Vol. 1 (London, 1890).

11. Albert Cousin and Daniel Suarin, *Annuaire du Maroc* (Paris: Comité du Maroc, 1905), 163–188. The *nazir* (supervisor) of the *hubus* would rent it out for a fixed sum called the *miftah* (key money). With the increase in land values at the end of the nineteenth century, a growing disparity opened up between the rent paid and the real value of property. This led holders of the *miftah* to sublet their property at many times the rent they had paid to the *hubus*, sometimes as much as twenty-five times greater. According to Ernest Waller, "The Jews especially made a great business of this," and some made "fortunes" by subletting *hubus* property. "A History of CIA Rentistica S.A. by Ernest Waller, "unpublished manuscript, unpaginated, author's personal archive. (Hereafter cited as "Waller manuscript.") To escape this situation, buyers sought property outside the walls. Yet this was also problematic, because it too was inalienable, being either *jaysh* (*guish*) land, given by the sultan as a gift in exchange for military service, or *hubus* land, belonging to the mosque. Nevertheless, this land too was eventually sold off, and many Jews and Europeans became landowners outside the town. The original landholders could transfer their property by getting a notarial act called a *mulkiya*, indicating it was neither *hubus* nor *jaysh*. The new owner had to actually occupy the land as a sign of his ownership; otherwise it could be resold. E. Michaux-Bellaire, *Tanger et sa zone, Villes et Tribus du Maroc* (Paris: Ernest Leroux, 1921), 2, 291.

12. *Times of Morocco*, 15 September 1888.

13. The Villa Idonia was the setting for the notorious kidnapping of Perdicaris and his son-in-law Cromwell Varley by the bandit al-Raysuni in 1904, later immortalized by Hollywood in *The Wind and the Lion*. For a popular account, see Barbara W. Tuchman, "Perdicaris Live or Raisuli Dead," in *A Sense of History: The Best Writing from the Pages of American Heritage* (New York: Houghton Mifflin, 1985), 548–560.

14. Temma Kaplan, *Anarchists of Andalusia, 1868–1903* (Princeton, N.J.: Princeton University Press, 1977), especially chapters 3, 4, and 5.

15. Decanat, Box 4, Folder 50 ("Voirie"), 4 January 1899, National Archives and Records Administration, Washington, D.C.

16. The "garden city" was a concept in urban planning developed by Ebenezer Howard at the turn of the last century in reaction to the brutal congestion of the industrialized city. In this scheme, individual houses were set in wooded lots within a curving street pattern. See Spiro Kostof, *The City Shaped: Urban Patterns and Meanings through History* (Boston: Little Brown, 1991), 75–77.

17. Claude Verdugo, "Ville de Tanger: enquête urbaine," *Bulletin économique et sociale du Maroc* 12, no. 78 (1958): 202.

18. Waller manuscript, n.p. On Anderson's Tangier portfolio, see McKinstry, *Rowand Anderson*, 144–146.

19. On Harris's friendship with Maclean, see Walter B. Harris, *Tafilet: The Narrative of a Journey of Exploration in the Atlas Mountains and the Oases of the North-West Sahara* (Edinburgh: W. Blackwood and Sons, 1895), 325.

20. On the Ghassal family, see Miège, *Maroc,* 3:31; and Michaux-Bellaire, *Tanger et sa zone,* 199.

21. "Tanger d'autrefois; La rue de Tetuan," *Journal du Tanger,* 5 May 1990.

22. Ibid.

23. Abraham I. Laredo, *Les Noms des Juifs du Maroc; Essai d'onomastique judéo-marocaine* (Madrid: Instituto B. Arias Montano, 1978), 450.

24. Isaac Laredo, *Memorias de un viejo Tangerino* (Madrid: C. Bermejo, 1935), 128.

25. Roy Strickland, "Between Party Walls," in *Rethinking [the] XIXth Century City,* vol. 2, ed. Attilio Petruccioli (Cambridge, Mass.: Agha Khan Program for Islamic Architecture, Massachusetts Institute of Technology, 1998), 75.

26. Archives of the Alliance Israélite Universelle, Paris, Series Maroc LI, E 830, 1889, Isaac Benchimol.

27. Mohamed Chekroun, "Les mutations urbaines à Tanger: Cas du Boulevard Pasteur," in *Tanger, 1800–1956* (Rabat: Jamiᶜat Muhammad al-Khamis, Kulliyat al-Adab wa-al-ᶜUlum al-Insaniya; Tangier: Jamiᶜat ᶜAbd al-Malik al-Saᶜidi, Madrasat Fahd al-ᶜUlya lil-Tarjama 1991), 77–84.

28. *Times of Morocco,* 28 February 1910.

29. *Times of Morocco,* 8 January 1914.

30. Waller manuscript, n.p. Henri Prost's plan for Tangier is found in Jean Royer, *L'urbanisme aux colonies et dans les pays tropicaux; communications et rapports du Congrès International de l'Urbanisme aux Colonies et dans les pays de latitude intertropicale,* 2 vols. (Nevers: Fortin, 1932), 1:106–108. Prost's urban planning in Morocco is discussed in Gwendolyn Wright, *The Politics of Design in French Colonial Urbanism* (Chicago: University of Chicago Press, 1991); Paul Rabinow, *French Modern: Norms and Forms of the Social Environment* (Chicago: University of Chicago Press, 1995); Abderrahmane Rachik, *Ville et pouvoirs au Maroc* (Casablanca: Afrique Orient, 1995); and Jean-Louis Cohen and Monique Eleb, *Casablanca: Colonial Myths and Architectural Ventures* (New York: Monacelli Press, 2002).

31. Michaux-Bellaire, *Tanger et sa zone,* 254.

32. Muhammad b. Muhammad Skirij, "Riyadh al-bahja fi akhbar Tanja," 1917, n.p., MS #1452, Bibliothèque Générale, Rabat.

33. On this period, and on the statute itself, see Graham H. Stuart, *The International City of Tangier,* 2nd ed. (Stanford, Calif.: Stanford University Press, 1955), chapters 6, 7, and 8.

34. C. A. Bayly, *The Birth of the Modern World, 1780–1914: Global Connections and Comparisons* (Malden, Mass.: Blackwell, 2004), 193.

35. Robert L. Heilbroner, *The Making of Economic Society,* 5th ed. (Englewood Cliffs, N.J.: Prentice Hall, 1975), 59.

36. Ibid.

37. Waller manuscript, n.p. After World War I, Waller joined forces with Lord Bute to form Rentistica, the largest real estate company in Tangier in the first half of the twentieth century.

The Fourth Marquess of Bute (1881–1947), one of Britain's richest men who owned vast estates throughout the British Isles, was Waller's silent partner in Rentistica's activities. His death coincided with the end of the international period in Tangier and the final sale and dissolution of the company's holdings.

38. Waller manuscript., n.p.

39. Chekroun, "Les mutations," 81. Later investments by the Toledano brothers proved to be less fortunate. Seriously overleveraged, their tea business suffered a serious crash in 1958 that led to a major reorganization of the tea trade in Morocco. This story is detailed by John Waterbury in "Tribalism, Trade and Politic: The Transformation of the Swasa of Morocco," in *Arabs and Berbers: From Tribe to Nation in North Africa,* ed. Ernest Gellner and Charles A. Micaud (Lexington, Mass.: Heath, 1972), 239–44.

40. Interview with Lucette Marques-Toledano, June 2002.

41. Chekroun, "Les mutations," 82.

42. It is tempting to speculate about why certain individuals and groups are less risk averse than others, but that topic is beyond the scope of this paper, reaching into a vast literature on religion, ethnicity, and business practices, in the forefront of which are the seminal writings of Max Weber. For an introduction to the topic, see *The International Encyclopedia of the Social and Behavioral Sciences,* ed Neli J. Smelser and Paul B. Baltes (Amsterdam, N.Y.: Elsevier, 2001), s.v. "Entrepreneurship."

43. Carlos de Nesry, *Le Juif de Tanger et le Maroc* (Tangier: Éditions Internationales, 1956), 64.

10

Muslim and Jewish Interaction in Moroccan Meat Markets, 1873–1912

Stacy E. Holden

On 23 September 1909, the chamberlain of Sultan Mawlay ʿAbd al-ʿAziz ordered Jewish butchers in Fez to send the lungs of their slaughtered animals to the palace. According to M. Elmaleh, who headed Fez's Alliance Israélite Universelle, a French educational organization dedicated to the betterment of Jews outside France, the sultan intended to feed these lungs to his cats, probably lions. Jewish butchers typically sold the lungs of slaughtered animals for one peseta. Arguing that they could not afford another tax, the butchers refused to part with the lungs. In response, the chamberlain sent all the Jewish butchers of Fez to jail.

In the mellah, Jewish butchers slaughtered according to Talmudic rites so as to render meat kosher. Lungs played an important role in this process. As the most delicate organ in an animal's body, lungs often provided evidence of internal damage that made meat *trefah*, or unfit for Jewish tables. If the lungs passed the test and were kosher, the Jews sold them at their own shops; if they were *trefah*, they sold them to Muslim butchers, whose religion permitted them to retail the meat to consumers of their faith.

Interpreting the tax as a violation of the Jews' rights, the diplomatic representatives of the French government rallied behind the butchers. Elmaleh negotiated the release of butchers within two days, just in time for Yom Kippur. He described the incident to the French chargé d'affaires, who in turn asked Consul Henri Gaillard to discuss the matter with royal officials. Through his grand vizir, Madani al-Glawi, the sultan denied abusing Moroccan Jews, pointing out that his subjects should bring their concerns to him and not to French officials.[1]

This incident highlights some important aspects of the political economy of Morocco just prior to the French protectorate. It points to interfaith interaction in local markets and to the influence of Europeans, who falsely assumed that a royal official's motivation was discriminatory. In precolonial Morocco, it is undeniable that crises such as Fez experienced during the famine of 1880 or the tribal block-ade of 1912 sometimes led to the victimization of Jews by hysterical mobs seek-ing a scapegoat for their woes.[2] Nevertheless, the French presumption that ten-sions persisted between the Muslim majority and the Jewish minority ignored everyday interactions in urban markets. Islam and Judaism impose strict guide-lines for the slaughter of animals and the preparation of meat, so butchers were central figures in the religious practices of both Muslims and Jews. And yet in Moroccan meat markets, Muslims and Jews engaged in intensive commercial ex-changes predicated on tolerance and understanding.

The Religious Work of Butchers

Religious laws regulated the purchase of livestock by both Muslim and Jew-ish butchers.[3] Muslims and Jews eat the meat of sheep, cattle, goats, and fowl. Muslims also eat camel meat. Jewish law, however, prohibits Jews from eating animals that do not have cloven hooves. Further, both Islam and Judaism pro-mote the consumption of healthy animals that are free of external and internal defects. Islamic law, for example, dictates that a Muslim should not purchase a ram with a missing eye or a limp. To check for disease, a buyer would take a ram's horns and shake its head. If the ram did not maintain its balance, then it was ill.

In nineteenth-century Morocco, butchers worked as independent craftsmen who purchased their own livestock. Butchers would bring their livestock to a designated site of slaughter, which Moroccans called a *gurna*. The term *gurna* does not translate as the modern concept of a "slaughterhouse," which connotes a complex of buildings managed by the state as a public facility.[4] A designated site of slaughter in a premodern Moroccan city had no features of an ordinary build-ing. For example, Fez's Sidi Abu Nafa *gurna* in the Fez Jadid quarter was an open space of about twelve meters by twenty meters.[5] Bounded by urban walls on its eastern and southern side and houses on its northern side, this site of slaughter was located at the margins of the city but still within a residential neighborhood.[6] In the nineteenth century, dirt covered Sidi Abu Nafa's floor. A whitewashing of lime and sand, or *dus*, often covered the floors of other Moroccan *gurnas*.[7] This *gurna*, like most others, had a sewage canal to carry away blood and intestinal contents, the only parts of an animal that were not eaten or otherwise used in precolonial Morocco.

Muslims and Jews usually worked at separate sites of slaughter in Morocco. In 1906, for example, a total of eighteen Muslim butchers and eleven Jewish butch-ers in Tangier worked at two separate *gurnas*, while six Catholic butchers from Spain slaughtered in their homes.[8] Together, they served at least 36,000 urban residents.[9] Neither Islam nor Judaism require that their butchers be physically isolated from each other. Muslim and Jewish butchers in Tangier in fact worked at the same *gurna* until 1889, when the city's booming population led to an enlargement of the butchers' work site.[10] Fez, in contrast, had 100,000 residents.[11] In this much larger imperial city, 150 butchers worked at four *gurnas*.[12] Some Muslim butchers worked at the Sidi Abu Nafa *gurna*. Others worked at a *gurna* near the northwestern gate of Bab Mahruk or at a *gurna* in Bayn al-Mudun, located in the center of the *madina*. Their Jewish colleagues worked at a *gurna* on the southern outskirts of the mellah.[13] Even in Fez, however, popular interpretations of religious codes permitted Muslims to work for Jewish butchers. Thus, the maternal uncles of a man named Oliel Makhluf, Jewish butchers who had been born around 1900, eventually hired a Muslim named Jillali al-Fakhir to assist them.[14]

Butchers of both faiths paid for the use of their work site. Muslim butchers paid a fee to officials that controlled the *hubus,* or charitable endowments, since their funds maintained canals, while Jewish butchers paid their fee to the local Jewish council.[15] Jewish butchers, however, suffered a heavier financial burden than their Muslim colleagues. In Tangier, Jewish butchers paid four pesetas for the use of the *gurna,* three times more than the 75 centimes paid by Muslims.[16]

At the *gurna,* a pious man performed the ritual act of slaughter, thereby ensuring that meat retailed in the market was either *hallal* for Muslims or kosher for Jews. An imam performed the ritual act of slaughter for Muslim butchers. This imam was not a religious specialist per se; he was an aging butcher esteemed for his piety. He would perform the ritual act of slaughter after leading *'isha',* the last of five required prayers each day, which takes place around 10 PM.[17] Then he would place each animal on its left side. With the animal's head facing northeast, toward Mecca, the imam would slit its throat from ear to ear. Stating "Bismillah Allahu Akbar," he would dedicate the slaughter to God. In return for this blessing, Muslim butchers would pay the imam a nominal fee, .125 pesetas in Tangier.[18]

Islamic law permits any practicing Muslim to perform the ritual act of slaughter, and a butcher did not need to be an imam to do so. In 1898, Muhammad b Ja'far b. Idris al-Kattani described a perfect butcher in a hagiography of Fez's saints. The butcher Abu Jabal Ya'la, whose brown skin suggested origins in the south, had died in 1107. In commemorating his professional honesty, al-Kittani revealed some occupational ruses prevalent in his own time. Ya'la, he noted, never slaughtered stolen rams and never charged clients for more meat than they had ordered. Further, Ya'la's work did not interfere with his religious devotion. While his assistants dressed the meat of slaughtered animals between the prayers of *subh* and *duha,* from about 3 AM until 9 AM, the master craftsman prayed in the mosque. It seems that God rewarded his piety and professional honesty, for Ya'la always gave money to those who deepened his understanding of the Quran. He worked as a butcher for twelve years, thereafter leaving Fez in order to voyage to holy places in southern Marrakesh and then Mecca.[19]

By the time al-Kattani recorded this saint's biography, Moroccans had begun questioning the piety of urban butchers. Butchers were often recent migrants and so were unknown to established residents of a city. In 1905, when Charles René-LeClerc traveled to Fez, he found that most butchers were freed slaves from the southern Oued Draa region.[20] The butcher Jillali Rabani, for example, had come to Fez from Tamur Sumt in the mid-nineteenth century, so he and his son Said, also a butcher, did not have deep roots in the urban community.[21] Legislation passed at the start of the protectorate suggests that some butchers in Fez engaged in impious activities. For example, the French banned gambling at Suq al-Khamis, the biweekly livestock market.[22] They also banned workers at Bayn al-Mudun's *gurna* from smoking marijuana.[23] Ahmed Sefrioui's fictional description of a butcher suggests that Fez's residents stereotyped these dark-skinned migrants as uncultured and fierce. Sefrioui, who was born ten years after René-LeClerc's visit, described "Selam, the Negro" as torn "between the desire to hurl [the axe] at the head of a disagreeable client and the need to continue serving his customers [*son monde*]."[24]

By insisting that an imam perform the ritual act of slaughter on the livestock of butchers, royal officials allayed public concerns about the purity of commercial meat. In 1876, for example, Essaouira's governor ʿAmara b. ʿAbd al-Sadiq condemned one butcher who refused to avail himself to the imam's services. According to ʿAbd al-Sadiq, Idris al-Harishi was a recent migrant who had turned to butchering because he had no training in skilled trades. The governor's description of al-Harishi suggests that he was not a pious Muslim. "He will leave at night," complained ʿAbd al-Sadiq, "and circulate in the city to exercise his craziness." Al-Harishi, a Spanish protégé, requested that Muhammad Bargash, the royal official who dealt with foreign consuls in Tangier, ask Spanish diplomats to intervene in this matter.[25] Official interpretations of Islamic law fostered distinctions between professional butchers, who were required to pay an imam for a ritual act of slaughter, and private residents, who were permitted to slaughter the animals themselves.

For Muslims, the performance of the ritual slaughter by a pious man vested a butcher's work site with religious meaning. In Meknes, forty-nine Muslim butchers slaughtered at three *gurnas*, while sixteen Jewish butchers worked in the mellah.[26] Urban scholars, even descendants of the Prophet, offered no complaints when some Muslim butchers set up a *gurna* inside an obsolete mosque. The historian Mawlay ʿAbd al-Rahman Ibn Zaydan, born in 1878, recorded that butchers in his hometown had adopted this mosque as a work site after its external fountain broke. (Since the fountain stopped bringing clean water to the mosque, it was impossible for worshippers to perform ablutions for prayers.)[27] Sometimes urban masses developed rituals that paid homage to the countless performances of a ritual slaughter at a *gurna*. In Fez, for example, ritual slaughter had occurred at the Bayn al-Mudun *gurna* since the sixteenth century.[28] By the turn of the twentieth century, women had begun visiting the *gurna* to find out the fate of absent or sick family members. Invoking the assistance of the spirit world, they would light incense and candles at the butchers' work site.[29]

For Jewish butchers, a shohet performed the ritual act of slaughter. Because a rabbinical authority was required to affirm the shohet's knowledge of slaughtering laws, he was an accredited religious specialist. Like an imam, he would dedicate an animal to God as he slit its throat, although in this case he would slit only the trachea and the esophagus. Judaism, like Islam, bans the undue suffering of an animal, so he would work quickly and with a sharp knife. Jews in Tangier paid shohets three pesetas for their services, twenty-four times as much as their Muslim counterparts received.[30] It seems likely that this cost differential stemmed from a key distinction between Judaic and Islamic law. Islam allows any practicing Muslim to perform the ritual act, whereas the Talmud required all Jews to eat only meat slaughtered by a shohet. Because the shohet had an absolute monopoly on ritual slaughter, he could charge more for his services.

Like their Muslim counterparts, Jewish butchers had a shady reputation, and ritual slaughter by the shohet ensured that butchers were retailing kosher meat. The Talmud suggests that butchering was one of seven occupations that can lead to the commission of sin.[31] Butchers, it warns, are tempted to avoid financial loss by selling meat that is not kosher. In Tangier, this scriptural prediction became reality at the end of the nineteenth century, when some Jewish butchers, often transplants from Fez, began selling impure meat.[32] These butchers avoided the costly services of a shohet, even though his services rendered meat kosher.

Religious law also regulated the butcher's dressing of a slaughtered carcass. Both Muslim and Jewish butchers hung slaughtered animals to drain their blood. Jewish law is more stringent than Islamic law with regard to dressing meat. Before declaring meat kosher, the shohet must examine the organs of the slaughtered animal for forty-seven possible defects. The perforation of a vital organ, for example, renders meat *trefah*. Jewish law also bans Jews from eating the fat covering the kidney and spleen as well as the sciatic nerve near the thigh vein. It is difficult to remove the sciatic nerve, so most Jewish butchers during this period disposed of the hindquarters. In accordance with Islamic law, many Jewish butchers sold *trefah* meat to Muslim butchers, who then sold it. Islamic law treats this meat the same as its own *hallal* meat.[33] In Tangier, however, Jewish butchers sold their hindquarters to Spanish butchers.[34]

Although both Muslim and Jewish butchers organized their work according to separate religious prescriptions, they interacted with each other in the secular realm. Muslims and Jews competed for livestock, for example. In 1880, the Muslim butcher al-Ghazi b. Sidi purchased livestock for the sultan's household in Fez. On one outing to Suq al-Khamis, al-Ghazi spotted an ideal ram the same time as the Jewish butchers Mimun al-Kharifi and ʿAyush b. ʿAyush did. Each butcher wanted this choice ram, and a struggle ensued. As al-Ghazi later explained to a royal official, he politely informed the Jewish butchers that he was purchasing the ram for the sultan. But he said that the Jewish butchers responded to his civility by hurling insults at his father and grandfather.[35] Al-Ghazi's tale provides no evidence of an interfaith workingman's paradise, but it does suggest that butchers, even if they were exasperated, did not resort to religious slurs.

At other times, Muslim and Jewish butchers cooperated with each other to pursue shared professional interests. In 1904, for example, the Sanitary Council in Tangier ruled that the French veterinarian Gabriel Dehors had to inspect all meat before it was sold in public markets. Butchers believed that his exacting appraisal of their meat was hurting their business, and they twice banded together to protest Dehors's interference.[36] At that time, Morocco was plagued with drought, and livestock, even emaciated livestock, was expensive. When the veterinarian condemned meat as unhealthy, butchers lost the return on a substantial investment. Muslim butchers also appealed to the *muhtasib*, a royal official who oversaw the price and quality of goods sold in urban markets.[37] He must have proved unresponsive, for they then began to undermine the veterinarian's work. Butchers were supposed to present their meat by 7:00 AM, but they began arriving closer to 10:00 AM (if at all), at great inconvenience to Dehors.[38] Within two years, the president of the Sanitary Council reported that many butchers in Tangier had begun to slaughter animals outside the *gurna*, breaking a law that prohibited such action.[39] In this way, the butchers avoided a municipal veterinarian whose job was to ensure that consumers were purchasing quality meat.

Retailing Meat: A Difficult Venture

The commercial activities of butchers began at the *gurna*. Each day, local peddlers came there to purchase the viscera of butchered animals. Neither Islam nor Judaism prohibits the consumption of bones or vital organs, such as brains, hooves, heart, lungs, liver, or intestines. Sometimes peddlers sold simple meals of the hooves, spleen, testicles, brains, and intestines to hungry travelers. At a market, the cry "Smells bad, but delicious!" might have advertised the sale of testicles boiled with chickpeas, just as it does today. Sometimes peddlers sold the viscera to urban residents, who cooked them at home. Moroccans, for example, often cook the fatty hooves of cattle or sheep in a sauce of chickpeas. Nevertheless, residents valued flesh more than they did organs. Thus, during the French protectorate, organs sold only at temporary stalls and not in shops, providing minimal profits for the peddlers.[40]

Butchers retailed meat at their own shops. An illustration by an Italian artist who visited Fez in 1875 shows a butcher shop that was a five-square-meter room.[41] Clients ordered meat from the street. Kosher meat, unlike its *hallal* counterpart, requires salting to draw out remaining blood, but this task was usually completed at home by the consumer, not by the butcher.[42] Moroccan butchers did not offer cuts of meat. Instead, they hung out dressed carcasses and cut meat according to weight. The weight used for meat was the *ratl*, which in Fez signified a half a kilogram.[43] In the Italian drawing, a man at the back, noting the butcher's shrinking carcass, shouts his order so as to be served before other customers. "The butcher, low status by definition," as Ianthe Maclagan points out in her study of Yemen, "has it in his power to decide the quality of every man's dinner."[44]

As a royal official representing the sultan, the *muhtasib* oversaw the quality and price of meat sold in urban markets.[45] In theory, he oversaw the markets in the Jewish and Muslim quarters, although royal officials or Jewish notables sometimes challenged his authority in the mellah. When examining meat markets, the *muhtasib* would make sure that a butcher had not mixed the meat of a lean animal with the meat of the more costly fatty animal or he would verify that a butcher had not mixed the less expensive meat of a goat with the meat of a ram.[46] The *muhtasib* did not control prices in the livestock market because he could not verify the cost of raising an animal in the countryside and transporting it to the city. Instead, he set a price for meat based on going rates for livestock, theoretically performing this task in consultation with an *'arif,* a proficient butcher acting as representative of his trade. In setting these prices, the *muhtasib* was prevented by Morocco's commercial laws from either doubling the costs entailed in purchasing and slaughtering livestock (thereby favoring butchers) or forcing the sale of meat at cost (thereby favoring customers).[47] Because he set prices based on the cost of production, this royal official—not market forces—decided a worker's profit margin.

Butchers sold a consumable luxury that provided a tangible indication of social class. The sultan would provide flour for impoverished subjects, but he did not consider meat a staple food. Instead, he used the income generated from the sale of meat to assist the poor. Mawlay ʿAbd al-ʿAziz, for example, granted a Jewish resident of Meknes the right to operate a royal property as a butcher shop. According to Ben Hayyim Ben Abu, this man's inheritor, the sultan asked him to set aside some of his income to help the poor in his community; in return, he exempted him from paying taxes.[48] In Morocco, however, social class was not necessarily a reflection of monetary wealth. Thus, to honor the *shurafa'*, the putative descendants of the Prophet, the sultan annually granted a sum to their poorest ranks so that they, too, like the rich, could prepare *khaliʿa,* dried meat in confit.[49]

Because meat was a luxury, butchers did not serve a steady clientele. In the sixteenth century, Leo Africanus observed that Fez's wealthy residents ate meat twice a day, but the urban majority ate it no more than twice a week.[50] By the late nineteenth century, a local proverb highlighted meat as a nonessential commodity. "If you pass the night without meat," North Africans advised, "you wake up without debt."[51] Many Moroccans could not afford meat, so its possession aroused popular envy. While protesting a gate tax in 1873, Fez's tanners pillaged a tax collector's house. Along with other transportable valuables, they took his entire stock of *khaliʿa.*[52] When the cost of living rose, Moroccans stopped buying meat. In 1910, the price of ram's meat doubled in Fez, as did staples such as clarified butter and oil. According to the scholar Muhamad al-Hajawi, all of the city's butcher shops closed as a result.[53]

Islamic law permits practicing Muslims to slaughter their own animals. Islamic jurists specify that practicing Muslims of sound mind can perform the rites of slaughter for the ʿId al-Kabir festival as well as for everyday meals. In this patriarchal society, private slaughter offered an assertion of masculinity and a demonstration of power. Some jurists acknowledged a woman's right to perform the ritual act of slaughter, but they deemed it *makruh,* an undesirable state that fell between the licit and the illicit.[54] North Africans believed that men should slaughter their own livestock. "If a man cannot slaughter his sheep or beat his wife," a proverb indicated, "then it is better for him to die than to live."[55] Thus, rich Muslims who could afford to purchase livestock did not always buy meat at a butcher's shop.

When drought caused famine, the butchers' sale of meat decreased. At first, starving peasants would sell off dying herds for rock-bottom prices, a temporary boon for their clientele. In 1878, for example, as drought caused wheat prices to increase by 300 percent, Europeans in Essaouira expressed amazement at low price of livestock.[56] During the next six years, however, as much as half of the kingdom's cattle and two-thirds of its sheep and goats died for want of grazing ground.[57] By 1880, livestock sold in Fez must have traveled long distances, for its hinterland could no longer supply the city. As the British consul Sir John Drummond-Hay passed through one village on his way to Fez, inhabitants cried out: "Give us some meat! In God's name, we have nothing to eat but grass."[58]

Drought increased the price of staples, so residents curtailed their consumption of luxuries. In 1878, for example, a tax collector in Meknes reported a 63 percent decrease in revenue collected from meat, while taxes collected at the wheat market had increased by 170 percent.[59] In Fez, the sultan periodically auctioned off the job of collecting taxes to the highest bidder. By 1880, however, Mawlay al-Hasan felt compelled to lower the income of Sharif Sidi Ahmad Dagga, who had purchased the right to collect taxes from Muslim butchers, by one-third. Dagga, like everyone else, had not anticipated the length of the drought when he purchased this right and did not take into consideration a decline in meat sales. Mawlay al-Hasan found no fault in the arrears, expressing instead a desire to "help him back on his feet."[60] Between the time of the Great Famine (1878–1884) and the establishment of the protectorate in 1912, Morocco suffered fifteen years of severe drought, which increased poverty levels and thus decreased the business activities of butchers.[61]

Butchers generally did not earn a lot of money. In 1901, Mawlay al-Hajj ʿAlawi moved from Fez to Casablanca to start a new life, although it is hard to imagine a butcher better positioned to earn his keep. Unlike other butchers in Fez, his title and surname suggest that he was from the *shurafaʾ* and a member of the sultan's extended family. ʿAlawi requested financial support, informing the grand vizir that he did not have enough money to feed his children during a period of "insufficiency." ʿAlawi, referring to the butcher's trade, insisted that "the industry is in crisis."[62] A local proverb that circulated at the time suggests that most butchers had trouble making ends meet. To indicate a contradictory situation, North Africans would state that "the butcher eats turnips for dinner."[63] Muslim and Jewish butchers were not content with their meager earnings, and they engaged in similar schemes to increase the sale of *hallal* and kosher meat.

Tax Evasion at the *Gurna*

When the sultan levied a tax on the *gurna*, he cut into the earnings of Moroccan butchers. To combat famine with social welfare programs, the sultan levied the *jarjuma*, more familiar to the Moroccans as *guerjouma* (its local pronunciation). This fiscal term signifies "the neck," and it was collected on each head of livestock commercial butchers slaughtered. The sultan established a fee based on the amount of meat an animal provided as well as its quality. For example, butchers paid more for the slaughter of cattle than for any class of ovine. The sultan also distinguished between white sheep and goats and black ones; the latter were more costly to slaughter than the former. To make sure that it was butchers that assumed this tax burden, not the local peddlers who purchased their viscera, the sultan specified that he would not tax feet, spleen, testicles, brains, intestines, and horns.[64] By the turn of the twentieth century, officials were collecting the *guerjouma* in Casablanca, Essaouira, Tangier, Larache and Fez.

The sultan intended for this tax revenue to serve the public interest by ensuring that city streets were cleaned regularly. In 1879, Mawlay al-Hasan explained to an official in Essaouira that removing garbage and waste from city streets eliminated the bad odors that caused disease, a statement that represented standard medical theory in Morocco and Europe at the time.[65] By specifying the purpose for *guerjouma* funds, the sultan distinguished that income from most other tax revenue, which he controlled as he saw fit.

When Mawlay al-Hasan instituted the *guerjouma* in Essaouira during the Great Famine, he was responding to epidemics of typhoid, cholera, and smallpox fostered by the environmental catastrophe. Drought caused malnourished peasants to migrate to the city, where they lived in the streets and were susceptible to disease. For example, in 1878, when the summer harvest failed and Essaouira's population doubled in a matter of weeks, at least 5,000 people in the city died of cholera from July of that year to January of the next.[66] Contemporary observers agreed that the epidemics took the highest toll on the malnourished poor. Thus, the *guerjouma* did more than institute a public service that was enjoyed equally by all urban residents. It also created a program of social assistance by which the sultan redistributed income from privileged Moroccans, those who could afford meat, to his poorest subjects who were living in the streets and thus were wracked by disease.

Sly butchers tried to avoid paying this tax, suggesting that they worried that this financial burden would decrease their sales. The Muslim butcher Idris' al-Haraishi, highlighted above for his refusal to pay an imam, used his status as a protégé to avoid taxes on slaughtered animals. Al-Haraishi was not the only butcher in Essaouira who schemed to minimize his tax burden. Governor Amara complained that al-Haraishi passed his exemption on to other butchers by pretending that their animals were his own livestock.[67] It seems that Essaouira's butchers had a shrewd understanding of the principle of decreasing returns. When Mawlay al-Hasan first implemented the *guerjouma* in 1879, protégés practicing the butcher's trade paid the tax. One week later, however, a royal official raised it by nearly a third, from twenty-nine *uqiyas* to forty *uqiyas*. It was only then that protégés refused to pay the *guerjouma*.[68] The collection of this tax reinforced the status of meat as an elite luxury.

Jewish notables, not the sultan, forced butchers who sold kosher meat to assume a higher tax burden than their Muslim colleagues. As Dehors recorded in 1906, the sultan collected a tax from both Muslim and Jewish butchers in Tangiers. The former paid the makhzan 1.125 pesetas, while the latter paid 1.15 pesetas. The Jewish council in that city, however, levied a separate tax on kosher meat, thereby making the production of kosher meat five times more expensive than its *hallal* counterpart. Jewish butchers paid eighteen extra pesetas for each animal slaughtered in Tangier. The *muhtasib* set a base price for meat, whether kosher or *hallal*, based on the cost of livestock. Because of the heavy tax burden of Jewish butchers, the *muhtasib* permitted them to increase the price of kosher meat.[69] In other cities, the Jewish council also collected a costly tax from butchers. When L. Martin visited Fez in 1908, for example, the revenue the council collected at the mellah's *gurna* enabled it to buy a tobacco farm.[70] Since meat played a secondary role in most household budgets, the cost of kosher meat must have decreased its sales.

Jewish butchers, like their Muslim colleagues, tried to evade taxes collected at the *gurna*. In Meknes, for example, the Jewish butcher Samuel Akoulid used his status as an Italian protégé to avoid paying taxes that cut into his profits. In 1894, notables from the mellah asked Akoulid to assume the same tax as other Jewish butchers. Once he began paying the tax, however, Akoulid reported that he "suffered damage." He would have known the financial burden when he agreed to the request of Jewish notables, so it can only be assumed that he had not anticipated a drop in meat sales once he factored the taxes into the price of meat. The Italian representative who wrote on his behalf to Muhammad al-Tarris [Torres] clearly felt that meat taxes were too high. He argued that most peoples in Europe considered meat a staple, so their butchers did not pay a lot of taxes.[71] Thus, he suggested that parity between Akoulid and other Jewish butchers would be better achieved if the Moroccan government lowered the tax burden of all butchers.[72]

The Slaughter of Female Animals and Muslim Consumption of Kosher Meat

Butchers wanted to increase their profits, but they needed to resolve a dilemma. Meat played a secondary role in most household budgets, and high prices led to a decline in meat sales that were already low. That is why some butchers asked their city's *muhtasib* to decrease meat prices. In 1887, for example, the *muhtasib* Muhammad b. al-ʿArabi Ajana set the price of ram's meat at 14 *uqiyas* per *ratl*[73] in the markets of Meknes. In response, forty-five butchers, all Muslim, petitioned him to reconsider the price. In consultation with the acknowledged head of the butchers (ʿarif) as well as other respected practitioners of the trade, the *muhtasib* decreased the price to 13.5 *uqiyas*.[74]

Cows and ewes sold more cheaply than bulls and rams, so slaughtering female animals permitted butchers to decrease their expenses and thus the price of meat. The preference of Moroccans for the meat of male livestock partially explains the price differential between the two sexes. Moroccans did not like the taste of a female animal's flesh, which, in their opinion, contained too much fat. Further, as a specifically Islamic influence, the Prophet had sacrificed a ram, so scholars proposed that it was better to slaughter male animals.[75] However, during times of drought, when there was no grazing ground, herders would sell off their animals, even fecund females, for the proverbial song. To safeguard the kingdom's livestock, Moroccan sultans banned butchers from slaughtering female animals for most of the late nineteenth and early twentieth centuries. Sly butchers, however, tried to get around this royal edict, especially protégés who did not need to heed set prices or pay royal taxes. When a Jewish butcher slaughtered a female animal, thus managing to undersell competitors, Muslim consumers would buy his kosher meat.

Because Judaism is a monotheistic religion, most schools of Islamic law permit Muslims to eat meat from animals sacrificed according to Jewish rites. Muslims could eat not only the meat declared *trefah* but also kosher meat intended for Jewish consumption. "It is not illegal," specified Ibn Jizzi, a fourteenth-century Andulusian scholar.[76] Islamic scholars deemed kosher meat *makruh*, and at least one commercial treatise from nineteenth-century Morocco indicates that Muslims there purchased kosher meat. Thus, when Abu al-ʿAbbas Ahmad b. Saʿid discussed commercial laws in 1894, he felt compelled to remind readers that Muslims should purchase *hallal* meat. Still, he argued, it was better for them to buy meat from a devout Jew than from an impious Muslim.[77]

When Muslim merchants or scholars traveled to Europe, they bought kosher meat. Muhammad al-Hajawi traveled to England in 1919 to visit merchants who had once done business with his father. But he could not find *hallal* meat, for few (if any) Muslim butchers were working in England. One merchant he encountered ate only meat slaughtered by Jews, refusing to eat meat slaughtered by Christians. This merchant, like al-Hajawi, was a native of Fez, so he had grown up alongside a large Jewish community; in 1879, one local rabbi counted 5,844 Jews in Fez.[78] Clearly, experiences in his hometown influenced this merchant's personal interpretation of Islam, for, when overseas, he frequented only Jewish butcher shops. Al-Hajawi felt that Christians and Jews were both "people of the book" and that he could eat meat slaughtered by either of them. By that time, al-Hajawi was overseeing the training of all of Morocco's religious scholars, so his opinion was irrefutable. Nevertheless, the merchant, fearing for his spiritual well-being, continued to eat only kosher meat while stationed in England.[79]

Muslim consumers also chose to frequent Jewish butcher shops in Moroccan cities. In Marrakesh, for example, Muslims purchased meat from a Jewish butcher who illegally slaughtered female livestock in 1879, the beginning of the Great Famine. The sister of this Jewish butcher, possibly a seamstress, was a frequent

visitor to the home of the city's Muslim magistrate. Counting on this royal official's protection, the Jewish butcher ignored the prohibition on female slaughter.
When the *muhtasib* learned of his criminal act, he reminded Marrakesh's rabbis
of the royal edict. After meeting with them, however, the *muhtasib* concluded that
the butcher's family, not a shohet, had slaughtered a cow that day in the mellah. If
that was the case, the meat would have been proscribed for both Jews and Muslims because it had not been slaughtered according to religious rites.

The disruption of the market during the Great Famine suggests that many
Muslims sought low prices and not high-quality *hallal* meat. As the *muhtasib* recounted, the Jewish butcher who slaughtered cows "did not sell meat according
to the fixed prices." He did not say that the butcher undercut competitors, but,
since this scofflaw had nothing to gain by artificially inflating the price of inferior meat, this must have been his meaning. The Jewish butcher slaughtered a
cow, not a ewe, which provides five times less meat than cows, so it seems that he
was counting on attracting a lot of customers. However, the *muhtasib* raided his
shop and shut it down. Afterward, the city's magistrate complained that he had
usurped his authority to implement law in the mellah. The *muhtasib* acknowledged
the city magistrate's jurisdiction, but he believed in this instance that it would
have slowed down his work, which involved preserving stability in urban markets, especially, as he himself admitted, in the Muslim quarters. For this reason, it
seems that the Jewish butcher, who was selling meat for less than the prices fixed
by the *muhtasib,* had stolen the customers of his law-abiding Muslim competitors.
Otherwise, the *muhtasib* would not have provoked the ire of the city's magistrate
by raiding a shop where his jurisdiction was in question.[80]

The strategy of slaughtering female animals appealed to other Jewish butchers in Marrakesh. Two years later, even though the prohibition on slaughtering
female animals was still in place, two Jewish butchers slaughtered cows. In this
instance, the butchers were protégés. Operating beyond the sultan's jurisdiction, they did not need to adhere to set prices or pay royal taxes. Once again,
Marrakesh's *muhtasib* found that butchers engaging in the illegal slaughter of female animals were selling meat "without [adhering to] the established price."
As a result, he stated, the butchers had "undermined the buying and selling of
their colleagues in the aforementioned trade." The *muhtasib* expressed concern for
law-abiding butchers, who, he worried, might be tempted to engage in a similar
strategy. Given these concerns, it is clear that butchers tried to lower prices by
selling inferior meat. In this way, they could expand their clientele, which, in
turn, would increase their income.[81]

In the 1880s, Jewish butchers in Meknes also tried to escape the sultan's authority as exercised by the *muhtasib,* Muhammad b. al-ʿArabi Ajana. There, Ajana's
authority irked many shopkeepers in the mellah, who argued that the *muhta-*

sib should not set prices for them as he did for the Muslim majority.[82] At that time, sixteen Jewish butchers worked in Meknes as well as forty-nine Muslim butchers.[83] In slaughtering cows, Jewish butchers Samuel Ben Harush and Yaʿqub Ohana deliberately resisted state interference in their commercial activities. Ajana found two cows slaughtered in Ohana's home. Because the shohet works at a designated site of slaughter, it seems possible that these butchers had not performed the ritual slaughter required to render their meat kosher. These Jews wanted commercial freedom. When called before the *muhtasib,* they insulted him and stated that they feared no one.[84]

Muslim butchers also schemed to decrease prices by slaughtering females. In Fez, for example, most Muslim butchers were managing to avoid the sultan's edict by 1890. The winter of 1889–1890 had been unusually cold and dry, causing a high mortality rate among Moroccan herds. The spring did not bring relief to the peasants, for swarms of locusts struck Fez's hinterland in March.[85] Many peasants must have brought cows to Suq al-Khamis so they could sell the animals before they died of starvation. The ban on female slaughter was still in place, so butchers needed authorization to leave the market with a cow. In this way, royal officials could verify that it was no longer capable of bearing young. According to the pasha Bushta b. al-Baghdadi, the official in Suq al-Khamis charged with verifying that an animal was no longer fertile was accepting money in exchange for proper documentation, no matter what the animal's condition. Al-Baghdadi did not use the word "bribe," but it is clear that he felt that the legality of this payment was dubious. Butchers—and some private residents preparing *khaliʿa*— offered this official a nominal fee of one riyal. Most butchers must have slaughtered female animals, for al-Baghdadi ordered their *ʿarif* to stop his colleagues from engaging in the illegal practice.[86]

Consistent efforts to violate the sultan's edict suggest that butchers calculated on earning sizable profits when they provided inferior-quality meat to local consumers. Because of the persistence of the drought, Mawlay ʿAbd al-ʿAziz continued his father's prohibition on slaughtering female animals, and protégés continued to use their special status to avoid this inconvenient regulation. In 1896, a royal official in Fez complained that a Muslim protégé named Ahmad Boussef offered his protected status to other butchers, thus permitting them to slaughter cows. That year, drought decimated Moroccan herds to an extent not seen since 1879.[87] Once again, peasants must have been anxious to sell off their livestock, while the sultan, in his turn, banned female slaughter in order to preserve the kingdom's herds. In Fez, the butchers could purchase female animals, which Bussif, who was outside the sultan's jurisdiction, could then claim as his own. The butchers' efforts to slaughter female animals drew the attention—and the censure—of the highest officials in the kingdom. The *muhtasib* complained of the business dealings of Bussif to Muhammad al-Tarris, who dealt with foreign consuls in Tangier. Al-Tarris, in turn, asked Bussif to write directly to the sultan highlighting the importance of this issue.[88]

Conclusion

Moroccan meat markets consistently preoccupied the makhzan as well as its subjects, whether they were Muslim or Jewish and whether they were producers or consumers of meat. From the purchase of animals to the dressing of meat, the sultan and his officials made sure that the kingdom's butchers organized their work according to religious codes. The practical concerns of butchers and their clients, however, hinged on other issues. Ordinary Moroccans wanted to eat more meat, while butchers hoped to earn more money. Meat played a secondary role in household budgets, so both Jewish and Muslim butchers pursued the same commercial strategies: they tried to cut the price of their commodity by evading taxes and slaughtering females. By offering protected status to Moroccans, Europeans often facilitated these commercial schemes, thereby fracturing established relations between the sultan and his Jewish and Muslim subjects. In this way, butchers increased their meat sales and their profits. If a Jewish butcher, perhaps a protégé who was exempt from the taxes of both the makhzan and the exacting Jewish Council, undercut competitors, then Muslim consumers purchased his meat. For buyer and seller, economic concerns outweighed considerations of religious identity. Moroccan meat markets theoretically define the separation between the Muslim majority and the Jewish minority, but in precolonial Morocco, they instead highlighted the intensity of interfaith interaction.

NOTES

1. For correspondence relating to this incident, see M. Elmaleh's report in *Bulletin de l'Alliance Israélite Universelle* (1909): 64. For four other letters, see Archives Diplomatiques de Nantes (ADN), Tanger, Serie A, 830.

2. For attacks against Jews in 1880, see British Parliament, *Correspondence Relative to the Conference Held at Madrid in 1880* (London: Government Printer, 1880). See also Ministère des affaires étrangères, *Documents diplomatiques: Question de la protection diplomatique et consulaire au Maroc* (Paris: Imprimerie Nationale, 1880). For attacks in 1912, see Edmund Burke, *Prelude to Protectorate in Morocco: Precolonial Protest and Resistance, 1860–1912* (Chicago: University of Chicago Press, 1976), 183–187.

3. For kosher meat, see Rabbi Gersion Appel, *The Concise Code of Jewish Law* (New York: Yeshiva University Press, 1977), 231–258. For a treatise on slaughter within the canon of Malikite jurisprudence, see Ibn Jizzi, *Al-Qawanin al-fiqhiya* (14th century; reprint, Casablanca: Dar Ma'arifa, 2000), 156–166. For a modern handbook, see Abou Bakr Djaber al-Djazairi, *Le pre-*

cepte du Musulman, trans. Mohamed al-Hamoui (1964; reprint, Casablanca: Librairie Es-Salam al-Jadida, 2000), 385–391.

4. *Gurna* must originate from *giran,* indicating a camel's neck. In Morocco, camels were a regular part of the Muslim diet until the twentieth century. For a discussion of *giran* based on Ibn Mandhur, who, in the late thirteenth and early fourteenth century "fathered" the Arabic dictionary, see Yusuf Khayat and Nadim Marʿashli, eds., *Lisan al-ʿarab al-muhit,* vol. 1 (Beirut: Dar Lisan al-ʿArab, n.d.), 447–448.

5. My description of Sidi Abu Nafa's *gurna* is based on a visit to the site in July 2001.

6. For a description of this *gurna* dating to 1889, see Bibliothèque Générale et Archives (BGA), Rabat, 136, Register 24, *Hawalat ahbas Fas al-aʿliya.*

7. Henri de la Caisinière, *Les municipalités marocaines: Leur développement, leur législation* (Casablanca: Imprimerie Marocaine, 1924), 159.

8. Gabriel Dehors, "Le commerce de la viande à Tanger," in *Renseignements coloniaux et documents,* supplement to *L'Afrique Française,* no. 9 (September 1905): 355.

9. Jean-Louis Miège, *Le Maroc et l'Europe (1822–1894),* 4 vols. (Paris: Presses universitaires de France, 1961–63; Rabat: Editions la Porte, 1996), 4: 402.

10. Direction des Archives Royales (DAR), Rabat, Portuguese diplomat (signature illegible) to Muhammad al-Tarris, *khalifa* in Tangier, 9 Safar 1307 (5 October 1889). I would like to thank Susan Miller for informing me that Jewish and Muslim butchers had worked together prior to that time.

11. Roger Le Tourneau, *Fès avant le protectorat* (1949; reprint, Rabat: Editions la Porte, 1987), 153–159.

12. Ibid., 329.

13. Ibid., 103.

14. Oelil Makhluf, interview with author, 9 July 2001.

15. BGA, A1074, note pour les Services Municipaux, 4 January 1914.

16. Dehors, "Le commerce de la viande à Tanger," 356.

17. Haj Mohamed Sharqi "Al-Sabay," interview with author, 19 July 2001.

18. Dehors, "Le commerce de la viande à Tanger," 356.

19. Muhammad b. Jaʿfar b. Idris al-Kattani, *Salwat al-anfas wa-muhadathat al-akyas bi-man uqbir mina al-ʿulama' wa-l-sulaha bi-Fas,* vol. 2 (Fez: Royal Lithograph, 1314/1896–1897), 162.

20. Charles René-LeClerc, "Le commerce et l'industrie à Fès, troisième partie," in *Renseignements coloniaux et documents,* supplement to *L'Afrique Française,* no. 9 (September 1905): 347.

21. Driss Rabani, interview with author, 12 July 2002

22. BGA, A753, arreté municipal, 28 October 1912.

23. BGA, A753, arreté municipal, 10 September 1913.

24. Ahmed Sefrioui, *La boîte à merveilles* (1954; reprint, Paris: Omnibus, 1996), 1063.

25. ʿAmara b. ʿAbd al-Sadiq to Muhammad Bargash, 10 Shaʿban 1293 (1 August 1876), quoted in *al-Watha'iq, Mudiriya al-Watha'iq al-Malikiya,* no. 5 (Rabat: al-Matbaʿat al-Malikiya, 1981), 99–100.

26. M. al-Lahya, "Al-Hayat al-iqtisadiya bi-madinat Miknas fi al-qarn al-tasiʿ ʿashar, 1850–1912" (Ph.D. diss., Université Mohamed V, 1984), 162

27. Mawlay ʿAbd al-Rahman Ibn Zaydan, *Ithhaf aʿlam al-nas bi-jamal akhbar hadirat Miknas,* vol. 1 (1931; reprint, Casablanca: Imprimerie Idéale, 1990), 283. The French constructed a slaughterhouse and turned the mosque-cum-*gurna* into offices.

28. Le Tourneau, *Fès avant le Protectorat,* 329.

29. Edward Alexander Westermark, *Ritual and Belief in Morocco,* vol. 2 (1926; reprint, New York: University Books, 1968), 358.

30. Dehors, "Le commerce de la viande à Tanger," 356.

31. Hershey H. Friedman, "Ideal Occupations: The Talmudic Perspective," *Jewish Law Articles* (2001), available at *www.jlaw.com/Articles/idealoccupa.html* (accessed 24 April 2004).

32. Susan Miller, e-mail to author, 10 February 2003.

33. Ibn Jizzi, *Al-Qawanin al-fiqhiya,* 157.

34. Dehors, "Le commerce de la viande à Tanger," 356

35. DAR, notarized document dating to 7 Jumadi II 1297 (17 May 1880).

36. DAR, unidentified representative of butchers to president of Sanitary Council, n.d.

37. DAR, unidentified representative of butchers to al-ʿArabi Abrudi, *muhtasib* of Tangier, 24 Ramadan 1322 (12 February 1904).

38. DAR, J. Liaberia, Spanish diplomat and president of Sanitary Council, to Muhamed b. al-Hajj al-ʿArabi al-Tarris, *khalifa* of Tangier, 14 November 1906.

39. DAR, diplomat representing Austria-Hungary and president of Sanitary Council to Muhammad b. al-Hajj al-ʿArabi al-Tarris, 13 Rabiʿa I (7 May 1906).

40. BGA, A753, Arreté municipal, 5 February 1914.

41. Edmondo de Amicis, *Morocco: Its People and Places,* trans. C. Rollin-Tilton (1882; reprint, London: A. Wheaton & Co. Ltd., 1985), 277.

42. Appel, *The Concise Code of Jewish Law,* 239.

43. Charles René-LeClerc, "Le commerce et l'industrie à Fès, deuxième partie," in *Renseignements coloniaux et documents,* supplement to *L'Afrique Française,* no. 8 (August 1905): 309.

44. Ianthe Maclagan, "Food and Gender in a Yemeni Community," in *Culinary Cultures of the Middle East,* ed. Sami Zubaida and Richard Tapper (London and New York: I. B. Tauris Publishers, 1994), 159–172.

45. For another analysis of the relationship between the *muhtasib* and butchers in the premodern era, see Amnon Cohen, *Economic Life in Ottoman Jerusalem* (Cambridge and New York: Cambridge University Press, 1989), 11–60, passim.

46. Bibliothèque Royale (BR), Rabat, 12453/4, Abu al-ʿAbbas Ahmad b. Saʿid, *Al-Taysir fi ahkam al-tasʿir,* 11 Jumadi I 1316 (27 September 1898), Folio 57.

47. Ibid., Folio 52.

48. DAR, Ben Hayyim Ben Abu to Ahmad b. Musa (Ba Ahmad), Grand Vizir, 16 Qaʿda 1316 (28 March 1899).

49. DAR, Mawlay Ahmad b. ʿAbd al-Salam b. ʿAbdallah b. Sulayman to Muhammad al-Mufaddal Gharit, Grand Vizir, 23 Jumada I 1324 (15 July 1906).

50. Léon l'Africain, *Description de l'Afrique,* trans. Epaulard (16th century; reprint, Paris: n.p., 1956), 208, quoted in Abderrahim Benhadda and Laila Benkirane, "Nourritures," in *Fès médiévale,* ed. Mohamed Mezzine (Paris: Editions Autrement, 1992), 158.

51. Mohamed ben Cheneb, *Proverbes arabes de l'Algérie et du Maghreb,* vol. 1 (Paris: Ernest Leroux, 1905), 52.

52. Ibn Zaydan, *Ithhaf aʿlam al-nas,* 2:137

53. BGA, H128, Muhammad b. al-Hasan al-Hajawi, *Kunash bi-hi taqayid ʿilmiya wa-tarikhiya,* 24 Rabiʿa II 1328 (5 May 1910), 51.

54. Ibn Jizzi, *Al-Qawanin al-fiqhiya,* 157.

55. Mohammed Ben Cheneb, *Proverbes populaires de l'Algérie et du Maghreb* (1905; repr., Paris: Maisonneuve & Larose, 2003), 89–90.

56. Miège, *Le Maroc et l'Europe,* 3:383.

57. Ibid., 3:403.

58. Philip Durham Trotter, *Our Mission to the Court of Morocco in 1880, under Sir John Drummond Hay* (Edinburgh: D. Douglass, 1881), 78–79.

59. Nicolas Michel, *Une économie de subsistance: le Maroc précolonial,* vol. 2 (Cairo: Institut Français d'Archéologie Orientale, 1997), 531.

60. DAR, Muhammad b. al-ʿArabi to Saʿid ʿAbdallah b. Ahmad, pasha of Fez, 29 Jumada I 1297 (9 May 1880).

61. For a year-by-year account of weather and crops in Morocco in the nineteenth century, see Nicolas Michel, "Bonnes et Mauvaises Années," Annex in *Une économie de subsistance: le Maroc précolonial* (Cairo: Institut Français d'Archéologie Orientale, 1997), 605–654.

62. BR, Dossier 570, Mawlay al-Hajj al-ʿAlawi to Muffadal Gharit, 14 Rajab 1319 (27 October 1901).

63. Ben Cheneb, *Proverbes populaires du Maghreb*, 1:177–178.

64. DAR, Mawlay ʿAbd al-ʿAziz to Hajj Radi al-Tahar al-Harraq, *muhtasib* of Larache, 26 Jumada II 1320 (30 September 1903).

65. ʿAmara b. ʿAbd al-Sadiq, governor of Essaouira, to Muhammad Bargash, royal *khalifa* in Tangier,10 Shaʿban 1293 (1 August 1876), quoted in *Al-Watha'iq, Mudiriya al-Watha'iq al-Malikiya*, no. 5 (Rabat: al-Matbaʿat al-Malikiya, 1981), 99–100. See also DAR, Mawlay al-Hasan to Muhammad Bargash, 30 Jumada I 1295 (1 June 1878).

66. Miège, *Les difficultés*, 385–388.

67. ʿAmara b. ʿAbd al-Sadiq, governor of Essaouira, to Muhamad Bargash, royal *khalifa* in Tangier,10 Shaʿban 1293 (1 August 1876), quoted in *Al-Watha'iq*, no. 5, 99–100. See also DAR, Mawlay al-Hasan to Muhamad Bargash, 30 Jumada I 1295 (1 June 1878).

68. DAR, Dossier ʿAmara, ʿAmara b. ʿAbd Sadiq, governor of Essaouria, to Muhammad Bargash, royal *khalifa* in Tangier, 2 Jumada II 1296 (24 May 1879).

69. Dehors, "Le commerce de la viande à Tanger," 356.

70. L. Martin, "Lettre de Fès," *Revue du Monde Musulman* 6 (1908): 713–715.

71. Massimo Montanari, *The Culture of Food*, trans. Carl Ipsen (Cambridge, Mass.: Basil Blackwell Inc., 1994).

72. DAR, Muhammad b. al-ʿArabi al-Tarris, *khalifa* in Tangiers, to Hamu b. al-Gillani, pasha of Meknes, 27 Jumada II 1312 (26 December 1894).

73. A *ratl* is about half a kilogram.

74. Al-Lahya, "al-Hayat al-iqtisadiya," 247.

75. Ibn Jizzi, *Al-Qawanin al-fiqhiya*, 163

76. Ibid., 156–157.

77. BR, folio 56, 12453/4, Abu al-ʿAbbas Ahmad b. Saʿid, *Al-Taysir fi ahkam al-tasʿir*, 11 Jumadi I 1316 (27 September 1898).

78. Y. D. Sémach, "Une chronique juive de Fès: Le 'Yahas Fès' de Ribbi Abner Hassarfaty," *Hespéris* 19 (1934): 87–91.

79. Muhammad Ibn al-Hasan al-Hajwi, *Voyage d'Europe: Le périple d'un Réformiste*, trans. Alain Roussillon and Abdellah Saâf (Casablanca: Afrique Orient, 2001), 124.

80. DAR, ʿAbdallah b. Ibrahim al-Bukili, *muhtasib* of Marrakesh, to Mawlay al-Hasan, 17 Muharam 1297 (31 December 1879), DAR; Mawlay al-Hasan to Mawlay ʿAbdallah b. Ibrahim al-Bukili, 7 Safar 1297 (20 January 1880).

81. DAR, Mawlay ʿAbdallah Bukili to Mawlay al-Hasan, 23 Rabiʿa I 1298 (23 February 1881.

82. al-Lahya, "al-Hayat al-iqtisadiya," 143.

83. Ibid., 162.

84. Ibid., 260.

85. Michel, *Une économie de subsistance*, 2:634.

86. DAR, Bushta b. al-Baghdadi to Mawlay al-Hasan, 25 Shawal 1307 (14 June 1890).

87. C. R. Pennell, *Morocco since 1830: A History* (New York: New York University Press, 2000), 116.

88. BR, Dossier 211, Ahmad b. Muhammad Abu Da'udi to Ahmad b. Musa (Ba Ahmad), 30 Safar 1314 (9 August 1896).

11

A Moment in Sephardi History

The Reestablishment of the Jewish Community of Oran, 1792–1831

SADDEK BENKADA

TRANSLATED BY ALLAN MACVICAR

O N 27 FEBRUARY 1792, the Algerian regency reconquered Oran and took it from the Spanish for the second time, an unprecedented event for that era and one that was closely related to the extraordinary figure of the bey, Muhammad al-Kabir. The bey's experience was unique in the Ottoman era in Algeria. His was not any ordinary military victory; rather, the war against the Spanish was undertaken under the banner of jihad, making it clearly religious in nature. It could be said that his was a countercrusade.

Despite the religious overtones of the victory, the eighteenth- and nineteenth-century Algerian historians/scribes who acted as Muhammad al-Kabir's chroniclers make virtually no mention of the bey's relationship to the non-Muslims with whom he was engaged, namely the Jewish communities in the main cities of the western *beylik* (Beylik al-Gharb), including Tlemcen, Nedroma, Mostaganem, Mascara, Mazouna, and Oran. As a result, our principal sources regarding the situation of the Jewish community in Oran after the Spanish withdrawal from the city in 1792 come entirely from historians of the colonial period, from the writings of local historians, and from traveling Jewish historians who were particularly interested in the history of the Jewish community of Oran during this time.[1]

The Oranian Jewish Community under Muslim Dynasties

Because of Oran's proximity to the Iberian Peninsula, it was long a preferred destination for Jewish refugees and exiles fleeing that region. It is highly likely that some of the Jews fleeing persecutions by Sisebot, king of the Goths, in 612–

613 landed on the North African coast and intermixed with the indigenous population, including the Azdaja and Ajissa Berber tribes of the Maghrawa confederation who lived in the area that would eventually become the city of Oran in 903. In any event, from the Islamic period onward, a native Jewish community clearly existed in Oran and was economically active. This community was less known for its intellectual activity than that of the western Algerian town of Tlemcen, where several rabbinical schools were founded in the tenth century. Talmudic studies experienced a period of significant expansion in the eleventh century, though this period of stability and development among Jewish communities in the main cities of the central Maghrib was soon followed by persecution at the hands of the Almohads beginning in 1132.

Persecution of the Jews in Tlemcen and Oran began in 1145. Oranian Jews were subject to relatively greater violence, perhaps because the Almoravid garrison, supported by the local population, fiercely resisted the Almohad siege of the city by ʿAbd al-Muʾmin b. ʿAli for a lengthy period of time. As was the case everywhere, those Jews who had somehow miraculously survived the massacre were faced with the choice of emigrating or converting to Islam.[2]

Once Almohad rule was established, however, Oran enjoyed a period of prosperity. ʿAbd al-Muʾmin constructed shipyards where he built approximately thirty vessels so he could maintain his connection to Andalusia, which he had just conquered and with which he had developed intimate commercial ties. The port quickly became one of the four main ports of the empire, along with Ceuta, Bejaïa, and Tunis. Oran became the central port of the Maghrib and the one most visited on a regular basis by European merchant ships from Barcelona, Marseille, and several Italian cities.

The return to a certain measure of political stability as well as the development of commercial exchanges with Christian nations made the presence of Jews in Oran all the more necessary. Economic and intellectual ties between Andalusian Jews and their counterparts in Oran were strengthened during the Almohad period, to the extent that after the horrific massacres of the Jewish communities in Castile in 1391, Oran became one of the destinations for Jewish refugees fleeing Spain. The demographic, economic, and intellectual importance of numerous Jewish communities in central North African cities was established at this time. The arrival of the *megorashim* (those who had been exiled from Spain) ensured that Algiers would become one of the principal centers of Judaism in North Africa, and the reconstitution of the Jewish community in Tlemcen in particular was made possible by the arrival of certain eminent rabbis from Spain.[3]

A century later, in 1492, the tragedy was repeated, but this time on a larger scale. A few months after the fall of the Grenada, the Spanish rulers signed the grievous edict ordering the expulsion of all Jews. Eventually both Jewish and Muslim Andalusians left for the shores of Africa (and farther east), where they were generally well received. The *toshavim* (native Jewish) communities, already fortified by the immigration of 1391, were revived by a significant supply "of men who were more evolved and better suited for the discipline of the mind."[4] The reinforcement of the Jewish community of Oran by successive waves of Andalusian immigrants brought about a period of prosperity and relative stability that lasted until the Spanish occupation of Oran in 1509.

The Expulsion of the Jews from Oran (1669)

Following the fall of Grenada in 1492, the Catholic monarchs of Spain planned to extend the *reconquista* to the Maghrib. Spain occupied Melilla in 1496, and Oran became the cornerstone of the *reconquista* strategy, first because of its proximity to the Spanish coast (weather permitting, the trip from Mers-el-Kebir to Almería could be made in less than a day) and second because of the ongoing maritime incursions by Oranian corsairs. On 13 September 1505, after a three-day siege, the Spanish seized control of the fortress at Mers-el-Kebir. A second expedition led by the cardinal Ximinés de Cisneros, archbishop of Toledo, ended with the occupation of Oran on 19 May 1509. Less than twenty years after the 1492 decree to expel all Jews, the cardinal's first act was to authorize the first Jewish families to settle in a city under the authority of the king of Spain. Jews were even permitted to establish a Jewish quarter (Juderia) and were recognized as Jewish vassals of the king. These were the origins of a genuine Jewish community.[5] Indeed, certain Oranian Jewish families developed and prospered in the shadow of the Spanish crown, such as the Cansinos, the Sasportas, the Maques, the El-Haïks, the Ballesteros, the Molhos, and the Navarros.[6]

During those 170 years, however, the king never actually guaranteed the safety of the Jews under his authority in Oran by issuing a decree of tolerance. The Jews' presence was only made possible by a reprieve in the persecutions in recognition of their usefulness to the Spanish possessions in North Africa. Amid rising interreligious tensions in the Mediterranean world in the latter half of the seventeenth century, the Spanish decided that expelling the Jews would in fact strengthen their position in the Maghrib. Thus, the reprieve from persecution ended on a fateful day in April 1669, when Queen Marie-Anne of Austria, widow of Philippe IV, signed a decree expelling the entire Jewish community of Oran, regardless of age, sex, or social status. In short, this was a kind of "final solution," as J. F. Schaub appropriately notes; "the Jewish presence in the city would be erased like a hidden vice to be forgotten forever."[7]

The Jewish Component of Bey Muhammad al-Kabir's Repopulation Policy

It is difficult to understand the development of Oran from 1792 on without taking into account Bey Muhammad al-Kabir's repopulation policy. The essential characteristics of this policy emerged well before the evacuation of Oran by the Spanish. The first steps were actually taken at the time of the siege of Oran (1788–1792) and involved maintaining the existing population outside the city and encouraging the establishment of new communities once the Spanish left.

Bey Muhammad al-Kabir was determined to look after the well-being of the Jews under his authority. His attitude greatly influenced the decisions of Jewish exiles to heed the call for Jews everywhere to come and live in Oran. The bey's first action after gaining possession of the city was to appeal to all social classes from other Algerian cities to repopulate Oran. Even though the call was apparently made to all people, regardless of social class, it seems that certain socio-professional categories were particularly sought after. These included craftsmen, merchants, and the educated, all recruited from among the townsfolk (*hadars*). In essence, the middle class was called upon to reinvigorate the city with their craftwork and their commercial and intellectual activity. It should also be noted that along with the Algerian *hadars*, Jews were among the first to be asked to settle in the city. Judging by the fact that the city was repopulated relatively quickly, apparently large segments of both the Muslim and Jewish populations of other cities responded to the bey's appeal.[8]

Among the first communities to respond favorably were the Jews from the cities of the western *beylik*. However, accounts differ concerning Jewish settlement in Oran in 1792, guided in part by the collective Jewish memory of the city. In the 1920s, the French military officer Gaston Pellecat was able to obtain a first-hand account from a Jew from Oran who was "descended from an old family originally from Tlemcen, which came to Oran during the time of Bey Muhammad al-Kabir." According to this account, "a Muslim delegation came to the bey and explained to him the need for Jews to come to Oran, as they had in Mostaganem, Tlemcen, and Mascara."[9] According to this same source, this request was apparently "well received by the bey who wrote to the *dayanim* [rabbinical judges] of all the cities to ask them to send Jewish families who would assist in the rapid repopulation of Oran and practice their trade or industry." Pellecat adds: "The bey required these delegates to promise beforehand that they were to respect the Jewish families that would settle among them, and who were somewhat fearful of this cohabitation among Muslims." Once assured of the protection of the bey, "the Jews flocked to Oran, primarily those who were close relatives of the *dayanim*."[10]

Characteristics of the New Jewish Community of Oran

Paradoxically, it is clear that in spite of the involvement of various groups in the repopulation of Oran, we are by far best informed about the Jews. The historical data indicates the geographical origin of Jewish immigrants to Oran, but also, and perhaps more importantly, it gives the key names of the first families to participate in the reconstitution of the Jewish community of Oran in 1792.[11] Due to Bey Muhammad al-Kabir's policy of protection and benevolence, Oran became an important and attractive center for the Jews of the time. Like the Muslims, the first group of Jews to settle in Oran came from Mascara. The Jewish community of Mascara, to whom Bey Muhammad al-Kabir showed great kindness, was one of the largest in the Oran region, after those of Tlemcen and Mostaganem.[12]

Leading the Mascaran Jewish settlers was the Darmon family, whose head, Mordechai Darmon, had been the rabbi of the Jewish community of Mascara as well as the official representative of Bey Muhammad al-Kabir there. As such, he was among the most intimate of the bey's entourage.[13] This family was almost immediately followed by families from other Algerian cities: the Shaloms and the Lascars from Miliana; the Abudarhans, the Bacris, the Bendahans, the Benichous, the Benamars, and the Benzaguens from Tlemcen, Nedroma, and Algiers;[14] and the Toledanos and the Masias, who were probably of Hispanic origin, as can be surmised from their names.[15]

An important contemporaneous event, but one that is rarely connected with the repopulation of Oran, was the extensive persecution of the Jews in Moroccan port cities. Most notable was the pillage of the mellah of Tetuan, which occurred after the death of the Moroccan sultan Sidi Muhammad b. ʿAbdallah in 1790. The installation of a new Moroccan ruler, Mawlay al-Yazid,[16] and the events that followed from 1790 to 1792 were apparently the reason that a large number of Jews left the country and took refuge in the Regency of Algiers. Tlemcen was the first stopping place, and many settled there in 1790, while the rest headed for other cities. Then, starting in 1792, Oran became a preferred destination for Moroccan Jews, who contributed a great deal to the reconstitution of the new Jewish community there. The Cabezas, who were of Hispano-Moroccan origin,[17] are but one example of this. Finally, along with the contingent of Moroccan Jews, Gibraltar also supplied a significant number of immigrants, made up primarily of the Tarueils, the Serruchas, the Benserias, the Benoliels, the Angels, the Gabissons, and the Tubianas.[18]

Muhammad al-Kabir had a twofold vision for Oran. First, he wanted to make the city a significant commercial port, and second, he sought to implement economic reforms. He planned to create both a cannon factory and a soap factory with the assistance of Spanish industrialists, which makes it easier to understand how collaboration with the Jews of Gibraltar, acting as intermediaries, could facilitate and help develop commercial relationships with other Mediterranean ports.[19]

The beys of Oran had private agents in Gibraltar, such as Aron Cardoso, the head of the Jewish "nation" there, and Salomon Pacifico. Although the English and French consular agents remained in contact with the Jews of Gibraltar who had settled in Oran, David Duran, head of the Jewish community in Gibraltar and consul general for the Republic of Ragusa, actively sought commercial ties with Oran. Beginning in 1832, these commercial dealings with Gibraltar by means of Jewish agents increased significantly when the *amir* ʿAbd al-Qadir fought the French in a war of resistance. His delegate at Fez, al-Hajj al-Talib b. Jallun, dealt with the merchants of Gibraltar through Ben Abby, a Jewish intermediary who was the chargé d'affaires of the sultan of Morocco. Many Jews also served the Algerian *amir* as consular agents, merchants, interpreters, and so forth, including Mordechai Amar and Judas Ben Duran (the famous "Bendran," as he was referred to in the literature of the time). A group of Oranian Jewish merchants that included Busnach (son of the associate of Bacri), Lasry, Podesta, Judas Sabah, and Makhluf Benaïm was protected by the *amir*. This group set up a firm to perform transactions between Gibraltar and the Algerian port of Rachgoun. It is most likely the extent of the Moroccan involvement and to a lesser degree the Hispanic contribution that led Nahum Slouschz to believe that Moroccan Jewish refugees were the exclusive source of the reconstitution of the communities of Tlemcen and Oran.[20]

It seems clear, however, that the melting pot that Oran became was brought about by an extraordinary fusion of elements, producing a new *qehilla* (Heb. "community") that in turn produced new Oranais families, such as the Darmons, the Karsentys, the Kanouis, the Farouzes, the Sananes, the Medionis, the Chouraquis, and the Parientés. The Oranian *qehilla* revered Judah Moatti, who died in Oran in 1826, as its patron saint.[21]

The Establishment of the Jewish Community

The "Ville-Neuve," founded by Bey Muhammad al-Kabir in 1792 on the right side of the Oued Ras-el-Aïn following the destruction of the Spanish city by the earthquake of 1790,[22] was not originally intended for the Jewish community exclusively. However, incidents that occurred after the first Jewish families settled in the old city caused the heads of certain families to ask the bey for their own quarter. Pellecat says that "the Jews went to see the bey, and essentially said: On the crest of the side of the Ras-el-Aïn ravine, there is a small, uninhabited plateau where we would do well and be at home. Please allow us to settle there."[23]

Bey Muhammad al-Kabir quickly responded to their request by choosing a site within the Ville-Neuve for the new Jewish quarter.

The vast piece of land designated for the creation of this quarter was sold to the Jewish community for the sum of 820 sultanis of Algiers.[24] This is how the Derb El Houd (darb al-Yahud, or street of the Jews) of Oran came into being.[25] According to Darmon, this land was marshy, which he claims indicated Bey Muhammad al-Kabir's contempt for the Jews.[26] Another Jewish observer, who seems more impartial in his observations than his Algerian compatriot (perhaps because he was from France), states that "the Jewish community held the favor of Bey Muhammad al-Kabir to a significant degree. This is demonstrated by the fact that they bought, at a very low price, the best-situated location within the city limits to build their quarter. The main street was given and still bears the name of Derb El Houd (street of the Jews)."[27] The original center of Derb El Houd was situated in the block bordered by the present-day rue de Ratisbonne, rue d'Austerlitz, and the adjacent streets. The first synagogue Mordechai Darmon built was located on rue de Ratisbonne.[28] On the same occasion, Bey Muhammad al-Kabir granted them free of charge another plot of land larger than three hectares outside the city for a cemetery.[29]

Until the death of the bey in 1799, however, the sale of the land and the granting of the cemetery remained a verbal agreement. His son and successor, Bey 'Usman, made the sale of the land and the granting of the cemetery official when he confirmed it in writing in front of both Muslim and Jewish witnesses, no doubt at the insistence of the Jewish community. As Isaac Bloch stresses, this document "is the true constitutional act of the community."[30]

In 1846, in order to conform with the new colonial legislation governing matters of property, Messaoud Darmon, chief rabbi of Oran, and Makhlouf Kalfon, his assistant, had the deed regarding the settlement translated by David Duran, a legal translator, and gave it to Mr. François Sauzède, a notary in Oran, for his consideration. This deed contained other clauses related to the Jewish neighborhood and was signed by religious leaders and the notary. Since then, the deed has belonged to the Jewish community of Oran.[31]

Conclusion

In 1792, after an absence of more than three centuries, Jewish communities that had been banned by the Spanish government and Muslims learned again how to live together as they had in the past. It goes without saying that for the Jewish community of Oran, the period from 1792 to 1831 is among the most important in its lengthy history on Algerian soil, because it was during this time that the community was reconstituted. As chance would have it, the rebirth of

Jewish culture and religion in this part of the Maghrib was contemporaneous with the great political upheaval taking place during the French Revolution, which had a profound impact on the emancipation of the Jews of France and eventually on Jews worldwide.

Moreover, Oran has continually revived its tradition of being a refuge for Hispanic Jews. It became the place where the Judeo-Hispanic language and culture were preserved after the arrival en masse of Jews from Tetuan in 1859–1860. This group formed the well-known Tetuani identity that distinguished all aspects of Jewish culture in colonial Oran, including language, cuisine, music, and literature. Eventually, many of these Oranian Jews took this identity with them as they settled in Brazil and other Latin American countries.

NOTES

1. See, in particular, Isaac Bloch, "Les Israélites d'Oran de 1792 à 1815, d'après des documents inédits," *Revue des Études Juives* 13 (1886): 85–104; and Daniel Lévy, "Souvenirs de l'Algérie: les Israélites d'Oran avant la conquête," *Archives Israélites* 20 (1859): 384–394, 464–468, 702–708.

2. André Chouraqui, *Les Juifs d'Afrique du Nord* (Paris: Presses universitaires de France, 1952), 60–61; H. Z. Hirschberg, *A History of the Jews in North Africa*, vol. 1, *From Antiquity to the Sixteenth Century* (Leiden: Brill, 1974), 118–119.

3. The eminent rabbis that emigrated to Tlemcen in 1391 included, among others, Isaac Ben Sheshet Barfat, called Ribach (1326–1408), and Simon Ben Semah Duran (1361–1442). Isaac Rouche, "Un grand rabbin à Tlemcen au XVe siècle," *Bulletin de la Société de Géographie et d'Archéologie d'Oran* 64 (1943): 43–72; Isadore Epstein, *The Responsa of Rabbi Simon B. Zemah Duran as a Source of the History of the Jews in North Africa* (London: Oxford University Press, H. Milford, 1930).

4. Chouraqui, *Les Juifs d'Afrique du Nord*, 66.

5. Regarding the development and eventual expulsion of the Jews of Oran under the Spanish, see Jean-Frédéric Schaub, *Les Juifs du roi d'Espagne: Oran 1509–1669* (Paris: Hachettes Littératures, 1999); Juan A. Sanchez Belen, "La expulsion de los Judíos de Orán en 1669," *Espacio, Tiempo, Forma*, serie 4, *Historia Moderna* 6 (1993): 155–198; Jonathan I. Israel, "The Jews of Spanish Oran and Their Expulsion in 1669," *Mediterranean Historical Review* 9 (1994): 235–255. For contemporary documentation of the expulsion of 1669, see Luis Joseph de Sotomayor y Valenzuela, *Brève relation de l'expulsion des Juifs d'Oran en 1669*, translation, presentation, and notes by J.-F. Shaub (Saint-Denis: Éditions Bouchène, 1998).

6. Schaub, *Les Juifs du roi d'Espagne*, 39.

7. Ibid., 7.

8. See Edouard Lapène, *Tableau historique de la province d'Oran depuis le depart des Espagnols, en 1791, jusqu'à l'élévation d'Abdelkader en 1831* (Metz: S. Lamort, 1842); and Ch. de Rotalier, *Histoire d'Alger et de la piraterie des Turcs dans la Méditerranée à dater du seizième siècle* (Paris: Paulin, 1841).

9. Société de Géographie et d'Archéologie d'Oran, archives of Commandant Gaston Pellecat, "Notes relatives à l'histoire du quartier israélite d'Oran," 1928.

10. Ibid.

11. For a primary source, see Bloch, "Les Israélites d'Oran."

12. Regarding the history of the Jewish community of Mostaganem, see the well-documented work of Norbert Bel-Ange: *Les Juifs de Mostaganem* (Paris: L'Harmattan, 1990).

13. Bloch, "Les Israélites d'Oran."

14. Lévy, "Souvenirs de l'Algérie."

15. René Lespes, "Oran, ville et port avant l'occupation française," *Revue Africaine* 75 (1934): 329.

16. Jacques Taïeb, *Être juif au Maghreb à la veille de la colonization* (Paris: Albin Michel, Présence du judaïsme, 1994), 24. On events during the reign of Mawlay al-Yazid, see Daniel J. Schroeter, *The Sultan's Jew: Morocco and the Sephardi World* (Stanford, Calif.: Stanford University Press, 2002), 26–29.

17. Lespes, "Oran, ville et port avant l'occupation française," 329.

18. Juan-Bautista Vilar, "Los Judios de Argel, Orán y Gibraltar, intermedarios del tráfico hispano-argelino entre 1791 y 1830: El asunto Bacri," *Miscelánea de Estudios Arabes y Hebráicos* 24, no. 2 (1975): 67–73.

19. Tayeb Chentouf, "Deux tentatives économiques du bey Mohamed El Kébir à la fin du XVIIIᵉ siècle en Algérie," *Cahiers de Tunisie* 29, nos. 3–4 (1981): 159–175.

20. Nahum Slousch, "La colonie des Maghrabim en Palestine," *Archives Marocaines* 2 (1904): 230–231.

21. "Mi-Kamokha," Hebrew poem in rhyme, written by the *dayan* of Oran, the revered Rabbi Messaoud Darmon, who died in 1866. Published in Oujda by Imprimerie Haloua in 5711/1951. For a translation, see Robert Attal, *Regards sur les Juifs d'Algérie* (Paris: L'Harmattan, 1996), 52–59.

22. Saddek Benkada, "Espace urbain et structures sociales à Oran de 1792 à 1831" (Dipôme d'études approfondies thesis, Université d'Oran, 1988)

23. Pellecat, "Notes relatives à l'histoire du quartier israélite d'Oran."

24. Bloch, "Les Israélites d'Oran."

25. In my opinion, the term "Derb-el-Houd," given to the Jewish quarter of Oran, originated in the history of the Jewish community in Tlemcen. It was then extended to include all Jewish neighborhoods in large cities in western Algeria. This was like the word "mellah," which originated in Fez and was applied to all Jewish quarters in Morocco. See Benkada, "Espace urbain et structures sociales à Oran." Touching on the question of "Darb el Houd" in 1950, André Chouraqui writes, "In Oran, the 'Jewish neighborhood' surrounds Maréchal Foch Square and Boulevard de la Révolution. The 'street of the Jews' is a hardly improved version of the spectacle of the Moroccan *mellahs*. It was from these same *mellahs* that a large segment of the population originated." Chouraqui, *Les Juifs d'Afrique du Nord*, 181.

26. Amram Darmon, "Origine et constitution de la communauté israélite de Tlemcen," *Revue Africaine* 14 (1870): 376–383.

27. Lévy, "Souvenirs de l'Algérie," 392.

28. Darmon, *Mi-Kamokha.*

29. Société de Géographie et d'Archéologie d'Oran, Archives of Commandant Gaston Pellecat, dossier "Cimetière juif."

30. "Acte de vente concernant les terrains servant d'assiette à l'établissement du quartier israélite (Derb el Houd). Écrit en arabe et date de 1801," reprinted in Bloch, "Les Israélites d'Oran," 85–104. Until 1962, the original of this document was kept in the archives of the Jewish Consistory of Oran. Presently, it is kept in the Jewish Consistory of Paris.

31. Société de Géographie et d'Archéologie d'Oran, Archives of Commandant Gaston Pellecat, dossier "Cimetière juif."

12

Crosscurrents

Trajectories of Algerian Jewish Artists and Men of Culture since the End of the Nineteenth Century

Hadj Miliani

Translated by Allan MacVicar

Introduction

This chapter focuses on several Algerian Jewish artists and cultural entrepreneurs who have not only influenced aesthetic evolutions but have originated artistic and cultural trends. The goal of this research is to reveal the role Jews played in the evolution of a common artistic heritage in North Africa and to demonstrate how artistic bridges can be built at the crossroads of three monotheistic religions of the Mediterranean in an effort to create a place for cultural sensitivity that is in step with modernity.

The approach used here emphasizes the dual program of conservation and innovation that Algerian Jewish musicians and singers have followed in North African music since the end of the nineteenth century. I trace the career of Edmond Nathan Yafil, who worked to rehabilitate and conserve Arabo-Andalusian music at the beginning of the twentieth century, and recount the tragic fate of Saoud Medioni to show how these artists, along with others, served as cultural mediators in a North African multicultural society deeply traumatized by colonization.

Despite the colorful Mediterranean friendliness and joie de vivre, this account is not a classic success story. Instead, it follows the social and political meanderings of a region, the Maghrib, that was permanently in a state of upheaval, and a country, France, that often fell prey to the worst of demons. Yet the story cannot be reduced to the sum of its parts, for it also demonstrates the power of individuality and subjectivity in an incredibly communitarian and holistic space.

Besides musicians and singers (Yafil, Mouzion, Saoud Medioni, Reinette, Ell Hallali, Raymond Leiris, Line Monty, Alice Fitoussi, Lili Labassi, Blond Blond, and others), I will also consider a few cultural entrepreneurs, such as record producers, managers, and show organizers. In my reexamination of several of the paths that they followed, I will combine general analysis with a more pointed assessment in order to reconstruct the sociopolitical context; this will enable me to analyze the part the Jewish community of Algeria played in the crosscurrents that lie at the foundation of what is today called multiculturalism.

A Cultural Tradition in Division

Between the end of the nineteenth and the first half of the twentieth century, many Jewish Algerian artists and entrepreneurs made their marks on the cultural landscape of the largest French colony. Writers and musicians established a pluralistic cultural space that highlighted both the local substrate (language, rhythms, traditions, rituals) and new perspectives on cultural creation that were emerging in Europe. Today, when the Jewish community has all but disappeared from the Algerian social and cultural landscape, it is these figures above all who live in collective memory in Algeria.

In 1861, when Alexandre Christanowitsch looked for Arabo-Andalusian musical performers in Algiers, he met only a few Jewish and Muslim musicians. He wrote, "Having learned that Arab music cafés existed in Algiers, I went one night to one of them on Citati Street. In these cafés Arabs and Moors would gather for coffee, while two or three Jews would play traditional songs, one playing the *rebab,* the second the *kemanche,* and the third the *tar* or the *darbuka.*"[1] The practitioners were in fact very numerous, but the number of venues for playing and performing was considerably smaller; it existed mainly in the form of very intimate exchanges at the heart of the Muslim population. Certain Jews were considered to be among the best players of this traditional folk music during the second half of the nineteenth century. Yossef Eni-Bel Kharraïa, Maqchiech (who died in 1899), and *muᶜallim* (master) Ben Farrachou (1833–1904), for example, had a decisive influence on the preservation and popularization of this music. Moreover, classical North African music owes its survival to the industriousness of certain weavers, babouche makers, and Jewish and Muslim merchants, as Jacques Taïeb has noted:

> Singing, musical professions, and dance were all despised activities left to the Jews and the Blacks (more precisely, to the Jews of the poorer classes). The high frequency of the family name Abitbol (drummer) and its variations Bitbol, Boutboul, Tabbali, Teboul, etc., demonstrates the extent of this

phenomenon. Jews, at least in the eastern Maghrib, were found much less frequently in bands that performed Andalusian plainsong, a classical music brought over from Spain beginning in the thirteenth century, a music for which they would have been at a disadvantage because they did not know standard Arabic and the particular pronunciation of dialectical Arabic, considered by Muslims as incorrect.[2]

Several observations reveal how collaboration between Muslims and Jews was vital for the preservation of this rich common cultural heritage; a cultural heritage that was greatly celebrated in Algeria, even to the point of being mythologized. The creation of this shared culture could have come about only through the solidarity and collaboration of Muslim and Jewish musicians. For example, in Tlemcen, the brothers Dib Ghaouti and Mohamed, both exceptional musicians, came to the aid of Jewish musicians Touati and Maqchich during the anti-Jewish violence of 1881 that was perpetrated by European settlers at the time of the legislative elections. It is worth noting that for many years, some Jewish musicians performed in Muslim orchestras, among them Liahou Benyoucef (1811–1856), Liahou el Ankri (1814–?), Mouchi Chloumou (1853–1898), Makhlouf Rouche, known as "Bettaira" (1868–1931), and Braham Edder'ai (1879–1964), and Eliahû Bensaïda (1893–1948), *hazzan* (cantor) at the large synagogue in Tlemcen, who was known for having one of the most beautiful voices for both religious and secular songs.[3]

We should not delude ourselves, however, for only a small segment of the Jewish community was involved in the indigenous musical culture and partnered with Muslims to preserve that culture, which drew part of its imaginary of wandering from a faraway and common Andalusian past. This shared elite culture, created by privileged and intimate ties and common points of reference between Muslims and Jews, was always fraught with tensions and distrust and was often stigmatized by a triumphant colonialism. Group identities were characterized by contrasts:

> The Mediterranean world can be thought of as a dialogical space in which one's identity is defined in a game of mirrors with the other. The relations between one group and the other in close proximity have oscillated throughout history from eros (love) to eris (hate) [to use a profound wordplay so dear to Jacques Berque] in very contrasting ways: crusade and holy war, conquest, tense cohabitation, peaceful and friendly coexistence.[4]

For example, in the eighteenth century, after noticing that a number of Arabo-Andalusian tunes and melodies had been lost and that Jewish musicians were competing with Muslim musicians, the Hanafi *muftis* of Algiers decided to adapt Andalusian styles to the writing of *mawludiyyat* (songs of praise of the prophet

Muhammad) that would be sung to tunes that differed from the Arabo-Andalusian traditions in order to better ensure their preservation, though in a different form.[5]

Jewish weavers, barbers, and managers of *cafés chantants* ("singing cafés") who depended on local customers (neighbors of the Jewish quarter or inhabitants of the *madina*), were often musicians with the savoir faire needed to modernize the common musical heritage as well as innovators and adaptors of musical styles. As soon as they plunged both legally and socially into the economic and cultural networks of colonial society, they would often let go of the cultural practices they shared with Muslims, even though they claimed nostalgia for those practices later.

Journeys and Musicians

In 1905, when Jules Rouanet presented the best performers of Arab music to an assembly of learned scholars gathered in Algiers, he included two of the most important Jewish musicians of the time, Mauzino and Laho Serror:

> You have before you the latest representatives of Arab music in Algiers, heirs of the last century's masters, Hadj Braham, his son Oulid, Ben Sellâm, Mennemesch, Ben Kaptan. They include M. Mohammed ben Ali Sfindja, *bachkiatri* (leader on guitar), the most well-known classical singer in Algiers; M. Mouzino, *kouas* (man of the bow), *rebab* and *kemanche* player, as well as [a] singer that recently had the honor of making a record; M. Laho Serror, one of my early collaborators, an excellent singer and kouitra player; M. Kaddour Oulid Ettebib, a rare *kanun* player; and M. Ali Maadi Mohammed ben Ali, known as Cherif, a *tar* player and drummer.[6]

In this group of renowned performers and respected masters, very few women are mentioned, except as singers. Women often had careers in all-female orchestras. This was the case of Soltana Daoud, for example. Known as Reinette, she mostly pursued her career in Algeria in the shadows of Cheikha Titma, Meriem Fekhaï, Fadela Dziria, and especially Alice Fitoussi (1916–1978).[7] The most emblematic of the Jewish women who set their sights on artistic performance was undoubtedly Marie Soussan. She was associated with the emergence of Algerian theater from the early 1930s (she first appeared in the magazine *Alger-Tunis* on 11 March 1929.) She was also the first "Arab" woman to appear in the theater; previously men had dressed in drag to play female roles. With Rachid Ksentini, she became part of one of the most popular theater couples during the interwar period. She was also a variety-show performer who recorded more than twenty 78 rpm records.

The other exemplary case, that of the writer Elissa Rhaïs (whose real name was Rosin Boumendil),[8] was more notorious and media-centered. Her notoriety was especially significant in the literary realm, contributing to the popularization among French readers of an "exoticism" associated with natives of the Maghrib. During the first quarter of the twentieth century, she became successful both in fashionable society and in French bookstores, in spite of the fact that it was later alleged that she used ghostwriters to create her novels.[9] Each of these women asserted their individuality through voluntary acculturation—that is, in the translation from one definite cultural space to another, from Jewish to Muslim in the case of Marie Soussan and from Jewish to French in the case of Elissa Rhaïss.

Jewish Algerian entrepreneurs and artists demonstrated their initiative and innovation by mediating between a space of legitimacy (France) and new forms of the distribution and performance of cultural practices. Two important popular Jewish Tunisian singers made a special impression on the cultural consciousness of Algerian Muslims during the interwar period. They were Habiba Messika, who came to Algiers to sing in 1923, and Cheikh El Afrit. Their records, along with those of Mohamed Abdelwahab and Umm Kulthum, were very influential in the musical scene of Arabic-language songs.

A conflicted modernity was inherent in the realm of Algerian music. From its small-scale beginnings as a local commodity, Algerian music grew into a cultural institution and a symbol of modern Algerian identity, yet it developed in a field that was dominated by colonial culture. Jewish performers were the first to distinguish themselves as "modern" by their Western dress, but Muslim musicians soon adopted the same type of clothing. Through the activities of a new breed of cultural entrepreneurs, music passed out of the private and amateur realm into the public and professional sphere during the colonial period.

As part of this process, Jewish musicians played a particularly important role in the spread of the recording industry. Edmond Nathan Yafil was the main consultant for Algerian record companies, which at the end of the nineteenth and the beginning of the twentieth century launched campaigns to record both traditional and modern music in Algeria and the Maghrib. Beginning in 1907, he created and recorded on the first label in Algeria.[10] This was also the case for Léon Mardoché Sasportes, who established the Algériaphone publishing house[11] in Algiers in May 1930. The role Jews played in the recording industry was well recognized in the 1930s:

> Jews in particular were the architects of this vogue in records. Operating generally as agents for the large labels, such as Gramophone, Pathé, Columbia, Odéon, Polyphone, etc., they were able to create an entire network of retailers in just a few years because of their well-known business sense. These retailers offered their merchandise at lower and lower prices, with easier and easier terms. Because of their knowledge of the local language, they have by now recorded, either locally or in studies of metropolitan

France, a large catalogue whose repertoire continues to grow with new [re-cordings].[12]

Edmond Nathan Yafil, known as Yafil Ibn Shbab, was born in 1874 in the Cas-bah, where his father who was nicknamed Makhlouf Loubia, ran a low-end res-taurant (Ar. lubia = beans, a cheap meal in North Africa). He earned his baccalau-reate as well as a diploma in Arabic. During the period 1904 to 1927, he published the essential works of the musical heritage of Algiers in Western musical nota-tion in twenty-nine installments. Around 1909, he founded the first Arabic music school in Algiers and then the first musical association, El Moutribia, in 1911. He died in 1928.

Yafil was one of the rare Algerian cultural personalities who was able to re-main at the crossroads of communities (Muslims, native Jews, and Europeans), cultural styles (Arabo-Andalusian and European), languages (Arabic, French), and musical styles (classical Arabo-Andalusian music and popular songs and the so-called Franco-Arabic song). He also distinguished himself by his profes-sional positioning. He was simultaneously a performer, a composer, an arranger, a producer, a manager, a show organizer, a publisher, and an anthologist. In short, because of him, Arabo-Andalusian music, which until that time had been transmitted from master to disciple in a guild-like system, was taken up by mu-sical associations and a methodology of apprenticeship developed in Algeria that was more open to the transcription of melodies. He tirelessly collected the texts of these songs and sought to record most of the ensembles and performers of his time. At the beginning of the 1920s, he helped France discover the classical music of the Maghrib.[13]

In contrast with his fellow Jews, who went to French schools and followed the general tendency toward integration into French culture, Edmond Nathan Yafil rooted himself within an indigenous cultural heritage in order to affirm his deep-seated and classical Arabo-Andalusian music traditions. He imitated European classical music in his staging with regard to dress and arrangement (particularly the presentation of concerts in the European style), and he made a mark for himself as an innovator in traditional practices by collecting the scat-tered corpus into anthologies and by transcribing songs.[14] Yafil established him-self within French modernity by introducing light musical forms that were actu-ally a compromise between the local background and French traditional music. Many Jewish artists and men of culture who did not have the necessary cultural capital gained entrance into the cultural scene of metropolitan France through minor forms of legitimate French culture (exotic novels, French-Arabic songs, etc.), which was also the case for Yafil. However, Jules Rouanet's opposition to this strategy and the beginnings of an autonomous cultural revival by Muslim scholars and artists prevented Edmond Nathan Yafil from moving seamlessly in all three segments of the musical world that had only been parallel to each other in colonial Algeria. This failure would cause Yafil to be excluded for a long time from both the Jewish community and the cultural world of French colonial Algeria and, to a lesser degree, from the cultural world of Muslim Algeria.

During the interwar period in Mostaganem, Pinhas Teboul, Meyer Reboah, and Issac Benghozi were the best of the Jewish musicians who actively participated both in the cultural ceremonies of their fellow Jews and at secular events for Muslim music lovers. Abdelkader Bentobdji, a poet from Mostaganem, complained in one of his poems from the 1930s that his fellow Muslims praised Meyer (Reboah) and Issac (Benghozi) as veritable sheikhs who were admired and praised by Muslim women:

> *yabaghdu shaʿar anabi wa-salihin   maya'tabru fasih du qawm al-fitna*
> *hazb Meyer wa Yaʿqub aʿda edin   yafarhu bih kulhum qawn ala'na*
> *hata alnsa yuluwlu bisawt azine   hadihi ouri lidik shaykh madmadinatina*
> atkhaltat wa satwat 'agba wa hdura[15]

While these musicians were intimately related to the social and cultural life of the Jewish community of the region through their art, "Moroccan Jews, like their counterparts in other North African and Middle Eastern communities, adapted Andalusian music to *piyyutim*, liturgical Hebrew-language poetry for important family celebrations, at the synagogue performing the equivalent of the *sama'*, an essentially religious song like that was sung in the mosque and at the *zawiya* glorifying the Prophet Muhammad in poems of praise and exalting Islam in edifying cantilenas. Following the example of the synagogal *piyyut*, they do not allow accompanying instruments."[16] The musicians also fully participated in events that affected their city. For example, after the flood of the wadi Aïn Sefra that devastated Mostaganem on 26 November 1927, Pinhas Teboul recorded a song dedicated to the tragedy while in Paris:

> *kayn safra yalas-lam   daratu qasa fida al-kam*
> *kihamlat fi du alyam   rah khbarha lilbuldan*
> *elkadlam mrah arrih   waldalma wa-al naw atih*
> *aqwiya wabdat atsih   filashcab mka elwadyan*
> *atlayam alma wafzak   wakla alaswar yadfak*
> *fi al-bazarat iqalak   kamalhum kala al-hitan*
> *atsarsab kala el-fandug   bayat fi-alard ikharag*
> *wali bayat tam ghraq   urah khabru lilbuldan*[17]

Saoud Medioni (El Wahrani, known as the Oranian), an orchestra leader and café manager in the Jewish quarter (*darb*) in Oran, welcomed Muslim artists such as Cheikh Hammada and Cheikh Madani. During the first third of the twenti-

eth century, he was a pivotal figure for Oranian music. As the driving force behind the main Arabo-Andalusian orchestras, he attracted disciples who pushed
the standard of music as far as their master did. Under Saoud Medioni's leadership, Oranian musicians won praise at important events at the end of the 1930s:

> The groups of Saoud, Zouzou, Mritakh and Ebiho were the most popular at
> that time and they were the most sought after for weddings. . . . There was a
> story that after the victory of the USMO in the Oran championship, Cheikh
> Saoud wrote a song in which he praised each player one by one. The chorus
> said: "*Khaluni nafrah awn-ghani, ʿala l'USMO champion d'Oranie.*"[18]

In 1938, Medioni emigrated to Marseille, where he managed a café. Then, on
23 March 1943, he was deported with his son from Drancy to the extermination
camp at Sobibor. There is no shortage of testimonies regarding his music and his
performances:

> As for the other Oranian Jewish singer, Saoud Medioni, he distinguished
> himself by his Andalusian interpretations and two magnificent Bedouin
> songs:
>
>> "It is for 'her' that I am taking care of you, keeping in mind the day
>> that I decide to leave;
>> By God, my horse, take me (to her)"
>> *Hraztak liha labbit nughda*
>> *Ya awdi lallah biya sir . . .*
>> And this one: "My heart leaps (and wants to see again) the pure-
>>   blooded girl, with blacks eyelashes
>> Let us go to her, O my horse"
>> *Galbi shash l-al huriya kahl alhdab,*
>> *Liha nrawhu ya awdi . . .* [19]

Another figure on the musical scene of Oran in the 1930s was *mu'allim* Zouzou
(Joseph Guenoun), known for his interpretation of the Bensoussan lament of a
man who is mourning his beloved, Maria Moreno, whom he has killed because
she left him for another.[20] There was also Lili Labassi (Elie Moyal, 1897–1969),
the son of an experienced musician, who continued the classical tradition but
also became particularly known for his lively songs, including "Kulshi ma'a al-
flus" (Everything with Money), "L'Orientale," "Ô ma gitane," "Les Yeux noirs,"
"Bombe Atomique," and "Wahran al-Bahia," in which he varied languages and
registers (between Arabic, French, and Franco-Arabic). He is one of the few modern singers to have published a collection of songs in both Arabic and Hebrew.
We can also include Cohen Sarriza, who recorded popular pieces of *hawzi* (local
Algerian popular music derived from the Andalusian tradition) during the 1930s
that were then taken up by Reinette the l'Oranais: "Sarriza is the stage name of
a Jewish Oranian woman from the upper middle class. Approximately 30 years

after the death of her husband, she went two or three times to Paris in 1935 and 1936 in order to record 'Chekoua' and 'Ana Loulei' with the Paris mosque orchestra at Polydor."[21] Until Algerian independence, she trained generations of musicians, particularly Muslim Algerians. Blond Blond, a recognized imitator of Maurice Chevalier and faithful disciple of Lili Labassi, demonstrated this mixed culture of classical music and lighter songs until after independence as she toured and recorded in France.

Elsewhere, in Constantine, the music scene[22] was forever dominated by the traditionalist Cheikh Raymond Leyris (1916–1961). A student of Omar Chaqleb, he gathered together the best instrumentalists of his era, among whom were Sylvain Ghenassia (the father of Enrico Macias), his faithful accompanist. Other singers and performers from this city include Bentari Nathan; Maurice Draï, a great lute player; Elbaz Bellara; Israel, an orchestra leader and a singer in the 1940s; Naccache Alexandre, known as Juda; and Allouche-Tammar Simone (1935–1984). For the most part, these musicians jealously guarded the established musical tradition of the *malouf.* They cultivated a kind of aristocratic culture of the emotions (*tarab*) that they knew how to popularize and make festive in the most mundane moments of daily life. I would be remiss, however, if I did not also mention Edmond Atlan, Line Monty, and Lili Bonniche, who energized the cultural life of the capital, Algiers. Their activities took place among those of dozens of other singers and musicians who for more than half a century worked to enliven and form musical associations and expand the circle of traditional North African music connoisseurs.

Universal Mediators

As I have emphasized throughout this chapter, most of these artists voluntarily undertook the formidable task of going beyond the limitations of language, community, genre, and geography. We can ascribe to them this wonderful statement by Jean Cohen: "We no longer seek the particular. We seek the universal."[23] While they followed very individual artistic paths, many of them also contributed to the establishment of new musical trends, to the safeguarding of a common heritage, and to the simple translation of a life ethic in the most beautiful expressions of artistic emotion.

NOTES

1. Alexandre Christianowitsch, *Esquisse historique de la musique arabe aux temps anciens, avec dessins d'instruments et 40 mélodies notes et harmonisées* (Cologne: Dumont-Schauberg, 1863),

2. He adds in a note: "In the past, according to the old inhabitants of Algiers, dancers from the country would go the Moorish cafés. It was also there that you could hear the tinny band, directed by Hamed-ben-Hamarra, and that you could see the Garagous (scandalous living paintings) that were shown behind oiled paper."

2. Jacques Taïeb, *Sociétés juives du Maghreb modern (1500–1900): un monde en mouvement* (Paris: Maisonneuve et Larose, 2000), 123.

3. Other names of Jewish musicians from Tlemcen, whose paths and true place in the musical sphere of their time remain unknown, include Saoûd Médiouni (1814–?), Lyahou L'âdri (1821–1851), Braham Ben Jacob (1827–?), Simah Teboul (1828–?), Braham Benkhobza (1828–?), Chaloum Touati (1829–1898), Ishac (Iscat) Bensaïd (1841–1911), Moché Mediouni (1842–?), Issac Sayagh (1845–1906), Issac Touati (1847–1912), Nessim Jian (1847–1881), Makhlouf Elbar (1848–1913), Israél Mediouni (1858–1879), and Moché Rouch (1865–1922).

4. Christian Bromberger and Jean-Yves Duran, "Fut-il jeter la Méditerranée avec l'eau du bain?" in *L'anthropologie de la Méditerranée*, ed. Dionigi Albera, Anton Blok, and Christian Bromberger (Paris-Aix: Maisonneuve et Larose/Maison Méditerranéenne des Sciences de l'Homme, 2001), 746.

5. By contrast, within the North African Jewish community, the same phenomenon of adapting (and thereby conserving) Arabo-Andalusian music to all the different forms of secular and religious songs was also occurring in the form of Hebrew liturgical poetry (*piyyutim*). See Haïm Zafrani, *Littératures dialectales et populaires juives en Occident musulman: l'écrit et l'oral*, part 3 of *Études et recherches sur la vie intellectuelle juive au Maroc. De la fin du 15è au début du 20è siècle* (Paris: Geuthner, 2003), 245.

6. Jules Rouanet, "La musique arabe," *Bulletin de la Société de Géographie d'Alger* (1905): 327. This conference took place on 20 April 1905 in the Hall du Palais Consulaire, during a conference of the Orientalistes et des Sociétés Savantes.

7. The daughter of Rahimou Fitoussi, who was also a renowned singer and violinist at the beginning of the twentieth century, debuted with him at the age of 13. She had the distinction of performing alternatively in a male band and a female band. She continued to host family celebrations after Algerian independence.

8. Her son, who signed his name Roland Rhaïs (and whose real name was Jacob Raymond Amar [1902–1988]) became involved in the Communist Party in 1934, then in the anticolonialist and Algerian independence struggles. He was imprisoned from 1955 to 1958. He became an Algerian citizen after independence and published several essays.

9. Elissa Rhaïs published *Saada la marocaine* (Paris: Plon-Nourrit & cie, 1919); *Le café chantant* (Paris: Plon,1920); and *Les juifs ou la fille d'Eléazar* (Paris: Plon-Nourrit & cie, 1921).

10. In Edmond Nathan Yafil's booklet *Majmuᶜ zahw al-anis al-mukhtasar bi-al-tabassi wa-l-qawadis* (Algiers, 1907), he also notes songs from the repertoire (in particular, *hawzi* and *ᶜarubi*) that were recorded on records and cylinders during the period 1900 to 1906.

11. Léon Mardoché Sasportes was imitated by Lili Labassi (Elie Moyal) on the Parlophone recording label in Algiers in the 1950s and by Raymond Leyris on Hess Moqnine at Constantine.

12. Bachagha Smati, *Causerie sur le disque de langue arabe* (1937), 3.

13. Praised and esteemed by Algerian Muslims during the 1920s, Yafil is still recognized today as having revived Arabo-Andalusian music in Algeria. A group of Algerian music aficionados have taken the name Le Groupe YAFIL and now publish a Web site under that name; see http//yafil.free.fr/groupe.htm.

14. Edmond-Nathan Yafil and Jules Rouanet, *Répertoire de musique arabe et maure: collection de mélodies, ouvertures, noubet, chansons, préludes, etc.* (Alger: Yafil & Seror, 1904); Edmond-Nathan Yafil, *Collection Yafil: répertoire de musique arabe et maure; collection d'ouvertures, mélodies, noubat, chansons, préludes, danses, etc.* (Mustapha: Imp. algérienne, 1900s).

15. An excerpt from the *qasida* on the "people of Mostaganem" by Abdelkader Bentobdji, kindly passed on by my colleague, Ahmed Amine Dellaï.

16. Zafrani, *Littératures dialectales,* 139.

17. According to Rashid Muhammad al-Hadi in *Nayl-al-Maghanim: min tarikh wa-taqalid Mustaghanim* (Mostaganem: al-Matba'a al-'Alawiya, 1998), 57.

18. For the testimony of an Orananian in keeping with the times, see the testimony of Guedda Zahar, known as Zahar "Essouâdji" (the watchmaker) in *La Voix de l'Oranie* (22 August 2002).

19. Mohamed Belhalfoui and Claude Roy, *La poésie arabe maghrébine d'expression populaire: défense et illustration d'une poésie classique d'expression "dialecticale"* (Paris: Maspéro, 1980), 24.

20. Bensoussan, a late-nineteenth-century young Algerian Jew who was in love with a Spanish woman in Oran, killed the woman because she preferred a toreador. He was arrested but spared death because of the chief rabbi's intercession. Instead, he was condemned to life in prison and deported to Cayenne. Geneviève Dermenjian describes the local reaction to these events: "At the end of 1888 and the beginning of 1889, there was an explosion of racial hatred in the city during the trial and then pardoning of the Jew, Bensoussan, passionate murderer of a young Spanish woman"; Geneviève Dermenjian, *La crise anti-juive oranaise (1895–1905): L'anti-sémitisme dans l'Algérie coloniale* (Paris: L'Harmattan, 1986), 57. Later, at the turn of the century, the song "Cheniet Bensoussan" was attributed to Rabbi Sadouni Bénichou.

21. Centre des Hautes Études d'Afrique et d'Asie Modernes (CHEAM), Paris, exposé no. 37, M. Delahaye, 22 December 1941.

22. For more about the music scene in Constantine, see Abdelmadjid Merdaci, *Dictionnaire des musiques et des musicians de Constantine* (Constantine: Simoun, 2002).

23. Jean Cohen, *Chronique d'une Algérie révolue. "Comme l'ombre et le vent"* (Paris: L'Harmattan, 1997), 17.

PART IV

Between Myth and History: Sol Hachuel in Moroccan Jewish Memory

13

Sol Hachuel in the Collective Memory and Folktales of Moroccan Jews

Yaëlle Azagury

IN THE COLLECTIVE imagination of Moroccan Jews, the heroic fate of Solika (Sol) Hachuel fascinates like no other historical figure from this community. A morality tale passed from generation to generation, Sol's story lives on in various guises, including in popular songs, eyewitness accounts, stage plays, and novels; her tomb in Fez remains a pilgrimage site to this day. She has not only acquired the status of a saint (*tsadiqa*) but her story has been elevated to the level of a myth. Fueling this fascination is the tragic, even sublime, nature of her story. But, as Mitchell Serels[1] observes, one has also to take account of the fact that Sol is a woman, which is, as we shall see, entirely pertinent to the matter.

The story is deceptively simple: it begins in 1834 in Tangier, where Sol was born.[2] She was the daughter of Haim and Simha Hachuel, and she had an older brother, Issachar. At the age of 17, the young girl was already an extraordinary beauty, and—according to Eugenio Mario Romero's 1837 account—complained constantly to her parents about being cloistered in the house.[3] She made friends with her neighbor, a Muslim girl named Tahra Masmoudi (and, in subsequent versions, with Tahra's brother ʿAli, who fell in love with Sol), but refused Tahra's offer to help her convert to Islam. Tahra didn't admit defeat but went to see the pasha, ʿArbi Esiudo, to denounce Sol. According to Tahra, Sol embraced Islam but later regretted her conversion.[4] Clearly Tahra's testimony is fake, but the accusation decided Sol's destiny nonetheless, sealing her fate forever like a Greek *fatum*, for in Islam, apostasy is a crime that is theoretically punishable by death. Rejecting the solutions the pasha proposed to Sol (including, among other things, a promise of riches and protection from parental authority if she would only confirm the fact of her conversion), Sol was beheaded in the town square in Fez, proclaiming her identity until the very end in a phrase that has become famous: *Hebrea naci y Hebrea quero [sic] morir* (I was born Jewish and I will die Jewish).[5] It serves, in effect, as her epitaph.

This version is just one of many history has bequeathed us, however. And plausible as it may seem to us today, it still raises a number of questions. As Sarah Leibovici asks: "So what age was she exactly? 14, 15, or 17? When, on what exact date, did the hellish process begin?"[6] Further questions that might engage us seem unanswerable in view of the differing versions. Did Sol have a mother or a stepmother? Are there any male figures to be taken into account? Which man, for instance, was it who fell desperately in love with her: the neighbor, Tahra's husband, Tahra's son, or Tahra's brother, who in certain accounts is named ʿAli? Was it the governor or, when she was finally taken to Fez, was it the sultan himself? Maybe it was his son the prince.

In this chapter, I would like to pursue the lines of inquiry Sarah Leibovici opened while also proposing a number of my own. What accounts for the imprecision and ambiguity that Sarah Leibovici finds so glaring in the versions of Sol's story handed down to us over the years? Leibovici reminds us of the silence or absence of Muslim sources and then cites a second version, recorded for us by Louis Voinot in 1948: "She [i.e. Sol] is supposed to have converted to Islam in Tangier, in order to marry a lover, but when this man dies, she reverts to the religion of her ancestors. Following this disavowal, she was sent to Fez, where the *qadi* had her tortured."[7] Sol is supposed to have converted out of love but also (perhaps) out of resentment, inasmuch as she was possibly mistreated by her mother and found in Tahra a consoling ear.

My goal here is less to deliver a historian's account with a view to proposing a definitive version of the facts than it is to come to grips with the relationship between the story and the workings of Moroccan Jewish collective memory. Examining this relationship, I suggest, is one way of accounting for the ambiguities that surround this particular tale. Why is Sol so fleeting and indistinct— a Protean figure par excellence? How does she evade the factual determinations of history? Moreover, we might wish to examine more closely what these different versions suggest to us. In particular, we might learn from the traces that history has deposited in the popular tale, particularly in Elisa Chimenti's text, titled "Sarita Benzaquen," which is included in her collection *Le Sortilège*.[8] Finally, we might in this general exploration interrogate Sarah Leibovici's approach, which is remarkable to be sure but oscillates between rigorous historical analysis and a laudatory idealization of Sol.

I am concerned to show that the true story of Sol has become legendary or even mythical because it is a means by which to think the unthinkable, in this case to imagine a specific type of sexual collusion—otherwise strictly forbidden— between two communities, the Muslim and the Jewish.[9] The story of Sol and her transformation in the collective memory and consciousness of Moroccan Jews codifies the symbolic map of social and affective spaces assigned to each of the two communities and articulates the terrible consequences if these boundaries are transgressed.[10] Collective memory, or rather the modalities by which it is diversely constituted and reconstituted, works to delimit a space of symbolic separation between Jews and Muslims, constructing a sort of imaginary mellah (let us remember that technically there wasn't a mellah in Tangier)[11] that functions as a cordon sanitaire to ward off the dangers and seductions of their Muslim neighbors. It is, in short, as if the confusion resulting from so many competing versions serves to obscure the following questions, each one thinking the unthinkable: What if Sol was truly in love with her neighbor ʿAli, or the sultan? What if her friendship with Tahra really was stronger than her religious and family ties? In other words, what happens when one passes "to the other side," to the side to which one does not belong? And once the border is crossed, how does one return?

To be clear, this is not an exercise in casting doubt on the facts as they are but rather an opportunity to look at the role of the imagination, taking into account its errors and uncertainties, in order to understand what it reveals about the collective fears of a community. Perhaps the existence of the ambiguities surrounding Sol's story (that is, the different versions generated by that collective imagination) tells us a great deal about the threatened and precarious situation of the Jewish community in this time and place. The story's aim would have been to create—using any and all possible means—protection against a threat, the threat of assimilation or the threat of destruction. And this is the task that falls to imagination and memory.

The theme of symbolic transgression (variously: religious transgression, the transgression of space when Sol goes to her neighbor Tahra, transgression against one's family when she refuses to adhere to her mother's ban on visiting Muslims) is revealed in a particular light when we study the relationships the different versions of Sol's story seem to have with the fairy tale, the mythological legend, and the popular folktale. The fairy tale first of all, for whatever the version, the story of Sol abounds in traditional motifs. We might observe Sol's extraordinary beauty, for instance, seeing her as a sort of Cinderella born to a poor family and mistreated by her mother or, according to other versions, by her cruel stepmother. But this much-vaunted beauty can only give rise to a mother's jealousy, whence the tensions between the two (remember Snow White and the queen, a maternal figure ceaselessly interrogating her mirror: "Mirror on the wall, who is the fairest of them all?").

The novelistic version of Sol's story by Robert Boutet, published in installments in *l'Avenir Illustré*,[12] introduces new characters, such as her brother Jacob and her sister Rachel—while it insists on Sol's isolation from her family (the romantic or Rousseauian theme of the exceptional individual pitted against family

or society) and, above all, on the tensions between mother and daughter, in particular when the latter reaches puberty: "At this dangerous time, Sulica [*sic*] was
more alone than she had ever been. Her sister Rachel had left for Rabat to marry a
rich merchant, her father still worked in his shop and her mother, older and more
cantankerous than ever, perpetually wore a frown."[13] Then, a little farther on,
when Soulika inadvertently tore her mother's party dress in the process of sewing it, thus unleashing the latter's fury, the conflict between mother and daughter
was openly declared: "In view of this disaster, her throat could not give proper
vent to all her fury, so she seized a broom to punish the wretch. . . . Shocked, the
young Jewess ran around the room to escape her mother[,] who pursued her mer-
cilessly. She flattened herself against the walls, pressing against them with her
hands. Suddenly behind her, an opening: the door, the corridor. An obstacle: a
step. The opening again: the street."[14]

In Ruben Tajouri's version, the same theme is underlined: "When the young
girl had reached the age of sixteen, her mother's surveillance became very severe, tyrannical even. . . . Her mother overwhelmed her with reprimands and
even went so far as to inflict bodily punishment."[15] By insisting on the lack of understanding between mother and daughter during Sol's puberty, Boutet is faithful to the fairy tale model where the heroine has to free herself from the family
domain in order to reach adulthood.[16] For in fairy stories, the theme of disobedience or filial rebellion is not always perceived as negative (witness, for instance,
Cinderella's disobedience when she goes to the ball) but can be viewed instead as
a rite of passage to adulthood. The umbilical cord, so to speak, has to be cut once
more. In this perspective, the bad mother, as far as the child is concerned, is only
a projection of his or her feelings of rebellion. The motif of the mother-daughter
conflict in the story of Sol declares, albeit in a muted way, the separation from the
mother, the mother of course being the privileged depository of religion in Judaism. In this way, then, the conflict discreetly prefigures the motif of religious
transgression. In Boutet's novel, this transition from disobedience—both with
regard to the mother and with regard to religion—is enacted by a change of domains. To escape her mother, Solika goes to her Muslim neighbor Tahra and does
so declaring that "your house will be my house." An eminently ambiguous formula, of course. This phrase—it serves as the heading to chapter 5 of the novel—
is ambiguous above all because we are to understand "your house" as "your religion." Tahras's reaction, for its part, is quite explicit: "She repudiated her God
in choosing my home."[17] In fact, it is a direct reference to the Book of Ruth. After
the death of her husband Elimelech, Ruth the Moabite decides to remain with her
mother-in-law Naomi in the land of Judah, thus relinquishing her native faith.
Her words are: "Your people shall be my people, and your God my God."[18]

If the story of Solika draws from the fairy tale genre in order to convey the motif of transgression, it also draws from mythology, in particular the Persephone legend, one of whose themes is the initiation of the young girl into adulthood. In the Persephone myth, reprised in the "Hymn to Demeter,"[19] Persephone, daughter of Demeter, disappears while on a walk. In despair, her mother discovers that she has been carried off by Hades, lord of the underworld, and is living now as his legitimate bride in the realm of the dead. Passing to the other side, Persephone is from then on in the universe of transgression. When Hades makes the young girl eat pomegranate seeds before she sees her mother, Persephone, now become a woman, does not refuse this token of her sexual belonging to her husband. Like Persephone, Solika also passes to the other side, the Muslim side in this case, and despite her initial resistances, different popular versions of the story suggest a sort of ambiguity about her will to transgress. Instead of pomegranate seeds, Boutet's version substitutes their North African equivalent: ʿAli, Tahra's brother, who is in love with Sol, tempts her with chickpeas. The moment of the Fall is preempted by the last-minute intervention of Simha, Sol's mother. But, as we have seen, this is not a definitive resolution, since Sol subsequently takes refuge with Tahra, seeking protection from her mother's wrath.

Let us finally note the remarkable absence of any paternal figure in most versions of the story. Psychologists remind us that the essential conflict of a pubescent young girl lies in relation to the mother, not the father. In the Persephone myth, the young girl does not return to her mother in any lasting way. She must choose between the biological link that ties her to her mother and the cultural and romantic link that ties her to her husband. The solution, in the Greek myth, is that of compromise: Persephone will pass two-thirds of the year with her mother and will stay the other third with her husband. In the Persephone tale, therefore, as to a certain degree in the tale of Sol, it is a matter of separating oneself from one's mother (and one's mother tongue) in order to find one's own voice, to find one's own way. Thus the insistence in the Boutet version on Sol's curiosity and her desire to see other worlds. Nevertheless, unlike Persephone, no compromise is possible for Sol between Islam and Judaism—one has simply to choose between the two.

Through the story of Sol, the collective memory of Moroccan Jews takes on the task of constructing, via the novelistic imagination, a cautionary tale that puts its readers on alert against the temptations of other worlds—in this case, that of Islam. We might therefore align this particular story with the general function of the morality tale. Concerning a related genre, the lives of the saints, André Elbaz writes that "besides simple entertainment, the narrator wants primarily to instruct, to teach an ethics; when, that is, he is not writing an outright moral sermon. . . . The legends of the saints thereby fulfill an essential pedagogical function."[20] This function is all the more explicit in a tale by Elisa Chimenti entitled "Sarita Benzaqen."[21] Ostensibly unrelated to Sol's story, the tale is nevertheless broadly inspired by it, insofar as it reactivates, not without a certain daring, the motif of religious transgression. Just like Sol, Sarita was "as beautiful as a divine *houri*" and came from a modest background (her father was a poor rabbi). One notices other striking similarities: the near total absence of the father and the same obsessive presence of the mother, with whom there is a palpable tension. To this list of similarities might be added the fact that the tale takes place in Tangier. Walking one day with two friends during the Jewish festival of Passover (and the choice of dates is germane here, since for Jews this holiday celebrates the liberation of the Jewish people from their Egyptian overlords), Sarita meets the handsome Muslim lord Si Mohammed El Marrakchi. They fall desperately in love. More explicitly than Sol's story, Sarita's tale explores the taboo of religious transgression. First Sarita resists and takes refuge in a synagogue in order to demonstrate that she is Jewish. As in the story of Sol, physical spaces are heavily invested with symbolic meaning. Thus, after Sarita and Si Mohammed meet for the second time to take a meal together in a garden of the Charf mountain—gardens being a secular, neutral space, and the traditional *locus amoenus* of romantic literature—Si Mohammed goes to the mosque. This is a way for him too not to forget who he is. Spaces are therefore significant, but not significant enough to keep Sarita safe from love. She will name the force that attracts her to Si Mohammed, the man who incarnates for her forbidden fruit, a bewitchment, as if the transgression could not find any name or justification in the rational order of things: "The mere sight of Si Mohammed was enough to make her madness return and strengthen the enchantment, she thought. More than ever, she was convinced that he had put a spell on her, that her struggle was in vain, that it would finish with her going to him whenever he asked for her."[22] Sarita succumbs, therefore, not without having fought a valiant fight against the forbidden man. For the motif of transgression is present throughout the tale, elaborated like so many warnings. First, there is the food that Sarita shares with her Christian friends: "I hope that you have only tasted food that is permitted, says the mother, anxiously." The phrase is readable on more than one level, of course. In a less ambiguous way, her friend Bettina the Christian warns her without mincing words: "I tell you again, Sarita, watch what you're doing. Think of your own kind, who would repudiate you if you married a man from a race other than your own."[23]

But all the warnings of her mother and friends fall on deaf ears. Sarita decides to flee with Si Mohammed. She knows, however, what this means: the renunciation of her faith to become a Muslim. She decides to escape during the night, but before leaving the family home, carries out the last gesture that still attaches her to her religion: she puts her hand on the mezuzah fixed to her bedroom door. But on the way to Mohammed, she suddenly meets a strange old man who asks her the way. Embarrassed, she takes him to his destination, the Jewish cemetery, only to suddenly find herself in front of the tomb of her parents, those whose home she has just left.

> But there must be some mistake, my parents are still alive, may the God of Israel yet grant them a long life.
> —They're still living but they will soon die in despair and shame, killed by you, daughter of Israel who forgets her faith and her race for the love of a goy. . . .
> —Is this my fault? A powerful spell spurs me on.
> —There is no power at work here other than your will. Do you want to join your handsome Muslim and cause the death of your parents?
> —No, no, heaven forbid that I suffer the fate of Sol the Sadika[,] who died by the executioner's hand on the field of kingly justice[,] were I to do such a thing.[24]

There is probably no more eloquent way of demonstrating that the story of Sarita is indeed a rewriting of Sol's story. Guided by the saint through a maze of streets, Sarita is diverted from a descent to hell and is now ready to reenter the family home. The story is edifying: it has an educational value and works as a warning to others. Let us especially note the motif of the *tsadiq* who "saves" Sarita: André Elbaz shows that it is a theme often found in Jewish Moroccan folktales.[25] In fact, the *tsadiq* serves as a privileged protection against outside attacks on the Jewish faith. As Issachar Ben-Ami explains, "The weak and scattered Jewish minority in Morocco saw in its *zaddikim* an important safeguard against the strong and sometimes hostile Muslim majority. Through the *zaddikim* individual Jews as well as whole communities were protected from Muslim threats."[26]

The story of Solika and her metamorphosis in the collective imagination of Moroccan Jews is a cautionary tale that serves both as a protection against external threats and as part of the moral glue of the community. As Mircea Eliade writes: "Historical truth is quickly transfigured through collective memory and revalued through poetic imagination, so that after some time it is reborn in the realm of myth."[27]

Armed with a collective mythology, a group strengthens itself; it consolidates its impermeability to attacks and threats from without. This is not without irony, for certain accounts remind us that Muslims also go to Sol's tomb to pray to have a daughter equal to her in virtue.[28] Using imagination and popular tales as armor against an exterior threat is an old story: for the Greeks, the conflict was between force (*bia*) and persuasion via words, language, and artifice (*dolos*). For Sol, in any case, the transformation of her story into an efficacious myth against assimilation and a shield against exterior threats attests to the fact—and this, I think, should well satisfy us—that language always has the last word.

NOTES

1. M. Mitchell Serels, *A History of the Jews of Tangier in the Nineteenth and Twentieth Centuries* (New York: Sepher-Hermon Press, 1991), 7.

2. I am referring here to the version offered in ibid., 7–10.

3. Eugenio María Romero, *El martirio de la joven Hachuel ó la heroína hebrea* (Gibraltar: Imprenta Militar, 1837), as quoted in Sarah Leibovici, "Sol Hachuel la Tsadikkah ou la force de la foi," *Pardès* 4 (1986): 134.

4. The problem of "abduction" (from one faith to another) is also at issue in the Mortara case in Bologna during roughly the same period. As in Sol's case, the details of the Mortara affair, which created a sensation in both Europe and America, are not fully known because the matter was never brought before an impartial court of justice. The following seems to be the most probable version: A child named Edgar Mortara was violently removed from the custody of his parents by papal guards in 1858. His nurse, a Catholic, had confessed to a priest that about four years before the abduction, when the child Edgar was very ill, she had secretly baptized him in order to save his soul if he should die. The priest to whom she confessed reported the matter to Rome, and the Congregation of the Inquisition gave orders that the child be taken forcibly from his parents and that he be educated as a Christian. The story became widely known and protest was aroused in nearly every European country. But the Vatican maintained that the question at issue was a spiritual one, outside the pope's temporal (political) jurisdiction. After the capture of Rome by Italian troops in 1870, Edgar Mortara had the opportunity to revert to Judaism but he refused to do so, and not long afterward he became an Augustinian. The Mortara case gave a strong impetus in Europe to the formation of the Alliance Israélite Universelle, an institution whose primary goal was the civil emancipation of Jews. By contrast, nothing similar occurred in Morocco as a result of Sol's travails. For a more detailed account of the Mortara case, see David I. Kertzer, *The Kidnapping of Edgardo Mortara* (New York: Alfred Knopf, 1997). A similar case occurred much later. The story of the twelve-year-old grandson of Rabbi Raphael Abensur who was abducted from Fez in 1910 and converted to Islam by the *qadi*, is eerily reminiscent of the story of Sol, although the ending is much happier, perhaps thanks to the precedent set by the tragic ending of Sol. The boy was released after the intervention of European diplomats. See Michael Menachem Laskier and Eliezer Bashan, "Morocco," in *The Jews of the Middle East and North Africa in Modern Times*, ed. Reeva Spector Simon, Michael Menachim Laskier, and Sara Reguer (New York: Columbia University Press, 2003), 481.

5. This version of Sol's epitaph is in Haketia, the Judeo-Spanish vernacular of Morocco.

6. Sarah Leibovici, "Sol Hachuel la Tsadikkah ou la force de la Foi (1834)," *Pardès* 4 (1986): 133.

7. Louis Voinot, *Pèlerinages judéo-musulmans du Maroc* (Paris: Larose 1948), quoted in Leibovici, "Sol Hachuel la Tsadikkah," 141.

8. Elisa Chimenti, *Le Sortilège et autres contes séphardites* (Tangier: Éditions Marocaines et Internationales, 1964).

9. *Editors' note:* The theme of the sultan seizing Jewish women and bringing them to the palace for sexual purposes is a common motif in some of the European literature on the Maghrib in the precolonial period. See, for instance, John Braithwaite, *The History of the Revolutions in the Empire of Morocco, upon the Death of the late Emperor Muley Ishmael* (London: Printed by J. Darby and T. Browne, 1729), esp. 210–216.

10. I am indebted to Susan Gilson Miller for suggesting this hypothesis to me.

11. *Editors' note:* Though technically there was no separate Jewish quarter in Tangier, the Jews nevertheless had a sense of separate space, a kind of "mellah of the imagination." See Susan Gilson Miller, "Apportioning Sacred Space in a Moroccan City: The Case of Tangier, 1860–1912," *City and Society* 13, no. 1 (2001): 57–83. Also, see chapter 9 by Miller in this volume.

12. Robert Boutet published a series of articles entitled "Soulika ou la vie de Sol Hachuel" in *L'Avenir Illustré* from 31 July 1929 to 16 January 1930.

13. Robert Boutet, "Sulika ou la vie de Sol Hatchuel," *L'Avenir Illustré,* 15 August 1929, 12–13.

14. Robert Boutet, "Sulika ou la vie de Sol Hatchuel," *L'Avenir Illustré,* 30 September 1929, 18.

15. Ruben Tajouri, "Sol la Sadica," *L'Avenir Illustré,* 30 April 1928.

16. Here I am drawing on Bruno Bettelheim's famous analyses of fairy tales in *The Uses of Enchantment: The Meaning and Importance of Fairy Tale* (New York: Knopf, 1976).

17. Robert Boutet, "Sulika ou la vie de Sol Hatchuel," 18.

18. Ruth 1:16, New Revised Standard Version.

19. "Hymn to Demeter," in *The Homeric Hymns,* trans. Apostolos N. Athanassakis (Baltimore, Md.: John Hopkins University Press, 1976).

20. André Elbaz, "Le culte des saints dans le conte populaire des Séphardim d'origine marocaine," *Fabula: Revue d'études sur le conte populaire* 23, nos. 1–2 (1982): 69.

21. Chimenti, *Le Sortilège et autres contes séphardites.*

22. Ibid., 54.

23. Ibid., 49.

24. Ibid., 60.

25. *"Souvent, le saint apparaît en songe au pélerin et lui révèle son remède, ou encore lui annonce que sa prière a été entendue, et qu'il peut rentrer chez lui.* Parfois, le saint prend l'aspect d'un vénérable vieillard vêtu de blanc. *On rencontre ce même motif (Mot. K. 1811: Saint déguisé qui rend visite à un mortel) dans les légendes musulmanes sur les marabouts"* (Often the saint appears in the pilgrim's dreams telling him what he should do to heal or announces to him that his prayer has been heard and that he may go home. *Sometimes the saint takes on the appearance of a venerable old man dressed in white.* We encounter the same motif [Mot. K. 1811: Disguised saint appearing to a mortal] in Muslim legends on maraboutic shrines). Elbaz, "Le culte des saints dans le conte populaire des Séphardim d'origine marocaine," 67–68, my emphasis.

26. Issachar Ben-Ami, "Beliefs and Customs," in *The Jews of the Middle East and North Africa in Modern Times,* ed. Reeva Spector Simon, Michael Menachim Laskier, and Sara Reguer (New York: Columbia University Press, 2003), 203.

27. *"La vérité historique ne tarde pas à être transfigurée par la mémoire collective et revalorisée par l'imagination poétique, de sorte qu'elle débouche de nouveau, au bout d'un certain temps, dans les catégories du mythe."* Mircea Eliade, "Littérature orale, mythologie, folklore, literature populaire," in *Histoire des Littératures,* vol. 1, *Littératures anciennes orientales et orales,* ed. Raymond Queneau (Paris: Gallimard 1955–1968), 3–26, quoted in Elbaz, "Le culte des saints dans le conte populaire des Séphardim d'origine marocaine," 69.

28. In fact, certain saints are "shared" by Jews and Muslims in Morocco: *"Le maraboutisme musulman, très populaire en Afrique du Nord, a nettement marqué le judaïsme local, au point qu'un véritable culte des saints juifs s'est répandu au Maroc, au mépris de toute orthodoxie juive. . . . D'ailleurs, de très nombreux cas de syncrétisme religieux ont été relevés au Maroc. Ainsi, L. Voinot signale l'existence d'une centaine de saints, juifs et musulmans, invoqués indifféremment par les pélerins des deux religions. Parfois le même saint est revendiqué par les juifs et les musulmans, qui l'invoquent sous des noms différents. Voinot cite en particulier Solika Hatsadika et Rabbi Amram Ben Diouane très présents dans les contes que nous avons recueillis au Canada"* (Muslim maraboutism, very popular in North Africa, has heavily influenced local Jewish practices to the point that a true cult of Jewish saints spread in Morocco, overlooking Jewish orthodoxy. Incidentally, several cases of religious syn-

cretism have been signaled in Morocco. L. Voinot, for instance, notes the existence of a hundred saints, Jewish and Muslim, invoked simultaneously by pilgrims of both religions. While the same saint is sometimes claimed by both Jews and Muslims, it is invoked under different names. Voinot cites in particular Solika Hatsadika and Rabbi Amram Ben Diouane, [who are] heavily present in the tales I have collected in Canada). Elbaz, "Le culte des saints dans le conte populaire des Séphardim d'origine marocaine," 69.

14

Sol Hachuel, "Heroine of the Nineteenth Century"

Gender, the Jewish Question, and Colonial Discourse

SHARON VANCE

T HE EXECUTION IN 1834 of Sol Hachuel, a young Jewish girl from Tangier, generated a great deal of attention and was the subject of numerous literary works and at least one French painting (Alfred Dehodencq, *L'exécution de la Juive*, 1852).[1] Sol, or Suleika, as she was also known, was written about both in Jewish and European languages.[2] There are two texts that can be considered primary historical sources because they rely on testimony from Sol's family. They are Eugenio María Romero, *El martirio de la joven Hachuel ó la heroína hebrea*, and M. Rey, *Souvenirs d'un voyage au Maroc*. Except for these two books, most of the texts considered here were not based on primary sources and do not reflect the perspective of Sol's family or her community. They should also not be interpreted as historically accurate accounts of Sol's martyrdom.[3] The Suleika texts I focus on here were selected for the light they shed on nineteenth- and early twentieth-century European discourses surrounding gender, the role of the Church and the nature of government, the "Jewish Question," representations of Muslims, and colonialism. Sometimes these issues are treated separately and at other times they intersect and overlap, as in gendered representations of Jews and Muslims in French and Spanish literature and in travel writing about Morocco.[4] Yet all reflect the discursive worlds in which they were created.

Suleika Texts and Contexts

Most versions of Sol's story begin when she was a teenager. The Jewish texts either play down or do not mention discord in the Hachuel household. All the European texts, however, narrate the fighting between Sol and her mother and

201

see it as a major catalyst for the drama that unfolded. These fights caused Sol to take refuge with her Muslim neighbors, who informed the *qadi* that she had converted to Islam. Sol was brought before the *qadi* and told that she had converted and that if she denied having done so she would be subject to the laws of apostasy. After spending some time in the women's prison in Tangier, she was sent to Fez. When all attempts to persuade her to accept a new life as a Muslim failed, she was publicly executed. In European versions, the rabbis of Fez tried to convince Sol to convert in order to avoid death. The ending of the story also varies from text to text, depending on the genre and the dominant themes of the text. The conversations between Sol and her Muslim captors, in particular Sol's speeches, allow the authors to present via their protagonist their own interpretations and messages. The European (Christian) texts differ from the Jewish texts in that their message has more to do with European politics and French and Spanish designs on Morocco than with concern for Sol's faith.[5] While these texts were no doubt motivated by humanitarian concerns over the status of the Jewish minority in Morocco and by shock at the martyrdom of a young Jewish girl because of her religious identity, they also advanced European colonial interests in Morocco. It is not difficult to detect polemics in the arenas of internal political debate and external propaganda in favor of colonialism.

The first author to publish a full-length work devoted exclusively to Sol was Eugenio María Romero, whose *El martirio de la joven hachuel, ó la heroína hebrea* was published in Gibraltar in 1837.[6] Romero met Issachar, Sol's brother, in Gibraltar, where the latter settled after his sister's execution.[7] He then traveled to Tangier and interviewed Sol's parents and other eyewitnesses. Romero's text is an invaluable historical source, given that it was published just three years after Sol's execution and relied on the testimony of her parents. I have analyzed his version of Sol's story as a historical source elsewhere.[8] Here I wish to focus on Romero's use of literary devices and on the political debates raging in Spain in the 1820s and 1830s, particularly the liberal political struggle against absolutism and the Inquisition. Romero provides the viewpoint of the characters, embellishes the voice of the narrator with his own literary style, and furnishes his own moral for the story according to liberal political ideology. Romero dedicated his work to the Duke of Rivas (Angel de Saavedra, 1791–1865), an Andalusian writer and politician who was also exiled in Gibraltar in 1823.[9] While nothing else is known of Romero, given the polemics he has Sol use, it seems likely that he, like Rivas, was part of the liberal Romantic movement in Spain. In Romero's hands, Sol's speech reverberates with French Enlightenment ideas, particularly the idea that religious sentiment is not a matter of divine truth but the product of upbringing from a tender age.[10] Romero attacks not only Islamic "barbarous legislation" but also Spanish Catholic decrees of forced conversion.[11] Even when his polemics are directed against the Muslim crowd of "fanatics" that called for Sol's execution, it is possible to see an indirect attack on religious intolerance in his own country, as in the speech where he drops the stance of omniscient narrator and addresses the crowd in his story directly:

> Barbarians! And, it is thus, you insult the Heroine of her age? Virtue you call impiety! And blaspheme her, whom you could not convince by reason?[12]

The language is reminiscent of the great orations of the French Revolution and the *exaltados* (Romantic republicans) in Spain's Revolution of 1820 with its exclamatory phrases and rhetorical questions.[13] Such a speech seems more at home in European parliamentary debates or in the pages of middle-class republican newspapers than in the streets of a public square in Morocco. Romero's outburst combines the specific oratory style of contemporary European politics with European Christian and even Roman pagan attacks against the Other as uncivilized and "barbarian." That Romero was able to go to Morocco and meet with other members of Sol's family was itself a result of the European conquests of Moroccan port cities that had been taking place since the fourteenth century and the continued European presence in Tangier. His own viewpoint thus combines both Christian animosities toward Islam dating back to medieval Spain with Romantic and liberal anticlerical polemics.[14]

Among the dramatic works written about Sol are Spanish-language plays that were performed in Gibraltar and in Seville.[15] That Sol's story was turned into a dramatic work may have been due to the popularity of the French opera *La Juive*[16] as well as a number of plays and operas in English based on Walter Scott's *Ivanhoe* that focused on the character of Rebecca, the "Jewess."[17] In 1901, Dr. Macé, a physician with the French military stationed in Morocco, also wrote and published a dramatic work based on Sol's story.[18] This text alters both Romero's and Jewish versions considerably, particularly in turning the character of Ali, Tahra's brother, into a chivalrous knight who falls in love with Sol. In Macé's rendition of the story, Ali declares that his religion is love and agrees to convert to Judaism, receiving Sol's love in return.[19] For Macé the story of Sol is also a plea for religious tolerance that is developed via the narrative of love between Sol and Ali. The influence of operatic conventions (Sol, Ali, Tahra, and a Muslim fortune-teller called "L'Arifa" enjoy an enchanted musical soirée) and references to *La Juive* (the Ali character recalls the role of Prince Leopold by attempting to save Sol and adhering to her "culte") is evident in Macé's version.[20] No doubt Sol's martyrdom, the role of the crowd in the final scene, and the attention she received from non-Jewish male suitors in prior versions of her story reminded Macé of the plot of *La Juive*, which was published and performed several times in the nineteenth century.[21]

A third publication exclusively devoted to Sol was a serialized novel by Robert Boutet that was published between 1929 and 1930 in the Casablanca-based journal *L'Avenir Illustré*.[22] In addition, Boutet also wrote for a French colonial newspaper in Morocco, *La Vigie Marocaine*. Unlike Macé and Romero, who were liberal and part of the anticlerical and Romantic movements, Boutet was a devout Catholic. In addition to his novel about Sol, he was the author of several articles on Moroccan Jewish customs and folklore in which he asserted that Christianity had preceded Berber culture.[23] His text devoted to Sol makes several direct and indirect references to Christianity. At the end of his version, Sol's martyrdom is subsumed under the martyrdom of four named Christian saints *"mort à Fez, captif de l'Islam!"*[24] This sublimation of Sol's text under the rubric of Christian martyrdom has a precedent in an earlier travel account of Morocco by Léon Godard, an *abbé* and a member of the Société historique algérienne. Godard included information on Jewish gravesites that were venerated by Muslims despite their alleged religious intolerance and "fanaticism." Godard writes: "We think that this great Sol belongs to the Church of Christ, of Moses and of the Patriarchs, and not to the Talmudic Synagogue."[25] Godard also claimed that Christianity had preceded other religions in Morocco, thus justifying France's right to colonize it.[26] Much of his book focuses on the "historical" Christian presence in Morocco, also advancing, as Boutet would over half a century later, the theory that many Imazighen were originally Christian.[27] While Boutet showed considerably more respect for Judaism than did Godard, in his version of Sol's story, the role that Christianity supposedly played in Morocco draws upon ideas that Godard had previously developed.

Prior to the official readmittance of Jews to Spain in the mid-nineteenth century, the Romantic movement and liberals used the plight of Jews and Muslims and the legacy of the Andalusian past to call for religious tolerance and political freedom. Many liberals attributed Spain's "decadence" and backwardness to the expulsion of Jews and Muslims.[28] Moreover, as Spaniards traveled to North Africa and the Ottoman Empire during the nineteenth century they encountered Spanish-speaking Sephardi Jews who provided them with linguistic models of pre-exilic Spanish and inspired a Romantic longing for a return to the *convivencia*.[29] Spanish liberals forced into exile during periods of royalist restoration found themselves identifying with Jewish exiles; they saw Sephardim as Spain's lost children who longed to return to the "Mother Country." Some Spaniards also imagined that Sephardi trading networks throughout the Mediterranean could be used to promote Spanish economic expansion.[30]

Several abridged versions of Sol's story by Spanish authors advance such claims. Felipe Ovilo y Canales, a Spanish military doctor who lived in Tangier, wrote a book titled *La mujer marroquí* in 1886, before the beginning of the Spanish protectorate, in which he argues that Spain's destiny was to colonize Morocco, impose Christianity, and liberate Moroccan women from the oppression of Islam.[31] Manuel Ortega, a journalist working in the Moroccan Spanish Zone, wrote about Moroccan Jews and Muslims. He stated that when Spaniards encounter Sephardim "it is as if a sister in infancy was snatched away from us whom we thought was lost forever. . . . We find her in the home of humble people."[32] However, despite this description of Sephardim as "humble people" (*gentes humildes*), Ortega felt that the loss of economic activity after their expulsion was the beginning of Spanish decadence.[33] For this reason he claimed that Spain should adopt a *"política sefardí"* that would grant Moroccan Jews Spanish citizenship, just as Crémieux had granted French citizenship to Algerian Jews. He stated that the Spanish government should organize trade visits to Spain for Sephardi merchants in order to encourage them to open Morocco's markets to Spanish products; he assumed that Moroccan trade was in exclusively Jewish hands.[34] For Ortega, Spain's involvement in Morocco and its "protection of Jews" was a "sacred duty of patriotism" because they were "our brothers, descendants of those who were expelled from the manorial home by a wicked act."[35] Thus, Ortega believed that Spain's "historical right" to Morocco was based in part on the presence of Sephardi Jews there whose ancestors had been expelled from Spain. In his book *El Raisuni* (1917), Ortega expresses the same claim in relation to Moroccan Muslim descendents of expelled Spanish Muslims.[36] This claim was also expressed in the publications of the Sociedad Española de Africanistas y Colonistas.[37]

In Ortega's discussion of Jewish religious customs, he offers Sol's story as an example of Jews who convert to Islam but always return to their "primitive beliefs,"[38] even at the risk of persecution and martyrdom. In this version of the story, Sol was persuaded by a certain Muslim woman to convert. Later she repented and decided to become a martyr. She was very beautiful, and the sultan tried to convince her not to renounce *mahometismo* (Mohammedanism) by bestowing presents and jewels upon her and offering to marry her and make her a sultana, but she declined. Even her executioners cried in the face of such faith and misfortune. According to Ortega, her burial site in Fez is a site of annual pilgrimage, and she is called "Sol la justa, Sol la mártir, la Saddi Ká [*sic*]."[39] Ortega uses Sol's story to make the argument that Jews cannot convert to another religion. He further states that *conversos* who are married to Christians continue to be *hebreos*, as they were before their conversion, because the heart "has not lost the faith in the mosaic creed."[40] Thus, Sol's story can be seen as a comment on the real beliefs and sentiments of the descendants of Spanish *conversos* as much as it is a comment on the fidelity of Jews to their ancestral beliefs. Despite Ortega's prior condemnation of the expulsion and his mentioning of the Inquisition as a possible obstacle to reestablishing relations between Spain and the Sephardim, this observation about the true nature of the *conversos* actually gives some credence to the claims made by the inquisitors that the *conversos,* or new Christians, were actually *"Judios judiazantes"*; that is, that they were really Jews secretly practicing Judaism. The idea that a Jew would always return to Judaism even after conversion was similar to Inquisition accusations in content, although Ortega and Juarros were sympathetic to such a return to Judaism. This probably has to do with a change in the intellectual climate from the period of the height of the Inquisition in the fourteenth through the sixteenth centuries to the period at the end of the nineteenth century when the Romantic movement, with its emphasis on cultural essence and national identity and liberal ideas of religious tolerance, gained ground among Spanish intellectuals such as these. However, for Ortega, the inability of Jews to convert does not pose an obstacle to a Spanish *política sefardí* because Spain had become "one of the most liberal countries in the world."[41] Ortega characterizes Spain as a liberal democratic imperial power capable of bringing civilization to Morocco, but its success was contingent upon its adopting his recommendations for the Sephardim,[42] and he admits that the only obstacle to such an adoption is the residual prejudice of Spaniards against Jews.[43]

Like Ovilo y Canales, César Juarros was a Spanish military doctor. He served during the period of the Spanish protectorate and was stationed in Tetuan. Juarros also wrote a book about Moroccan women,[44] which starts off with a detached scientific discourse but rapidly transforms into a romantic sentimental travelogue. Juarros declared that his mission was to penetrate the secret soul of the indigenous Jewish and Muslim woman. *"Ojos bellos"* (beautiful eyes) is a recurring trope throughout the text. The work begins with an observation, seemingly devoid of any emotion, of the form of a Moroccan woman on the street and the need to penetrate the "secret soul" hidden behind the veil to expose the pent-up "desire" and reveal both to the Spanish reader. It ends with a declaration of the impossibility of this mission and even of Spain's colonial civilizing mission in Morocco.[45] In the course of Juarros's work there is also an abrupt change from a focus on the psychosexual and the feminine to the social and the political. In the first part of the book, when Juarros is focusing on the psychosexual and the feminine, his work can be seen as an answer to Ovilo y Canales's book *La mujer marroquí.* He adamantly rejects the latter's notions that Christianity and Spanish culture are superior to Islam or Judaism. He valorizes the segregation of women, their confinement to the home, and their exclusion from public religious participation, contrasting Moroccans' deep religiosity with the growing secularism in Spain. He attributes the latter to the feminization of religious life in Spain, where only women continue to attend religious service and go to confession on a regular basis.[46] Despite his disagreement with Ovilo y Canales over the role of

Islam and Moroccan traditional culture and its treatment of women, his writing on this subject can be seen, like the writing of Ovilo y Canales, as an answer to the nascent feminist movement that was developing in Spain and a rejection of the increasing public presence of women in Spanish society.[47]

Juarros adopts virtually the same position as Ortega regarding politics and society, advocating the same *política sefardí*. His Suleika text can be seen in the context of his interest in the soul and psychology of Moroccan Muslims and Jews. He categorizes the story of Sol as a romance and focuses on the general characteristics of melancholy, resignation, and sacrifice he sees as typical of Moroccan Jewish women.[48] Unlike Ortega, who stated that Spaniards were deeply moved by Sephardi romances, seeing in them the resurrection of Old Spain, Juarros dismisses the literary merits of the ballads dedicated to Sol and states that they are "poor, infantile and vulgar."[49] However, he does find some merit in one of the ballads, "El Rey Arrepentido," which he quotes in full. This ballad, which focuses on the regret of the king after Sol's execution, describes "a rare veil of sexuality that smells of nard and dark-skinned flesh."[50] According to Juarros, although it lacks meter and literary merit, it enchants and when performed causes the throat of the listener to tighten and disturbs the heart. He quoted only a few stanzas of a ballad to Sol that he had earlier dismissed that expressed Sol's suffering in prison, her faith in God, her praise of Judaism, her rejection of Islam, and the moral lesson to not trust Muslim women. In contrast, he provides the whole text of "El Rey Arrepentido," which focuses on the king's longing for Sol and his regret at killing "that which my soul adored."[51] Juarros was extremely moved, even aroused by the performance of this ballad, which, he stated, "appears as if the veins of the *Enemy* were opened and in them fell the words like molten lead."[52] Thus, Juarros was most stimulated by the imaginary interreligious coupling and romantic longing expressed in the second ballad. While Juarros stated that the ballad reminded him of the Song of Songs, perhaps it also reminded him of the role that Jewish women played in Spanish literature, from the legend of "la Judía de Toledo" and King Alfonso VIII to the role they played as courtesans in picaresque novels written after the Reconquista.[53] For Juarros, "El Rey Arrepentido" and this aspect of Sol's story offer the opportunity to look under the veil and witness (and perhaps experience in the imaginary) the secret sexual longing of the Jewish woman.

The two additional texts I will consider are also parts of larger works. One is an 1885 biography by Gabriel Séailles of the painter Alfred Dehodencq,[54] who painted *La exécution de la Juive*, a visual representation of Sol's execution.[55] The other is contained in Henri de la Martinière's reminiscence of his stay in Morocco when he was the French chargé des affaires in Tangier.[56] Both Séailles and de la Martinière tell Sol's story in versions similar to those of Ovilo y Canales and

Ortega, who claimed that she converted after falling in love with the male relative of her Muslim neighbor. Both also add another story about the fate of Dehodencq's first painting on the subject. According to Séailles, Dehodencq's biog-
rapher, the artist's first painting was destroyed by Jewish "fanatics" who were
upset because he had painted a visual image of the saint. This was not the first
time Dehodencq's painting of religious subjects in Morocco had gotten him into
trouble and aroused negative reactions; Séailles also tells a story of Dehodencq
being chased by a crowd after attempting to paint a religious figure, a *marabout*,
whom he painted as *le Fou* (the madman). Séailles characterizes Dehodencq as
a painter infatuated with Morocco and as an Orientalist documentarian who
wanted to paint the type, the physiognomy of the Moroccans before they were
"annihilated." It appears from these incidents that he had not obtained permission to paint living Moroccans and religious processions.[57]

At the end of his work, Séailles comes to the conclusion that it is better to
leave the world of Jewish and Muslim fanatics and return to the superior world of
Western art. This world allows one to be transported to different times, virginal
dances, wandering rhapsodies, and even to the world of "primitive music"—that
is, back to the world of the "Orient." However, through Western art this world
is cleansed of the immediacy of the "bloody conflict" between "Mahomet" and
"Jehovah."[58] Séailles's account of Sol's story is accompanied by a combination of
elaborate praise for the legendary young beautiful Moroccan Jew and a description of the harm caused by Muslim fanaticism. This account also stresses the historical animosity between Muslims and Jews. Sol falls in love with "an enemy of
her race, forgetting the persecutions," and marries him, "negating her blood and
her God." Her Muslim husband is quickly carried off by death as a punishment
by a jealous God. Alone and remorseful, she finds herself at the door to a synagogue and collapses inside. This return infuriates the Muslims, who regard Jews
as "worse than Christians" and "dogs."[59] His account is an Orientalist fantasy of
beauty, passion, violence, and fanaticism, where neither Jews nor Muslims evoke
any sympathy.

De la Martinière gives a different version of the fate of Dehodencq's first
painting. He states that the painter had constructed an artist's workshop with a
platform near the French consulate. While he was paying a visit to the consulate, the platform collapsed and destroyed the painting.[60] Like de la Martinière's
account of the first painting, his account of Sol's story is also less inflammatory
and dramatic. The main events are the same, but they are told in a more abbrevi-
ated and less histrionic manner without Séailles's descriptions of Jews and Muslims and their primordial hatred for each other. He gives a very brief version of
the story, adding that it was regrettable that the European consulates had not
done more to save her. This conception of the benevolent or potentially benevo-

lent role of the European consulates fits well with the rest of his *mémoire*. In it, he discusses the beneficial effects of the French *mission civilisatrice* and its protectorate.[61] The admission that European consulates could have done more asserts both a political power and the right to exercise that power as well as a moral lapse, for this power was often exercised not so much in the service of humanitarian concerns as it was in the service of programs to gain economic and political advantages.[62]

In all of these texts there is an interweaving of assertions and claims that Europeans had influence over Morocco. Both women and Jews are used as arguments for European intervention in Morocco. This is evident in the use of Sol's story, which is altered to fit the cultural claims and political agenda of the authors, many of whom were under the employ of their governments, particularly their military institutions, prior to and during the protectorate. The next sections will consider the affinity between these texts and Spanish and French writings on the "Jewish Question" and literary images of Jews and Muslims, paying attention to the points where these images overlap with colonial and gender discourses.

Representing Women in the Colonial Context

Understanding the different tellings of Sol's story requires us to pay attention to the political context of internal debate in Spain and France, the role female images played in this debate, and the specific context of the colonial relationship and attitudes toward Jewish and Muslim men and women. As Pura Fernández has pointed out, Sol's story served Romero in his attacks on religious fanaticism and forced conversion.[63] In his version, Sol serves as the beautiful "heroine of the nineteenth century" who was martyred for the sake of religious tolerance and a liberal education. The term *la hermosa Sol* (the beautiful Sol) is used repeatedly almost as a metanymic phrase. Romero describes Sol's beauty using images and tropes very similar to the poetry of the Duke of Rivas, who some have argued gives women an elevated and highly esteemed status.[64] In many cases, the beauty of the duke's women was a reflection of their virtue, morality, and comportment. His descriptions at times reach the heights of hyperbole, as does Romero's exaltation of Sol as the "Goddess of Virtue." Some of the same images, such as "hand of snow" and "black and long tresses negligently fastened," are encountered in both Rivas's poems and Romero's description of Sol.[65] This attitude toward women has its origins in courtly love poetry.[66] Romero's combination of Romanticism with the poetic conventions of courtly love is apparent in his descriptions of Sol, as it was in the writings of Rivas and in the Romantic movement in general.[67]

In Macé's text one can also see the Romantic and liberal sentiment, this time filtered through operatic conventions and intertextual references to Scribe's and Halevy's *La Juive*. Here too Sol is a symbol of beauty, of liberal tolerance and ecumenicalism, and loyalty to Judaism. Like *La Juive*, the message is a denunciation of religious intolerance. Added to this is a more specific lament at the passing of "La belle Andalousie," where "harmony reigns."[68] There is a scene of ecumenical piety, with each character representing a different religion, including Asaia, a Jewish friend of Sol, and Ali, whose religion is his love for Sol, each praying to his respective deity. Ali's prayer reveals his religious devotion to Sol:

> God who commands the elements, Who makes one love, who makes one smile, Near this Spring flower, I feel your breathe and radiance. Divine creator, improve my heart. . . and make me love you in your creature.[69]

Ali affirms to his sister that Sol is "my idol."[70] Because of her brother's hopeless love for Sol, Tahra, who disappears shortly after the first act, agrees to trick Sol into converting. After Sol is taken to prison, Ali declares that he will save her and accompanies her to Fez. After he advises her to flee to France, where "tolerance reigns," and Sol refuses, Ali declares his love for her, describing her physical ("your rosy mouth") and spiritual qualities ("this noble sentiment, your most beautiful ornament").[71] Macé celebrates Sol's beauty using Romantic ideals of spiritual love. In both Romero's and Macé's texts, the political message of religious tolerance is the same and the celebration of Sol's beauty combines physical description with spiritual virtue. In Macé, the embodiment of religious tolerance is also developed in the character of Ali, who becomes a gallant lover willing to convert to Judaism in order to marry Sol. However, this is not rabbinic Judaism, the Judaism of the "unemancipated," but an enlightened Judaism of *culte israélite*; that is, a reformed Judaism under French tutelage.[72] Ali denounces Islamic fanaticism and celebrates the age of Averroès and Andalusian Spain. Sol and her beauty become symbols of tolerance, ecumenical existence, and the power of love to overcome separation and difference.

Sol's story was also taken up by devout Catholics, who saw it as an example of devotion to God, religious martyrdom, and Islamic cruelty. In the Spanish texts, Ovilo y Canales illustrates this approach,[73] in which Spain's civilizing mission in Morocco was centered on rescuing Moroccan women from Islamic misogyny. Like Macé, Ovilo y Canales served as a doctor in his country's military mission just prior to the establishment of the protectorate. He felt that Morocco was a decadent country whose culture was destined to be obliterated. The source of decadence was Islam itself and the proof of this decadence was the status and treatment of women in Morocco. Ovilo y Canales presents Sol's story as an example of Islamic cruelty toward women and sees her execution as the public execution of another female, one who was a potential member of the sultan's harem.[74] In Ovilo y Canales's text, Catholicism's superiority to Islam is proven by its worship of women.[75] Correspondingly, Ovilo y Canales stresses Sol's identity as a female over her identity as a Jew. In his version of her story, Sol converted to Islam in a "moment of insanity and weakness." Given the author's religious leanings he could not conceive of any other motivation for such a conversion. After the moment passed, Sol repented her conversion but was publicly executed in Meknes (rather than Fez). The crowd that watched her execution was moved by her faith and valor. According to Ovilo y Calanes, Sol rejected the rabbis, who officially sanctioned her conversion in order to spare her life, as "hypocritical and disloyal."[76] This characterization of the rabbis was also taken up by Macé and by Boutet, as will be shown below. In Ovilo y Canales's estimation, Judaism does not fare much better than Islam in the area of the treatment of women, particularly in its marriage and divorce laws. Ovilo y Canales's claim that Christianity valorizes women does not extend to independent women; it extends only to women who fulfill roles as wives and mothers.[77] Given that there were some feminist writings and agitation in Spain[78] at the time and that Catholicism was being blamed for holding back Spain's progress toward modernization and gender equality, his work can be seen as being a part of this internal political debate as much as it was a claim for a Christian civilizing mission in Morocco.

Boutet illustrates French Catholic sentiment in his version of Sol's story. In the opening of his serialized novel, he declares his own love for Sol because she represents beauty and saintliness, two things that embody, for him, "the absolute of the world and the infinity of heaven."[79] Boutet begins his narration of Sol's life with her birth and infancy. He describes her as a beautiful, innocent infant whose parents loved her but did not celebrate her birth, as they would have done for a male child.[80] Boutet describes Jewish customs in detail and with sympathy, but there is also a barely veiled criticism of Jewish male chauvinism similar to that of Ovilo y Canales, albeit not as intense and as vitriolic. His descriptions of the poverty of Sol's family, her wicker cradle, her nursing at her mother's breast, her small hands and feet, recall paintings of the infant Jesus. In another intertextual reference, Tahra, like Judas, kisses Sol on the lips before she betrays her. In her testimony before the pasha of Tangier, Sol is transformed from the *petite juive* who was seduced by Andalusian music into a being who represents "all of her race, animated by prophetic survival. The same wind that blew over Sinai on the day of the Revelation passed on her soul and swept up all the foreign influences."[81] Sol, like Jesus, belongs to God but is prepared to be judged by men. In the author's graphic description of Sol's final moments, it is the sword that penetrates her body, but Boutet gets into her skin, her lungs, her throat, and experiences her agony and delirium as she dies for God.

In Boutet's text, the roles of Ali and Andalusia are also transformed. Ali becomes a *kif*-smoking heartless seducer who uses the Andalusian songs Sol's mother sang to her to intoxicate and overcome her, and the shared Andalusian culture becomes a foreign influence that leads to Sol's downfall. In another Christian reference, this time to early Christian virgin martyrs, Sol becomes the dominant, impassioned, sexually charged, aggressive virgin martyr: "She had in her the beauty of a virgin warrior."[82] Daniel Boyarin's study of martyrdom in Judaism and early Christianity analyzes the sexual politics of the *virago*, the active, aggressive virgin martyr of early Christian texts.[83] For the purpose of this analysis it is enough to note the existence of a figure such as the virago or warrior virgin martyr to see Boutet's as yet another Christianization of Sol's story.

Another aspect of the gendered discourse is the comparison of Sol with Tahra. Two of these texts make direct contrasts between Sol and Tahra. In Romero, as stated above, *la hermosa Sol* is often contrasted with the "crafty," "fanatic," "deceitful Mooress."[84] Ironically enough, in European literature these same adjectives have been used to characterize Jews.[85] In Macé, Ali makes the contrast between Sol and Moorish women, dismissing the latter as baby machines who lack education and knowledge.[86] English travel literature of the period described Jewish women of Tangier in a similar manner.[87] In such dichotomies, the women of one ethnic or religious group are juxtaposed with women in another group in a hierarchy of spirituality versus physicality, goodness and virtue versus malice and vice. In these comparisons, gender discourse becomes divided along ethnic, religious, or racial lines.

In all of these texts Sol's beauty becomes a symbol for the political or religious perspective of the author. She can represent a plea for religious tolerance or be seen as a symbol of the power of faith and religious fervor. She can be used to advocate liberal ecumenical politics or transform into a religious crusader dying for God. In the process, Andalusia either becomes an ideal lost paradise, as in Macé, or a foreign influence that leads to corruption and death. Ali is also transformed from a gallant knight to a *kif*-smoking seducer. The character of Tahra also varies slightly. In Macé and Boutet, she is merely a helpmate to her brother who does his bidding. In Romero, she acts almost alone because the character of Ali is not mentioned. Here it is Tahra, who is constantly contrasted to Sol, who plays the role of the treasonous, fanatical "Mooress."

A dominant current in Ovilo y Canales, which Macé shares despite their differences, is the idea of colonizer as liberator. This notion is also seen in the role Boutet gives the French consul in Tangier, who tries unsuccessfully to intimidate the corrupt pasha in an attempt to get him to release Sol. Another French character, an anguished renegade who has converted to Islam, also offers to help Sol and her brother flee to Gibraltar on a boat. Sol refuses his offer, stating that her family in Morocco would be put in danger if she fled. The local Moroccan authorities had demanded that Sol's father either pay for her transport to Fez or be flogged. In Romero, José Rico, the Spanish vice-consul, plays the role of the savior of Sol's father by loaning him 40 duros so he can pay for Sol's transport to Fez and thus avoid a flogging. This portrayal of European and colonizer as savior also appears in Ortega's and Juarros's descriptions of the Spanish occupation of Tetuan in the mid-nineteenth century and in their depictions of Spain's "benevolent" protectorate over northern Morocco. Juarros, who is more equivocal about Spain's ability to modernize Morocco, given its social problems, mentions the problem of Spanish *colons,* who exhibit prejudiced attitudes toward both Jews and Muslims, and their uncouth behavior.[88] Of all the texts dealt with here, Juarros's is the only one to question the consistency and benevolence of the colonizing mission; he offers testimonials from Muslims who believed that Spain's only ambition was to enrich itself at their expense. Juarros wrote his work in the midst of the Rif War, before France's intervention turned the tide in favor of the colonial powers. In the end, however, Juarros affirms Spain's colonial mission, stating that the future of Spain was in Morocco and that Spain had an obligation to modernize both itself and its "little brother" at the same time.[89] Despite an initial doubt, in the end he affirms Spain's Moroccan policy as articulated two decades earlier by the Spanish pro-colonial institutions. In his opinion, Spain could still play the gallant, paternal savior despite its shortcomings.

Juarros's *"ojos bellos"* and other ocular attempts to penetrate the veil of Moroccan women during the Spanish protectorate period and expose their secret desires informed his interpretation of Sephardi ballads about Sol, particularly "El Rey Arrepentido." Juarros's musings about women was aided by his medical practice, which gave him access to Moroccan women via his female patients that would have been otherwise unavailable, but such an interest in Moroccan women was already visible in the Spanish illustrated press at the end of the nineteenth century. Illustrations of the harem and of the reclining "odalisque"; comparisons between women of the West, women of Spain, and women of the secluded Eastern harem; and representations of the sexual superiority of the turbaned Arab sheik surrounded by beautiful veiled women were all part of the illustrated weeklies that were accompanied by descriptions of "Oriental life."[90] This idealized male fantasy can be contrasted to the debates in Spain about the steadily increasing presence of Spanish women in public places.[91] This is evident in Juarros's disparaging comments regarding Spanish women, with their "exposed" bodies, in contrast to the mystery and allure of veiled Muslim women.[92] His "valorization" and objectification of the veiled and secluded woman responded to polemics against feminist claims in Spain but were situated in a colonial context. Looking at the gender discourse in these texts, one can see that the images

of beauty and the message the authors inserted into Sol's story were closely related to their political and religious perspectives and to the political struggles in
Spain and France at the time. In addition, a nascent feminist movement in Spain
may account for the number of Spanish texts devoted to Moroccan women. Colonial discourse was thus also a gendered discourse, with the colonizer as doctor, savior, psychologist, and voyeur. But gender discourse also must be seen in
the context of European attitudes toward Jews and Muslims, such as the image of
the *belle juive,* the different images of the *moro* and *mora* Muslim men and women.
The colonial gaze of Juarros's text was fixated on both Muslim and Jewish female
bodies and the images and writings about them were in turned deployed to put
Spanish women in their place at home. But these images need to be placed in the
context of how these authors characterized both Judaism and Islam, which in
many ways were quite similar.

The "Jewish Question"

In most discussions of the "Jewish Question," Jewish emancipation in Europe, and anti-Semitism, gender receives little consideration. Yet discussions about
Jews in this period were hardly gender neutral.[93] In order to understand how images of Jewish women were recycled in these Suleika texts, it is important to discuss the evolution of the image of the *belle juive,* a well-known character type of
nineteenth-century European literature and drama. Klein discusses the history
of the different types of *juives* in French literature, making the connection between them and European ambivalence toward Judaism itself.[94] The Christianization of ancient Judaism and the practice of reading the Old Testament in light
of the New provided the background for the development of the beautiful, virtuous, and even self-sacrificing "Jewess," as in the opera *La Juive.* This image was
closely related to the idea that Jewish women and children were exempt from
the crime of Judas and were more easily converted to Christianity.[95] This notion
can be seen in the character type of the Jewish daughter who converts and reb-
els against her father in the works of Marlowe (*The Jew of Malta*) and Shakespeare.
Shakespeare's *Merchant of Venice* was translated into French in the 1820s, as was
Walter Scott's *Ivanhoe,* and these became important sources for the development
of *la belle juive.* As the century progressed, this literary type evolved, sometimes
in negative ways. In the context of growing secularization and anti-clericalism
and the diffusion of Enlightenment ideas, the Bible began to be seen in some
quarters in a more negative light, and this resulted in a more critical and even
negative evaluation of *la belle juive.*[96] Toward the end of the nineteenth century,
the ideas of Edouard Drumont and Charles Maurras began influencing some
French writers, such as Daudet. Anti-Semitism and Orientalism were at times

united in the *origine asiatique* of Jewish characters, and such origins were attributed to Jewish politicians and celebrities in France.[97] The *belle juive* as an exotic, Oriental courtesan also combined the images of the *belle juive* and the *asiatique*.

In the French texts discussed here we can see both the benevolent and virtuous *belle juive* and the coquettish *belle juive*. Not surprisingly, the first type is found in Boutet's Christianized, beatified Sol and the second in Macé's operatic Sol. I have already discussed Boutet's intertextual references to Christianity, in particular to the life of Jesus. Placing these in the larger context of the literary and theological conception of ancient Judaism as nascent Christianity, we can see where these ideas came from. The relationship between the *belle juive* as coquette and Macé's operatic Sol remains to be shown. Unlike most other Suleika texts, Macé's text does not allow Sol to carry her own message. This message is conveyed by her two male companions, Ali and Asaia. In fact much of her dialogue, particularly in the beginning of the work, consists of flirtatious interchanges with Ali.[98] By singing, entertaining, and leading the chorus in the soirée of the first act, Macé's Sol comes close to the Orientalist singing courtesan.[99]

It is possible to find commonalities in Macé's Sol and Boutet's Sol despite the radically different worldviews of the authors. Before her radical transformation into the virgin warrior, Boutet's Sol was also a frivolous *petite juive* whom Ali easily seduced as he played and sang her mother's Andalusian love songs. Without this radical transformation and self-sacrifice, she could well have become a singing courtesan of Ali's harem. In Macé, Ali himself becomes the agent of transformation, both of himself (from noble Arab to enslaved lover and gallant knight) and of Sol (from singing coquette to pure angel and beloved object of veneration). Despite the differences in plots and worldviews, both Macé's singing Sol and Boutet's saintly Sol incorporate the dual nature and ambivalent character of *la belle juive* of French literature.

In these French texts, Sol's story is used either as a liberal plea for religious tolerance and as anticlerical polemics or it is subsumed under the rubric of Catholic martyrdom. Throughout the nineteenth century and into the twentieth, both Spain and France were engaged in political struggles over the role of the Catholic Church in the state. While the French Revolution granted Jews citizenship, their struggle for social acceptance and access to public institutions continued for a long time. The Dreyfus affair and the prior publication of Drumont's *La France Juive* in 1886 as well as anti-Semitic agitation by the Catholic press from the time of the Second Empire show that French citizens by no means unanimously accepted Jews. Although Jews were able to integrate successfully into the Republic, debates over its legitimacy continued up until the Union Sacrée, the political movement that allowed republicans and Catholic monarchists to put aside their differences during World War I. In the 1920s, membership in anti-republic, anti-

Jewish organizations dwindled for a time and some Catholics began to repudiate anti-Semitism.[100] This probably accounts for the differences between the attitudes toward Jews of Godard, who wrote during the Second Empire, and those
of Boutet, who wrote in 1929.

Spanish literature offers a different set of textual references, including the
legend of the Judía of Toledo and Alfonso VIII and the *"conversa/Marrana"* prostitutes of picaresque novels. In seventeenth-century Spanish drama, Esther became a noble character that prefigured Mary during the period of Muslim expulsion from Spain (1609) and the auto-da-fé. Such works can be seen as a veiled
way of criticizing the Inquisition.[101] In the nineteenth century, Romanticism combined with exoticism and a turn to biblical themes in a number of novels, some
of which included female characters from the Hebrew Bible and the New Testament, such as Judith, Esther, and Mary Magdalene. The works of Romantic
writers contrasted the nobility and morals of biblical figures with the degener-
acy of modern writers such as Byron and George Sand.[102] At the end of the nineteenth century a Spanish anti-Semitic work based on Drumont appeared (*La España judía,* by P. Casabó y Pagés) that attacked *conversos* (new Christian men)
especially *conversas* (new Christian women). Similar themes of the noble "Jewess" of the Bible and the Jewish courtesan appear in Spanish literature but in the
context of different cultural and historical influences and different literary texts.
The feminine ideals of nobility, virtue, and beauty were united in the biblical
dramatic heroines of the Spanish literary "golden age" and nineteenth-century
romantic novels. Romero's Sol fits into this conception. As the conflicts between
clerics and anti-clerics intensified, the Bible and its heroines became part of the
contested zone. Anti-clerics pointed to the Song of Songs as a source of eroticism
and even pornography.[103] Starting in 1834, with the publication of J. de Espron-
ceda's *Sancho Saldaña, El castellano de Cuéllar,* the literary type of the *heroína hebrea*
appeared, a slave to her passions who was carried away by fatal attractions to
Christian heroes, who dominate her and lead her to a sad end.[104] One could certainly see an analogue to Sol's story in these literary types. In Romero's version of
Sol's story, she does not succumb to any temptation to convert or marry out of her
faith. In contrast, Ovilo y Canales and Ortega have Sol follow the plotline of the
stereotypical *heroína hebrea.* Perhaps this Spanish literary type led them to prefer a conversionist rendition of Sol's story. Juarros shows a marked preference for
this literary type in his valorization of the romance, which focuses on the longings of the non-Jewish king for his dead Jewish beloved. Perhaps this is why he
deprecated the romance that celebrated Sol's rejection of conversion and her devotion to her natal faith rather than to carnal love.

Another literary "Jewess" type, stemming from *The Jew of Malta* and *The Merchant of Venice,* is the virtuous daughter of an evil Jewish father. The latter some-

times appears as a rabbi. The virtuous daughter represents Christianized and valorized biblical Judaism or the Jewish qualities of the mother of Jesus and of Mary Magdalene, while the fanatical Jewish father or rabbi represents the often-vilified Talmud.[105] Godard was perhaps the first to apply this theoretical framework to Sol's story. In Boutet and Macé, it is integrated into the plot and dramatized in an anti-Semitic diatribe from Sol herself, directed at the rabbis of Fez:

> Boutet: It is not the Mishna [Talmud] / that inspires these rabbis, but the gold of Sidna [i.e., the Sultan]. / Their dishonest speech / preaches to me, I blush for them! The mental restriction / What shame! This scandal![106]

> Macé: Enough of trying to tempt me; am I attached to my religion by the sons of these veins from which the forms of your bodies are boastful, your bodies that tomorrow will be nothing?[107]

The authors seem unaware of the irony of having Sol die for a faith while at the same time attacking its leaders. We can see the potential for this even in Romero, when Sol rejects the arguments of the rabbis trying to save her life, but in Romero she does this respectfully. Romero also makes it clear that if the rabbis had not tried to convince her to convert, they would have been threatened with the destruction of the entire Jewish community of Fez.[108] In contrast, in both Macé and Boutet, the motivation is pure monetary greed. One can see the workings of nineteenth-century anti-Semitic stereotypes, which intensified over the course of the century. That such stereotypes would show up in works that praised a Jewish heroine for being faithful to her religion is not without precedent. One can see anti-Semitic stereotypes even in defenders of Jews among nineteenth-century European writers, including Ortega and Juarros, who both used the stereotypes of Jewish commercial power and monetary "genius" to advocate Spain's adoption of their *política sefardí*.[109] The motivation for such a policy was not simply to right a historical wrong or reunite with long-lost Spanish blood but also to promote Spanish economic, political, and colonial interests.

This contrast between the ideal and the real can also be seen in the notion that the European was the savior of the Jew. This savior appeared in the form of Boutet's Christian renegade and in Romero's vice-consul and contrasts with the reality of increasing instability in Morocco as the European presence increased. The French invasion of Algeria four years before Sol was executed,[110] European gunboat diplomacy in the mid-nineteenth century, and the growing intensity of European anti-Semitism at the end of the nineteenth century all make the claim that Europeans would be the salvation of the Jews equivocal. While the protégé system may have helped some Jews escape the debilities of *dhimmi* status, the situation in the countryside and for the vast majority of Jews outside the protégé system was a lot more volatile.[111] The corollary to the notion of the European as the savior of the Jew was the idea that the Muslim was the oppressor of the Jew. This conception was part of the larger depiction of the Muslim in European writings.

Conclusion

The foregoing discussion highlights the overlap in discourses on gender, the "Jewish Question," and the colonial "mission" in the Suleika texts and beyond. Clearly, a number of similarities exist between images of Jews and Muslims and between Orientalism and anti-Semitism in these works. These texts characterized both Jews and Muslims as fanatical, primitive, crafty, and treacherous. Moreover, these discourses are also inevitably gendered even when they only discuss men. In the context of the Suleika texts and in the portrayals of *la belle juive* or *la heroína hebrea* and the *mora* or *mauresque,* gender issues are particularly transparent. As a coquette and courtesan, the *origine asiatique* of the *belle juive* is closely related to the Oriental female entertainer or the odalisque in terms of their physical portrayal (black eyes and long black hair) and their supposed sexual desires and knowledge. In the portrayal of the *mora* in Spanish literature, the *belle juive* in French literature, and even the "Jewess" in English literature,[112] the more Christian-like the character is, the more positive the portrayal is.

When comparing the representations by writers from different European countries it is important to note both similarities and differences. There are a number of contextual similarities between Spain and France in the nineteenth century. Some of these include political instability, fights between anti-clerics and Catholic monarchists, a Romantic movement that looked to its medieval past for inspiration, and a medieval history of armed conflict with Muslims on French and Spanish soil. There are also important differences. France was the first European nation to grant citizenship to Jews. In Spain there was the long medieval history of Andalusia and the *convivencia,* on the one hand, and the Inquisition, the expulsion, and blood purity laws, on the other. These historical differences help in part to account for the variations in the portrayal of Jews and Muslims in French and Spanish literature. Historically Muslim characters, both positive and negative, have a much larger presence in Spanish literature than Jewish characters. At the same time the rediscovery of the Sephardi Jewish communities of the Mediterranean in the nineteenth century led to an unprecedented valorization of Sephardi culture and literature. Colonial desires and the perceived need to make up for the humiliation of the final loss of the Americas in 1898 by colonizing Morocco led to mistrust and direct conflict with Muslims. There is a greater prominence of Jewish characters in French literature than in Spanish. These characters underwent changes that were related to the incorporation of French Israélite citizens into the institutions of the Republic and the resentment about this incorporation and toward the Republic itself, particularly on the part of Catholic monarchists.[113] While there is no direct correspondence between political history and literature, the literary images in the Suleika texts, taken as they are from European literary character types and images, correspond closely with depictions of Jews and Muslims in works of nonfiction, including European works of nonfiction about Morocco. These works had direct political intentions; their authors advocated and later celebrated colonial rule over Morocco. Some of the justifications for European countries' increased involvement in Morocco included the ways Muslim men treated women and a stereotype of Muslims as the oppressor and sworn enemies of Jews. While the authors who wrote these accounts may have been moved by genuine humanitarian concerns, they often failed to consider how Jews were treated in their own countries and their own anti-Semitic stereotypes and prejudices in their portrayal of Jews. In addition, these texts did not tell and interpret Sol's story in the same way as the Jewish texts but instead used her martyrdom to advance their own political concerns.[114] Both Juarros and Boutet were presented with Jewish versions of her story, Juarros with at least two ballads and Boutet with stories he heard while in Morocco, and both rejected these. Juarros preferred to focus on interreligious carnal love and Boutet on Catholic martyrdom.[115]

Evaluating the literary merit of these texts as a corpus,[116] one can see that none of the authors discussed were particularly original. Their works were derivative, drawing on the stereotypical treatments of Jews and Muslims available in European discourse. Familiar images of the fanatical Jewish or Muslim believer or the beautiful Tangier "Jewess" found their way from travelogues and memoirs of the early nineteenth century into these texts. Their portrayal of Sol's story and of the situation of Jews in Morocco in general combined humanitarian concerns with colonial designs. A literary historical study focusing on comparative analysis of both Jewish and Muslim portrayals reveals a considerable overlap with the primary sources of nineteenth century European anti-Semitism and Orientalism. It is especially ironic to consider similarities between Orientalist and anti-Semitic portrayals of Muslims and Jews in texts that consistently portrayed relations between Muslims and Jews as characterized by animosity and violence. Any negative incident that took place in Morocco was used to reinforce arguments that Europeans should intervene. But looking closely at these discourses reveals that the portrayal of both Jews and Muslims and of both Judaism and Islam was mostly negative. Although these texts valorized Sol, they valorized a Christianized Sol or a liberal Romantic Sol, not a Jewish Sol. In these discourses neither Judaism nor Islam are validated as positive identities. Hopefully more attention will be paid to the ways that both Judaism and Islam have been portrayed in anti-Semitic and Orientalist writings and discourse and to the historical similarities of their images in the West.

NOTES

1. According to a French traveler who heard Sol's story from one of her brothers, news about her arrest in Tangier spread throughout the Moroccan Empire. See M. Rey, *Souvenirs d'un Voyage au Maroc* (Paris: Au Bureau du Journal L'Algérie, 1844), 152.

2. For a full listing of Suleika texts and references, see Sharon Vance, "Sol ha-Ṣaddiqah: Historic Figure, Saint, Literary Persona" (Ph.D. diss., University of Pennsylvania, 2005); and Sara Leibovici, "Sol Hachuel, la Tsaddikkah ou la force de la Foi (1834)," *Pardès*, no.4 (1984): 133–146. See also citations to works in Robert Attal, *Les Juifs d'Afrique du Nord: Bibliographie* (Jerusalem: Yad Izhak Ben-Zvi et Université Hébraïque, 1993). *Editors' Note:* See also the recent publication by Saïd Sayagh: *l'Autre Juive* (Paris: Ibis Press, 2009).

3. See Eugenio María Romero, *El martirio de la joven Hachuel, ó la heroína hebrea* (Gibraltar: Imprenta Militar, 1837); and Rey, *Souvenirs d'un voyage au Maroc*, I analyzed and compared these texts for their historical accuracy in my dissertation. Here I will be focusing on Romero's rhetoric as a reflection of his political perspective and the historical events that took place in Spain when he published his work on Sol. Other works about Sol were written by Moroccan Jewish authors; see Yaʿakov Berdugo, *Kol Yaʿakov: Ve-nikra shemo be-Yisra'el maʿavar yabok* (London, 1844), 10–11; David Pinto, "Kissa Di Solika a-Sadikah," in *Tefilah*, Oran, Algeria (ms. 582, Bar-Ilan University, Ramat Gan); Hayyim Halewa, "'Am Asher Nivharu," in Berdugo, *Kol Yaʿakov*, 129–131; Shemu'el Elbaz, "Shimkha yah kidshah," in *mi-Ginze shirat ha-Kedem: Piyyut ve-hikre piyyut*, ed. Y. Ratzaby (Jerusalem: Misgav Yerushalayim, ha-Makhon le-heker moreshet Yahadut Sefarad ve-ha-Mizrah, 1990), 83–87; Yaʿakov Abihatsira, *Sefer Yagel Yaʿakov* (Tunis: Kastro, [1902]); Yaʿakov Mosheh Toledano, *Ner ha-maʿarav* (Jerusalem: A. M. Lunts, 1911); Yosef Ben-Na'im, *Malkhe Rabanan* (Jerusalem: Y. Abikatsits, 1930); Moshe Ben-Saʿadon, "Kissat Solika," in *Kissot le-Tishʿah be-Av* (ms. 537, Bar-Ilan University, Ramat Gan). I analyzed the published works in Hebrew in my dissertation and will discuss the manuscripts in Judeo-Arabic by Ben-Saʿadon and Pinto in a forthcoming book.

4. Mrinalini Sinha points out the interconnections between gender and other group identities, stating that "all aspects of reality are engendered." However gender itself is a category that operates within other categories of "class/caste, race, nation and sexuality." Mrinalini Sinha, *Colonial Masculinity: The "Manly Englishman" and the "Effeminate Bengali" in the Late Nineteenth Century* (New York: St. Martin's Press, 1995), 11.

5. In contrast to the texts discussed here, all the Jewish texts emphasize Sol's defense of Judaism (particularly in her polemics) and her willingness to die—not for liberal principles of religious tolerance, which go unmentioned, but for her faith and identity as a Jew.

6. Two years later an English translation was published in London: *The Jewish Heroine of the Nineteenth Century: A Tale, Founded on Fact* (London: L. Thompson, 1839).

7. Romero, *El martirio de la joven Hachuel ó la heroina hebrea* , ix, 105. According to the version of Sol's story in *La Epoka*, Issachar settled in Gibraltar after Sol's death. "Sol La Saddeket," Folioton Numero 2, *Folieton de La Epoca* (1902): 16.

8. See Vance, "Sol ha-Ṣaddiqah: Historic Figure, Saint, Literary Persona," where I compare Romero's version with Rey's account, which was based on the testimony of Sol's brother.

9. Rivas was an early supporter of liberal republican politics in Spain but later became a monarchist. He went into exile in Gibraltar on 3 October 1923. See Gabriel H. Lovett, *The Duke of Rivas* (Boston: Twayne, 1977), 11.

10. Romero, *El martirio de la joven Hachuel ó la heroíina hebrea,* 86–88. Romero's book was translated as Eugenio Maria Romero, *The Jewish Heroine of the Nineteenth Century: A Tale Founded on Fact* (London: L. Thompson, 1839); the corresponding page numbers in this version are 67–69. This shift in focus from culture and belief to nature and race intensified throughout the nineteenth century along with the ideological popularity of ethnonationalism; see Eric Hobsbawm, "The Rise of Ethno-Linguistic Nationalisms," in *Nationalism,* ed. John Hutchinson and Anthony D. Smith (Oxford: Oxford University Press, 1994), 178.

11. Romero, *El martirio de la joven Hachuel ó la heroina hebrea,* 20.

12. Ibid., 116 (p. 90 in the English version).

13. Raymond Carr, *Spain, 1808–1939* (Oxford: Clarendon Press, 1966), 132–133.

14. Kenneth Baxter Wolf, "Muhammad as Antichrist in Ninth-Century Córdova," in *Christians, Muslims, and Jews in Medieval and Early Modern Spain,* ed. Mark D. Meyerson and Edward D. English (Notre Dame, Ind.: University of Notre Dame Press, 1999), 3–19.

15. Antonio Calle, *El martirio de la joven Hachuel o la heroína hebrea, drama historice en cinco actos, en prosa y verso* (Seville: Imprenta D.G. Camacho, 1858); Enrique Sumel, *La heroína hebrea* (Gibraltar: 1858), cited in Sarah Leibovici, "Sol Hachuel," 135.

16. *La Juive* was first performed at the Paris Opera on 23 February 1835; music by Jacques François Fromental Halévy, libretto by Eugène Scribe. The libretto for *La Juive* was published in Nico Castel, *French Opera Libretti,* 3 vols. (Geneseo, N.Y.: Leyerle Publications, 1999), 2:167–269.

17. W. T. Moncrieff, *Ivanhoe! or, The "Jewess": A Chivalric Play in Three Acts; Founded on the Popular Romance of Ivanhoe* (London: Printed for J. Lowndes by F. Marshall, 1820). For an opera based on *Ivanhoe,* see the libretto *The Templar and the "Jewess": A Grand Romantic Opera from Sir W. Scott's Novel of Ivanhoe* (London: [1841?]).

18. Ch. Macé, *Sol Hachuel: Melodrame En 4 Actes* (Rome: Impr. de I. Artero, 1901).

19. Ibid., 70–71.

20. Ibid., 70. In *La Juive,* Prince Leopold pretends to be a Jew so he can have a rendezvous with Rachel (Castel, *French Opera Libretti,* 185). In *Sol Hachuel,* Ali is known as *"le Maure"* (44). Sol calls him *"ce Maure si beau"* (this Moor so beautiful) and wonders, *"Que sera cet Ali? Pacha a l'air sévère? Ou caïd ou cadi qu'on craint et qu'on révère?"* (What will Ali be? A pasha with a stern manner? Or a *qa'id* or a *qadi* that one fears and reveres?) (20).

21. *La Juive* was performed throughout the nineteenth century. It was reprinted in Paris in 1859, 1861, and 1870.

22. *L'Avenir Illustré* was a pro-Zionist journal published in Casablanca by Jonathan Thursz during the period 1926–1940; Michael M. Laskier, *The Alliance Israèlite Universelle and the Jewish Communities of Morocco, 1862–1962* (Albany: State University of New York Press, 1983), 203.

23. See, e.g., Robert Boutet, "Notes sur le Judaïsme dans l'extrême-sud marocain," *L'Avenir Illustré,* 31 March 1936, 3–5; *L'Avenir Illustré,* 30 April 1936, 3–5.

24. Robert Boutet, "'Sulika' ou la vie de Sol Hatchuel," *L'Avenir Illustré,* 16 January 1930, 6.

25. Léon Godard, *Description et histoire de Maroc* (Paris: E. Donnaud, 1860), 83–84.

26. Ibid., 111.

27. Ibid., 301.

28. Manuel L. Ortega, *Los Hebreos en Marruecos* (Madrid: Editorial Hispano Africana, 1919), 306.

29. Ibid., 221; Isidro Gonzales, *El Returno de los Judios* (Madrid: NEREA, 1991), 11–13, 59.

30. Ortega, *Los Hebreos en Marruecos,* 298; Gonzalez, *El Returno de los Judios,* 14.

31. Felipe Ovilo y Canales, *La mujer marroquí* (Madrid: M. G. Hernández, 1881), 8, 26.

32. Ortega, *Los Hebreos en Marruecos,* 221.

33. Ibid., 300.

34. Ibid., 221.

35. Ibid., 325.

36. Manuel L. Ortega, *El Raisuni* (Madrid: Tipografía Moderna, 1917), vii–viii.

37. Francisco Coello, Joaquín Costa, Gabriel Rodríguez, Gumersindo de Azcárate, Eduardo Saaverda, and José de Carvajal, *Intereses de España en Marruecos discursos pronunciados en el meet-*

ing de la sociedad española de africanistas y colonistas celebrado en el Teatro de La Alhambra el Dia 30 de Marzo de1884 (Madrid: Instituto de Estudios Africanos, 1951).

38. *"Siempre acaban por volver públicamente a sus creencias primitivas"* (They always finish by returning publicly to their primitive beliefs); Ortega, *Los Hebreos en Marruecos,* 159.

39. Ibid.

40. Ibid., 159–160.

41. Ibid., 337.

42. He also recommended taking over Sephardi education for the benefit of Spain. His educational policy expressed both the liberalism of religious tolerance and the "patriotic" imperial desires of reestablishing Spain as a great power, pervaded by a sense of urgency about Spain establishing itself in Morocco and competition with France, Britain, and Zionism. Ibid., 276–280, 345.

43. Ibid., 338–339.

44. César Juarros, *La Cuidad de los ojos bellos (Tetuan)* (Madrid: Editorial Mundo Latino, 1922). Juarros also wrote works in the areas of medicine, psychiatry, and psychology, including works on love and sexuality.

45. See ibid., 9–22, 25, 298–305, for both Spain and Morocco.

46. Ibid., 197.

47. Ibid., 13–14. For debates over women's public presence in Spain and the transition from the nineteenth-century prohibition against women appearing in public alone to a society in which women increasingly appeared in public in the early part of the twentieth century, see Elizabeth Munson, "Walking on the Periphery: Gender and the Discourse of Modernization," *Journal of Social History* 36, no. 1 (2002): 63–75.

48. Juarros, *La Cuidad de los ojos bellos (Tetuan),* 164, 225, 293, 298.

49. Ibid., 225.

50. *"El poeta sigue mostrándose tan desconocedor de los secretos de la métrica como antes, mas hay aquí un rato velo de sexualidad que huelo a nardo y carne morena"* (The poet continues to demonstrate a lack of knowledge of the secrets of meter as before; rather, there is here a rare veil of sexuality that smells of nard and dark-skinned flesh); ibid., 226.

51. Ibid., 228.

52. Ibid., 226.

53. Edna Aizenberg, "'Una judía muy fermosa': The 'Jewess' as Sex Object in Medieval Spanish Literature and Lore," *La Cornica: A Journal of Medieval Spanish Language & Literature* 12, no. 2 (1984): 187–194; Sanford Shepard, "Prostitutes and Picaros in Inquisitional Spain," *Neohelicon* 3, nos. 1–2 (1975): 365–372

54. Gabriel Séailles, *Alfred Dehodencq: Histoire d'un coloriste* (Paris: P. Ollendorff, 1985).

55. Rey, *Souvenirs d'un voyage au Maroc,* 140–176.

56. Henri de la Martinière, *Souvenirs du Maroc* (Paris: Plon, 1919).

57. Séailles, *Alfred Dehodencq,* 141–142, 145–146, 148.

58. Ibid., 151–152.

59. Ibid., 146–148.

60. De la Martinière, *Souvenirs du Maroc,* 8.

61. Ibid., iv.

62. C. R. Pennell, *Morocco since 1830* (New York: New York University Press, 2000), 110.

63. Pura Fernández, "La Literature del siglo xix y los orígenes del contubernio judeo-masônico-comunista," in *Judíos en La Literature Espaõla,* ed. Iacob M. Hasséan and Ricardo Izquierdo Benito (Cuenca: Ediciones de la Universidad de Castilla-La Mancha, 2001), 301–351.

64. Bernier Blanco, Juan Antonio, and Francisco Onieva Ramírez, "La dama en los 'Romances históricos' de Rivas: función de un tópico," in *Los Románticos y Andalucía,* ed. Diego Martínes Torrón (Córdova: Servicio de Publicaciones de la Universidad de Córdova, 1997), 119–148.

65. Romero, *El martirio de la joven Hachuel ó la heroína hebrea,* 63 (p. 51 in the English version); Blanco, Antonio, and Ramírez, "La dama en los 'Romances históricos' de Rivas," 126–127.

66. Blanco, Antonio, and Ramírez, "La dama en los 'Romances históricos' de Rivas," 121.

67. Ibid., 157–166.

68. Macé, *Sol Hachuel*, 50.

69. Ibid., 59.

70. Ibid., 22.

71. Ibid., 44.

72. See Miriam Hoexter, "Les Juifs français et l'assimilation politique et institutionelle de la communauté juive en Algérie (1830–1870)," in *Les Relations intercommunautaires juives en Méditerranée occidentale xiiie–xxe siècles*, ed. Jean Louis Miège (Paris: Editions du Centre National de la Recherche Scientifique, 1984), 154–162; and Macé, *Sol Hatchuel, mélodrame*, 65. Sol declares, *"Mes pères pleuraient Sion, je pleure ma ville natale"* (My parents cried for Zion, I cry for my hometown).

73. Ovilo y Canales, *La Mujer maroqui* (Madrid: Impr. de M.G. Hernández, 1886).

74. Ibid., 8–10, 114.

75. Ibid., 142–143.

76. Ibid., 115.

77. Ibid., 85–86, 91–92.

78. Mary Nash, "The Rise of the Women's Movement in Nineteenth Century Spain," in *Women's Emancipation Movements in the Nineteenth Century: A European Perspective*, ed. Sylvia Paleschek and Bianka Pietrow-Ennker (Stanford, Calif.: Stanford University Press, 2004), 243–262.

79. Boutet, "'Sulika' ou la vie de Sol Hatchuel," *L'Avenir Illustré*, 31 July 1929, 7.

80. Ibid., 8.

81. Boutet, "'Sulika' ou la vie de Sol Hatchuel," *L'Avenir Illustré*, 11 April 1929, 10.

82. Ibid.

83. Daniel Boyarin, *Dying for God: Martyrdom and the Making of Christianity and Judaism* (Stanford, Calif.: Stanford University Press, 1999), 76–78. The virago was also associated with masculine traits and was altered to a more passive and (what was perceived to be) a more feminine characterization in later Christian martyrdom texts.

84. Romero, *The Jewish Heroine*, 13, 16, 23.

85. Albert I. Bagby, Jr., "The Figure of the Jew in the Cantigas of Alfonso X," in *Studies on the Cantigas de Santa Maria: Art, Music and Poetry Proceedings of the International Symposium on the Cantigas de Santa Maria of Alfonso X, el Sabio (1221–1284)*, ed. Israel J. Katz and John E. Keller (Madison, Wis.: Hispanic Seminary of Medieval Studies, 1987), 235–245; Fernández, "La Literatura del siglo xix y los orígenes del contubernio judeo-masónico-comunista," 292.

86. Macé, *Sol Hachuel*, 11.

87. John H. Drummond-Hay, *Western Barbary: Its Tribes and Savage Animals* (London: John Murray, 1844), 66; Elizabeth Murray, *Sixteen Years of an Artist's Life in Morocco, Spain and the Canary Islands*, 2 vols. (London: Hurst and Blackett, 1859), 1:36.

88. Juarros, *La Cuidad de los ojos bellos (Tetuan)*, 243–244.

89. Ibid., 305.

90. Lou Charnon-Deutch, *Fictions of the Feminine in the Nineteenth-Century Spanish Press* (University Park: Pennsylvania State University Press, 2000), 182.

91. Munson, "Walking on the Periphery."

92. Juarros, *La Cuidad de los ojos bellos (Tetuan)*, 13–14.

93. Abbé Grégoire's call for Jewish emancipation during the French Revolution paints a picture of the unhealthy, effeminate Jewish male and nymphomaniac Jewish female of the pre-emancipation ghetto. Such negative cultural traits and Jewish cultural and religious differences would be eliminated, according to Grégoire, with the achievement of Jewish emancipation and assimilation. See Alyssa Goldstein Sepinwall, "Eliminating Race, Eliminating Difference: Blacks, Jews and the Abbé Grégoire," in *The Color of Liberty: Histories of Race in France*, ed. Sue Peabody and Tyler Stovall (Durham, N.C.: Duke University Press, 2003), 28–41.

94. Luce A. Klein, *Portrait de la Juive dans la littérature française* (Paris: Nizet, 1970), 16.

95. In Spanish literature, the *mora* sometimes played this role. See David H. Darst, *Converting Fiction: Counter Reformation Closure in the Secular Literature of Golden Age Spain* (Chapel Hill, N.C.: U.N.C. Department of Romance Languages, 1998).

96. Klein, *Portrait de la Juive dans la littérature française,* 69, 95.

97. Carol Ockman, "When Is a Jewish Star Just a Star? Interpreting Images of Sarah Bernhardt," in *The Jew in the Text: Modernity and the Construction of Identity,* ed. Linda Nochlin and Tamar Garb (London: Thames and Hudson, 1995), 121–139; Pierre Birnbaum, *Anti-Semitism in France: A Political History from Léon Blum to the Present,* trans. M. Kochan (Oxford: Blackwell, 1992), 101 (originally published as *Un mythe politique: La "Republique juive,"* by Librarie Arthème Fayard in 1988).

98. Macé, *Sol Hachuel,* 20.

99. See Edward Said, *Orientalism* (New York: Vintage Books, 1978), for an analysis of Flaubert's description of Orientalist female characters such as the Queen of Sheba, Salomé, and Kuchuk Hanem, "a famous Egyptian dancer and courtesan he encountered in Wadi Haifa" (186). See also Julia Clancy-Smith, "The Colonial Gaze: Sex and Gender in the Discourses of French North Africa," in *Franco-Arab Encounters,* ed. L. Carl Brown and Matthew Gordon (Beirut: American University of Beirut Press, 1996), 201–228. For an analysis of Salomé and stereotypes of the Jewish woman in French literature, see Klein, *Portrait de la Juive dans la littérature française,* 49–56.

100. Natalie Isser, *Antisemitism during the French Second Empire* (New York: Peter Lang, 1991), 100–101; Birnbaum, *Anti-Semitism in France,* 19, 263–264.

101. Felipe B. Pedraza Jiménez, "Los Judíos en el teatro del siglo xvii: la comedia y el entremés," in *Judíos en la literatura española,* ed. Iacob M. Hassán and Ricardo Izquierdo Benito (Cuenca: Ediciones de la Universidad de Castilla-La Mancha, 2001), 152–211. Pedraza Jiménez discusses the cases of Godínez (1585–1659) and Enríquez Gomez (1600–1663), two writers of Jewish origin who were victims of the Inquisition (172–174). The author points that the publication on Lope de Vega's *La Hermosa Ester* (1610) came on the heels of the expulsion of the Moriscos from Spain and can be seen as a protest against this act (165–166).

102. Fernández, "La Literature del siglo xix y los orígenes del contubernio judeo-masônico-comunista," 303–304.

103. Ibid., 304.

104. This theme also appeared in C. Z. Barnett's English drama *The Dream of Fate, or, Sarah, the 'Jewess'! A Drama, in Two Acts* (London: J. Duncombe & Co., [1838?]).

105. *La Juive* also characterizes the father as a fanatic. Fernández, after discussing Romero's Sol, gives an example of another *heroína hebrea,* this time a Jewish girl of Gibraltar who converts to Catholicism and then suffers her father's torture. This story was told by the Augustinian priest C. Muiñoz in a work entitled *Sima la hebrea, Relato histórico* (1889). Unlike Romero's work, which was only published once in a very limited edition, this work went through many editions and was translated into several languages; see Fernández "La Literature del siglo xix y los orígenes del contubernio judeo-masônico-comunista," 310.

106. Boutet, "Sulika," *L'Avenir Illustré,* 19 December 1929, 7.

107. Macé, *Sol Hachuel,* 68.

108. Romero, *El martirio de la joven Hachuel ó la heroína hebrea,* 101–107.

109. Ortega, *Los Hebreos en Marruecos,* 298, Juarros, *La Cuidad de los ojos bellos (Tetuan),* 248–249.

110. On the destabilizing impact of the French conquest of Algeria on Morocco, see Mohammed Kenbib, "The Impact of the French Conquest of Algeria on Morocco (1830–1912)," *Hespéris-Tamuda* 19, Fasc. 1 (1991): 47–60.

111. Mohammed Kenbib, *Juifs et Musulmans au Maroc 1859–1948,* (Rabat: Université Mohammed V, Publications de la Faculté des Lettres et des Sciences Humaines, 1994), see esp. 311–312, 617–618, and 702.

112. Michael Galchinsky, *The Origin of the Modern Jewish Woman Writer: Romance and Reform in Victorian England* (Detroit, Mich.: Wayne State University Press, 1996); Alide Cagideme-

trio, "A Plea for Fictional Histories and Old-Time 'Jewesses,'" in *The Invention of Ethnicity,* ed. William Sollors (New York: Oxford University Press, 1989); Michael Ragussis, "The Birth of a Nation in Victorian Culture: The Spanish Inquisition, the Converted Daughter, and the 'Secret Race,'" *Critical Inquiry* 20, no. 3 (1994): 477–508; Mildred Starr Witkin, "The 'Jewess' in English Literature: A Mediating Presence" (Ph.D. diss., City University of New York, 1988).

113. Birnbaum, *Anti-Semitism in France,* 19.

114. For a discussion of Hebrew, Moroccan, Judeo-Arabic, and Judeo-Spanish versions of Sol's story, see Vance, "Sol ha-Ṣaddiqah: Historic Figure, Saint, Literary Persona."

115. I discuss Juarros's rejection of one of the ballads above. Boutet also stated he could not believe the stories about Sol and that she did not believe in his God. See Boutet, "Sulika," *L'Avenir Illustré,* 31 July 1929, 7.

116. It is important to remember that the works discussed here represent only a fraction of the total number of texts devoted to Sol Hachuel, both published and in manuscript form. The vast majority of Suleika texts were written and continue to be written by Jews. Some of these works in English include I. J. Benjamin, *Eight Years in Asia and Africa from 1846–1855* (Hanover, [Germany]: The author, 1859), 273–277; Henry Iliowizi, *Sol, An Epic Poem* (Minneapolis: Tribune Print, 1883); and Ruth Knafo Setton, *The Road to Fez: A Novel* (Washington D.C.: Counterpoint, 2001). Suleka also continues to inspire writers in Hebrew: Erez Biton, "Kasidat Sulikah," in *Naʿnaʿ: Shirim* (Tel Aviv: ʿEked, 1979), 27–29; Sarah Shalom, *Haguʾel: o, ha-sipur ʿal Sulikah ha-yafah* ([Givʿatayim]: Masadah, 1995).

15

Searching for Suleika

A Writer's Journey

RUTH KNAFO SETTON

FIERCE AFRICAN SUN burns on my head as I weave my way between tiny white tombs packed helter-skelter, nearly on top of each other, half-hidden by stray grasses and tall weeds blowing in the hot wind. A white dome about eight feet high rises above Suleika's tomb. The inscription is painted in childlike black letters. The first four lines, shaped in a rainbow arc, are in Hebrew. Underneath, in French, are these words:

> *Ici repose Mlle Solica Hatchouel*
> *Née à Tanger en 1817*
> *Refusant de rentrer*
> *Dans la religion is-*
> *lamisme les Arabes*
> *L'ont assassinée a Fez*
> *en 1834 Arrachée de sa*
> *Famille tout le monde*
> *Regrette cette enfant*
> *Sainte*

(Here rests Mlle Solica [Suleika] Hatchouel, born in Tangiers, in 1817. Refusing to enter the Islamic religion, the Arabs assassinated her in Fez in 1834. Torn from her family, all the world mourns this holy child.)

It is July of 1981. I am four months pregnant as I stand before her tomb. I cannot explain the urgent desire that led me here to the Jewish cemetery of Fez. A name in a book had suddenly illuminated the page as if it were a medieval manuscript. The letters shone with the promise of mystery, magic, secret. I touched her name on the page the way I used to touch pictures in books as a child, hoping to get sucked into that other world, already wanting to penetrate every border, open every door.

* * *

Which Suleika do I show you? Bad girl or good girl? Muslim, Christian, Jewish: take your pick. Over 300, at last count. I will recount two versions: one Muslim and one Jewish. Here is a popular Muslim account. Suleika was a rebellious girl. Her mother couldn't stand the sight of her. When she laughed, her mother wanted to shut her up. When she dreamed about the future, her mother swore there wouldn't be one. But Suleika was no angel. She knew her mother hated her, and she figured "I can't do anything right anyway, and whatever I do, I get beaten, so I might as well do what I want." She got into trouble every day and hung around with the Arabs. In Tangier, Jews and Arabs lived side by side, but still, there was a high wall that separated them. It was dangerous for Jews to break through the wall. Only someone desperate like Suleika would take the chance. Once you crossed over to the other side, you were in their hands— completely. The risk was the only thing that made her feel alive. By the time she turned 17, she was hard and bitter. She'd been beaten so many times it left her numb. She didn't care about anything anymore. Then her mother sold her in an arranged marriage to her cousin, a 60-year-old widower with six kids. Ugly as a sardine, with bulging eyes and a red nose that dripped snot down his shirt.

The wedding was coming closer and closer. She got wilder. There was only one thing that kept her going. In the evenings, she sat in her courtyard and listened to the music that came from the courtyard next door, where an Arab family lived. She heard the sound of an oud and a man's voice singing in Spanish or Arabic, sometimes just humming the melody. The music made her cry. It made her dream. One night, about a week before her wedding, her mother realized she was going to lose her slave, and she beat the hell out of her with a broom, a leather belt, everything she could lay her hands on. Crying, Suleika ran to the courtyard. The music was coming from next door. She went to the stone wall, feeling with her fingers for a hole. She saw a gap in the wall where a stone had fallen out and looked through. Taleb sat cross-legged, oud upright between his legs. His eyes were closed, and he was singing. This was the first time she'd really seen him. He'd been away at boarding school. When he was home, he didn't go out with the others; instead, he spent his time playing music in the courtyard. He was about her age but different, quiet. And very handsome. Every day after that, she watched him. I want this boy, she thought. I'm going to mess with him. But her plan backfired. One day she whispered his name through the hole in the wall and he saw her. He came to the wall and stared at her for a long time. Did I tell you she was beautiful? The kind of beauty that makes you ache. He left her standing there and went back in his house. She stood at the wall. She couldn't move. She was in love. That night he sang a new song. She pressed her face against the hole in the wall and watched him. Every string he strummed vibrated inside her. When he finished, he came to the wall and touched her face with the same fingers that had played through her. "That was for you," he told her. "From now on, they'll all be for you."

After that, it was impossible to stay in her old life. Her mother's beatings, the old dripping cousin. She begged Taleb to run away with her. He was engaged to be married too. Another arranged marriage. He'd never seen the bride, but it was too late: there was no room in his heart for anyone but Suleika. One morning, very early, they ran away to the casbah of Tangier, where people who have secrets go to hide. They got married. The only way they could do it was if she recited the *shahada,* the Formula of Conversion: *La ilaha illa Allah, Muhammadu rasul Allah.* There is no God but Allah, and Muhammad is His Prophet. She recited the words, and she and Taleb moved into a beat-up old shack, but they were happy. They were together. He played his music at a nearby club, and when he was done, he came home to her.

After a month, he was on his way home from the club when two men jumped him. The brothers of the girl he'd jilted. Suleika was at home, waiting for him. She knew something was wrong when he didn't show up. At dawn she went to look for him. She found him on the ground, oud smashed at his side. She threw herself on him, covered his body with hers. She howled like a beast in pain. People came running. She clung to him, but they pulled her away. She stood and looked around and realized that she was completely alone. Lost. She didn't know what to do, where to go. She wanted to die with Taleb, to go with him wherever he went. She stood alone that day, waiting for a sign from him. After a long time she heard a low hum. Taleb's hum. It came from far away, and it drew her. It led her back to her family's *sla* (synagogue) in the Fuente Nueve. All the Jews were there, praying. When they saw her, most of them threw stones at her. They called her a whore and a traitor. Her mother threw the most stones. "I've come home," she told them. But the Arabs from the casbah had followed her. "We don't think so," they said. "Did you forget the words you spoke? You're ours now." A fight broke out. They nearly tore her in half. In the end, the Arabs beheaded her.

*   *   *

Not happy with that version? Want her to be dragged against her will next door to the Arab house? Then go with the Jews and Christians. Their Suleika is an angel, a martyr in the making. One writer memorably calls her "a white rose of virginity." Another puts words in her mouth: "Dying is the only good I wish for!" Not exactly my idea of a fun date. But the Arab next door wants her. He's old and fat and in the market for a second wife. No, we can do better than that. He's young and handsome, and he tells his mother: "Yo Mama, get me one of those." Too hackneyed, too Romeo and Juliet? Get Tahra in here. She's the Arab woman next door, an actress of unusual range and passion. Whether she's the widow yearning for a daughter or Jealous Wife #1 or the mother who wants to make her son happy or a girl the same age as Suleika, she throws herself into the part and carries it to its utmost limits.

She needs a worthy adversary. Most Suleikas are too flat and passive, sleep-walking toward death ("the only good I wish for"). Enter Simha: bitch-mama extraordinaire. Mommy Dearest is Simha on a good day. She gave Cinderella's wicked stepmother advice on how to raise her daughter. The husband, as in all these stories, is weak, inconsequential. He's holed up somewhere studying the Torah and arguing with dead rabbis while the drama of life unfolds around him. "You know best, dear," he says and returns to his texts as Simha chases Suleika through the house with a weapon of her own invention: a stick to which she's attached a donkey tail. Her goal: to slap the unearthly beauty off Suleika's face. Some commentators, unable to comprehend the extent of Simha's viciousness, transform her with four letters: from mother into stepmother, a worthy addition to any fairy tale.

So here's the scene: you've got Suleika in the middle, between these two Amazons of jealousy, selfishness, brutality. The climactic moment occurs during Pesach, 1834. Suleika is 17, daydreaming at her chores. Simha finds her, and with a scream that chills the heart races after her. Exhausted and desperate, Suleika runs outside the house and stops for a second. Where to go? What to do? Mom is gaining ground, sounds like Godzilla tramping down the stairs. Tahra opens her door, beckons: "Suleika, come to me! I'll be your mother, sister, best friend, _____ (fill in the blank)."

One night in a dream, I counted the steps between the Jewish house and the Arab house. There were twenty-two. Twenty-two steps that span an eternity, a Sahara of yearning and ignorance.

Suleika hesitates between the two houses. Behind her, the inevitable beat-ing. Before her, who knows? She cries: "Your house will be my house!" and runs to Tahra, who pulls her inside and slams the door.

The next time we see Suleika she's facing the *qa'id* of Tangier, swearing she did *not* say the words. "I was born a Jew," she insists, "and I will die a Jew." Tahra steps in: "No way. The girl's a liar. She converted, and now she's recanting."

What do we do with a recanting Jew? Throw her in the dungeon, of course. And that's where she'd have languished and died, if rumors of her beauty hadn't traveled to the sultan in Fez. This jaded, restless ruler sent for her.

The voyage from Tangier to Fez takes a few hours today. For Suleika in 1834, on mule, it took six days. She wasn't allowed to speak (the danger of words, espe-cially a woman's words). Twice a day the guards allowed her to get off the mule, get down on all fours, and lap milk from a bowl like a cat. This voyage parallels the fairy tale heroine's journey into the woods. She emerges at the end of the journey, *changed*. When Suleika arrives in Fez, she's no longer a passive, bland, gorgeous teenager. She's Joan of Arc for the Jews, Esther defending her people, Ruth embracing the God of the Jews and refusing to return to the wilderness. She is now a gorgeous parable.

Now here's the choice. Play the game and see what you would choose if the price was right for you. Door #1 or Door #2: you be the judge. Behind Door #1 is the sultan, Mawlay ʿAbd al-Rahman. In his 40s, with a vast harem to choose from, he sees you and falls instantly, irrevocably, in love. He promises you everything. Jewels, silks, and brocades; a life of ease; power. And most important, love. He asks you to marry him. He vows to take care of you forever. Still not enough? Let's up the ante. You fall in love with him too. Why not? He's good-looking, gentle in the way only the truly powerful can be. He wants you the way no one has ever wanted you before. His nearness makes you tremble. Stack the deck a touch more. He gets the grand rabbi of Fez, Rabbi Serfaty, to come in and talk to you. The rabbi himself tells you to play the *converso* game. Survival, it's called in various corners of the world. Convert on the outside; believe what you want inside.

Wealth, security, love, your own faith in private. Count me in. Oh, you have to pay an entrance fee? How much? A pittance, a trifle, seven words to be exact. It takes less than a minute to say. And does God really care if you call Him Yahweh or Allah?

Behind Door #2 is—what? The void our words attempt to cover? A cold, sharp wind blowing from beyond. The edge of a cliff. Is God waiting for you there? Arms open, saying: "Come home, my child. Come here and be warm." Or is there nothing? A long tunnel that opens onto endless night?

The moment of truth. Sol Hachuel, come on down! Which will it be? Door #1 or Door #2? And you in the audience: which door do you choose?

* * *

I'm about 3 in the last photo taken of me before my parents and I leave Morocco for the United States. Curly blonde hair pulled back in a ponytail. Tiny white dress, sturdy bare legs. Light eyes that look questioningly at the photographer or at the street ahead of me. A small wanderer through life, I clutch a black purse and pause, only for an instant, on my journey. I am resolute, firmly rooted, feet in black patent-leather shoes gripping the tiled outdoor corridor. My lips are dark, as if I've just eaten a plum and traces of the juice have stained my lips. Unsmiling, confident that in a moment I will continue on my path to the future, I can afford to let the photographer freeze me. What he doesn't know, what I don't yet know, is that in another moment, my patent-leather shoes will be lifted from

Figure 15.1. Ruth Knafo Setton's maternal family (Cohen and Cabessa) in Fez, 1938. Ruth Knafo Setton.

the tiles, will dangle in the air, as I hover between two worlds—the New and the Old, belonging to neither, clinging to both.

What happened to that girl? Did she live a parallel life to mine in the dim, powerful Morocco of my memory? Did she study? Was she married off early, as soon as her blood came? Was she afraid of the Arabs? Mistreated for being a Jew? Did she fall in love with a boy at school? Sneak out to meet him at the *souk*? Did she walk along the sea with him? I want that girl, I want to smell her flesh, to kiss the back of her knee, to see if her ears are dainty whorled seashells like mine, her eyes as wide, her hands as yearning. What became of her? I feel the pain of exile. I was ripped from her. The girl who crossed the ocean is already the shadow of myself. Right now when you think I am looking at you, I'm looking for her—across the mountains and seas—wondering if she even knows I exist, if she misses me at all.

Sometimes I think I've been writing *her* story all along, the girl I might have been, the girl who could have been me. Which door would she have chosen? Which would I choose?

* * *

When I first began writing my novel *The Road to Fez*, I created my own Suleika Hall of Mirrors: the reckless rebel, the goddess of virginity, the disobedient daughter—adding in the handsome boy next door, treacherous Tahra—everyone, everything—until I'd created a swollen shapeless Suleika, pregnant with all her stories, too ungainly to move.

I began the novel again, choosing the most striking elements of each version. Still she felt lopsided. I rewrote again and again, squeezing her life into a semi-coherent narrative, the way I tried to squeeze mine, eliminating the hyphens and inconsistencies in my own identity, immigrant memories, dreams and longings that made no rational sense, the search for a home that didn't seem to exist in daylight, the key that unlocked my grandparents' house in Morocco, and even earlier, the house we had abandoned in Spain during the Inquisition. In my search for Suleika I discovered my own family: rabbis, Kabbalists, and philosophers—and a grandfather who composed poetry in classical Arabic and played his oud on a roof terrace against the sea wind.

As a Sephardi-Jewish writer in America, I found no models, no peers, and was almost ritualistically turned away by publishers in a manner that seemed eerily reminiscent of the way the board of the synagogue of our town in Pennsylvania turned away my father when we had first arrived in America: "A Jew from Africa? Go home. There's nothing for you here."

Go back home, publishers wrote me. *Or join us and write about the "real Jews."*

Who was I to dispute the numbers? When I began teaching Jewish literature, I couldn't find another Sephardic-American writer for the life of me. It never occurred to me that she was probably banging on the back door of American Judaism, same as I was, but that our frantic knocking betrayed our ignorance of the Ashkenazi password that would allow us to enter.

Dark lean years passed during which I taught and wrote. No matter how much I struggled against it, by Chapter Three of the current American novel-in-process that I worked on—usually set in rural Texas, starring a rancher named Old Sam and his horse, Gus—inevitably a Moroccan family moved to town, name of Abitbol or Aflalo, and before you knew it, the whole town was taken over by these melodramatic, passionate Mediterranean cousins. "Go home," I told them sternly, crossing them out as they appeared: "There's nothing for you here."

But irrepressible, undaunted, they returned, banged on the back door, broke through windows, cooked me couscous, serenaded me at night—strains of Enrico Macias singing the eternal song of the exile—and lo and behold, one night I weakened and sat under a purple-streaked sky, imagining the shade of palm trees tracing my bare (black) feet, and I realized that they had nowhere else to go but to me, no one to tell their story to but me. When the writing finally began to flow and I let the Abitbols and their extended family move to town, I felt as if I constructed a memory-house on sand, one that disintegrated as I wrote. The world I described—the rich, complex, smoldering tapestry of Moroccan Jews—exiles and immigrants no matter where they went—was vanishing, dispersing, diffusing, and scattering, like the fabled Kabbalistic holy sparks. In order to attain *tikkun,* or restoration and harmony, the holy sparks had o be found and gathered. As Papa Naphtali tells his granddaughter, Brit, in *The Road to Fez:* "Holy sparks . . . don't come announced, or gift-wrapped, or labeled. You trip over them and see them glittering in the dirt. When you find your holy spark, you grab it and hold tight."

In a sense, these sharp-edged sparks—holy and profane—jagged pieces of a puzzle that will never fit together, are my Sephardi-Jewish identity: unavoidable and essential as the sun that burns through my memory, the sea that crashes against my heart, the house that must be rebuilt every morning, word by word. Like my Suleika.

* * *

On a July day in 1981, I hurry across the square on my way to the Jewish cemetery, as fast as I can move, considering how hot it is, how pregnant I feel, how I'm dreading the moment of seeing her grave. I'm still an innocent, haven't pondered the complex questions of life and death yet, haven't drowned in the quicksand of Suleika's story, where every possibility, every version, opens yet another door, until it's not merely choosing between Door #1 and Door #2 but between infinite doors, each opening onto another, each offering another choice, yet another way to be or not to be.

The square is bounded on all sides. In one corner a man has set up a tired flea market: old appliances, used clothes, a broken chair toppling on three legs. The large brass doors of the Sultan's Palace gleam, touched by the long fingers of the afternoon sun. Next to the palace is the entrance to the mellah, a gaping mouth that swallowed centuries of Moroccan-Jews. Deceptively large and light, the mellah hides its dark decaying heart, like a woman wearing makeup to conceal ravages of time and grief. At the end of the square is the Jewish cemetery. Beggars claw and shriek like raucous seagulls. The iron-carved Hebrew letters twist and wail to the sky. About fifty years after Suleika's death, they moved the cemetery. Witnesses swear she smelled like fresh-baked bread when they dug her up. They also swear a white dove flew up at the instant of her death. And that the sultan couldn't move his arm until he went to her tomb in the mellah and rubbed his arm against the cool stone.

Yeah, well.

I don't even have to close my eyes to see the square filling with the curious and bloodthirsty. Mountain men, warriors from the Rif, Berbers from the Atlas

Mountains, Blue Men from the Sahara, dancers, sword swallowers, and storytellers. Here come the Jews—barefoot and in black, as the law required then. Guards lead in a mule on which sits Suleika. Gone are the satin and silk dresses the sultan lavished on her. She wears the same coarse white *haik* worn on the journey from Tangier to Fez. She dismounts from the mule. The executioner slices the air with his sword. Slashes the veil from her face. The crowd gasps at her beauty. She asks for water to pray and *sarwal* to cover her legs. Then she kneels at the block. The executioner teases the back of her neck with the point of his sword. "The sultan asked that you be given one last chance to change your mind."

She can't move her head. She's pinned to the block. But her voice rises: "*Shema Isra—*"

Her head flies at least ten feet away.

* * *

In one of the many odd notes in her tale, Muslim women worship her today as a saint. They come to her tomb in the Jewish cemetery in Fez, bringing plates of couscous (even a dead girl needs to keep up her strength), bunches of wild flowers, a lucky *hamsa*, a magic coin. Meanwhile the Jewish women light a candle and place it in one of the niches in the white dome over her tomb. The niches are filled with remnants of white candles, burned prayers. The women chant, pray, sing, cry, beg her to listen. Usually they ask her for a baby or for help in getting pregnant or avoiding a miscarriage. Our Suleika, who never had a child of her own, is the secret ingredient for successful pregnancies. She has become a woman's saint. In saint hierarchy, that means a saint too minor (too female) to have her own *hillulah* (or festive pilgrimage on Lag ba'Omer), relegated to granting conception, preventing illness in the family or menstrual cramps, you know: women's stuff. "Her *baraka* is still strong," the caretaker of the cemetery assures me. "She is still as powerful as ever. The women never stop coming to her."

Muslim women. Jewish women. Side by side. Praying to a dead teenage girl. In death obliterating the border that in life she couldn't cross.

* * *

Suleika's story is about testing, breaking through, penetrating, and transcending borders She is the ultimate trespasser who enters a world in which she doesn't belong and once there, cannot find her way home. I see her in that cold dark lonely place, backed against the wall by the powerful, those who hold all the cards, saying, "Words won't change what I am." No wonder everyone relates to her. We all look into her story and see ourselves reflected. When I give readings from the novel, people come to me—Korean, gay, Muslim, refugees—and tell me: *Her story is my story.*

When I finally abandoned Old Sam and returned to Suleika, I began writing again with the understanding that there is no *one* Suleika, no simple answer. Her stories deepen, complicate, diffuse, end up connecting us all—Arab, Jew, Christian, male, female. Over a century after her death I may be as close to the truth or truths as the earliest commentators in 1834. In the beginning I prayed for a scrap of her clothing, a piece of her life I could touch, yearning to *feel* her truth and bring her justice. She'd been killed once. I didn't want to kill her a second time by choking her in a stifling narrative, forcing her to follow my agenda. My Suleika is a mosaic: fragments, puzzle pieces, holy sparks, tales that contradict each other, overlap, imagine, explore. On one level, reading *The Road to Fez* is the actual process of piecing together a life that will always be greater than its parts. In setting Suleika free, I set myself free—and hopefully, set the reader free as well.

* * *

I break an unwritten rule as I stand before Suleika's grave. "Never enter a cemetery when you are pregnant," my aunt warns me. "The souls are waiting there, desperate to live again. They steal into the fetus and take over the baby's life." I don't know yet that the child I'm carrying is a girl, that she will grow up to be as wild and rebellious as the Suleika of Arab legend, that I will look back at this moment with longing and pain. The moment before she kicks inside me for the first time: sign of life in the house of death. The moment before I hug the tomb as if it were a living, breathing woman. The moment before I choose to follow her to the inevitable promised end. Twenty-two steps. An eternity. Or a breath on the back of my neck. I wheel around. The door opens.

PART V

*Gender, Colonialism, and
the Alliance Israélite Universelle*

16

Corresponding Women

Female Educators of the Alliance Israélite Universelle in Tunisia, 1882–1914

Joy A. Land

THE WOMEN EDUCATORS of the Alliance Israélite Universelle (AIU) fulfilled many roles in the complex Muslim-Jewish environment of Tunisia during the period 1882–1914.[1] Trained in Paris, teachers and principals were sent to far-flung destinations of the AIU educational system. Beginning in the mid-nineteenth century, the AIU established a network of schools in the Ottoman Empire, its Arab provinces, Iran, Egypt, and North Africa. The period 1880–1914 represents the "golden age"[2] of the AIU's establishment of an expanding transregional educational enterprise whose center was France. The first AIU school, founded in Tetuan, Morocco, in 1862, served as a model for other schools throughout the Balkans, the Middle East, and North Africa.[3]

When the founders of the AIU made their first appeal for funds in 1860, their stated purpose included the right "to help effectively all those who suffer because they are Jews."[4] But the AIU also shared many goals with the French colonial power. Among them was *la mission civilisatrice*, which was to be accomplished through the use of the French language and the transmission of Enlightenment culture in AIU schools. Indeed, many of the educators of the AIU viewed themselves as cultural missionaries.[5] However, the primary aims of the schools, as stated in the AIU's protocols, were to work on the emancipation and "moral progress" of the local Jewish population and the "regeneration" of their co-religionists.[6] These goals, easy to disparage with postcolonial hindsight, were a product of their time.

In 1878, a school for boys was established in Tunis, and one for girls followed in 1882.[7] The founding of the girls' school took place during particularly tumultuous times: the French had occupied Tunisia in 1881 and established a protectorate there in 1883. In 1880, the *Bulletin* of the AIU announced that the most im-

239

portant school of the AIU in terms of enrollment was unquestionably the one in Tunis.[8] By 1884, the girls' school in Tunis could boast that it had the highest enrollment among AIU girls' schools.[9]

The teachers of the AIU, both men and women, spearheaded the formation of a largely urban elite that was educated and "Westernized." But it was the women educators who were truly revolutionary: they were the first Jewish professional females in the Middle East.[10] That is not to say that theirs was an isolated case. In Tunisia, for instance, the first primary school for Muslim girls opened in Tunis in 1900.[11] But what was especially unique about the AIU schools was that they accepted rich and poor, girls and boys, Jews and non-Jews. According to AIU statistics for 1895, the non-Jewish student population included ninety-five Catholics, forty-three Protestants, thirty-nine Greek Orthodox, twenty-one Armenians, and thirty-seven Muslims.[12] The total school enrollment of 12,050 was dispersed among fifty-nine schools. Of the 12,050 students, 4,900 were girls.[13] The teachers were also of a diverse background.

This chapter, which is based on the correspondence of the women educators, explores the nature of the newly emancipated, modernizing Jewish elite of AIU female teachers and principals in the multireligious and multiethnic environment of North Africa. In analyzing the writings of these women, several questions regarding correspondence and authorship emerge. For example, what role does correspondence play in transmitting the views, attitudes, or social constraints of the women educators/authors? Or to what extent is the correspondence indicative of issues of "age, gender, rank and power"?[14]

On the one hand, the women teachers and *directrices* (female directors) held positions of power and certain degrees of autonomy within the confines of the school system. On the other hand, their status as educated women limited their marital choices: they stayed single, married their male counterparts at the AIU, which they were encouraged to do, or left the school system altogether, possibly to find suitable mates. In addition to information about marital options, the content of the correspondence of the educators reveals gender differences. According to one researcher,[15] women teachers were more likely to comment on pedagogical issues in their correspondence than on the broader political and social conditions; male teachers were more apt to comment on the latter in their letters. In order to understand the role of women as possible agents of social change in the hybrid Muslim-Jewish culture of Tunisia, the correspondence of both the women and their male counterparts in the boys' school requires thorough investigation. We cannot understand the role of female AIU educators in the hybrid Muslim-Jewish culture of Tunisia without a thorough analysis of the letters they wrote to their superiors in Paris and the letters of their male counterparts.

In a recent essay, Cheryl Johnson-Odim and Margaret Stroebel ask: "How does the clustering of women, apart from men, empower and/or limit women?"[16] Continuing their discussion of women in cross-cultural contact, they assert:

> Women are important intermediaries of cultural exchange. . . . Women may become empowered by their intermediary position: it may give them pivotal control of information or material resources. On the other hand, as intermediaries they are sometimes marginal within their society of origin.[17]

This analysis was made in the context of indigenous women who had sexual relations with European men, a far cry from the women teachers who were exhorted to be exemplars of moral rectitude for an impressionable group of youngsters. Even so, my analysis of the correspondence of female teachers in AIU schools finds that these women were in fact cultural intermediaries. Nevertheless, even though they were empowered professionally, their social roles were limited.

Correspondence as an Historical and Literary Genre

Archival sources for this study are based on the correspondence of women educators, focusing on the *directrices* of the AIU primary school in Tunis. Since the nursery school in Tunis was attached to the primary school building, the same individual usually (though not always) served as the directress of both institutions.[18] This study will not discuss nursery schools but will rather focus on the education and educators of girls aged 7 to 14. The *directrices* left complete sets of correspondence, and their letters and reports constitute the bulk of the AIU's archival material for Tunisia. (Similar sets of correspondence are not available for the teaching staff.) The directresses, writing far from home to the AIU Central Committee in Paris in penmanship perfected in European classrooms, provide a unique source about the social and educational history of Tunisia. Where relevant, I have supplemented their letters and reports with the correspondence of the male principal of the boys' school of Tunis.

What does the genre of *correspondance,* including that of a business or administrative nature, reveal about the attitudes and social conventions of the French-educated authors? First is the role of letter-writing in the literary canon, where the *Bibliographie de la France* (1830–1839) seems to place it. According to Cecile Dauphin,

> The *Bibliographie de la France* dispenses with "epistolary style" in its "Belles-Lettres" section. It lumps together editions of the correspondence of Madame de Sévigné or Voltaire, love letters, *secrétaires* great, small, modern,

new, universal ... and a variety of commercial and administrative formu-
laries. Everything, that is, that has anything to do with letter-writing.[19]

In this definition, even mundane letters warrant classification among works of
literature. This is perhaps indicative of the importance ascribed to letter-writing
as a society becomes literate.

The *Grande Encyclopédie du XIXe siècle* offers this definition of correspondence:

> A letter is a conversation between people who are absent from one another.
> ... To succeed at it imagine that you are in the presence of whomever you
> are addressing, that they can hear the sound of your voice and that their
> eyes are fixed on yours.[20]

This definition, "related to prayer in its effort to transcend absence and in the de-
termination to think one's way into the other person's presence,"[21] has its shortcomings. It denotes correspondence as an "illusion of oral communication" while
denying the social distancing[22] implicit in a relationship between, for example,
an employer and an employee, an administrator in Paris and an educator in Tunis.

A French-English edition of the *Nouveau Manuel Epistolaire*, or *The New Universal Letter Writer* (1890), offers a definition similar to that of the *Grande Encyclopédie*: "A letter is a written conversation."[23] It continues: "Excellence in the art of
correspondence supposes a good education, talent, an extensive general knowledge, a facility of expression and above all tact."[24] Tact, or, put another way, the
need to maintain job security could account for which issues were discussed and
which were overlooked in the correspondence of AIU male and female educators.

The AIU provided guidelines to its teachers on letter-writing. The *Instructions générales pour les professeurs* echo the epistolary manuals of the nineteenth
century:

> In his correspondence with the Central Committee, an AIU teacher must,
> in general, avoid the use of any terms which are not in keeping with a tone
> appropriate to administrative matters or which might signal a lack of re-
> spect for his superiors. ...
>
> The teacher should concentrate on the style of his letters and make ev-
> ery effort to convey in them the polite, urbane, educated tone which must
> be maintained in all administrative correspondence. He must seek a han-
> dling of the French language and will arrive at a mastery of that language
> especially through the careful reading and rereading of a few authors who
> number among the great writers.[25]

Style and content and types of subjects were to a large extent dictated by the *Instructions* from the Central Committee in Paris. While the *Instructions* directly ad-

dress male teachers, women and men shared the same letter-writing responsibilities. What is constant is that the correspondence keeps flowing, from Tunis to Paris and back, recording, in various amounts of detail, the functioning of the school and the lives lived in it.

Population statistics for Tunisia in the late nineteenth century are at best estimates. The first official census was taken in 1921,[26] and earlier figures appear exaggerated in retrospect.[27] According to one source, in 1870 it was estimated that Tunisia consisted of one million inhabitants, of which 30,000 were Jews.[28] Another source claims that in 1882 there was a total population of about 1,300,000 in Tunisia and that the population of Tunis was between 60,000 and 80,000.[29] The Jewish sector was not more than 3 percent of the total population of Tunisia. Most of the Jews lived in the urban centers on the littoral, and more than 50 percent resided in Tunis.[30]

The AIU attempted to maintain statistics on the Jewish communities in its network. From 1882 to 1912, the *Bulletin* of the AIU states, with unvarying consistency, that the Jewish population of Tunis comprised a total of "40,000 souls." The *Bulletin* of the AIU for the same period for Sfax, the only other town in Tunisia to establish an all-girl AIU school, constantly cites a Jewish population of 2,600.[31] Fluctuations in population due to births or deaths are not recorded. Nor do the statistics indicate years of severe epidemics that might have lowered the population levels, especially among young children. Thus, other than providing the relative size of one community in comparison to another, these statistics are of limited value.

The *Bulletin* of the AIU also includes school enrollment figures in the statistics for each community. These figures were derived from the correspondence of the directors. One of the tasks of the *directrice,* for instance, was to report on the progress of the school. Invariably, the first sentence of each report states enrollment figures, noting that it had increased dramatically and stating that insufficient staff had drastically hindered the progress of the school. Part of this statement, no doubt, was a ploy to receive more funding and more teachers, and part of it represented genuine need. However, the statistics presented by the *directrices* could have been inflated and were subject to inspection by the male principal of the local school or the French inspector from the Department of Public Education in Tunis.[32] Any figures presented in the *Bulletin* should therefore be treated cautiously.

The AIU student population was not representative of the entire school-aged Jewish community in Tunis. The Jews who originated from Leghorn (Livorno, Italy) preferred to send their children to the Italian schools; hence it was primarily the "indigenous" Jews, the Twansa (Ar. *tawānisa,* Tunisians), who sent their children to the AIU schools.[33] These families were the artisans, the merchants, or the indigent of the *hara* (Ar., *harat al-yahud*, the Jewish quarter), whose children were precisely the target of the AIU's efforts at "regeneration" through European-style education.

The AIU Schools in Tunisia

The first AIU boys' school in Tunis was established on Malta Sghira (Little Malta) Street outside the *hara* in 1878. It remained in operation until 1976. In addition to its male teaching staff, the boys' school also employed women teachers. Because their educational training was modeled on the French curriculum, the women teachers could, and did, transfer to other schools, either in the AIU system or at French public schools. For instance, the woman who became the sixth *directrice* of the School for Girls in Tunis, Mme. Sidi Oro Tahar (1926 to 1946), began her career at the Malta Sghira School for Boys in 1911. In a report on her first day at the boys' school, she mentioned the astonishment of her students on seeing a woman teacher in front of the classroom for the first time.[34] The early women educators of the AIU not only caused surprise but engendered change within their students and indirectly within their host communities.[35]

In addition to its boys' school, the AIU established other educational institutions for boys in Tunisia. These included additional primary schools as well as a school for commerce, which operated briefly in the period 1899–1902.[36] A rabbinical school opened in 1907 with the goal of training rabbis in religious and secular studies; it closed in 1914. These ventures were short lived. In contrast, the first boys' school on Malta Sghira Street was so successful that the AIU opened a second school inside the *hara* of Tunis on Hafsia Street that remained in operation from 1910 to 1964. The school on Hafsia soon became coeducational (*une école mixte*), first admitting girls in January 1913,[37] but it was headed by a male *directeur*, Albert Saguès.

Outside Tunis, primarily in the north of the country, the AIU founded more schools for boys, including a farm school. The farm school was established in 1895 but was closed for a period during World War I (1917). It reopened briefly after the war but soon closed because of low enrollment.[38] In addition, AIU schools for boys in Tunisia were founded in Sfax (1905–1963) and Sousse (1885–1965).[39] While the northern communities of Tunisia accepted the AIU schools, communities in the south were much more resistant. On the island of Jerba, a stronghold of traditional Jewish scholarship and religious conservativism, attempts to establish an AIU school in 1905 were rejected by local Jewish leaders and townsmen alike.[40] This was a unique rebuff to the AIU's endeavors in Tunisia. By the 1970s, the two Jewish communities of Jerba, the larger Hara Kebira and the smaller

Hara Sghira, had "emerge[d] as a repository of a vanished culture."[41] Thus, unlike the Jewish communities in the North, the Jerbans in the South never accepted the AIU or its version of modernity.

When the girls' school of Tunis opened in 1882, it shared a building with the boys' school on Malta Sgrira Street, finally moving to larger quarters in the *hara* on al-Meshnaka (Ar. *mishnaqa,* gallows) Street in December 1890. In 1891, a nursery school (*école maternelle*) on al-Meshnaka Street was founded; it accepted its first pupils in 1892. Intended as a coeducational institution but primarily serving girls between the ages of 4 and 6, the nursery school functioned until 1937. The girls' school on al-Meshnaka Street remained open until 1976. A second AIU School for Girls in Tunisia was established in 1905 in the coastal town of Sfax. It closed its doors in 1963.

The Roles of the *Directrice* and Her Colleagues

The *directrice* in Tunis served as an intermediary between a variety of cultural groups: the Twansa (indigenous Tunisian Jews), Grana (descendants of Jews from Livorno),[42] Ashkenazi teachers from northern and central Europe, and Sephardi teachers and students from different parts of the Mediterranean Basin. The *directrice* also had to mediate the cultural divide between Jews and non-Jews and (perhaps most important), between the secularizing tendencies of the Enlightenment and the traditional culture of North African Jewry. She often also served as a link between the sexes, bridging the female environment of the girls' school and the male-dominated world of education and employment.

Mlle. Louise Bornstein, fourth *directrice* of the School for Girls in Tunis who served from 1900 to 1905,[43] aptly described the role of the woman educator in Tunis at the turn of the last century. She stated that teachers affect a transformation in the minds of their students.[44] Thanks to these "agents of this transformation," Bornstein noted, by the end of the academic year 1900–1901, the school was characterized by discipline, cleanliness, and regular attendance, a place where an "awakening of the spirit" and the "development of intelligence" took place.[45] These are qualities the AIU had invoked in its original appeal. But "love of work" and "the spirit of observation"[46] are more difficult to quantify than the number of hot meals served or the number of apprentices employed. Yet over the decades the influence of women educators was limited. Even at the end of the protectorate, the number of Jewish or Muslim women from the *hara* who were employed outside the home was minimal.[47]

The *directrice* and the *directeur* served in many capacities: teacher, administrator, social worker, protector of the abused, fund-raiser, public relations agent, representative to the community, correspondent to Paris, and role model of French

Figure 16.1. Tunisian schoolgirls at the Alliance Israélite
Universelle School for Girls, Tunis, ca. 1903. In author's
possession.

Enlightenment civilization.[48] Many of the functions of the *directeur* and *directrice*
were parallel, since they faced many of the same challenges: overenrollment and
(later) retention of pupils, overcrowding, understaffing, and providing nourish-
ment, clothes, and shoes for the poorest of the students.

Along with these pressing responsibilities, the *directrice* and *directeur* had
many other obligations. The *directrice*, for instance, lived and worked in the school
building with her teaching staff and family, if she had one. The AIU required
reports on the religious practices and moral behavior of its teachers; AIU instructions in 1903 specified the details of religious observance it required of the
teaching staff. Moreover, the *directrice* was to report on the "religious, moral, and
intellectual discipline" of her *adjointes* (assistants) in her annual report.[49] The *directrice* could provide firsthand information about the activities of teachers if she
chose to divulge the information. However, she often did not.[50] As far as the level
of religious observance was concerned, the second directress, Mme. Chimènes,
said that since Jewish women did not traditionally attend services in Tunis, she
could not comment on her teachers' synagogue attendance.[51] But the Catholic
teacher, Mme. Duchesne, went to church every day at 6:00 AM.[52]

Raising children in Tunisia was a challenge for a *directrice* with a family. When
her children were sick, Mme. Chimènes would stay home to take care of them.[53]
Since substitute teachers did not exist (the AIU women educators were in the vanguard and had no trained replacements), an older child or a *monitrice* would have
to tend to the lower classes.[54] When two or three teachers were absent, the *directrice* would spend much of her day supervising and teaching classes.

When the girls' school was located in the same building as the boys' school, as on Malta Sghira Street, disciplinary problems often arose at the beginning or end of the day, when the boys and girls would jostle against each other, leading to "disorder."[55] It was the role of the teacher to maintain order.

In addition, the *directrice* was a female role model for the girls in her school and the mothers in the community. First she influenced the girls to change their style of dress. The girls from wealthier families requested that their mothers bring fabric to school for dressmaking and the mothers proudly complied.[56] Their daughters sewed European clothes for themselves, for their sisters,[57] and for the boys in the AIU school.[58] However, even those girls who switched to European dress outside the house continued to wear traditional clothing at home to please their grandparents.[59]

School officials hoped that the girls who sewed European clothes in their dressmaking workshop would take their knowledge home and influence their mothers. And that is what happened; by the beginning of the twentieth century, the schoolgirls had become catalysts for change within their families. In January 1900 the third *directrice*, Hortense Gelbmann, wrote that the mothers of her students wanted to wear European clothes.[60] Thus, the *directrice* was not just an administrator or teacher; she was also an important catalyst for social change.

The AIU was concerned about sewing dresses and lingerie or mending and ironing for several reasons. Aside from fulfilling a requirement of the curriculum, these were occupations that even the very poorest girls could practice at home or in the shops of Tunis. However, these trades were also the least lucrative and therefore were unlikely to affect much of a transformation in the established social order or in perceptions about the roles of women in the family or society.

One of the earliest plans of the first *directrice*, Sara Ungar, was to open a workshop for dressmaking (*atelier de couture*) to enable her students to earn a livelihood or at least contribute financially to the household. But a problem arose: while the boys could easily walk to an apprenticeship in town, it would have been considered inappropriate for the girls to do the same. Thus in her letter of 22 February 1884, Ungar asked that the workshops for girls be attached to the school.[61] When the school moved to larger quarters in 1891, the second *directrice* was able to open workshops that conformed to Ungar's proposal.[62]

The Viewpoint of the *Directeur*

The correspondence of the director, David Cazès, a native of Tetuan, Morocco, reveals the underlying social conditions that warranted the creation of classes and workshops for girls in several related trades.[63] The poverty and abject misery of the population prompted Cazès to write a confidential letter on 22 February 1884 to headquarters in Paris. Cazès wrote critically of the dress and morality of Jewish women in Tunisia.[64] To Western Europeans, the dress of the Jewish women of Tunis was strange and indecent. The account of a European traveler to Tunisia, published in 1882 reflects what Cazès said. He noted in a discussion of Tunis that Jewish women's "tight fitting trousers and . . . stockings" and hiplength silk tunics reminded him of "the costume of ballet-girls." The outfit included an embroidered velvet jacket and black leather slippers or high wooden sandals. It was topped by the conical embroidered-velvet head covering of Tunisian Jewish females.[65]

While Cazès acknowledged that the dress of Jewish women was actually the same as that of Muslim women, he noted that Muslim women rarely went out and that when they did, they were wrapped in a *haik* (Ar. *hayik,* cloak)[66] that covered them completely. Cazès maintained that since Jewish women no longer submitted to the absolute rules of seclusion but also did not wear a *haik,* their dress struck foreign travelers as indecent. The remedy, Cazès noted, was to make it obligatory for girls to study pattern cutting and the construction of European garments in school.

This part of the letter reveals that in the hybrid Muslim-Jewish culture of Tunisia, Muslim and Jewish women wore similar dress at home. It also reveals that when Jewish women began entering the public world, it was deemed necessary to Europeanize their clothes, if not their outlook, through schooling. The second part of the letter provides other valuable information. As a native North African Jew, David Cazès had insight into local social conditions and was thus able to suggest reasons for instituting vocational training programs in the School for Girls. Finally, Cazès's correspondence discloses the nature of his relationship with the *directrice* and, by extension, the functioning of the school. A closer investigation of Sara Ungar's tenure will illustrate the last point.

Sara Ungar, First *Directrice* of the School for Girls, Tunis

Mlle. Sara Ungar (1849–1911) arrived in Tunisia in May of 1882 and stayed for five years.[67] Her task was to organize an AIU school for girls, the first of its kind in Tunisia. The school opened its doors on 1 June 1882.[68] In January 1883, the school hosted several parties to celebrate the opening. Ungar remarked that invitations were sent to "ladies only" according to the custom of the country, noting that an event would be held "for the gentlemen" at a later date. Most of the women who attended her party were the mothers of the students. At the party, they saw an exhibit of notebooks and handiwork and listened to performances by the children.[69] The party is evidence that in Ungar's role of forging positive community relations, she gathered the most influential women in the Jewish community to publicize and support the work of the school.

Sara Ungar was an unusual woman for the late nineteenth century. As Elizabeth Antébi, a grandchild of AIU directors, notes, Ungar had a spirit of adventure and a certain sangfroid.[70] Ungar remained single for much of her life in a world where most of the *directrices* were married.[71] She was of German origin, born in Bonn, an unusual circumstance; many of her colleagues originated in Alsace-Lorraine, the region France had recently lost to Germany in the Franco-Prussian War of 1870–1871. Memory of this bitter defeat by the Germans was to haunt her years in Tunis.[72]

On a purely educational level, the *directrice* faced difficult curricular and pedagogical issues. On a social level, she confronted powerful men and women: the *directeur* of the school for boys, members of the local AIU committee in Tunis, members of the Central Committee in Paris, male and female officials from the French protectorate, other women teachers in her school, and the parents of her students. Her relationship with the *directeur* of the boys' school in particular warrants further attention.

Sara Ungar became embroiled in a contest for power with the director of the Boys' School, David Cazès (1850–1913). Cazès, a native of Tetuan and a bachelor, was one of the first students at the AIU's teacher training school in Paris for men, the Ecole Normale Israélite Orientale (ENIO). Lauded by ENIO director A. H. Navon as *"le doyen des maîtres formés par l'école,"* Cazès was also a knight of the Legion of Honor.[73] As a native North African, he may have resented a German woman carving out a piece of his domain to create a school for girls. Did David Cazès truly resent Ungar or were her reports of his animosity a distortion of the truth? Were her descriptions of the situation embellished in order to gain sympathy from her Paris employers? As with any correspondence, the author was "performing" for an audience, in this case Jacques Bigart, her Alsatian supervisor in Paris and secretary of the AIU. It is possible that the *directrice* implied that Cazès was to blame for her own shortcomings as an administrator.

Ungar's struggles as a single professional woman are an important feature in her correspondence. She lamented how difficult it was socially for her to meet with members of the AIU regional committee to discuss business: although a *directeur* might accidentally meet an associate on the street or in the cafés, social conventions prevented her from meeting a man in public, even to discuss the administration of the school. She had to request an invitation to be received by the man's wife in his home instead.[74] Moreover, she complained, no one listened to women in Tunis;[75] officials of the French protectorate did not receive her or recognize her in any official capacity and people in town were under the impression that Cazès was the director of both schools.[76] Ungar felt marginalized or even erased outside the domain of her school.

Cazès's letters to the AIU in Paris regarding the inauguration of the school for girls reads quite differently from Ungar's.[77] Since he (and not Ungar) was in charge of the budget,[78] he carefully noted the amount of money donated to the school through a collection. He barely noted the two parties Ungar held to celebrate the opening of the girls' school. His public statement at the inauguration of the school, presumably delivered at the party for men only, proudly touted the goals of female education but never mentioned the *directrice*.[79] He got all the publicity in the *Bulletin* of the AIU; her views, if she publicly enunciated them, were not published.

Corroborating evidence exists to support Sara Ungar's claim that Cazès was suspicious of her.[80] Ungar reported that a member of the AIU local committee believed that Cazès was "hostile" to her school. She thought that Cazès was "indifferent" if not harboring "bad faith" toward the school.[81] Perhaps the most telling statement from Cazès, the only one in his correspondence that even alluded to Ungar's existence as the *directrice*, is in a letter from June 1887 in which he discussed a replacement for Ungar, specifying that such a person should, above all, be French.[82] Here he signaled his disdain for Ungar and her German background. She, on the other hand, was somewhat more gracious: she cited his "ambiguity"[83] as an explanation for his behavior.

The relationship of the two principals was caught in a nexus of conflicting dualities: male/female, French/German, North African/European, (*indigène/ Européene*), Sephardi/Ashkenazi (or *portugais/allemand*).[84] The correspondence of Ungar and Cazès reveals their starkly contrasting lives. While it was the role of the principals to maintain a respectful working relationship with each other, they operated in separate orbits. In her domain Ungar had the authority to hire and fire staff members, amend the curriculum, initiate new courses, and maintain order, discipline, and cleanliness. In the male-dominated realm outside the School for Girls, her claim to authority in Tunis, even her existence, was all but denied. Cazès, on the other hand, received praise and recognition wherever he turned. Sara Ungar's life conformed to the model of women as intermediaries who may become socially marginalized within their society of origin. In this case, her society of origin is the Jewish world. However, in the academic framework of the AIU, she went on to become an outstanding *directrice* and a successful member of an emerging female Jewish professional elite.[85]

*   *   *

The lives of the women educators of the AIU point to a need to define (before re-defining) the role of Jewish women in educating North African Jewry and by extension their implicit influence on the surrounding non-Jewish population. The *institutrices* and the *directrices* were the first secularizing women teachers in the region, and although they served as cultural intermediaries to their students in the classroom, the same cultural complexities their students faced could impose self-censorship and isolation on the teachers in their own personal lives.

The similarity between the lives of the *directrices,* as gleaned from the letters they wrote, indicates the need to expand our understanding of how these educators understood social change. Their correspondence often focuses on visible change, such as apparel or student enrollment. The principals address changes in the attitudes of their students less frequently. The attitudes they brought from the metropole in Paris to Tunis may originally have been similar to the attitudes that French teachers took into French classrooms. But as they faced the daily realities of life in the *hara,* the goals, attitudes, and expectations of female AIU teachers were no doubt altered.

Finally, the letters reveal points of congruence in the lives of Muslim and Jewish women in Tunisia. For instance, they shared the same style of dress in the home and the same need for education outside the home. The correspondence provides an enduring legacy to the tenacity of the female educators and the strength of the AIU school system. Moreover, the role of women in the AIU expands our notions of perceived cultural boundaries by asking us to rethink Jewish culture and society in North Africa.

NOTES

1. The bibliography on women educators and female education at AIU schools includes Esther Benbassa, "L'éducation feminine en Orient: L'école de filles de l'Alliance Israélite Universelle à Galata, Istanbul (1879–1912)," *Histoire, Economie et Société* 4 (1991): 529–559; Esther Benbassa, "Education for Jewish Girls in the East: A Portrait of the Galata School in Istanbul, 1879–1912," *Studies in Contemporary Jewry* 9 (1993):163–173; Annie Benveniste, "Le rôle des institutrices de l'Alliance Israélite à Salonique," *Combat pour la Diaspora* 8 (1982): 13–26; Joy A. Land, "Corresponding Lives: Women Educators of the Alliance Israélite Universelle School for Girls in the City of Tunis, 1882–1914" (Ph.D. diss., University of California, Los Angeles, 2006), available at http://escholarship.org/uc/item/6dr950wk; Frances Malino, "The Women Teachers of the Alliance Israélite Universelle, 1872–1940," in *Jewish Women in Historical Perspective,* ed. Judith Baskin, 2nd ed. (Detroit, Mich.: Wayne State University Press, 1998), 248–269; Frances Malino, "Prophets in Their Own Land? Mothers and Daughters of the AIU," *Nashim* 3 (2000): 56–73; Susan G. Miller, "Gender and the Poetics of Emancipation: The Alliance Israélite Universelle in Northern Morocco, 1890–1912," in *Franco-Arab Encounters: Studies in Memory of David C. Gordon,*

ed. L. Carl Brown and M. Gordon (Syracuse, N.Y.: Syracuse University Press, 1996), 229–252; Rachel Simon, *Change within Tradition among Jewish Women in Libya* (Seattle: University of Washington Press, 1992), 108–126; and Rachel Simon, "Jewish Female Education in the Ottoman Empire, 1840–1914," in *Jews, Turks, Ottomans: A Shared History, Fifteenth through the Twentieth Century,* ed. Avigdor Levy (Syracuse, N.Y.: Syracuse University Press, 2002), 127–152. See also Keith Walters, "Education for Jewish Girls in Nineteenth- and Early Twentieth-Century Tunis and the Spread of French in Tunisia," in this volume.

2. Aron Rodrigue, *Jews and Muslims: Images of Sephardi and Eastern Jewries in Modern Times* (Seattle: University of Washington Press, 1993), 13.

3. Ibid., 12–21; Norman Stillman, *The Jews of Arab Lands in Modern Times* (Philadelphia, Pa.: The Jewish Publication Society, 1991), 23–25.

4. English translation in Rodrigue, *Jews and Muslims,* 7. The AIU was founded in 1860 by a group of French Jews, guided by Enlightenment principles, who sought the "regeneration" of "backward" Jewish communities to set them on the road to emancipation and citizenship. This was to be accomplished through the establishment of a network of schools in territories from Morocco to Persia as well as in Ottoman Turkey and the Balkans. The appeal "to all Jews" for funds and support was a document published by the AIU in 1860.

5. Elizabeth Antébi, *Les Missionnaires Juifs de la France, 1860–1939* (Paris: Calmann-Lévy, 1999). It should be noted that the documentation on which Antébi's study is based is relatively weak.

6. André Chouraqui, *Cent ans d'histoire: l'Alliance Israélite Universelle et la renaissance juive contemporaine, 1860–1960* (Paris: Presses universitaires de France, 1965), 196–200, 38–39, 188–190, 408; A. Rodrigue, *French Jews, Turkish Jews: The Alliance Israélite Universelle in Turkey, 1860–1914* (Bloomington: Indiana University Press, 1990), xi–xiii, 22, 72.

7. Rodrigue, *Jews and Muslims,* 19–20.

8. "The most important school of the Alliance, in terms of student population figures, is, without question, that of Tunis. Eight hundred children, almost all poor, are nourished daily and receive some clothing as well"; *Bulletin de l'Alliance Israélite Universelle,* IIe sem. (1880): 37.

9. In the first semester of 1884, the enrollment of the girls' school was 280 pupils. "Écoles primaires, tableaux récapitulatifs des écoles et de l'oeuvre d'apprentissage; II. Écoles de fílles," *Bulletin de l'Alliance Israélite Universelle,* second series, Ie sem., 8 (1884): 43.

10. Rodrigue, *French Jews, Turkish Jews,* 74; Rodrigue, *Jews and Muslims,* 49.

11. Souad Bakalti, *La femme tunisienne au temps de la colonisation, 1881–1956* (Paris: L'Harmattan, 1996), 124; Julia Clancy-Smith, "Envisioning Knowledge: Educating the Muslim Woman in Colonial North Africa, c. 1850–1915," in *Iran and Beyond: Essays in Middle Eastern History in Honor of Nikki R. Keddie,* ed. Rudolph Mathee and Beth Baron (Costa Mesa, Calif.: Mazda Publishers, 2000), 106.

12. AIU, *L'Alliance Israélite Universelle, 1860–1895* (Paris: Maréchal et Montorier, [1895]) 17.

13. Ibid., 16–17.

14. Epistolary manuals and correspondence of the nineteenth century mirrored the social order, which was based on age, gender, rank, and power. See Cécile Dauphin, "Letter-Writing Manuals in the Nineteenth Century," in Roger Chartier, Alain Boureau, and Cécile Dauphin, *Correspondence: Models of Letter-Writing from the Middle Ages to the Nineteenth Century,* trans. C. Woodall (Oxford: Polity Press, 1997), 140. Also see the more comprehensive French edition: R. Chartier, *La Correspondance, les usages de la lettre au XIXe siècle* (Paris: Fayard, 1991).

15. Rodrigue, *Jews and Muslims,* 82.

16. Cheryl Johnson-Odim and Margaret Stroebel, "Conceptualizing the History of Women in Africa, Asia, Latin America and the Caribbean, and the Middle East and North Africa," in *Women in the Middle East and North Africa: Restoring Women to History,* ed. Guity Nashat and Judith E. Tucker (Bloomington: Indiana University Press,1999), lv.

17. Ibid., lvi.

18. The first *directrice* of the *école maternelle* on al-Meshnaka Street, the widow Mme. Léonie

Féraud, served from 1892 until her early death at age 45 in 1894; AIU Tunisie, XXXI E, 7 July 1894. The third *directrice* of the School for Girls, Mme. Hortense Gelbmann (1896–1900), shouldered the responsibility of supervising the nursery school as well as the primary school; AIU Tunisie, XXXI E, 27 November 1898.

19. As quoted in Dauphin, "Letter-Writing Manuals in the Nineteenth Century," 113.

20. Ibid., 132.

21. Ibid.

22. Ibid.

23. J. McLaughlin, *The New Universal Letter Writer in English and French: Theory, Practice, Models* (Paris: Garnier Frères, 1890), 3.

24. Ibid., 5.

25. AIU, *Instructions générales pour les professeurs,* 13–14, as translated by A. Rodrigue in *Jews and Muslims,* 55–56.

26. Official census figures for Tunisia's Jewish population can be found in Robert Attal and Claude Sitbon, *Regards sur les Juifs de Tunisie,* (Paris: Albin Michel, 1979), 289–292. The maximum estimated Jewish population of Tunis in 1901 was 24,000; the 1921 census registered 19,029.

27. Claude Hagège, "La communauté de Tunisie à la veille du protectorat français," *Le Mouvement Social* 110 (January–March 1980): 35.

28. Ibid.

29. Henri de Montety, "Enquête sur les veilles familles et les nouvelles élites en Tunisie" (1939), as quoted in François Arnoulet, "Les problèmes de l'enseignement au début de Protectorat français en Tunisie (1881–1900)," *Revue de l'Institut des Belles Lettres Arabes* 54, no. 167 (1991): 41.

30. Claude Hagège, "Les Juifs de Tunisie et la colonisation française jusqu'à la première guere mondiale" (Doctoral thesis, Ecole Pratique des Hautes Etudes, Paris, 1973); and Hagège, "La communauté de Tunisie," 35.

31. The following statement provides proportional estimates of the total Jewish population and (I assume) the (Jewish) school-age population in Tunis in 1890: "The [Jewish] population of Tunis is approximately 40,000; therefore there are about 5–6000 school-aged children. Several excellent schools exist in Tunis but more than 1000 girls do not attend any." *Bulletin de l'Alliance Israélite Universelle,* 2nd Series, I^e and IIe sem., 15 (1890): 44.

32. See the report by S. Pariente (second director of the AIU boys' school in Tunis) on the girls' school in Tunis under the direction of Mme. H. Gelbmann, the third directress: AIU Tunisie, XXXVIII E, 23 June 1899.

33. Hagège, "La communauté de Tunisie à la veille du protectorat français," 38, 49.

34. Sidi Oro Tahar wrote, "It was not without emotion that I entered the classroom where the students were waiting impatiently for the arrival of the new teacher. As they had not had a female teacher until then, a feeling of astonishment and curiosity could be read on their faces." AIU Tunisie, XXV E 56, 18 December 1911.

35. See Land, "Corresponding Lives," 231–236.

36. AIU Tunisie, XIX E, *Rapport Annuel,* 27 August 1902, Clément Ouziel.

37. AIU Tunisie, XXIV E, 16 January 1913, Albert Saguès.

38. Narcisse Leven, *Cinquante ans d'Histoire: L'Alliance Israélite Universelle, 1860–1910,* 2 vols. (Paris: F. Alcan, 1911–1920), 2:321–332; Paul Silberman," An Investigation of the Schools Operated by the Alliance Israélite Universelle from 1862 to 1940 (Ph.D. diss., New York University, 1974), 148–151.

39. For dates for the schools, see G. Weill, *Emancipation et progrès* (Paris: Editions du Nadir, 2000), 194.

40. Shlomo Deshen, "Southern Tunisian Jewry in the Early Twentieth Century," in *Jews among Muslims: Communities in the Precolonial Middle East,* ed. S. Deshen and W. P. Zenner (London: Macmillan Press,1996), 136.

41. Abraham L. Udovitch and Lucette Valensi, *The Last Arab Jews: The Communities of Jerba, Tunisia* (Chur: Harwood, 1984), 5.

42. For additional material on the Twansa and Grana of Tunis, see Itzhaq Avrahami, ed., *Le Memorial de la communauté Israélite Portugaise de Tunis: Les Granas, 1710–1944* (Lod: Institut de recherches, 1997); H. Z. Hirschberg, *History of the Jews in North Africa*, vol. 2, *From the Ottoman Conquests to the Present Time* (Leiden: Brill, 1981), 82–83, 97–100, 118, 137–139; Paul Sebag, *Histoire des Juifs de Tunisie: des origines à nos jours* (Paris: L'Harmattan, 1991); Jacques Taieb, "Israélites de Tunisie sous le règne de l'Islam," *Les Nouveaux Cahiers* 42 (August 1975); and J. Vehel, *Grana et Touannsa-ou: les deux communautés juives de Tunis*, AIU, ms. 544, 1921.

43. See AIU Tunisie, XIV E, Louise Bornstein. For Bornstein's correspondence from the period following her marriage to a teacher from the boys' school, Lazare Guéron, see AIU Tunisie, XVI E, 1905–1911, Louise B. Guéron.

44. AIU Tunisie, XIV E, 9 October 1901, Louise Bornstein,.

45. Ibid.

46. Ibid.

47. For census figures for 1956, see Paul Sebag and Robert Attal, *L'évolution d'un ghetto nord africain, la Hara de Tunis* (Paris: Presses universitaires de France, 1959), 33–45. Of those responding, 283 Jewish women and 101 Muslim women were employed as salaried or independent wage earners. In 1956 the female population of the *hara* included 3,362 "Tunisian" Jews, 453 "French" Jews, 73 "foreign" Jews, and 1,093 "Tunisian and other" Muslims.

48. Leven, *Cinquante ans d'histoire*, mentions the multiple duties of the director (2:21). Silberman, "An Investigation of the Schools," devotes a chapter to "The Roles of the Teacher," that is, the *directeur*, which included "protector of the Jews, administrator, community leader and social worker" (185–198).

49. "Règles de discipline religieuse, morale, et intellectuelle," in AIU, *Instructions générales pour les professeurs*, 16.

50. AIU Tunisie, XXXIV E, 16 October 1885, Jacques Bigart, and 23 October 1885, Sara Ungar.

51. AIU Tunisie, XXX E, 2 April 1889 and 1 May 1890, Mme. Chimènes.

52. AIU Tunisie, XXX E, 2 April 1889, Mme. Chimènes.

53. AIU Tunisie, XXX E, 16 May 1890, Mme. Chimènes.

54. AIU Tunisie, XXX E, 22 March 1892, Mme. Chimènes.

55. AIU Tunisie, XXXIV E, 30 June 1882 and 14 November 1883, Sara Ungar; AIU Tunisie, XXX E, 1 May 1890, Mme. Chimènes.

56. AIU Tunisie, XXXIV E, 2 March 1892, Mme. Chimènes.

57. AIU Tunisie, XXX E, 8 March 1893, Mme. Chimènes.

58. AIU Tunisie, XXX E, 7 March 1894 and 2 April 1894, Mme. Chimènes.

59. AIU Tunisie, XXXIV E, 22 February 1884, Sara Ungar.

60. "Our clientele is composed of the Tunisian element almost exclusively; of young girls, whose mothers dress in the Arab manner, [who] wish to give up this clothing in order to sport European clothes, and of young women who, for the most part, have already renounced the indigenous style." AIU, Tunisie XXXI E, 29 January 1900, Hortense Gelbmann.

61. AIU Tunisie, XXXIV E, 22 February 1884, Sara Ungar.

62. AIU Tunisie, XXX E, 2 March 1891, Voley Chimènes.

63. Cazés was the director of the AIU from 1879 to 1893.

64. "Let us speak of dress first. To begin, allow me dispel a widespread error. There is an almost legendary belief that Jewish dress is indecent and disgraceful. But there is no [special] Jewish dress for women. What is acknowledged as such is worn just as much by Arab women as by Jewesses. It is only that Muslim women hardly venture out and when they do they are wrapped in a 'haïk' which covers everything. Jewish women, in contrast, no longer submit to the absolute rules of seclusion to which they earlier conformed, and which still apply to Muslim women; such that when they go out, their dress strikes travelers . . . as indecent even though it is acceptable. . . . What we can do is to prohibit the teaching of how to make traditional clothing while making it obligatory to study pattern cutting and the construction of European garments in school"; AIU Tunisie, XXVIII E, 22 February 1884, David Cazès.

65. Ernest von Hesse-Wartegg, *Tunis: The Land and the People* (London: Chatto and Windus, 1882), 124–129. It should be noted that Hesse-Wartegg's account was derogatory. Yet it was David Cazès, the director of the School for Boys in Tunis, who provided the cultural context for this mode of dress.

66. R. P. A. Dozy, *Dictionnaire détaillé des noms des vêtements chez les Arabes* (Beirut: Librairie du Liban, 1969), 147–152.

67. According to Elizabeth Antébi, Ungar came from a different social milieu than most of the other teachers. Ungar's family connections included her brother-in-law, M. Kopf, a well-off jurist from Nuremberg, who had access to the founding members of the AIU, including the president of the AIU, banker Solomon Goldschmidt. After Ungar's five years in Tunis, Goldschmidt helped raise funds from the German Jewish community to help her relocate to Andrinople (Edirne) in (pro-German) Ottoman Turkey, where she again served as an AIU *directrice*. Antébi, *Les Missionnaires Juifs*, 150–151.

68. The AIU *Bulletin mensuel* of June 1882 indicates that Ungar received pedagogical training at the Bischoffsheim School, an AIU institute for women in Paris (p. 131). For recent research on Sara Ungar's career using German sources, including a thwarted attempt to join the German public school system after she left Tunis and her highly successful comeback in Andrinople, see Carsten L. Wilke, "Competing for Mendelssohn's Legacy: German Jewish Pedagogy within the Alliance Israélite Universelle," 4–5, paper presented at the Annual Conference of the Association for Jewish Studies, Los Angeles, California, 21 December 2009. See also Joy Land, "Ungar, Sara," in *Encyclopedia of Jews in the Islamic World,* ed. Norman A. Stillman (Leiden: Brill, 2010).

69. During Ungar's tenure, the AIU schools of Tunis won awards at the Amsterdam International Colonial Exhibition (1883), the International Health Exhibition in London (1884), and the Exposition Internationale d'Anvers in France (1885), as noted in Leven, *Cinquante Ans d'histoire,* 2:115n1. See also "Ecoles Primaries, Tunisie," *Bulletin de l'Alliance Israélite Universelle,* 2nd series, no. 9 (2e sem. 1884–1e sem. 1885): 35. In her correspondence, Ungar mentions the awards only in passing.

70. Antébi, *Les Missionnaires Juifs,* 149.

71. Ungar married Jacques Danon, also affiliated with the AIU, in December of 1896. Their marriage took place during her tenure as *directrice* in Adrianople. Karsten L. Wilke has informed me that this information is available at Paris, AIU, Archives de Moscou, fiches des instituteurs, "Ungar, Sara"; conversation with the author, 21 December 2009.

72. Antébi, *Les Missionnaires Juifs,* 149.

73. A. H. Navon, *Les 70 Ans de l'Ecole Normale Israélite Orientale (1865–1935)* (Paris: Durlacher, 1935), 117.

74. AIU, Tunisie XXIV E 73, 22(?) September 1885, Sara Ungar.

75. "Tunis appears to be the country par excellence where women are not heard; this habit even seems to extend to the school *directrices.* The fact is that I could never obtain official information"; AIU Tunisie, XXXIV E, 24 November 1882, Sara Ungar.

76. AIU Tunisie, XXIV E, 16 July 1885, Sara Ungar.

77. "The inauguration of the Girls' School took place this week. The women were invited for Sunday; they came in great number. A collection, made on this occasion by the widow Mme. Cardoso, produced close to 300 piasters. The next day, Monday, was the men's turn. Only Mr. [Raymond] Valensi was present"; AIU Tunisie, XXVIII E, 2 February 1883, David Cazès, In 1883, 1.10 piasters equaled 1 franc; advertisement in *Le Journal Officiel Tunisienne,* 29 November 1883.

78. AIU Tunisie, XXVIII E, 12 February 1884, David Cazès. His letter states that the expenses for the girls' school for 1883 were 6,231.20 francs. The school was subsidized by subventions of the AIU (3,526.20 F) and local school fees and donations (710.30 F). The shortfall (1,994.70 F) was covered by funds from the boys' school.

79. *Bulletin de l'Alliance Israélite Universelle,* 2e sem. (1883), 29.

80. "She received a baptism by fire at Tunis, excluded from French society in the Tunisian capital (because of the recent war between France and Germany), and prey to the suspicions

of the director of the Boys' School, David Cazès, who found her stiff and scarcely adaptable to the mentality of North Africa"; Antébi, *Les Missionnaires Juifs*, 149.

81. AIU Tunisie, XXXIV E, 16 July 1885, Sara Ungar.

82. "I do not have anyone on hand to recommend to you for the post of *directrice* of our Girls' School . . . [which] is absolutely secular and for we would much prefer to have a capable Christian woman than a Jewess who would not be her equal. What is necessary, above all, is that we have a Frenchwoman . . . but I believe it would be absolutely necessary to rule out the young girls from Bischoffsheim"; AIU Tunisie, XXIX E, 20 June 1887, David Cazès.

83. AIU Tunisie, XXXIV E, 16 July 1885, Sara Ungar.

84. The Jews of France referred to the two rites of the Jewish community as "Portuguese" (Sephardi) and "German" (Ashkenazi).

85. Antebi, *Les Missionnaires Juifs*, 149–162; Wilke, "Competing for Mendelssohn's Legacy," 4–5; Rodrigue, *Jews and Muslims*, 51.

17

Education for Jewish Girls in Late Nineteenth- and Early Twentieth-Century Tunis and the Spread of French in Tunisia

KEITH WALTERS

SINCE AT LEAST the time of the Phoenicians, Tunisia has been multilingual, and from the time Jews first arrived there, they have contributed to that multilingualism. Enjoined to use Hebrew as a liturgical language, Jewish communities have necessarily been bilingual to varying degrees as they came to speak whatever languages were used in daily life while continuing to use Hebrew in religious contexts. In a very real sense, because Tunisia and North Africa more broadly have always been multilingual, debates—public and private, institutional and individual—about specific languages (or varieties of language) are in many ways constitutive of North Africanness: to be North African is to have a particular stake in any of several debates about language and languages going on at any given time.

Despite this fact, scholars of the region have very little systematic information about the social histories of the languages of North Africa, including those used in or by Jewish communities. In other words, we know little about the mechanisms by which specific languages came to North Africa, the institutions through which knowledge and use of them were spread or encouraged, the perceived social motivations (whether incentives or disincentives) for learning or using them, or the details of how the spread took place or why it took the form it did. The existing documentation of what we might term arguments about specific languages is deliberative in nature. It looks toward the future and asks what a community or nation should do (or allow to be done to it) with respect to the languages it uses rather than to the past to evaluate how and why a specific language spread as it did. Thus, these discussions teach us much more about the symbolic valences a specific language represented at a specific historical moment than about the social history of the languages being used, especially as they came to define one another relationally.

This chapter focuses on one very small part of the social history of language in Tunisia and more particularly in its Jewish communities. It seeks to explore the role that formal education for Jewish girls in nineteenth- and early twentieth-century Tunis played in the language shift that took place in the Jewish community there during the period between the two world wars, when community members came to use French rather than Judeo-Arabic as the primary language of daily life and as the native language—that is, the first or primary language—they passed on to the next generation. Neither Muslim communities nor Jewish communities elsewhere in Tunisia adopted French as their primary language. What set of circumstances and events might have led to such a language shift in the Jewish community of Tunis? What can an examination of this situation teach us about that community and its role in Tunisian history, about Jewish culture and society in North Africa more broadly, or about language and languages as social signifiers? As Benedict Anderson has noted, "The most important thing about languages is their capacity for generating imagined communities."[1] This chapter seeks to examine the ways that language created Jewish communities, real and imagined, in colonial Tunisia.

To achieve these goals, I provide information about the complex nature of the Jewish community in Tunis in the nineteenth century and sketch the history and nature of education for Jewish children, especially girls, during the nineteenth and twentieth centuries. I then examine factors that encouraged the Jews of Tunis to learn to speak French, to speak it well (i.e., "without an accent," which, of course, means speaking it with the accent associated with educated Parisians), and to use the language, considering specifically the ways French functioned as various kinds of financial, cultural, and symbolic capital. Particular attention is paid to the expectations regarding matrimony for Jewish and Muslim families and their daughters and to assimilation and naturalization. Finally, I conclude by contextualizing the historical role the Jewish community of Tunis likely played in helping create the social context for a particularly robust contemporary language ideology in Tunisia, one that associates the speaking of French with women.

I focus on the Jewish community of Tunis for two major reasons. First, Tunis was home to the largest number of Jews in the country and served as the primary destination of Jewish migrants from the countryside and smaller towns during the first half of the twentieth century. In 1948, for example, there were some 105,000 Jews in Tunisia, 65,000 of whom lived in Tunis. In 1931, the population of Tunis was about 9 percent Jewish, 38 percent European, and 53 percent Muslim, ratios that more or less held for much of the first half of that century. Today there are only some 1,300 Jews in the country, mostly in Jerba or Tunis. Not surprisingly, the history of the Jewish community of Tunis is far better documented than that of other Tunisian Jewish communities.

Second, from the perspective of sociolinguistic practice, Tunis remains quite distinct from the rest of the country. Despite the fact that Tunisian children across the Republic today study French beginning in the third grade of primary school and that many older Tunisians received most of their education in French, it is in Tunis that one is most likely to hear languages other than Arabic in the streets (especially among Tunisians speaking to one another) and to hear widespread codeswitching between Arabic and French and other languages speakers might know. (Codeswitching is the use of more than one language within the same speech exchange, often within a single sentence.) I attribute these practices to the earlier history of the city and its continuing influence. A century ago, for example, as census data amply demonstrate, Tunis was home to native and non-native speakers of many languages to a degree that other areas of the country were not. Further, the French colonial government paid bonuses to *fonctionnaires* who studied Arabic. In addition, the colonial government, religious organizations, and other groups staffed schools for the children of the colonized and the colonizers that used a language other than Arabic as the medium of instruction. Finally, as speakers of Arabic in Tunis (including speakers of Judeo-Arabic) began to learn French, they engaged in codeswitching, which is sometimes part of the larger process of language spread or even shift. As Carol Myers-Scotton has noted, the elite in many contexts engage in such switching to mark their social status: by codeswitching between a local language and another language—one to which all members of the community do not have access—bilinguals embody the very marker of their social distinction, to use metaphors associated with the work of Pierre Bourdieu.[2] From the perspective of sociolinguistics, researchers would be surprised if such codeswitching did not occur in a place like Tunis, especially because the ability to speak more than one language there often indexes education and cosmopolitanism today, much as it did in the last century and even earlier.

The Jewish Community in Nineteenth-Century Tunis

The social organization of the Jewish community in nineteenth-century Tunis was extremely complex, as shown in Table 17.1, which provides information about the various groups that made up that community at the time.[3]

Without too much oversimplification, one can think of the Jewish community of Tunis at the time as composed of layers with status defined in terms of chronological order of arrival. Thus, those with lowest status, the overwhelming

Table 17.1. The Jewish Community in Nineteenth-Century Tunis

	Twansa	Grana	
Name in Tunisian Arabic (singular/plural)	Tunsi/Twansa[1]	Gorni (Livorno [Italian])/Grana	
		Old Livournais	New Livournais
Origin	Autochthonous Jews;[2] Berbers who had converted at various times; Jews expelled from Spain/Portugal, 1391–1496	Jews who came to Tunis from Livorno, Italy (also victims of the Inquisition), beginning in the last decade of the 1500s	After Treaty of 1822,[3] Jews from Livorno and later from all of Italy, most Italian in origin. Included Jews from France, Gibraltar, and Malta. Likely included some Spanish/Portuguese families not arabized the previous century
Status	*Dhimmi* (religious minority that paid special taxes to the Muslim ruler)	*Dhimmi*	Same as Europeans; not subject to the bey
Names	Hebrew names and naming patterns	Spanish/Portuguese surnames	Italian surnames
Location	The *hara,* or Jewish quarter	The Jewish quarter	The European neighborhoods, among Christians
Clothing	Comparable to that of Muslim Tunisians with minor modifications; subject to sumptuary laws indicating that they were Jewish	Nearly identical to that of Twansa; in some cases, subject to sumptuary laws	Retained European clothing; not subject to sumptuary laws

Table 17.1. *Continued*

	Twansa	Grana	
		Old Livournais	New Livournais
Language(s) (All groups used Hebrew as liturgical language.)	Judeo-Arabic, which was written using Hebrew characters.	Over time became Arabized; some retained Spanish or Italian; originally kept their account books in Portuguese	Italian; learned Judeo-Arabic and later French; helped re-Italianize the Old Livournais

Notes

1. "Tunsi" is Arabic for Tunisian; "Twansa" is the plural noun form. In discussions of the Jewish community of Tunis, it stands in contrast to "Gorni," a Jew of Italian or European origin, and "Grana."

2. There is debate about when Jews first came to Tunisia. Perhaps they arrived as early as the founding of Carthage (814 bc) or the destruction of the First or the Second Temple (586 bc and 70 ce, respectively), but certainly they were present by early in the second century ce. See Sebag, *Histoire des Juifs de Tunisie*.

3. The treaty (and its later expansion in 1846) gave Tuscan Jews (and after unification, all Italian Jews) the same rights as Tuscan Christians: the right to retain their status in perpetuity and not become subjects of the Tunisian bey. France and Britain ensured that Jews of French and British nationality, respectively, received similar rights. Jews from Gibraltar and Malta held British citizenship.

majority of the community, were Twansa, whose ancestors had been in Tunisia for centuries or even millennia. The remaining Jews were Grana, whose ancestors had fled Spain or Portugal during the Inquisition by way of the port of Livorno, Italy, or some other part of Europe. By 1710, the two communities had split, each having its own governing structures, synagogues, schools, butchers, and cemetery. Following an agreement between the two communities in 1741, Jews newly arriving from a predominantly Muslim country became Twansa while those arriving from a predominantly Christian country became Grana. Historical discussions of the Livournais, as the Grana are termed in the French-language research on Tunisia, divide this group in the Old and New Livournais, depending on when they arrived, the latter group having arrived during the nineteenth century. As Table 17.1 demonstrates, with respect to status, location of residence, and clothing, the Old Livournais patterned with the Twansa. They were *dhimmis*—so-called protected religious minorities who lived under a Muslim ruler and resided in the Jewish quarter. They were generally subject to sumptuary laws, as had been the Christians and all Twansa for several centuries. In contrast, the status of the New Livournais was in many ways comparable to that of European Christians, who were protected by the European powers.

These distinctions had consequences of all sorts, and they are certainly relevant in considering the spread of schooling and of French. An individual's status within the Jewish community and the city was determined by his or her way of life: where he or she lived, the kind of lodging he or she had, and the clothing he or she wore or did not wear. As Sebag and others have repeatedly observed, inside and outside the community, where an individual lived, what he or she wore, and what language(s) he or she used were read as indices of status and what the French would term *mentalité*. Worth noting as well is that discussions of the Jewish community make clear that at any given time, its elite was composed of the New Livournais and members of the Old Livournais or the Twansa who had the financial, cultural, and symbolic capital to be accepted by the New Livournais. As is often the case, status was socially constructed and contingent despite an individual's legal status as either a subject of the bey or a protégé of a European power.[4] The languages an individual had mastered no doubt played a role in this construction.

The Advent of "Modern" Schooling in Tunisia

Although a growing number of writers treat the history of modern education in Tunisia, the subject still awaits thorough investigation, especially one that includes the education of Tunisian Jewish as well as European Jewish and Christian children. Julia Clancy-Smith has commented about education for girls that "there is surprisingly little research on female education in Tunisia . . . for the entire colonial era."[5] In the context of North African history, "modern" schools are contrasted with traditional or religious schools. Thus, prior to 1831, schooling for Jews or Muslims was limited to religious schools, which taught boys from each community the language of their respective religious texts, either biblical Hebrew or Quranic Arabic, as part of teaching the texts themselves. Additional education was also religious in nature and included requisite knowledge about the sacrosanct texts and their traditions. A very small minority of the daughters of elite families might have received private tutoring in these same subjects as well. In contrast, "modern schools" took as their focus what we might term today the humanities, mathematics, and the sciences. The language of instruction was always a European language.

The first "modern" school in the country was opened in Tunis in 1831 by Pompeo Sulema and his sister, Esther Sulema, who were New Livournais.[6] This school later merged with one opened in 1845 by Abbé François Bourgade, who opened a kindergarten in 1846 under his direction and that of a Jewish primary-school teacher, Madame Malah.[7]

In 1840, the Sisters of Saint Joseph of the Apparition opened the first girls' schools in Tunis—one that charged tuition and another that was free.[8] Additional girls' schools were started by the same religious order in a suburb of Tunis where many Europeans and New Livournais lived and in three other Tunisian towns. Among the other religious orders that likewise opened schools were the Catholic nuns and sisters who opened girls' schools in conjunction with the clinics, orphanages, and other institutions they developed. Some were free, while others charged tuition. Secondary sources that discuss these schools make clear that Jewish girls frequently attended them.[9] Soon thereafter, the Italians in Tunis (of whom the New Livournais would have been a part), with the assistance of the Italian government, opened one secondary school for boys and another for girls there, strong evidence that education was being made available to Italian girls as well as boys. Commenting on the schools, Sebag writes:

> The "Livournais" Jews who had come from Italy at a relatively recent date were the first to send their children to these schools. Their example was followed by the Livournais Jews who had been in the country for many years and by the more fortunate of the Tunisian Jews [i.e., the Twansa]. Thus, during the course of the nineteenth century, a number of Jews of both sexes were able to acquire a modern primary-school education along with the knowledge of a European language, either Italian or French. There were even those who received a secondary education that enabled them to continue their studies at the university level in Europe.[10]

These comments reflect a larger pattern of the diffusion of social innovations and the hierarchical nature of social status in the Jewish community. The New Livournais, who could also claim membership in the European community, served as a model for the Old Livournais, who, in turn, served as a model for Twansa of means, who became models to be emulated at a distance by poorer Twansa who wanted to improve their social standing.

The Catholics were joined by the London Society for Promoting Christianity amongst the Jews in contributing to the education of Jews in Tunis and in Tunisia more broadly.[11] The organization's goals were clearly evangelical: it distributed tracts, Hebrew translations of the New Testament, and copies of the Bible in a range of languages as part of its efforts to convert Jews worldwide to Christianity and demonstrated little concern for adherents of other non-Christian faiths. Despite the organization's goals and clear evidence of the Christian orientation of any schooling it offered, the desire of Jews in Tunisia and elsewhere for education was obviously greater than fears they might have had about losing their children to Christianity. Reverend F. C. Ewald established the society in 1834 but had to return home to Britain in 1841 because of illness. Ewald reported the baptism of one Jew, a Livournais, a fact that may be taken as evidence that the society's appeal was not merely to the poor and destitute. Later missionaries reported a very limited number of baptisms and a slightly larger number of Jewish converts to Christianity, but by and large Jews felt that they could not risk the social stigma and isolation within the Jewish community that inevitably followed baptism. In fact, most of the baptisms did not take place in Tunis but elsewhere, even out of the country.

In 1855, a year before he passed away, E. A. Page opened a mission school for boys in Tunis. The school was reestablished in 1861 by Reverend W. Fenner.[12] The following year, a school for girls was opened. Of this school, Reverend W. T. Gidney, the author of the centennial history of the society, wrote, "This shewed great advance in missionary activity, for no class stood in greater need of moral and spiritual elevation."[13] Gidney's comments provide evidence of how British missionaries, at least, saw the situation of Jewish girls then living in the *hara*, where the society's work was centered. The society also operated a school in Sousse from 1876 to 1881. The volume devoted to the society's history does not specify the language(s) used in the mission's schools or the linguistic ability of most of its missionaries. However, one missionary's "profound knowledge of Arabic" is the subject of comment—evidence that such knowledge was unusual. We might assume that a European language, likely English, was used as the language of instruction. During certain periods, religious services were held in English on Sunday with an "evangelical" service in French on a weeknight. All the missionaries reportedly spoke frequently with Jews, interactions that would have taken place via an interpreter or in Judeo-Arabic or a European language. One can expect that many of the society's missionaries had studied biblical Hebrew as part of their training for the ministry.

Table 17.2 gives available information on enrollment at the society's school in Tunis for the years reported in Gidney's history of the society.

As is evident, the school for girls educated a larger number of Jewish children than did the school for boys. Gidney noted that in addition to the usual school program, there was a Sunday school (though he provided no information about which age groups attended or what the focus of the program was) and sewing classes for mothers and older girls. This reminds us that representatives of Christian organizations, whether Catholic or Protestant, interacted with Tunisians in contexts other than the formal classroom and that the curricula inside and outside formal classrooms were often highly gendered. Many curricula for girls, initially at least, taught sewing and other domestic arts in addition to lim-

Table 17.2. Enrollment in Schools Operated by the Tunis Mission of the
London Society for Promoting Christianity amongst the Jews (1861–1900)

Year	Boys	Girls	Total
1861	33	0	33
1862	NA[1]	85	85
1863	NA	119	119
1874	72	93	165
1881	180	320	500
1897	100	161	261
1900	112	NA	112
Cumulative totals 1861–1878	960	1,600	2,560

Notes
   1. NA = not available.
Source: Gidney, *The History of the London Society for Promoting Christianity amongst the Jews,* passim.

ited literacy and numeracy skills. Such differences in the content of education reflected cultural assumptions about gender complementarity: because women and men played very different roles in society, girls and boys needed very different kinds of education and socialization more broadly.

As early as 1864, a committee made up of French and Italian Jews was set up in Tunis in order to seek permission for a school operated by the Alliance Is-raélite Universelle (AIU). The school would be supported by a tax Jews paid to their butchers, but the bey refused. Founded in Paris in 1860, the AIU took as its goal "the emancipation and the moral progress of the Jews" around the world.[14] It represented what might be termed French Jewry's *mission civilisatrice* with regard to their North African and Middle Eastern brothers and sisters. Members of the AIU saw North African Jews as being in need of civilizing in matters ranging from education to hygiene in addition to emancipation, and they used rhetoric not unlike that of the French colonial government when they commented on anything outside the West. These schools were targeted at poor Jews rather than those of means. Several sources demonstrate that a very small number of Muslim students also attended AIU schools. It should also be noted that while AIU schools were concerned with teaching Hebrew, they were far more committed to teaching French and French ways.[15]

As Rachel Simon points out, because AIU schools were run by Jews, they could not be accused of any efforts to convert students, a fact that made them especially appealing to many within the Jewish community. In some senses, however, AIU schools presented a greater threat to existing patterns of Jewish education and traditional communities than did Christian or foreign secular schools, because the Western-style education the AIU offered, fully legitimated within a Jewish context, inculcated systems of belief and behavior, including aspirations, that had previously not existed.[16] The Jews of Jerba, for example, refused to permit an AIU school to be set up there because community leaders feared they would lose their influence and were concerned about the potential for the community to fall away from its traditional religious practices.

The first AIU school in Tunisia, a school for boys, was finally opened in 1878 in a Tunis neighborhood called Little Malta. A girls' school was opened in the same neighborhood four years later in 1882, the year after Tunisia became a French colony. Over the next twenty-eight years, the AIU opened six other schools across Tunisia, one of which was for girls. These schools clearly filled a need the Jewish community recognized. When the boys' school opened in 1878, its enrollment was over 1,000: 750 from the Talmud-Torah or traditional religious schools of the Twansa, 125 from the Talmud-Torah of the Livournais, and 150 from "various backgrounds."[17]

In addition to schools established and run by Christian organizations (whether Catholic or Protestant) and the AIU of Paris, the French colonial government set up public schools, which were often frequented by Jewish students, including girls. In discussing these schools, Patrick Cabanel comments:

> The fact that the Jewish children were divided nearly equally between the public schools (41% of the Jewish boys and 54% of the girls) and the schools of the Alliance could be attributed to the division between the more traditional Twansa, present in the country for a very long time, who sent their children to the schools of the Alliance, and the Grana, who had come from Livorno, enjoyed a higher social and educational level, one closer to the Western model, and sent their children to public schools. Additionally, some Jewish children, but no Muslims, attended the Catholic schools.[18]

Although Cabanel's claim about the total absence of Muslim youth, including Muslim girls, in schools run by various religious groups is a very slight exaggeration, he is correct in noting that long-standing distinctions within the Jewish community had become salient once again with respect to education, including education for girls.

Thus, by the late nineteenth century, educational opportunities presented themselves to Jewish girls in Tunis in several forms. Each school brought with it particular kinds of experiences: schools run by Protestant missionaries or Catholic orders, "secular" schools run by the French colonial government, schools created specifically for Jews by the AIU, and no doubt private schools of various sorts run by individuals or groups in the Italian or other European communities there. Obviously, much remains to be learned at the most basic level about schools for girls (including Jewish girls) during the colonial era.

Creating the Necessary Conditions for Language Shift

In this section, I discuss how the several kinds of schools in Tunis that educated Jewish children contributed to language shift in that community. Table 17.3 gives information on school enrollment among Tunisian Jews from 1889 (eight years after Tunisia became a French colony) until 1955 (a year before Tunisia's independence).

Several observations about these figures are important. First, they represent the entire country, not just Tunis, though, as noted, the overwhelming majority of Jews lived in Tunis and the vast majority of educational establishments set up for Jewish students—or students from any background—were located there.

Second, and surely more striking, is the near balance in Jewish girls and boys who attended school; the number of girls was close to and sometimes exceeded the number of boys. Yet, the near-equal numbers of boys and girls did not ultimately translate into any sort of gender equity with respect to achievement. Sebag presents an example of fifteen Jewish boys who finished secondary school in 1916 and could enroll in university; only one such Jewish girl did so. In 1939, ninety-three Jewish boys finished secondary school but only thirty-two such Jewish girls—a vast improvement, but nothing like equity.[19]

However, this near balance between Jewish girls and boys attending school is especially impressive when one considers the situation of Muslim girls vis-à-vis Muslim boys. According to Bakalti, in 1885 six Muslim girls were attending primary school in all of Tunisia—and they would surely have been in Tunis. In 1903, thirty-seven Muslim girls were attending school, comprising 1.2 percent of the total population of Muslim children attending school. The situation improved when the French opened a school for Muslim girls in 1909; the percentage of girls among Muslim children attending school rose to 10.4 percent. Just before World War II, in 1939, Muslim girls made up 15.3 percent of the Muslim population in school. By 1954, Muslim girls accounted for 26.1 percent of the Muslim children attending school. By that time, they also represented nearly 63.9 percent of the girls of any confessional background being schooled, although it should be noted that Muslims in general represented a much larger proportional segment of the population than school-aged Jewish or Christian girls.[20] In the overwhelming number of cases, French was the primary language of instruction in the schools Muslim girls attended. By 1896, French had become the language

Table 17.3. School Enrollment for Jews in Tunisia (1889–1955)

Year	Males	Females	Totals	Females as Percentage of Total
1889	1,887	1,187	3,074	38.6
1895	2,201	1,713	3,914	43.8
1905	2,922	2,611	5,533	47.2
1912	4,141	3,764	7,905	47.6
1913	4,347	4,069	8,416	48.3
1914	4,419	4,289	8,708	49.3
1921	4,960	4,690	9,650	48.6
1926	5,663	5,434	11,097	49.0
1931	5,929	6,021	11,950	50.4
1936	6,475	6,193	12,668	48.9
1939	6,343	6,313	12,656	49.9
1940	6,766	6,777	13,543	50.0
1946	6,903	7,150	14,053	50.9
1951	7,653	7,306	14,959	48.8
1955	7,399	7,042	14,441	48.8

Source: Data in this table are derived from Sebag, *Histoire des Juifs de Tunisie,* 142, 191, and 263.

of instruction in all schools except traditional religious schools or schools run by the Italian community.[21] Muslim girls were not permitted to attend Quranic schools until 1944.[22]

In contrast, the near balance in the Jewish community in number of boys and girls attending school is especially important for language there and in Tunisia for two reasons. First, it made language shift possible within the Jewish community. Language shift to French could not have taken place in Jewish communities elsewhere across the country because so few Jewish women and girls would have spoken French. Obviously, it could not have taken place in Muslim communities because almost no Muslim women or girls spoke French. Second, as I explain below, this use of French by girls and women likely served as a model of *local* origin for Muslim Tunisian girls and women and for Muslim Tunisian families wanting to improve their own status, a fact that helps account for the relationship Tunisian women, who are overwhelmingly Muslim, have with the language even today.

In seeking to understand cases of language shift and why they come about, researchers from various fields are wise to remember the obvious but sometimes forgotten fact that languages in bilingual situations never offer merely different ways of saying the same thing. Rather, each language indexes or "points to" value orientations associated with situated acts, activities, and stances, to use Elinor Och's formulation. Hence, a speaker's choosing among languages in a multilingual situation and using a specific language in performing a particular act (e.g., disagreeing), engaging in a particular activity (e.g., participating in a faculty meeting), or taking a particular stance (e.g., being assertive) necessarily gives rise to contestable social meanings. This situation applies not only in the local immediate context but also in larger, more abstract, and often transnational systems of meaning.[23] Ochs's claim certainly holds for colonial and independent Tunisia. In other words, it is not the case that (mastery of) French always and eternally indexes (or symbolizes) modernity or education or "the West" in all social contexts (though knowledge of French sometimes indexes these things in Tunisia even today). Such meanings are historically and socially contingent; they depend, as Ochs contends, on specific and repeated acts. Hence, today, by choosing to speak French in a professional context, an educated Tunisian women in her 50s indirectly reminds her male colleagues that she should not be treated as, say, their mothers or hers, who are likely monolingual speakers of Tunisian Arabic and illiterate.

Similarly, when I read Sebag and other historical accounts of the Jewish community of Tunis, I am struck by how frequently the shift from Judeo-Arabic (and even Italian) to French is the subject of commentary, though all the writers are historians, not students of language. Equally important, these writers consistently associated the increasing use of French with modernization (always defined as Westernization and most often as "Frenchification") and the spread of "modern" ways of thinking. Thus, in commenting on the last years of the protectorate—from the end of World War II until 1956, Sebag noted that "the education of boys and girls in modern schools translated into greater and greater use of French as the language of everyday interaction and of culture, and language shift to French was accompanied by a greater and greater acculturation that influenced customs and manners."[24] A few pages later, he added:

> An education that extended to nearly all of the school-aged population of both sexes led to a knowledge of French among all social classes. For those whose parents had attended a French school, French replaced, in part or in whole, Arabic as the native language. The use of French expanded, supplanting Arabic more and more as the language of interaction. It was only in the [Jewish] communities of the rural areas, where life was closely linked to the life of the Muslim population, that Arabic continued to be used. In the capital and the nearby large towns, where life was more tightly linked to that of the European population, the use of Arabic continued to decline.

It is likewise worth noting that many of those who still used Arabic no
longer mastered it and that their vocabulary was reduced more and more
to the requirements of everyday life.[25]

What Sebag describes in this passage is communal language shift, where
within a generation or two, individuals move from being bilingual in Judeo-
Arabic and French to being monolingual (or nearly so) in French. As his larger
discussion makes clear, the shift to the French language was accompanied by
changes in patterns of naming (or referring to) children, in manner of dress,
and in place and style of residence. In other words, it represented a shift in con-
ceptions of individual and communal identity at the local, national, and transnational levels, indexed unmistakably by patterns of language choice and use.

Knowledge of a European Language as Capital of Several Sorts

As analysts, we should be able to make more concrete observations about the
meanings of French and why learning and using French came to have the importance it did for the Jews of Tunis than merely linking it to modernity or Westernization. Such abstractions are rarely sufficient motivation for individual social
actors to muster the effort necessary to master a language and especially to develop native-like proficiency in it, as many of the Jews of Tunis did. The work of
Pierre Bourdieu[26] is helpful in this regard. Using the metaphor of markets, Bourdieu often analyzes language, and especially the ability to use it and to speak it
"without an accent," as several overlapping and often mutually reinforcing kinds
of capital. As symbolic capital, knowledge of a language can bring its "owners"
prestige or honor. Most immediately, it permits those with such knowledge to
claim membership in various groups—whether as natives of a region or members
of the social group whose life circumstances have afforded them the opportunity
to learn a particular language, especially one they do not speak natively or those
not required of them. Indeed, the ability to use a language represents a particular
kind of symbolic capital, one that cannot be bought as one might buy a consumer
item such as a vehicle or a dwelling or a piece of jewelry because knowledge of a
language and more particularly the ability to use it and do so appropriately are
the result of a long process of socialization through which knowledge of the language becomes literally embodied.

Knowledge of a language likewise represents a kind of cultural capital: an
acquisition or qualification that has particular values in local contexts. This fact
is no less true of knowledge of nonstandard dialects than of the most elevated
registers of a standardized language. Such knowledge opens certain doors while
ensuring that others are slammed shut. Finally, knowledge of a language has the

potential to become economic capital, that is, material wealth, as when someone uses that knowledge or is required to have it to get certain jobs. For example, Arabization campaigns across North Africa after independence, whether they involved Arabizing school curricula or legal systems, left many who had received their schooling in French scrambling for other posts or lessons in Modern Standard Arabic.

Let us consider the kinds of capital that French likely represented for members of the Jewish community of Tunis and how the potential for having such capital might have functioned as motivation to learn the language. First, Sebag noted that while institutionalizing the teaching of Hebrew and Jewish culture, the first boys' school of the AIU, which opened in 1878, ensured the teaching of French and the curriculum that characterized the primary schools of France at the time. Thus, the schools served as a site for the inculcation of French and the ways of seeing the world promulgated by the French institution of schooling during this period. As he later commented, "Thanks to this new institution, knowledge of French was spread among the Jewish masses, and with it, new ways of thinking."[27]

The potential value of education and especially a "modern" education in the language of the colonizer was not lost on the Jewish community in Tunis or elsewhere across the Middle East. Scholars of earlier periods have repeatedly noted that knowledge of a European language, however obtained, was often very valuable to Jews living across the Middle East. By using a European language in their work with or for Europeans, whether as interpreters, translators, or multilingual employees, Jews were sometimes able to gain certain kinds of legal protection for themselves and their families in contrast to the continuing disadvantages of remaining *dhimmi*s. In the modern era, as Sara Reguer observes: "Knowledge of languages enabled young Jewish men and women to expand their economic opportunities as civil service officials and bank and commercial company clerks; women could take jobs as secretaries, teachers, pharmacists, and nurses by the twentieth century."[28]

Reeva Spector Simon explains how education in an AIU school positioned Jews across the Middle East vis-à-vis their fellow Muslim citizens:

> Educated to be Europeans, Jews who attended AIU schools emerged a generation or so ahead of Muslims in the race to westernization. Muslims mostly attended the state public schools and later entered the state bureaucracy in the Ottoman Empire, Egypt, and Tunisia, but Jews and Christians filled the new niches in the professions. Jews were also tied to European powers as business agents for foreign companies and the new colonial bureaucracies, so that during the later struggles between nationalism and colonialism, they were caught in the middle politically.[29]

Laskier and Simon contend further that the creation of a "new haute bourgeoisie that considered itself European" among the Jewish communities of North
Africa and elsewhere created opportunities for those who had received modern
educations and hence spoke European languages.[30] These scholars' comments
regarding the graduates of AIU schools apply no less to those educated in other
French-language contexts.

Third, AIU schools and education for girls more broadly played a significant role in the emancipation and reformation of women, sometimes consciously,
other times less so. Rodrigue, who has analyzed letters AIU teachers wrote to the
home office in Paris, describes the gendered difference in letters female and male
teachers in these schools wrote. Whereas male teachers often wrote about politics
in the host country or the local Jewish community, female teachers wrote about
pedagogy and the liberation of local Jewish women.

> Letter after letter [from female teachers] painted a very somber picture in
> which the liberation of local women would be realized only through the
> Alliance. The female teachers constituted the first cohort of educated Jew-
> ish women of . . . North African origin and were the first professional Jew-
> ish women in the region. The westernizing zeal in their discourse, like that
> of their male counterparts, was deeply rooted in legitimation and valida-
> tion of their own trajectories.[31]

Elsewhere, Rodrigue adds that "the education of girls was . . . deemed essential by the Alliance because of its potential impact on future generations."[32] In
other words, as is often the case, education was offered to girls not because it was
"the right thing to do" or because they had a right to be educated; rather, the primary stated motivation was that Jewish girls should be educated because they
would become mothers of future generations. The gendered nature of this motivation is noteworthy: the reasons given for educating Jewish (or Muslim or Christian) boys was never that they would become the fathers of future generations of
children.[33]

In her discussion of education for Jewish women across the Middle East,
Reguer notes that in many places, economic need led poor Jewish women to work
outside the home, a fact that encouraged vocational education for Jewish girls.
She explains that education and the desire for it influenced not only poor women
but those of the middle class as well.

> Economic necessity may have been the starting point, but education was
> the key to the new world. Economics was also the driving force behind
> the modernization of women from the middle class. In this case it was be-
> cause of the father's exposure to the modern world. For their own prestige

they sent their daughters to the new schools available to them. Educating daughters became a sign of status, and sending them to the colonial European schools meant that daughters might even socialize with the daughters of the Europeans. Here too education would be the main modernizing force.[34]

The schools associated with various Christian groups and the colonial government's public schools in Tunis were clearly sites where students from different cultural and confessional communities interacted. In writing of the Collège Allaoui, which prepared European and Tunisian students who hoped to teach in colonial schools for Tunisian youth and therefore studied both French and Tunisian Arabic, Cabanel cites one of its headmasters, Benjamin Buisson, who characterized the institution as "the major site of meeting and mixing among the nationalities for Tunisian youth of school age."[35]

In addition to these motivations for learning French, another emerges—the marriage market for Jewish and Muslim families and their daughters. With regard to status issues in the Muslim community, I have noted elsewhere that marriage during this period in the Muslim communities was considered an economic relationship between families, and a young woman who married a man of higher social status helped improve the status of her entire family.[36] Rodrigue notes that French played such a role in the marriage market of the Jewish communities of the North Africa and the Middle East during the colonial period: "It was perceived as beneficial for the acquisition of new manners and ways that would add polish and hence facilitate marriage in societies that had come to culturally value the outer accoutrements of Western mores."[37]

Assimilation, Naturalization, and Westernization

An important issue that is relevant to the topic of the spread of French, especially in the Jewish community, is the complex issue of naturalization, which presumed assimilation, including linguistic assimilation.[38] Understandably, nationalists, including nearly all Tunisian Muslims and some Jews, believed that Tunisian Jews should remain loyal to the cause of independence; in other words, Jews should privilege their Tunisianness (or their status as "colonized" individuals) over any other part of their identity. However, not everyone within the Jewish community agreed. Predictably, both the French and Tunisian Muslims questioned the loyalty of the Jews. The French suspected that Tunisian Jews were closely aligned with Tunisian Muslim nationalists while the latter suspected that Tunisian Jews had become too Europeanized and hence sympathized too greatly with the goals of the French.

Yet it is clear that the historically marginal status of Jews in Tunisia served as a motivation to assimilate and naturalize, when possible, though France had its own history of anti-Semitism. Abdelkarim Allagui has argued that the Jewish elite believed that the secularism associated with France, despite that history, was a safer bet than whatever they might be able to negotiate in Muslim Tunisia during or after the colonial era.[39] Haim Saadoun describes the situation in this way:

> The main problem for the Jews in this colonial society was that they were living within a Muslim society that had set patterns for Jewish existence. In the past a Jew had been obliged to be part of an autonomous Jewish community, living side by side with, yet in the shadow of, Islam. The new colonial society gave Jews the freedom, within certain limitations, to choose how to live or identify themselves. French culture presented the Jews with a challenge that was irresistible. French rule was both the source of the Jews' security and their means of release from the degradation of Islam. Consciously, then, but not necessarily by overt choice, the Jews tied their fate to that of French colonial rule, which eventually distanced them even more from the Muslim majority in Tunisia.[40]

Tunisian Jews were never afforded automatic citizenship, as Algerian Jews had been, but the possibility of naturalization during a certain period was certainly high motivation for many Tunisian Jews to identify with the French, as shown by the data in Table 17.4, which provides information on Tunisian naturalizations during the period 1881–1948.

These figures provide evidence of the multilingual nature of Tunisia—and most assuredly Tunis—to which I referred earlier. They likewise demonstrate that during this period, nearly 18 percent of those who became French citizens were Tunisian Jews.[41] The issue of naturalization also reminds us that in this case (and no doubt in many others), questions of gender as they relate to matters of language choice and shift cannot be separated from issues often discussed as part of nationalism and the creation of national identities. As noted above, especially in multilingual situations, language choice becomes indexical, and the social meanings of specific languages or language varieties can often not be divorced from transnational symbolical and political economies. Thus, the shift to the French language and assimilation to French ways should be seen as consequences, likely unintended in certain ways, of the colonial project. At the same time, cultural assimilation and language shift facilitated naturalization as the law at various times allowed, and they had clear consequences for the future of Tunisian Jews after 1948, when they began leaving Tunis in large numbers.

Religious Confession, Gender, and Language Shift in Tunisia

In this chapter, I have tried to give the briefest outline of Jewish girls' access to education in late nineteenth- and early twentieth-century Tunis, linking it with the spread of French there and in Tunisia more broadly. I hope to have contributed to the study of the Jewish community in Tunis by beginning to document language shift from Judeo-Arabic to French in that community and noting the role this community played in the social history of Tunisian multilingualism. Clearly, the education of Jewish girls in Tunis received cannot be separated from the medium of instruction—first Italian, but by 1896 almost uniquely French (with Hebrew or Arabic taught as a subject in some schools). The specific history of the language shift that took place in the Jewish community of Tunis is tied to the complexity of the nineteenth-century Jewish community there, where the New Livournais maintained strong ties with the larger Italian community, one of the major supporters of the creation of modern schools in Tunisia.

Nor should the schooling these girls received be divorced from its colonial context, which marginalized girls in multiple ways. Indeed, by the late nineteenth century, it was the curriculum of France that was taught in these schools, and by 1910, even the exams were those used in France.[42] This education fostered and made possible language shift to French in the Jewish community of Tunis even as it contributed to the use of French more broadly in Tunis.

The observations made here are in line with a rethinking of scholars' understanding of multilingualism, language learning, and gender. While research in the study of language and gender traditionally suffers from a monolingual bias, nearly all of the research on language learning, whether formal or informal, is militantly asexual, as if the gendered social self had no influence on learning or using languages other than the native language. The community treated here, the Jewish community in pre-Independence Tunis, was defined in and by its relationship to the larger Muslim and European communities, and like all the communities found there it subscribed heartily to the notion of gender complementarity. Its members could not help but "respond symbolically to relations of power between their group and the dominant group[s] in society."[43] Within each of these communities, females and males led highly gendered lives, and females, despite whatever agency they might find, were disadvantaged in many ways. Within this context, Jewish girls and women were subject to the patriarchies of all three communities. It should not be surprising that education and mastery of French represented new and important kinds of economic, political, and symbolic capital for them and their families, both their families of origin and the families they created. Mastery, indeed embodiment, of the French language

Table 174. Naturalizations to French Citizenship in Tunisia, 1881–1948

Nationalities/Religion	1891–1898	1899–1910	1911–1930	1931–1935	1936–1940	1941–1946	1946	1947	1948	Total	Percent
Italian	142	881	10,892	4575	3549	201	457	3777	2198	26,672	65.3
Maltese	42	225	1,561	290	235	NA1	6	30	49	2,438	6.0
Swiss	18	36	104	35	28	NA	NA	3	NA	224	0.5
German	28	30	43	66	32	NA	3	14	1	217	0.5
Austrian	10	44	45	2	1	NA	NA	4	7	113	0.3
Spanish	3	27	201	36	17	NA	2	9	16	311	0.8
Greek	20	8	238	61	18	NA	NA	7	12	364	0.9
Dutch	2	9	7	2	2	NA	NA	NA	NA	22	0.1
English	NA	NA	14	2	NA	1	NA	NA	NA	17	0.0
Portuguese	NA	3	14	6	3	NA	NA	NA	3	29	0.1
Belgian	6	1	29	9	19	NA	NA	7	2	73	0.2
Norwegian & Swedish	NA	4	NA	2	1	NA	NA	NA	NA	7	0.0
Czechoslovak	NA	NA	8	16	23	NA	NA	NA	NA	47	0.1
Bulgarian	NA	2	4	3	1	NA	NA	NA	NA	10	0.0
Hungarian	NA	NA	7	6	6	2	NA	11	2	34	0.1
Romanian	NA	NA	8	6	2	NA	NA	4	NA	20	0.0
Yugoslavian	NA	NA	7	10	8	NA	NA	4	NA	29	0.1
Turkish	NA	11	186	20	9	1	NA	5	2	234	0.6
Albanian	NA	NA	12	11	NA	NA	NA	NA	2	25	0.1
Polish	NA	NA	37	22	44	1	NA	12	7	123	0.3
Russian	3	6	310	421	139	3	1	27	14	924	2.3

Luxemburger	2	NA	1	3	NA	NA	NA	1	NA	7	0.0
Algerian											
Catholic	NA	NA	34	6	1	NA	5	NA	NA	46	0.1
Muslim	3	5	193	3	1	NA	NA	NA	NA	205	0.5
Jewish	NA	NA	67	4	3	NA	NA	3	NA	77	0.2
Tunisian											
Catholic	NA	NA	NA	17	5	NA	1	4	NA	27	0.1
Muslim	17	80	1037	12	4	5	NA	10	2	1,167	2.9
Jewish	NA	NA	5569	1312	205	28	27	101	69	7,311	17.9
Moroccan	NA	NA	18	NA	NA	NA	NA	NA	NA	18	0.0
Syrian	NA	NA	18	NA	NA	NA	NA	11	1	30	0.1
Other	NA	NA	2	1	1	3	5	7	2	21	0.1
Total	296	1,372	20,666	6,959	4,357	245	507	4,051	2,389	40,842	100.0

Notes

1. NA = not available.

Source: Régence de Tunis, Protectorat Français, Service Tunisien des Statistiques, *Annuaire statistique de la Tunisie, Année 1948* (Tunis: Imprimerie S.A.P.I.), 23.

became a tangible symbol in the renegotiation of identity and the imagining of community that took place among the Jews of Tunis.

Even as the gendered linguistic practices described here shaped Tunisia's linguistic past, they continue to influence the small Jewish community that remains there today. Specifically, I wish to contend that the linguistic practices of these Jewish girls and women encouraged Muslim girls and women to invest in mastering French, a tradition that continues to this day across Tunisia. Importantly, these models were local in origin rather than imported directly from France (or other European countries). Thus, in addition to the native speakers of French and to Europeans who were becoming French by naturalization (and thus almost assuredly speaking French), Muslim Tunisian girls and women saw locally born Tunisian Jewish girls and women receiving educations and creating families and homes that were quite different from either traditional Jewish or Muslim families or homes. Such models likely encouraged the spread of the use of French among Muslim Tunisian girls and women seeking alternatives to traditional ways of being that were available to Muslim women in Tunisia, a sociolinguistic practice that continues to this day, when the use of French by women, especially *tunisoises,* is associated with education, urbanity, and cosmopolitan attitudes. In short, speaking French amounts to a rejection of certain traditional definitions of what it means to be a woman. Tunisian historian Abdelhamid Larguèche reports that during the colonial period, the Muslim community saw the local Jewish community as a "laboratory" for understanding the possible consequences of becoming modern, and issues relating to changing roles for women, including education for girls, were among those Muslims debated.[44] Those who supported education for girls found evidence to support their position in what was occurring in the Jewish community, while those who opposed such education or the renegotiation of gender roles more broadly found evidence there to support that position.[45]

In one of the most influential recent papers on language ideology, Susan Gal and Judith Irvine contend that such ideologies are best understood in terms of three related processes.[46] The first of these is iconization, or the identification of a language or language variety with some social attribute, often in an essentializing way, much as contemporary Tunisians generally link the speaking of French with women there. The second process, fractal recursivity, involves the projection of a difference at one level of social organization onto another one. With respect to the case described here, although it is clear that while Tunisian women *and* men sometimes speak French, engage in codeswitching, and use the uvular *r,* such intraspeaker variability is projected onto and reified as intergroup variation: French has come to be associated with women, an ideological move that thus associates Arabic with men. Finally, for these two processes to occur there must be a great deal of erasure, whereby the complex details of synchronic variability and past history are ignored or minimized. Contemporary discussions of women's use of French in Tunisia, whether they occur on the sidewalk or in academic journals,[47] generally ignore the role that French might have played or continues to play in local language patterns. In this chapter, I have begun reinscribing the perhaps limited but nevertheless important role that the Jewish community in Tunis, especially its girls and women, played in the spread of French there and in Tunisia more broadly, a role that has generally been forgotten or erased.

NOTES

1. Benedict Anderson, *Imagined Communities: Reflections on the Origin and Spread of Nationalism,* rev. ed. (London: Verso, 1991), 133.

2. Carol Myers Scotton, "Elite Closure as Boundary Maintenance: The Evidence from Africa," in *Language Policy and Political Development,* ed. Bruce Weinstein (Norwood, N.J.: Ablex, 1990), 25–41; and Carol Myers Scotton, *Social Motivations for Codeswitching: Evidence from Africa* (Oxford: Oxford University Press, 1993). The most relevant works of Pierre Bourdieu are *Language and Symbolic Action,* trans. Gino Raymond and Matthew Adamson (Cambridge, Mass.: Harvard University Press, 1991); and Pierre Bourdieu, *Distinction: A Social Critique of the Judgement of Taste,* trans. Richard Nice (Cambridge, Mass.: Harvard University Press, 1984). John B. Thompson's "Editor's Introduction" to *Language and Symbolic Action* is especially useful in offering an overview of Bourdieu's thinking on language.

3. Relevant sources on the Jewish community of Tunis include Paul Sebag, *Histoire des Juifs de Tunisie: Des origines à nos jours* (Paris: L'Harmattan, 1991); Paul Sebag, *Tunis: Histoire d'une ville* (Paris: L'Harmattan, 1998); Haim Saadoun, "Tunisia," in *The Jews of the Middle East and North Africa in Modern Times,* ed. Reeva Spector Simon, Michael Menachem Laskier, and Sara Reguer (New York: Columbia University Press, 2003), 444–457; and Jacques Taïeb, "Les Juifs Livournais de 1600 à 1881," in *Histoire communautaire, histoire plurielle: La communauté juive de Tunisie, Actes du colloque de Tunis organisé les 25–27 Février 1998 à la Faculté de la Manouba* (Tunis: Centre de Publications Universitaire, 1999), 153–164.

4. For the "modern transnational Jewish merchant elite" in the region, see Michael Menachem Laskier and Reeva Spector Simon, "Economic Life," in *The Jews of the Middle East and North Africa in Modern Times,* ed. Reeva Spector Simon, Michael Menachem Laskier, and Sara Reguer (New York: Columbia University Press, 2003), 29–48. The authors discuss the case of Eugenio Lumbroso, an Italian citizen who resided in Tunisia and built one of the earliest olive-oil refining factories there in 1892. "This elite was composed of Italian and Sephardic Jews, many of whom had married into the local Jewish merchant elite of North Africa" (42).

5. Julia Clancy-Smith, "Envisioning Knowledge: Educating the Muslim Woman in Colonial North Africa, c. 1850–1918," in *Iran and Beyond: Essays in Middle Eastern History in Honor of Nikki R. Keddie,* ed. Rudi Mathee and Beth Baron (Costa Mesa, Calif.: Mazda, 2000), 101. Other sources on the history of education for girls in Tunisia include Souad Bakalti, *La femme tunisienne au temps de la colonization 1881–1956* (Paris: L'Harmattan, 1996); Selwa Khaddar Zangar, "Une école pionnière, l'école de la rue du Pacha," in *La femme tunisienne à travers les âges* (Tunis: Ministère de la Culture, Institut National du Patrimoine, 1997), 176–180; and Keith Walters, "Considering the Meanings of Literacy in a Postcolonial Setting: The Case of Tunisia," in *Women and Literacy: Inquiries for a New Century,* ed. Beth Daniell and Peter Mortensen (Mahwah,

N.J.: Lawrence Earlbaum and NCTE, 2007), 294–320. On the history of education in Tunisia, especially from a nationalist perspective, see Nourredine Sraïeb, *Le Collège Sadiki de Tunis, 1875–1956: Enseignement et nationalisme* (Tunis: Alif, n.d.); and Mokhtar Ayachi, *Écoles et société en Tunisie 1930–1958* (Tunis: Centre de CERES, 2003).

6. Sebag, *Histoire des Juifs de Tunisie,* 127.

7. Ibid.; Bakalti, *La femme tunisienne,* 117.

8. Bakalti, *La femme tunisienne,* 116. On schools in Tunisia run by various Catholic orders, see François Dornier, *Les Catholiques en Tunisie au fils des ans* (Tunis: Imprimerie Finzi, 2000); and Pierre Soumille, "Les activités et les œuvres des congrégations religieuses catholiques en Tunisie à l'époque du protectorat français (fin XIXᵉ-milieu XXᵉ siècle)," in *La Tunisie mosaïque: Diasporas, cosmopolitisme, archéologies de l'identité,* ed. Jacques Alexandropoulos and Patrick Cabanel (Toulouse: Presses universitaires du Mirail, 2000), 319–346.

9. See, e.g., Dornier, *Les Catholiques en Tunisie au fils des ans,* 398–578; Sebag, *Histoire des Juifs de Tunisie,* 127.

10. Sebag, *Histoire des Juifs de Tunisie,* 127–128.

11. The London Society for Promoting Christianity amongst the Jews was associated with the Anglican Church. Although several discussions of the history of education in Tunisia mention the society, which was founded in 1809, and a school the society operated, none provides any detail. Information here comes from W. T. Gidney, *The History of the London Society for Promoting Christianity amongst the Jews from 1809 to 1908* (London: London Society for Promoting Christianity amongst the Jews, 1908). For a contemporary historian's account of the founding of the organization, see Reeva Spector Simon, "The Case of the Curse: The London Society for Promoting Christianity amongst the Jews and the Jews of Baghdad," in *Altruism and Imperialism: Western Cultural and Religious Missions in the Middle East,* ed. Eleanor H. Tejirian and Reeva Spector Simon (New York: Middle East Institute, Columbia University, 2002), 46–65. The organization's name has changed several times: in addition to the original name, we find "Church Mission to Jews," "The Church's Ministry among the Jews," and, since 1995, "The Church's Ministry among Jewish People."

12. Fenner also ran a night program where fifty Jews—males, we might imagine—received instruction in the New Testament.

13. Gidney, *The History of the London Society for Promoting Christianity amongst the Jews,* 389.

14. Aron Rodrigue, *Jews and Muslims: Images of Sephardi and Eastern Jewries in Modern Times* (Seattle: University of Washington, 2003), 7.

15. Aron Rodrigue's *Jews and Muslims* includes a chapter on "the war of languages," about the proper role of Hebrew and French in AIU schools across North Africa and the Middle East. French was obviously the victor. See Rodrigue, *Jews and Muslims,* 125–134.

16. Rachel Simon, "Education," in *The Jews of the Middle East and North Africa in Modern Times,* ed. Reeva Spector Simon, Michael Menachem Laskier, and Sara Reguer (New York: Columbia University Press, 2003), 132–164.

17. Sebag, *Histoire des Juifs de Tunisie,* 128.

18. Patrick Cabanel, "L'école laïque française en Tunisie (1881–1914): La double utopie," in *La Tunisie mosaïque: Diasporas, cosmopolitisme, archéologies de l'identité,* ed. Jacques Alexandropoulos and Patrick Cabanel (Toulouse: Presses Universitaires du Mirail, 2000), 264.

19. Sebag, *Histoire des Juifs de Tunisie,* 191, Table VII.

20. Bakalti, *La femme tunisienne,* 145–146.

21. Sebag, *Histoire des Juifs de Tunisie,* 281n11.

22. Bakalti, *La femme tunisienne,* 144.

23. Elinor Ochs, "Indexing Gender," in *Rethinking Context: Language as an Interactive Phenomenon,* ed. Alessandro Duranti and Charles Goodwin (Cambridge: Cambridge University Press, 1992), 336–358.

24. Sebag, *Histoire des Juifs de Tunisie,* 253.

25. Ibid., 264.

26. See, e.g., Bourdieu, *Language and Symbolic Action*. See also note 2 above.

27. Sebag, *Histoire des Juifs de Tunisie*, 128.

28. Sara Reguer, "The World of Women," in *The Jews of the Middle East and North Africa in Modern Times*, ed. Reeva Spector Simon, Michael Menachem Laskier, and Sara Reguer (New York: Columbia University Press, 2003), 242–243.

29. Reeva Spector Simon, "Europe in the Middle East," in *The Jews of the Middle East and North Africa in Modern Times*, ed. Reeva Spector Simon, Michael Menachem Laskier, and Sara Reguer (New York: Columbia University Press, 2003), 24.

30. Laskier and Simon, "Economic Life," 43. These authors note further, "In North Africa, despite increasing Jewish literacy in French and the creation of a Gallicized Jewish elite, most jobs went to the French and Italian settlers" (43). A few generations later, following independence, Tunisian Muslims who were literate in French took such posts.

31. Rodrigue, *Jews and Muslims*, 82.

32. Ibid., 81.

33. On the arguments offered for educating Tunisian Muslim girls now and in the past, see Walters, "Considering the Meanings of Literacy in a Postcolonial Setting."

34. Reguer, "The World of Women," 242.

35. Ferdinand Buisson, "Tunisie," in *Nouveau dictionnaire de pédagogie et d'instruction primaire* (Paris: Hachette, 1909), cited in Cabanel, "L'école laïque française en Tunisie," 266.

36. Walters, "Considering the Meanings of Literacy in a Postcolonial Setting." See also Keith Walters, "Gendering French in North Africa: Language Ideologies and Nationalism," *International Journal of the Sociology of Language* (forthcoming).

37. Rodrigue, *Jews and Muslims*, 80. On marriage as an economic relationship between Jewish families, see also Reguer, "The World of Women."

38. On the topic of naturalization, see Sebag, *Histoire des Juifs de Tunisie*; Sebag, *Tunis*; Saadoun, "Tunisia"; Abdelkarim Allagui, "Les Juifs face à la naturalization dans le Tunis colonial," in *Histoire communautaire, histoire plurielle: La communauté juive de Tunisie, Actes du colloque de Tunis organisé les 25–27 Février 1998 à la Faculté de la Manouba* (Tunis: Centre de Publications Universitaire, 1999), 204–215; and Colette Zytnicki, "Les Juifs de Tunisie à l'heure des choix," in *La Tunisie mosaïque: Diasporas, cosmopolitisme, archéologies de l'identité*, ed. Jacques Alexandropoulos and Patrick Cabanel (Toulouse: Presses universitaires du Mirail, 2000), 157–169.

39. Allagui, "Les Juifs face à la naturalization dans le Tunis colonial."

40. Saadoun, "Tunisia," 447.

41. It is likely the case that there are Jews to be found among other populations listed here, especially the Italians, who constituted the majority of Europeans in Tunisia until the census of 1931, when, thanks to naturalization, they were outnumbered by the French for the first time.

42. Bakalti, *La femme tunisienne*, 139.

43. Ingred Piller and Aneta Pavlenko, "Introduction: Multilingualism, Second Language Learning, and Gender," in *Multilingualism, Second Language Learning, and Gender*, ed. Aneta Pavlenko, Adrian Blackledge, Ingrid Piller, and Marya Teutsch-Dwyer (Berlin: Mouton de Gruyter, 2001), 5.

44. Personal communication.

45. Note the parallels between the Larguèche's claims and those of Reeva Spector Simon in "Europe in the Middle East," quoted above at note 29.

46. Susan Gal and Judith Irvine, "Language Ideology and Linguistic Differentiation," in *Regimes of Language: Ideologies, Polities, and Identities*, ed. Paul Kroskrity (Santa Fe, N.M.: School of American Research, 2000), 35–83.

47. Mahmoud Dhaouadi, "Des racines du franco-arabe féminin au Maghreb," *Arab Journal of Language Studies* 2 (1984): 145–162; Chedia Trabelsi, "De quelques aspects du langage des femmes de Tunis," *International Journal of the Sociology of Language* 87 (1991): 87–98. For further analysis of this process of erasure involved in this specific language ideology, see Walters, "Gendering French in North Africa."

18

"Les Temps Héroïques"

The Alliance Israélite Universelle in Marrakesh on the Eve of the French Protectorate

JONATHAN G. KATZ

IN 1998, AT THE age of 91 Alfred Goldenberg published a memoir recounting the decades he spent in Marrakesh as an Alliance Israélite Universelle (AIU) teacher and school director. The AIU had operated in the city for almost thirty years by the time of Goldenberg's arrival in 1927. In part owing to his efforts, the AIU's presence over the next three decades expanded from a pair of boys' and girls' primary schools in the mellah, the traditional Jewish quarter, to include a school for boys and girls in the *ville nouvelle* and an agricultural training center.[1] Despite these accomplishments, there is a clear sense of nostalgia and regret when Goldenberg writes of Marrakesh before his arrival. For Goldenberg and other relative "latecomers," the pioneering aspect of the AIU's mission—what its teachers referred to as *l'Oeuvre*—had long passed. During much of Goldenberg's tenure, the AIU was a relatively uncontroversial fixture of Jewish life in Marrakesh and an institution deeply rooted in the French protectorate.

Goldenberg's experience is not irrelevant to my purposes here. To borrow a phrase from José Bénech's *Essai d'explication d'un mellah*, AIU activities in Morocco before the establishment of the protectorate in 1912 constituted *les temps héroïques*.[2] Drawing on reports sent to the AIU's Central Committee in Paris, this chapter offers a microhistory of the AIU's operations in Marrakesh during the volatile first decade of the twentieth century. The chapter illustrates how, in a period characterized by political turmoil, economic dislocation, and famine, the AIU's emissaries attempted to negotiate a path between the factions of the local Jewish community and at the same time meet the demands and constraints placed upon them by the AIU's Central Committee and local Moroccan authorities.

Even in Goldenberg's narrative one sees glimpses of continuity from that earlier time. At the start of his career, Goldenberg had an opportunity to reenact the heroic days of the AIU when he was called upon to establish a new school in

Demnat, some eighty kilometers from Marrakesh. In many ways, the year Goldenberg and his wife spent among the Berber Jews of the Atlas Mountains resembled the pioneering experience of the olden days, but one particularly telling episode illustrates the entirely different sense of esprit that characterized this later venture. As a bemused Goldenberg remembered it, a local Jew approached him bearing gifts in an effort to induce the school director to intervene on his behalf with the authorities. The man's son had been arrested for fishing before the season had officially opened. Could Goldenberg ask the French *hakim* or official to release his son in time to attend the Passover Seder? Goldenberg declined, saying it was beyond his authority, and the man reclaimed his gifts.[3]

How unlike the response we might have anticipated from a pugnacious AIU teacher during the so-called heroic times. As the examples in this chapter demonstrate, AIU teachers during the pre-protectorate phase of its mission did not hesitate to challenge existing political and institutional authorities, whether they were *qa'ids* of the makhzan, French consular officials, or members of the local Jewish council. This was not the case thirty years later when Goldenberg was given the opportunity to test his mettle. Goldenberg saw it as beyond his job description to argue the case of an individual Jew's plight before French officialdom.

Indeed, with the creation of the protectorate and the AIU's gradual institutionalization within it, the role of the AIU director was transformed. Directors in the field were no longer by definition intermediary figures between local Jews and external authorities. Joan Gardner Roland describes the transition to the protectorate as follows: "As the French now protected all Moroccan subjects, the Jews, as a community and as individuals, had less need for the AIU representatives to defend their rights."[4] Roland attributes these changes on the ground to a change in policy at the top. With the establishment of the protectorate, the AIU pursued—albeit without success—a campaign to award Morocco's Jews French citizenship, as had occurred with Algerian Jews in 1870 with the Crémieux Decree.[5]

While Moroccan nationalist historians might portray the AIU and its schools as instruments of French colonial policy, prior to the establishment of the protectorate the circumstances were far more complicated. At its inception the AIU was not in any official sense an organ of French colonialism. The AIU took the "universal" aspect of its name seriously and received no government funding prior to 1914, when the AIU schools in Morocco began to receive a subvention from the protectorate.[6] Not until 1924—when the AIU, by an arrangement with the protectorate government, took primary responsibility for educating Morocco's Jewish children—did the AIU teachers become de facto employees of the state.[7]

In the days before the protectorate, the AIU deliberately sought to maintain its independence. Thus the AIU's Central Committee early on explicitly forbade one of its teachers from seeking an appointment as French consul in Tangier.[8] More-

over, the AIU was not under the protection of the French state, and school directors in the field could not necessarily count on the support of French diplomats
in their disputes with local makhzan authorities. And yet despite the separation
that existed between the AIU and the French government, the aims of the former
undeniably coincided with French colonial ambitions, especially as the AIU's educational mission was framed within the discourse of *la mission civilisatrice.*[9]

In September 1912, when French troops under the command of Colonel Charles
Mangin marched into Marrakesh, the students of the Alliance Israélite Universelle greeted them waving French flags. Writing in the 1930s, José Bénech gave
the AIU an important supporting role in the French takeover of Morocco. AIU
students aided French penetration in Morocco, Bénech writes, by furnishing "a
contingent of secretaries, employees, bookkeepers and interpreters. . . . At the beginning of this century, at a time when the destiny of Morocco still stood in the
balance, the Alliance school formed in Marrakesh a veritable small French post."[10]

Nevertheless, at times even the French government could be seen as a rival
to the AIU. Such was the case when the legation in Tangier encouraged the creation of Alliance Française and Franco-Muslim schools, which the AIU viewed as
potentially serious competitors.[11] As an autonomous organization separate from
the French government, the AIU pursued its own agenda first and foremost, giving priority to improving the material lot of Morocco's Jews, and it did so even
when its position on a particular issue might put it in opposition to policies advocated by France and the other European powers.

But to those outside the AIU, the distinctions between it and the French government were not always so apparent. Despite the fact that the AIU was neither
an arm of the Quai d'Orsay nor the recipient of French governmental funding,
the AIU and its schools was the symbolic presence of France for many Moroccan Jewish communities at the turn of the century. This was especially the case
in Marrakesh, which lacked official French consular representation before 1911.
Moreover, the teachers of the AIU discovered that their role extended far beyond
their classroom duties. Both the schools and other AIU-initiated humanitarian
projects became lightning rods for controversy. Their commitment to an assimi-
lationist ideology—with its potential to alienate young Moroccan Jews from their
communal traditions—often put idealistic French schoolmasters in conflict with
conservative elements of the local community. On the other hand, in times of
crisis even opponents of the AIU program looked to the organization and its
teachers to represent Jewish interests vis-à-vis the makhzan and local governmental officials. As Morocco entered an extended period of political uncertainty
that lasted from the death of the regent Ba Ahmed in 1900 to the establishment
of the protectorate in 1912, the AIU undertook a role of ever-increasing advocacy
for Morocco's Jews.

The Founding of the Marrakesh Schools and the Work of Moïse Lévy

Although the Alliance Israélite Universelle had operated schools in Morocco since 1862, the Paris-based philanthropic organization did not open schools in Marrakesh until 1901.[12] This relatively late start is somewhat surprising given the size of Marrakesh's Jewish community. With a Jewish population of 15,700 (according to a 1905 AIU statistic), Marrakesh constituted the largest Jewish community in Morocco.[13] In part, the relative isolation of Marrakesh contributed to the delay, but factors within the Marrakesh community also played a role the AIU's decision to hold back. In his 1920 history of the AIU, Narcisse Leven, the organization's president, remarked on the lack of strong communal institutions in Marrakesh compared to other Jewish centers such as Fez and Tetuan.[14] Although the AIU was an instrument of European philanthropy, the success of its mission depended upon the support of the local community. The AIU not only expected parents to pay tuition for their children but it also looked to the community as a whole for financial support from its communal coffers.

The AIU's interest in Marrakesh dated back to 1876 when the French Orientalist Joseph Halévy visited the city on the AIU's behalf. Like other visitors before and after him, Halévy depicted the mellah as a place of desperate poverty and disease. Despite the protecting presence of the sultan in Marrakesh (the city served as his primary residence through the 1890s), Jews were subjected both individually and communally to occasional humiliation and persecution. In 1893, for example, leaders of the Marrakesh community wrote to the AIU in the hope that the European organization could pressure the makhzan to address its complaints.[15]

At the end of the nineteenth century a new sultan, ʿAbd al-ʿAziz, acceded the throne, and the AIU deemed the time ripe for expanding its efforts.[16] In July 1896, the AIU asked Abraham Ribbi, a veteran instructor and school director in Tangier, to submit a detailed report on prospects for new schools. Ribbi made his initial contacts with the Jewish community in Marrakesh in 1899, but his subsequent recommendations were colored by an incident that occurred in Fez the following year. There a Moroccan-born Jew who was a naturalized American citizen was killed during an altercation in the street with a Muslim.[17] Ribbi complained of the weak response of the American diplomats.[18] Writing to his superiors in Paris, Ribbi introduced a theme that would continue to echo throughout the following decade in the correspondence of the AIU instructors in Marrakesh, namely the need for respect and security for the AIU's staff and schools. "Our teacher in Marrakesh," Ribbi wrote, "our schools even, absolutely need the prestige of autonomy [*l'émancipation*]. It will only be assured them if an authorized voice—that of a representative of a Great Power—makes the Sharifian government understand that our teachers and our schools must be shielded from the fanaticism and rudeness of the natives."[19]

Even without the benefit of a French consul, the AIU was determined to establish a school in Marrakesh. Its first teachers were Moïse Lévy and Messody Coriat, Moroccan-born graduates of the AIU's preparatory school in Paris, l'École Normale Israélite Orientale (ENIO).[20] The school soon reported an enrollment of 116 boys, of whom 38 were paying students. Of the 61 girls enrolled, 27 paid tuition. These numbers would double to 255 boys and 135 girls five years later in 1906, although the proportion of paying students would decline owing to the increasingly difficult financial situation in Marrakesh.[21] Moreover, many parents withdrew their students from AIU schools in times of communal tension between Muslims and Jews. In February 1904, Lévy contemplated closing the girls' school, which suffered from low enrollment and took away resources from the boys' school. The deteriorating political situation also continued to affect the school, forcing it to close temporarily, as we will see below, in 1907 following the murder of the French medical missionary Émile Mauchamp.

In addition to operating the school, the young AIU representatives in Marrakesh responded to humanitarian crises as they arose. In 1902 an outbreak of smallpox took the lives of 300 children in the mellah. Lévy solicited and received a shipment of vaccines from the AIU.[22] He and his co-workers also set about establishing a variety of social reforms. With the aid of Judah Holzmann, a German-educated Palestinian-born doctor who lived in Marrakesh, and with local contributions from 100 members, Lévy organized the Bikur Holim, a charitable institution to take care of the indigent sick.[23] A fellow teacher, Joseph Souessia, another Moroccan-born graduate of the ENIO, established a student choir. Its performance contributed to the success of Passover services organized by the school and led to contributions from the more affluent members of Marrakesh's Jewish community. The teachers also pressured the notables to organize a trash collection service to clear the streets of the mellah of refuse. The success of these initial efforts was encouraging, but Lévy's successors were unable to sustain enthusiasm for the Bikur Holim and the street-cleaning efforts.[24]

When the AIU schools opened in Marrakesh, local Jews quickly turned to the schools' director for political support. In a letter to Paris dated 13 August 1902 Lévy described how local Jews had called on him to confront a local pasha who had ordered that Jews remove their shoes when they left the mellah.

> In this country, it suffices to be called European or to be known as a protégé of some Western power to command a certain measure of respect on the part of the indigenous population. This is enough to guarantee the security of a foreigner in Marrakesh. But by our title of Alliance teachers, we are called to the more humanitarian task of guaranteeing the security of the great majority of our fellow Jews, who find no favor with the pasha.[25]

Lévy himself had no authority, and lacking a local consular official to which to apply, he appealed to the AIU's Central Committee in Paris. The committee in turn wrote directly to Si Muhammad al-Turris, the sultan's representative in Tangier. According to Lévy, this application of pressure from on high had the desired effect; the AIU was instrumental in forcing the pasha of the casbah to rescind an order and to offer an apology for requiring that Jews remove their shoes when they left the mellah.

At the beginning of 1904, following a period of drought and monetary inflation, the situation again worsened for the Jewish community in Marrakesh. Calling the days that followed disturbances on 19 January "very sad for our unfortunate *mellah*," Lévy described how a protest over the makzhan's introduction of copper coins—which many merchants would not accept as payment—escalated into a violent attack on the Jewish quarter. Order was restored by the sultan's brother and viceroy Mawlay Hafidh. Lévy praised Mawlay Hafidh, who four years later would supplant his brother on the throne, as "a man of remarkable intelligence, very learned, just and vigilant over all his subjects."[26]

Lévy concluded his 1904 report by outlining the various costs the community had incurred in the wake of the violence. These included paying the soldiers who guarded the mellah and providing assistance to those who were wounded or too frightened to go to their work in the *madina*. Lévy asked the AIU's Central Committee for additional funds to aid the community as well as new monies to hire guards for the boys' school.[27]

Nissim Falcon's Career in Marrakesh

As December 1904 came to an end, Lévy and his wife were transferred to Tetuan. He was replaced by Nissim Falcon.[28] Morocco's southern capital was not a happy assignment for Falcon. He filled his letters to his superiors in Paris with complaints about the inadequacy of his pay, the cost of setting up a household, and his and his wife's recurrent health problems.[29] He also had to deal with the gruesome death of his friend and compatriot, Dr. Émile Mauchamp, who was murdered by a mob in March 1907.[30]

With Falcon as headmaster, Joseph Souessia continued as the adjunct director of the boys' school. A Mademoiselle Garzon served as the adjunct director for girls. The staff also included four locally hired Hebrew instructors, two monitors, and two housekeepers. Despite the westernizing mission of the school, much of the school's curriculum for boys remained dedicated to teaching Hebrew so the school could compete more effectively with Marrakesh's traditional yeshivas.

In March 1905, Falcon sent off the first of his bimonthly reports to Paris. His long, 16-page letter was filled with despondency. While the students were generally in good health, he lamented the lack of hygiene. Falcon said he was reluctant to devote the first hour or two of the school day to the children's *toilette* and that he had installed a small bathroom with towels and hot water, which was another unanticipated expense. The students were intelligent but lazy, he said. They approached the study of French like they approached Hebrew—that is, they saw both as dead languages. Not least, the teachers were prone to corporal punishment despite his admonitions against the practice.[31]

The AIU was in a tenuous position in Marrakesh. Older members of the community viewed the boys' and girls' schools with suspicion, seeing them as a contaminating influence on the youth. Meanwhile, Falcon reported, "everybody believes that the Alliance, after having obtained permission to open the schools, will take charge of supporting the mellah." Some, according to Falcon, anxiously worried that the AIU would require them to pay dues.

More than outright hostility, what Falcon bemoaned, however, was indifference. "*Voilà,* we've been here three months and not one notable has come to see the schools, to interest himself in what we do, to encourage us with a good word." The Jews of Marrakesh, Falcon complained, were blind to their own best interests and excelled at only one thing, making a profit from the smallest transaction. "Incomparable quibblers [*chicaneurs*] . . . they appreciate only the power of the god Mammon and know how to use this power in their relationship with the Makhzan."[32]

In subsequent reports, Falcon described the plight of the mellah's Jews in increasingly desperate terms. Marrakesh was hit with another famine in June 1905, and the price of wheat had doubled. The community chest was exhausted, and the *ma'amad,* the community council, was unable to alleviate the general distress or see to the distribution of bread.[33] In August, Falcon again applied to the Central Committee of the AIU to provide aid. The demand for people seeking community assistance had tripled; the supplicants were no longer ordinary indigents but now included workers, he said.[34]

In the mellah's Hobbesian world of hunger and desperation, one Jew was the community's uncrowned king. This was Yeshu'a Corcos, the mellah's most powerful and richest man, president of the community council and banker to Viceroy Mawlay Hafidh.[35] If the AIU's efforts were to succeed in Marrakesh, they could do so only with the support of Corcos. José Bénech, an early observer, attributed the establishment of the AIU schools in Marrakesh to the "energetic intervention" of Corcos.[36] In contrast, Emily Gottreich argues that the AIU faced an uphill battle in Marrakesh owing to Corcos's resistance.[37] While the relationship between the AIU directors and the school's wealthy benefactor was not always smooth, Corcos nonetheless took evident pride in his own family's success at the school. The writer Eugène Aubin described a Shabbat dinner at the home of the wealthy banker in 1902. "At the house of M. Josua [Yeshu'a] Corcos, the women, faithful to the ancient custom, did not appear at the meal. Only his youngest daughter, educated at the school of the Jewish Alliance, and dressed in European clothes, inaugurated the new *régime* by sitting down at the table."[38] Corcos showed his support of the schools when it counted most. In the summer of 1907, when Falcon and the other European schoolteachers sought refuge on the coast, Corcos undertook a commitment to keep the schools open.[39] While the schools did in fact close, he used his influence the following year to secure from Mawlay Hafidh and his minister Si Madani al-Glawi a pledge to reopen them.

Despite his wealth and position, Corcos was not without rivals for authority. One particular rival was another wealthy notable of Marrakesh, Samuel Turjman. Quite early on, the AIU schools became a political football caught between "le parti Corcos" and "le parti Turjman." The rivalry manifested itself in unanticipated ways, and Nissim Falcon found the schools at the mercy of political processes beyond his control. During the famine of 1905 and the desperate economic crisis, Falcon reported an increase in prostitution.[40] According to his account, the community's chief rabbi had done nothing to remedy the situation and was even said to encourage it because he had been paid to maintain his silence. Youths from good families were profiting from the relaxation in morals and having relations with their maids. When a girl became pregnant, they had her accuse someone innocent. The accused was then brought before the rabbinic court; either he was forced to marry the girl and provide her with a dowry or swear his innocence upon the Torah scroll. Those who refused to swear could pay the rabbis and the girl would be sent back to her parents or even to prison.

Falcon learned of the system's corruption the hard way when a maid at the school who was only 14 years old became pregnant. Falcon's wife made inquiries and identified the father as a friend of the prominent Turjman and Rosilio families. When, at Falcon's insistence, the *ma'amad* (community council) met to render judgment, Corcos was absent and a peremptory ruling was made by those present in only five minutes. The boy was found innocent and the girl condemned to prison. Falcon protested in vain. He had brought charges against the girl in order to protect the good name of his school, but he had expected that the young man would be punished as well. "Our words displeased these gentlemen and immediately they asked us to leave saying they had had enough of our schools, of our continual intervention in the communal affairs, etc. etc."[41]

The campaign against the AIU schools continued into the autumn. Going over Falcon's head, Turjman wrote letters to a variety of important persons, including Benjamin Baruch Braunschvig, head of a Tangier-based commercial firm. Turjman was Braunschvig's protégé and representative in Marrakesh.[42] In December 1905, Falcon brought news of Turjman's meddling to the attention of his superiors. Judah Holzmann, the German-trained physician, had paid him a visit and informed him that Turjman was circulating a letter among the Jewish notables of Marrakesh requesting that they stop their financial support of the school. This news astonished Falcon, who wrote that he had just come from a meeting with Corcos and other notables. All had assured him that the schools provided a great service to the community. Taking up his pen, Falcon wrote to Braunschvig in an effort to set the record straight. He encouraged him to "counsel his friend and representative in Marrakesh to cease his hostilities," and he asked that Turjman give him the satisfaction of enrolling his two children in the school.

Holzmann came on several more occasions to talk to Falcon about the community's dissatisfaction with the schools and in particular to demand the removal of his assistant, Souessia. The reasons given were vague, but evidently Souessia had displeased the notables solely because he was a Moroccan Jew. He had allegedly displayed his disloyalty to the conservative Jewish leadership of the mellah by taking the interests of the school and its European teachers over theirs. Falcon—with the support of Corcos and Jacob Hazan, the local director of the French postal service—stuck by his adjutant.[43]

A contributing factor to Holzmann's disaffection with the AIU was the arrival in the autumn of 1905 of Émile Mauchamp, a French doctor sent by the Quai d'Orsay to open a clinic in the *madina*.[44] Holzmann had once provided valuable and much-appreciated services to the AIU schools and the wider Jewish community; after Mauchamp's arrival, his relationship with the AIU turned sour. For Falcon, the arrival of a French government doctor was particularly welcome. He wrote approvingly of Mauchamp to his Paris superiors. Although "all the doctors sent by the government have been ordered to attend in particular only to the Muslims," Mauchamp admitted poor Jews to the free consultations given thrice weekly. And, finding the AIU students to be thin and sickly, Mauchamp also offered to examine and care for several students "without distinction to fortune." Falcon wrote, "We hope that with the aid of Dr. Mauchamp and with the student excursions that I've instituted that our students will present less suffering faces."[45]

In a city without French consular representation, Falcon naturally viewed the French doctor as another ally in his effort to represent the Jews to the makhzan. In mid-March 1906, a fracas broke out on the school grounds involving the school's janitor and two black slaves who belonged to the sultan's brothers. According to Falcon, a fisherman was chasing three boys in the street, claiming that they had stolen some fish from him. He caught one of the boys and burst into the schoolgrounds with his prey in tow. The school's janitor tried to separate the man and the boy, going so far as to offer to pay the fisherman for the stolen fish. When the boy got away, the fisherman seized the janitor. At that very moment, two black men happened by—one a slave of Mawlay Taher, another a slave of Mawlay ʿAli, brothers of the sultan. The fisherman enlisted their support and together they began to beat the janitor and a student who was standing nearby. When the two victims tried to escape, the slaves followed them into the boys' school. They continued their beating, stopping only when their victims escaped and took refuge in the girls' school next door.

Neither the *qaʾid* of the mellah nor Ibn Kabbur, the pasha of the casbah, treated the incident seriously, and no punishment was meted out to the offending slaves. Falcon appealed to Mauchamp for support and reported the incident to Jeannier, the French vice-consul in Essaouira (Mogador).[46] Eventually the pressure on Ibn Kabbur bore fruit, and, from Falcon's vantage point, the story had a satisfactory ending. At the end of May, the two slaves were brought before the *qaʾid* of the mellah, the French consular agent, and the assembled students and staff of the school. There, in a public demonstration, they requested "pardon for their cowardly aggression."[47]

In June 1906, Falcon again turned to Mauchamp in his efforts to represent the interests of the Jewish community. In the midst of a typhus epidemic, Viceroy Mawlay Hafidh cut off water to the mellah so he could irrigate his adjacent gardens. With Mauchamp in tow, Falcon made a successful representation to Hajj ʿAbd al-Islam Fijij, the *qaʾid* of the *madina*. As Mauchamp had remonstrated, "if the *mellah* lacked water, he [Mauchamp] would not be responsible for the spread of the epidemic."[48]

As 1906 came to an end, Falcon felt that the AIU school was a great success, and he spoke of plans to add a little museum that he said would display the range of human endeavor. Much, however, remained to be done within the Jewish community. No doubt hoping for a greater financial contribution from the AIU's Central Committee, Falcon painted a desperate portrait of the mellah.[49] Falcon's work was abruptly interrupted, however, when, Émile Mauchamp was fatally assaulted by a mob outside his home in the *madina* on 19 March 1907. The hapless French doctor had provoked the attack by erecting a pole on his roof. At a time when rumors were circulating throughout Morocco about French efforts to establish wireless telegraph stations, Mauchamp had intended the faux antenna to be joke. The repercussions of Mauchamp's *petite plaisanterie* extended far beyond Marrakesh. French troops occupied the Moroccan city of Oujda as a reprisal, while an escalation of violence against European nationals later that summer led to the French bombardment of Casablanca and outright war in the Shawiya. In the ensuing turmoil, Mawlay Hafidh proclaimed himself sultan in August 1907 and embarked on a successful campaign to dislodge his brother, the reigning monarch ʿAbd al-ʿAziz.[50]

On the fateful day when Mauchamp was murdered, it appeared for a moment that the twenty or so Europeans living in Marrakesh might also come un-

der attack. The head of the local association of former AIU students, a man by
the name of Edhery, proposed hiding the Europeans in Jewish homes throughout the mellah. They declined the offer for fear of putting the Jewish community
at risk.[51] Tensions were further heightened when the French occupied Oujda, and
the small European colony in Marrakesh planned a general evacuation. Falcon
and his family fled to Safi.[52] In the weeks that followed, local Moroccan Jews, led
by the head of the French-sponsored post office, Hazan, and the banker Corcos,
attempted to keep the schools open in the absence of the European teachers. But
in July, Falcon expressed concern. "The schools cannot be eternally confided to
inexpert hands," he wrote from Safi, and, in fact, Hazan and Corcos did temporarily close the schools.[53]

Falcon and his wife finally returned to Marrakesh in November 1908, eventually reopening the schools the following April.[54] "My arrival in the *mellah* was
welcomed with enthusiasm by our co-religionists who considered my presence
as a gauge of durable security," he wrote to Paris.[55] From his own personal stand-
point, however, the return to the mellah was anything but fortuitous. Writing to
the AIU's Central Committee, Falcon alternately pleaded for permission to remove
his family to the coast for medical attention and for a new posting altogether. In
June 1909 Falcon wrote, "Despite all our goodwill and intentions to do well, we
cannot spend out entire lives in Marrakesh."[56] Finally, in October 1910, a grateful
Falcon and his family were reassigned to the more salubrious Tetuan. Despite all
the hardships he and his family endured, Falcon had succeeded in keeping the
AIU schools in Marrakesh alive through difficult times.

Mawlay Hafidh's Ascendancy and Raphaël Danon's Tenure

As much as Falcon complained about his personal life in Marrakesh, his return in fact coincided with a consolidation of the AIU schools' position both there
and throughout Morocco. The ascendancy of Mawlay Hafidh to the throne inaugurated what Michael Laskier has called a "political honeymoon" between the
AIU and the makhzan. Having provided financial backing for Mawlay Hafidh's
bid for the sultanate, Yeshuʿa Corcos had unparalleled access to the new sultan
and his ministers. Through Corcos's good graces, Narcisse Leven, the president
of the AIU, began a correspondence in October 1908 with Si Madani al-Glawi,
Mawlay Hafidh's prime minister. In it he raised concerns about the harassment
of Jews and demanded that the Marrakesh schools be reopened.[57] In his reply,
Madani al-Glawi, assured Leven: "Send your teachers," he wrote, "they will be
welcomed."[58] Falcon enthusiastically confirmed al-Glawi's words: "With the arrival of Si Madani, everything has changed as if by magic."[59] Banking on the support of the new prime minister, Falcon proposed in February 1910 that a new
building be purchased in the mellah.[60]

The fact that Mawlay Hafidh made warm overtures to the AIU is not surprising. At the start of his reign, the European press reviled him as the leader of a "holy war." Moreover, the harsh treatment he meted out to his political enemies earned him a reputation for cruelty. By lending support to the AIU's efforts, Mawlay Hafidh sought to present himself as a benign and tolerant ruler. Makhzan support for the AIU's efforts in Marrakesh were further confirmed in 1911 when Si Madani's ambitious younger brother Thami became pasha of Marrakesh. In May of that year the future "grand seigneur" of southern Morocco granted Falcon's replacement Raphaël Danon an audience. Referring to an earlier exchange of letters, Thami called himself a friend of France and reaffirmed his support for the schools.[61]

The AIU was forced temporarily to close its schools again in the summer of 1912. The political situation had changed; the French had recently appointed a new sultan, Mawlay Yusuf, to replace the recalcitrant Mawlay Hafidh. But Saharan tribesmen led by El Hiba, a son of the late Mauritanian leader Ma al-ʿAynayn, briefly occupied the city and took a number of Frenchmen hostage. El Hiba declared Mawlay Yusuf illegitimate and raised the specter of jihad against the French occupation. The threat did not last long. On 6 September 1912, El Hiba's 10,000-man force was decimated at Sidi Bou Othman by 5,000 French troops led by Colonel Mangin. The following day a French column entered Marrakesh to the sounds of the Marseillaise sung by the assembled students of the AIU schools.[62]

After the French established the protectorate, the AIU turned directly to the French government for support. In 1912, Danon reported a conversation in which he sought the aid of the leader of the French forces in Marrakesh, Colonel Charles Mangin, in acquiring a parcel of land for the erection of a new school. His report also noted that the resident general, Louis-Hubert Lyautey, who toured Marrakesh soon after the French occupied it, had donated 500 francs to the schools.[63] Shortly afterward, Lyautey proposed a parcel of 3,000 hectares located close to the mellah as the new school's site. But the local Jewish leaders refused, "fearing that their children would not be secure beyond the walls of their quarter."[64]

In his interactions with Thami al-Glawi and Mangin, Danon appears to have been something of an opportunist. When the father of one of Danon's teachers ended up in jail for nonpayment of a debt (he was awaiting payment from Thami for the purchase of a large jewel), Danon took it upon himself to plead the jeweler's case. It was an opportunity, he noted, to gain access to the pasha.[65]

Danon was also willing to champion the cause of the Jews even when it meant opposing the French. In the previously mentioned conversation with Mangin, Danon called upon Mangin to launch an investigation and issue a statement regarding an incident that had occurred in the village of Chichaoua. There the local Jews had refused to sell to the French troops forage for their animals out of fear that doing so would provoke reprisals from their Arab neighbors who were hostile to the French. In response, Mangin imposed a 3,000-peseto fine that the Jews refused to pay. When an altercation broke out between the Jews and the French troops, the French troops ransacked Jewish homes, defiled sacred objects, and set fire to the brambles that formed a fence around the Jewish quarter. Two sick children and a woman died in the melée. Danon called upon Mangin to launch an investigation and issue a statement.[66]

Danon's political interference annoyed General Lyautey, who had been installed as resident general of French Morocco. Lyautey wrote to Narcisse Leven, Danon's AIU superior, to complain. The protectorate conferred certain rights on France, Lyautey insisted. In response, according to Joan Roland, the AIU "promised to remind its instructors that their main role was to teach." In fact, the establishment of the protectorate in Morocco, like that in Tunisia, gave the work of the AIU in Morocco a new focus. "The Alliance," writes Roland, "could turn its attention from the defense of the Jews to the struggle for their legal assimilation. The task was no longer to assure the Jews of equality with the Muslim subjects of the Bey or Sultan. On the contrary, the goal was to make them French citizens."[67]

The AIU had difficulty staffing its schools during World War I, and in 1918 the schools in Marrakesh were again temporarily closed. In 1920, Nissim Falcon, by that point a widower but with his grown daughter at as his aide, returned to Marrakesh to direct the schools once again. Finally, in 1924, the AIU signed an agreement with France in regard to the education of Morocco's Jewish children. The AIU would furnish the teaching staff and the protectorate government would pay a subvention to cover salaries and operating expenses.[68] The long engagement the AIU had entered into with the French government at the founding of the protectorate was at last consummated.

Conclusion

The foregoing discussion has focused on the role of the teachers of the AIU in Marrakesh as political intermediaries prior to the establishment of the protectorate. While the seeds of the subsequent history of Morocco's Jews—in particular, their alienation from their Moroccan identity and their exodus to Israel, France, and other countries—owes much to the work of the AIU, it would be difficult to argue that these outcomes were solely the result of the AIU's activities. As Norman A. Stillman has pointed out, the attraction of the AIU and its schools for the Jews of the Middle East and North Africa was symptomatic of a broad process of modernization.[69]

The primary motivation of the AIU's efforts was humanitarian. Nevertheless, as an institution, the AIU was an obvious beneficiary of the colonial takeover of Morocco. To what degree was it a contributing factor as well? The pre-protectorate miseries of the Marrakesh mellah as described by Falcon and others were hardly an exaggeration. Similar accounts had been a staple of European writing about Morocco for decades. Although the material and judicial plight of ordinary Moroccans was often hardly better, proponents of colonialism frequently cited the degradation of Jewish life in the Sharifian empire and the second-class legal status that Islamic law placed upon Jews as *dhimmis*—a tolerated but unequal minority—as justifications for France's intervention in Morocco's affairs. This stance, however, ignored the complexity of Jewish-Muslim communal relations; in many instances the traditional restrictions on Jews no longer applied or were honored only in the breach.[70]

The first decade of the twentieth century saw an acceleration of earlier disruptive trends in Moroccan society. These included the weakening of the economy and the breakdown of traditional markets. As land increasingly concentrated in the hands of city-dwellers, displaced rural people (including rural Jews flocking to the mellah) flooded the already teeming cities. And in the context of increased lawlessness, urban dwellers held Jews responsible for selling contraband weapons to surrounding tribes. Not surprisingly, in Morocco's subsequent political struggle against the French, Jews suffered to the extent that they were identified with the foreigners.[71] In particular, many Jewish merchants—together with their counterparts among the Muslim notables—benefited from and often abused their status as European protégés. Yet as Mohammed Kenbib argues, in those instances of civil unrest in which the French refrained from direct involvement, Jews were just as often ignored. "Contrary to the image spread at the time in the papers of 'the Jews as the first victims of trouble,' most of the *mellah*s were in fact spared even during the most pointed phases of the agitation, not least where there was no intervention of foreign troops."[72]

The opinions of Moroccan Jews were far from uniform regarding European intervention. In a letter to Narcisse Leven sent on 2 September 1907, Falcon cautioned the AIU president not to be "taken in" by Moroccan Jewish fears over security. For all the noise he makes, Falcon wrote, "the Jew, as much as the Muslim, fears the intervention of Europe." With the installation of Europeans in the country, Falcon observed, the Jews would relinquish their traditional role as middlemen.[73]

Morocco's Jews might have been reluctant to abandon their familiar social role, but the AIU and its directors imagined that they knew what was best for them. Echoing Falcon's words, José Bénech wrote that "the directors of the Alliance forever cherish the dream of tearing away the Jew away from his eternal occupation of middleman, which condemns him to insolent fate or to extreme misery."[74]

The AIU in fact succeeded in its goal of providing new occupations and opportunities for the Jews of Morocco, but success also brought unanticipated social
and political consequences. In 1955, on the eve of Moroccan independence, the
eighty-three schools of the AIU in Morocco enrolled 33,000 Jewish children. A far
greater proportion of Jewish children were attending school than Muslim children. AIU enrollment also cut across a wide range of social classes. As a result,
the schools' graduates, including those from humble origins, tended to identify
for the most part with the European colonial elite. As Michael Laskier writes,

> The educational progress of the Jews before and after 1912, the social con-
> sequences of the cultural and educational diversity among Muslims and
> Jews, the policies of the colonial systems, and the activities of the AIU in all
> aspects of communal and educational activities, deepened the already ex-
> isting divisions between these two peoples [i.e., Muslims and Jews].[75]

Zionism and the establishment of Israel also had profound repercussions for Morocco's Jews.

At the beginning of the twentieth century, AIU teachers such as Moïse Lévy,
Nissim Falcon, and Raphaël Danon entertained a vision of the future that was
simultaneously down to earth and idealistically high-minded. In their role as
privileged outsiders, they time and again fought to improve the day-to-day lot
of their fellow Jews of Marrakesh. All the while, they held tightly to the AIU's
ideal that Jews everywhere—including their co-religionists in Morocco—should
participate in the modern world that was emerging. The teachers seem to have
been unaware that these goals were fraught with contradictions. Indeed, from
the vantage point of Marrakesh in the decade before the protectorate, the wholesale exodus of the city's Jews a half-century later was unimaginable.

NOTES

1. Alfred Goldenberg, *Souvenirs d'Alliance: Itinéraire d'un instituteur de l'Alliance Israélite
Universelle au Maroc* (Paris: Éditions du Nadir, 1998). On the agricultural training center, see
Michael M. Laskier, *The Alliance Israélite Universelle and the Jewish Communities of Morocco: 1862–
1962* (Albany: State University of New York Press, 1983), 263–265; and Meir Ben Abraham, "The
Impact of the 'Alliance Israélite Universelle' on Change and Modernization of the Jewish Communities of Morocco: 1912–1956" (Ph.D. diss., Anglia Polytechnic University, 2000), 165–167.
The AIU's role in Morocco is discussed in André Chouraqui, *Cent ans d'histoire: L'Alliance Israélite Universelle et la renaissance juive comtemporaine (1860–1960)* (Paris: Presses universitaires
de France, 1965); Élias Harrus, *L'Alliance en action: Les écoles de l'Alliance Israélite Universelle dans
l'Empire du Maroc (1862–1912)* (Paris: Nadir, 2001); Mohammed Kenbib, *Juifs et Musulmans au
Maroc, 1859–1948:* (Rabat: Université Mohammed V, Publications de la Faculté des Lettres et
des Sciences Humaines 1994); Susan G. Miller, "Gender and Poetics of Emancipation: The Al-

liance Israélite Universelle in Northern Morocco, 1890–1912," in *Franco-Arab Encounters: Studies in Memory of David C. Gordon*, ed. L. Carl Brown and Matthew S. Gordon (Beirut: American University of Beirut, 1996), 229–252; Aron Rodrigue, *Images of Sephardi and Eastern Jewries in Transition: The Teachers or the Alliance Israélite Universelle, 1860–1939* (Seattle: University of Washington Press, 1993); and Norman A. Stillman, *The Jews of Arab Lands in Modern Times* (Philadelphia, Pa.: Jewish Publication Society, 1991).

2. José Bénech, *Essai d'explication d'un mellah (ghetto marocain): Un des aspects du Judaïsme* (Paris: Éditions Larose, 1940).

3. Goldenberg, *Souvenirs d'Alliance*, 74; and Ben Abraham, "The Impact of the 'Alliance Israélite Universelle,'" 184–185.

4. Joan Gardner Roland, "The Alliance Israélite Universelle and French Policy in North Africa, 1860–1918" (Ph.D. diss. Columbia University, 1969), 183.

5. See Narcisse Leven to Lyautey, 14 February 1913, in Chouraqui, *Cent ans d'histoire*, Annexe no. 6, 440–442. For a critique of this policy see Michel Abitbol, "The Encounter between French Jewry and the Jews of North Africa: Analysis of a Discourse (1830–1914)," in *The Jews in Modern France*, ed. Frances Malino and Bernard Wasserstein (Hanover and London: University Press of New England, 1985), 31–53.

6. Ben Abraham, "The Impact of the 'Alliance Israélite Universelle,'" 198–207.

7. On the Alliance's relationship with the French government prior to 1912, see ibid., 116–129. Although Alliance teachers eventually received state pensions, their salaries were lower than those of instructors at other French schools for many years. Goldenberg, *Souvenirs d'Alliance*, 123.

8. Laskier, *The Alliance Israélite Universelle and the Jewish Communities of Morocco*, 44; and Ben Abraham, "The Impact of the 'Alliance Israélite Universelle,'" 131–133 cite the example of Bernard Lévy, founder of the AIU boys' school in Tangier, who unsuccessfully argued that he could better represent the interests of the Jewish community if he were appointed French consul.

9. For French visitors to Marrakesh at the turn of the century, a visit to the schools was obligatory, and they often recorded favorable impressions. On Louis Gentil's visit, see AIU Maroc, XXVI.E.398–416, 16 January 1905, Falcon to Leven. Eugène Aubin recounted his visit in *Morocco of To-day* (London: J. M. Dent, 1906), 303. Christian Houel, a reporter for the French paper *Le Matin*, later recalled being overcome with emotion at hearing a young student recite from La Fontaine's fables in 1908; see Houel, *Mes aventures marocains* (Casablanca: Éditions Maroc-Demain, 1954), 54.

10. Bénech, *Essai d'explication d'un mellah*, 294.

11. Laskier, *The Alliance Israélite Universelle and the Jewish Communities of Morocco*, 72–73.

12. Narcisse Leven, *Cinquante ans d'histoire: L'Alliance israélite universelle (1860–1910)*, vol. 2 (Paris: Libraire Félix Alcan, 1920), 99. The secondary literature reflects confusion over the actual date of the founding of the schools in Marrakesh. Moïse Lévy arrived in Marrakesh in November 1900, but the schools did not actually open for another three months. See Bénech, *Essai d'explication d'un mellah*, 289.

13. The next largest concentrations of Jews were in Essaouira (Mogador) and Fez, with Jewish populations there at 10,000 each. On the Jewish urban population in Morocco prior to the protectorate, see Laskier, *The Alliance Israélite Universelle and the Jewish Communities of Morocco*, Table 14, 147; and Shlomo Deshen, *The Mellah Society: Jewish Community Life in Sherifian Morocco* (Chicago: University of Chicago Press, 1989), 30–45. A comprehensive discussion of the Jewish demography of Marrakesh can be found in Emily R. Gottreich, *The Mellah of Marrakesh: Jewish and Muslim Space in Morocco's Red City* (Bloomington: Indiana University Press, 2007), 39–70.

14. Leven, *Cinquante ans d'histoire*, 2:99. Leven's negative impression of Marrakesh undoubtedly owes much to Abraham Ribbi, who wrote following his visit that "the rabbis of Marrakesh are from the poor people, servile, fanatical, and stripped of all moral authority." *Bulle-*

tin de l'Alliance Israélite Universelle, IIe semester (1900), quoted in Bénech, *Essai d'explication d'un mellah,* 154.

15. The letter told of an incident in which a Jewish woman and her children were seized by makhzan soldiers after her husband had converted to Islam and the community failed to redeem them. In the same letter the correspondents reported that a Jew had been beaten to death by a Muslim. See Laskier, *The Alliance Israélite Universelle and the Jewish Communities of Morocco,* 56, 66n78; and AIU Maroc, XXXIV.E582(a), Jewish community leaders in Marrakesh to AIU, 20 November 1893 (in Hebrew), reproduced in Laskier, *The Alliance Israélite Universelle and the Jewish Communities of Morocco,* 57. The leaders in Marrakesh also appealed in this case to the British Board of Jewish Deputies. Gottreich, *The Mellah of Marrakesh,* 97 and 170n27.

16. The reform-minded ʿAbd al-ʿAziz ascended the throne in 1894 while in his teens. He assumed full leadership after the death of the regent Ba Ahmad in 1900.

17. The incident involved Marcus Azzagui, who managed the local affairs of the French commercial firm Braunschvig. When the perpetrators were not punished, Ribbi foresaw future difficulties for the Marrakesh school. Elizabeth Antébi erroneously places the Azzagui incident in Marrakesh; see *Les Missionnaires Juifs de la France (1860–1939)* (Paris: Calmann-Lévy, 1999), 47.

18. According to the *New York Times,* the United States demanded an indemnity of 1,000 pounds; *New York Times,* 13 October 1900, 6.

19. Ribbi, Marrakesh, 2 December 1900, quoted in Antébi, *Les Missionnaires Juifs de la France,* 47. In Ribbi's report on Marrakesh he estimated there to be about 600 households in the mellah; *Bulletin de l'Alliance Israélite Universelle* 25 (1900), 9, cited in Gottreich, *The Mellah of Marrakesh,* 58 and 159n124. Gottreich believes this figure was "possibly an exaggeration to justify the opening of an AIU school in Marrakesh" (159n24).

20. Messody Coriat was born in Tetuan in 1881; A. H. Navon, *Les 70 Ans de l'École Normale Israélite Orientale (1865–1935)* (Paris: Librairie Durlacher,1935), 164. On AIU women teachers, see Frances Malino, "The Women Teachers of the Alliance Israélite Universelle, 1842–1940," in *Jewish Women in Historical Perspective,* ed. Judith R. Baskin, 2nd ed. (Detroit: Wayne State University Press, 1998), 248–269. See also the chapter by Joy Land in this volume.

21. Leven, *Cinquante ans d'histoire,* 2:99. According to another account, the school for boys had 350 students in 1904, of whom only twenty-four paid tuition, the remaining 326 receiving their education for free. The girls' school, under the direction of Falcon's wife, had 117 students, of whom twenty paid and the remainder attended for free. A subvention from the Alliance accounted for some 93 percent of the budget. *Bulletin de l'Alliance Israélite Universelle,* 3ème série, 30 (1905): 127–142. Relying on information provided by Falcon, Bénech described the enrollment figures for 1904 as "very elastic," varying from 250 to 350 boys and from 150 to 175 girls; Bénech, *Essai d'explication d'un mellah,* 293.

22. Harrus, *L'Alliance en action,* 81.

23. These are outlined in a letter dated 13 August 1902, published as M. Lévy, "Social Reforms Initiated by an Alliance Director, Marrakesh, 1902," in Rodrigue, *Images of Sephardi and Eastern Jewries in Transition,* 183–185.

24. Drunkenness was another problem that plagued the mellah. During the school's first year of operation, Lévy was obliged to hire a special guard for Saturdays after Jews who had consumed too much alcohol attacked the school. AIU Maroc, XXVII.E.417–442, 30 December 1901, Lévy, cited in Gottreich, *The Mellah of Marrakesh,* 79 and 164n37.

25. AIU France, XIV.F.25, 13 August 1902, Lévy, quoted in translation in Rodrigue, *Images of Sephardi and Eastern Jewries in Transition,* 206–207.

26. AIU Maroc, microfilm VII.B, 1904 report, received 15 February 1904, Moïse Lévy. An extract of this letter appears in Harrus, *L'Alliance en action,* 131–132.

27. On 19 January 1904, a hundred or so shoemakers demonstrated before the house of the governor, ʿAbd al-Salam al-Warzazi. The following day, their ranks supplemented from Berbers from the countryside, the demonstrators marched on the mellah, chanting, according to Lévy,

"We'll eat the mellah." The mellah guards shut the quarter's gates in time, but that did not prevent panic from breaking out. Nearly fifty Jews who had been working outside the mellah were assaulted and wounded. The Christian cemetery was also desecrated. Lévy, 1904 report. Gottreich, *The Mellah of Marrakesh*, 85 and 167n83 cites additional correspondence related to this incident from Direction des Archives Marocaines, Marrakesh 12, Dhu al-Qaʿda 1321/25 January 1904, Muhammad Znibar.

28. Falcon was born in Smyrna in 1878 and educated at the ENIO. His first assignment was in Tangier in 1901. He held posts in several cities over the course of the next three decades, eventually finding service under the French protectorate in 1927 as director of the École Franco-Israélite Albert Sonsol in Fez. Despite his long career, Falcon's record was not entirely without blemish. In Tetuan in May 1903, when the city was threatened with attack from revolting tribes in the Rif, Falcon was accused of abandoning his post when he joined the community's wealthier members as they evacuated the city. AIU Maroc, I.C.1–2, May 1903, Bigart to Carmona, quoted in Rodrigue, *Images of Sephardi and Eastern Jewries in Transition*, 211.

29. "We suffer enough from a thousand little things in this somber land of misery," he wrote soon after his arrival. AIU Maroc, XXVI.E.398–416, 15 January 1905, Falcon to Leven.

30. AIU Maroc, XXVI.E.398–416, "Rapport," received 23 January 1906, Falcon. The first page of this report is missing.

31. AIU Maroc, XXVI.E.398–416, "Rapport bimestriel" (January to February 1905), 5 March 1905, Falcon.

32. "If at least the *Marrakeschiotes* knew enough to interest themselves in something useful!" Falcon lamented. "In a large community like this there is no organization outside the burial society and some funds for the rabbis and for maintaining the tomb of some saint." Falcon, "Rapport bimestriel," 5 March 1905.

33. AIU Maroc, XXVI.E.398–416, 22 June 1905, Falcon to Leven, Marrakesh. Part of this text is quoted in Gottreich, *The Mellah of Marrakesh*, 65.

34. Falcon wrote, "Everywhere the processions of the miserable, the paralyzed, everywhere beings with cadaverous faces with feverish and haggard eyes, half-naked, trailing their limbs, dry, all skin and bones, in the dust under an implacable sky; everywhere the lamentable cries, the women who tug on you to stop you by force to demand your offering. Our school is entirely invaded by beggars, and our students are attacked by the hungry who want to rob them of the morsel of bread we have for them." AIU Maroc, XXVI.E.398–416, 9 August 1905, Falcon to Leven.

35. For portraits of this Moroccan "Rothschild," see Aubin, *Morocco of To-day*, 296–298; Jérôme and Jean Tharaud, *Marrakech ou les seigneurs de l'Atlas*, in *Maroc: Les villes impériales* (Paris: Omnibus, 1996), 794–795, 814; and Bénech, *Essai d'explication d'un mellah*, 260–270.

36. According to Bénech, Corcos had broken through the barrier of resistance put up by the rabbis, who "saw religious danger and no practical utility in profane education." He was the first to enroll his own children. Bénech, *Essai d'explication d'un mellah*, 265.

37. "Although his monetary contributions to the Alliance were consistently larger than those of his fellow Jews, and he himself was a French protégé, his reluctance to abandon strong patronage ties to the local Muslim authorities made him untrustworthy in the eyes of the AIU. Corcos's relations with the first AIU director in Marrakesh, Moïse Lévy[,] were especially difficult, with the latter accusing Corcos of 'selling out' his co-religionists." In subsequent disagreements with the Alliance directors, Corcos accused the AIU of "Christianizing Jewish children and inculcating them with 'irreligion.'" Gottreich, *The Mellah of Marrakesh*, 89 and 168nn109–111, citing AIU Maroc, III.C.10, 20 December 1910, Lévy; AIU Maroc, XXVI.E.398–416, 12 April 1907, Falcon; and AIU Maroc XXVI.E.398–416, 5 May 1905, Falcon.

38. Aubin, *Morocco of To-day*, 298.

39. Concerned about the safety of the city's Jews, Corcos encouraged Falcon and the other Europeans to leave. AIU Maroc, XXVI.E.398–416, 14 May 1907, Falcon. The partial text of Falcon's letter detailing Corcos's request is reprinted in Gottreich, *The Mellah of Marrakesh*, 189n139.

Corcos made his promise to keep the schools open after Falcon returned temporarily to Marrakesh later that summer. AIU Maroc, XXVI.E.398–416, 10 July 1907, Falcon to Leven. Corcos died in 1929, and in 1948 the AIU converted his home into a school for boys. Goldenberg, *Souvenirs d'Alliance*, 108.

40. On the mellah's historical association with prostitution, see Gottreich, *The Mellah of Marrakesh*, 79–82.

41. AIU Maroc, XXVI.E.398–416, 20 August 1905, Falcon to Leven.

42. In 1875, Braunschvig, an Alsatian-born Jew, established himself in Tangier, where he became one of principal stockholders in la Société Immobilière du Maroc; Kenbib, *Juifs et Musulmans au Maroc*, 322–323.

43. AIU Maroc, XXVI.E.398–416, 9 December 1905, copied 23 January 1906, Falcon to Leven.

44. See Jonathan G. Katz, *Murder in Marrakesh: Émile Mauchamp and the French Colonial Adventure* (Bloomington: Indiana University Press, 2006); and Jonathan G. Katz, "The 1907 Mauchamp Affair and the French Civilizing Mission," *Journal of North African Studies* 6 (2001): 143–166.

45. AIU Maroc, XXVI.E.398–416, "Rapport," received 23 January 1906, Falcon.

46. Archives diplomatique de Nantes (hereafter ADN), Tangier A 342, Marrakesh, 19 March 1906, Falcon to Mauchamp; AIU Maroc, XXVI.E.398–416, Marrakesh, 15 March 1906, 18 April 1906, Falcon to Leven, and copy of 15 March 1906, Falcon to Jeannier, Marrakesh. Falcon later presented the pasha of the casbah with a letter from the vice-consul of Mogador demanding that he arrest the two slaves. The pasha refused to take action, and (according to Falcon) "launched into less than friendly reflections on all the French in Marrakesh, the consular agent, the doctor, the schoolteachers. He called us all *liars* and declared that he would start legal proceedings against all those who had written to the consul on the subject of this affair and demand from all of us public apologies toward him!" The AIU was in a difficult position. The vice-consul in Mogador expressed reluctance to work energetically in this affair in light of the fact that the AIU was not officially protected by the legation. AIU Maroc, XXVI.E.398–416, Marrakesh, 18 April 1906, Falcon to Leven.

47. Ibn Kabbur remained hostile to the schools. Had they not been authorized by the Makhzan, he told Falcon, "I would send twenty soldiers to close them down and expel all the personnel from Marrakesh." AIU Maroc, XXVI.E.398–416, 29 May 1906, Falcon to Leven.

48. ADN, Tangier A 342, undated, Falcon to Mauchamp; and AIU Maroc, XXVI.E.398–416, 21 June 1906, Falcon to Leven.

49. "The crisis of the preceding years has left profound traces of moral distress in the bosom of our community. The rich have become more egotistical, the authorities more greedy, the starving crowd freely supports itself by theft and debauchery." AIU Maroc, XXVI.E.398–416, "Rapport bimestriel" (October to December 1906), Falcon. In 1906, Moïse Nahon also visited Marrakesh on behalf of the AIU. See "Les israélites du Maroc," *Revue des Etudes Ethnographiques et Sociologique* 2 (1909): 38–55.

50. For details regarding the Hafidhiyya movement, see Edmund Burke, III, *Prelude to Protectorate: Precolonial Protest and Resistance, 1860–1912* (Chicago: University of Chicago Press, 1976). On Yeshuʿa Corcos's role in Hafidh's accession, see Gottreich, *The Mellah of Marrakesh*, 127–130.

51. ADN, Tangier A 269, 23 April 1907, Gentil to Pichon.

52. "Our presence in the quarter could lead the Arabs to use the opportunity to pillage the Jewish homes. As for us, we have lost all influence with the authorities, we are suspect and our co-religionists even ardently wish that we would leave Marrakesh as soon as possible." AIU Maroc, XXVI.E.398–416, 1 April 1907, Falcon to Leven.

53. AIU Maroc, XXVI.E.398–416, 10 July 1907, Falcon to Leven.

54. AIU Maroc, XXVI.E.398–416, "Report bimestriel de Janvier à Avril 1909," Falcon's report to Leven. Also see AIU Maroc, XXVI.E.398–416, 2 May 1909, Mme. C. Falcon to Leven.

55. Falcon to Central Committee, 27 November 1908, quoted in Goldenberg, *Souvenirs d'Alliance*, 49.

56. AIU Maroc, XXVI E.398–416, 27 June 1909, Falcon to Leven. A year later, in July 1910, Falcon reluctantly acknowledged the Central Committee's decision that he and his wife stay in Marrakesh another two months. AIU Maroc, XXVI.E.398–416, 11 July 1910, Falcon to Leven.

57. Laskier, *The Alliance Israélite Universelle and the Jewish Communities of Morocco*, 57–58. Narcisse Leven published the letter dated 26 October 1908 in Leven, *Cinquante ans d'histoire*, 1:370. Also see "Israélites du Maroc," *Bulletin de l'Alliance Israélite Universelle*, Ie sem. (1909): 78–87; and Leven to Madani al-Glawi, 16 October 1908, in Leven, *Cinquante ans d'histoire*, 2:82.

58. Quoted in Chouraqui, *Cent ans d'histoire*, 120–21. Also see Bénech, *Essai d'explication d'un mellah*, 295–296.

59. AIU Maroc, XXVI.E.398–416, 8 December 1908, Falcon to Leven.

60. AIU Maroc, XXVI.E.398–416, 6 February 1910, Falcon to Leven.

61. AIU Maroc, Microfilm VII.B.2514/5, 17 May 1911, Danon to Leven.

62. Goldenberg, *Souvenirs d'Alliance*, 50.

63. AIU Maroc, Microfilm VII.B.4651/1, 17 November 1912, Danon to Leven.

64. Goldenberg, *Souvenirs d'Alliance*, 50–51.

65. AIU Maroc, MicrofilmVII.B.1752/2, 2 March 1911, Danon to Leven; and AIU Maroc, Microfilm VII.B.1852/2, 12 March 1911, Danon to Leven. Also see Gottreich, *The Mellah of Marrakesh*, 171n45.

66. AIU Maroc, XXVI.E.398–416, 17 November 1912, Danon to Leven.

67. AIU Maroc, I.J.2, Lyautey to Leven, 7 May 1913, 29 July 1913, and 6 May 1913, Leven to Lyautey, cited in Roland, "The Alliance Israélite Universelle and French Policy in North Africa," 183–184.

68. Goldenberg, *Souvenirs d'Alliance*, 51. At the outset AIU teachers received less pay than other French protectorate teachers. Ibid., 123.

69. "For better or worse, [Oriental Jewries] saw their fortunes tied to the rising star of European political, economic, and cultural power long before the AIU came with its mission of *régénération*"; N. Stillman, "Middle Eastern and North African Jewries," 65.

70. Following a memorandum by the Jewish banker Jacob Schiff on the alleged mistreatment of Jews, the secretary of the American delegation to Algeciras, Lewis Einstein, submitted a report countering Schiff's claims point by point. Kenbib, *Juifs et Musulmans au Maroc*, 333–335.

71. Some historians have pointed to the socioeconomic and political contradictions colonial pressure created as the principal reason for the increase in tension between Morocco's Jews and Muslims. The longstanding debate regarding the nature of Jewish-Muslim relations in Morocco is beyond the scope of this study. Shlomo Deshen labels the two opposing viewpoints as the "integrationist" and "conflict" models. As an example of the first case, Deshen points to the work of Lawrence Rosen, which stresses individual and personal interactions between Jews and Muslims. In the second instance, Deshen cites Norman Stillman, who "marshaled literary sources that demonstrate the humiliation to which Jews were categorically subjected in traditional Morocco." Deshen, *The Mellah Society*, 123. See also Laskier, *The Alliance Israélite Universelle and the Jewish Communities of Morocco*, 13–14.

72. Kenbib, *Juifs et Musulmans au Maroc*, 309. Kenbib's assertion is true in the case of Marrakesh following Mauchamp's death. In that instance the governor and the viceroy succeeded in preventing violence against the mellah. Whether this was later the case when El Hiba's forces occupied the city in 1912 is a matter of dispute. Bénech writes that El Hiba's forces spared the mellah in recognition of services Yeshuʿa Corcos had earlier rendered his family. Bénech, *Essai d'explication d'un mellah*, 260. Gottreich, on the other hand, cites Danon's report of victimization of the Jews during the El Hiba occupation. The report, dated 12 November 1912, is in AIU Maroc, III.C.10; it is cited in Gottreich, *The Mellah of Marrakesh*, 178–179n80.

73. AIU Maroc, Microfilm VII.B.188/2, 2 September 1907, Falcon to Leven. Part of this letter is reproduced in Gottreich, *The Mellah of Marrakesh*, 86–87.

74. Bénech, *Essai d'explication d'un mellah*, 311.

75. Laskier, *The Alliance Israélite Universelle and the Jewish Communities of Morocco*, 307, 312.

North African Jews and Political Change in the Late Colonial and Post-Colonial Periods

PART XI

19

Jewish-Muslim Relations in Tunisia during World War II

Propaganda, Stereotypes, and Attitudes, 1939–1943

FAYÇAL CHERIF

TRANSLATED BY ALLAN MACVICAR

Introduction

For many centuries, different ethnic and religious communities have co-existed in the geographical area known today as Tunisia. After the region was conquered by the Arabs and it became the vanguard of the Muslim conquest of the Maghrib, Muslims came to form the majority. Archaeological and historical evidence reveals that Jews were strongly anchored in the area, surviving the various transformations this region underwent. From time to time, the generally peaceful coexistence between the Muslim and Jewish communities was threatened by the repercussions of political changes, crises, and fallout from events taking place both inside and outside of the area. These periodic upheavals tested the mutual understanding between the two communities.

This chapter seeks to understand how the relationship between Tunisia's Muslim and Jewish communities was affected during a pivotal yet controversial period in Tunisian history: World War II, from the outbreak of the war in Europe in 1939 to the end of the German campaign and the occupation of Tunisia on May 13, 1943.

The Situation of Tunisian Jews before the War (April 1938–May 1943)

While tensions existed between Jews and Muslims, until the period of the French occupation, which began in 1881, they remained submerged and confrontations between the two communities occurred only occasionally. Tensions rose to the surface, however, as a consequence of French colonial policies in Tunisia and the positions Tunisian nationalists took regarding the Palestinian question, which reverberated in both the local and broader Arabic press. Because radio propaganda was only beginning at this time, radio was not a major source of information for Tunisians in 1938. In 1939, however, with the establishment of several different stations, propaganda began to play an important, even decisive role, as will be discussed further below.

Paul Azan, *commandant supérieur* of French troops of Tunisia in 1936, offered this reflection on the situation of the Jewish community of Tunisia at the time:

> In the Regency of Tunisia, the indigenous Jews are in a better situation than in Algeria or Morocco. They are not conspicuously despised by the Muslim population and live in harmony with them. They even enjoy some of the same privileges. They can wear a red fez and yellow babouches, which would not be tolerated in Algeria or Morocco. During the early days of the protectorate, the Jews of Tunisia devoted themselves to industry and commerce. Presently, they tend in fairly large numbers to choose professional careers, such as law or medicine, and they fill them up. Some possess considerable fortunes and therefore enjoy a certain influence, but many are very poor and are assisted by Jewish aid. Generally, they quickly adapt to Western civilization. As they become French, thanks to naturalization, which has, in the main, been granted to them, they exert a growing influence on the appointments of elected bodies, and consequently on the general policies of the Regency.[1]

Azan's observations suggest that despite evidence of rising tensions between Muslims and Jews and the social transformation of the Jewish community, the rapport between the two communities remained strong. The relatively harmonious relationship continued even after the radicalization of the Tunisian national movement. The Néo-Destour, the political party that led Tunisia to independence, advocated showing no mercy in its struggle against colonization. This warlike attitude culminated in the bloody events of 9 April 1938, which resulted in the deaths of 150 Tunisians and the imprisonment of the main political leaders of Néo-Destour, apparently the most popular party at the time. These events seriously influenced Muslim opinion about French colonialism, yet ties between the Jewish and Muslim communities were not greatly affected.

More consequential in the relationships between colonized and colonizer and between Muslims and Jews was the new conflict between the French colonizing power and the fascist states of Europe. The latter held out the promise of a different and decidedly seductive alternative to colonization characterized by liberation, the unity of the Arab-Muslim world, and a new order based on friendship rather than force. This came at a time when the French offered no overarching political plan for Tunisia; the meager reforms of June 1938 had not succeeded in appeasing those who were agitating for independence. Another important factor was the imprisonment of prominent political leaders and the introduction of repressive measures that restricted public and private freedoms. The mobilization of Tunisian troops for the war and the simultaneous exemption of Tunisian Jews from military service gave Muslims reason to believe that the authorities of the protectorate were showing favoritism toward the Jews and disfavor toward the Muslims. It was in this tense situation that a propaganda war began.

Foreign Propaganda and the Staking out of Positions: The Split between Jewish and Muslim Communities

Before the outbreak of World War II, a parallel war was begun by the various rival powers, a war of propaganda intended for Arab populations. Its main outlet was the radio, arguably the most powerful political weapon in the world at that time. Hitler's Germany, Mussolini's Italy, and later Great Britain each established Arabic-language radio stations: Radio-Berlin, Radio-Bari, and the BBC, respectively. Each country broadcast programs that sought to embellish its own image and denounce the other side's reasons for making war. These programs sought to undermine the morale of the "enemy" and to win the psychological war that was sometimes more important than the physical one. In this war of propaganda, what messages were directed toward Arab populations and Tunisia? What were the true goals of the fascist dictatorships for the Tunisian people, and to what degree did Tunisians accept or reject this propaganda?

Hitler's Germany and to a lesser degree Mussolini's Italy allied against the French and British by presenting themselves as protectors of Islam and friends of Arabs. Germany's Arabic propaganda was much more skillful and believable than that of Italy. The establishment of the ministry of propaganda under the direction of Joseph Goebbels in 1933 indicated the importance Nazi Germany gave to this crucial tool. In the eyes of Muslims, Italian propaganda was much less credible. The negative Tunisian reaction to Mussolini's propaganda was vindicated when the Italian army colonized Tripoli and then invaded Albania in April 1938, events that left bitter memories in the minds of many Tunisians. Refugees from Tripoli in Tunisia helped dispel the image of Italy that Mussolini sought to promote among Muslim populations. Italian foreign policy was greatly discredited in Tunisia by Italy's use of force against Muslims and its poor treatment of Libyans in particular as well as by denouncements in the local French, Arabic, and even Italian (antifascist) press. A fierce campaign led by Libyan nationalists in Tripoli worked to expose fascist dogma, with the result that Muslim public opinion came to view Mussolini's Italy in an unfavorable light. (When Italy signed the armistice with the Allied forces in 1943, some Tunisians were worried that their country might eventually be conceded to Italy.)

Radio Berlin seemed more credible because of its support for national self-determination (in theory). It relied on emotionally charged messages that were thought to appeal to Muslims, and its broadcasts repeatedly stressed that Germany's colonial ambitions were directed toward Eastern Europe. The Germans thought that this was the best way to impede the mobilization of North Africans against Germany should conflict break out. German propaganda was intended to contrast with the Italian program, which sought to annex Tunisia, Corsica, and the area around Constantine in order to rebuild the lost glory of the Roman Empire in *Africa Romana*.

Tunisians generally believed Younes Bahri, the newscaster on Radio Berlin. His exaltation of the extraordinary German military only reinforced the already positive impressions people had. It should be noted that in Tunisia, there were only 1,000 radio receivers for a population of 2.3 million people (an average of one receiver for every 2,300 inhabitants). However, the habit of listening to the radio (which was banned once hostilities began) spread easily, and important news reached even the most remote villages. In September 1939, as Allied forces declared war on Germany, the French authorities in Tunisia banned listening to foreign programs, particularly ones emanating from Italy and Germany. It even requisitioned radios in the Italian community as a preventative gesture. The French believed that the psychological effect of this propaganda was harmful to the morale of the population. A report on radio propaganda recovered by the Contrôle Postal Métropolitain (a censorship committee) is quite instructive:

> The programs of German radio seem to have made a particular impression on indigenous circles in Tunisia. Judging by the effects on individuals questioned regarding this topic, one has to acknowledge that German broadcasting demonstrated a certain adroitness. It would start by reciting the Quran. Respect for the Holy Book obliged the listeners who might have tuned into another station to continue listening. They would then transmit a poem, often religious in nature, which would encourage the listeners to not change channels. They would then read the news, which constituted the *piece de resistance*, with eloquent, inflammatory, and tendentious commentary. The newscaster seems to have been held in some esteem. He could be persuasive and touch the sensitive side of Muslims. After the news, prisoners would speak, and this was followed by musical programming, including the Palestinian anthem and a national Pan-Arab song. Muslim circles within the Regency that listened to German radio seemed to have allowed

themselves to be impressed by the themes developed: legendary history, the bravery of Arabs.[2]

German propaganda directed toward North Africa and the Arab world during this period and even after rarely mentioned race. Moreover, Hitler's *Mein Kampf* had not been translated into Arabic in its entirety, and those extracts that circulated in the Arab world had been expunged of racist theories. The plan to publish a full Arabic translation of *Mein Kampf* for the purpose of denouncing Nazism was halted in 1934 because the Editions Latines (which had translated the work in 687 pages) had not obtained the permission of the author and editor beforehand. The publisher was ordered to pay token damages and withdraw the book from circulation.[3] The first Arab-Muslim denunciation of the book came from the perspective of an Egyptian lawyer, Hamid Maliji, in May 1937 in a 67-page pamphlet in Arabic, published in Cairo, entitled *Revelation of the Theory of Supremacy of Certain Races and the Place of North Africans in This Theory.*[4] Maliji, with the paltry resources available to him, tried to denounce the racist German theories and the entire German bibliography that was inspired by the notion of the supremacy of the Aryan race. His response relied on Islamic theology and jurisprudence. He also used philosophy to acerbically criticize the fact that such ideas were incompatible with human reason. His attempt at denouncing these theories to the general public, however, only reached Cairo and never attained the hoped-for impact in the rest of the Arab world because of poor distribution. Faced with the fact that no unabridged Arabic-language version of *Mein Kampf* was available, an especially terrible circumstance given the public's ignorance of Nazi ideology, Maliji wrote:

> Arab friends: . . . The Arabic copies of *Mein Kampf* distributed in the Arab world do not conform to the original German edition since the instructions given to Germans regarding us have been removed. In addition, these excerpts do not reveal his [Hitler's] true opinion of us. Hitler asserts that Arabs are an inferior race, that the Arabic heritage has been pillaged from other civilizations, and that Arabs have neither culture nor art, as well as other insults and humiliations that he proclaims concerning us.[5]

Tunisian Jews of course saw nothing positive in the arrival of Nazism and fascism. On the contrary, these two ideologies clearly threatened the very existence of the community. The Nuremberg laws and the anti-Jewish measures adopted in Italy only heightened their concerns that one day Hitler's Germany and Mussolini's Italy would expel Jews from Tunisia altogether.[6]

The difference between the reactions of the Jewish and Muslim communities stemmed from their expectations of the political programs of the colonial powers. While Muslims expected some kind of vague "new order" to arrive through the so-called emancipation from the yoke of French colonialism in North Africa and English colonialism in the Middle East, the Jews took this "new order" as a direct threat and preferred to stay on the side of the established powers, France and Great Britain. At the time, Muslims considered these powers to be their "hereditary enemies." Here then lies the fundamental split between two visions and two programs, and this caused much dispute and unease between the two communities throughout the war.

The defeat of France in 1940 and the subsequent establishment of the Vichy government, resulting in the promulgation of anti-Jewish measures in October 1940,[7] further intensified the differences between Muslims and Jews, striking an additional blow to their already precarious relationship.

The Impact of the Measures of October 1940 on Jewish-Muslim Relations

With the signing of the Franco-German armistice and the Franco-Italian armistice in June 1940, the Tunisian Jewish community grew increasingly nervous. Marechal Pétain came to power and the Vichy government was installed with Pierre Laval as prime minister. Both men were advocates of a "new order" that was partly inspired by the German model and extreme right-wing ideologies. Vichy indictments against Léon Blum and the communists were clear signs that accounts would also be settled with the Jews. The Montoire talks between Hitler and Laval on 24 October 1940 established the basis for collaboration between the Nazi regime and Vichy France. Shortly thereafter, new legislation was put forth to counter the supposedly "excessive" influence of the Jewish community on political and economic life in both metropolitan France and its North African holdings.

The new measures targeted the personal status of Tunisian Jews. Jewish newspapers published in Tunisia—the most important of which were *La Justice, L'Égalité, La Nouvelle Aurore, Le Réveil Juif, La Gazette d'Israël,* and *Es Sabbah* (the latter a Judeo-Arabic publication)—were suppressed. The only periodical that was allowed to publish freely was *Le Petit Matin,* but only with the notice that it was a "Jewish newspaper." Tunisian Jews were dismissed from their posts in several sectors, including medicine, law, and official administrative positions. A *numerus clausus* restricted their ability to function to a large degree.[8] The repeal of the Crémieux Decree in Algeria (the 1870 law that had granted Algerian Jews French citizenship) signaled that the process of naturalization for Tunisian Jews would stop. From then on, some property of the Jewish community of Tunisia was seized. It is worth noting that anti-Jewish legislation in Tunisia was actually the least rigorous of such laws in the three North African countries since the new legislation had to be submitted to the bey for signing, which proved a lengthy process. Also, the moderating influence of the resident general, Admiral Esteva, a fervent Christian; Ahmed Pacha (d. 1942), bey of Tunisia; and his successor Moncef Bey greatly contributed to slowing the implementation of these measures. "The Admiral," writes Michel Abitbol, "was not particularly zealous in carrying out the anti-Jewish decrees, since he waited until March 1942 to promulgate the principal implementation orders regarding the Jewish Statute. At the same time, he sought to pay particular attention to the Tunisian community, even visiting the old synagogue of Jerba and making donations to the poor on the eve of Pessah in 1941 and 1942. . . . There were no indications of a similar concern in Morocco or Algeria."[9] Meanwhile, the Italian fascist authorities strenuously sought to avoid implementing these measures among Jewish Italians, who were for the most part from Livorno.[10]

In any case, most of the gains Tunisian Jews had made during the protectorate period were undone. Education and the professions were hit especially hard. For example, a decree issued on 16 October 1941 limited the proportion of Jewish doctors to 5 percent. Its strict application had disastrous consequences on the health of the population. When the decree was issued, 123 of the total of 425 physicians registered in the local physicians' association were Jews. This directive reduced their number to around twenty. Because this measure provoked a strong reaction within the Jewish community, an amendment was made to the legislation of the *numerus clausus* on 24 November 1941 that stated that the physicians who had been removed because of the new regulation would be authorized to care for the Jewish population, but only for that population.[11]

The situation increased Jewish support for British and Gaullist arguments for full struggle against the Vichy government and Nazi Germany. The resident general, Marcel Peyrouton, who was in office only from June to 24 July 1940, received an anonymous letter written in a Judeo-Arabic pidgin. Whether or not the letter was authentic, its tone served to confirm to the Vichy authorities the attitude of the Jewish population:

> Mr. Resident: We swear to you that we Jews will remain with powerful England, because France wants to side with a Germany that is killing us and persecuting our race. You know that we have money and business at our disposal, which are unequaled in their power. The tactics of the Marechal Pétain will not work. France will see with what kind of money it will pay Hitler. . . . France belongs to no one. All those who own property have the right to determine justice and to lead politics.
>
> The Jews will not die since they possess all the riches and control the levers of power in France and in North Africa. England will always defend us. In addition, it acted properly at Mers el-Kébir, for if it had not, the Germans and Italians would have taken over the fleet.[12]

For the Tunisian Jewish community, which had been stripped of all its civil rights and its administrative and economic positions by French policies, Great Britain provided the only recourse for revenge against Nazism and fascism, the centers of European anti–Semitism. It should be pointed out Muslims did not look upon this attitude favorably because Great Britain was a colonial power and an ally of colonial France. Not only did Great Britain dampen any possibility for independence, its position regarding the question of Palestine further discredited it in the opinion of Arabs and Muslims. The measures Vichy undertook, however, prompted mixed reactions among these same Arabs and Muslims.

Even before the anti-Jewish measures were passed, several incidents took place throughout Tunisia that were indicative of some Muslims' attitudes. During the week of 2 to 9 August 1940, while crowds gathered for weekly marches in different villages around the Souk el-Arba, bands of individuals pillaged Jewish stores. Admiral Esteva reported his superior in France that "the most serious [events] took place yesterday [8 August 1940] in Thala and Sliana. . . . The Muslim mob pillaged the Jewish stores and even [their] foodstocks. . . . The police were forced to use their weapons. Eleven Muslims were killed and the funerals took place this morning."[13] By this point, the economic situation in Tunisia had become intolerable: there was a lack of basic necessities, a decline in purchasing power after the devaluation of the local currency (in July 1940, it reached 40 percent of its prewar value), and an astronomical increase in unemployment as a result of the halt of the war industry. These violent demonstrations as well as the attempted murder of the superintendent (*amin*) of the Moknine supplies (on 23 July 1940) showed the depth of the crisis.

Most Muslims believed that Jews were a kind of privileged caste united by religion, since they appeared to own the wholesale and retail trade and most handicrafts, particularly the precious metal industry, including the jewelry trade. In the collective imagination of the Muslim population, Jews were associated with usury, a widespread practice in colonial Tunisia given the insurmountable difficulty in obtaining credit from the bank. While the Quran formally forbids the practice of lending money with interest and the Tunisian civil code condemned such practices, a good number of moneylenders still existed, and some of them were Jews. Muslims held these moneylenders responsible for the lack of foodstuffs and the decrease in the quality of life, and moneylending practices gained some notoriety in the press. In addition, the nationalists used the slogan of the pauperization of the masses to denounce French colonization. "In the news weekly, *L'Avenir du Centre*, there were 126 auctions by order of the court in 1931, behind which usury loans undoubtedly lay hidden: in 72 cases, the plaintiffs were Jewish creditors."[14] Jews, of course, did not have exclusive rights or a monopoly on these practices; Italians and Maltese were also involved. Moneylending practices tested a large number of *fellahs*, especially the most destitute, who were forced to pawn their belongings in order to meet their urgent need for money. Rural people especially resented these hardships. Some Muslims pillaged and destroyed Jewish property in part to eliminate pawnbroker contracts. Several anti-Jewish incidents were thus the product of purely personal vengeance.

During the economic crisis, especially in 1940–1941, the level of popular exasperation caused by the economic restrictions rose, as a police official noted:

> Complaints concerning the high price of living are ongoing. The government is accused of tolerating the rapid increase in the price of essential foodstuffs: milk, eggs, sugar, meat, coal, etc. Examples can be found of neighborhoods and towns where eggs are sold for 10 francs per dozen or more (a Jew from La Goulette sells them for 12 francs). Coal is being sold at 5 francs per kilo, and milk is becoming very rare, because of the production of cheese.[15]

Yet these restrictions are not enough to explain the anti-Jewish tendencies of popular opinion. Rather, internal as well as external propaganda contributed to the hostile attitude toward Jews and to increased xenophobia more generally. It originated with the Italian community, which had rejoiced at the apparent defeat of France and the signing of the Franco-Italian armistice on 24 June 1940. Within this context of military rivalry, Italophobia grew, and Muslims were more than ever concerned that Tunisia would be subjected to outright annexation by Italy. In fact, Italians formed the largest European community in Tunisia (96,000 according to French statistics; 120,000 according to Italian authorities), and if one adds to this number the Italians who had been granted French nationality, they undoubtedly formed the largest community. Muslims also accused the 13,000 Maltese of Tunisia of being the lackeys of British imperialism. Tunisians in general expressed satisfaction with the defeat of colonial France, which had used draconian measures to silence nationalist voices after April 1938.

In this context, extreme right parties such as the Parti Populaire Français (PPF) began to extend its activities into Tunisia in mid-July of 1940. At the same time, veterans' leagues were being formed that attributed responsibility for the military defeat to Jews and communists.

> A tract entitled "Protocol of Zion," typed in French and reproduced by a duplicating machine[,] is circulating among certain indigenous groups in the capital. It is a synthesis of the policy of world domination by the Jews. It can definitely be considered the time for anti-Jewish propaganda. . . .

> —The Jews are appalled by the wave of anti-Semitism breaking out over Europe.

—The P.P.F. has begun activities in Tunis and will publish a manifesto. It has not ceased leading the struggle against interior enemies: communism, Judeo-Marxism, and freemasonry.[16]

This upsurge in anti–Semitism was spurred in part by political events, beginning with the Montoir talks on 24 October 1940, which established the basis for Franco-German collaboration, as well as the meeting between Il Duce and the Führer in Florence. This diplomatic activity revealed the degree of agreement between the Axis powers and Vichy France. The political situation and questions of complicity came together in the accusations leveled against "international Jewry," an idea clearly informed by Nazi propaganda. Many Tunisians admired Hitler's boldness and the success of his initiatives. Germany had long been popular for its victories against Great Britain and France, but pro-German sentiment grew into Germanophilia as Hitler won spectacular victories that were replayed on Radio Berlin and echoed by demobilized soldiers or those who had been liberated by the German army. Students returning to Tunisia from Europe also unknowingly (and sometimes knowingly) spread elements of German propaganda.

As indicated above, Muslims often negatively associated the name of Great Britain with the Palestinian question. Their resentment was focused on the Jews' use of ties to Great Britain to facilitate immigration to Palestine and therefore the dispossession of Palestinian Arabs of their land. For the Muslim masses, Palestine implied Jerusalem (al-Quds), which added a religious element to their resentment. The Archéo-Destour, a party with religious leanings, never failed to discuss events in Palestine in the columns of *al-Nahda*.[17]

After the armistice, while the more enlightened elements of society were preoccupied with political questions, the masses remained focused on the cost of living and economic stagnation after the defense industry closed and maritime traffic was temporarily stopped between France and its colonies, all of which had been imposed by the Franco-German armistice of 1940. Those deemed responsible for the situation were systematically targeted by some of the Muslim population. First, the protectorate administration itself was blamed. But no unified political or union action was possible, since Vichy had eliminated all such organizations. Collective frustration of the Muslim masses was thus vented through occasional attacks against the Jewish community. Not only were Jews active in the strategic sectors of the economy, the fact that they chose to remain outside of the nationalist struggle further inflamed hatred toward them. Several had acquired French nationality and some sat on the Grand Counsel. For Jews, especially those who held degrees, naturalization (which the Muslim population did not pursue for the most part) was a way to escape from the sovereignty of the bey and to benefit from the advantages of French nationality (e.g., the "colonial third"

awarded to civil servants, which was reduced from 33 percent to 28 percent under Peyrouton). From 1911 to 1940, the year that marked the end of the granting of
French nationality, 7,160 Jews were naturalized, approximately 12 percent of the
total number of those granted French nationality in Tunisia.[18] The Néo-Destour
party latched on to the issue of naturalization as a way of entering the political
scene. Even though his own beliefs were secular, Habib Bourguiba, the leader of
the Néo-Destour, proclaimed that naturalized persons should not be buried in
Muslim cemeteries. Popular opposition to naturalization grew to the point that
its beneficiaries were considered renegades.

Such attitudes were among the sources of latent anti-Judaism, as the chief
prefect of Tunisian security services noted:

> The animosity of Muslims against Jews is very much alive. All sectors of
> the population are concerned about an intervention by the R.A.F. in Tuni-
> sia and blame the Jews for being the only present defenders of the English
> cause. Jewish negotiators were also accused of having broken off all busi-
> ness relations with Muslim merchants and of being responsible for the eco-
> nomic crisis in all sectors.[19]

The backdrop for all this was of course the major political transformations as the
Vichy government tried desperately to hold onto its colonial possessions. Vichy
also had to face the fact that from the perspective of the population in the protectorates (particularly in North Africa, the "jewel of the empire"), France had suffered a humiliating defeat.

Putting the Conflict into Perspective

In 1940, five Jewish speculators were convicted in the court of the city of
Driba; they were sanctioned with high fines and their goods were confiscated. A
faction composed of M'hammed Bourguiba, Bahri Guiga, and Ezzedine Cherif
accused their colleague, Hassen Guellaty, of "having agreed to ensure the defense of the speculators at the exact moment when almost all the European nations were reacting against the grip of the 'Jewry.'" M. Guellaty responded that
he separated himself from his political opinions in order to carry out his profession and that in any case he was not in favor of racism.[20] If Guellaty's feelings
are any indication, antisemitism never became overly popular in Tunisia. However, the reaction can be explained by the reemergence of the nationalist movement since the advent of the Vichy government. While the religious rancor between Jews and Muslims remained strong, the two communities continued to
cooperate in business and commerce and separated themselves from their political opinions and religious beliefs in the public sphere. For example, in Ta-

touine, "there was noticeable collusion between Muslim producers and Jewish merchants, who encouraged smuggling and the black market by becoming the moneychangers for the smugglers. Any crackdown becomes difficult when the parties are in accord."[21] On the whole, tensions were low and coexistence was not affected; disagreements occurred only occasionally and were temporary. Also, the two main Tunisian nationalist parties never promoted gratuitous racism in their publications. Instead, tensions were driven primarily by political, economic, and social forces.

Moncef Bey and the Jewish Community of Tunisia

On 19 June 1942, Moncef Bey acceded to the throne. He quickly became popular among his subjects. He hoped to be a unifier and sought to reestablish the social and national cohesion of his country that had been compromised by the anti-Jewish legislation of October 1940 and the events that followed. He made no attempt to hide his opposition to such measures. A police report indicates that he "did not hesitate to dramatically proclaim several times that the Tunisian Jews are his children like the Muslims, and that he will not allow them to be harmed. He says, however, that he is little interested in those who become naturalized French citizens. Such proclamations have echoed strongly among the masses."[22]

At the time of his accession, Moncef Bey visited the town of Ariana, a northern suburb of Tunis, an event that provided an opportunity for a visible rapprochement between the sovereign prince and the Tunisian Jewish community. The Jews loudly proclaimed their friendship and pledged their support for the bey. Jews wanted to demonstrate to Muslims that they greatly appreciated the political reform of a bey who demonstrated feelings of humanity and warmth toward them. Nationalist circles as well welcomed the new bey's willingness to develop closer ties with the Muslim masses and to protect them from threats to their status. Admiral Esteva noted this support for the bey in a report to Pierre Laval:

> In spite of his relatively short visit through the town [of Ariana], people reacted by demonstrating strong support for the Bey's actions. A few words of welcome were expressed at the Sidi Amara mausoleum where His Highness made a very brief stop. Several sport and music clubs enhanced the splendor of the ceremony by their presence and their parades, most notably, "La Naceuria et La Musulmane." His Highness was welcomed by cries of "Long live the King," "Long live our Lord," "Long live Tunisia," by lengthy "Youyous" of Muslim women, and by the crowds' wild clapping along the road.[23]

The enthronement of Moncef Bey stimulated a kind of relaxation of social tensions, and the Tunisian Jewish community was comforted by the monarch's moderate positions. He did everything he could to restore the social cohesion that had been entirely missing from 1939 to 1942.[24]

Tunisian Jews during the German-Italian Occupation of Tunisia

The German campaign in North Africa led to the occupation of Tunisia from 9 November 1942 to 7 May 1943. On 6 December 1942, the Service du travail obligatoire (STO) imposed forced labor upon the Jewish population of Tunisia, and more particularly on the Jews of Tunis. This time, the Tunisian Jews were accused of being Anglo-American accomplices. From the time Rudolf Rahn arrived in Tunis as Plenopotentiary Minister of the Reich, he indicated to Admiral Esteva that the Jewish question would be his jurisdiction. On 23 November 1942, a detachment of SS troops arrested a number of Jewish figures, among whom were Moïse Borgel, president of the Jewish community's administration committee, and Félix Samama, former president of the Jewish community. On the same day, a communiqué from Von Arnim, commander of the German forces in Tunisia, detailing Allied bombings denounced the war that was "sought by international Jewry."[25]

It should be noted that the measures adopted by the German military were not applied to Italian Jews. The Italian government energetically intervened to separate them from other Tunisian Jews "as if their Italianness was more important than their Jewishness."[26] Italy had also opposed the Aryanization of the property of Livornese Jews since the time that the anti-Jewish measures were promulgated in October 1940.

The German authorities quickly expanded their plan of action against the Jews of Tunisia. Although the Jewish question had not been at the heart of discussions at the German-Italian meetings in Rome or in diplomatic correspondence, Germany had raised the issue with increasing frequency since the beginning of the war in order to demonstrate Germany and Italy's support for the Arab cause against the "Judeo-Bolshevik" or, alternately, the "Judeo-Democratic" coalition. Rahn wanted to punish the Jewish community for its active support of the Allies and at the same time bolster the themes German propaganda had developed. It was also a question of profiting from the human and financial resources of the community; it was understood that in the context of the war, neither the Vichy government nor the Italian authorities would challenge anti-Jewish measures. As a whole, neither the Tunisian Muslim population nor the French showed much enthusiasm for these policies, apart from a few isolated cases in which individuals took advantage of the almost universal confusion and economic depression to pillage Jewish goods. There were some cases of Jews who found refuge with Muslims and were able to escape German repression.[27] This repression increased as the Germans subjected Tunisian Jews, who were already subject to the October measures, to even more repressive measures that included supplying workers for the occupation authorities, paying collective fines (the Germans held the Jews responsible for the Allied bombings), and finally the deportation of certain Jews of French nationality to metropolitan France, from where they were sent on to Germany.

In order to justify their severe policies with regard to Tunisian Jews, German authorities promoted the idea that the Jewish community had a monopoly on merchandise and was engaged in speculation. Admiral Esteva tried to intervene by directly appealing to the German authorities for the liberation of certain Jewish figures. On 6 December, the Kommandatur sent word to the president of the community and to the chief rabbi of Tunisia of a decision to dissolve the administrative committee of the Jewish community. The same day, a new committee was introduced, and the next day, it presented a list of 2,000 Jews who were condemned to forced labor. The new committee was responsible for providing supplies, clothing, and subsidies to the families of forced laborers. Faced with such a difficult task, Borgel, the president of the committee, asked Esteva to intervene again to gain more time, since the resident had been unable to oppose German demands outright. After much effort, the committee was able to assemble only 125 workers, which provoked the wrath of Colonel Rauff.[28]

The opposition of the resident general and of Moncef Bey to the discriminatory measures the Germans took against Tunisian Jews continued when the Kommandatur insisted that the Jews pay "the price of the war." However, the Allied landing ignited much hope among Tunisian Jews that Tunisia would soon be freed from the German occupation and that the Vichy government would be replaced by the French resistance forces. The acceleration of military operations and the beginning of the rout of Axis armies after the fall of the Cyrenaica on 21 January 1943 sounded the toll of an imminent defeat. The successive defeats of the Axis armies at Mareth on 6 April, the fall of Sfax on 10 April, and the fall of Sousse on 12 April 1943 clearly signaled the Allied victory in North Africa.

The Tunisian Jewish community suffered greatly from the Germano-Italian occupation. To the same degree that Muslims had hoped for an Axis victory to help bring about a new political order, the Jews hoped to be delivered by the Allies. Despite these contradictory interests, only a minimal number of anti-Jewish acts by Muslims occurred during the six months that Germano-Italian forces were present.[29] During this period, some Jews found refuge among Muslims who opposed racial policies.[30]

After the war ended, the Tunisian Muslim population found itself accused of collaboration with the Axis armies by Anglo-American and Gaullist interests and mired in a rendering of accounts. For them, the Allied victory was simply another chapter in their ongoing saga of colonization.

Conclusion

The tensions between Jews and Muslims during the war are instructive in many ways and offer us the possibility to analyze several factors that affected the relationship between the two communities—the experience of colonialism, the rising tide of nationalism, the Palestine question—all against the backdrop of a long history of coexistence in Tunisia. Even though this study focused on the relatively short period of time during the war years, these factors converged in a sequence of major politico-military events during this uncertain time that accentuated and highlighted interethnic tensions in Tunisia as well as the enduring aspects of Muslim-Jewish coexistence. This study has also tried to gather together, from a long historical perspective, the contradictions in the Tunisian cultural mosaic while stressing major events that constituted a crucial turning point in the Jewish-Muslim relationship in Tunisia and more broadly in North Africa.

NOTES

1. Paul Azan, "Les problèmes de la Tunisie actuelle," *Revue des Deux Mondes,* 15 March 1936, 388.

2. Archives Générales du Gouvernement Tunisien (AGGT), carton 35, dossier 1, Note non signée n° 52, 19 January 1940.

3. H. Roussou, "Mein Kampf, le best-seller des années trente," in *L'Allemagne d'Hitler, 1933–1945* (Paris: Seuil, 1991), 47–48.

4. Hamid Maliji, *Kashf al-sitar ʿan nazariyat imtiyaz baʿd al-ajnas* (Cairo, 1937).

5. Ibid., 26.

6. For more background on the relationship between Italian fascism and Tunisian Jews, see Daniel Carpi, *Between Mussolini and Hitler: The Jews and the Italian Authorities in France and Tunisia* (Hanover, N.H.: University Press of New England, 1994).

7. Michael M. Laskier, *North African Jewry in the Twentieth Century: The Jews of Morocco, Tunisia, and Algeria* (New York: New York University Press, 1994), 72–73.

8. Paul Sebag, *Histoire des Juifs de Tunisie des origins à nos jours* (Paris: L'Harmattan, 1992), 224.

9. Michel Abitbol, *Les Juifs d'Afrique du Nord sous Vichy* (Paris: Maisonneuve, 1983), 81.

10. Carpi, *Between Mussolini and Hitler*, 208–227.

11. Sebag, *Histoire des Juifs de Tunisie*, 226; Claude Nataf, "Les Juifs de Tunisie face à Vichy et aux persecutions allemands," *Pardès* 16 (1992): 213–214.

12. Archives du Ministère des Affaires Etrangères, Paris (AEP), série P (Vichy-Tunisia), carton 6, dossier 1, letter no. 699, 24 July 1940, Marcel Peyrouton (General Resident) to Paul Baudouin, Minister of Foreign Affairs (Paris).

13. AEP, série P (Vichy-Tunisie), dossier 18, telegram dated 9 August 1940, Admiral Esteva to Paul Baudouin.

14. Ali Nouredine, "Le phénomène de l'usure et la recrudescence des pratiques usuraires au Sahel au début des années 1930," *Les Cahiers de Tunisie* 32, nos. 129–130 (1984): 85.

15. AGGT, série: Histoire du Mouvement National, Carton 33, D:1, Commissariat de police, note dated 26 December 1940. To give a sense of the standard of living: The daily salary of a construction worker did not exceed 25 francs per day. A dozen eggs represented half a day's work. After the defeat and the armistice, the economic difficulties were due in part to the stoppage of wartime industries and the extremely rapid increase in unemployment. In July 1940, inflation reached 40 percent.

16. Archives Nationales d'Histoire d'Outre-Mer (Aix-en-Provence), Série 77, sous série 26h21, dossier 3, Bulletin d'information, 27 July 1940.

17. The daily paper *Al-Nahda* began publication in 1923. For the position it took during the 1948 Arab-Israeli war, see Mohsen Hamli, "*Nekba* or Boon: When the 1948 Arab-Israeli War Unveils the Unsaid in Tunisia," *Journal of North African Studies* 10 (2005): 61–76.

18. *Annuaire statistique de la Tunisie, années 1940–1946* (Tunis: Service des statistiques, 1948), 62.

19. AGGT, Série Histoire du Mouvement National, carton 38, dossier 3, 8 July 1940, chief prefect of the security services to the secretary general of the Tunisian government.

20. Ibid.

21. Archives Nationales d'Histoire d'Outre-Mer (Aix-en-Provence), série 72, sous série 26H 21, Rapport du service de l'information, November 1941.

22. AEP, série Vichy-Tunisie, telegram dated 18 August 1942, Esteva to Laval.

23. Ibid.

24. Robert Satloff, *Among the Righteous: Lost Stories from the Holocaust's Long Reach into Arab Lands* (New York: Public Affairs, 2006), 111–113.

25. The text of the communiqué, reproduced in French, Italian, and Arabic, reads (in English translation): "The war was sought after and prepared by international Jewry: The people of Tunisia—French, Italian, and Muslim—have greatly suffered from recent bombings. That is why I have decided to impose a fine of 20 million francs upon the Jewish fortunes of Tunisia, and to use the money to offer immediate assistance to the civilian victims of the bombings. The distribution of aid has been entrusted to the Committee of Immediate Aid (C.O.S.I.) that will directly assist all who have materially suffered from the criminal Anglo-American bombings of unarmed people. Therefore, all the French, Italian, or Muslim inhabitants of Tunis who have suffered because of the Anglo-American aggression need only to make a request with a detailed justification." Quote in Jacques Sabille, *Les Juifs de Tunisie sous Vichy et l'occupation* (Paris: Éditions du Centre, 1954), 147.

26. Sebag, *Histoire des Juifs de Tunisie*, 232.

27. Satloff, *Among the Righteous*, 111–137; Sebag, *Histoire des Juifs de Tunisie*, 245.

28. Sebag, *Histoire des Juifs de Tunisie*, 233–236

29. See Nataf, "Les Juifs de Tunisie face à Vichy," 225.

30. Ibid., 244–248.

20

The Emigration of Moroccan
Jews, 1948–1956

Jamaâ Baïda

Translated by Allan MacVicar

I N THE HISTORY of every people, painful wounds exist that historians, particularly those writing about their own nations, have a tendency to avoid as themes of study. The emigration of Moroccan Jews falls into this category. In just a few years, Morocco was stripped of one of its essential ethnic and religious components. The country's cultural diversity and economic potential were diminished by the Jews' departure. Except in some rare instances, this subject has not always received the attention it deserves in academic circles.[1] In the end, in Morocco as elsewhere, time has diminished such hesitations, whatever the motives behind them might have once been.

After World War II, and especially beginning in 1948, Morocco experienced an unprecedented event in its history: part of its population, whose roots in that land ran deep, emigrated in large numbers to take up residence in other countries, such as Israel, France, the United States, and Canada. To offer just a few telling statistics: in 1948, the Moroccan Jewish population numbered approximately 250,000 out of a total of about 8 million inhabitants; in 1960, there were 160,000 Jews left in Morocco; and toward the end of 1967, there were only 40,000.[2] Today, fewer than 4,000 Jews still live in Morocco. This leads us to conclude that Moroccan Judaism today is more evident outside rather than inside Morocco itself.

The point of this chapter is not to present an exhaustive study of this hemorrhage by examining the multiple facets of its development. The process of emigration of Moroccan Jews was the result of the convergence of many factors: decolonization, the clash of national identities, the poverty of the Jewish masses, and the uncertainties of the political and economic future of Jews in an independent Morocco. My aim is more modest: I seek to understand Jewish emigration, within a fixed time period, through the reactions of and statements made by the main political entities. These statements would most likely have had an impact on local public opinion and on the process of emigration itself.

Before proceeding, however, it is worth noting that the emigration of Moroccan Jews, particularly to Palestine, began before World War I. Even during the interwar period, foreign Zionist activists made appeals for emigration and tried to cultivate the idea of a return to Eretz Israel among the Jewish communities in Morocco. These attempts were countered by official representatives of Moroccan Judaism as well as by French authorities and Moroccan nationalists. During the 1930s, this last group campaigned against Zionism, which it considered to be disruptive and incompatible with the Moroccan nationality of the Jews in the Sharifian Empire.[3] Thus, prior to World War II, appeals for emigration garnered little success. The attraction to Palestine had not yet diverged from traditional views, which were above all mystical-religious.

The circumstances of World War II, the birth of the State of Israel, and the beginnings of Moroccan independence finally disrupted this situation. With these exigencies in mind, Jews from Morocco and from the Maghrib in general sensed more than ever the need to emigrate to locales where they hoped to find friendlier living conditions. Their bitter experience under the Vichy government's racist laws as well as the diminution of France's prestige as a protecting power are elements to be considered in seeking to understand this phenomenon. They in fact help explain, at least in part, the pro-American sentiment prevalent in the Jewish Maghribi communities after the Normandy landings. Once the news of the birth of Israel arrived in these communities, a strong political conception of emigration converged with the mystical-religious attraction the Holy Land had always held. This provided a favorable setting for Zionist propaganda, which urged emigration as a means of consolidating the newly created state in the Middle East.

In addition to these eternal factors, what was happening within Morocco must also be considered. The general discursive strategy of the Moroccan nationalist movement was to appeal to Islam and Arabism, references that had considerable impact among the bulk of the Muslim majority. In January 1944, when the Istiqlal Party published its famous Manifesto of Independence engaging it in a power struggle with the French protectorate powers, the vast majority of Moroccan Jews were skeptical, preferring to wait and see what would result. The nationalists, without saying very much publicly, probably thought that connecting the Jewish elite to their struggle would be fruitless. This elite, in the nationalists' estimation, was seeking to integrate itself into the heart of Western civilization after having served as a local auxiliary to the colonial powers. The Moroccan Jewish communities, while continuing to swear allegiance to the sultan, felt themselves to be more or less outside the struggle for national liberation.

This feeling intensified in 1947, one year before the birth of Israel, when the primary political forces in Morocco embraced the direction offered by the Arab League (an organization founded in 1945 that promoted independence and unity of Arab states and opposition to a Jewish state) after the famous speech by Sultan Mohammed Ben Youssef in Tangier (in April 1947) that supported independence, national unity, and bringing Morocco into the Arab League. The Jews' feeling of marginalization from the nationalist struggle was further reinforced when the leader of the Rif war and symbol of Moroccan national resistance, Muhammad b. ʿAbd al-Karim al-Khattabi, in exile in Réunion, escaped to Cairo where he became chair of the Maghrib Arab Liberation Committee and rallied supporters to participate in the Arab struggle in Palestine. While Muslim political movements were reinforcing their connections to pan-Arabism with the goal of ousting the colonial presence, Moroccan Jews were turning their backs on these movements[4] and instead heeding the appeals of Zionist groups that were organizing *aliyah* (the Zionist term for immigration to Eretz Israel).

Clandestine Emigration

While Jewish emigration from Morocco for religious, economic, and political reasons did not begin in the postwar period, the Jews' desire to leave was nonetheless galvanized by the war. This phase of their departure took place clandestinely or semi-clandestinely. French authorities tolerated emigration for various reasons but were officially opposed to it so as not to upset the Moroccan nationalist groups, who supported the Palestinian cause. In addition, the French authorities, at least until 1948, had to take into account the fact that the British had banned Jewish settlement in Palestine beyond a fixed quota.

Zionist groups began organizing the *aliyah* from Morocco at the beginning of 1947. The nationalist movement looked very unfavorably on Jewish emigration to Palestine, seeing it as both treasonous to the mother country and as reinforcement for the Zionist project. It was in such a spirit that Ahmed Bouhelal (under the pseudonym Abou Khalil) wrote a scathing article in the Arabic edition of *Le Jeune Maghrébin* entitled "The Zionist Poison in Morocco."[5] It was a harsh indictment of the Jews, the majority of whom, according to the author, were the lackeys of Zionism and ingrates toward their country, all because of their love of money. This article provoked a reaction by the Alumni Federation of the Alliance Israélite Universelle of Morocco, whose president, Isaac Dahan, wrote a letter of protest to the French resident general. Dahan accused the editor of *Le Jeune Maghrébin* of anti–Semitism and alleged that the paper was using the question of Zionism in Morocco as "a pretext to call for a campaign of incitement and hatred against Moroccan Judaism."[6]

The Birth of Israel and the Riots in Eastern Morocco

When the UN passed a resolution supporting the partition of Palestine in November 1947, Moroccan nationalists held several demonstrations to proclaim their solidarity with the Palestinian Arabs. Participants in these campaigns sometimes made a dangerous conflation between Zionists and Jews, particularly when they made calls to boycott the businesses and services of Moroccan Jews.[7]

The day after the proclamation of the birth of Israel on 14 May 1948, the sultan personally intervened in order to warn his subjects, both Muslim and Jewish, against any action that would disrupt law and order and undermine a secular tradition of friendly relations between the two communities on Moroccan soil. The sovereign reminded Jewish Moroccans in particular that they were Moroccans first and that they should "abstain from any act that might support or demonstrate their solidarity with the Zionist aggression, for in so doing, they would undermine both their particular rights as well as the Moroccan nationality."[8]

While Moroccan Jews could not openly express their enthusiasm for the birth of Israel, they channeled their reaction into an ever-increasing clandestine emigration, particularly via Oujda, which is located close to the Moroccan border with Algeria. In June 1948, this region was witness to bloody riots (in Oujda and Jerada) in which forty-four people died and dozens more were injured, the majority of whom were Jews. The official version of these events, based in most part on reports by Brunel, the French authority in the region, located their origin in the Palestinian issue. Early on, however, the Ligue Française des Droits de l'Homme et du Citoyen, among other groups, took note of the complexity of events and particularly of the French authorities' lax control in the Oujda region.[9] Many things continue to remain unclear regarding this painful episode in the history of Morocco, an episode that has not yet been subjected to rigorous inquiry. The available archives and testimonies about this tragedy weave a confusing web that only dispassionate academic study can untangle.[10]

Despite all the work that remains to be done, we can see that the effects of the events in the Oujda region stimulated the Jewish migration. From 1948 on, a deep unease and climate of suspicion dominated relations between the two communities. The idea of *aliyah* no longer needed the encouragement of zealous Zionist propagandists to make headway for members of the Jewish community, among whom a certain sense of panic was growing. In addition, the resident general, Alphonse Juin, who had been officially opposed to Jewish emigration, was forced to make concessions because of pressure from the West, particularly from France and the United States, countries that had been affected by the seriousness of the events in eastern Morocco.

In 1948, Marc Jarblum, president of the Zionist Federation of France, visited Morocco. Jarblum, reporting a few months later on the results of his visit and his talks with Resident-General Alphonse Juin, stated to a Parisian newspaper:

> For a few months now, we have been met with genuine understanding. Soon, neither the French nor the Sharifian authorities will have any reason to cause us problems. The desire to leave is so strong that no restriction could impede its coming to pass. And the Residency knows very well that one cannot fight against a spiritual longing with prisons.[11]

Jarblum's optimism was confirmed in April 1949, when the residency granted Jews permission to create Cadima, an organization whose goal was to organize the Jewish emigration to Israel. With this new structure in place, it was through Casablanca, not Oujda, that almost all Jewish emigration took place thereafter.

The residency's flexibility regarding emigration did not, however, extend to allowing an overt, visible Zionist campaign; that might have provoked a strong reaction by the nationalist movement. On 28 January 1949, the authorities banned several foreign Zionist publications, including *Le Journal de Jérusalem, La Nouvelle Renaissance, La Riposte, L'Appel,* and *Le Monde Juif.* In France, the Conseil représentatif des institutions juives de France strongly protested this action.[12] In April 1949, *La Riposte,* which claimed to have never received the order of prohibition, reported on what had happened to the copies it had continued to ship to Morocco. Under the headline "*La Riposte* Is Banned in Morocco. Our Parcels Are Burned at the Casablanca Airport," the Zionist newspaper invoked a recent event that would undoubtedly provoke a reaction: "Do not these *auto-da-fés* remind us of something? The smoke that rises from them cannot help but recall the smoke that arose from the Nazi pyres where it was fashionable to incinerate Jewish works and other subversive literature."[13]

The Reaction of Nationalist Groups

Nationalist groups were called upon by various actors in the new postwar environment to issue a statement regarding Moroccan Jews. Because authorities arrested several nationalist militants and Muslim unionists during their investigation surrounding the riots in Oujda and Jerrada, these groups were directly implicated in the tragedy in eastern Morocco. A few even appeared before a military tribunal in Casablanca in February 1949.

Let us examine the three principal nationalist discourses relating to the Jews:

1. The Istiqlal Party. After the riots in Oujda and Jerada, the Istiqlal Party, the most influential Moroccan political group, adopted the same at-

titude as the sultan and relayed the sovereign's appeal for peace and calm. In addition, it rejected the accusations made concerning its militants and attributed the responsibility for what had occurred to the French authorities. According to Istiqlal spokesmen, the French were the ones who were most interested in sowing discord in the Jewish-Muslim relationship in Morocco. Finally, the party also criticized Moroccan Jews for having undermined the possibility for peace by supporting Israel and Zionism, especially through fund-raising and emigration. The Istiqlal Party deemed emigration a military act because it felt that the goal was to reinforce Israel against its Arab neighbors. It was for this reason that the party reminded its Jewish compatriots that they were first "Moroccan and then Jewish" and said that they should not demonstrate solidarity with Israel simply because they were Jewish.[14]

2. The Democratic Party of Independence (PDI). In its newspaper *Er-Raï El-Amm* (The Public Opinion), the PDI was less prudent than the Istiqlal Party regarding Moroccan Jewry. It made no distinction between Jews and Zionists, a position that, considering the context, clearly endangered Jewish-Muslim relations in Morocco.[15] The writers of articles in *Er-Raï El-Amm* often let themselves be carried away by their own wit and eloquence without considering the consequences of their words and allusions.[16]

3. The Moroccan Communist Party (PCM). Significant numbers of Jews were members of the PCM: in 1948, 500 Jewish members stood alongside 3,000 Muslims. Since the birth of the Arab League, the Communists had been especially open about their mistrust of what they called the "league of pashas and beys." The discourse of *Espoir* (the voice of the PCM) and *L'Action Syndicale* (voice of the Confédération Générale du Travail, a French trade union) diverged completely from that of the Istiqlal Party and the PDI's support of pan-Arabism. The Communists did, however, agree with the Istiqlal Party that the colonial authorities were to blame for the June 1948 riots in eastern Morocco. Yet the primary concern of the PCM was to prevent its militants from falling into the "Palestinian trap" set by what it saw as Anglo-Saxon imperialism. The party urged its members to remain "vigilant" and "united" and to continue the class struggle at any cost. According to the PCM, the duty of Moroccan Jews was to carry out the struggle on their native soil,[17] not in Israel or elsewhere.

Moroccan Jews Face a Dilemma: Integration or Emigration?

After the wave of emigration that followed the proclamation of Israel and the events at Oujda, fervor lessened on both the Jewish and Muslim sides. On the Jewish side, the flexibility demonstrated by the French authorities reassured those who saw exile as the only way to escape the danger. As for the Muslim side, Israel's defeat of Arab armies and the failure of the Arab League's slogans had wounded the pride of some and subdued the pan-Arabist fervor of others. For nationalist leaders, who were preoccupied by the escalation of the Franco-Moroccan conflict under the fist of General Juin, the problem of Moroccan Judaism became secondary. This was especially the case after Sultan Mohammed Ben Youssef was deposed and went into exile to Madagascar. In light of such developments, most Jews, uncertain of what their place would be in an independent Morocco, adopted a wait-and-see attitude. Not until a solution to the Franco-Moroccan conflict was being sketched out, most notably during the negotiations at Aix-les-Bains, did the official leaders of Moroccan Judaism—who up to then had supported France—make their grievances known. A Jewish elite also existed that understood the historical implications of independence well before this point, although this group was certainly in the minority. Its members had taken a position on the Franco-Moroccan conflict and maintained contact with the primary nationalist movements. Let us cite a few examples of these initiatives, however limited their actual impact may have been:

Since its inception in March 1951, the Amitiés Marocaines association (Moroccan Friendships), led by Félix Nataf, had tried to forge a dialogue between the Muslim, Jewish, and Christian communities in order to find appropriate solutions to the various difficulties facing the country.[18]

Meyer Tolédano,[19] through his writings in both the Jewish newspaper *Noar,* where he was the editor, and the liberal daily *Maroc-Presse,*[20] attempted to persuade Morocco's Jews to abandon their wait-and-see attitude and come out of "isolation" and connect with world Jewry. Locally, he also tried to push the Moroccan Jewish community to fully accept its responsibility during this crucial phase in the history of Morocco. In 1951, he wrote in *Noar:*

> Our leaders think that the Franco-Moroccan problem does not concern them. They deliberately ignore the social reality that has been set in motion. They wash their hands of it. This is a dangerous error. The Jewish community is an integral part of the country; this community counts and as a result, it has a say in things.[21]

On the eve of independence, Tolédano discredited a rumor that apocalypse awaited the Jews of Morocco after the departure of the French as "pernicious" and "untruthful."[22]

Joe Ohana, who had just formed the Mouvement National Marocain and who had been received by the sultan in Paris on 2 November 1955 and then in Rabat on 1 December 1955, called for the suppression of the Conseil des Communautés (Council of Communities), the Comités des Communiuatés (Committees of Communities), and the entire separatist apparatus that was primarily responsible for the isolation of Jews in the Moroccan nation. He also wanted to repeal the dahirs of 1918 and 1945.[23] For Ohana, once these fetters were removed, Jews could participate in the public sector in the same ways as Muslims. The Federation of Jewish Alumni of the AIU, which gathered on 4 December 1955, expressed the same views.

Along these same lines, in an article in *Maroc-Presse* entitled "Réalités juives" ("Jewish Realities"), David Berdugo criticized the fact that there were so many Jewish institutions in Morocco; in his opinion, this had created a "Jewish kingdom" within the Sharifian Empire, a "state within a state." According to Berdugo, these institutions, which had been created neither by Jews nor for their well-being, were the product of a politics of division carried out by the colonial regime. As this regime was on its way out, it was necessary for the Jews to become fully integrated into the national governing bodies: "Through our militants within the political parties, through our elected officials in all the national governing bodies, through our active participation in the central national trade union, we will very quickly become worthy of our country and we will fully realize our duty as Moroccans, our duty as free people."[24]

Let me cite one last example that illustrates the patriotic awakening of the Jewish Moroccan elite: in May 1955, approximately fifty Jewish Moroccan students in Paris published a communiqué supporting their country's independence.[25]

Moroccan Jews, like their Muslim compatriots, joyfully celebrated Sultan Mohammed Ben Youssef's return to Morocco and the country's independence. During this decisive period, nationalist leaders could not ignore the issue of Moroccan Judaism. They were constantly called upon, particularly by the World Jewish Congress, to make their stand clear regarding the future of Moroccan Jews and to make gestures that would assuage the concerns of those who felt their situation to be precarious. But these efforts did not have the hoped-for effect. In 1955, the official figures for foreign emigration were quite telling: 2,008 in June, 2,329 in July, 2,527 in August, and 2,748 in September.[26] Furthermore, many rural Jewish families moved from the countryside to urban centers as a stepping-stone to emigration. Faced with this unpleasant reality on the eve of Moroccan independence, the Istiqlal Party and the PDI tried to outdo one another in their declarations of good intentions and gestures of good will toward the Jewish community.

In December 1955, the Istiqlal Party held a special conference that focused, among other matters, on the issue of Moroccan Judaism. The motion it adopted was unequivocal: Jews and Muslims should have the same rights, with no distinction based on class, religion, or race.[27] To encourage a rapprochement between the two communities, an association called Wifaq (Understanding) was created under the aegis of the Istiqlal Party. It consisted of a training unit for future Jewish Istiqlal activists, since it would not have been easy to simply drop uninitiated Jews into a struggle that was for the most part unfamiliar to them. Among the goals of Wifaq was the dissemination of Arabic-language literacy among the Jewish masses. In January 1956, Joe Ohana's Mouvement National Marocain called on its militants to join the Istiqlal Party.

As for the PDI, it denounced Jewish emigration and reasserted that all Moroccans, regardless of race or religion, would be full citizens. Emphasizing Moroccan unity, the PDI declared that "any propaganda, regardless of its origin, that is inspired by retrograde considerations that would hinder this unity, constitutes . . . a crime against the homeland."[28]

During the conference at Aix-les-Bains in August 1955, the lawyer Abdelkader Benjelloun, one of the leaders of the PDI and the future minister of finance, made several declarations to the press defending the need for Jews to have representatives in the next government. The declaration that garnered the most interest, however, was an interview that he gave to the Paris correspondent of the London newspaper *The Jewish Chronicle* on 23 September 1955. Large extracts were reported on by the Moroccan press, in particular *Maroc-Presse* and *La Voix des Communautés*. Most notably, Benjelloun told the British newspaper:

> The P.D.I. was the first party to wish for a Moroccan of the Jewish confession to participate in the negotiating government of negotiation. This would then accustom the citizens of our country to the idea that no distinction based on religion should exist among them. . . . We consider that the emigration of Moroccan Jews to Israel is due in part to a lack of confidence in the future, and we believe that this emigration is encouraged by improper propaganda.[29]

Although Benjelloun's declarations might have been sufficient to calm anxieties within some Jewish Moroccan circles, they also provoked conservative militants within the PDI. This was the case with Driss Kettani, who opposed any Jewish participation in the government and accused his colleague of having succumbed to Zionist pressures and to the influence of his wife, who was originally from an Austrian Jewish family.[30] This type of opposition within the PDI did not stop the party from moving forward with its policy concerning the integration of Moroccan Jews. It expanded its recruitment campaigns and formed a Jewish-Muslim youth movement called The Democratic Union of Moroccan Youth in January 1956 under the aegis of the PDI. Its board of directors was comprised of Driss Jaï, Saadali Cohen, and André Cohen.

The integration of Moroccan Jews seemed to be under way. On both the Muslim and the Jewish sides, several initiatives attempted to highlight the principle that "religion belongs to God, the homeland belongs to all." On 18 November 1955, during his speech from the throne, the sultan emphasized that "Jewish Moroccans have the same rights and the same duties as other Moroccans."[31] The nomination of the Jewish Dr. Léon Benzaquen to the government as minister of the Postal Telecommunication Service and Broadcasting seemed to guarantee this integration. Disillusionment quickly set in, however, and the integration process lasted only during the initial euphoria of independence. It did not take long for it to be undermined by both internal and external factors. These included the violent partisan struggles between the PDI and the Istiqlal Party, Morocco's membership in the Arab League, the Suez Crisis and the solidarity that Muslim Moroccans felt with Nasser's Egypt, and finally (and especially) the dissolution of Cadima's office and the imposition of restrictions on Jewish emigration on 10 June 1956.

Contrary to expectations, the banning of Cadima created a climate of anxiety and feelings of uncertainty within the Jewish community. International Zionist organizations and their local activists cleverly exploited this situation. Once again, the field was opened for clandestine emigration, resulting in the loss of some of the country's future potential, right at the moment when it needed it most. The following years confirmed this tendency.

The majority of Moroccan Jews wanted to reconcile their Moroccan nationality with supranational ties, but this was an equation that Moroccan political parties did not want to acknowledge. Here lay the heart of the problem. Once the economic and political uncertainties of recent independence were added to the mix, all the elements were in place to provoke Jewish emigration in full.

Carlos de Nesry, a Jew from Tangier, was an important witness to these events, having lived through the gut-wrenching moment when "Jewish Moroccans had to choose" (as his book was entitled). His assessment provides a poignant conclusion:

> Emigration is reverberating through all levels of the Jewish population. In fact, the exodus of Moroccan Jews has begun imperceptibly and surreptitiously, an exodus that no one truly desires, but that is often rendered inevitable due to economic necessity. This exodus does not indicate a particular political stance, but, given the circumstances, has become essential to survival. The people are not fleeing Morocco, but their own misery. They are reluctantly leaving a country that is made for them, that remains a part of them, and that they will never forget. They are torn as they abandon this land, a land where they have lived, struggled, and prayed, a land where their generations built an earthly residence, a land where their dead lie at rest.[32]

NOTES

1. *Editors' note:* The most in-depth study on the question of Moroccan emigration to date is the recent state doctorate by Mohammed Hatmi (supervised by Professor Jamaâ Baïda): "Al-Jamaʿat al-yahudiyat al-maghribiya wa-l-khiyar al-saʿb bayn nida' al-sahyuniya wa-rihan al-Maghrib al-mustaqil: 1947–1961" (Université de Fès-Sais, 2007). Until recently, research on the emigration of Moroccan Jews has been studied largely by non-Moroccan historians. See especially Michael M. Laskier, *Yisra'el veha-ʿaliyah me-Tsefon Afrika, 1948–1970* (Sede Boker: Makhon Ben Guryon le-Heker Yisra'el, Universitat Ben-Guryon be-Negev, 2006); Michael M. Laskier, *North African Jewry in the Twentieth Century: The Jews of Morocco, Tunisia, and Algeria* (New York: New York University Press, 1994), 158ff; and Yaron Tsur, *Yehude Maroko veha-le'umiyut, 1943– 1954* (Tel Aviv: Am Oved, 2001), 237ff.

2. Arlette Berdugo, "Maroc: la source vive," in *Les Juifs du Maroc: images et texts,* ed. André Goldenberg (Paris: Éditions du Scribe, 1992), 11; Goldenberg, "L'Alyah des Juifs du Maroc," in Goldenberg, *Les Juifs du Maroc,* 102; Simon Lévy, "La communauté juive dans le contexte de l'histoire du Maroc: du XVIIème siècle à nos jours," in *Juifs du Maroc: identité et dialogue* (Paris: La Pensée Sauvage, 1980), 137–148 passim.

3. See Jamaâ Baïda, "La presse juive au Maroc entre les deux Guerres," *Hespéris-Tamuda* 37 (1999): 171–189.

4. Only within the ranks of the communist party, the PCM, was there a significant number of Jews. In 1948, it had 500 Jewish and 3,000 Muslim members. Robert Rézette, *Les parties politiques marocains* (Paris: Armand Colin, 1955), 339. See below for more on the PCM.

5. *Le Jeune Maghrébin,* no. 1, 20 June 1947.

6. Archives Diplomatiques de Nantes (ADN), Maroc—Cabinet civil, liasse 163, Rabat, 30 June 1947, copy of Isaac Dahan's letter to the residency. Before this article, which provoked Dahan's indignation, Bouhelal's *Le Jeune Maghrébin* had already shown its colors in the 4 June 1948, issue (French edition): "Modern crusades. They are not Christian this time round! They are Hebrew and Zionist. Survivors of the central European ghettos, determined survivors of totalitarian regimes, errant Jews, anarchist believers, Marxist bankers, international racists, freemasons of different lodges, and revolutionaries are struggling to beat each other to what they claim is the 'promised' land." Quoted in Georges Oved, *La gauche française et le nationalisme marocain* (Paris: L'Harmattan, 1984), 2:492n244.

7. See the call made by the PDI newspaper *Erraï El-Amm,* on 12 January 1948. Cited in Robert Assaraf, *Mohammed V et les Juifs du Maroc* (Paris: Plon, 1997), 185.

8. Declaration made on 23 May 1948. Quoted in André Chouraqui, *La Condition juridique de l'Israélite marocain* (Paris: Presses du livre français, 1950), 221.

9. *"Le chef de la Région, M. Brunel, bien qu'informé des bruits qui couraient et de l'état des esprits se serait absenté de son poste le 7 juin. Au moment où éclate l'émeute, aucun fonctionnaire n'aurait pris l'initiative de requérir la troupe pour aider la police débordée à retablir l'ordre"* (The head of the region, Mr. Brunel, though well informed of the rumors circulating and of the state of affairs, was absent from his post on June 7. At the moment that the riot erupted, no official took the initiative to require the troops to help the overwhelmed police restore order); Archives Diplomatiques du Quai d'Orsay, Paris (ADP), Maroc, 1944–1955, vol. 75, Ligue Française des Droits de l'Homme et du Citoyen to Ministre Français des Affaires Etrangères, n.d. Albert Ayache's account of the shortcomings of the regional authorities, based on the testimony of various witnesses, is in *Le Mouvement syndical au Maroc,* vol. 2 (Casablanca: Wallada, 1990), 278.

10. For more details and somewhat differing accounts of the events in Oujda and nearby Jerada, see Mohammed Kenbib, *Juifs et musulmans au Maroc, 1859–1948* (Rabat: Université Mohammed V, Publications de la Faculté des Lettres et des Sciences Humaines, 1994), 677–687; Yvette Katan, *Oujda, une ville frontière du Maroc (1907–1956): Musulmans, Juifs et Chrétiens en mi-*

lieu colonial (Paris: L'Harmattan, 1990), 599–614; and Michael M. Laskier, *North African Jewry in the Twentieth Century: The Jews of Morocco, Tunisia, and Algeria* (New York: New York University Press, 1994), 91–101.

11. *La Terre Retrouvée* (Paris), 15 April 1949.

12. ADN, Maroc, Cabinet Civil, liasse 133, 9 May 1949, Léon Meiss, president of the CRIF, to Robert Schuman, French minister of Foreign Affairs (copy).

13. *La Riposte* (Paris), 20 April 1949. In the same issue, an article by Réuben Halévy emphasized the need to take on "a question of utmost importance: the repatriation of North-African Jews."

14. See *L'Opinion du Peuple*, 20 May 1948.

15. See *Erraï El-Amm*, 12 May 1948, 26 May 1948, and 16 June 1948.

16. See *Erraï El-Amm*, 4 February 1948, 16 June 1948, February 1950.

17. *Espoir*, 19 March 1948.

18. Nataf was a Tunisian Jew who settled in Morocco and converted to Christianity. See Félix Nataf, *Juif maghrébin: une vie au Maghreb racontée à ma fille* (Paris: Fayolle, 1978).

19. Meyer Tolédano was a Jewish lawyer who practiced in Casablanca. For his activities as the head of *Noar*, see Jamaâ Baïda, *La presse marocaine d'expression française des origins à 1956* (Rabat: Université Mohammed V. Publications de la Faculté des Lettres et des Sciences Humaines, 1996), 339ff.

20. For example, see "Raisons d'une emigration," *Maroc-Presse*, 7 October 1955, 1–2; and "Les tâches de demain," *Maroc-Presse*, 8 November 1955, 1–2. In his article of 7 October, Tolédano recalled how Moroccan Jews had always lived in a spirit of tolerance in Morocco: "The native Moroccans' spirit of religious tolerance is well known. Numerous Berber tribes lived as Jews or Christians in Morocco for many centuries, before embracing Islam. During the time of the Inquisition, thousands of Spanish Jews, faced with having to choose between exile and conversion, found refuge in Morocco and were able to practice their religion here. From 1940 to 1943, during which time antisemitic laws threatened their persons and property, Moroccan Jews were treated with dignity and respect by their Muslim fellow countrymen."

21. *Noar*, 1 October 1951, 1.

22. "To claim that current emigration is a result of anxiety caused by future Moroccan political transformations is to spread a lie." *Maroc-Presse*, 7 October 1955, 2.

23. Joe Ohana, "Conscience nationale," *Maroc-Presse*, 22 November 1955. The *dahirs* of 1918 and 1945 refer to important new policies promulgated to reorganize Jewish institutions in Morocco. See Joseph Chetrit and Daniel J. Schroeter, "Emancipation and Its Discontents: Jews at the Formative Period of Colonial Rule in Morocco," *Jewish Social Studies* 13, no. 1 (2006): 170–206.

24. *Maroc-Presse*, 17 December 1955.

25. Lévy, "La communauté juive dans le contexte de l'histoire du Maroc," 139.

26. Résidence Générale, Direction de l'Intérieur, *Bulletin de Renseignements Politiques*, September 1955 (official publication of the Résidence Générale).

27. Motion regarding Moroccan Jews:

"The special conference of the Istiqlal Party, assembled in plenary session,

CONSIDERING THAT the principles and doctrine of the Istiqlal Party anticipate the establishment of a political, economic, and social democracy, on the basis that all Moroccan nationals are considered to be equal without distinction of race or denomination;

CONSIDERING THAT Moroccan Jews are nationals of the country in the full meaning of the historical and juridical term;

That it matters, therefore, that they enjoy and exercise the rights and freedoms accorded to their Muslim fellow citizens in complete equality;

CONSIDERING THAT they must, therefore, be an integral part of the Moroccan community;

CONSIDERING THAT this integration should not in any way affect their ability to worship or their personal status,

REQUESTS

That the equality of all Moroccan citizens without distinction of class or religion be openly proclaimed and sanctioned in the texts of law;

That Moroccan Jews enjoy all political and civic rights, especially that they would have the right to vote and to be represented in all Moroccan assemblies;

That their right of access to all functions of the Moroccan State be expressly recognized under the same conditions as their Muslim fellow citizens;

SUGGESTS

That the Executive Committee of the Istiqlal Party encourage contact between Muslims and Jews, to organize and promote common activities in different areas, in order to overcome any absurd prejudices and to favor to the best of its ability a true and fraternal rapprochement."

Archives de l'Institut d'Histoire du Temps Présent, Paris, Fonds Paret, carton 7, brochure of the Istiqlal Party.

28. Communiqué by the PDI, in *Maroc-Presse*, 12 September 1955, 2.

29. *Maroc-Presse*, 1 October 1955, 4.

30. Idris al-Kattani, *al-Maghrib al-Muslim didda ʿala diniya* [The Moroccan Muslim against Atheism] (1958), 129.

31. *La Voix des Communautés*, novembre 1955, 8, cited in Doris Bensimon-Donath, *Evolution du judaïsme marocain sous le Protectorat français (1912–1956)* (Paris and The Hague: Mouton, 1968), 116.

32. Carlos de Nesry, *Les Israélites marocains à l'heure du choix*, 2nd ed. (Tangier: Éditions Internationals, 1958), 98–99.

21

Zouzef Tayayou (Joseph the Tailor), a Jew from Nedroma, and the Others

Belkacem Mebarki

THIS PORTRAIT RELIES almost exclusively on the testimony of the Muslim inhabitants of a city they cohabited with Jews.[1] While working on this project, I was surprised by how extensive and important the Jewish presence was in the memory of this city's inhabitants. This is also my city and my memory, even if my memory is slightly truncated for obvious ideological reasons that I could not overcome. For this reason, I promised myself that I would study this passionate subject in greater depth. In the course of my research, I realized that this topic also fit into my field of research, since Jewishness constitutes a peripheral aspect of Maghribi Algerian expression, which I qualify as limited or deterritorialized.[2]

Since 1988 and the collapse of a single socialist ideal, Algerians have become more aware of their pluralism and diversity. Before this time, the focus for most Algerians was on building a viable state and assuring social cohesion; therefore, only the Arabo-Muslim character of the country was acknowledged in a way that was connected to the socialist and revolutionary "dimension." Even the Berbers remained, for the most part, hidden.

After the "earthquake" of 5 October 1988,[3] Algeria awoke to deep and age-old realities. It discovered that it was in fact an ethnic and cultural mosaic whose imaginary extended beyond the limits sketched by a political discourse that had trouble situating itself in the East-West conflict. Algeria also discovered that those who laid claim to the title "North African" included more than Algerians living in Algeria who expressed themselves in relation to this political discourse by defending or critiquing its tenets. Other groups were also politically, historically, and emotionally connected to this region, such as the Beurs (children of North African immigrants in France), political exiles, and even the *pieds-noirs* and the Jews.

Unlike the *pieds-noirs,* who were forced to flee Algeria after the activities of the Organisation de l'Armée Secrète (OAS),[4] some Jews, even though they had been granted French nationality by the Crémieux Decree of 1870, preferred to remain in what they considered to be the country of their ancestors. It is clear that many Jews followed close behind the fleeing *pied-noirs,* but it is important to emphasize that some of them did not leave, either because they were unable to or because they loved their native soil.

Some claim that several thousand Jewish Algerian partisans remained, others say the numbers reached tens of thousands, and some Algerian Jews say it was only several hundred. These individuals lived as full Algerians, with all the rights and responsibilities this identity implied. As was suggested in a history of Algerian Jewry, "these Jews know all about Algeria, while Algeria knows nothing about them."[5] This contradicts the assertion that the Jews enjoy all rights, at least on the level of religion, since, to the best of my knowledge, Judaism is not practiced openly in Algeria. If Jews practice their religion in Algeria today, they do so in the utmost secrecy.

The ongoing existence of Jews in Algeria was revealed in the early 1990s, when Raymond Benhaim, Claude Berbi, and Benhamou assumed high-level positions within the Ministry of Finance in Mouloud Hamrouche's government.[6] But while the existence of Jews in Algeria came as a surprise to some, particularly those in the big cities, it was considered perfectly normal by others, particularly in the smaller towns such as Nedroma. Why did Jews settle in Nedroma, and why did a few refuse to leave after 1962?

Nedroma is a small city in Western Algeria. It is part of the Wilaya (province) of Tlemcen, approximately 50 kilometers from the provincial capital; it is approximately the same distance from Oujda in Morocco. The city is nestled in the north side of Filaoucen Mountain overlooking the beautiful plain of Mezarou with the Mediterranean on the horizon, six kilometers away.

Nedroma is constructed in medieval style. The houses of the *madina* are generally two stories and are grouped around the old mosque, whose minaret was constructed toward the end of the tenth century. The alleyways are so narrow that only three or four people can walk abreast; in order to pass, you have to angle your body. There are some advantages to such narrow streets; the most significant of which is contact with others. If, perhaps, you pass by someone ten times in a day, you greet them ten times and of course exchange the customary salutations each time.

It takes little time for a visitor to Nedroma to understand that this city has withdrawn into itself geographically, socially, and culturally. Very few outsiders settle there and there are very few "mixed" couples. The city, set apart from the main roads between Tlemcen and the cities of Oran, Oujda, and Ghazaouet, was not greatly influenced by these large centers in terms of language, cuisine, or style of dress.

Many scholarly works have been written regarding this kind of "autarchy." A Nedromi's accent, vocabulary, and even (some would think) complexion and physiognomy are clearly distinct. They are very unlike those of the residents of Fez, Tlemcen, or Constantine, cities that share common Andalusian traits.

The paradox is that this enclosed urban space, whose only contact with outsiders—even those in the surrounding countryside—is in the form of commerce, has produced important figures for Algeria and the Maghrib, people that made and continue to make history. These include writers, singers, theologians, ministers, a prime minister, and even the current president of the republic, Abdelaziz Bouteflika, as well as the founder of the great Almohad dynasty, ʿAbd al-Muʾmin b. ʿAli.

Of course, there are reasons for this kind of fruitfulness. In my estimation, the most significant is the origin of the city's population. The Berbers come to mind, even though they did not really emerge onto the national scene until after 1962 by taking advantage of the democratization of education. There were also certain large tribes that settled in this city during the era of the Almohads, such as the tribes of Rahal, Sanhaja, and Zarhun. In addition, there are the "Andalusian" families—Gharnati, Sabili, Andalusi—who brought the arts of cuisine, clothing, and particularly song along with them, making Nedroma known throughout Algeria and even all of North Africa.

Those who know Nedroma know that among these "Andalusians" there was a large number of Jews. We are not entirely sure why they chose this city. Perhaps it was because it offered the necessary security for a minority community. The style of the city might have reminded them of Andalusian cities such as Benidorm or Cordova and might have eased the pain of exile. Perhaps they came simply because the city was hospitable.

Such hospitality was not new in the history of the city. First, in the past Nedroma had been an important political, religious, and cultural Muslim center, and there were likely also indigenous Jews there. Second, according to tradition, Jews settled in Algeria after their deportation by Titus,[7] and some arrived in the area at that time. Since there is a tradition in the Maghrib whereby one respects or even venerates the foreigner, especially if he arrives from a holy land or one that is apparently holy, some Jews rose to the rank of saint and were recognized as such by the indigenous populations.

This is the reason why there is a village, a seaside resort at Nedroma beach, that bears the name Sidi (or Sidna) Youchâa (our lord Joshua). A few kilometers away, on a hillside that overlooks the ocean, there is another village that bears the name of a Jew: Sidi Noun (Nun). Sidi Noun is venerated as the father of Sidi Youchâa.[8]

According to the Nedromi collective imagination, these contemporaries of Moses chose to exile themselves to this faraway land in order to flee the persecution to which they had been subjected as true believers. It matters little whether this was a true story or not. The essential point, which is nonetheless odd, is that these individuals were accepted as Jews and were considered to be saints and were venerated as such and with the same fervor as Muslim saints were venerated. This was especially the case with Sidi Youchâa, to whom a mausoleum was erected in the courtyard of the village mosque. The tomb of Sidi Youchâa was a pilgrimage site for both Muslims and Jews.

Every year in May, the Muslim inhabitants of the region arrange a *waʿada*, a popular religious celebration to remember and honor Sidi Youchâa. Certainly no one would consider entering the mosque in swimming attire; proper dress is expected. This Jewish saint may be worshipped with such sincerity because the North African Muslim tradition accepts Jewish prophets as true prophets and encourages respect for all saints regardless of their original monotheistic religion.

To the best of my knowledge, there are no longer any Jews in Nedroma. This is rather striking in a city that was home to some 551 Jews according to the census of 1911, a time when the total population was only 6,000.[9] Around 1970, when the population of Nedroma passed 50,000 inhabitants, only one Jew remained. He was a unique character, a kind of "last of the Mohicans." His first name was Joseph, and he was a tailor by profession. Everyone called him Zouzef Tayayou. Compelled by the events taking place in the Middle East, Zouzef finally left Nedroma in the mid-1970s, probably evacuated, according to most accounts, by the Zionist movement.

The last time that I had the opportunity to meet him was in 1972, when he must have been in his 50s. He was of medium height and always wore his *berreta* (or *barrita*, as it was pronounced locally), a distinctive hat worn by Algerian Jews. Let me take a moment here to recall the story of the Jews and their *berretas*.

There is a tradition that during the Ottoman period, a group of corsairs inspected a European ship loaded with velour berets. Not knowing what to do with the cargo, they forced the Jews to buy the berets and to wear them. What began as an obligation became a tradition. This is how in Nedroma, as elsewhere, the *berreta* became a distinctive trait of being Jewish in Algeria.

Three things struck me with regard to Zouzef: the pleasant smells coming from his cooking, his indelible smile, and the fact that he spoke in Arabic. He seemed to be such a "normal" Arab from Nedroma that I could not help questioning if he was really Jewish. In my mind, a Jew was "different," which should have translated as a difference in religion, of course, but also perhaps in dress and language. Joseph, however, spoke Arabic. Physically, he looked like everyone else, but the fact that he spoke to me in Arabic is what really surprised me.

Zouzef lived alone, without a wife or children, which for me at the time was another oddity. Apparently, however, he did not live in solitude. He had an adopted family. Clearly he lacked for nothing with them, and especially not for friendship or affection. His larger family, as the older ones could attest, included all the inhabitants of Nedroma, who considered him as one of their own. No one was allowed to speak ill of Zouzef.

It should be noted that economically he had a position in the city as an accomplished tailor. Even though he himself only dressed in European attire, he made the traditional or ceremonial clothes for Nedroma's elderly and notable citizens.

Joseph and many others like him could not understand why Algerian society no longer functioned according to the foundations of traditional and Maraboutic beliefs.

Traditional points of reference were being redrawn by the ideology of the political party in power. This power, like all political powers in the world, needed a real or fabricated enemy in order to maintain social coherence. From the end of the 1960s the enemy was there: the Jews, either in Israel or elsewhere.

In 1967, during the Six-Day War, the local politicians of Nedroma decided to demonstrate their membership in the Arab nation that had been "attacked" and to show their solidarity with it. How? By deporting Zouzef from Algeria to Marseilles. The trouble was that Zouzef was Nedromi, not Marseillais. He was born in Nedroma and had never left it in his whole life. Despite this fact, it was quite a surprise to the inhabitants of Nedroma to find that their Zouzef had returned home just ten days after his deportation to Marseille.

The most touching part of this story, or the most dramatic, occurred when Joseph told those who no longer wanted him to kill him that if they still so desired, they had to do it in Nedroma. "I was born in Nedroma, I have always lived in Nedroma, and I want to be buried in Nedroma," he said. Unfortunately, his wish was not granted. In 1973, after the October War, Joseph disappeared and was never seen again in Nedroma. He was driven out of his native land, but he continues to live on in the memory of those who knew him and adopted him and his differences. Because of his profession, he was very active in Nedroma, as were many others before him, like the Taubias, the Chemaouns, and others, who were butchers, tailors, bricklayers, carpenters, grocers, jewelers, and, of course, rabbis and sellers of anisette.

Historically, not many Jews of Nedroma were rich and few held administrative positions, with the exception of two or three policemen, a mail carrier, and a rural policeman. As a whole, Jews were normal people who were an integral part of society and who enriched the city by their lifestyle and their adoption of the city's customs in almost perfect harmony.

Differences, however, did exist. First, the Jews of Nedroma and all Algeria wanted to show that they had accepted the Crémieux Decree, which made them "French." They sought to distinguish themselves by building their homes in a European architectural style. In the neighborhood that was reserved for them, they owned houses with two or three stories, which they painted blue or beige, with balconies and French doors that opened outward, as if to show that they were not as poor as the Muslims and that they were more inclined to become Westernized.

It was perhaps their willingness to abandon their ancestral lifestyle for a Western one, which they showed off ostentatiously, combined with other unforgivable behavior, such as their neutrality in the war of independence or their open support for colonization, that led to their being condemned later on. They were seen as being ungrateful toward a nation that had adopted them centuries earlier.

Differences were also visible in their style of clothing. The Jews of Nedroma were known for their particular clothing, and for the most part they wore black. Their North African style of Arabic dress was the *sirwal* (jacket and vest) or the *jellaba* and turban. Their headgear was often yellow, which distinguished them from Muslims, who wore white turbans. If they dressed in the European style, they wore pants, jacket, vest, and a hat or *berreta*, black of course. According to some accounts, Jews sometimes wore a white *burnous* over their black clothes, but this was only for special religious or social occasions. For a long time, the Jewish women did not dress very differently from Muslim women, except that they did not veil their faces. For special occasions, however, they wore their traditional dresses that had been brought over from Andalusia.

With regard to social and religious practices, the Jews of Nedroma became well known for their excessive veneration of saints, regardless, strangely enough, of their religious origin. In the city and its vicinity, two saints in particular drew large crowds who came on a kind of pilgrimage. This gave Nedroma the false reputation of having sheltered a large number of Jews, even though there really were far fewer than in medium-sized cities in western Algeria, such as Tlemcen, Maghnia, or Relizane.

The most well known saint was undoubtedly Sidi Youchâa, who the Jews associated with Rabbi Simeon Bar Yohai, the legendary author of the Book of Zohar from the Holy Land of the second century CE. The people of the region, however, believed that he had lived much earlier (they associated him with the biblical Joshua). A *waʿada* took place each year near the mausoleum of this saint on 18 May. While this commemoration was primarily religious in the morning, by the afternoon it would become a kind of fair, and by the evening, probably due to the anisette, it would become a dancing party.

The Muslim inhabitants of the area continue to carry on this tradition, and every year they organize the *waʿada* of Sidi Youchâa on the Thursday closest to 18 May (Friday being a day of rest). This event always leads to the same type of religious contemplation and popular celebration as before, even without the anisette.

Zouzef Tayayou has left Nedroma. He did, however, hold on for a long time, like a child who refuses to be weaned and separated from his mother. In the end, he gave in, following the footsteps of the numerous others that went before him in their exodus.

What did he and the others leave behind in the city that sheltered them for centuries?

Perhaps they left their homes and their shops; certainly, they left a little of their style of living; but especially, they left many, many memories, for these "people of the book" remain a part of the collective memory of this city and the surrounding area.

NOTES

1. *Editors' note:* For the construction of memory of Jews and Muslims cohabiting in colonial Algeria, compare Joëlle Bahloul, *The Architecture of Memory: A Jewish-Muslim Household in Colonial Algeria 1937–1962* (Cambridge: Cambridge University Press, 1996).

2. This expression comes from exiled Algerians, both from *pied-noirs* and from Jews.

3. The social revolt that put an end to the socialist regime in Algeria.

4. The OAS was an organization of French military and *pied-noirs* who rejected Algerian independence and laid waste to the country, causing the colonists to depart in massive numbers.

5. Fawzi Saʿdallah, *Yahud al-Jazaʾir: haʾulaʾ al-majhulun* (Algiers: Dar al-Umma, 1996), 5.

6. Ibid.

7. The two main works on this topic are André Chouraqui, *Histoire des Juifs en Afrique du Nord* (Paris: Hachette Littérature, 1985); and Richard Ayoun and Bernard Cohen, *Les Juifs d'Algérie, 2000 ans d'histoire* (Paris: J. C. Lattès, 1982).

8. *Editors' note:* See the essay by Farid Benramdane in this volume.

9. Simon Schwarzfuchs, *Tlemcen: mille ans d'une communauté juive* (Paris: La Fraternelle, Union Nationale des Amis de Tlemcen, 1995), 178.

22

The Real Morocco Itself

Jewish Saint Pilgrimage, Hybridity, and the Idea of the Moroccan Nation

Oren Kosansky

Jewish pilgrimages to the shrines of saints have often been recognized as having roots in a North African cultural milieu that cuts across confessional distinctions. The ideological and ritual similarities between Jewish and Muslim pilgrimage in Morocco attracted the attention of twentieth-century commentators, writing across a wide range of disciplines and genres, who emphasized the religious hybridity of these traditions. This hybridity has been formulated in the idea that Moroccan pilgrimage is a Judeo-Muslim phenomenon, emerging at the intersection of two religious histories. As elaborated in scholarly articles, ethnographic reports, tourist guidebooks, and international newspapers, this claim often refers to both the sociological parameters and the cultural features of saint pilgrimages in Morocco. At the sociological level, much has been made of the veneration of common saints and the participation of Muslims and Jews in pilgrimages that cross religious boundaries. At the cultural level, the similarities between the cosmologies, hagiographies, and rituals of Jewish and Muslim pilgrimage traditions have often been taken as evidence of a common historical source and longstanding cultural interactions.[1]

Here, however, I put aside the problem of how to gauge significant points of ritual commonality or historical convergence between Jewish and Muslim pilgrimages in Morocco. I am concerned, instead, with the conditions under which commonality and convergence have been interpreted as the most salient features of such traditions. By tracing a selective genealogy of twentieth-century discourses about Jewish pilgrimage, I argue that the representation of Judeo-Muslim hybridity has been instrumental in the successive projects of constituting colonial Morocco as a national object of French control and imagining independent Morocco as a liberal nation-state.[2]

Two texts, each emphasizing pilgrimage hybridity, mark endpoints on a genealogy of representations that span the colonial and postcolonial periods. The
first is *Pèlerinages judéo-musulmans du Maroc* (1948), written by the French colonial
ethnographer Louis Voinot.[3] In his introduction, Voinot approvingly quotes another major voice in French colonial ethnography, Edmond Michaux-Bellaire, as
follows:

> The question of Judeo-Muslim pilgrimage has, in my opinion, considerable
> importance. It can permit us to retrace the role that Jews have played in Mo-
> roccan history since antiquity and to account not only for present Jewish
> survivals, but also pagan ones that during a certain epoch might have been
> placed in a Jewish envelope. I seek the real Morocco itself [*le vrai Maroc lui-
> même*], beyond the Muslim Morocco that I take to be opposed to it and that
> in my opinion is somewhat artificial.[4]

For Voinot and the ethnographic enterprise he represented, Judeo-Muslim pilgrimage appears as an emblem of nothing less than the real Morocco itself.

The second text comes from the public oratory at Jewish saint pilgrimage as
it became institutionalized in postcolonial Morocco, especially from the 1970s
onward.[5] During the annual communal events (as *hillulot,* sing. *hillulah*) involving pilgrimages to the shrines of deceased Jewish saints, speeches are commonly
delivered by representatives of the official Moroccan Jewish community. The
speeches are intended for an audience that includes devotees living in Morocco
and those who have returned from abroad as well as local delegates of the Moroccan state. The text of the speeches is also eventually disseminated to a wider public via the Moroccan press.[6] Over the past three decades, this mode of discourse
has been relatively consistent, to the extent that speeches are in some measure recycled from year to year and event to event. During this period, a version of the
following statement, delivered at the shrine of Rebbi Amram Ben Diwan in 1980,
has been repeated at numerous pilgrimages:

> This ceremony, which is the mark of a tradition common to all Moroccans,
> is the symbol of a mystical convergence rooted in this land. Each year this
> ancient rite brings us, Muslims and Jews, to this holy place. Here, we con-
> firm the link between our two religions, both issuing from the same divine
> source, but also establishing above our obvious differences the proof of our
> Moroccanness [*marocanité*].[7]

Despite the significant differences between this characterization and the example from the colonial era cited earlier, what remains relatively constant is the
rhetorical construction of pilgrimage as an authentic national tradition shared by
Muslims and Jews as Moroccans. The colonial presentation of pilgrimages as a

window into the real Morocco (*le vraie Maroc*) is mirrored in post-independence characterizations of pilgrimages as proof of "Moroccanness" (*marocanité*) that transcends religious boundaries. How is it that the symbol of saint pilgrimage has been harnessed to represent Morocco within the divergent projects of colonialism, on the one hand, and post-independence nationalism, on the other? In addressing this question, I want to emphasize the resilience of hybridity in discourses through which Jewish pilgrimage has been made to stand for the Moroccan nation. More specifically, I trace the theme of hybridity as follows: first, in the colonial era, when pilgrimage was characterized as a syncretic site of chaos, impurity, and transgression; second, in a transitional moment when pilgrimage was hesitantly recuperated as a fulcrum of humanistic sentiment, national patrimony, and monotheistic piety; and third, in the postcolonial period when pilgrimage was made to represent symbiosis, indicating fraternity, tolerance, and transcendence.

Social Chaos, Colonial Hybridity, and Religious Syncretism

Jewish saint pilgrimage in the colonial era can productively be viewed in light of what Hobsbawm and Ranger famously called the invention of tradition.[8] To be sure, the Jewish practice of visiting shrines preceded the colonial period, as did hagiographic discourses in which saints incarnate divine sanctity and intercede with God on behalf of devotees in search of health, wealth, fertility, and good fortune.[9] Nevertheless, *hillulot* were radically transformed in size, scope, and significance under the French protectorate (1912–1956). Facilitated by the development of information and transportation infrastructures, several shrines throughout Morocco emerged as major pilgrimage destinations that attracted thousands of devotees from the immediate environs, the broader region, the colonial territory, and beyond.[10]

The growth of shrines and pilgrimages was not merely an unintended consequence of colonial development, however. As *hillulot* became one of the major Jewish social manifestations of the period, mass pilgrimages provided an audience for which the beneficence, authority, and power of the French colonial state could be performed. In this context, the French protectorate directly supported pilgrimage events in a variety of ways. Roads were built explicitly for the purpose of facilitating travel to shrines. Security services were provided to ensure the safety of pilgrims. Protectorate representatives authorized the events and were welcomed at official receptions. In this venue, as in others, the colonial administration showed that it encouraged local patterns of life, albeit under the protectorate's watchful eye and subject to its modernizing reform.[11]

Jews themselves were most responsible for rethinking and refashioning pilgrimage events in the colonial image, either as direct agents of the protectorate or as local social actors associated with the Francocentric institutions of the Alliance Israélite Universelle (AIU).[12] Much of the colonial ethnography dealing with pilgrimage, for example, was written by Jewish authors who were highly critical of pilgrimage, which they took to be an exemplar of a wider range of persistent superstitious practices (e.g. the use of amulets, cures, and magical rituals) from which Jews might be liberated.[13] Such Jewish colonial voices, both European and Moroccan, recognized the entrenched nature of pilgrimage traditions and often called for their reform rather than their wholesale rejection.

Shrines, for example, were represented in colonial discourse as epitomizing essential aspects of Moroccan residential space (like the ancient walled *madinas,* for example) that would benefit from colonial intervention without being destroyed.[14] Colonial accounts depicted shrines as exceptionally unsanitary places and thus as targets for the introduction of modern hygiene. To emphasize this point, some colonial commentators pointed to what they viewed as a great irony in Moroccan Jewish pilgrimages: although pilgrims often made their way to shrines in order to find cures for illness, the physical conditions of *hillulot*— overcrowding, lack of proper sewage systems, the absence of potable water, and so forth—actually promoted the spread of disease.[15] Against this background, modernist Jewish reformers successfully introduced running water, electricity, and sewage systems at some of the major shrines.[16]

Hillulot also became a potential site for the enactment of colonial control over the throbbing social disorder of Moroccan society, as represented by the imagined unruliness of pilgrimage masses that were concentrated in close quarters, were swept away in religious ecstasy, and drank to excess. Toward this end, the colonial administration and its allies among the Moroccan Jewish elite instituted a series of regulations aimed at reforming and bureaucratizing major pilgrimage events. The shrine of Rebbi Amram Ben Diwan in Asjen, which emerged as one of the most important pilgrimage destinations in the colonial era, provides a case in point. The shrine was placed under the auspices of state-sanctioned commissions that were authorized to regulate pilgrimage finances, logistics, and behavior. Begging was to be prohibited in order to funnel charity through a rationalized communal treasury and to expunge what was considered to be the retrogressive behavior of the poor. Pilgrimage finances were rationalized and subjected to modern accounting procedures. Regular fees were to be imposed at the entrance to the shrine for parking, for animals bought for slaughter, for camping, for meals, and so forth. While such reforms were partially aimed at monopolizing pilgrimage income, shrine commissions were also concerned with controlling what their members viewed (and what they feared the French administration would view) as social chaos and cultural degradation within the Jewish community.[17]

The social chaos and cultural backwardness of pilgrimage communities was further indexed by the indiscriminate intermingling of social elements and strata. Noting that the wealthy and the poor alike attended pilgrimages, critics depicted the former as ostentatious poseurs who cared little for the plight of the Jewish masses they encountered at shrines.[18] Religious-minded reformers viewed the intimate mingling of men and women at shrines as being contrary to Jewish law.[19] Colonial ethnographers, Louis Voinot included, viewed the common veneration of saints by both Muslims and Jews as demonstrating the inability of natives to understand the heterogeneous and foreign sources of their folk practices.[20] Colonial ethnographers informed their readers that what each confessional community took to be an authentic expression of its own religious tradition was in fact the product of indiscriminate syncretic accretions—Jewish, Muslim, Berber, Christian, and so forth—through the centuries. The colonial discourse on Judeo-Muslim pilgrimages thus became a medium through which to identify the disorderly aspects of Moroccan society and then to introduce proper socioreligious distinctions and relations between the wealthy and the poor, men and women, and Jews and Muslims. In this regard, rabbinical and modernist reformers proposed (and occasionally enacted) reforms aimed at effacing obvious discrepancies of wealth, rationalizing the distribution of charity, enforcing the religious separation of men and women, and regulating pilgrimage activities to conform with rabbinically authorized Jewish practices.[21]

The colonial approach to Jewish shrines, *hillulot,* and pilgrimage communities was also part of a larger strategy that played itself out in the ambiguous relationship between the French administration and the socioreligious institutionalization of saint veneration (*maraboutism*).[22] In colonial literature, *maraboutism* represented the social phenomena of competing saintly lineages and religious brotherhoods that, by throwing into relief the internal divisions of Moroccan society, might hamper collective political action against the French. As a political phenomenon that represented alternative centers of social authority, *maraboutism* provided a strategic resource and set of alliances the French administration could use to temper the potentially resurgent power of the Moroccan monarchy. Although the sociology and politics of Jewish sainthood were quite different—living Jewish saints did not wield significant political power and corporate Jewish religious groups did not exist on anything near the scale of the Sufi brotherhoods—Jewish sainthood and pilgrimage provided another example of the diversity of Moroccan society. Jewish pilgrimages further underscored the religious and ethnic diversity of Moroccan society and thus bolstered French efforts to undermine the potential of Islamic and Arab identity to serve as a force of nationalist unity.[23]

It is in this colonial context that Voinot's characterization of Judeo-Muslim pilgrimage takes its rhetorical force:

> The question of Judeo-Muslim pilgrimage has, in my opinion, considerable importance. It can permit us to retrace the role that Jews have played in Moroccan history since antiquity and to account not only for present Jewish survivals, but also pagan ones that during a certain epoch might have been placed in a Jewish envelope. I seek the real Morocco itself [*le vrai Maroc lui-même*], beyond the Muslim Morocco that I take to be opposed to it and that in my opinion is somewhat artificial.[24]

This passage suggests that the study of Judeo-Muslim pilgrimage is significant because it displaces Islam as the foundation of Moroccanness, the essence of which therefore must be found elsewhere. That essence is pagan, which refers here both to a paradigmatic other in the discourses of Christian Europe and, more specifically, to Berber religion and society as framed by French colonial ethnographers. The substitution of paganism for Islam or Berbers for Arabs as the core of the real Morocco itself represents a well-established trope in colonial ethnography. As Edmund Burke, III, argues, the ethnographic figure of the Berber emerged in the dialectical space between representations of Moroccan national purity and Moroccan social heterogeneity. Berbers symbolized the singularity of Moroccan historical origins and cultural essence and helped sustain one strand of contradictory colonial ideology, namely that Morocco was essentially Berber and thus not deeply an Arab and Islamic domain. In addition, Berbers (as other than Arab and only superficially Muslim) symbolized the ethnic and religious heterogeneity of Moroccan society, which thereby ought not to become united in nationalist resistance. The figure of the Berbers was summoned (with equivocal success at best) both to represent the non-Arab and non-Islamic core of Morocco's identity and the heterogeneous composition of Moroccan society.[25] By rooting Judeo-Muslim pilgrimage in an antecedent Berber tradition, Voinot harnessed cultural hybridity to the broader colonial project of displacing the Arab and Islamic identity of Morocco.

Voinot's statement also construed a variety of hybridities that characterize the contemporaneous features (and not just the historical origins) of saint pilgrimage as a twentieth-century phenomenon. The most prominent hybridity is marked by the hyphenation Judeo-Muslim, which Voinot justified in several ways. First was the fact that some pilgrimages were undertaken by both Jews and Muslims who shared certain saints in common. The author also noted that in some cases the religious identity of saints was contested by pilgrims of the different confessions. Finally, Voinot claimed that Jewish and Muslim pilgrims share a common belief system that underpins their devotion (i.e., beliefs in saintly miracles, intercession, cures, curses, etc.). Voinot concluded that saint pilgrimage is neither purely Jewish nor purely Muslim and he characterizes the phenomenon as syncretic.[26]

The foregrounded hybridity of Judeo-Muslim pilgrimage was part of a larger trope of Moroccan intermixings with regard to race, belief, ritual, and language. Thus, while Berbers were put forward as the original Moroccans, their racial stock, society, religion, and language were often portrayed as being drawn from multiple sources (pagan, Roman, Christian, Jewish, etc.). Berbers themselves were hybrid beings, and thus even the putatively original source of saint pilgrimage was hybrid.[27] Pilgrimages, as I have noted, were often classed in the larger category of superstition, which included other forms of cures, curses, rituals, and beliefs. Moroccans, in turn, were seen as indiscriminately mixing religion and superstition, and the difference between the two was not discernable to the average native.[28] In the realm of language, colonial linguists made much of the lexical hybridity of Moroccan Judeo-Arabic which draws on both Hebrew and Arabic words.[29]

In these ways, the idea of Judeo-Moroccan pilgrimage represented the hybridity of Moroccan society as compared to the purity and homogeneity of idealized French society. While Moroccan minds confused and combined superstition and religion, rational French minds did not. While Moroccan religion confused and combined elements of Judaism, Islam, and Berber religion, refined European religion did not. In a Morocco that appeared to be rife with boundary transgressions against which the French defined themselves and their colonial project, the idea of Judeo-Muslim pilgrimage served its purpose.[30] The socioreligious hybridity of Judeo-Muslim pilgrimage represented the mental, social, and political chaos that defined Morocco as an object of colonial imagination, control, and rationalization.

Prognosticating Pilgrimage

Voinot and others drew a sharp contrast between monotheistic orthodoxy encoded in fixed and limited canonical texts and saint veneration realized in the popular practices of the ignorant masses. Saint veneration was understood to be at best incongruent with and at worst prohibited by Islam and Judaism.[31] It was by virtue of this imputed incompatibility, made reasonable partly by the idea of a hybrid Judeo-Muslim tradition, that the potential demise of Jewish pilgrimage in Morocco could be cast not only as a turn toward modernity—a leaving behind of outdated superstition—and as a return to a historically authentic Judaism. From this perspective, there would be no place for Jewish pilgrimage in a modern Moroccan future. This is precisely what some Moroccan Jewish reformers demanded and what some colonial ethnographers predicted.[32]

The future of pilgrimage was, however, subject to diverse speculations, and the alternative fates predicted for it registered various approaches to the colonial project more generally. If Morocco were to be subject to *la mission civilisatrice* through the strategic diffusion of French culture and the attendant demise of indigenous traditions, then the future of saint pilgrimages would seem to be in question. Because Jews were, in fact, ambiguous objects of *la mission civilisatrice*, largely through the efforts of the AIU, the vexing persistence of pilgrimage was often noted in colonial representations of Jewish Morocco. As one AIU teacher remarked in 1910, "Our institutions should be a place to uproot these beliefs [in saints and miraculous cures], but students are absent from school on [pilgrimage days]."[33] Another AIU commentator assessed the matter two decades later:

> It is a commonplace to recall the rapid movement that carries the Moroccan Jewish masses towards modern progress and civilization. . . . The notable fact is this forward march, this will to turn away from the past, to forget forever times of disgrace and oppression, to let go of ancient customs, of all the ridiculous superstitions. . . . In this general commotion, the cult of saints . . . is maintaining itself and even growing to a significance unknown in the past.[34]

Some critics saw stubborn faith and ignorance as sufficient explanations for the continuance of pilgrimages despite the efforts of the modernizing Jewish elite.

Protectorate policy, however, was often antithetical to *la mission civilisatrice*, aiming instead to strengthen and reform indigenous institutions in order to further French objectives.[35] Jewish pilgrimage in colonial Morocco was not always represented as an antiquated superstition whose termination was desirable. The perseverance of Jewish pilgrimages in the present and extended future was cast in a variety of terms. In fact, some colonial commentators were able to recuperate pilgrimages for the discourses of modernity, and although early efforts in this direction relied more on themes of faith and humanism than on idioms of hybridity, such efforts nevertheless foreshadowed postcolonial strategies of claiming pilgrimages for the present.

To the extent that pilgrimages could be regulated by modern administrative forms, the events could become models of the ordering effects of the colonial project: the improvements to local roads to shrines, the establishment of sanitary conditions for pilgrims, the efforts to ensure safety of the pilgrimage masses, and the freedom of Jewish expression were all to be celebrated by colonial advocates as evidence of the paternal efforts of the French administration. The benefits of the protectorate regime for the Jewish community could be communicated by pointing to the persistence of pilgrimage traditions rather than their demise. Consider, for example, this 1932 account of the *hillulah* of Rebbi Amram Ben Diwan:

> I saw affirmed during the course of this moving event, the always tenacious and vibrant faith of these Jews who used to be oppressed for their beliefs, and who today enjoy, under the protection of France the liberator, religious peace, peace itself, this Shalom that is our dream and the dream of all humanity.[36]

Stripped of references to Jewish oppression, these themes of protection, freedom, and peace would come to dominate in postcolonial pilgrimage discourse. Similarly, the blind faith that some critics read as ignorance on the part of pilgrims could be recast in more humanistic and romantic terms, for example as a counterpoint to the excesses of modernity. "This pilgrimage," wrote one chronicler in 1957, "demonstrates the power of faith upon which depends, perhaps, the well-being of our world torn apart and ravaged by hatred and war."[37] Moroccan Jews in the late twentieth century, as we will see, similarly used the platform of pilgrimage to speak out against hatred and war in the Middle East.

Nationalizing Pilgrimage

Jewish pilgrimages in Morocco did indeed survive the onslaught of colonial and postcolonial modernity. The reasons for this survival were multiple, but of importance here is the continued relevance of pilgrimage in the discourses of an independent and modern Moroccan nation.[38] The hybridity of pilgrimage remained a central theme of nationalist representations, but the significance of that theme was radically altered over time.

Through the end of the protectorate period, annual Jewish pilgrimages were venues for colonial officials to demonstrate their protection of, control over, and affection for the Jewish community.[39] In return, representatives of the Moroccan Jewish community offered declarations of loyalty to the French project. This pageantry carried over into the early national period (1956 and after), when the newly independent royal state sent invited representatives to Jewish pilgrimages, which emerged as one of the key sites for situating Jews in the emergent postcolonial Moroccan nation.[40] These sites were of importance to both the Moroccan state and the Jewish community as they colluded in manufacturing narratives that situated Jews as productive national subjects, symbols, and resources.

Though some early efforts were made to include Jews in the postcolonial Moroccan nation and its state apparatus, a variety of circumstances converged to limit the presence of Jews in public national life. The ascent of pan-Arab nationalism, the mass migrations of Moroccan Jews to Israel, and the memory of Jewish collaboration with the colonial regime were among the factors that made it precarious to emphasize the Jewish constituency of the Moroccan nation in the 1950s and 1960s. It was not until the late 1970s, with the waning of mass migrations of Moroccan Jews and the political warming between Morocco and Israel, that the official Jewish community reasserted a significant public presence in national life.[41] It was at this point as well that Jewish pilgrimages came to be more widely represented as an emblem of the independent Moroccan nation.

Following trends toward the centralization of Moroccan Jewish communal organization that had begun in the colonial period, a single national pilgrimage to be held each year for the entirety of Morocco emerged in 1978. The new national pilgrimage did not displace other local ones. It did, however, provide an official stage for representing Moroccan Jews as loyal citizens and grateful subjects of the Moroccan state and for representing the Moroccan nation as inclusive of its Jewish constituents. In these efforts, the idea of Judeo-Muslim pilgrimage in Morocco was transformed from evidence of pagan origins and sociocultural chaos into an emblem of interfaith congruence, religious tolerance, and common heritage. Where the hybridity of Jewish pilgrimage was once characterized primarily as syncretic, it increasingly was presented as symbiotic.[42] Pilgrimage hybridity would no longer point to a past to be superseded but rather to an enduring present that could also represent the future of the Moroccan nation.[43]

This shift can be traced to the rise of national Jewish pilgrimages and the associated forms of official promotion, publicity, and oratory that were a calculated part of pilgrimage development. This process was largely initiated by Jewish elites, institutionalized in the Conseil des Communautés Israélites du Maroc (CCIM). Just as earlier Jewish reformers had engaged in colonial discursive forms, these nationalist elites may be viewed as mediating agents of the Moroccan state. Late-twentieth-century discourses of pilgrimage have been authorized by and propagated through state-sanctioned institutions such as the CCIM, the national press, and government ministries. The image of the Moroccan nation that emerges in this context represents the collusion between elite Jewish perspectives and state-centered nationalist ones.[44]

The promotional materials the CCIM distributed for the inaugural national pilgrimage, held at the shrine of R. Amram Ben Diwan, were among the first to move toward Moroccan nationalist representations of Judeo-Muslim pilgrimage hybridity. Among these materials was a press release in which old colonial and new nationalist discourses coexisted in transitional tension. For the most part, the press release relied upon and responded to colonial themes in the representation of Jewish pilgrimage. Thus, for example, the competence of the increasingly centralized national Jewish community to ensure the hygiene and orderliness of the events is asserted: "Everything has been put in place with the cooperation of the local officials, so that the event will be a complete success. The housing of pilgrims in tents, sanitation services, and the necessary restorations have been assured."[45] Over the ensuing decades, the CCIM consolidated its administrative control over pilgrimages. Yet in the transformation of pilgrimages into an exemplar of new forms of Moroccan authenticity, there was no place for the reiteration of colonial tropes that implied that indigenous society was disorderly.

The 1978 press release also recalls themes of syncretism as they were developed in colonial literature:

> Resulting from a long coexistence between Jews and Arabs, the Cult of the Saints, which impregnated Sephardi Judaism, is obviously derived from Maraboutism and constitutes one of the religious rites most distinctive to the Maghribi Jewish Community. In fact, the Jews of the biblical epoch did not practice the Cult of the Saints, but made pilgrimage in order to render homage directly to God.[46]

Following the colonial pattern, the press release used Judeo-Muslim hybridity to establish the exteriority of Moroccan pilgrimage traditions to Judaism proper, as represented here by a pure Andalusian/European heritage (i.e., Sephardi Judaism) and biblical sources. *Maraboutism* remains a key point of reference for the "Cult of Saints." The geopolitical frame of these comments also indexes colonial sensibilities more than nationalist ones. It is the Maghribi Jewish community (here referring to the entire extent of French colonial domains in North Africa rather than the specifically Moroccan one) that is invoked.[47]

Although the public representation of pilgrimage was still constrained by colonial terms, the refashioning of Jewish pilgrimage into a nationalist image had begun. In this transitional document there are elements of the emergent nationalist discourse that would come to dominate public representations of pilgrimage hybridity. There is no mention, for example, of any Berber influences on Jewish pilgrimage. In line with the official Arab identity of independent Morocco, the coexistence of Jews and Arabs is taken as the salient point of reference. Furthermore, despite the lingering efforts to situate pilgrimage beyond the pale of essential Judaism, the religious content of the rituals is not entirely dismissed. "These manifestations of piety," the press release continues, "illustrate the singular character of the encounter between two monotheisms, Jewish and Muslim, and many saints are recognized and celebrated by the two religious communities."[48] What in colonial representations was often cast as superstition is here recognized as piety. If the events are not entirely orthodox, then neither are they bereft of all religious merit. Finally, there is a move toward specifying such pilgrimages in distinctively national terms: "In Morocco alone, it has been noted that 31 saints are invoked by Jews and Muslims in common devotion. The most celebrated example of this mystical convergence is the cult devoted to the memory of R. Amram Ben Diwan."[49] While the specific reference to saints invoked by both Jews and Muslims echoes colonial discourses, this common devotion would be quickly appropriated within nationalist frames that have come to dominate the public discourse of Jewish pilgrimage in Morocco.

Religious Tolerance, Ritual Symbiosis, and National Transcendence

The watershed *hillulah* of 1978 was not the first time a pilgrimage was used to situate Jews as constituents of the new nation. Since national independence such events had provided a public stage for the Moroccan state and its Jewish constituency to exchange reciprocal declarations of loyalty and patronage, humility and protection, commitment and inclusion. When the Moroccan Jewish community began its renewal in the 1970s, saint pilgrimages were recentered as nationalist performances. Far from distinguishing Jews from the Muslim counterparts, these performances relied on the very idioms used in numerous domains to construe the entire Moroccan citizenry as subject to royal control, beneficence, and protection.[50]

Jews are well suited to represent the productive tension between constitutional citizens and royal subjects in the postcolonial Moroccan body politic.[51] As the only recognized indigenous religious minority, Jews can stand for a national society in which all citizens have the same rights and responsibilities regardless of religious confession. Freedom of religious expression is among the virtues of the Moroccan nation on display at *hillulot*. The state and the Jewish community have joined together to mobilize Jewish pilgrimage as a symbolic vehicle to emphasize the inclusiveness, tolerance, and plurality of the Moroccan nation.

These representations are nowhere more evident than in the battery of official speeches that Jewish community officials and representatives of the Moroccan state deliver during pilgrimage events. Beginning in the early 1980s, this collusive oratory has been characterized by a national-constitutional discourse in which a liberal Moroccan nation-state is represented as the authentic inheritor of longstanding traditions of national tolerance, liberty, and diversity. The official speeches given by Jewish leaders and government officials have regularly celebrated tolerance, liberty, and freedom as Moroccan national virtues that are on display at pilgrimage shrines. "The absolute equality of Muslim and Jewish citizens in the constitution and collection of texts that constitute our nation as a functioning democracy," for example, has emerged as a constant refrain in pilgrimage speeches.[52]

Because the executive power of the state is vested in monarchical institutions, however, the postcolonial Moroccan nation is also framed in official discourse as the collective subject of royal protection. In this guise the Jewish community is a part that illuminates a condition of the national whole. Insofar as Jews may be considered as being among the most politically marginal and potentially fragile of Moroccan constituencies, the celebrated Jewish reliance on the palace for protection represents, writ small, a crucial relationship that defines the nation writ large.[53] Jews, that is, are the quintessential protected subjects in a national imaginary that is broadly constituted through idioms of royal protection. In this regard, the ritual form of saint pilgrimage, based on the acceptance of the existential weakness of a supplicant who relies on the personified power of the saint, makes the events into more than merely a vehicle for frankly political discourse. The cultural logic of pilgrimage, in which devotees and saints are brought together in relationships of supplication and protection (from illness, poverty, infertility, etc.), corresponds with discourses on the relationship of the Moroccan populace to the crown.

Hillulah oratory, in sum, casts Jews as distinctively useful subjects and citizens who embody the royal and republican idioms through which the Moroccan state represents its relationship to the national citizenry. These idioms are, to some degree, carried over from the protectorate period. Just as colonial ethnographers and colonized Jews exploited *hillulot* to represent French tolerance and the patronage of the Jewish community, postcolonial Moroccan Jewish citizens and state officials have agreed to reiterate a similar message vis-à-vis the independent Moroccan state. The notion that pilgrimage is situated at the intersection of Jewish and Muslim traditions has likewise been recuperated from colonial discourse. Judeo-Muslim pilgrimage has remained a symbol of the real Morocco itself, but the ritual's hybrid character is now meant to index the liberal pluralism, inclusive unity, and sacred transcendence of the Moroccan nation.

The stirrings of this transformation were already present in the press release for the first national *hillulah* in 1978. There, new forms of nationalist representation were evident in the erasure of Berbers from the historical narrative of Judeo-Muslim pilgrimage. By emphasizing Arab-Islamic influences and ignoring Berber-pagan ones, this discourse about Jewish pilgrimage reinforced dominant portraits of Morocco as an Arab and Islamic nation. The idea of Judeo-Muslim pilgrimage persisted from an earlier era, but the dominant intention of colonial representation was turned on its head. For the Jewish elite and the communal interests they represented, the characterization of Jewish pilgrimage as being directly derived from Arab influences provided evidence that Moroccan Jews partook of a common cultural patrimony shared by all Moroccans and that Jews were thus part of the national community. For the Moroccan state, the characterization of that patrimony as Arab contributed to a broader nationalist discourse that opposed itself to colonial notions that Morocco was only superficially Arabized.[54]

By the 1980s, the hybridity of Jewish pilgrimage was cast in predominantly religious (i.e., Judeo/Muslim) rather than ethnic (i.e., Arab/Berber) terms. Moreover, rather than giving historical precedence to either Islam or Judaism in the discourse of pilgrimage, the official rhetoric shifted toward a historically transcendent frame of reference. The speech drafted by the CCIM leadership and delivered at the national *hillulah* in 1980 was formative in the development of this rhetoric. It included these remarks:

> This ceremony, which is the mark of a tradition common to all Moroccans, is the symbol of a mystical convergence rooted in this land. Each year this ancient rite brings us, Muslims and Jews, to this holy place. Here, we confirm the link between our two religions, both issuing from the same divine source, but also establishing above our obvious differences the proof of our Moroccanness.[55]

Here, Judeo-Muslim pilgrimage represents an authentic and enduring Moroccan heritage that is neither external to Judaism nor antithetical to Islam. Though the reference to a "mystical convergence" suggests a certain notion of irrationality, this idiom conforms more to late colonial romantic sentiments of productive spirituality than to early twentieth-century notions of superstition. Judeo-Muslim pilgrimage, moreover, represents the divine source of the religions that nurture saint pilgrimages rather than the pagan antecedents of parochial traditions. In this statement pilgrimage symbolizes a nation that transcends both history (insofar as it is rooted in a divine source) and internal social differences in that both Muslim and Jewish communities participate.

The hybridity of Judeo-Muslim pilgrimage is no longer offered up as a window onto the heterogeneous and heterodox origins of Moroccan religion or the disorder of Moroccan society. Rather, this hybridity now serves as evidence of a transcendent Moroccan heritage that is both divine and pluralistic. As expressed by the Jewish elite who fashion pilgrimage oratory, this idea of Morocco as a nation that authentically incorporates its religious minorities has its strategic value. In this vein, the language of influence is replaced by the claim of a common source in describing Judeo-Muslim hybridity. Jewish pilgrimage traditions are said to be authentically Moroccan not only because they bear the marks of Berber, Arab, or Islamic influences but also because Jewish and Muslim traditions, both of which issue from the same divine source, are placed on an equal footing. Judeo-Muslim pilgrimage is thereby forwarded as an authentic Moroccan tradition that in some measure transcends even Islam.

The idea that Moroccanness is grounded in a divine source that transcends Islam has an obvious appeal for the Jewish minority; in the face of countervailing ideologies, this Moroccanness does not require a Muslim identity. Yet, as I am suggesting, the idea of Morocco that emerges in this oratory has always also been tied to broader discourses of the nation. Indeed, it was precisely as *hillulot* were undergoing public revitalization that King Hassan II was galvanizing the religious legitimacy of the royal state at an institutional level. As a descendent of the prophet (*sharif*), the king had officially been declared the leader of the Moroccan Islamic community and the "commander of the faithful" (*amīr al-mu'minīn*) in the national constitution of 1962. In the 1970s and 1980s, the state apparatus extended and confirmed its status as the legitimate domain of Islamic scholarship and stewardship, for example through the establishment of the Conseils des Oulémas and the creation of a ministry of pious endowments (*hubus*).[56] Insofar as official *hillulah* oratory proclaimed the divine source of Moroccanness, it also confirmed the efforts of the royal Moroccan state, as the authentic representative of the Moroccan nation, to legitimize itself on religious grounds.

Conclusion

> We would have hoped that Muslim-Jewish fraternity had occurred other than in pagan veneration of the dead and in the degeneration towards idolatry, but we cannot control history.[57]
> —AIU teacher, 1909

> We have been able to reinforce the long-standing cohabitation of our two communities, Muslim and Jewish, above all tribulations, because of mutual respect, tolerance, and because of the civilization of Morocco and of the Alawi Monarchy. This respect of others and this tolerance account for the profound and fraternal relationships that have tied our communities together over the centuries.[58]
> —Public address at the *hillulah* of Moualine Dad, 1981

Jewish pilgrimages in Morocco show no signs of fading in the near future. The revitalization of pilgrimage that began in the final quarter of the twentieth century continues into the present: shrines are being renovated, new dates are being added to the pilgrimage calendar, and *hillulot* continue to be featured in the national media. Now, as before, *hillulah* oratory extols pilgrimage as part of the national patrimony in which Jews partake as authentic contributors. Pilgrimages also remain reciprocal venues for the Jewish community to voice its support of government positions, ranging from Moroccan claims on the Western Sahara to support for the Palestinian nationalist cause, and for the state to demonstrate national consensus on these issues. As a tradition that demonstrates interfaith commonality and respect, Judeo-Muslim pilgrimage has over the past several decades been used to emblemize the possibility of a peaceful resolution to the Arab-Israeli conflict.[59]

The changing terrain of ethnic politics in Morocco, especially with respect to the burgeoning intensity of Berber cultural activism, has also created renewed possibilities for representing hybridity. Postcolonial discourses that give precedence to the Arab identity of the nation are being challenged across a range of domains. Berber activists have continued (with growing success) to institutionalize the presence of Berber language, history and identity in newspapers, televisions, and schools. In the process of contesting Arab hegemony in Morocco, activists have pointed toward Moroccan Jewish patrimony, which the emergent Berber press features prominently, as further evidence of the heterogeneity of the nation. Among those most interested in my research have been Berber activists who have informed me that pilgrimages are in essence and origin Judeo-Berber, like Morocco itself. And in fact, in this opening decade of the twenty-first century, official *hillulah* oratory is once again recognizing Berberness as an authentic aspect of pilgrimage hybridity in Morocco.

My approach in this chapter has been to rethink the Judeo-Muslim hybridity of pilgrimages not as a fact to be tested but rather as a rhetorical trope that has been elaborated in specific historical contexts and deployed toward specific ends. To establish this point I have focused on the ways that pilgrimage hybridity has been instrumental in constituting the idea of Morocco, first as the object of colonial control and second as a liberal nation-state that recognizes and transcends internal pluralism. On the whole, recent scholarship on Jewish pilgrimage in Morocco has not been wedded to the colonial and nationalist projects I have examined here. Nor, however, has this scholarship been immune to an interpretative framework that takes Judeo-Muslim hybridity as one of the notable features of pilgrimage traditions in Jewish Morocco. Taking into account the historical contexts in which this framework has been established and identifying the interested agents responsible for its elaboration helps us comprehend the resilience of hybridity as a key frame in the representation of Moroccan Jewish pilgrimage. After this kind of accounting we are in a better position to rethink the frame and consider alternatives.

NOTES

Earlier versions of this essay were presented at the American Institute for Maghrib Studies Conference (2004), the Twelfth Annual Maghrebi Area Studies Symposium for U.S. Fulbright Grantees (2005), the University of Arizona (2005), and the University of Kansas (2007). This chapter was completed with the support of a Fulbright Scholar Award for Research in Morocco. Jonathan Boyarin, Majid Hannoum, Julie Hastings, Hassan Rachik, Lawrence Rosen, and Daniel Schroeter provided critical feedback at various stages of writing. My thanks to all who contributed to the realization of this essay.

1. The adjective Judeo-Muslim, for example, appears in the title of numerous articles and at least two books on the topic: L. Voinot, *Pèlerinages judéo-musulmans du Maroc* (Paris: Éditions Larose, 1948); and Issachar Ben-Ami, *Cultes des saints et pèlerinage judéo-musulmans au Maroc* (Paris: Maisonneuve & Larose, 1990). For an example of references to pilgrimages in tourist guidebooks, see Nina Banon, *Morocco: A Guide and History* (Casablanca: Société Nouvelle des Impressions et Cartonnages Idéale, 1991), 428. For differing views on the substantive relationship between Jewish and Muslim hagiographic and pilgrimage traditions in Morocco, see Norman Stillman, "Saddiq and Marabout in Morocco," in *The Sephardi and Oriental Jewish Heritage*, ed. Issachar Ben Ami (Jerusalem: Magnes Press, 1982), 489–500; André N. Chouraqui, *Between East and West: A History of the Jews of North Africa* (New York: Atheneum, 1973); and Ben-Ami, *Cultes des saints*.

2. The significance of Muslim saint pilgrimage in the representation of the Moroccan nation has been addressed by historians and anthropologists. See, for example, Abdallah Laroui, "Marche verte et conscience historique," in Abdallah Laroui, *Esquisses historiques* (Casablanca: Centre Culturel Arabe, 1993), 147–158; and Fenneke Reysoo, *Pèlerinages au Maroc: Fête, politique et échange dans l'islam populaire* (Paris: Éditions de la Maison des Sciences de l'Homme, 1991).

3. Voinot, *Pèlerinages judéo-musulmans du Maroc*, 1. Voinot was a prolific writer who published many works under the auspices of the Institut des Hautes Etudes Marocaines, the academic arm of the French protectorate. See Jadda M'Hamed Jadda, *Bibliographie analytique des publications de L'Institut des Hautes Etudes Marocaines* (Rabat: Publications de la Faculté des Lettres et des Sciences Humaines, 1994). I deal primarily with Voinot, but themes of pilgrimage hybridity are extensive throughout the colonial ethnography of Morocco. See also Edmond Doutté, *Notes sur l'Islâm maghribin: Les Marabouts* (Paris: E. Leroux, 1900), 68–69; Louis Brunot and Elie Malka, *Textes judéo-arabes de Fès* (Rabat: Ecole du Livre, 1939), 276–281; and Pierre Flamand, *Un mellah en pays berbère: Demnate* (Paris: Librarie Générale de Droit & de Jurisprudence, 1952), 93–122.

4. Voinot, *Pèlerinages judéo-Musulmans du Maroc*, 1.

5. For a history of this institutionalization, see Oren Kosansky, "All Dear unto God: Saints, Pilgrimage, and Textual Practice in Jewish Morocco" (Ph.D. diss., University of Michigan, 2003).

6. For an example of press coverage, see "La Haïloula, ou le pèlerinage des sept saints des Ouled Ben-Zmirou à Safi," *Le Matin du Sahara*, 27 August 1995.

7. The full text of the speech is in the archives of the Conseil des Communautés Israélites du Maroc, Casablanca. See also "De centaines d'Israelites du Maroc d'Europe et d'Amérique présents à la Hiloula de Rabbi Amram Ben Diouane," *Matin Maroc Soir*, 6 May 1980. The same passage appears in subsequent speeches at various shrines. See, for example, "Célébration de la 'Hilloula de Moualine Dad,'" *Le Matin du Sahara et du Maghreb*, 27 May 1981.

8. Eric J. Hobsbawm and Terence Ranger, eds., *The Invention of Tradition* (Cambridge: Cambridge University Press 1989).

9. See Shlomo Deshen, *The Mellah Society: Jewish Community Life in Sherifian Morocco* (Chicago: University of Chicago Press 1989), 83.

10. Harvey E. Goldberg, "Introduction," in *Sephardi and Middle Eastern Jewries: History and Culture in the Modern Era*, ed. Harvey E. Goldberg (Bloomington: Indiana University Press, 1996), 26–28.

11. Y. D. Semach (Dasey), "Pèlerinage à Ouezzan," *L'Univers Israélite* 83 (1928): 301–302; Lazare Conquy, "Les miracles du pèlerinage d'Ouezzan," *Paix et Droit* (1 January 1932): 9–10.

12. On the AIU in Morocco, see Michael M. Laskier, *The Alliance Israélite Universelle and the Jewish Communities of Morocco* (Albany: State University of New York Press, 1983). For a detailed account of the AIU and its role in facilitating reformist voices in Turkey, see Aron Rod-

rigue, *French Jews, Turkish Jews: The Alliance Israélite Universelle and the Politics of Jewish Schooling in Turkey, 1860–1925* (Bloomington: Indiana University Press, 1990).

13. Elie Malka, *Essai d'ethnographie traditionnelle des mellahs: Ou croyances, rites de passage et vieilles pratiques des Israélites marocains* (Rabat: École du Livre 1946).

14. See Janet Abu-Lughod, *Rabat: Urban Apartheid in Morocco* (Princeton, N.J.: Princeton University Press 1980).

15. See, for example, Haïm Zafrani, *Le Judaïsme maghrébin: Le Maroc, terre des rencontres des cultures et des civilisations* (Rabat: Marsam, 2003); AIU Maroc, I.B.5/Fès, Sarah Behar, "Les saints du Maroc," (10 March 1934); "La veille du conseil annuel des rabbins du Maroc: La Hilloula," *La Voix des Communautés* 14 (1 October 1951): 3.

16. See, for example, Flamand, *Un mellah en pays berbère,* 112.

17. For an example of colonial representations of social chaos at pilgrimages, see N. Levy, "Dernière echos de la Helloula," *L'Union Marocaine* 10 (1932). On efforts at pilgrimage reform in the late colonial period, see Samuel Youssef Benaim, *Le pèlerinage juif des lieux saints au Maroc: Etude de tous les tsadiquimes dont les tombe aux sont éparpillés dans tout le Maroc* (Casablanca: Auteur, 1980), 6–10. For a detailed analysis of the colonial rationalization of pilgrimage, see Kosansky, "All Dear unto God." Rabbinic critics, it is worth noting, also joined the chorus of those condemning pilgrimage chaos insofar as it led to such religiously prohibited activities as traveling on the Sabbath, ostentatious expenditures, and the intermingling of men and women. See Yehudah Messas, *Mayim hayyim* (Fez: 1934), 169–170, as quoted in Ben-Ami, *Cultes des saints,* 136.

18. I. D. Abbou, "L'Exploitation de l'ignorance: Les fêtes de la 'Hilloula' ou le jour des saints au Maroc," *Noar,* Nouvelle Serie, 15 (1950): 2.

19. Messas, *Mayim hayyim,* 169–170.

20. Voinot, *Pèlerinages judéo-musulmans du Maroc,* 6.

21. Benaim, *Le pèlerinage juif des lieux saints au Maroc.*

22. On the colonial politics of *maraboutism,* see Dale F. Eickelman, *Moroccan Islam: Tradition and Society in a Pilgrimage Center* (Austin: University of Texas Press: 1976), 59–60, 218–228; and Abdellah Hammoudi, *Master and Disciple: The Cultural Foundations of Moroccan Authoritarianism* (Chicago: University of Chicago Press, 1997), 101–107.

23. Edmund Burke, III, "The Image of the Moroccan State in French Ethnological Literature: A New Look at the Origin of Lyautey's Berber Policy," in *Arabs and Berbers,* ed. Ernest Gellner and Charles Micaud (Lexington, Mass.: Lexington Books, 1972), 188–199.

24. Voinot, *Pèlerinages judéo-musulmans du Maroc,* 1.

25. Burke, "The Image of the Moroccan State," 188–189.

26. Voinot, *Pèlerinages judéo-musulmans du Maroc,* 125.

27. For a related discussion of colonialists' emphasis on the multiple sources of Berber rituals, see Abdellah Hammoudi, *The Victim and Its Masks: An Essay on Sacrifice and Masquerade in the Maghreb* (Chicago: University of Chicago Press, 1993), 23–27.

28. Malka, *Essai d'ethnographie traditionnelle des mellahs,* 5–11.

29. Brunot and Malka, *Textes judéo-arabes de Fès,* i–viii.

30. Establishing and policing proper boundaries, especially between *colons* and *indigènes,* was of paramount concern. Abu-Lughod, *Rabat,* 142–150.

31. Colonial accounts scarcely noticed the fact that Jewish devotees of saints and pilgrimages were astute at situating their practices in univocally Judaic terms by informed reference to the same range of biblical and rabbinic textual genres that colonial ethnographers and reformist critics harnessed to demonstrate the incompatibility of saint pilgrimage with Judaism. Several genres of rabbinic texts that legitimized sainthood and pilgrimage in classical Judaic terms were circulated in Morocco during the twentieth century. These genres included bibliographic-biographical dictionaries, e.g. Ya'akov Abihatsira, *Sefer Yagel Ya'akov* (Jerusalem: Mosadot Ner Yitshak 5755 1994/1995); and hagiographic collections, e.g. Moshe Pinto, *Shanot Hayyim* (Casablanca: David Amar, 1961).

32. See, for example, "Pèlerinage de Hilloula au cimetière de Salé (sur la tombe du Grand Rabbin Raphaél Encaoua)," *Noar* (1 July 1946): 9.

33. AIU Maroc, VI.B.27/Divers, R. Danon, "Coutumes de pèlerinage/Ouazan" (1910).

34. AIU Maroc, III.B.15/Ouezzane, Y. D. Semach, "Le Saint d'Ouezzan, Ribbi Amram Ben Diwan" (1935).

35. Paul Rabinow, *French Modern: Norms and Forms of the Social Environment* (Cambridge, Mass.: MIT Press, 1989), 286.

36. AIU Maroc, II.B.9/Marrakech, Léon Ninio, "La Hiloula à Marrakech" (1932). See also Z. El. H., "Autour du pèlerinage d'Asjen," *L'Union Marocaine* 7 (1932): 1.

37. Jacob Elhadad, "Le saint d'Ouezzane: Rabbi Amram Ben Diouane," *Les Cahiers de l'A.I.U.* 109 (1957): 5–6.

38. For a detailed account of Jewish pilgrimage in postcolonial Morocco, see Kosansky "All Dear unto God."

39. "Boujad: La fête de la hiloula," *La Voix des Communautés* 31 (1953): 3.

40. Representatives of the Moroccan state (the makhzan) were also included in colonial era ceremonies, so the transition was not entirely discontinuous. Ibid. Other key sites for the public performance of Jewish inclusion in and loyalty to the nation include the Fête du Throne (see Hassan Rachik, *Symboliser la nation: Essai sur l'usage des identités collectives au Maroc* [Casablanca: Editions le Fennec, 2002], 107) and Yom Kippur (see Salomon Benbaruk, *Trois-Quarts de siècle pêle-mêle* [Lachine, Quebec: Imprimeurs du 21e Siècle, 1990]), 5–7.

41. On the diplomatic context of these developments, see Mark Tessler, "Moroccan-Israeli Relations and the Reasons for Moroccan Receptivity to Contact with Israel," *The Jerusalem Journal of International Relations* 10, no. 2 (1988): 76–108.

42. This shift toward symbiosis as a key metaphor was a feature of earlier postcolonial scholarship on Jewish-Muslim relations more generally. See, for example, *Juifs du Maroc: Identité et dialogue* (Paris: La Pensée Sauvage, 1980); Haim Zafrani, *Milles ans de vie juive au Maroc* (Paris: Maisonneuve & Larose, 1983). Recent scholarship has attended more fully to the complicated and ambivalent relationships between Muslims and Jews in Moroccan history, especially in the context of European colonization. See, for example, Mohammed Kenbib, *Juifs et Musulmans au Maroc: 1859–1948* (Rabat: Université Mohammed V, Publications de la Faculté des lettres et des Sciences Humaines, 1994); Daniel J. Schroeter, *The Sultan's Jew: Morocco and the Sephardi World* (Stanford, Calif.: Stanford University Press, 2002); and André Levy, "Notes on Jewish-Muslim Relationships: Revisiting the Vanishing Moroccan Jewish Community," *Cultural Anthropology* 18, no. 3 (2003): 365–397. This recent scholarly turn toward examining the varieties and complexities of Jewish-Muslim relationships has not surfaced in official representations of Jewish pilgrimage.

43. Cultural resources, previously deemed to be archaic counterpoints to a national future, have been recuperated by postcolonial nationalisms and state projects throughout the Middle East and North Africa. The appropriation of "tribalism" provides a case in point. See, for example: Linda L Layne, "The Dialogics of Tribal Self-Representation in Jordan," *American Ethnologist* 16, no. 1 (1989): 24–39; and Andrew J. Shryock, "Popular Genealogical Nationalism: History Writing and Identity among the Balqa Tribes of Jordan," *Comparative Studies in Society and History* 37, no. 2 (1995): 325–357.

44. The relationship between the monarch (sultan/king), the royal state (makhzan), and the nation (*watan*) in Morocco has never been stable. Indeed, certain forms of nationalism in colonial and postcolonial Morocco have been arrayed against royal authority and governance. See Abdallah Laroui, *Les origines sociales et culturelles du nationalisme marocain, 1830–1912* (Paris: F. Maspero, 1977); William I. Zartman, ed., *The Political Economy of Morocco* (New York: Praeger, 1987); and Rahma Bourqia and Susan G. Miller, eds., *In the Shadow of the Sultan: Culture, Power, and Politics in Morocco* (Cambridge: Harvard University Press, 1999). I am concerned here primarily with the forms of nationalism wedded most closely to the royal state.

45. Conseil des Communautés Israélites du Maroc, Archive, "Sous l'egide du conseil des

Communautés Israélites du Maroc: célébration de la Hiloula de Rabbi Amram Ben Diouane. Les 24 3t 25 Mai (1978) à Ouazzane."

46. Ibid.

47. As I will develop below, Morocco rather than the Maghrib soon emerged as the point of reference in nationalist discourse. On the challenges and tensions regarding Moroccan and broader Maghribi forms of nationalist representation, see Benjamin Stora, "Algeria/Morocco: The Passions of the Past. Representations of the Nation that Unite and Divide," *The Journal of North African Studies* 8, no. 1 (2003): 14–42.

48. "Sous L'Egide du Conseil des Communautés Israélites du Maroc." This emphasis on interconfessional celebration obscures the ways that the identity of saints as Jewish or Muslim continues to be contested in local contexts. See, for example, Lawrence Rosen, *The Culture of Islam: Changing Aspects of Contemporary Muslim Life* (Chicago: University of Chicago Press, 2002), 7–87.

49. "Sous L'Egide du Conseil des Communautés Israélites du Maroc."

50. Hammoudi, *Master and Disciple,* 12–24, 75–80.

51. On Jews as royal subjects in colonial and postcolonial contexts, see Daniel J. Schroeter, "From Dhimmis to Colonized Subjects: Moroccan Jews and the Sharifian and French Colonial State," in *Jews and the State: Dangerous Alliances and the Perils of Privilege,* ed. Ezra Mendelson (Jerusalem: Oxford University Press, 2003), 104–123.

52. Official speeches developing nationalist themes can be found, for example, in "Pèlerins juifs étrangers et marocains ont prié pour le repos de l'âme des chouhada de notre intégrité territoriale au cours de la Hiloula de Rabbi David Ben Baroukh dans le région de Taroudant," *Le Matin du Sahara et du Maghreb,* 30 December 1979; "En marge de la commémoration de la hiloula par la commune juive marocaine. Des espoirs communs pour la réalisation d'une société de valeurs morales et de respect de l'homme," *Maroc Soir,* 4 May 1980; "La tolérance religieuse est une composante de notre civilisation," *Maroc Soir,* 27 May 1986; and "Hilloula à la mémoire des "Sebâa des Ouled Ben-Zmirou" à Safi," *Le Matin du Sahara,* 7 August 1993.

53. Although no direct mention is made in *hillulah* oratory to the past legal status of Jews as *dhimmis* in the precolonial Moroccan polity, the idea of *dhimma* as the status of tolerated and protected subjects provides one frame for situating this relationship as an extension of the precolonial national heritage. This frame is indicated in recent *hillulah* oratory in references to Jews as "People of the Book," i.e. as recipients of divine revelation, which is an idiom closely associated with the status of *dhimmi.*

54. See Stora, "Algeria/Morocco: The Passions of the Past," 18–21; and John P. Entelis, *Culture and Counterculture in Moroccan Politics* (New York: University of America Press, 1996), 11.

55. See note 7 above.

56. M. Soukri, "Quelle réforme du champ religieux," *La Verité,* 13–19 May 2005, 17.

57. Moïse Nahon, "Saints et sanctuaires judéo-musulmans," *Revue des Ecoles de l'Alliance Israélite* 5 (Avril–Juin 1902): 332–336.

58. "Célébration de la 'Hilloula de Moualine Dad,'" *Le Matin du Sahara et du Maghreb,* 27 May 1981, 3.

59. Ibid.

Contributors

Yaëlle Azagury is Adjunct Lecturer in French Literature and Humanities at State University of New York (SUNY Purchase) (United States).

Jamaâ Baïda is Professor of History at the Université Mohammed V-Agdal in Rabat and a founding-member and coordinator of the Study and Research Group on Moroccan Judaism ("GREJM") (Morocco).

Philippe Barbé is Assistant Professor of Sociology at Fatih University, Istanbul (Turkey).

Saddek Benkada is Senior Fellow at the Centre de Recherche en Anthropologie Sociale et Culturelle (CRASC), Assistant Director of the publication *Insaniyat* in Oran, and Mayor of Oran (Algeria).

Farid Benramdane is Dean of the Faculté des Lettres et des Arts at the Université de Abdelhamid Ibn Badis, Mostaganem (Algeria).

Aomar Boum is Assistant Professor in the Department of Near Eastern Studies and the Program of Religious Studies at the University of Arizona in Tucson, Arizona (United States).

Fayçal Cherif is Assistant Professor at the Institut Supérieur d'Histoire du Mouvement National (ISHMN), Université de Manouba, Tunis (Tunisia) and a researcher at the Unit for Archival Research (l'Unite d'Etudes et des Recherches Archivistiques).

Emily Benichou Gottreich is Associate Adjunct Professor in the Department of History and Middle Eastern Studies and Vice Chair of the Center for Middle Eastern Studies at the University of California, Berkeley. She also serves as President of the American Institute for Maghrib Studies (AIMS) (United States).

Stacy E. Holden is Assistant Professor in the Department of History at Purdue University in West Lafayette, Indiana (United States).

Jonathan G. Katz is Professor and Chair of the Department of History at Oregon State University in Corvallis, Oregon (United States).

Mohammed Kenbib is Professor of Contemporary History at the Université Mohammed V and a member of the editorial board of Hespéris-Tamuda, Rabat (Morocco).

Oren Kosansky is Assistant Professor of Anthropology in the Department of Sociology and Anthropology at Lewis & Clark College in Portland, Oregon (United States).

Joy A. Land is Adjunct Professor in the Department of History at the University of Connecticut in Stamford, Connecticut (United States).

Abdellah Larhmaid received his Ph.D. in History from the Université Mohammed V, Rabat, and currently serves as First Secretary, Ministry of Foreign Affairs and Cooperation (Morocco).

Mabrouk Mansouri is Assistant Professor in the Department of Arabic at the Faculty of Arts and Humanities, University of Sousse (Tunisia).

Belkacem Mebarki is Professor of French in the Département des Langues Latines at the Université d'Oran, Es-Sénia (Algeria).

Hadj Miliani is Professor of Comparative Literature at the Université de Mostaganem and Associate Director of Research at the Centre de Recherche en Anthropologie Sociale et Culturelle (CRASC) (Algeria).

Susan Gilson Miller is Associate Professor in the Department of History at the University of California, Davis (United States).

Daniel J. Schroeter is Professor in the Department of History, the Deinard Memorial Chair in Jewish History, and Director of the Center for Jewish Studies at the University of Minnesota, Twin Cities, Minnesota (United States).

Ruth Knafo Setton is Writer-in-Residence at the Berman Center for Jewish Studies and Professor of Practice in the Department of English at Lehigh University in Bethlehem, Pennsylvania (United States).

Yaron Tsur is Associate Professor in the Department of Jewish History, Director of the Jews of Islamic Countries Research Unit at Tel Aviv University, and founder and co-director of the Historical Jewish Press project (www.jpress.org.il), (Israel).

Sharon Vance is Assistant Professor in the Department of History at Northern Kentucky University in Highland Heights, Kentucky (United States).

Keith Walters is Professor in the Department of Applied Linguistics at Portland State University, Oregon (United States).

INDEX

Index

ethnography, 6, 8, 9, 18, 26, 38, 74, 75, 79, 80, 83, 88, 89, 341, 342, 344–346, 348, 353
Europe: attitudes of, 16, 111, 131, 159, 160, 178, 198n4, 201–203, 214, 217, 219, 248, 312, 315, 346; and colonialism, 79, 101, 111, 113, 117, 124n15, 128, 130–132, 147n11, 179, 202, 203, 269, 286, 295, 296, 308, 313, 359n42; commerce of, 14, 65, 67, 69, 69, 94–97, 100, 129, 141, 144, 164, 285, 169; culture of, 41, 128, 130, 132, 135, 137, 139, 145, 182, 247, 248, 289, 338, 339; education in, 241, 244, 245, 263, 267, 271, 273, 289, 290, 292; emigration to, 4; fascism in, 306; Islam in, 93, 161; Jews of, 11, 13, 16, 19, 27, 98, 99, 107, 109, 114, 123n13, 146, 214, 217, 261, 262; languages of, 6, 201, 262–264, 270–272; literature of, 26, 74, 93, 198n9, 201, 202, 212, 214, 217–219, 295; powers of, 97, 99, 100, 262, 271, 284; press, 293; travelers from, 14, 73, 75, 80, 81, 83–86, 116, 133, 157, 248, 291, 292; travel narratives of, 73, 75, 79, 80, 82, 87; war in, 305
evolués, 27, 28
exorcism, 110, 120, 121
exoticism, 9, 18, 181, 182, 215, 216
expulsion, 7, 8, 97, 107, 123n1, 170, 204, 205, 216, 218. *See also* 1492; Inquisition

Faculté des Lettres (Rabat), 24
Falcon, Nissim, 287–296
famine, 68, 81, 131, 151, 157–159, 161, 162, 282, 288, 289
fanaticism, 84, 203, 204, 208–210, 212, 217–219, 286
Fanon, Frantz, 116
Fantar, Mhamed, 38
Farhi (family), 97, 98
Farrachou, Ben, 178
fascism, 306–309, 311, 312
Fatimid (dynasty), 51–53
fatwa, 25, 53
feminism, 207, 211, 213, 214
Fernández, Pura, 209
Fertile Crescent, 94
Fez, 15, 26, 81, 85, 122, 150–161, 163, 173, 191, 192, 202, 204, 205, 210, 211, 213, 217, 226, 229–235, 285, 336
Filippini, Jean-Pierre, 96, 97
Fitoussi, Alice, 180
Fleg, Edmond, 118
folklore, 16, 63, 87, 121, 191–197, 204, 229, 230, 234, 234
Foucauld, Charles de, 14, 26, 62, 75, 81, 84, 86–89
1492 (year), 15, 27, 93, 94, 97, 169, 170. *See also* expulsion; Inquisition
France, 3, 4, 177, 181, 182, 185, 218, 249, 278, 293; attitudes in, 209, 210, 214, 215, 284; colonialism, 83, 84, 87, 206, 213, 222n42, 294, 295, 312, 314, 349; commerce of, 140; education, 7, 8, 239, 271, 275; Jewish relationship with, 4, 7, 12, 18, 150, 218, 274, 284, 294, 310, 318, 321,

324, 327, 334, 347; Jews of, 28, 77, 99, 107, 118, 174, 175, 215, 260, 261, 274, 325; Moroccans in, 4; Second Empire, 215, 216; Tunisians in, 122, 123; Vichy, 310, 311, 313–315, 318, 322
Francos, 97–99, 101
French (language), 3, 6, 16, 17, 27, 35, 41, 122, 133, 181, 182, 184, 201, 209, 214, 215, 218, 226, 239, 242, 258, 259, 261–265, 267–275, 278, 279, 288, 307, 313
French Revolution, 175, 203, 215
frontier, 15, 115, 116. *See also* border

Gaillard, Henri, 150
Gal, Susan, 278
Gaudí, Antonio, 129
Geertz, Clifford, 8, 9, 47
Germany, 140, 249, 307, 308, 309, 311, 314, 317, 318
ghetto. *See hara; mellah*
Gibralter, 15, 172, 173, 202, 203, 212, 260, 261
Gidney, W.T. (Reverend), 264, 265
Gimenez, Don Diego, 145
Glawi, Madani al-, 150, 289, 292
Godard, Léon, 204, 216, 217
Goebbels, Joseph, 307
Goitein, S. D., 13
Goldberg, Harvey, 8
Goldenberg, Alfred, 282, 283
Gottreich, Emily, 288
government. *See* authority
Grana, 96, 245, 260, 261, 266. *See also* Livorno
Great Britain, 81, 161, 264, 307, 310, 311, 312, 314
Great Mosque (Tangier), 128, 132
Greek Orthodox (religion), 240
Guérin, Victor, 116

Habsburg Empire, 97
Hachuel, Suleika (Sol), 16, 17, 191–197, 201–205, 207–219, 226–230, 232–235
Hafidh, Mawlay. *See* 'Abd al-Hafidh (Sultan)
Halevy, Eliahu, 100
Halévy, Joseph, 285
Hajawi, Muhammad, 157, 161
Hamburg (Germany), 98
Hamrouche, Mouloud, 335
Hannoum, Abdelmajid, 75
hara (Tunisian Jewish quarter), 108–111, 113–115, 116, 119, 120, 122, 244, 245, 251, 260, 264. *See also mellah*
harem, 211, 213, 215, 230
Harris, Walter, 81
Hasan, al- (Sultan), 67, 68, 158, 159
Hasidism, 18
Hassan, Salvadore, 134
Hassan II (King), 4, 355
Hassoun, Jacques, 115
Hazan, Jacob, 290, 292
hazaqa, 63, 69
Hebrew (language), 3, 6, 10, 25, 47, 54, 98, 130,